TCP/IP Network Administration

TCP/IP Network Administration

Second Edition

Craig Hunt

O'REILLY®

Beijing · Cambridge · Farnham · Köln · Paris · Sebastopol · Taipei · Tokyo

TCP/IP Network Administration, Second Edition
by Craig Hunt

Copyright © 1998, 1992 Craig Hunt. All rights reserved.
Printed in the United States of America.

Published by O'Reilly & Associates, Inc., 101 Morris Street, Sebastopol, CA 95472.

Editor: Mike Loukides

Update Editor: Gigi Estabrook

Production Editor: Nicole Gipson Arigo

Printing History:

August 1992:	First Edition.
March 1993:	Minor corrections.
September 1993:	Minor corrections.
January 1994:	Minor corrections.
May 1994:	Minor corrections.
January 1998:	Second Edition.

ISBN: 1-56592-322-7   [12/99]

[M]

Table of Contents

Preface

The protocol wars are over and TCP/IP won. TCP/IP is now universally recognized as the pre-eminent communications protocol for linking together diverse computer systems. The importance of interoperable data communications and global computer networks is no longer debated. But that was not always the case. When I wrote the first edition of this book, IPX was far and away the leading PC communications protocol. Microsoft did not bundle communications protocols in their operating system. Corporate networks were so dependent on SNA that many corporate network administrators had not even heard of TCP/IP. Even UNIX, the mother of TCP/IP, nursed a large number of pure UUCP networks. Back then I felt compelled to tout the importance of TCP/IP by pointing out that it was used on thousands of networks and hundreds of thousands of computers. How times have changed! Today we count the hosts and users connected to the Internet in the tens of millions. And the Internet is only the tip of the TCP/IP iceberg. The largest market for TCP/IP is in the corporate "intranet." An intranet is a private TCP/IP network used to disseminate information within the enterprise. The competing network technologies have shrunk to niche markets where they fill special needs—while TCP/IP has grown to be the communications software that links the world.

The acceptance of TCP/IP as a worldwide standard and the size of its global user base are not the only things that have changed. In 1991 I lamented the lack of adequate documentation. At the time it was difficult for a network administrator to find the information he or she needed to do the job. Since that time there has been an explosion of books about TCP/IP and the Internet. However, there are still too few books that concentrate on what a system administrator really needs to know about TCP/IP administration and too many books that try to tell you how to surf the Web. In this book I strive to focus on TCP/IP and UNIX, and not to be distracted by the phenomenon of the Internet.

I am very proud of the first edition of *TCP/IP Network Administration*. In the second edition, I have done everything I can to maintain the essential character of the book while making it better. The Domain Name Service material has been updated to cover the latest version of the BIND 4 software. The email configuration is now based on sendmail version 8, and the operating system examples are from the current versions of Solaris and Linux. The routing protocol coverage has been expanded to include Open Shortest Path First (OSPF) and Border Gateway Protocol (BGP). I have also added new topics such as one-time passwords and configuration servers based on Dynamic Host Configuration Protocol (DHCP) and Bootstrap Protocol (BOOTP). Despite the additional topics, the book has been kept to a reasonable length.

The bulk of this edition is derived directly from the first edition of the book. To emphasize both that times have changed and that my focus on practical information has not, I have left the introductory paragraphs from the first edition intact.

Foreword from the First Edition

The Internet, the world's largest network, grew from fewer than 6,000 computers at the end of 1986 to more than 600,000 computers five years later.* This explosive growth demonstrates the incredible demand for network services. This growth has taken place despite a lack of practical information for network administrators. Most administrators have been forced to content themselves with **man** pages, or protocol documents and scholarly texts written from the point of view of the protocol designer. For practical information, most of us have relied on the advice of friends who had already networked their computers. This book addresses the lack of information by providing practical, detailed network information for the UNIX system administrator.

Networks have grown so extravagantly because they provide an important service. It is in the nature of computers to generate and process information, but this information is frequently useless unless it can be shared with the people who need it. The network is the vehicle that enables data to be easily shared. Once you network your computer, you'll never want to be stuck on an isolated system again.

The common thread that ties the enormous Internet together is TCP/IP network software. TCP/IP is a set of communications protocols that define how different types of computers talk to each other. This is a book about building your own network based on TCP/IP. It is both a tutorial covering the "why" and "how" of TCP/IP networking, and a reference manual for the details about specific network programs.

---

* These figures are taken from page 4 of RFC 1296, *Internet Growth (1981–1991)*, by M. Lottor, SRI International. Read this book and you'll learn what an RFC is, and how to get your own free copy!

Audience

This book is intended for everyone who has a UNIX computer connected to a TCP/IP network.* This obviously includes the network managers and the system administrators who are responsible for setting up and running computers and networks, but it also includes any user who wants to understand how his or her computer communicates with other systems. The distinction between a "system administrator" and an "end user" is a fuzzy one. You may think of yourself as an end user, but if you have a UNIX workstation on your desk, you're probably also involved in system administration tasks.

In recent years there has been a rash of books for "dummies" and "idiots." If you really think of yourself as an "idiot" when it comes to UNIX, this book is not for you. Likewise, if you are a network administration "genius," this book is probably not suitable. If you fall anywhere between these two extremes, however, you'll find this book has a lot to offer.

We assume that you have a good understanding of computers and their operation, and that you're generally familiar with UNIX system administration. If you're not, the Nutshell Handbook *Essential System Administration* by Æleen Frisch (published by O'Reilly & Associates) will fill you in on the basics.

Organization

Conceptually, this book is divided into three parts: fundamental concepts, tutorial, and reference. The first three chapters are a basic discussion of the TCP/IP protocols and services. This discussion provides the fundamental concepts necessary to understand the rest of the book. The remaining chapters provide a "how-to" tutorial. Chapters 4–7 discuss how to plan a network installation and configure the basic software necessary to get a network running. Chapters 8–10 discuss how to set up various important network services. The final chapters, 11–13, cover how to perform the ongoing tasks that are essential for a reliable network: troubleshooting, security, and keeping up with changing network information. The book concludes with a series of appendices that are technical references for important commands and programs.

This book contains the following chapters:

Chapter 1, *Overview of TCP/IP*, gives the history of TCP/IP, a description of the structure of the protocol architecture, and a basic explanation of how the protocols function.

---

* Much of this text also applies to non-UNIX systems. Many of the file formats and commands, and all of the protocol descriptions apply equally well to Windows 95, Windows NT, and other operating systems. If you're an NT administrator, don't worry. I'm currently writing an NT version of this book.

Chapter 2, *Delivering the Data*, describes addressing and how data passes through a network to reach the proper destination.

Chapter 3, *Network Services*, discusses the relationship between clients and server systems, and the various services that are central to the function of a modern internet.

Chapter 4, *Getting Started*, begins the discussion of network setup and configuration. This chapter discusses the preliminary configuration planning needed before you configure the systems on your network.

Chapter 5, *Basic Configuration*, describes how to configure TCP/IP in the UNIX kernel, and how to configure the Internet daemon that starts most of the network services.

Chapter 6, *Configuring the Interface*, tells you how to identify a network interface to the network software. This chapter provides examples of Ethernet, SLIP, and PPP interface configurations.

Chapter 7, *Configuring Routing*, describes how to set up routing so that systems on your network can communicate properly with other networks. It covers the static routing table, commonly used routing protocols, and gated, a package that provides the latest implementations of several routing protocols.

Chapter 8, *Configuring DNS Name Service*, describes how to administer the name server program that converts system names to Internet addresses.

Chapter 9, *Configuring Network Servers*, describes how to configure the most common network servers. The chapter discusses the BOOTP and DHCP configuration servers, the LPD print server, the POP and IMAP mail servers, the Network Filesystem (NFS), and the Network Information System (NIS).

Chapter 10, *sendmail*, discusses how to configure sendmail, which is the daemon responsible for delivering electronic mail.

Chapter 11, *Troubleshooting TCP/IP*, tells you what to do when something goes wrong. It describes the techniques and tools used to troubleshoot TCP/IP problems, and gives examples of actual problems and their solutions.

Chapter 12, *Network Security*, discusses how to live on the Internet without excessive risk. This chapter covers the security threats brought by the network, and the plans and preparations you can make to meet those threats.

Chapter 13, *Internet Information Resources*, describes the information resources available on the Internet and how you can make use of them. It also describes how to set up an information server of your own.

Appendix A, *PPP Tools*, is a reference guide to the various programs used to configure a serial port for TCP/IP. The reference covers **dip**, **pppd**, and **chat**.

Appendix B, *A gated Reference*, is a complete reference guide to the configuration language of the **gated** routing package.

Appendix C, *A named Reference*, is a reference guide to the Berkeley Internet Name Domain (BIND) name server software.

Appendix D, *A dhcpd Reference*, is a reference guide to the Dynamic Host Configuration Protocol Daemon (**dhcpd**).

Appendix E, *A sendmail Reference*, is a detailed reference to sendmail syntax, options and flags. It also contains sections of the *sendmail.cf* configuration file developed in the step-by-step examples in Chapter 10.

Appendix F, *Selected TCP/IP Headers*, contains detailed protocol references, taken directly from the RFCs, that support the protocol troubleshooting examples in Chapter 11.

UNIX Versions

Most of the examples in this book are taken from Linux 2.0.0, which is a freely available UNIX-like operating system, and from Solaris 2.5.1, which is the Sun operating system based on System V UNIX. Fortunately, TCP/IP software is remarkably standard from system to system. Because the TCP/IP software is so uniform, the examples should be applicable to any Linux, System V, or BSD-based UNIX system. There are small variations in command output or command-line options, but these variations should not present a problem.

Some of the ancillary networking software is identified separately from the UNIX operating system by its own release number. Many such packages are discussed, and when appropriate are identified by their release numbers. The most important of these packages are:

BIND

Our discussion of the BIND software is based on version 4.9.5 running on a Slackware 96 Linux system. This version of BIND supports all of the standard resource records and there are relatively few differences between it and the current releases of BIND provided by computer vendors.

sendmail

Our discussion of sendmail is based on release 8.8.5. This version should be compatible with other releases of sendmail v8. However, sendmail has been changing rapidly in recent years.

Conventions

This book uses the following typographical conventions:

Italic

> is used for the names of files, directories, hostnames, domain names, and to emphasize new terms when they are first introduced.

Bold

> is used for command names.

`Constant width`

> is used to show the contents of files or the output from commands. Keywords are also in `constant width`.

`Constant bold`

> is used in examples to show commands or text that you would type.

`Constant italic`

> is used in examples and text to show variables for which a context-specific substitution should be made. (The variable *`filename`*, for example, would be replaced by some actual filename.)

%, #

> When we demonstrate commands that you would give interactively, we normally use the default C shell prompt (%). If the command must be executed as root, then we use the default superuser prompt (#). Because the examples may include multiple systems on a network, the prompt may be preceded by the name of the system on which the command was given.

[*option*]

> When showing command syntax, we place optional parts of the command within brackets. For example, **ls** [-l] means that the -l option is not required.

We'd Like to Hear from You

We have tested and verified all of the information in this book to the best of our ability, but you may find that features have changed (or even that we have made mistakes!). Please let us know about any errors you find, as well as your suggestions for future editions, by writing:

> O'Reilly & Associates, Inc.
> 101 Morris Street
> Sebastopol, CA 95472
> 1-800-998-9938 (in the U.S. or Canada)

        1-707-829-0515 (international/local)
        1-707-829-0104 (FAX)

You can also send us messages electronically. To be put on our mailing list or to request a catalog, send email to:

        info@ora.com   (via the Internet)

To ask technical questions or comment on the book, send email to:

        bookquestions@ora.com (via the Internet)

Acknowledgments

I would like to thank the many people who helped in the preparation of this book. All of the people who contributed to the first edition—John Wack, Matt Bishop, Wietse Venema, Eric Allman, Jeff Honig, Scott Brim, and John Dorgan—deserve thanks because so much of their input lives on in this edition.

The second edition has benefited from many contributors. Bryan Costales and Eric Allman did their best to set me straight about sendmail V8. Cricket Liu and Paul Albitz provided many comments that improved the sections on Domain Name Service. Ted Lemon provided insights about the technical details of DHCP and **dhcpd**. Elizabeth Zwicky's and Brent Chapman's insights on security were very helpful. Simson Garfinkel also commented on the security chapter. (You can't be too careful about security!) Jeff Sedayao reviewed the entire book and provided improvements for almost every chapter. And finally Æleen Frisch showed me the gaps that needed to be filled in. All of these people helped me make this book better than the first edition. Thanks!

All the people at O'Reilly & Associates have been very helpful. Mike Loukides, my editor, deserves a special thanks. Mike keeps me pointed in the right direction when my enthusiasm fades. Gigi Estabrook handled the very hectic job of editing the second edition. Nicole Gipson Arigo was the production editor and project manager. Nancy Wolfe Kotary and Jane Ellin performed quality control checks. Elissa Haney provided production assistance. Bruce Tracy wrote the index. Edie Freedman designed the cover, and Nancy Priest designed the interior format of the book. Lenny Muellner implemented the format in troff. Chris Reilley's handiwork from the first edition has been updated by Robert Romano, who created the illustrations for this edition.

Finally, I want to thank my family—Kathy, Sara, David, and Rebecca. They keep my feet on the ground when the pressure to meet deadlines is driving me into orbit. They are the best.

1

Overview of TCP/IP

All of us who use a UNIX desktop system—engineers, educators, scientists, and business people—have second careers as UNIX system administrators. Networking these computers gives us new tasks as network administrators.

Network administration and system administration are two different jobs. System administration tasks such as adding users and doing backups are isolated to one independent computer system. Not so with network administration. Once you place your computer on a network, it interacts with many other systems. The way you do network administration tasks has effects, good and bad, not only on your system but on other systems on the network. A sound understanding of basic network administration benefits everyone.

Networking computers dramatically enhances their ability to communicate—and most computers are used more for communication than computation. Many mainframes and supercomputers are busy crunching the numbers for business and science, but the number of such systems pales in comparison to the millions of systems busy moving mail to a remote colleague or retrieving information from a remote repository. Further, when you think of the hundreds of millions of desktop systems that are used primarily for preparing documents to communicate ideas from one person to another, it is easy to see why most computers can be viewed as communications devices.

The positive impact of computer communications increases with the number and type of computers that participate in the network. One of the great benefits of TCP/IP is that it provides interoperable communications between all types of hardware and all kinds of operating systems.

This book is a practical, step-by-step guide to configuring and managing TCP/IP networking software on UNIX computer systems. TCP/IP is the software package that dominates UNIX data communications. It is the leading communications software for UNIX local area networks and enterprise intranets, and for the foundation of the worldwide Internet.

The name "TCP/IP" refers to an entire suite of data communications protocols. The suite gets its name from two of the protocols that belong to it: the Transmission Control Protocol and the Internet Protocol. Although there are many other protocols in the suite, TCP and IP are certainly two of the most important.

The first part of this book discusses the basics of TCP/IP and how it moves data across a network. The second part explains how to configure and run TCP/IP on a UNIX system. Let's start with a little history.

TCP/IP and the Internet

In 1969 the Advanced Research Projects Agency (ARPA) funded a research and development project to create an experimental packet-switching network. This network, called the *ARPANET*, was built to study techniques for providing robust, reliable, vendor-independent data communications. Many techniques of modern data communications were developed in the ARPANET.

The experimental ARPANET was so successful that many of the organizations attached to it began to use it for daily data communications. In 1975 the ARPANET was converted from an experimental network to an operational network, and the responsibility for administering the network was given to the Defense Communications Agency (DCA).* However, development of the ARPANET did not stop just because it was being used as an operational network; the basic TCP/IP protocols were developed after the ARPANET was operational.

The TCP/IP protocols were adopted as Military Standards (MIL STD) in 1983, and all hosts connected to the network were required to convert to the new protocols. To ease this conversion, DARPA† funded Bolt, Beranek, and Newman (BBN) to implement TCP/IP in Berkeley (BSD) UNIX. Thus began the marriage of UNIX and TCP/IP.

About the time that TCP/IP was adopted as a standard, the term *Internet* came into common usage. In 1983, the old ARPANET was divided into MILNET, the

---

* DCA has since changed its name to Defense Information Systems Agency (DISA).

† During the 1980s and early 1990s, ARPA, which is part of the U.S. Department of Defense, was named Defense Advanced Research Projects Agency (DARPA). Currently known as ARPA, the agency is again preparing to change its name to DARPA. Whether it is known as ARPA or DARPA, the agency and its mission of funding advanced research has remained the same.

unclassified part of the Defense Data Network (DDN), and a new, smaller ARPANET. "Internet" was used to refer to the entire network: MILNET plus ARPANET.

In 1985 the National Science Foundation (NSF) created NSFNet and connected it to the then-existing Internet. The original NSFNet linked together the five NSF super-computer centers. It was smaller than the ARPANET and no faster—56Kbps. Nonetheless, the creation of the NSFNet was a significant event in the history of the Internet because NSF brought with it a new vision of the use of the Internet. NSF wanted to extend the network to every scientist and engineer in the United States. To accomplish this, in 1987 NSF created a new, faster backbone and a three-tiered network topology that included the backbone, regional networks, and local networks.

In 1990, the ARPANET formally passed out of existence, and the NSFNet ceased its role as a primary Internet backbone network in 1995. Still, today the Internet is larger than ever and encompasses more than 95,000 networks worldwide. This network of networks is linked together in the United States at several major inter-connection points:

- The three Network Access Points (NAPs) created by the NSF to ensure contin-ued broad-based access to the Internet.

- The Federal Information Exchanges (FIXs) interconnect U.S. government net-works.

- The Commercial Information Exchange (CIX) was the first interconnect specifi-cally for commercial Internet Service Providers (ISPs).

- The Metropolitan Area Exchanges (MAEs) were also created to interconnect commercial ISPs.

The Internet has grown far beyond its original scope. The original networks and agencies that built the Internet no longer play an essential role for the current net-work. The Internet has evolved from a simple backbone network, through a three-tiered hierarchical structure, to a huge network of interconnected, distributed net-work hubs. It has grown exponentially since 1983—doubling in size every year. Through all of this incredible change one thing has remained constant: the Inter-net is built on the TCP/IP protocol suite.

A sign of the network's success is the confusion that surrounds the term *internet*. Originally it was used only as the name of the network built upon the Internet Protocol. Now *internet* is a generic term used to refer to an entire class of net-works. An internet (lowercase "i") is any collection of separate physical networks, interconnected by a common protocol, to form a single logical network. The Inter-net (uppercase "I") is the worldwide collection of interconnected networks, which grew out of the original ARPANET, that uses *Internet Protocol* (IP) to link the various physical networks into a single logical network. In this book, both "internet" and "Internet" refer to networks that are interconnected by TCP/IP.

Because TCP/IP is required for Internet connection, the growth of the Internet has spurred interest in TCP/IP. As more organizations become familiar with TCP/IP, they see that its power can be applied in other network applications. The Internet protocols are often used for local area networking, even when the local network is not connected to the Internet. TCP/IP is also widely used to build enterprise networks. TCP/IP-based enterprise networks that use Internet techniques and World Wide Web tools to disseminate internal corporate information are called *intranets*. TCP/IP is the foundation of all of these varied networks.

TCP/IP Features

The popularity of the TCP/IP protocols did not grow rapidly just because the protocols were there, or because connecting to the Internet mandated their use. They met an important need (worldwide data communication) at the right time, and they had several important features that allowed them to meet this need. These features are:

- Open protocol standards, freely available and developed independently from any specific computer hardware or operating system. Because it is so widely supported, TCP/IP is ideal for uniting different hardware and software, even if you don't communicate over the Internet.

- Independence from specific physical network hardware. This allows TCP/IP to integrate many different kinds of networks. TCP/IP can be run over an Ethernet, a token ring, a dial-up line, an FDDI net, and virtually any other kind of physical transmission medium.

- A common addressing scheme that allows any TCP/IP device to uniquely address any other device in the entire network, even if the network is as large as the worldwide Internet.

- Standardized high-level protocols for consistent, widely available user services.

Protocol Standards

Protocols are formal rules of behavior. In international relations, protocols minimize the problems caused by cultural differences when various nations work together. By agreeing to a common set of rules that are widely known and independent of any nation's customs, diplomatic protocols minimize misunderstandings; everyone knows how to act and how to interpret the actions of others. Similarly, when computers communicate, it is necessary to define a set of rules to govern their communications.

In data communications these sets of rules are also called *protocols*. In homogeneous networks, a single computer vendor specifies a set of communications rules designed to use the strengths of the vendor's operating system and hardware architecture. But homogeneous networks are like the culture of a single country—only the natives are truly at home in it. TCP/IP attempts to create a heterogeneous network with open protocols that are independent of operating system and architectural differences. TCP/IP protocols are available to everyone, and are developed and changed by consensus—not by the fiat of one manufacturer. Everyone is free to develop products to meet these open protocol specifications.

The open nature of TCP/IP protocols requires publicly available standards documents. All protocols in the TCP/IP protocol suite are defined in one of three Internet standards publications. A number of the protocols have been adopted as *Military Standards* (MIL STD). Others were published as *Internet Engineering Notes* (IEN)—though the IEN form of publication has now been abandoned. But most information about TCP/IP protocols is published as *Requests for Comments* (RFCs). RFCs contain the latest versions of the specifications of all standard TCP/IP protocols.* As the title "Request for Comments" implies, the style and content of these documents is much less rigid than most standards documents. RFCs contain a wide range of interesting and useful information, and are not limited to the formal specification of data communications protocols.

As a network system administrator, you will no doubt read many of the RFCs yourself. Some contain practical advice and guidance that is simple to understand. Other RFCs contain protocol implementation specifications defined in terminology that is unique to data communications.

A Data Communications Model

To discuss computer networking, it is necessary to use terms that have special meaning. Even other computer professionals may not be familiar with all the terms in the networking alphabet soup. As is always the case, English and computer-speak are not equivalent (or even necessarily compatible) languages. Although descriptions and examples should make the meaning of the networking jargon more apparent, sometimes terms are ambiguous. A common frame of reference is necessary for understanding data communications terminology.

An architectural model developed by the International Standards Organization (ISO) is frequently used to describe the structure and function of data communications protocols. This architectural model, which is called the *Open Systems Interconnect Reference Model* (OSI), provides a common reference for discussing

---

* Interested in finding out how Internet standards are created? Read *The Internet Standards Process*, RFC 1310.

communications. The terms defined by this model are well understood and widely used in the data communications community—so widely used, in fact, that it is difficult to discuss data communications without using OSI's terminology.

The OSI Reference Model contains seven *layers* that define the functions of data communications protocols. Each layer of the OSI model represents a function performed when data is transferred between cooperating applications across an intervening network. Figure 1-1 identifies each layer by name and provides a short functional description for it. Looking at this figure, the protocols are like a pile of building blocks stacked one upon another. Because of this appearance, the structure is often called a *stack* or *protocol stack*.

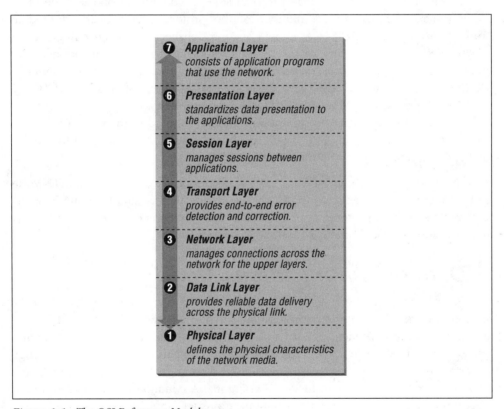

Figure 1-1: The OSI Reference Model

A layer does not define a single protocol—it defines a data communications function that may be performed by any number of protocols. Therefore, each layer may contain multiple protocols, each providing a service suitable to the function of that layer. For example, a file transfer protocol and an electronic mail protocol both provide user services, and both are part of the Application Layer.

Every protocol communicates with its peer. A *peer* is an implementation of the same protocol in the equivalent layer on a remote system; i.e., the local file transfer protocol is the peer of a remote file transfer protocol. Peer-level communications must be standardized for successful communications to take place. In the abstract, each protocol is concerned only with communicating to its peer; it does not care about the layer above or below it.

However, there must also be agreement on how to pass data between the layers on a single computer, because every layer is involved in sending data from a local application to an equivalent remote application. The upper layers rely on the lower layers to transfer the data over the underlying network. Data is passed down the stack from one layer to the next, until it is transmitted over the network by the Physical Layer protocols. At the remote end, the data is passed up the stack to the receiving application. The individual layers do not need to know how the layers above and below them function; they only need to know how to pass data to them. Isolating network communications functions in different layers minimizes the impact of technological change on the entire protocol suite. New applications can be added without changing the physical network, and new network hardware can be installed without rewriting the application software.

Although the OSI model is useful, the TCP/IP protocols don't match its structure exactly. Therefore, in our discussions of TCP/IP, we use the layers of the OSI model in the following way:

Application Layer

> The Application Layer is the level of the protocol hierarchy where user-accessed network processes reside. In this text, a TCP/IP application is any network process that occurs above the Transport Layer. This includes all of the processes that users directly interact with, as well as other processes at this level that users are not necessarily aware of.

Presentation Layer

> For cooperating applications to exchange data, they must agree about how data is represented. In OSI, this layer provides standard data presentation routines. This function is frequently handled within the applications in TCP/IP, though increasingly TCP/IP protocols such as XDR and MIME perform this function.

Session Layer

> As with the Presentation Layer, the Session Layer is not identifiable as a separate layer in the TCP/IP protocol hierarchy. The OSI Session Layer manages the sessions (connection) between cooperating applications. In TCP/IP, this function largely occurs in the Transport Layer, and the term "session" is not used. For TCP/IP, the terms "socket" and "port" are used to describe the path over which cooperating applications communicate.

Transport Layer

Much of our discussion of TCP/IP is directed to the protocols that occur in the Transport Layer. The Transport Layer in the OSI reference model guarantees that the receiver gets the data exactly as it was sent. In TCP/IP this function is performed by the *Transmission Control Protocol* (TCP). However, TCP/IP offers a second Transport Layer service, *User Datagram Protocol* (UDP), that does not perform the end-to-end reliability checks.

Network Layer

The Network Layer manages connections across the network and isolates the upper layer protocols from the details of the underlying network. The Internet Protocol (IP), which isolates the upper layers from the underlying network and handles the addressing and delivery of data, is usually described as TCP/IP's Network Layer.

Data Link Layer

The reliable delivery of data across the underlying physical network is handled by the Data Link Layer. TCP/IP rarely creates protocols in the Data Link Layer. Most RFCs that relate to the Data Link Layer discuss how IP can make use of existing data link protocols.

Physical Layer

The Physical Layer defines the characteristics of the hardware needed to carry the data transmission signal. Features such as voltage levels, and the number and location of interface pins, are defined in this layer. Examples of standards at the Physical Layer are interface connectors such as RS232C and V.35, and standards for local area network wiring such as IEEE 802.3. TCP/IP does not define physical standards—it makes use of existing standards.

The terminology of the OSI reference model helps us describe TCP/IP, but to fully understand it, we must use an architectural model that more closely matches the structure of TCP/IP. The next section introduces the protocol model we'll use to describe TCP/IP.

TCP/IP Protocol Architecture

While there is no universal agreement about how to describe TCP/IP with a layered model, it is generally viewed as being composed of fewer layers than the seven used in the OSI model. Most descriptions of TCP/IP define three to five functional levels in the protocol architecture. The four-level model illustrated in Figure 1-2 is based on the three layers (Application, Host-to-Host, and Network Access) shown in the DOD Protocol Model in the *DDN Protocol Handbook—Volume 1*, with the addition of a separate Internet layer. This model provides a reasonable pictorial representation of the layers in the TCP/IP protocol hierarchy.

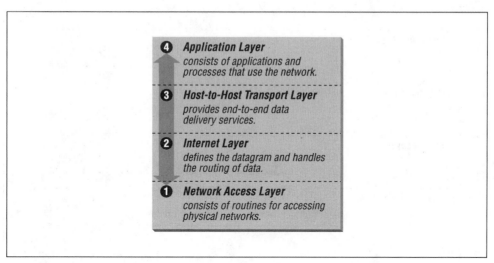

Figure 1-2: Layers in the TCP/IP protocol architecture

As in the OSI model, data is passed down the stack when it is being sent to the network, and up the stack when it is being received from the network. The four-layered structure of TCP/IP is seen in the way data is handled as it passes down the protocol stack from the Application Layer to the underlying physical network. Each layer in the stack adds control information to ensure proper delivery. This control information is called a *header* because it is placed in front of the data to be transmitted. Each layer treats all of the information it receives from the layer above as data and places its own header in front of that information. The addition of delivery information at every layer is called *encapsulation*. (See Figure 1-3 for an illustration of this.) When data is received, the opposite happens. Each layer strips off its header before passing the data on to the layer above. As information flows back up the stack, information received from a lower layer is interpreted as both a header and data.

Each layer has its own independent data structures. Conceptually, a layer is unaware of the data structures used by the layers above and below it. In reality, the data structures of a layer are designed to be compatible with the structures used by the surrounding layers for the sake of more efficient data transmission. Still, each layer has its own data structure and its own terminology to describe that structure.

Figure 1-4 shows the terms used by different layers of TCP/IP to refer to the data being transmitted. Applications using TCP refer to data as a *stream*, while applications using the User Datagram Protocol (UDP) refer to data as a *message*. TCP calls data a *segment*, and UDP calls its data structure a *packet*. The Internet layer views all data as blocks called *datagrams*. TCP/IP uses many different types of

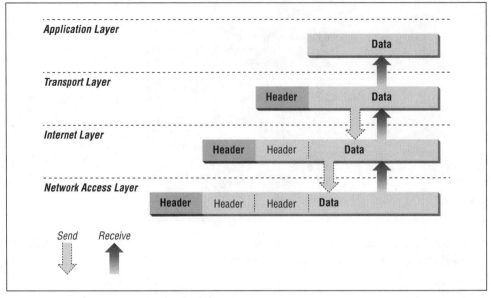

Figure 1-3: Data encapsulation

·underlying networks, each of which may have a different terminology for the data it transmits. Most networks refer to transmitted data as *packets* or *frames*. In Figure 1-4 we show a network that transmits pieces of data it calls *frames*.

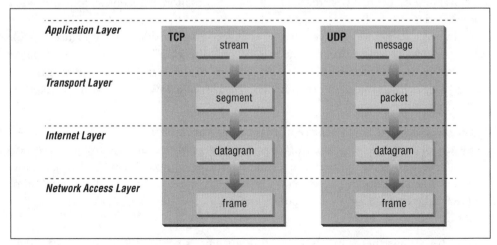

Figure 1-4: Data structures

Let's look more closely at the function of each layer, working our way up from the Network Access Layer to the Application Layer.

Network Access Layer

The *Network Access Layer* is the lowest layer of the TCP/IP protocol hierarchy. The protocols in this layer provide the means for the system to deliver data to the other devices on a directly attached network. It defines how to use the network to transmit an IP datagram. Unlike higher-level protocols, Network Access Layer protocols must know the details of the underlying network (its packet structure, addressing, etc.) to correctly format the data being transmitted to comply with the network constraints. The TCP/IP Network Access Layer can encompass the functions of all three lower layers of the OSI reference Model (Network, Data Link, and Physical).

The Network Access Layer is often ignored by users. The design of TCP/IP hides the function of the lower layers, and the better known protocols (IP, TCP, UDP, etc.) are all higher-level protocols. As new hardware technologies appear, new Network Access protocols must be developed so that TCP/IP networks can use the new hardware. Consequently, there are many access protocols—one for each physical network standard.

Functions performed at this level include encapsulation of IP datagrams into the frames transmitted by the network, and mapping of IP addresses to the physical addresses used by the network. One of TCP/IP's strengths is its universal addressing scheme. The IP address must be converted into an address that is appropriate for the physical network over which the datagram is transmitted.

Two examples of RFCs that define network access layer protocols are:

- RFC 826, *Address Resolution Protocol (ARP)*, which maps IP addresses to Ethernet addresses

- RFC 894, *A Standard for the Transmission of IP Datagrams over Ethernet Networks*, which specifies how IP datagrams are encapsulated for transmission over Ethernet networks

As implemented in UNIX, protocols in this layer often appear as a combination of device drivers and related programs. The modules that are identified with network device names usually encapsulate and deliver the data to the network, while separate programs perform related functions such as address mapping.

Internet Layer

The layer above the Network Access Layer in the protocol hierarchy is the *Internet Layer*. The Internet Protocol, RFC 791, is the heart of TCP/IP and the most important protocol in the Internet Layer. IP provides the basic packet delivery service on which TCP/IP networks are built. All protocols, in the layers above and below IP, use the Internet Protocol to deliver data. All TCP/IP data flows through IP, incoming and outgoing, regardless of its final destination.

Internet Protocol

The Internet Protocol is the building block of the Internet. Its functions include:

- Defining the datagram, which is the basic unit of transmission in the Internet
- Defining the Internet addressing scheme
- Moving data between the Network Access Layer and the Host-to-Host Transport Layer
- Routing datagrams to remote hosts
- Performing fragmentation and re-assembly of datagrams

Before describing these functions in more detail, let's look at some of IP's characteristics. First, IP is a *connectionless protocol.* This means that IP does not exchange control information (called a "handshake") to establish an end-to-end connection before transmitting data. In contrast, a *connection-oriented protocol* exchanges control information with the remote system to verify that it is ready to receive data before any data is sent. When the handshaking is successful, the systems are said to have established a *connection.* Internet Protocol relies on protocols in other layers to establish the connection if they require connection-oriented service.

IP also relies on protocols in the other layers to provide error detection and error recovery. The Internet Protocol is sometimes called an *unreliable protocol* because it contains no error detection and recovery code. This is not to say that the protocol cannot be relied on—quite the contrary. IP can be relied upon to accurately deliver your data to the connected network, but it doesn't check whether that data was correctly received. Protocols in other layers of the TCP/IP architecture provide this checking when it is required.

The datagram

The TCP/IP protocols were built to transmit data over the ARPANET, which was a *packet switching network.* A *packet* is a block of data that carries with it the information necessary to deliver it—in a manner similar to a postal letter, which has an address written on its envelope. A packet switching network uses the addressing information in the packets to switch packets from one physical network to another, moving them toward their final destination. Each packet travels the network independently of any other packet.

The *datagram* is the packet format defined by Internet Protocol. Figure 1-5 is a pictorial representation of an IP datagram. The first five or six 32-bit words of the datagram are control information called the *header*. By default, the header is five words long; the sixth word is optional. Because the header's length is variable, it includes a field called *Internet Header Length (IHL)* that indicates the header's length in words. The header contains all the information necessary to deliver the packet.

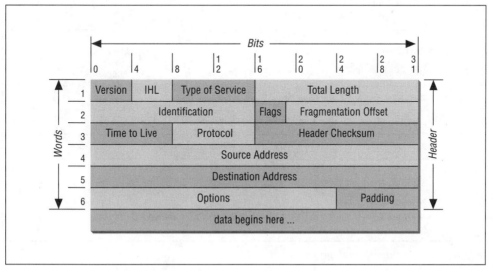

Figure 1-5: IP datagram format

The Internet Protocol delivers the datagram by checking the *Destination Address* in word 5 of the header. The Destination Address is a standard 32-bit IP address that identifies the destination network and the specific host on that network. (The format of IP addresses is explained in Chapter 2, *Delivering the Data*.) If the Destination Address is the address of a host on the local network, the packet is delivered directly to the destination. If the Destination Address is not on the local network, the packet is passed to a gateway for delivery. *Gateways* are devices that switch packets between the different physical networks. Deciding which gateway to use is called *routing*. IP makes the routing decision for each individual packet.

Routing datagrams

Internet gateways are commonly (and perhaps more accurately) referred to as *IP routers* because they use Internet Protocol to route packets between networks. In traditional TCP/IP jargon, there are only two types of network devices—*gateways* and *hosts*. Gateways forward packets between networks, and hosts don't. However, if a host is connected to more than one network (called a *multi-homed host*), it can forward packets between the networks. When a multi-homed host forwards packets, it acts just like any other gateway and is considered to be a gateway.

Current data communications terminology makes a distinction between gateways and routers,* but we'll use the terms *gateway* and *IP router* interchangeably.

Figure 1-6 shows the use of gateways to forward packets. The hosts (or *end systems*) process packets through all four protocol layers, while the gateways (or *intermediate systems*) process the packets only up to the Internet Layer where the routing decisions are made.

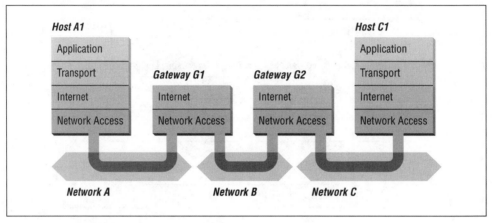

Figure 1-6: Routing through gateways

Systems can only deliver packets to other devices attached to the same physical network. Packets from *A1* destined for host *C1* are forwarded through gateways *G1* and *G2*. Host *A1* first delivers the packet to gateway *G1*, with which it shares network *A*. Gateway *G1* delivers the packet to *G2* over network *B*. Gateway *G2* then delivers the packet directly to host *C1*, because they are both attached to network *C*. Host *A1* has no knowledge of any gateways beyond gateway *G1*. It sends packets destined for both networks *C* and *B* to that local gateway, and then relies on that gateway to properly forward the packets along the path to their destinations. Likewise, host *C1* would send its packets to *G2*, in order to reach a host on network *A*, as well as any host on network *B*.

Figure 1-7 shows another view of routing. This figure emphasizes that the underlying physical networks that a datagram travels through may be different and even incompatible. Host *A1* on the token ring network routes the datagram through gateway *G1*, to reach host *C1* on the Ethernet. Gateway *G1* forwards the data through the X.25 network to gateway *G2*, for delivery to *C1*. The datagram traverses three physically different networks, but eventually arrives intact at *C1*.

---

* In current terminology, a gateway moves data between different protocols and a router moves data between different networks. So a system that moves mail between TCP/IP and OSI is a gateway, but a traditional IP gateway is a router.

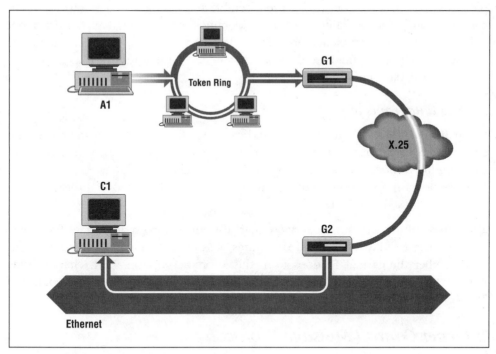

Figure 1-7: Networks, gateways, and hosts

Fragmenting datagrams

As a datagram is routed through different networks, it may be necessary for the IP module in a gateway to divide the datagram into smaller pieces. A datagram received from one network may be too large to be transmitted in a single packet on a different network. This condition occurs only when a gateway interconnects dissimilar physical networks.

Each type of network has a *maximum transmission unit* (MTU), which is the largest packet that it can transfer. If the datagram received from one network is longer than the other network's MTU, it is necessary to divide the datagram into smaller *fragments* for transmission. This process is called *fragmentation*. Think of a train delivering a load of steel. Each railway car can carry more steel than the trucks that will take it along the highway; so each railway car is unloaded onto many different trucks. In the same way that a railroad is physically different from a highway, an Ethernet is physically different from an X.25 network; IP must break an Ethernet's relatively large packets into smaller packets before it can transmit them over an X.25 network.

The format of each fragment is the same as the format of any normal datagram. Header word 2 contains information that identifies each datagram fragment and provides information about how to re-assemble the fragments back into the original datagram. The Identification field identifies what datagram the fragment belongs to, and the Fragmentation Offset field tells what piece of the datagram this fragment is. The Flags field has a "More Fragments" bit that tells IP if it has assembled all of the datagram fragments.

Passing datagrams to the transport layer

When IP receives a datagram that is addressed to the local host, it must pass the data portion of the datagram to the correct Transport Layer protocol. This is done by using the *protocol number* from word 3 of the datagram header. Each Transport Layer protocol has a unique protocol number that identifies it to IP. Protocol numbers are discussed in Chapter 2.

You can see from this short overview that IP performs many important functions. Don't expect to fully understand datagrams, gateways, routing, IP addresses, and all the other things that IP does from this short description. Each chapter adds more details about these topics. So let's continue on with the other protocol in the TCP/IP Internet Layer.

Internet Control Message Protocol

An integral part of IP is the *Internet Control Message Protocol* (ICMP) defined in RFC 792. This protocol is part of the Internet Layer and uses the IP datagram delivery facility to send its messages. ICMP sends messages that perform the following control, error reporting, and informational functions for TCP/IP:

Flow control
> When datagrams arrive too fast for processing, the destination host or an intermediate gateway sends an ICMP Source Quench Message back to the sender. This tells the source to stop sending datagrams temporarily.

Detecting unreachable destinations
> When a destination is unreachable, the system detecting the problem sends a Destination Unreachable Message to the datagram's source. If the unreachable destination is a network or host, the message is sent by an intermediate gateway. But if the destination is an unreachable port, the destination host sends the message. (We discuss ports in Chapter 2.)

Redirecting routes
> A gateway sends the ICMP Redirect Message to tell a host to use another gateway, presumably because the other gateway is a better choice. This message can be used only when the source host is on the same network as both gateways. To better understand this, refer to Figure 1-7. If a host on the X.25 network sent a datagram to *G1*, it would be possible for *G1* to redirect that host

to *G2* because the host, *G1*, and *G2* are all attached to the same network. On the other hand, if a host on the token ring network sent a datagram to *G1*, the host could not be redirected to use *G2*. This is because *G2* is not attached to the token ring.

Checking remote hosts

A host can send the ICMP Echo Message to see if a remote system's Internet Protocol is up and operational. When a system receives an echo message, it replies and sends the data from the packet back to the source host. The **ping** command uses this message.

Transport Layer

The protocol layer just above the Internet Layer is the *Host-to-Host Transport Layer*. This name is usually shortened to *Transport Layer*. The two most important protocols in the Transport Layer are *Transmission Control Protocol* (TCP) and *User Datagram Protocol* (UDP). TCP provides reliable data delivery service with end-to-end error detection and correction. UDP provides low-overhead, connectionless datagram delivery service. Both protocols deliver data between the Application Layer and the Internet Layer. Applications programmers can choose whichever service is more appropriate for their specific applications.

User Datagram Protocol

The User Datagram Protocol gives application programs direct access to a datagram delivery service, like the delivery service that IP provides. This allows applications to exchange messages over the network with a minimum of protocol overhead.

UDP is an unreliable, connectionless datagram protocol. As noted previously, "unreliable" merely means that there are no techniques in the protocol for verifying that the data reached the other end of the network correctly. Within your computer, UDP will deliver data correctly. UDP uses 16-bit *Source Port* and *Destination Port* numbers in word 1 of the message header, to deliver data to the correct applications process. Figure 1-8 shows the UDP message format.

Why do applications programmers choose UDP as a data transport service? There are a number of good reasons. If the amount of data being transmitted is small, the overhead of creating connections and ensuring reliable delivery may be greater than the work of re-transmitting the entire data set. In this case, UDP is the most efficient choice for a Transport Layer protocol. Applications that fit a *query-response* model are also excellent candidates for using UDP. The response can be used as a positive acknowledgment to the query. If a response isn't received within a certain time period, the application just sends another query. Still other

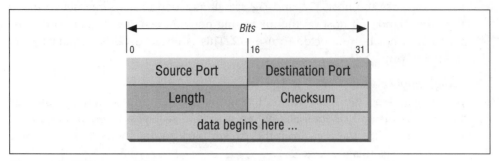

Figure 1-8: UDP message format

applications provide their own techniques for reliable data delivery, and don't require that service from the transport layer protocol. Imposing another layer of acknowledgment on any of these types of applications is inefficient.

Transmission Control Protocol

Applications that require the transport protocol to provide reliable data delivery use TCP because it verifies that data is delivered across the network accurately and in the proper sequence. TCP is a *reliable, connection-oriented, byte-stream* protocol. Let's look at each of the terms—reliable, connection-oriented, and byte-stream—in more detail.

TCP provides reliability with a mechanism called *Positive Acknowledgment with Re-transmission* (PAR). Simply stated, a system using PAR sends the data again, unless it hears from the remote system that the data arrived okay. The unit of data exchanged between cooperating TCP modules is called a *segment* (see Figure 1-9). Each segment contains a checksum that the recipient uses to verify that the data is undamaged. If the data segment is received undamaged, the receiver sends a *positive acknowledgment* back to the sender. If the data segment is damaged, the receiver discards it. After an appropriate time-out period, the sending TCP module re-transmits any segment for which no positive acknowledgment has been received.

TCP is connection-oriented. It establishes a logical end-to-end connection between the two communicating hosts. Control information, called a *handshake*, is exchanged between the two endpoints to establish a dialogue before data is transmitted. TCP indicates the control function of a segment by setting the appropriate bit in the Flags field in word 4 of the *segment header*.

The type of handshake used by TCP is called a *three-way handshake* because three segments are exchanged. Figure 1-10 shows the simplest form of the three-way handshake. Host *A* begins the connection by sending host *B* a segment with the "Synchronize sequence numbers" (SYN) bit set. This segment tells host *B* that

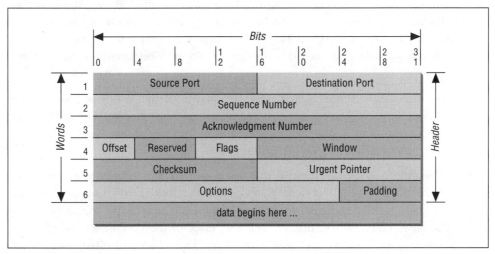

Figure 1-9: TCP segment format

A wishes to set up a connection, and it tells *B* what sequence number host *A* will use as a starting number for its segments. (Sequence numbers are used to keep data in the proper order.) Host *B* responds to *A* with a segment that has the "Acknowledgment" (ACK) and SYN bits set. *B*'s segment acknowledges the receipt of *A*'s segment, and informs *A* which Sequence Number host *B* will start with. Finally, host *A* sends a segment that acknowledges receipt of *B*'s segment, and transfers the first actual data.

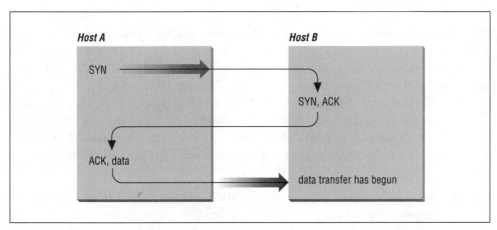

Figure 1-10: Three-way handshake

After this exchange, host *A*'s TCP has positive evidence that the remote TCP is alive and ready to receive data. As soon as the connection is established, data can be transferred. When the cooperating modules have concluded the data transfers, they will exchange a three-way handshake with segments containing the "No more data from sender" bit (called the *FIN* bit) to close the connection. It is the end-to-end exchange of data that provides the logical connection between the two systems.

TCP views the data it sends as a continuous stream of bytes, not as independent packets. Therefore, TCP takes care to maintain the sequence in which bytes are sent and received. The Sequence Number and Acknowledgment Number fields in the TCP segment header keep track of the bytes.

The TCP standard does not require that each system start numbering bytes with any specific number; each system chooses the number it will use as a starting point. To keep track of the data stream correctly, each end of the connection must know the other end's initial number. The two ends of the connection synchronize byte-numbering systems by exchanging SYN segments during the handshake. The Sequence Number field in the SYN segment contains the *Initial Sequence Number* (ISN), which is the starting point for the byte-numbering system. For security reasons the ISN should be a random number, though it is often 0.

Each byte of data is numbered sequentially from the ISN, so the first real byte of data sent has a sequence number of ISN+1. The Sequence Number in the header of a data segment identifies the sequential position in the data stream of the first data byte in the segment. For example, if the first byte in the data stream was sequence number 1 (ISN=0) and 4000 bytes of data have already been transferred, then the first byte of data in the current segment is byte 4001, and the Sequence Number would be 4001.

The Acknowledgment Segment (ACK) performs two functions: *positive acknowledgment* and *flow control*. The acknowledgment tells the sender how much data has been received, and how much more the receiver can accept. The Acknowledgment Number is the sequence number of the next byte the receiver expects to receive. The standard does not require an individual acknowledgment for every packet. The acknowledgment number is a positive acknowledgment of all bytes up to that number. For example, if the first byte sent was numbered 1 and 2000 bytes have been successfully received, the Acknowledgment Number would be 2001.

The Window field contains the *window*, or the number of bytes the remote end is able to accept. If the receiver is capable of accepting 6000 more bytes, the window would be 6000. The window indicates to the sender that it can continue sending segments as long as the total number of bytes that it sends is smaller than the window of bytes that the receiver can accept. The receiver controls the flow of bytes from the sender by changing the size of the window. A zero window tells the sender to cease transmission until it receives a non-zero window value.

Figure 1-11 shows a TCP data stream that starts with an Initial Sequence Number of 0. The receiving system has received and acknowledged 2000 bytes, so the current Acknowledgment Number is 2001. The receiver also has enough buffer space for another 6000 bytes, so it has advertised a window of 6000. The sender is currently sending a segment of 1000 bytes starting with Sequence Number 4001. The sender has received no acknowledgment for the bytes from 2001 on, but continues sending data as long as it is within the window. If the sender fills the window and receives no acknowledgment of the data previously sent, it will, after an appropriate time-out, send the data again starting from the first unacknowledged byte.

In Figure 1-11, re-transmission would start from byte 2001 if no further acknowledgments are received. This procedure ensures that data is reliably received at the far end of the network.

TCP is also responsible for delivering data received from IP to the correct application. The application that the data is bound for is identified by a 16-bit number called the *port number*. The *Source Port* and *Destination Port* are contained in the first word of the segment header. Correctly passing data to and from the Application Layer is an important part of what the Transport Layer services do.

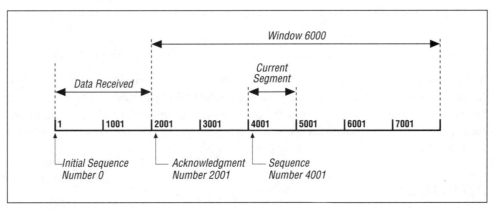

Figure 1-11: TCP data stream

Application Layer

At the top of the TCP/IP protocol architecture is the *Application Layer*. This layer includes all processes that use the Transport Layer protocols to deliver data. There are many applications protocols. Most provide user services, and new services are always being added to this layer.

The most widely known and implemented applications protocols are:

telnet
>   The Network Terminal Protocol, which provides remote login over the network.

FTP
>   The File Transfer Protocol, which is used for interactive file transfer.

SMTP
>   The Simple Mail Transfer Protocol, which delivers electronic mail.

HTTP
>   The Hypertext Transfer Protocol, which delivers Web pages over the network.

While HTTP, FTP, SMTP, and telnet are the most widely implemented TCP/IP applications, you will work with many others as both a user and a system administrator. Some other commonly used TCP/IP applications are:

Domain Name Service (DNS)
>   Also called *name service*, this application maps IP addresses to the names assigned to network devices. DNS is discussed in detail in this book.

Open Shortest Path First (OSPF)
>   Routing is central to the way TCP/IP works. OSPF is used by network devices to exchange routing information. Routing is also a major topic of this book.

Network Filesystem (NFS)
>   This protocol allows files to be shared by various hosts on the network.

Some protocols, such as telnet and FTP, can only be used if the user has some knowledge of the network. Other protocols, like OSPF, run without the user even knowing that they exist. As system administrator, you are aware of all these applications and all the protocols in the other TCP/IP layers. And you're responsible for configuring them!

Summary

In this chapter we discussed the structure of TCP/IP, the protocol suite upon which the Internet is built. We have seen that TCP/IP is a hierarchy of four layers: Applications, Host-to-Host Transport, Internet, and Network Access. We have examined the function of each of these layers. In the next chapter we look at how the IP packet, the datagram, moves through a network when data is delivered between hosts.

2

Delivering the Data

In Chapter 1, *Overview of TCP/IP*, we touched on the basic architecture and design of the TCP/IP protocols. From that discussion, we know that TCP/IP is a hierarchy of four layers. In this chapter, we explore in finer detail how data moves between the protocol layers and the systems on the network. We examine the structure of Internet addresses, including how addresses route data to its final destination, and how addressing rules are locally redefined to create subnets. We also look at the protocol and port numbers used to deliver data to the correct applications. These additional details move us from an overview of TCP/IP to the specific implementation details that affect your system's configuration.

Addressing, Routing, and Multiplexing

To deliver data between two Internet hosts, it is necessary to move the data across the network to the correct host, and within that host to the correct user or process. TCP/IP uses three schemes to accomplish these tasks:

Addressing
> IP addresses, which uniquely identify every host on the network, deliver data to the correct host.

Routing
> Gateways deliver data to the correct network.

Multiplexing
> Protocol and port numbers deliver data to the correct software module within the host.

Each of these functions—addressing between hosts, routing between networks, and multiplexing between layers—is necessary to send data between two cooperating applications across the Internet. Let's examine each of these functions in detail.

To illustrate these concepts and provide consistent examples, we use an imaginary corporate network. Our imaginary company sells packaged nuts to the Army. Our company network is made up of several networks at our packing plant and sales office, as well as a connection to the Internet. We are responsible for managing the Ethernet in the computing center. This network's structure, or *topology*, is shown in Figure 2-1.

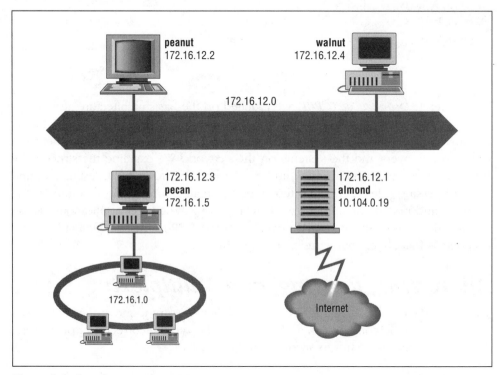

Figure 2-1: Sample network

The icons in the figure represent computer systems. There are, of course, several other imaginary systems on our imaginary network. You'll just have to use your imagination! But we'll use the hosts *peanut* (a workstation) and *almond* (a system that serves as a gateway) for most of our examples. The thick line is our computer center Ethernet and the circle is the local network that connects our various corporate networks. The cloud is the Internet. What the numbers are, how they're used, and how datagrams are delivered are the topics of this chapter.

The IP Address

The Internet Protocol moves data between hosts in the form of datagrams. Each datagram is delivered to the address contained in the Destination Address (word 5) of the datagram's header. The Destination Address is a standard 32-bit IP address that contains sufficient information to uniquely identify a network and a specific host on that network.

An IP address contains a *network part* and a *host part*, but the format of these parts is not the same in every IP address. The number of address bits used to identify the network, and the number used to identify the host, vary according to the prefix length of the address. There are two ways the prefix length is determined: by address class or by a CIDR address mask. We begin with a discussion of traditional IP address classes.

Address Classes

Originally, the IP address space was divided into a few fixed-length structures called *address classes*. The three main address classes are *class A*, *class B*, and *class C*. By examining the first few bits of an address, IP software can quickly determine the class, and therefore the structure, of an address. IP follows these rules to determine the address class:

- If the first bit of an IP address is 0, it is the address of a *class A network*. The first bit of a class A address identifies the address class. The next 7 bits identify the network, and the last 24 bits identify the host. There are fewer than 128 class A network numbers, but each class A network can be composed of millions of hosts.

- If the first 2 bits of the address are 1 0, it is a *class B network* address. The first 2 bits identify class; the next 14 bits identify the network, and the last 16 bits identify the host. There are thousands of class B network numbers and each class B network can contain thousands of hosts.

- If the first 3 bits of the address are 1 1 0, it is a *class C network* address. In a class C address, the first 3 bits are class identifiers; the next 21 bits are the network address, and the last 8 bits identify the host. There are millions of class C network numbers, but each class C network is composed of fewer than 254 hosts.

- If the first 4 bits of the address are 1 1 1 0, it is a multicast address. These addresses are sometimes called *class D* addresses, but they don't really refer to specific networks. Multicast addresses are used to address groups of computers all at one time. Multicast addresses identify a group of computers that share a common application, such as a video conference, as opposed to a group of computers that share a common network.

- If the first four bits of the address are 1 1 1 1, it is a special reserved address. These addresses are sometimes called *class E* addresses, but they don't really refer to specific networks. No numbers are currently assigned in this range.

Luckily, this is not as complicated as it sounds. IP addresses are usually written as four decimal numbers separated by dots (periods).* Each of the four numbers is in the range 0–255 (the decimal values possible for a single byte). Because the bits that identify class are contiguous with the network bits of the address, we can lump them together and look at the address as composed of full bytes of network address and full bytes of host address. If the value of the first byte is:

- Less than 128, the address is class A; the first byte is the network number, and the next three bytes are the host address.

- From 128 to 191, the address is class B; the first two bytes identify the network, and the last two bytes identify the host.

- From 192 to 223, the address is class C; the first three bytes are the network address, and the last byte is the host number.

- From 224 to 239, the address is multicast. There is no network part. The entire address identifies a specific multicast group.

- Greater than 239, the address is reserved. We can ignore reserved addresses.

Figure 2-2 illustrates how the address structure varies with address class. The class A address is 10.104.0.19. The first bit of this address is 0, so the address is interpreted as host 104.0.19 on network 10. One byte specifies the network and three bytes specify the host. In the address 172.16.12.1, the two high-order bits are 1 0 so the address refers to host 12.1 on network 172.16. Two bytes identify the network and two identify the host. Finally, in the class C example, 192.168.16.1, the three high-order bits are 1 1 0, so this is the address of host 1 on network 192.168.16—three network bytes and one host byte.

The IP address, which provides universal addressing across all of the networks of the Internet, is one of the great strengths of the TCP/IP protocol suite. However, the original class structure of the IP address has weaknesses. The TCP/IP designers did not envision the enormous scale of today's network. When TCP/IP was being designed, networking was limited to large organizations that could afford substantial computer systems. The idea of a powerful UNIX system on every desktop did not exist. At that time, a 32-bit address seemed so large that it was divided into

---

* Addresses are occasionally written in other formats, e.g., as hexadecimal numbers. However, the "dot" notation form is the most widely used. Whatever the notation, the structure of the address is the same.

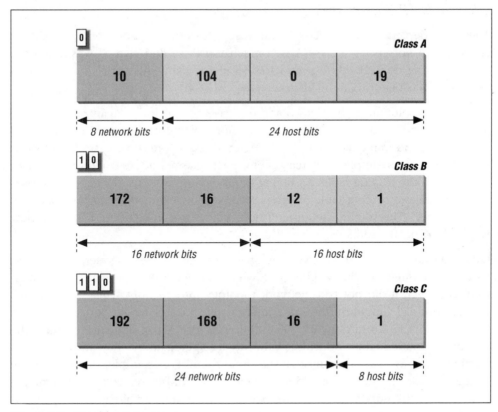

Figure 2-2: IP address structure

classes to reduce the processing load on routers, even though dividing the address into classes sharply reduced the number of host addresses actually available for use. For example, assigning a large network a single class B address, instead of six class C addresses, reduced the load on the router because the router needed to keep only one route for that entire organization. However, an organization that was given the class B address probably did not have 64,000 computers, so most of the host addresses available to the organization were never assigned.

The class-structured address design was critically strained by the rapid growth of the Internet. At one point it appeared that all class B addresses might be rapidly exhausted.* To prevent this, a new way of looking at IP addresses without a class structure was developed.

---

* The source for this prediction is the draft of *Supernetting: an Address Assignment and Aggregation Strategy*, by V. Fuller, T. Li, J. Yu, and K. Varadhan, March 1992.

Classless IP Addresses

The rapid depletion of the class B addresses showed that three primary address classes were not enough: class A was much too large and class C was much too small. Even a class B address was too large for many networks but was used because it was better than the alternatives.

The obvious solution to the class B address crisis was to force organizations to use multiple class C addresses. There were millions of these addresses available and they were in no immediate danger of depletion. As is often the case, the obvious solution is not as simple as it may seem. Each class C address requires its own entry within the routing table. Assigning thousands or millions of class C addresses would cause the routing table to grow so rapidly that the routers would soon be overwhelmed. The solution required a new way of assigning addresses and a new way of looking at addresses.

Originally network addresses were assigned in more or less sequential order as they were requested. This worked fine when the network was small and centralized. However, it did not take network topology into account. Thus only random chance would determine if the same intermediate routers would be used to reach network 195.4.12.0 and network 195.4.13.0, which makes it difficult to reduce the size of the routing table. Addresses can only be aggregated if they are contiguous numbers and are reachable through the same route. For example, if addresses are contiguous for one service provider, a single route can be created for that aggregation because that service provide will have a limited number of routes to the Internet. But if one network address is in France and the next contiguous address is in Australia, creating a consolidated route for these addresses does not work.

Today, large, contiguous blocks of addresses are assigned to large network service providers in a manner that better reflects the topology of the network. The service providers then allocate chunks of these address blocks to the organizations to which they provide network services. This alleviates the short-term shortage of class B addresses and, because the assignment of addressees reflects the topology of the network, it permits route aggregation. Under this new scheme, we know that network 195.4.12.0 and network 195.4.13.0 are reachable through the same intermediate routers. In fact, both of these addresses are in the range of the addresses assigned to Europe, 194.0.0.0 to 195.255.255.255. Assigning addresses that reflect the topology of the network enables route aggregation, but does not implement it. As long as network 195.4.12.0 and network 195.4.13.0 are interpreted as separate class C addresses, they will require separate entries in the routing table. A new, flexible way of defining addresses is needed.

Evaluating addresses according to the class rules discussed above limits the length of network numbers to 8, 16, or 24 bits—1, 2, or 3 bytes. The IP address,

however, is not really byte-oriented. It is 32 contiguous bits. A more flexible way
to interpret the network and host portions of an address is with a *bit mask*. An
address bit mask works in this way: if a bit is on in the mask, that equivalent bit in
the address is interpreted as a network bit; if a bit in the mask is off, the bit
belongs to the host part of the address. For example, if address 195.4.12.0 is interpreted as a class C address, the first 24 bits are the network number and the last 8
bits are the host address. The network mask that represents this is 255.255.255.0,
24 bits on and 8 bits off. The bit mask that is derived from the traditional class
structure is called the *default mask* or the *natural mask*. However, with bit masks
we are no longer limited by the address class structure. A mask of 255.255.0.0 can
be applied to network address 195.4.0.0. This mask includes all addresses from
195.4.0.0 to 195.4.255.255 in a single network number. In effect, it creates a network number as large as a class B network in the class C address space. Using bit
masks to create networks larger than the natural mask is called *supernetting*, and
the use of a mask instead of the address class to determine the destination network is called *Classless Inter-Domain Routing* (CIDR).*

CIDR requires modifications to the routers and routing protocols. The protocols
need to distribute, along with the destination addresses, address masks that define
how the addresses are interpreted. The routers and hosts need to know how to
interpret these addresses as "classless" addresses and how to apply the bit mask
that accompanies the address. Older routing protocols, such as *Routing Information Protocol* (RIP), and older operating systems do not support CIDR address
masks. As the incorporation of the mask information in the routing table shows,
new operating systems like Linux 2.0.0 do support CIDR.

```
# route
Kernel routing table
Destination  Gateway      Genmask          Flags MSS   Window Use Iface
172.16.26.32 *            255.255.255.224  U     1500  0        2 eth0
195.4.0.0    129.6.26.62  255.255.0.0      UG    1500  0        0 eth0
loopback     *            255.0.0.0        U     3584  0        1 lo
default      129.6.26.62  *                UG    1500  0        3 eth0
```

Specifying both the address and the mask is cumbersome when writing out
addresses. A shorthand notation has been developed for writing CIDR addresses.
Instead of writing network 172.16.26.32 with a mask of 255.255.255.224, we can
write 172.16.26.32/27. The format of this notation is *address/prefix-length*, where
prefix-length is the number of bits in the network portion of the address. Without
this notation, the address 172.16.26.32 could easily be interpreted as a host
address. RFC 1878 list all 32 possible prefix values. But little documentation is
needed because the CIDR prefix is much easier to understand and remember than
are address classes. I know that 10.104.0.19 is a class A address, but writing it as

---

* CIDR is pronounced "cider."

10.104.0.19/8 shows me that this address has 8 bits for the network number and therefore 24 bits for the host number. I don't have to remember anything about the class A address structure.

CIDR is an interim solution, though it is capable of providing address and routing relief for many more years. The long-term solution is to replace the current addressing scheme with a new one. In the TCP/IP protocol suite addressing is defined by the IP protocol. Therefore, to define a new address structure, the Internet Engineering Task Force (IETF) created a new version of IP called IPv6.* IPv6 has a very large 128-bit address, so address depletion is not an issue. The large address also makes it possible to use a hierarchical address structure to reduce the burden on routers while still maintaining more than enough addresses for future network growth. Other benefits of IPv6 are:

- Improved security built into the protocol

- Simplified, fixed-length, word-aligned headers to speed header processing and reduce overhead

- Improved techniques for handling header options

IPv6 has several good features, but it is still a few years from widespread availability. In the meantime, the current generation of TCP/IP should be more than adequate for your network needs. On your network you will use IP and standard IP addressing.

Final notes on IP addresses

Not all network addresses or host addresses are available for use. We have already said that the addresses with a first byte greater than 223 cannot be used as host addresses. There are also two large pieces of the address space, 0.0.0.0/8 and 127.0.0.0/8, that are reserved for special uses. Network 0 designates the *default route* and network 127 is the *loopback address*. The default route is used to simplify the routing information that IP must handle. The loopback address simplifies network applications by allowing the local host to be addressed in the same manner as a remote host. We use these special network addresses when configuring a host.

There are also some host addresses reserved for special uses. In all network classes, host numbers 0 and 255 are reserved. An IP address with all host bits set to 0 identifies the network itself. For example, 10.0.0.0 refers to network 10, and 172.16.0.0 refers to network 172.16. Addresses in this form are used in routing table listings to refer to entire networks. An IP address with all host bits set to 1 is

---

* The current release of IP is IP version 4 (IPv4). IP version 5 is an experimental Stream Transport (ST) protocol used for real-time data delivery.

a *broadcast address.** A broadcast address is used to simultaneously address every host on a network. The broadcast address for network 172.16 is 172.16.255.255. A datagram sent to this address is delivered to every individual host on network 172.16.

IP addresses are often called host addresses. While this is common usage, it is slightly misleading. IP addresses are assigned to network interfaces, not to computer systems. A gateway, such as *almond* (see Figure 2-1), has a different address for each network to which it is connected. The gateway is known to other devices by the address associated with the network that it shares with those devices. For example, *peanut* addresses *almond* as 172.16.12.1, while external hosts address it as 10.104.0.19.

Systems can be addressed in three different ways. Individual systems are directly addressed by a host address, which is called a *unicast address*. A unicast packet is addressed to one individual host. Groups of systems can be addressed using a *multicast address*, e.g., 224.0.0.9. Routers along the path from the source to destination recognize the special address and route copies of the packet to each member of the multicast group.† All systems on a network are addressed using the broadcast address, e.g., 172.16.255.255. The broadcast address depends on the broadcast capabilities of the underlying physical network.

IP uses the network portion of the address to route the datagram between networks. The full address, including the host information, is used to make final delivery when the datagram reaches the destination network.

Subnets

The structure of an IP address can be locally modified by using host address bits as additional network address bits. Essentially, the "dividing line" between network address bits and host address bits is moved, creating additional networks, but reducing the maximum number of hosts that can belong to each network. These newly designated network bits define a network within the larger network, called a *subnet*.

Organizations usually decide to subnet in order to overcome topological or organizational problems. Subnetting allows decentralized management of host addressing. With the standard addressing scheme, a central administrator is responsible for managing host addresses for the entire network. By subnetting, the administrator can delegate address assignment to smaller organizations within the overall

---

* Unfortunately, there are implementation-specific variations in broadcast addresses. Chapter 5, *Basic Configuration*, discusses these variations.

† This is only partially true. Multicasting is not supported by every router. Sometimes it is necessary to tunnel through routers and networks by encapsulating the multicast packet inside of a unicast packet.

organization—which may be a political expedient, if not a technical requirement. If you don't want to deal with the data processing department, assign them their own subnet and let them manage it themselves.

Subnetting can also be used to overcome hardware differences and distance limitations. IP routers can link dissimilar physical networks together, but only if each physical network has its own unique network address. Subnetting divides a single network address into many unique subnet addresses, so that each physical network can have its own unique address.

A subnet is defined by changing the bit mask of the IP address. A *subnet mask* functions in the same way as a normal address mask: an "on" bit is interpreted as a network bit; an "off" bit belongs to the host part of the address. The difference is that a subnet mask is only used locally. In the outside world the address is still interpreted as a standard IP address.

Assume we have been assigned network address 172.16.0.0/16. The subnet mask associated with that address is 255.255.0.0. The most commonly used subnet mask, and the one we use in most of our examples, extends the network portion of the address by an additional byte, e.g., 172.16.0.0/24. The subnet mask that does this is 255.255.255.0; all bits on in the first three bytes, and all bits off in the last byte. The first two bytes define the original network; the third byte defines the the subnet address; the fourth byte defines the host on that subnet.

Many network administrators prefer byte-oriented masks because they are easy to read and understand when addresses are written in dotted decimal notation. However, limiting subnet masks to byte boundaries does not take advantage of their true power. The subnet mask is bit-oriented. We could subdivide 172.16.0.0/16 into 16 subnets with the mask 255.255.240.0, i.e. 172.16.0.0/20. Applying this mask defines the four high-order bits of the third byte as the subnet part of the address, and the remaining 12 bits—four bits of the third byte and all of the fourth byte—as the host portion of the address. This creates 16 subnets that each contain more than four thousand host addresses, which may well be better suited to our network and organization. For example, we may have a small number of large subdivisions. Table 2-1 shows the subnets and host addresses produced by applying this subnet masks to network address 172.16.0.0/16.

Table 2-1: Effect of a Subnet Mask

Network Number	First Address	Last Address
172.16.0.0	172.16.0.1	172.16.15.254
172.16.16.0	172.16.16.1	172.16.31.254
172.16.32.0	172.16.32.1	172.16.47.254
172.16.48.0	172.16.48.1	172.16.63.254

Table 2-1: Effect of a Subnet Mask (continued)

Network Number	First Address	Last Address
172.16.64.0	172.16.64.1	172.16.79.254
172.16.80.0	172.16.80.1	172.16.95.254
172.16.96.0	172.16.96.1	172.16.111.254
172.16.112.0	172.16.112.1	172.16.127.254
172.16.128.0	172.16.128.1	172.16.143.254
172.16.144.0	172.16.144.1	172.16.159.254
172.16.160.0	172.16.160.1	172.16.175.254
172.16.176.0	172.16.176.1	172.16.191.254
172.16.192.0	172.16.192.1	172.16.207.254
172.16.208.0	172.16.208.1	172.16.223.254
172.16.224.0	172.16.224.1	172.16.239.254
172.16.240.0	172.16.240.1	172.16.254.254

You don't have to manually calculate a table like Table 2-1 to know what subnets and host addresses are produced by a subnet mask. The calculations have already been done for you. RFC 1878 lists all possible subnet masks and the valid addresses they produce.

Organizations have been discouraged from subnetting class C addresses because of the fear that subnetting reduces the number of host addresses to increase the number of network addresses. A class C network is limited to fewer than 255 host addresses. Further limiting the number of hosts would reduce the utility of a class C address. The mask 255.255.255.192 divides a class C address into four subnets of 64 host addresses. The fear is that the subnet address of all 0s and the subnet address of all 1s will not be usable. This leaves only two subnets; and because host addresses of all 1s and all 0s are also unusable, the remaining two subnets can only address 62 hosts. Therefore the address space of this class C network number is reduced from 254 hosts to 124 hosts. The fear of subnetting class C addresses is no longer justified.

Originally, the RFCs implied that you should not use subnet numbers of all 0s or all 1s. However, RFC 1812, *Requirements for IP Version 4 Routers*, makes it clear that subnets of all 0s and all 1s are legal and should be supported by all routers. Some older routers do not allow the use of these addresses despite the newer RFCs. Updating router software or hardware should make it possible for you to reliably subnet class C addresses.

Class C subnets are used when very small networks are needed for specialized network equipment, such as terminal servers, cluster controllers or routers. In some configurations an entire subnet may be consumed for the link between two routers. In this case only two host addresses are needed, one for the router at each end of the link. A subnet mask of 255.255.255.252 applied to a class C address creates 64 subnets each containing four host addresses. In a special case this might be just what is needed.

Internet Routing Architecture

Chapter 1 described the evolution of the Internet architecture over the years. Along with these architectural changes have come changes in the way that routing information is disseminated within the network.

In the original Internet structure, there was a hierarchy of gateways. This hierarchy reflected the fact that the Internet was built upon the existing ARPANET. When the Internet was created, the ARPANET was the backbone of the network: a central delivery medium to carry long-distance traffic. This central system was called the *core*, and the centrally managed gateways that interconnected it were called the *core gateways*.

In that hierarchical structure, routing information about all of the networks in the Internet was passed into the core gateways. The core gateways processed the information, and then exchanged it among themselves using the *Gateway to Gateway Protocol* (GGP). The processed routing information was then passed back out to the external gateways. The core gateways maintained accurate routing information for the entire Internet.

Using the hierarchical core router model to distribute routing information has a major weakness: every route must be processed by the core. This places a tremendous processing burden on the core, and as the Internet grew larger the burden increased. In network-speak, we say that this routing model does not "scale well." For this reason, a new model emerged.

Even in the days of a single Internet, core groups of independent networks called *autonomous systems* (AS) existed outside of the core. The term "autonomous system" has a formal meaning in TCP/IP routing. An autonomous system is not merely an independent network. It is a collection of networks and gateways with its own internal mechanism for collecting routing information and passing it to other independent network systems. The routing information passed to the other network systems is called *reachability information*. Reachability information simply says which networks can be reached through that autonomous system. The *Exterior Gateway Protocol* (EGP) was the protocol used to pass reachability information between autonomous systems and into the core (see Figure 2-3).

The new routing model is based on co-equal collections of autonomous systems, called *routing domains*. Routing domains exchange routing information with other domains using *Border Gateway Protocol* (BGP). Each routing domain processes the information it receives from other domains. Unlike the hierarchical model, this model does not depend on a single core system to choose the "best" routes. Each

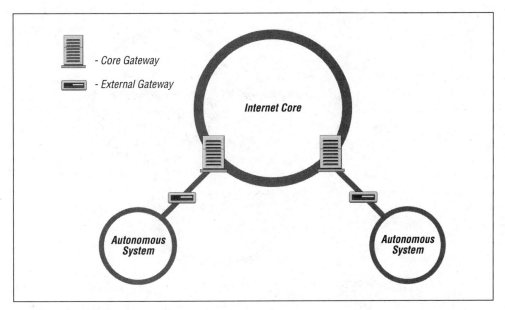

Figure 2-3: Gateway hierarchy

routing domain does this processing for itself; therefore, this model is more expandable. Figure 2-4 represents this model with three intersecting circles. Each circle is a routing domain. The overlapping areas are border areas, where routing information is shared. The domains share information, but do not rely on any one system to provide all routing information.

The problem with this model is: how are "best" routes determined in a global network if there is no central routing authority, like the core, that is trusted to determine the "best" routes? In the days of the NSFNET, the *policy routing database* (PRDB) was used to determine whether the reachability information advertised by an autonomous system was valid. But now, even the NSFNET does not play a central role.

To fill this void, NSF created the *Routing Arbiter* (RA) servers when it created the *Network Access Points* (NAPs) that replaced the role of the NSFNET. A route arbiter is located at each NAP. The server provides access to the *Routing Arbiter Database* (RADB), which replaced the PRDB. Internet Service Providers can query servers to validate the reachability information advertised by an autonomous system.

Many ISPs do not use the route servers. Instead they depend on formal and informal bilateral agreements. In essence, two ISPs get together and decide what reachability information each will accept from the other. They create, in effect, local routing policies. This is a slow manual process that probably will not be flexible enough for a rapidly growing Internet.

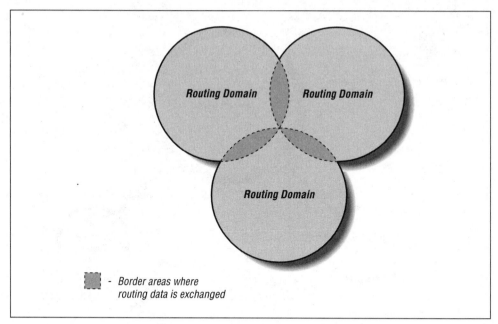

Figure 2-4: Routing domains

The RADB is only part of the *Internet Routing Registry* (IRR). As befits a distributed routing architecture, there are multiple organizations that validate and register routing information. Europeans were the pioneers in this. The Reseaux IP Europeens (RIPE) Network Control Center (NCC) provides the routing registry for European IP networks. Big network carriers, like MCI and ANS, provide registries for their customers. All of the registries share a common format based on the RIPE-181 standard.

Creating an effective routing architecture continues to be a major challenge for the Internet that will certainly evolve over time. No matter how it is derived, eventually the routing information winds up in your local gateway, where it is used by IP to make routing decisions.

The Routing Table

Gateways route data between networks; but all network devices, hosts as well as gateways, must make routing decisions. For most hosts, the routing decisions are simple:

- If the destination host is on the local network, the data is delivered to the destination host.

- If the destination host is on a remote network, the data is forwarded to a local gateway.

Because routing is network-oriented, IP makes routing decisions based on the network portion of the address. The IP module determines the network part of the destination's IP address by applying the network mask to the address. If the destination network is the local network, the mask that is applied may be the local subnet mask. If no mask is provided with the address, the address class determines the network portion of the address.

After determining the destination network, the IP module looks up the network in the local *routing table.** Packets are routed toward their destination as directed by the routing table. The routing table may be built by the system administrator or by routing protocols, but the end result is the same; IP routing decisions are simple table look-ups.

You can display the routing table's contents with the **netstat −nr** command. The **−r** option tells **netstat** to display the routing table, and the **−n** option tells **netstat** to display the table in numeric form. It's useful to display the routing table in numeric form because the destination of most routes is a network, and networks are usually referred to by network numbers.

On a Solaris system, the **netstat** command displays the routing table with the following fields:

Destination
> The destination network (or host).

Gateway
> The gateway to use to reach the specified destination.

Flags
> The flags describe certain characteristics of this route. The possible flag values are:
>
> *U*   Indicates that the route is up and operational.
>
> *H*   Indicates this is a route to a specific host (most routes are to networks).
>
> *G*   Means the route uses a gateway. The system's network interfaces provide routes to directly connected networks. All other routes use remote gateways. Directly connected networks do not have the G flag set; all other routes do.
>
> *D*   Means that this route was added because of an ICMP Redirect Message. When a system learns of a route via an ICMP Redirect, it adds the route to

---

* This table is also called the *forwarding table.*

its routing table, so that additional packets bound for that destination will not need to be redirected. The system uses the D flag to mark these routes.

Ref

The number of times the route has been referenced to establish a connection.

Use

The number of packets transmitted via this route.

Interface

The name of the network interface* used by this route.

The only two fields important for our current discussion are the destination and gateway fields. The following is a sample routing table:

```
% netstat -nr
Routing Table:
Destination  Gateway      Flags  Ref   Use    Interface
-----------  -----------  -----  ----  -----  ---------
127.0.0.1    127.0.0.1    UH     1     298    lo0
default      172.16.12.1  UG     2     50360
172.16.12.0  172.16.12.2  U      40    111379 le0
172.16.2.0   172.16.12.3  UG     4     1179
172.16.1.0   172.16.12.3  UG     10    1113
172.16.3.0   172.16.12.3  UG     2     1379
172.16.4.0   172.16.12.3  UG     4     1119
```

The first table entry is the *loopback route* for the local host. This is the loopback address mentioned earlier as a reserved network number. Because every system uses the loopback route to send datagrams to itself, this entry is in every host's routing table. The H flag is set because it is a route to a specific host (127.0.0.1), not a route to an entire network (127.0.0.0). We'll see the loopback facility again when we discuss kernel configuration and the **ifconfig** command. For now, however, our real interest is in external routes.

Another unique entry in the routing table is the entry with the word "default" in the destination field. This entry is for the *default route*, and the gateway specified in this entry is the *default gateway*. The default route is the other reserved network number mentioned earlier: 0.0.0.0. The default gateway is used whenever there is no specific route in the table for a destination network address. For example, this routing table has no entry for network 192.168.16.0. If IP receives any datagrams addressed to this network, it will send the datagram via the default gateway 172.16.12.1.

---

* The network interface is the network access hardware and software that IP uses to communicate with the physical network. See Chapter 6, *Configuring the Interface*, for details.

You can tell from the sample routing table display that this host (*peanut*) is directly connected to network 172.16.12.0. The routing table entry for that network does not specify an external gateway; i.e., the routing table entry for 172.16.12.0 does not have the G flag set. Therefore, *peanut* must be directly connected to that network.

All of the gateways that appear in a routing table are on networks directly connected to the local system. In the sample shown above this means that, regardless of the destination address, the gateway addresses all begin with 172.16.12. This is the only network to which *peanut* is directly attached, and therefore it is the only network to which *peanut* can directly deliver data. The gateways that *peanut* uses to reach the rest of the Internet must be on *peanut*'s subnet.

In Figure 2-5 the IP layer of each host and gateway on our imaginary network is replaced by a small piece of a routing table, showing destination networks and the gateways used to reach those destinations. When the source host (172.16.12.2) sends data to the destination host (172.16.1.2), it first determines that 172.16.1.2 is the local network's official address and applies the subnet mask. (Network 172.16.0.0 is subnetted using the mask 255.255.255.0.) After applying the subnet mask, IP knows that the destination's network address is 172.16.1.0. The routing table in the source host shows that data bound for 172.16.1.0 should be sent to gateway 172.16.12.3. Gateway 172.16.12.3 makes direct delivery through its 172.16.1.5 interface. Examining the routing tables shows that all systems list only gateways on networks they are directly connected to. Note that 172.16.12.1 is the default gateway for both 172.16.12.2 and 172.16.12.3. But because 172.16.1.2 cannot reach network 172.16.12.0 directly, it has a different default route.

A routing table does not contain end-to-end routes. A route points only to the next gateway, called the *next hop*, along the path to the destination network.* The host relies on the local gateway to deliver the data, and the gateway relies on other gateways. As a datagram moves from one gateway to another, it should eventually reach one that is directly connected to its destination network. It is this last gateway that finally delivers the data to the destination host.

Address Resolution

The IP address and the routing table direct a datagram to a specific physical network, but when data travels across a network, it must obey the physical layer protocols used by that network. The physical networks that underlay the TCP/IP network do not understand IP addressing. Physical networks have their own addressing schemes, and there are as many different addressing schemes as there

---

* As we'll see in Chapter 7, *Configuring Routing*, some routing protocols, such as OSPF and BGP, obtain end-to-end routing information. Nevertheless, the packet is still passed to the next-hop router.

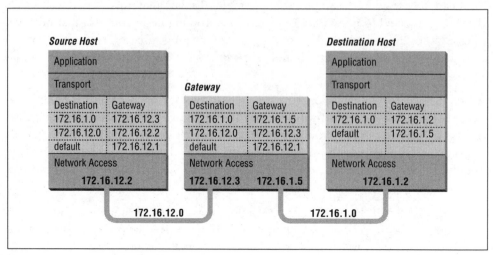

Figure 2-5: Table-based routing

are different types of physical networks. One task of the network access protocols is to map IP addresses to physical network addresses.

The most common example of this network access layer function is the translation of IP addresses to Ethernet addresses. The protocol that performs this function is *Address Resolution Protocol* (ARP), which is defined in RFC 826.

The ARP software maintains a table of translations between IP addresses and Ethernet addresses. This table is built dynamically. When ARP receives a request to translate an IP address, it checks for the address in its table. If the address is found, it returns the Ethernet address to the requesting software. If the address is not found in the table, ARP broadcasts a packet to every host on the Ethernet. The packet contains the IP address for which an Ethernet address is sought. If a receiving host identifies the IP address as its own, it responds by sending its Ethernet address back to the requesting host. The response is then cached in the ARP table.

The **arp** command displays the contents of the ARP table. To display the entire ARP table, use the **arp –a** command. Individual entries can be displayed by specifying a hostname on the **arp** command line. For example, to check the entry for *peanut* in the ARP table on *almond*, enter:

```
% arp peanut
peanut (172.16.12.2) at 8:0:20:0:e:c8
```

Checking all entries in the table with the **–a** option produces the following output:

```
% arp -a
Net to Media Table
```

```
Device    IP Address                   Mask       Flags  Phys Addr
------    ------------------           ---------------   -----  ---------------
le0       peanut.nuts.com              255.255.255.255          08:00:20:00:0e:c8
le0       acorn.nuts.com               255.255.255.255          08:00:02:05:21:33
le0       almond.nuts.com              255.255.255.255 SP       08:00:20:22:fd:51
le0       pecan.nuts.com               255.255.255.255          00:20:af:1e:7e:5f
le0       BASE-ADDRESS.MCAST.NET 240.0.0.0           SM       01:00:5e:00:00:00
```

This table tells you that when *almond* forwards datagrams addressed to *peanut*, it puts those datagrams into Ethernet frames and sends them to Ethernet address 08:00:20:00:0e:c8.

Three of the entries in the sample table (*peanut*, *acorn*, and *pecan*) were added dynamically as a result of queries by *almond*. Two of the entries (*almond* and *BASE-ADDRESS.MCAST.NET*) are static entries added as a result of the configuration of *almond*. We know this because both of these entries have an S, for "static," in the Flags field. The special *BASE-ADDRESS.MCAST.NET* entry is for all multicast addresses. The M flag means "mapping" and is only used for the multicast entry. On a broadcast medium like Ethernet, the Ethernet broadcast address is used to make final delivery to a multicast group.

The P flag on the *almond* entry means that this entry will be "published." The "publish" flag indicates that when an ARP query is received for the IP address of *almond*, this system answers it with the Ethernet address 08:00:20:22:fd:51. This is logical because this is the ARP table on *almond*. However, it is also possible to publish Ethernet addresses for other hosts, not just for the local host. Answering ARP queries for other computers is called *proxy ARP*.

For example: assume that *acorn* is the server for a remote system named *hazel* connected via a dial-up telephone line. Instead of setting up routing to the remote system, the administrator of *acorn* could place a static, published entry in the ARP table with the IP address of *hazel* and the Ethernet address of *acorn*. Now when *acorn* hears an ARP query for the IP address of *hazel*, it answers with its own Ethernet address. The other systems on the network therefore send packets destined for *hazel* to *acorn*. *acorn* then forwards the packets on to *hazel* over the telephone line. Proxy ARP is used to answer queries for systems that can't answer for themselves.

ARP tables normally don't require any attention because they are built automatically by the ARP protocol, which is very stable. However, if things go wrong, the ARP table can be manually adjusted. See Chapter 11, *Troubleshooting TCP/IP*, the section called "Troubleshooting with the arp Command."

Protocols, Ports, and Sockets

Once data is routed through the network and delivered to a specific host, it must be delivered to the correct user or process. As the data moves up or down the TCP/IP layers, a mechanism is needed to deliver it to the correct protocols in each layer. The system must be able to combine data from many applications into a few transport protocols, and from the transport protocols into the Internet Protocol. Combining many sources of data into a single data stream is called *multiplexing*.

Data arriving from the network must be *demultiplexed*: divided for delivery to multiple processes. To accomplish this task, IP uses *protocol numbers* to identify transport protocols, and the transport protocols use *port numbers* to identify applications.

Some protocol and port numbers are reserved to identify *well-known services*. Well-known services are standard network protocols, such as FTP and telnet, that are commonly used throughout the network. The protocol numbers and port numbers allocated to well-known services are documented in the *Assigned Numbers* RFC. UNIX systems define protocol and port numbers in two simple text files.

Protocol Numbers

The protocol number is a single byte in the third word of the datagram header. The value identifies the protocol in the layer above IP to which the data should be passed.

On a UNIX system, the protocol numbers are defined in */etc/protocols*. This file is a simple table containing the protocol name and the protocol number associated with that name. The format of the table is a single entry per line, consisting of the official protocol name, separated by whitespace from the protocol number. The protocol number is separated by whitespace from the "alias" for the protocol name. Comments in the table begin with #. An */etc/protocols* file is shown below:

```
% cat /etc/protocols
#ident  "@(#)protocols 1.2    90/02/03 SMI"    /* SVr4.0 1.1   */

#
# Internet (IP) protocols
#
ip      0       IP      # internet protocol, pseudo protocol number
icmp    1       ICMP    # internet control message protocol
ggp     3       GGP     # gateway-gateway protocol
tcp     6       TCP     # transmission control protocol
egp     8       EGP     # exterior gateway protocol
pup     12      PUP     # PARC universal packet protocol
udp     17      UDP     # user datagram protocol
hmp     20      HMP     # host monitoring protocol
```

```
xns-idp 22      XNS-IDP # Xerox NS IDP
rdp      27     RDP     # "reliable datagram" protocol
```

The listing shown above is the contents of the */etc/protocols* file from a Solaris 2.5.1 workstation. This list of numbers is by no means complete. If you refer to the Protocol Numbers section of the *Assigned Numbers* RFC, you'll see many more protocol numbers. However, a system needs to include only the numbers of the protocols that it actually uses. Even the list shown above is more than this specific workstation needed, but the additional entries do no harm.

What exactly does this table mean? When a datagram arrives and its destination address matches the local IP address, the IP layer knows that the datagram has to be delivered to one of the transport protocols above it. To decide which protocol should receive the datagram, IP looks at the datagram's protocol number. Using this table you can see that, if the datagram's protocol number is 6, IP delivers the datagram to TCP. If the protocol number is 17, IP delivers the datagram to UDP. TCP and UDP are the two transport layer services we are concerned with, but all of the protocols listed in the table use IP datagram delivery service directly. Some, such as ICMP, EGP, and GGP, have already been mentioned. You don't need to be concerned with the minor protocols.

Port Numbers

After IP passes incoming data to the transport protocol, the transport protocol passes the data to the correct application process. Application processes (also called *network services*) are identified by port numbers, which are 16-bit values. The source port number, which identifies the process that sent the data, and the destination port number, which identifies the process that is to receive the data, are contained in the first header word of each TCP segment and UDP packet.

On UNIX systems, port numbers are defined in the */etc/services* file. There are many more network applications than there are transport layer protocols, as the size of the table shows. Port numbers below 256 are reserved for well-known services (like FTP and telnet) and are defined in the *Assigned Numbers* RFC. Ports numbered from 256 to 1024 are used for UNIX-specific services, services like **rlogin** that were originally developed for UNIX systems. However, most of them are no longer UNIX-specific.

Port numbers are not unique between transport layer protocols; the numbers are only unique within a specific transport protocol. In other words, TCP and UDP can, and do, both assign the same port numbers. It is the combination of protocol and port numbers that uniquely identifies the specific process to which the data should be delivered.

A partial */etc/services* file from a Solaris 2.5.1 workstation is shown below. The format of this file is very similar to the */etc/protocols* file. Each single-line entry starts with the official name of the service, separated by whitespace from the port number/protocol pairing associated with that service. The port numbers are paired with transport protocol names, because different transport protocols may use the same port number. An optional list of aliases for the official service name may be provided after the port number/protocol pair.

```
peanut% head -20 /etc/services
#ident   "@(#)services   1.13    95/07/28 SMI"   /* SVr4.0 1.8   */

#
# Network services, Internet style
#
tcpmux          1/tcp
echo            7/tcp
echo            7/udp
discard         9/tcp           sink null
discard         9/udp           sink null
systat          11/tcp          users
daytime         13/tcp
daytime         13/udp
netstat         15/tcp
chargen         19/tcp          ttytst source
chargen         19/udp          ttytst source
ftp-data        20/tcp
ftp             21/tcp
telnet          23/tcp
smtp            25/tcp          mail
```

This table, combined with the */etc/protocols* table, provides all of the information necessary to deliver data to the correct application. A datagram arrives at its destination based on the destination address in the fifth word of the datagram header. Using the protocol number in the third word of the datagram header, IP delivers the data from the datagram to the proper transport layer protocol. The first word of the data delivered to the transport protocol contains the destination port number that tells the transport protocol to pass the data up to a specific application. Figure 2-6 shows this delivery process.

Despite its size, the */etc/services* file does not contain the port number of every well-known application. You won't find the port number of every *Remote Procedure Call* (RPC) service in the *services* file. Sun developed a different technique for reserving ports for RPC services that doesn't involve registering well-known port numbers. When an RPC service starts, it picks any unused port number and registers that number with the **portmapper**. The **portmapper** is a program that keeps track of the port numbers being used by RPC services. When a client wants to use an RPC service, it queries the **portmapper** running on the server to discover the port assigned to the service. The client can find **portmapper** because it is assigned

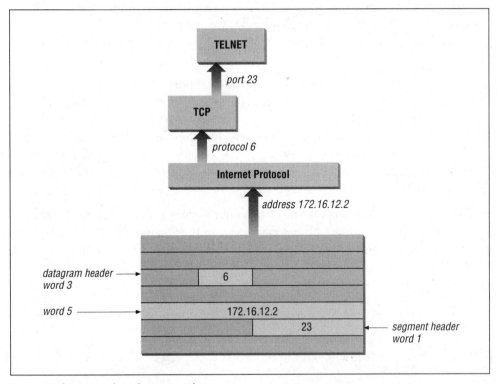

Figure 2-6: Protocol and port numbers

well-known port 111. **portmapper** makes it possible to install well-known services
without formally obtaining a well-known port.

Sockets

Well-known ports are standardized port numbers that enable remote computers to
know which port to connect to for a particular network service. This simplifies the
connection process because both the sender and receiver know in advance that
data bound for a specific process will use a specific port. For example, all systems
that offer telnet do so on port 23.

There is a second type of port number called a *dynamically allocated port*. As the
name implies, dynamically allocated ports are not pre-assigned. They are assigned
to processes when needed. The system ensures that it does not assign the same
port number to two processes, and that the numbers assigned are above the range
of standard port numbers.

Dynamically allocated ports provide the flexibility needed to support multiple
users. If a telnet user is assigned port number 23 for both the source and

destination ports, what port numbers are assigned to the second concurrent telnet user? To uniquely identify every connection, the source port is assigned a dynamically allocated port number, and the well-known port number is used for the destination port.

In the telnet example, the first user is given a random source port number and a destination port number of 23 (telnet). The second user is given a different random source port number and the same destination port. It is the pair of port numbers, source and destination, that uniquely identifies each network connection. The destination host knows the source port, because it is provided in both the TCP segment header and the UDP packet header. Both hosts know the destination port because it is a well-known port.

Figure 2-7 shows the exchange of port numbers during the TCP handshake. The source host randomly generates a source port, in this example 3044. It sends out a segment with a source port of 3044 and a destination port of 23. The destination host receives the segment, and responds back using 23 as its source port and 3044 as its destination port.

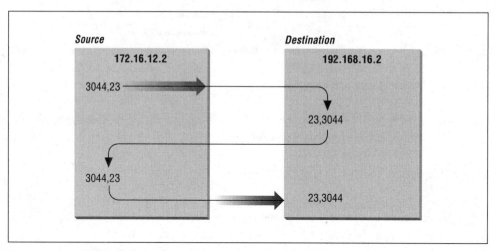

Figure 2-7: Passing port numbers

The combination of an IP address and a port number is called a *socket*. A socket uniquely identifies a single network process within the entire Internet. Sometimes the terms "socket" and "port number" are used interchangeably. In fact, well-known services are frequently referred to as "well-known sockets." In the context of this discussion, a "socket" is the combination of an IP address and a port number. A pair of sockets, one socket for the receiving host and one for the sending host, define the connection for connection-oriented protocols such as TCP.

Let's build on the example of dynamically assigned ports and well-known ports. Assume a user on host 172.16.12.2 uses telnet to connect to host 192.168.16.2. Host 172.16.12.2 is the source host. The user is dynamically assigned a unique port number—3382. The connection is made to the telnet service on the remote host which is, according to the standard, assigned well-known port 23. The socket for the source side of the connection is 172.16.12.2.3382 (IP address 172.16.12.2 plus port number 3382). For the destination side of the connection, the socket is 192.168.16.2.23 (address 192.168.16.2 plus port 23). The port of the destination socket is known by both systems because it is a well-known port. The port of the source socket is known, because the source host informed the destination host of the source socket when the connection request was made. The socket pair is therefore known by both the source and destination computers. The combination of the two sockets uniquely identifies this connection; no other connection in the Internet has this socket pair.

Summary

This chapter shows how data moves through the global Internet from one specific process on the source computer to a single cooperating process on the other side of the world. TCP/IP uses globally unique addresses to identify any computer in the world. It uses protocol numbers and port numbers to uniquely identify a single process running on that computer.

Routing directs the datagrams destined for a remote process through the maze of the global network. Routing uses part of the IP address to identify the destination network. Every system maintains a routing table that describes how to reach remote networks. The routing table usually contains a default route that is used if the table does not contain a specific route to the remote network. A route only identifies the next computer along the path to the destination. TCP/IP uses hop-by-hop routing to move datagrams one step closer to the destination until the datagram finally reaches the destination network.

At the destination network, final delivery is made by using the full IP address (including the host part) and converting that address to a physical layer address. An example of the type of protocol used to convert IP addresses to physical layer addresses is *Address Resolution Protocol* (ARP). It converts IP addresses to Ethernet addresses for final delivery.

The first two chapters described the structure of the TCP/IP protocol stack and the way in which it moves data across a network. In the next chapter we move up the protocol stack to look at the type of services the network provides to simplify configuration and use.

3

Network Services

Some network servers provide essential computer-to-computer services. These differ from application services in that they are not directly accessed by end users. Instead, these services are used by networked computers to simplify the installation, configuration, and operation of the network.

The functions performed by the servers covered in this chapter are varied:

- Name service for converting IP addresses to hostnames

- Configuration servers that simplify the installation of networked hosts by handling part or all of the TCP/IP configuration

- Electronic mail services for moving mail through the network from the sender to the recipient

- File servers that allow client computers to transparently share files

- Print servers that allow printers to be centrally maintained and shared by all users

Servers on a TCP/IP network should not be confused with traditional PC LAN servers. Every UNIX host on your network can be both a server and a client. The hosts on a TCP/IP network are "peers." All systems are equal. The network is not dependent on any one server. All of the services discussed in this chapter can be installed on one or several systems on your network.

We begin with a discussion of name service. It is an essential service that you will certainly use on your network.

Names and Addresses

The Internet Protocol document* defines names, addresses, and routes as follows:

A name indicates what we seek. An address indicates where it is.
A route indicates how to get there.

Names, addresses, and routes all require the network administrator's attention. Routes and addresses are covered in the previous chapter. This section discusses names and how they are disseminated throughout the network. Every network interface attached to a TCP/IP network is identified by a unique 32-bit IP address. A name (called a *hostname*) can be assigned to any device that has an IP address. Names are assigned to devices because, compared to numeric Internet addresses, names are easier to remember and type correctly. The network software doesn't require names, but they do make it easier for humans to use the network.

In most cases, hostnames and numeric addresses can be used interchangeably. A user wishing to **telnet** to the workstation at IP address 172.16.12.2 can enter:

```
% telnet 172.16.12.2
```

or use the hostname associated with that address and enter the equivalent command:

```
% telnet peanut.nuts.com
```

Whether a command is entered with an address or a hostname, the network connection always takes place based on the IP address. The system converts the hostname to an address before the network connection is made. The network administrator is responsible for assigning names and addresses and storing them in the database used for the conversion.

Translating names into addresses isn't simply a "local" issue. The command **telnet peanut.nuts.com** is expected to work correctly on every host that's connected to the network. If *peanut.nuts.com* is connected to the Internet, hosts all over the world should be able to translate the name *peanut.nuts.com* into the proper address. Therefore, some facility must exist for disseminating the hostname information to all hosts on the network.

There are two common methods for translating names into addresses. The older method simply looks up the hostname in a table called the *host table*.† The newer technique uses a distributed database system called *Domain Name Service* (DNS) to translate names to addresses. We'll examine the host table first.

---

* RFC 791, *Internet Protocol*, Jon Postel, ISI, 1981, page 7.

† Sun's Network Information Service (NIS) is an improved technique for accessing the host table. NIS is discussed in a later section.

The Host Table

The *host table* is a simple text file that associates IP addresses with hostnames. On most UNIX systems, the table is in the file */etc/hosts*. Each table entry in */etc/hosts* contains an IP address separated by whitespace from a list of hostnames associated with that address. Comments begin with #.

The host table on *peanut* might contain the following entries:

```
#
# Table of IP addresses and hostnames
#
172.16.12.2        peanut.nuts.com peanut
127.0.0.1          localhost
172.16.12.1        almond.nuts.com almond loghost
172.16.12.4        walnut.nuts.com walnut
172.16.12.3        pecan.nuts.com pecan
172.16.1.2         filbert.nuts.com filbert
172.16.6.4         salt.plant.nuts.com salt.plant salt
```

The first entry in the sample table is for *peanut* itself. The IP address 172.16.12.2 is associated with the hostname *peanut.nuts.com* and the alternate hostname (or alias) *peanut*. The hostname and all of its aliases resolve to the same IP address, in this case 172.16.12.2.

Aliases provide for name changes, alternate spellings, and shorter hostnames. They also allow for "generic hostnames." Look at the entry for 172.16.12.1. One of the aliases associated with that address is *loghost*. *loghost* is a special hostname used by the syslog daemon, **syslogd**. Programs like **syslogd** are designed to direct their output to the host that has a certain generic name. You can direct the output to any host you choose by assigning it the appropriate generic name as an alias. Other commonly used generic host names are *lprhost*, *mailhost*, and *dumphost*.

The second entry in the sample file assigns the address 127.0.0.1 to the hostname *localhost*. As we have discussed, the class A network address 127 is reserved for the loopback network. The host address 127.0.0.1 is a special address used to designate the loopback address of the local host—hence the hostname *localhost*. This special addressing convention allows the host to address itself the same way it addresses a remote host. The loopback address simplifies software by allowing common code to be used for communicating with local or remote processes. This addressing convention also reduces network traffic because the *localhost* address is associated with a loopback device that loops data back to the host before it is written out to the network.

Although the host table system has been superseded by DNS, it is still widely used for the following reasons:

- Most systems have a small host table containing name and address information about the important hosts on the local network. This small table is used when DNS is not running, such as during the initial system startup. Even if you use DNS, you should create a small */etc/hosts* file containing entries for your host, for *localhost*, and for the gateways and servers on your local net.

- Sites that use NIS use the host table as input to the NIS host database. You can use NIS in conjunction with DNS; but even when they are used together, most NIS sites create host tables that have an entry for every host on the local network. Chapter 9, *Configuring Network Servers*, explains how to use NIS with DNS.

- Very small sites that are not connected to the Internet sometimes use the host table. If there are few local hosts and the information about these hosts rarely changes, and there is no need to communicate via TCP/IP with remote sites, then there is little advantage to using DNS.

The old host table system is inadequate for the global Internet for two reasons: inability to scale and lack of an automated update process. Prior to adopting DNS, the Network Information Center (NIC) maintained a large table of Internet hosts called the *NIC host table*. Hosts included in the table were called *registered hosts*, and the NIC placed hostnames and addresses into this file for all sites on the Internet.

Even when the host table was the primary means for translating hostnames to IP addresses, most sites registered only a limited number of key systems. But even with limited registration, the table grew so large that it became an inefficient way to convert host names to IP addresses. There is no way that a simple table could provide adequate service for the enormous number of hosts in today's Internet.

Another problem with the host table system is that it lacks a technique for automatically distributing information about newly registered hosts. Newly registered hosts can be referenced by name as soon as a site receives the new version of the host table. However, there is no way to guarantee that the host table is distributed to a site. The NIC didn't know who had a current version of the table, and who did not. This lack of guaranteed uniform distribution is a major weakness of the host table system.

Some versions of UNIX provide the command **htable** to automatically build */etc/hosts* and */etc/networks* from the NIC host table. **htable** and the NIC host table are no longer used to build the */etc/hosts* file. However, the command is still useful for building */etc/networks*. The */etc/networks* file is still used to map network addresses to network names because many network names are not included in the

DNS database. To create the */etc/networks* file, download the file *ftp://rs.internic.net/netinfo/networks.txt* into a local work directory. Run **htable networks.txt**. Discard the *hosts* file and the *gateways* file produced by **htable**, and move the *networks* file to the */etc* directory.

This is the last we'll speak of the NIC host table: it has been superseded by DNS. All hosts connected to the Internet should use DNS.

Domain Name Service

The Domain Name System (DNS) overcomes both major weaknesses of the host table:

- DNS scales well. It doesn't rely on a single large table; it is a distributed database system that doesn't bog down as the database grows. DNS currently provides information on approximately 16,000,000 hosts, while less than 10,000 are listed in the host table.

- DNS guarantees that new host information will be disseminated to the rest of the network as it is needed.

Information is automatically disseminated, and only to those who are interested. Here's how it works. If a DNS server receives a request for information about a host for which it has no information, it passes on the request to an *authoritative server*. An authoritative server is any server responsible for maintaining accurate information about the domain being queried. When the authoritative server answers, the local server saves (*caches*) the answer for future use. The next time the local server receives a request for this information, it answers the request itself. The ability to control host information from an authoritative source and to automatically disseminate accurate information makes DNS superior to the host table, even for networks not connected to the Internet.

In addition to superseding the host table, DNS also replaces an earlier form of name service. Unfortunately, both the old and new services are commonly called *name service*. Both are listed in the */etc/services* file. In that file, the old software is assigned UDP port 42 and is called *nameserver* or *name*. DNS name service is assigned port 53 and is called *domain*. Naturally, there is some confusion between the two name servers. This text discusses DNS only; when we refer to "name service," we always mean DNS.

The Domain Hierarchy

DNS is a distributed hierarchical system for resolving hostnames into IP addresses. Under DNS, there is no central database with all of the Internet host information. The information is distributed among thousands of name servers organized into a hierarchy similar to the hierarchy of the UNIX filesystem. DNS has a *root domain* at the top of the domain hierarchy that is served by a group of name servers called the *root servers*.

Just as directories in the UNIX filesystem are found by following a path from the root directory, through subordinate directories, to the target directory, information about a domain is found by tracing pointers from the root domain, through subordinate domains, to the target domain.

Directly under the root domain are the *top-level domains*. There are two basic types of top-level domains—geographic and organizational. Geographic domains have been set aside for each country in the world, and are identified by a two-letter code. For example, the United Kingdom is domain UK, Japan is JP, and the United States is US. When US is used as the top-level domain, the second-level domain is usually a state's two-letter postal abbreviation (e.g., WY for Wyoming). US geographic domains are usually used by state governments and K–12 schools and are not widely used for other hosts within the United States.

Within the United States, the most popular top-level domains are organizational— that is, membership in a domain is based on the type of organization (commercial, military, etc.) to which the system belongs.* The top-level domains used in the United States are:

com
> Commercial organizations

edu
> Educational institutions

gov
> Government agencies

mil
> Military organizations

net
> Network support organizations, such as network operation centers

int
> International governmental or quasi-governmental organizations

org
> Organizations that don't fit in any of the above, such as non-profit organizations

---

* There is no relationship between the organizational and geographic domains in the U.S. Each system belongs to either an organizational domain *or* a geographical domain, not both.

Several proposals have been made to increase the number of top-level domains. The proposed domains are called *generic top level domains* or gTLDs. The proposals call for the creation of additional top-level domains and for the creation of new registrars to manage the domains. All of the current domains are handled by a single registrar—the InterNIC. One motivation for these efforts is the huge size of the *.com* domain. It is so large some people feel it will be difficult to maintain an efficient *.com* database. But the largest motivation for creating new gTLDs is money. Now that it charges fifty dollars a year for domain registration, some people see the InterNIC as a profitable monopoly. They have asked for the opportunity to create their own domain registration "businesses." A quick way to respond to that request is to create more official top-level domains and more registrars. The best known gTLDs proposal is the one from the *International Ad Hoc Committee* (IAHC). The IAHC proposes the following new generic top-level domains:

firm
> businesses or firms

store
> businesses selling goods

web
> organizations emphasizing the World Wide Web

arts
> cultural and entertainment organizations

rec
> recreational and entertainment organizations

info
> sites providing information services

nom
> individuals or organizations that want to define a personal nomenclature

Will the IAHC proposal be adopted? Will it be modified? Will another proposal win out? I don't know. There are several other proposals, and as you would expect when money is involved, plenty of controversy. At this writing the only official organizational domain names are: *com, edu, gov, mil, net, int,* and *org.*

Figure 3-1 illustrates the domain hierarchy by using the organizational top-level domains. At the top is the root. Directly below the root domain are the top-level domains. The root servers only have complete information about the top-level domains. No servers, not even the root servers, have complete information about all domains, but the root servers have pointers to the servers for the second-level domains.* So while the root servers may not know the answer to a query, they know who to ask.

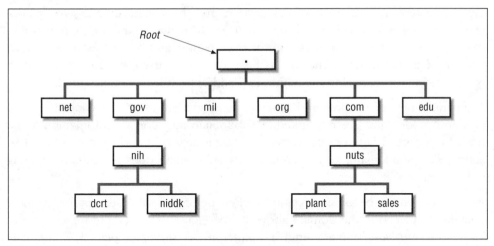

Figure 3-1: Domain hierarchy

Creating Domains and Subdomains

The Network Information Center has the authority to allocate domains. To obtain a domain, you apply to the NIC for authority to create a domain under one of the top-level domains. Once the authority to create a domain is granted, you can create additional domains, called *subdomains*, under your domain. Let's look at how this works at our imaginary nut packing company.

Our company is a commercial profit-making (we hope) enterprise. It clearly falls into the *com* domain. We apply to the NIC for authority to create a domain named *nuts* within the *com* domain. The request for the new domain contains the hostnames and addresses of at least two servers that will provide name service for the new domain. (Chapter 4 discusses the domain name application.) When the NIC approves the request, it adds pointers in the *com* domain to the new domain's name servers. Now when queries are received by the root servers for the *nuts.com* domain, the queries are referred to the new name servers.

The NIC's approval grants us complete authority over our new domain. Any registered domain has authority to divide its domain into subdomains. Our imaginary company can create separate domains for the sales organization (*sales.nuts.com*) and for the packing plant (*plant.nuts.com*) without consulting the NIC. The decision to add subdomains is completely up to the local domain administrator.

---

* Figure 3-1 shows two second-level domains: *nih* under *gov* and *nuts* under *com*.

Name assignment is, in some ways, similar to address assignment. The NIC assigns a network address to an organization, and the organization assigns subnet addresses and host addresses within the range of that network address. Similarly, the NIC assigns a domain to an organization, and the organization assigns subdomains and hostnames within that domain. The NIC is the central authority that delegates authority and distributes control over names and addresses to individual organizations. Once that authority has been delegated, the individual organization is responsible for managing the names and addresses it has been assigned.

The parallel between subnet and subdomain assignment can cause confusion. Subnets and subdomains are not linked. A subdomain may contain information about hosts from several different networks. Creating a new subnet does not require creating a new subdomain, and creating a new subdomain does not require creating a new subnet.

A new subdomain becomes accessible when pointers to the servers for the new domain are placed in the domain above it (see Figure 3-1). Remote servers cannot locate the *nuts.com* domain until a pointer to its server is placed in the *com* domain. Likewise, the subdomains *sales* and *plant* cannot be accessed until pointers to them are placed in *nuts.com*. The DNS database record that points to the name servers for a domain is the NS (*name server*) record. This record contains the name of the domain and the name of the host that is a server for that domain. Chapter 8, *Configuring DNS Name Service*, discusses the actual DNS database. For now, let's just think of these records as pointers.

Figure 3-2 illustrates how the NS records are used as pointers. A local server has a request to resolve *salt.plant.nuts.com* into an IP address. The server has no information on *nuts.com* in its cache, so it queries a root server (*terp.umd.edu* in our example) for the address. The root server replies with an NS record that points to *almond.nuts.com* as the source of information on *nuts.com*. The local server queries *almond*, which points it to *pack.plant.nuts.com* as the server for *plant.nuts.com*. The local server then queries *pack.plant.nuts.com*, and finally receives the desired IP address. The local server caches the A (address) record and each of the NS records. The next time it has a query for *salt.plant.nuts.com*, it will answer the query itself. And the next time the server has a query for other information in the *nuts.com* domain, it will go directly to *almond* without involving a root server.

Figure 3-2 is an example of a non-recursive query. In a *non-recursive* query, the remote server tells the local server who to ask next. The local server must follow the pointers itself. In a *recursive* search, the remote server follows the pointers and returns the final answer to the local server. The root servers generally perform only non-recursive searches.

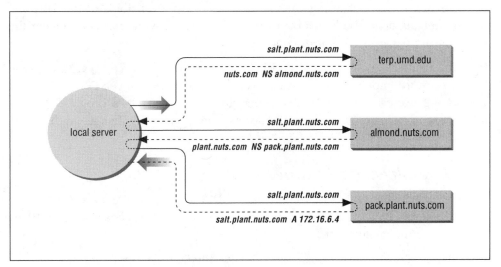

Figure 3-2: Non-recursive query

Domain Names

Domain names reflect the domain hierarchy. Domain names are written from most specific (a hostname) to least specific (a top-level domain), with each part of the domain name separated by a dot.* A fully qualified domain name (FQDN) starts with a specific host and ends with a top-level domain. *peanut.nuts.com* is the FQDN of workstation *peanut*, in the *nuts* domain, of the *com* domain.

Domain names are not always written as fully qualified domain names. Domain names can be written relative to a *default domain* in the same way that UNIX pathnames are written relative to the current (default) working directory. DNS adds the default domain to the user input when constructing the query for the name server. For example, if the default domain is *nuts.com*, a user can omit the *nuts.com* extension for any hostnames in that domain. *almond.nuts.com* could be addressed simply as *almond*. DNS adds the default domain *nuts.com*.

This feature is implemented in different ways on different systems, but there are two predominant techniques. On some systems the extension is added to every hostname request unless it *ends* with a dot, i.e., is qualified out to the root. For example, assume that there is a host named *salt* in the subdomain *plant* of the *nuts.com* domain. *salt.plant* does not end with a dot, so *nuts.com* is added to it giving the domain name *salt.plant.nuts.com*. On most systems, the extension is added only if there is no dot embedded in the requested hostname. On this type of system, *salt.plant* would not be extended and would therefore not be resolved

---

* The root domain is identified by a single dot; i.e., the root name is a null name written simply as ".".

by the name server because *plant* is not a valid top-level domain. But *almond*, which contains no embedded dot, would be extended with *nuts.com*, giving the valid domain name *almond.nuts.com.*

How the default domain is used and how queries are constructed varies depending on software implementation. It can even vary by release level. For this reason, you should exercise caution when embedding a hostname in a program. Only a fully qualified domain name or an IP address is immune from changes in the name server software.

BIND, resolver, and named

The implementation of DNS used on most UNIX systems is the *Berkeley Internet Name Domain* (BIND) software. Descriptions in this text are based on the BIND name server implementation.

DNS name service software is conceptually divided into two components—a resolver and a name server. The *resolver* is the software that forms the query; it asks the questions. The *name server* is the process that responds to the query; it answers the questions.

The resolver does not exist as a distinct process running on the computer. Rather, the resolver is a library of software routines (called the "resolver code") that is linked into any program that needs to look up addresses. This library knows how to ask the name server for host information.

Under BIND, all computers use resolver code, but not all computers run the name server process. A computer that does not run a local name server process and relies on other systems for all name service answers is called a *resolver-only* system. Resolver-only configurations are common on single user systems. Larger UNIX systems run a local name server process.

The BIND name server runs as a distinct process called *named* (pronounced "name" "d"). Name servers are classified differently depending on how they are configured. The three main categories of name servers are:

Primary

    The *primary server* is the server from which all data about a domain is derived. The primary server loads the domain's information directly from a disk file created by the domain administrator. Primary servers are *authoritative*, meaning they have complete information about their domain and their responses are always accurate. There should be only one primary server for a domain.

Secondary

> *Secondary servers* transfer the entire domain database from the primary server. A particular domain's database file is called a *zone file*; copying this file to a secondary server is called a *zone file transfer*. A secondary server assures that it has current information about a domain by periodically transferring the domain's zone file. Secondary servers are also authoritative for their domain.

Caching-only

> *Caching-only servers* get the answers to all name service queries from other name servers. Once a caching server has received an answer to a query, it caches the information and will use it in the future to answer queries itself. Most name servers cache answers and use them in this way. What makes the caching-only server unique is that this is the only technique it uses to build its domain database. Caching servers are *non-authoritative*, meaning that their information is second-hand and incomplete, though usually accurate.

The relationship between the different types of servers is an advantage that DNS has over the host table for most networks, even very small networks. Under DNS, there should be only one primary name server for each domain. DNS data is entered into the primary server's database by the domain administrator. Therefore, the administrator has central control of the hostname information. An automatically distributed, centrally controlled database is an advantage for a network of any size. When you add a new system to the network, you don't need to modify the */etc/hosts* files on every node in the network; you modify only the DNS database on the primary server. The information is automatically disseminated to the other servers by full zone transfers or by caching single answers.

Network Information Service

The *Network Information Service* (NIS)* is an administrative database system developed by Sun Microsystems. It provides central control and automatic dissemination of important administrative files. NIS can be used in conjunction with DNS, or as an alternative to it.

NIS and DNS have similarities and differences. Like DNS, the Network Information Service overcomes the problem of accurately distributing the host table, but unlike DNS, it provides service only for local area networks. NIS is not intended as a service for the Internet as a whole. Another difference is that NIS provides access to a wider range of information than DNS—much more than name-to-address conversions. It converts several standard UNIX files into databases that can be queried over the network. These databases are called *NIS maps*.

---

* NIS was formerly called the "Yellow Pages," or *yp*. Although the name has changed, the abbreviation *yp* is still used.

NIS converts files such as */etc/hosts* and */etc/networks* into maps. The maps can be stored on a central server where they can be centrally maintained while still being fully accessible to the NIS clients. Because the maps can be both centrally maintained and automatically disseminated to users, NIS overcomes a major weakness of the host table. But NIS is not an alternative to DNS for Internet hosts, because the host table, and therefore NIS, contains only a fraction of the information available to DNS. For this reason DNS and NIS are usually used together.

This section has introduced the concept of hostnames and provided an overview of the various techniques used to translate hostnames into IP addresses. This is by no means the complete story. Assigning host names and managing name service are important tasks for the network administrator. These topics are revisited several times in this book and discussed in extensive detail in Chapter 8.

Name service is not the only service that you will install on your network. Another service that you are sure to use is electronic mail.

Mail Services

Users consider electronic mail the most important network service because they use it for interpersonal communications. Some applications are newer and fancier. Other applications consume more network bandwidth. Others are more important for the continued operation of the network. But email is the application people use to communicate with each other. It isn't very fancy, but it's vital.

TCP/IP provides a reliable, flexible email system built on a few basic protocols. These are: *Simple Mail Transfer Protocol* (SMTP), *Post Office Protocol* (POP), and *Multipurpose Internet Mail Extensions* (MIME). There are other TCP/IP mail protocols. *Interactive Mail Access Protocol*, defined in RFC 1176, is an interesting protocol designed to supplant POP. It provides remote text searches and message parsing features not found in POP. We will touch only briefly on IMAP. It and other protocols have some very interesting features, but they are not yet widely implemented.

Our coverage concentrates on the three protocols you are most likely to use building your network: SMTP, POP, and MIME. We start with SMTP, the foundation of all TCP/IP email systems.

Simple Mail Transfer Protocol

SMTP is the TCP/IP mail delivery protocol. It moves mail across the Internet and across your local network. SMTP is defined in RFC 821, *A Simple Mail Transfer Protocol*. It runs over the reliable, connection-oriented service provided by *Trans-*

mission Control Protocol (TCP), and it uses well-known port number 25.* Table 3-1 lists some of the simple, human-readable commands used by SMTP.

Table 3-1: SMTP Commands

Command	Syntax	Function
Hello	HELO *<sending-host>*	Identify sending SMTP
From	MAIL FROM:*<from-address>*	Sender address
Recipient	RCPT TO:*<to-address>*	Recipient address
Data	DATA	Begin a message
Reset	RSET	Abort a message
Verify	VRFY *<string>*	Verify a username
Expand	EXPN *<string>*	Expand a mailing list
Help	HELP [*string*]	Request online help
Quit	QUIT	End the SMTP session

SMTP is such a simple protocol you can literally do it yourself. **telnet** to port 25 on a remote host and type mail in from the command line using the SMTP commands. This technique is sometimes used to test a remote system's SMTP server, but we use it here to illustrate how mail is delivered between systems. The example below shows mail manually input from Daniel on *peanut.nuts.com* to Tyler on *almond.nuts.com*.

```
% telnet almond.nuts.com 25
Trying 172.16.12.1 ...
Connected to almond.nuts.com.
Escape character is '^]'.
220 almond Sendmail 4.1/1.41 ready at Tue, 29 Mar 94 17:21:26 EST
helo peanut.nuts.com
250 almond Hello peanut.nuts.com, pleased to meet you
mail from:<daniel@peanut.nuts.com>
250 <daniel@peanut.nuts.com>... Sender ok
rcpt to:<tyler@almond.nuts.com>
250 <tyler@almond.nuts.com>... Recipient ok
data
354 Enter mail, end with "." on a line by itself
Hi Tyler!
.
250 Mail accepted
quit
221 almond delivering mail
Connection closed by foreign host.
```

The user input is shown in bold type. All of the other lines are output from the system. This example shows how simple it is. A TCP connection is opened. The sending system identifies itself. The *From* address and the *To* address are

---

* Most standard TCP/IP applications are assigned a well-known port in the *Assigned Numbers RFC*, so that remote systems know how to connect the service.

provided. The message transmission begins with the **DATA** command and ends with a line that contains only a period (.). The session terminates with a QUIT command. Very simple, and very few commands are used.

There are other commands (**SEND, SOML, SAML,** and **TURN**) defined in RFC 821 that are optional and not widely implemented. Even some of the commands that are implemented are not commonly used. The commands **HELP, VRFY,** and **EXPN** are designed more for interactive use than for the normal machine-to-machine interaction used by SMTP. The following excerpt from a SMTP session shows how these odd commands work.

```
HELP
214-Commands:
214-   HELO    MAIL    RCPT    DATA    RSET
214-   NOOP    QUIT    HELP    VRFY    EXPN
214-For more info use "HELP <topic>".
214-For local information contact postmaster at this site.
214 End of HELP info
HELP RSET
214-RSET
214-     Resets the system.
214 End of HELP info
VRFY <jane>
250 <jane@brazil.nuts.com>
VRFY <mac>
250 Kathy McCafferty <<mac>>
EXPN <admin>
250-<sara@pecan.nuts.com>
250 David Craig <<david>>
250-<tyler@nuts.com>
```

The **HELP** command prints out a summary of the commands implemented on the system. The **HELP RSET** command specifically requests information about the **RSET** command. Frankly, this help system isn't very helpful!

The **VRFY** and **EXPN** commands are more useful, but are often disabled for security reasons because they provide user account information that might be exploited by network intruders. The **EXPN <admin>** command asks for a listing of the email addresses in the mailing list *admin*, and that is what the system provides. The **VRFY** command asks for information about an individual instead of a mailing list. In the case of the **VRFY <mac>** command, *mac* is a local user account and the user's account information is returned. In the case of **VRFY <jane>**, *jane* is an alias in the */etc/aliases* file. The value returned is the email address for *jane* found in that file. The three commands in this example are interesting, but rarely used. SMTP depends on the other commands to get the real work done.

SMTP provides direct end-to-end mail delivery. This is unusual. Most mail systems use *store and forward* protocols like UUCP and X.400 that move mail toward its destination one hop at a time, storing the complete message at each hop and then forwarding it on to the next system. The message proceeds in this manner until final delivery is made. Figure 3-3 illustrates both store and forward and direct delivery mail systems. The UUCP address clearly shows the path that the mail takes to its destination, while the SMTP mail address implies direct delivery.*

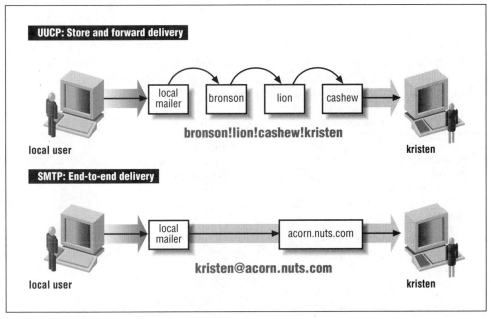

Figure 3-3: Mail delivery systems

Direct delivery allows SMTP to deliver mail without relying on intermediate hosts. If the delivery fails, the local system knows it right away. It can inform the user that sent the mail or queue the mail for later delivery without reliance on remote systems. The disadvantage of direct delivery is that it requires both systems to be fully capable of handling mail. Some systems cannot handle mail, particularly small systems such as PCs or mobile systems such as laptops. These systems are usually shut down at the end of the day and are frequently offline. Mail directed from a remote host fails with a "cannot connect" error when the local system is turned off or offline. To handle these cases, features in the DNS system are used to route the message to a mail server in lieu of direct delivery. The mail is then moved from the server to the client system when the client is back online. The protocol most TCP/IP networks use for this task is POP.

---

* The address doesn't have anything to do with whether or not a system is store and forward or direct delivery. It just happens that UUCP provides an address that helps to illustrate this point.

Post Office Protocol

There are two versions of POP in widespread use: POP2 and POP3. POP2 is defined in RFC 937 and POP3 is defined in RFC 1725. POP2 uses port 109 and POP3 uses port 110. These are incompatible protocols that use different commands, but they perform the same basic functions. The POP protocols verify the user's login name and password, and move the user's mail from the server to the user's local mail reader.

A sample POP2 session clearly illustrates how a POP protocol works. POP2 is a simple request/response protocol, and just as with SMTP, you can type POP2 commands directly into its well-known port (109) and observe their effect. Here's an example with the user input shown in bold type:

```
% telnet almond.nuts.com 109
Trying 172.16.12.1 ...
Connected to almond.nuts.com.
Escape character is '^]'.
+ POP2 almond POP2 Server at Wed 30-Mar-94 3:48PM-EST
HELO hunt WatsWatt
#3   ...(From folder 'NEWMAIL')
READ
=496
RETR
{The full text of message 1}
ACKD
=929
RETR
{The full text of message 2}
ACKD
=624
RETR
{The full text of message 3}
ACKD
=0
QUIT
+OK POP2 Server exiting (0 NEWMAIL messages left)
Connection closed by foreign host.
```

The **HELO** command provides the username and password for the account of the mailbox that is being retrieved. (This is the same username and password used to log into the mail server.) In response to the **HELO** command the server sends a count of the number of messages in the mailbox, three (#3) in our example. The **READ** command begins reading the mail. **RETR** retrieves the full text of the current message. **ACKD** acknowledges receipt of the message and deletes it from the server. After each acknowledgment the server sends a count of the number of bytes in the new message. If the byte count is zero (=0) it indicates that there are no more messages to be retrieved and the client ends the session with the **QUIT** command. Simple! Table 3-2 lists the full set of POP2 commands.

Table 3-2: POP2 Commands

Command	Syntax	Function
Hello	**HELO** *user password*	Identify user account
Folder	**FOLD** *mail-folder*	Select mail folder
Read	**READ** [*n*]	Read mail, optionally start with message *n*
Retrieve	**RETR**	Retrieve message
Save	**ACKS**	Acknowledge and save
Delete	**ACKD**	Acknowledge and delete
Failed	**NACK**	Negative acknowledgement
Quit	**QUIT**	End the POP2 session

The commands for POP3 are completely different from the commands used for POP2. Table 3-3 shows the set of POP3 commands defined in RFC 1725.

Table 3-3: POP3 Commands

Command	Function
USER *username*	The user's account name
PASS *password*	The user's password
STAT	Display the number of unread messages/bytes
RETR *n*	Retrieve message number *n*
DELE *n*	Delete message number *n*
LAST	Display the number of the last message accessed
LIST [*n*]	Display the size of message *n* or of all messages
RSET	Undelete all messages; reset message number to 1
TOP *n* *1*	Print the headers and *1* lines of message *n*
NOOP	Do nothing
QUIT	End the POP3 session

Despite the fact that these commands are different from those used by POP2, they can be used to perform similar functions. In the POP2 example we logged into the server and read and deleted three mail messages. Here's a similar session using POP3:

```
% telnet almond 110
Trying 172.16.12.1 ...
Connected to almond.nuts.com.
Escape character is '^]'.
+OK almond POP3 Server Process 3.3(1) at Mon 15-May-95 4:48PM-EDT
user hunt
+OK User name (hunt) ok. Password, please.
pass Watts?Watt?
+OK 3 messages in folder NEWMAIL (V3.3 Rev B04)
stat
+OK 3 459
retr 1
```

```
+OK 146 octets
```
The full text of message 1
dele 1
```
+OK message # 1 deleted
```
retr 2
```
+OK 155 octets
```
The full text of message 2
dele 2
```
+OK message # 2 deleted
```
retr 3
```
+OK 158 octets
```
The full text of message 3
dele 3
```
+OK message # 3 deleted
```
quit
```
+OK POP3 almond Server exiting (0 NEWMAIL messages left)
Connection closed by foreign host.
```

Naturally you don't really type these commands in yourself, but experiencing hands-on interaction with SMTP and POP gives you a clearer understanding of what these programs do and why they are needed.

Multipurpose Internet Mail Extensions

The last email protocol on our quick tour is MIME.* As its name implies, *Multipurpose Internet Mail Extensions* is an extension of the existing TCP/IP mail system, not a replacement for it. MIME is more concerned with what the mail system delivers then it is with the mechanics of delivery. It doesn't attempt to replace SMTP or TCP; it extends the definition of what constitutes "mail."

The structure of the mail message carried by SMTP is defined in RFC 822, *Standard for the Format of ARPA Internet Text Messages*. RFC 822 defines a set of mail headers that are so widely accepted they are used by many mail systems that do not use SMTP. This is a great benefit to email because it provides a common ground for mail translation and delivery through gateways to different mail networks. MIME extends RFC 822 into two areas not covered by the original RFC:

*   Support for various data types. The mail system defined by RFC 821 and RFC 822 transfers only 7-bit ASCII data. This is suitable for carrying text data composed of US ASCII characters, but it does not support several languages that have richer character sets and it does not support binary data transfer.

*   Support for complex message bodies. RFC 822 does not provide a detailed description of the body of an electronic message. It concentrates on the mail headers.

---

* MIME is also an integral part of the Web and HTTP.

MIME addresses these two weaknesses by defining encoding techniques for carrying various forms of data, and by defining a structure for the message body that allows multiple objects to be carried in a single message. The RFC 1521, *MIME (Multipurpose Internet Mail Extensions) Part One: Mechanisms for Specifying and Describing the Format of Internet Message Bodies*, defines two headers that give structure to the mail message body and allow it to carry various forms of data. These are the *Content-Type* header and the *Content-Transfer-Encoding* header.

As the name implies, the Content-Type header defines the type of data being carried in the message. The header has a Subtype field that refines the definition. Many subtypes have been defined since the original RFC was released. A current list of MIME types can be obtained from the Internet.* The original RFC defines seven initial content types and a few subtypes:

text

> Text data. RFC 1521 defines text subtypes *plain* and *richtext*. Several subtypes have since been added, including *enriched* and *html*.

application

> Binary data. The primary subtype defined in RFC 1521 is *octet-stream*, which indicates the data is a stream of 8-bit binary bytes. One other subtype, *PostScript*, is defined in the standard. Since then more than 90 subtypes have been defined. They specify binary data formatted for a particular application. For example, *msword* is an application subtype.

image

> Still graphic images. Two subtypes are defined in RFC 1521: *jpeg* and *gif*. More than 10 additional subtypes have since been added, including widely used image data standards such as *tiff*, *cgm*, and *g3fax*.

video

> Moving graphic images. The initially defined subtype was *mpeg*, which is a widely used standard for computer video data. A few others have since been added, including *quicktime*.

audio

> Audio data. The only subtype initially defined for audio was *basic*, which means the sounds are encoded using pulse code modulation (PCM).

multipart

> Data composed of multiple independent sections. A multipart message body is made up of several independent parts. RFC 1521 defines four subtypes. The primary subtype is *mixed*, which means that each part of the message can be

---

* Go to *ftp://ftp.isi.edu/in-notes/iana/assignments/media-types* and retrieve the file *media-types*.

data of any content type. Other subtypes are: *alternative*, meaning that the same data is repeated in each section in different formats; *parallel*, meaning that the data in the various parts is to be viewed simultaneously; and *digest*, meaning that each section is data of the type *message*. Several subtypes have since been added, including support for voice messages (*voice-message*) and *encrypted* messages.

message

Data that is an encapsulated mail message. RFC 1521 defines three subtypes. The primary subtype, *rfc822*, indicates that the data is a complete RFC 822 mail message. The other subtypes, *partial* and *External-body*, are both designed to handle large messages. *partial* allows large encapsulated messages to be split among multiple MIME messages. *External-body* points to an external source for the contents of a large message body, so that only the pointer, not the message itself, is contained in the MIME message. Two additional subtypes have been defined: *news* for carrying network news, and *http* for HTTP traffic formatted to comply with MIME content typing.

The Content-Transfer-Encoding header identifies the type of encoding used on the data. Traditional SMTP systems only forward 7-bit ASCII data with a line length of less than 1000 bytes. To ensure that the data from a MIME system is forwarded through gateways that may only support 7-bit ASCII, the data can be encoded. RFC 1521 defines six types of encoding. Some types are used to identify the encoding inherent in the data. Only two types are actual encoding techniques defined in the RFC. The six encoding types are:

7bit

US ASCII data. No encoding is performed on 7-bit ASCII data.

8bit

Octet data. No encoding is performed. The data is binary, but the lines of data are short enough for SMTP transport; i.e., the lines are fewer than 1000 bytes long.

binary

Binary data. No encoding is performed. The data is binary and the lines may be longer than 1000 bytes. There is no difference between *binary* and *8bit* data except the line length restriction; both types of data are unencoded byte (octet) streams. MIME does not handle unencoded bitstream data.

quoted-printable

Encoded text data. This encoding technique handles data that is largely composed of printable ASCII text. The ASCII text is sent unencoded, while bytes with a value greater than 127 or less than 33 are sent encoded as strings made up of the equal sign followed by the hexadecimal value of the byte. For example: the ASCII form feed character, which has the hexadecimal value of 0C, is sent as *=0C*. Naturally there's more to it than this—for example, the literal equal sign has to be sent as *=3D*, and the newline at the end of each line is not encoded. But this is the general idea of how *quoted-printable* data is sent.

base64

Encoded binary data. This encoding technique can be used on any byte-stream data. Three octets of data are encoded as four 6-bit characters, which increases the size of the file by one-third. The 6-bit characters are a subset of US ASCII, chosen because they can be handled by any type of mail system. The maximum line length for *base64* data is 76 characters. Figure 3-4 illustrates this 3 to 4 encoding technique.

x-token

Specially encoded data. It is possible for software developers to define their own private encoding techniques. If they do so, the name of the encoding technique must begin with *X–*. Doing this is strongly discouraged because it limits interoperability between mail systems.

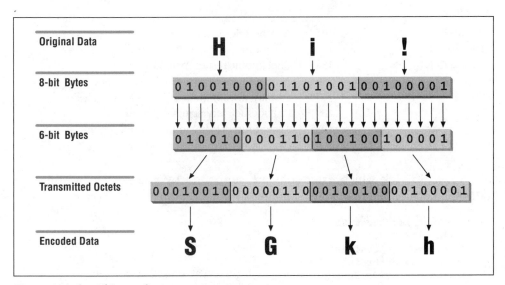

Figure 3-4: base64 encoding

The number of supported data types and encoding techniques grows as new data formats appear and are used in message transmissions. New RFCs constantly define new data types and encoding. Read the latest RFCs to keep up with MIME developments.

MIME defines data types that SMTP was not designed to carry. To handle these and other future requirements, RFC 1869, *SMTP Service Extensions*, defines a technique for making SMTP *extensible*. The RFC does not define new services for SMTP; in fact, the only service extensions mentioned in the RFC are defined in other RFCs. What this RFC does define is a simple mechanism for systems to negotiate which SMTP extensions are supported. The RFC defines a new *hello* command (**EHLO**) and the legal responses to that command. One response is for the receiving system to return a list of the SMTP extensions it supports. This response allows the sending system to know what extended services can be used, and to avoid those that are not implemented on the remote system. SMTP implementations that support the **EHLO** command are called Extended SMTP (ESMTP).

Several ESMTP service extensions have been defined for MIME mailers. Table 3-4 lists some of these. The table lists the **EHLO** keyword associated with each extension, the number of the RFC that defines it, and its purpose. These service extensions are just the beginning. Undoubtedly more will be defined to support MIME and other SMTP enhancements.

Table 3-4: SMTP Service Extensions

Keyword	RFC	Server Extension
8BITMIME	1652	Accept 8bit binary data
CHUNKING	1830	Accept messages cut into chunks
CHECKPOINT	1845	Checkpoint/restart mail transactions
PIPELINING	1854	Accept multiple commands in a single send
SIZE	1870	Display maximum acceptable message size
DSN	1891	Provide delivery status notifications
ETRN	1985	Accept remote queue processing requests
ENHANCEDSTATUSCODES	2034	Provide enhanced error codes

It is easy to check which extensions are supported by your server by using the **EHLO** command. The following example is from a sendmail 8.8.5. system:

```
> telnet localhost 25
Trying 127.0.0.1...
Connected to localhost.
Escape character is '^]'.
220 peanut ESMTP Sendmail 8.7.5/8.7.3; Tue, 11 Nov 1997 15:22:34 -0500
ehlo peanut
250-peanut Hello craig@localhost [127.0.0.1], pleased to meet you
250-EXPN
250 HELP
250-8BITMIME
250-SIZE
250-DSN
250-ETRN
250-VERB
```

```
250-ONEX
250-XUSR
quit
221 peanut closing connection
Connection closed by foreign host.
```

The sample system lists nine commands in response to the **EHLO** greeting. Two of these, **EXPN** and **HELP**, are standard SMTP commands that aren't implemented on all systems (the standard commands are listed in Table 3-1). 8BITMIME, SIZE, DSN, and ETRN are ESMTP extensions, all of which are described in Table 3-4. The last three keywords in the response are VERB, ONEX, and XUSR. All of these are specific to sendmail version 8. None is defined in an RFC. VERB simply places the sendmail server in verbose mode. ONEX limits the session to a single message transaction. XUSR is as yet unimplemented, but it will be equivalent to the –U sendmail command-line argument.* As the last three keywords indicate, the RFCs allow for private ESMTP extensions.

The specific extensions implemented on each operating systems are different. For example, on a Solaris 2.5.1 system only three keywords (EXPN, SIZE, and HELP) are displayed in response to **EHLO**. The purpose of **EHLO** is to identify these differences at the begining of the SMTP mail exchange.

ESMTP and MIME are important because they provide a standard way to transfer non-ASCII data through email. Users share lots of application specific data that are not 7-bit ASCII. Many users depend on email as a file transfer mechanism.

SMTP, POP, and MIME are essential parts of the mail system, but other email protocols may also be essential in the future. The one certainty is that the network will continue to change. You need to track current developments and include helpful technologies into your planning. In the next section we look at the various types of TCP/IP configuration servers. Unlike DNS and email, configuration servers are not used on most networks. This is changing, however. The demand for easier installation and improved mobility may make configuration servers part of your network's future.

Configuration Servers

The powerful features that add to the utility and flexibility of TCP/IP also add to its complexity. TCP/IP is not as easy to configure as some other networking systems. TCP/IP requires that the configuration provide hardware, addressing, and routing information. It is designed to be independent of any specific underlying network hardware, so configuration information that can be built into the hardware in some network systems cannot be built-in for TCP/IP. The information

---

* See Appendix E, *A sendmail Reference*, for a list of the sendmail command-line arguments.

must be provided by the person responsible for the configuration. This assumes that every system is run by people who are knowledgeable enough to provide the proper information to configure the system. Unfortunately, this assumption does not always prove correct.

Configuration servers make it possible for the network administrator to control TCP/IP configuration from a central point. This relieves the end user of some of the burden of configuration and improves the quality of the information used to configure systems.

TCP/IP has three protocols that simplify the task of configuration: RARP, BOOTP, and DHCP. We begin with RARP, the oldest and most basic of these configuration tools.

Reverse Address Resolution Protocol

RARP, defined in RFC 903, is a protocol that converts a physical network address into an IP address, which is the reverse of what Address Resolution Protocol (ARP) does. A Reverse Address Resolution Protocol server maps a physical address to an IP address for a client that doesn't know its own IP address. The client sends out a broadcast using the broadcast services of the physical network.* The broadcast packet contains the client's physical network address and asks if any system on the network knows what IP address is associated with the address. The RARP server responds with a packet that contains the client's IP address.

The client knows its physical network address because it is encoded in the Ethernet interface hardware. On most systems you can easily check the value with a command. For example, on a Solaris system the superuser can type:

```
# ifconfig le0
le0: flags=63<UP,BROADCAST,NOTRAILERS,RUNNING>
        inet 128.66.12.1 netmask ffffff00 broadcast 128.66.12.255
        ether 8:0:20:e:12:37
```

The **ifconfig** command can set or display the configuration values for a network interface.† le0 is the device name of the Ethernet interface. The Ethernet address is displayed after the *ether* label. In the example, the address is 8:0:20:e:12:37.

The RARP server looks up the IP address that it uses in its response to the client in the */etc/ethers* file. The */etc/ethers* file contains the PC's Ethernet address followed by the PC's hostname. For example:

---

* Like ARP, RARP is a *Network Access Layer* protocol that uses physical network services that reside below the *Internet Layer*. See the discussion of TCP/IP protocol layers in Chapter 1, *Overview of TCP/IP*.

† See Chapter 6, *Configuring the Interface*, for information about the **ifconfig** command.

```
2:60:8c:48:84:49        hazel
0:0:c0:a1:5e:10         hickory
0:80:c7:aa:a8:04        acorn
8:0:5a:1d:c0:7e         cashew
8:0:69:4:6:31           pistachio
```

To respond to a RARP request, the server must also resolve the host name found in the */etc/ethers* file into an IP address. Domain name service or the *hosts* file is used for this task. The following *hosts* file entries could be used with the *ethers* file shown above.

```
hazel           172.16.3.10
hickory         172.16.3.16
acorn           172.16.3.4
cashew          172.16.3.7
pistachio       172.16.3.21
```

Given these sample files, if the server receives an RARP request that contains the Ethernet address, 0:80:c7:aa:a8:04, it matches it to *acorn* in the */etc/ethers* file. The server uses the name *acorn* to look up the IP address. It then sends the IP address 172.16.3.4 out as its RARP response.

RARP is a useful tool, but it provides only the IP address. There are still several other values that need to be manually configured. BOOTP is a more flexible configuration tool that provides more values than just the IP address and can deliver those values via the network.

Bootstrap Protocol

Bootstrap Protocol (BOOTP) is defined in RFCs 951 and 1532. The RFCs describe BOOTP as an alternative to RARP, and when BOOTP is used RARP is not needed. BOOTP, however, is a more comprehensive configuration protocol than RARP. It provides much more configuration information and has the potential to offer still more. The original specification allowed vendor extensions as a vehicle for the protocol's evolution. RFC 1048 first formalized the definition of these extensions, which have been updated over time and are currently defined in RFC 2132. BOOTP and its extensions became the basis for the Dynamic Host Configuration Protocol (DHCP). (More on DHCP later.)

The BOOTP client broadcasts a single packet called a *BOOTREQUEST* packet that contains, at a minimum, the client's physical network address. The client sends the broadcast using the address 255.255.255.255, which is a special address called the *limited broadcast address.** The client waits for a response from the server. If a response is not received within a specified time interval, the client retransmits the

---

* This address is useful because, unlike the normal broadcast address, it doesn't require the system to know the address of the network it is on.

request. BOOTP uses UDP as a transport protocol and, unlike RARP, it does not require any special Network Access Layer protocols.

The server responds to the client's request with a *BOOTREPLY* packet. BOOTP uses two different well-known port numbers. UDP port number 67 is used for the server and UDP port number 68 is used for the client. This is very unusual. Most software uses a well-known port on the server side and a randomly generated port on the client side.* The random port number ensures that each pair of source/destination ports identifies a unique path for exchanging information. A BOOTP client, however, is still in the process of booting. It may not know its IP address. Even if the client generates a source port for the *BOOTREQUEST* packet, a server response that is addressed to that port and the client's IP address won't be read by a client that doesn't recognize the address. Therefore, BOOTP sends the response to a specific port on all hosts. A broadcast sent to UDP port 68 is read by all hosts, even by a system that doesn't know its specific address. The system then determines if it is the intended recipient by checking the physical network address embedded in the response.

The server fills in all of the fields in the packet for which it has data. BOOTP can provide every essential TCP/IP configuration value. Chapter 9 provides a tutorial on setting up a BOOTP server, as well as a complete list of all of the configuration parameters that BOOTP can provide. In the next section we look at DHCP, which is based on BOOTP.

Dynamic Host Configuration Protocol

Dynamic Host Configuration Protocol (DHCP) is defined in RFCs 2131 and 2132. It's designed to be compatible with BOOTP. RFC 1534 outlines interactions between BOOTP clients and DHCP servers, and between DHCP clients and BOOTP servers. But interoperability problems are possible; many network administrators limit DHCP servers to DHCP clients. That's not necessary. See Chapter 9 and Appendix D for information on supporting BOOTP clients with DHCP servers.

DHCP uses the same UDP ports, 67 and 68, as BOOTP and the same *BOOTREQUEST* and *BOOTREPLY* packet format. But DHCP is more then just an update of BOOTP. The new protocol expands the function of BOOTP in two areas:

- The configuration parameters provided by a DHCP server include everything defined in the *Requirements for Internet Hosts* RFC. DHCP provides a client with a complete set of TCP/IP configuration values.
- DHCP permits automated allocation of IP addresses.

---

* How and why random source port numbers are used is described in Chapter 1.

DHCP uses the portion of the BOOTP packet originally set aside for vendor extensions to indicate the DHCP packet type and to carry a complete set of configuration information. DHCP calls the values in this part of the packet *options* instead of *vendor extensions*. This is a more accurate description because DHCP defines how the options are used and does not leave their definition up to the vendors. To handle the full set of configuration values from the *Requirements for Internet Hosts* RFC, the Options field is expanded to 312 bytes from the original 64 bytes of the BOOTP Vendor Extensions field.

You don't usually need to use this full set of configuration values. Don't get me wrong. The parameters are needed for a complete TCP/IP configuration. It's just that you don't need to define values for them. Default values are provided in most TCP/IP implementations, and the defaults only need to be changed in special circumstances. Frankly, you don't need most of the parameters defined by BOOTP, let alone any additional parameters. The expanded configuration parameters of DHCP make it a more complete protocol than BOOTP, but they are of only marginal value.

For most network administrators, automatic allocation of IP addresses is a more interesting feature. DHCP allows addresses to be assigned in three ways:

Manual allocation
> The network administrator keeps complete control over addresses by specifically assigning them to clients. This is exactly the same way that addresses are handled under BOOTP.

Automatic allocation
> The DHCP server permanently assigns an address from a pool of addresses. The administrator is not involved in the details of assigning a client an address.

Dynamic allocation
> The server assigns an address to a DHCP client for a limited period of time. The limited life of the address is called a lease. The client can return the address to the server at any time, but must request an extension from the server to retain the address longer than the time permitted. The server automatically reclaims the address after the lease expires if the client has not requested an extension.

Dynamic allocation is useful in a large distributed network where many systems are being added and deleted. Unused addresses are returned to the pool of addresses without relying on users or system administrators to take action to return them. Addresses are only used when and where they're needed. Dynamic allocation allows a network to make the maximum use of a limited set of addresses. It is particularly well-suited to mobile systems that move from subnet to subnet and therefore must be constantly reassigned addresses appropriate for their current network location.

Dynamic address allocation does not work for every system. Name servers, email servers, login hosts and other shared systems are always online, and they are not mobile. These systems are accessed by name, so a shared system's domain name must resolve to the correct address. Shared systems are manually allocated permanent, fixed addresses.

Dynamic address assignment has major repercussions for DNS. DNS is required to map hostnames to IP addresses. It cannot perform this job if IP addresses are constantly changing and DNS is not informed of the changes. To make dynamic address assignment work for all types of systems, we need a new DNS that can be dynamically updated by the DHCP server. The IETF is currently working on a standard for *Dynamic DNS*. When fully operational, it will help make dynamic addresses available to systems that provide services and to those that use them.

Given the nature of dynamic addressing, most sites assign permanent fixed addresses to shared servers. This happens through traditional system administration and is not handled by DHCP. In effect, the administrator of the shared server is given an address and puts that address in the shared server's configuration. Using DHCP for some systems doesn't mean it must be used for all systems.

Many DHCP servers can support BOOTP clients. However, a DHCP client is needed to take full advantage of the services offered by DHCP. BOOTP clients do not understand dynamic address leases. They do not know that an address can time out and that it must be renewed. BOOTP clients must be manually or automatically assigned permanent address. True dynamic address assignment is limited to DHCP clients.

Therefore, most sites that use DHCP have a mixture of:

- Permanent addresses assigned to systems that can't use DHCP or BOOTP
- Manual addresses assigned by DHCP to BOOTP clients
- Dynamic addresses assigned to all DHCP clients

We conclude this chapter with a discussion of file and print servers.

File and Print Servers

The last two network services, file and print services, make the network more convenient for users. Not long ago, disk drives and high-quality printers were relatively expensive, and diskless workstations were common. Today every system has a large hard drive and many have their own high-quality laser printers, but the demand for resource-sharing services is higher than ever.

File Sharing

File sharing is not the same as file transfer. It is not simply the ability to move a file from one system to another. A true file-sharing system does not require you to move entire files across the network. It allows files to be accessed at the record level so that it is possible for a client to read a record from a file located on a remote server, update that record, and write it back to the server—without moving the full file from the server to the client.

File sharing is transparent to the user and to the application software running on the user's system. Through file sharing, users and programs access files located on remote systems as if they were local files. In a perfect file-sharing environment, the user neither knows nor cares where files are actually stored.

File sharing didn't exist in the original TCP/IP protocol suite. It was added to support diskless workstations. Unlike a proprietary LAN where one vendor defines the official file-sharing protocol, TCP/IP is an open protocol suite and anyone can propose a new protocol. That's why there are three TCP/IP protocols for file sharing:

Remote File System
> RFS was defined by AT&T for UNIX System V. It is offered on many UNIX systems, but rarely used.

Andrew File System
> AFS is a file-sharing system developed at Carnegie Mellon University. AFS has several performance enhancements that make it particularly well-suited for wide area network (WAN) use. AFS has evolved into *Distributed File System* (DFS). Despite its features, it is not the most widely used file sharing system.

Network File System
> NFS was defined by Sun Microsystems to support their diskless workstations. NFS is designed primarily for LAN applications and is implemented for all UNIX systems and many other operating systems.

You will probably use NFS, as it is the most widely used TCP/IP file-sharing protocol. For a detailed discussion, see Chapter 9.

Print Services

A print server allows printers to be shared by everyone on the network. Printer sharing is not as important as file sharing, but it is a useful network service. The advantages of printer sharing are:

- Fewer printers are needed, and less money is spent on printers and supplies.

- Reduced maintenance. There are fewer machines to maintain, and fewer people spending time fiddling with printers.

- Access to special printers. Very high-quality color printers and very high-speed printers are expensive and needed only occasionally. Sharing these printers makes the best use of expensive resources.

There are two techniques commonly used for sharing printers on a TCP/IP network. One technique is to use the network's file sharing services. The other approach is to use the traditional UNIX **lpr** command and an **lpd** server. Print server configuration is covered in Chapter 9.

Summary

TCP/IP provides some network services that simplify network installation, configuration, and use. Name service is one such service and it is used on every TCP/IP network.

Name service can be provided by the host table, Domain Name Service (DNS), and Network Information Service (NIS). The host table is a simple text file stored in */etc/hosts*. Most systems have a small host table, but it cannot be used for all applications because it is not scalable and does not have a standard method for automatic distribution. NIS, the Sun "yellow pages" server, solves the problem of automatic distribution for the host table but does not solve the problem of scaling. DNS, which superceded the host table as a TCP/IP standard, does scale. DNS is a hierarchical, distributed database system that provides hostname and address information for all of the systems in the Internet.

Simple Mail Transfer Protocol (SMTP), Post Office Protocol (POP), and Multipurpose Internet Mail Extensions (MIME) are the building blocks of a TCP/IP email network. SMTP is a simple request/response protocol that provides end-to-end mail delivery. Sometimes end-to-end mail delivery is not suitable and the mail must be routed to a mail server. TCP/IP mail servers can use POP to move the mail from the server to the end system where it is read by the user. SMTP can only deliver 7-bit ASCII data. MIME extends the TCP/IP mail system so that it can carry a wide variety of data.

Many configuration values are needed to install TCP/IP. These values can be provided by a configuration server. Three protocols are popular for distributing configuration information:

RARP

> *Reverse Address Resolution Protocol* tells a client its IP address. The RARP server does this by mapping the client's Ethernet address to its IP address. The Ethernet to IP address mappings are stored on the server in the */etc/ethers* file.

BOOTP

> *Bootstrap Protocol* provides a wide range of configuration values.

DHCP

> *Dynamic Host Configuration Protocol* extends BOOTP to provide the full set of configuration parameters defined in the *Requirements for Internet Hosts* RFC. It also provides for *dynamic address* allocation, which allows a network to make maximum use of a limited set of addresses.

Network File System (NFS) is the leading TCP/IP file sharing protocol. It allows server systems to export directories that are then mounted by clients and used as if they were local disk drives. The UNIX LPD/LPR protocol can be used for printer sharing on a TCP/IP network.

This chapter concludes our introduction to the architecture, protocols, and services of a TCP/IP network. In the next chapter we begin to look at how to install a TCP/IP network by examining the process of planning an installation.

4

Getting Started

In this chapter, our emphasis shifts from how TCP/IP functions to how it is configured. While Chapters 1–3 describe the TCP/IP protocols and how they work, now we begin to explore the network configuration process. The first step in this process is planning. Before configuring a host to run TCP/IP, you must have certain information. At the very least, every host must have a unique IP address and hostname. You should also decide on the items below before configuring a system:

Default gateway address

If the system communicates with TCP/IP hosts that are not on its local network, a default gateway address may be needed. Alternatively, if a routing protocol is used on the network, each device needs to know that protocol.

Name server addresses

To resolve hostnames into IP addresses, each host needs to know the addresses of the domain name servers.

Domain name

Hosts using the domain name service must know their correct domain name.

Subnet mask

To communicate properly, each system on a network must use the same subnet mask.

Broadcast address

To avoid broadcast problems, the broadcast address of every computer on a network must be the same.

If you're adding a system to an existing network, make sure you find out the answers from your network administrator before putting the system online. The network administrator is responsible for making and communicating decisions about overall network configuration. If you have an established TCP/IP network, you can skip several sections in this chapter, but you may still want to read about selecting hostnames, planning mail systems, and other topics that affect mature networks as much as they do new networks.

If you are creating a new TCP/IP network, you will have to make some basic decisions. Will the new network connect to the Internet? If it will, how is the connection to be made? How should the network number be chosen? How do I register a domain name? How do I choose hostnames? In the following sections, we cover the information you need to make these decisions.

Connected and Non-Connected Networks

First, you must decide whether or not your new network will be directly connected to the Internet. The Internet's administration makes a distinction between networks connected to the Internet and those that are not connected. A *connected network* is directly attached to the Internet and has full access to other networks on the Internet. A *non-connected network* is not directly attached to the Internet, and its access to Internet networks is limited. An example of a non-connected network is a TCP/IP network that attaches to the outside world via a mail gateway at America Online (AOL). Users on the network can send mail to Internet hosts but they cannot directly **rlogin** to one of them.*

Many TCP/IP networks are not connected to the Internet. On these networks, TCP/IP is used for communication between the organization's various networks. Private networks that interconnect the various parts of an organization are often called *enterprise networks*. When those private networks use the information services applications that are built on top of TCP/IP, particularly Web servers and browsers, to distribute internal information, those networks are called *intranets*.

There are a few basic reasons why many sites do not connect to the Internet. One reason is security. Connecting to any network gives more people access to your system. Connecting to a global network with millions of users is enough to scare any security expert. There is no doubt about it: connecting to the Internet increases the security risks for your computer. Chapter 12, *Network Security*, covers some techniques for reducing this risk.

Cost versus benefit is another consideration. Many organizations do not see sufficient value in an Internet connection. For some organizations, low use or limited requirements, such as only needing email access, make the cost of an Internet connection exceed the benefit. For others, the primary reason for an Internet connection is to provide information about their products. It is not necessary to

---

* **rlogin** is covered in Chapter 9, *Configuring Network Servers.*

connect the entire enterprise network to the Internet to do this. It is often sufficient to connect a single Web server to the local Internet Service Provider (ISP) or to buy Web services from the ISP to provide information to your customers.

Other organizations consider an Internet connection an essential requirement. Educational and research institutions depend on the Internet as a source of information. Many companies use it as a means of delivering service and support to their customers.

You may have both types of networks: a "non-connected" enterprise network sitting behind a security firewall, and a small "connected" network that provides services to your external customers and proxy service for your internal users.

Unless you have carefully determined what your needs are and what an Internet connection will cost, you cannot know whether an Internet connection is right for your organization. Your local Internet service provider (ISP) can give you the various cost and performance alternatives. The next section offers ways to locate appropriate ISPs. Regardless of whether or not you decide to connect your network to the Internet, one thing is certain: you should build your enterprise network using the TCP/IP protocols.

Network Contacts

Choosing an ISP for your network can be confusing. Currently more than 5,000 ISPs operate in the United States alone. No attempt is made to list them all here. Instead we provide pointers to where you can obtain information on ISPs via email, newsgroups, the Web, and in print.

Readers who want basic information about the Internet can start by reading a book about the Internet. My favorite is *The Whole Internet Users' Guide and Catalog,* by Ed Krol (O'Reilly & Associates). It provides a user-oriented focus on the Internet and a substantial list of ISPs. Another book that provides a business focus on "getting connected" is *Getting Connected: Establishing a Presence on the Internet,* by Kevin Dowd (O'Reilly & Associates).

If you can send email to the Internet, request information about the ISPs in your area by sending email to *zahner@aimnet.com* with the words "MY AREA CODE =" followed by your area code in both the subject line and the body of the message. Here is an example for mail sent from a Solaris system to inquire for service providers for the 301 area code:

```
% Mail zahner@aimnet.com
Subject: MY AREA CODE = 301
MY AREA CODE = 301
^D
EOT
```

Use network news to obtain information about ISPs from the newsgroups *alt.internet.services* and *alt.internet.services.wanted.* Monitor *alt.internet.services* for announcements. Post a query to *alt.internet.services.wanted* asking if anyone knows of a good ISP in your area. Generally people in newsgroups have strong opinions and are willing to share them!

A good source of information about service providers is *The List* from Mecklermedia, which is accessible on the Web at *http://thelist.iworld.com.* The List contains information on thousands of ISPs. The information is sorted into country code and telephone area code lists to make it more useful.

Ask prospective ISPs about services as well as prices. Some ISPs specialize in providing low-cost service to home users. They emphasize price. However, if you are connecting a full network to the Internet, you may want an ISP that can provide network address, name service, Web services, and other features that your network might need.

Basic Information

Regardless of whether or not your network is connected to the Internet, you must provide certain basic information to configure the physical TCP/IP network interface. As we see in Chapter 6, *Configuring the Interface,* the network interface needs an IP address and may also need a subnet mask and broadcast address. In this section we look at how the network administrator arrives at each of the required values.

Obtaining an IP Address

Every interface on a TCP/IP network must have a unique IP address. If a host is part of the Internet, its IP address must be unique within the entire Internet. If a host's TCP/IP communications are limited to a local network, its IP address only needs to be unique locally. Administrators whose networks will not be connected to the Internet select an address from RFC 1918, *Address Allocation for Private Internets,* which lists network numbers that are reserved for private use.* The private network numbers are:

- Class A network 10.0.0.0 (10/8 prefix and a 24-bit block of addresses).

- Class B networks 172.16.0.0 to 172.31.0.0 (172.16/12 prefix and a 20-bit block of addresses).

---

* The address (172.16.0.0) used in this book is an address set aside for use by non-connected enterprise networks. Feel free to use this address on your network if it will not be connected to the Internet.

- Class C network 192.168.0.0 to 192.168.255.0 (192.168/16 prefix and a 16-bit block of addresses).

Networks connecting to the Internet must obtain official network addresses. An official address is needed for every system on your network that *directly* exchanges data with remote Internet hosts.* Obtain the address from your ISP. Your ISP has been delegated authority over a group of network addresses, and should be able to assign you a network number. If your local ISP doesn't offer this service, perhaps the ISP's upstream provider does. Ask your local ISP who it receives service from and ask that organization for an address. If all else fails, you may be forced to go directly to an Internet registry. The box *Internet Registries* provides information about the Internet registry services. The form required for registering an address is available at *ftp://rs.internic.net/templates/internet-number-template.txt*. Use the application as a last resort to obtain an address.

The advantages to choosing a network address from RFC 1918 are that you do not have to apply for an official address and you save address space for those who do need to connect to the Internet.† The advantage to obtaining your address from an Internet registry is that you will not have to change your address in the future if you do connect to the Internet.

If you do choose an address from RFC 1918 it is still possible to connect to the Internet without renumbering all of your systems. But it will take some effort. You'll need a *network address translation* (NAT) box or a proxy server. NAT is available as a separate piece of hardware or as an optional piece of software in some routers and firewalls. It works by converting the source address of datagrams leaving your network from your private address to your official address. Address translation has several advantages.

- It conserves IP addresses. Most network connections are between systems on the same enterprise network. Only a small percentage of systems need to connect to the Internet at any one time. Therefore far fewer official IP addresses are needed than the total number of systems on an enterprise network. NAT makes it possible for you to use a large address space from RFC 1918 for configuring your enterprise network while using only a small official address space for Internet connections.

- It eliminates address spoofing, a security attack in which a remote system pretends to be a local system. The addresses in RFC 1918 cannot be routed over the Internet. Therefore, even if a datagram is routed off of your network toward the remote system, the fact that the datagram contains an RFC 1918

---

* Hosts that communicate with the Internet through a firewall or proxy server may not need official addresses. Check your firewall/proxy server documentation.

† See Chapter 2, *Delivering the Data.*

destination address means that the routers in the Internet will discard the datagram as a *martian.*[*]

* It eliminates the need to renumber your hosts when you connect to the Internet.

Network address translation also has disadvantages:

Cost
NAT may add cost for new hardware or optional software.

Performance
Address translation adds overhead to the processing of every datagram. When the address is changed, the checksum must be recalculated. Furthermore, some upper-layer protocols carry a copy of the IP address that also must be converted.

Reliability
NAT is a new technology and there is very little experience with it in the network. Routers never modify the addresses in a datagram header, but NAT does. This might introduce some instability. Similarly, no one has much experience in determining how many addresses should be kept in a NAT address pool or how long an address should be held by a connection before it is released back to the pool.

Security
NAT limits the use of encryption and authentication. Authentication schemes that include the header within the calculation do not work because NAT changes the addresses in the header. Encryption does not work if the encrypted data includes the source address.

Proxy servers provide many of the same advantages as NAT boxes. In fact, these terms are often used interchangeably. But there are differences. Proxy servers are application gateways originally created as part of firewall systems to improve security. Internal systems connect to the outside world through the proxy server, and external systems respond to the proxy server. Unlike routers, even routers with network address translation, the external systems do not see a network of internal systems. They see only one system—the proxy server. All **ftp**, **telnet**, and other connections appear to come from one IP address: the address of the proxy server. Therefore, the difference between NAT boxes and proxy servers is that NAT uses a pool of IP addresses to differentiate the connection between internal and external systems. The true proxy server has only one address and therefore must use protocol numbers and port numbers to differentiate the connections.

---

[*] A martian is a datagram with an address that is known to be invalid.

Internet Registries

The original network information center was the SRI NIC, *sri-nic.arpa*. In 1992 the NIC moved to *nic.ddn.mil* and became the DDN NIC. Then in April 1993 the registration, directory, and information services it provided for the Internet moved to the new Internet NIC, *internic.net*. The InterNIC still provides these services but it does not do so alone.

Almost every large network has its own network information center. Most of these NICs provide access to all the RFCs, FYIs, and other TCP/IP documentation. A few provide registration services. For the Internet to work properly, IP addresses and domain names must be unique. To guarantee this addressing, authority is carefully delegated. Authority to delegate domains and addresses has been given to the Internet Resource Registries (IRR). Currently these are: RIPE for Europe, APNIC for Asia and the Pacific, CA*net for Canada, RNP for Brazil, and InterNIC for the rest of us. More registries may be created at any time. (See the discussion of generic top-level domains (gTLDs) in Chapter 3.) Additionally large groups of addresses have been delegated to ISPs so that they can assign them to their customers.

The place to start looking for registry services is your ISP. If it does not provide these services, contact the InterNIC. You can contact the InterNIC at the postal address:

> Network Solutions
> InterNIC Registration Services
> 505 Huntmar Park Drive
> Herndon, VA 22070

You can also reach the InterNIC via telephone at 703-742-4777 or via fax at 703-742-4811.

All of the forms needed to register an address, domain name, or other essential value can be obtained from the InterNIC using either anonymous FTP or a Web browser. Obtain the forms via anonymous FTP from *rs.internic.net*, where they are stored in the *templates* directory. Via the Web, connect to the Registration Template Guide at *http://rs.internic.net/help/templates.html*. It provides links to all of the forms and descriptions of when they are used and how they are filled in.

Proxy servers often have added security features. Address translation can be done at the IP layer. Proxy services require the server to handle data up to the application layer. Security filters can be put in proxy servers that filter data at all layers of the protocol stack.

Given the differences discussed here, network address translation servers should scale better than proxy servers, and proxy servers should provide better security. Proxy servers are frequently used in place of address translation for small networks. Before you decide to use either NAT or proxy services, make sure they are suitable for your network needs.

Assigning host addresses

So far we have been discussing *network numbers*. Our imaginary company's network (*nuts-net*) was assigned network number 172.16.0.0/16. The network administrator assigns individual host addresses within the range of IP addresses available to the network address; i.e., the *nuts-net* administrator assigns the last two bytes of the four-byte address.* The portion of the address assigned by the administrator cannot have all bits 0 or all bits 1; i.e., 172.16.0.0 and 172.16.255.255 are not valid host addresses. Beyond these two restrictions, you're free to assign host addresses in any way that seems reasonable to you.

Network administrators usually assign host addresses in one of two ways:

One address at a time
> Each individual host is assigned an address, perhaps in sequential order, through the address range.

Groups of addresses
> Blocks of addresses are delegated to smaller organizations within the overall organization, which then assign the individual host addresses.

The assignment of groups of addresses is most common when the network is subnetted, and the address groups are divided along subnet boundaries. But assigning blocks of addresses does not require subnetting. It can be just an organizational device for delegating authority. Delegating authority for groups of addresses is often very convenient for large networks, while small networks tend to assign host addresses one at a time. No matter how addresses are assigned, someone must retain sufficient central control to prevent duplication and to ensure that the addresses are recorded correctly on the domain name servers.

Addresses can be assigned statically or dynamically. Static assignment is handled through manually configuring the boot file on the host computer, or through a server such as BOOTP. Dynamic address assignments are always handled by a server, such as PPP or DHCP. Before installing a server for dynamic addressing, make sure it is useful for your purposes. Dynamic PPP addressing is useful for servers that handle many remote dial-in clients that connect for a short duration. If the PPP server is used to connect together various parts of the enterprise network

---

* The range of addresses is called the *address space*.

and has long-lived connections, dynamic addressing is probably unnecessary. Likewise, the dynamic address assignment features of DHCP are of most use if you have mobile systems in your network that move between subnets and therefore need to frequently change addresses. See Chapter 6 for information on PPP, and Chapters 3 and 9 for details of DHCP.

Clearly, you must make several decisions about obtaining and assigning addresses. In the next section we look at the subnet mask, which changes how the address is interpreted.

Defining the Subnet Mask

Chapter 2 describes the structure of IP addresses and touches upon the reasons for subnetting. Unless you wish to change the interpretation of your assigned network number, you do not have to define a subnet mask. The decision to subnet is commonly driven by topological or organizational considerations.

The topological reasons for subnetting include:

Overcoming distance limitations
> Some network hardware has very strict distance limitations. Ethernet is the most common example. The maximum length of a "thick" Ethernet cable is 500 meters; the maximum length of a "thin" cable is 300 meters; the total length of an Ethernet, called the maximum diameter, is 2500 meters. If you need to cover a greater distance, you can use IP routers to link a series of Ethernet cables. Individual cable still must not exceed the maximum allowable length, but using this approach, every cable is a separate Ethernet. Therefore the total length of the IP network can exceed the maximum length of an Ethernet.

Interconnecting dissimilar physical networks
> IP routers can be used to link together networks that have different and incompatible underlying network technologies. Figure 4-1 later in this chapter shows a central token ring subnet, 172.16.1.0, connecting two Ethernet subnets 172.16.6.0 and 172.16.12.0.

Filtering traffic between networks
> Local traffic stays on the local subnet. Only traffic intended for other networks is forwarded through the gateway.

Subnetting is not the only way to solve topology problems. Networks are implemented in hardware and can be altered by changing or adding hardware, but subnetting is an effective way to overcome these problems at the TCP/IP software level.

Of course, there are non-technical reasons for creating subnets. Subnets often serve organizational purposes such as:

Simplifying network administration

Subnets can be used to delegate address management, troubleshooting, and other network administration responsibilities to smaller organizations within the overall organization. This is an effective tool for managing a large network with a limited staff. It places the responsibility for managing the subnet on the people who benefit from its use.

Recognizing organizational structure

The structure of an organization (or simply office politics) may require independent network management for some divisions. Creating independently managed subnets for these divisions is preferable to having them go directly to an ISP to get their own independent network numbers.

Isolating traffic by organization

Certain organizations may prefer to have their local traffic isolated to a network that is primarily accessible only to members of that organization. This is particularly appropriate when security is involved. For example, the payroll department might not want their network packets on the engineering network, where some clever person could figure out how to intercept them.

Isolating potential problems

If a certain segment is less reliable than the remainder of the net, you may want to make that segment a subnet. For example, if the research group puts experimental systems on the network from time to time, or experiments with the network itself, this part of the network will be unstable. You would make it a subnet to prevent experimental hardware or software from interfering with the rest of the network.

The network administrator decides if subnetting is required and defines the subnet mask for the network. The subnet mask has the same form as an IP address mask. As described in Chapter 2, it defines which bits form the "network part" of the address and which bits form the "host part." Bits in the "network part" are turned *on* (i.e., 1), while bits in the "host part" are turned *off* (i.e., 0).

The subnet mask used on *nuts-net* is 255.255.255.0. This mask sets aside 8 bits to identify subnets, which creates 256 subnets. The *nuts-net* administrator has decided that this mask provides enough subnets and that the individual subnets have enough hosts to effectively use the address space of 253 hosts per subnet. Figure 4-1 later in this chapter shows an example of this type of subnetting. Applying this subnet mask to the addresses 172.16.1.0 and 172.16.12.0 causes them to be interpreted as the addresses of two different networks, not as two different hosts on the same network.

Once a mask is defined, it must be disseminated to all hosts on the network. There are two ways this is done: manually, through the configuration of network interfaces; and automatically, through routing protocols. Old routing protocols cannot distribute subnet masks, and old operating systems cannot store the masks in the routing table. In an environment that contains these old systems, every device on the network must use the same subnet mask because every computer believes that the entire network is subnetted in exactly the same way as its local subnet.

New routing protocols distribute address masks for each destination, and new operating systems store those masks in the routing table. This makes it possible to use variable-length subnet masks (VLSM). Using variable-length subnet masks increases the flexibility and power of subnetting. Assume you wanted to divide 192.168.5.0/24 into three networks: one network of 110 hosts, one network of 50 hosts, and one network of 60 hosts. Using traditional subnet masks, a single subnet mask would have to be chosen and applied to the entire address space. At best this would be a compromise. With variable length subnet masks you could use a mask of 255.255.255.128, which creates subnets of 126 hosts, for the large subnet and a mask of 255.255.255.192 to create subnets of 62 hosts for the smaller subnets. VLSMs, however, require UNIX kernels that know how to store and use the masks and routing protocols that can transmit them. See Chapter 7, *Configuring Routing*, for more information on routing.

Specifying the broadcast address

The need to specify a broadcast address may not be as clear as, for example, the need to specify a subnet mask. The standard broadcast address is an address where all host bits are set to 1s. This means the standard broadcast address on subnet 172.16.12.0 is 172.16.12.255. We want to use the standard broadcast address, so why worry about it?

The problem arises because some devices use the wrong broadcast address. The BSD 4.2 UNIX release used a broadcast address where the host bits were all set to 0, and there was no facility for changing it. The problem did not exist in BSD 4.3 and later releases; however, some systems still default to the wrong broadcast address. If you have systems on your network that use the wrong broadcast address, fix the address.

In Chapter 6, *Configuring the Interface*, we discuss how the IP address, subnet mask, and broadcast address are used to configure the physical network interface. Another essential part of a TCP/IP network is routing.

Planning Routing

In Chapter 2, we learned that hosts communicate directly only with other computers connected to the same network. Gateways are needed to communicate with systems on other networks. If the hosts on your network need to communicate with computers on other networks, a route through a gateway must be defined. There are two ways to do this:

- Routing can be handled by a *static routing table* built by the system administrator. Static routing tables are most useful when the number of gateways is limited. Static tables do not dynamically adjust to changing network conditions, so each change in the table is made manually by the network administrator. Complex environments require a more flexible approach to routing than a static routing table provides.

- Routing can be handled by a *dynamic routing table* that responds to changing network conditions. Dynamic routing tables are built by routing protocols. Routing protocols exchange routing information that is used to update the routing table. Dynamic routing is used when there are multiple gateways on a network, and is essential when more than one gateway can reach the same destination.

Many networks use a combination of both static and dynamic routing. Some systems on the network use static routing tables, while others run routing protocols and have dynamic tables. While it is often appropriate for hosts to use static routing tables, gateways usually run routing protocols.

The network administrator is responsible for deciding what type of routing to use and for choosing the default gateway for each host. Make these decisions before you start to configure your system. Here are a few guidelines to help you plan routing. If you have:

A network with no gateways to other TCP/IP networks
> No special routing configuration is required in this case. The gateways referred to in this discussion are IP routers that interconnect TCP/IP networks. If you are not interconnecting TCP/IP networks, you do not need an IP router. Neither a default gateway nor a routing protocol needs to be specified.

A network with a single gateway
> If you have only one gateway, don't run any routing protocols. Specify the single gateway as the default gateway in a static routing table.

A network with internal gateways to other subnets and one gateway to the world
> Here there is a real choice. You can statically specify each subnet route and make the gateway to the world your default route, or you can run a routing protocol. Decide which you want to do based on the effort involved in

maintaining a static table versus the slight overhead of running a routing protocol on your hosts and networks. If you have more than a few hosts, running a routing protocol is probably easiest.

A network with multiple gateways to the world

If you have multiple gateways that can reach the same destination, use a routing protocol. This allows the gateways to adapt to network changes, giving you redundant access to the remote networks.

Figure 4-1 shows a subnetted network with five gateways identified as *A* through *E*. A central subnet (172.16.1.0) interconnects five other subnets. One of the subnets has a gateway to an external network. The network administrator would probably choose to run a routing protocol on the central subnet (172.16.1.0) and perhaps on subnet 172.16.12.0, which is attached to an external network. Dynamic routing is appropriate on these subnets because they have multiple gateways. Without dynamic routing, the administrator would need to update every one of these gateways manually whenever any change occurred in the network—for example, whenever a new subnet was added. A mistake during the manual update could disrupt network service. Running a routing protocol on these two subnets is simpler and more reliable.

On the other hand, the administrator would probably choose static routing for the other subnets (172.16.3.0, 172.16.6.0, and 172.16.9.0). These subnets each use only one gateway to reach all destinations. Changes external to the subnets, such as the addition of a new subnet, do not change the fact that these three subnets still have only one routing choice. Newly added networks are still reached through the same gateway. The hosts on these subnets specify the subnet's gateway as their default route. In other words, the hosts on subnet 172.16.3.0 specify *B* as the default gateway, while the hosts on subnet 172.16.9.0 specify *D* as the default, no matter what happens on the external networks.

Some routing decisions are thrust upon you by the external networks to which you connect. In Figure 4-1, the local network connects to an external network that requires that Border Gateway Protocol (BGP) be used for routing. Therefore, gateway *E* has to run BGP to exchange routes with the external network.

Obtaining an autonomous system number

The Border Gateway Protocol (BGP) requires that gateways have a special identifier called an *autonomous system number* (ASN). (Refer to the section "Internet Routing Architecture" in Chapter 2 for a discussion of autonomous systems.) Most sites do not need to run BGP. Most sites do not need a unique ASN, even when they do run BGP. Usually those sites can select one of the ASNs that have been set aside for private use, which are the numbers from 64512 to 65535. Select a number and coordinate your selection with your border gateway peers to avoid any

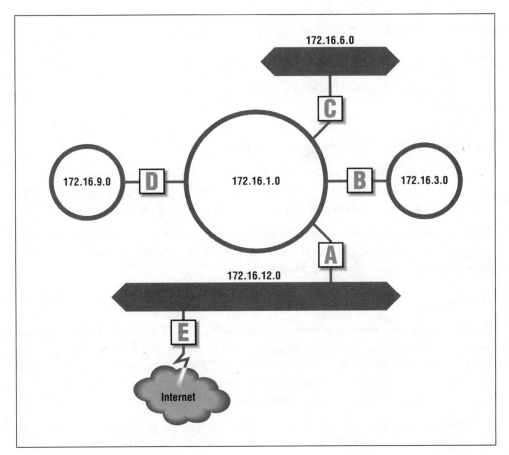

Figure 4-1: Routing and subnets

possible conflicts. If you connect to the Internet through a single ISP, you almost certainly do not need an official ASN. If after discussions with your service provider you find that you must obtain an official ASN, obtain the application form at *ftp://rs.internic.net/templates/asn-template.txt*. (See the "Internet Registries" sidebar earlier in this chapter.)

If you submit an application, you're asked to explain why you need a unique autonomous system number. Unless you are an ISP, probably the only reason to obtain an ASN is that you are a *multi-homed site*. A multi-homed site is any site that connects to more than one ISP. Reachability information for the site may be advertised by both ISPs, confusing the routing policy. Assigning the site an ASN gives it direct responsibility for setting its own routing policy and advertising its own reachability information. This doesn't prevent the site from advertising bad routes, but it makes the advertisement traceable back to one site and ultimately to one technical contact. (Once you submit an ASN application, you have no one to blame but yourself!)

All of the items we have discussed so far (addressing, subnetting, and routing) are required to configure the basic physical network on top of which the applications and services run. Now we begin planning the services that make the network useful and usable.

Planning Naming Service

To make your network user-friendly, you need to provide a service to convert hostnames into IP addresses. Domain name service (DNS) and the host table, explained in Chapter 3, perform this function. You should plan to use both.

To configure her computer, a network user needs to know the domain name, her system's hostname, and the hostname and address of at least one name server. The network administrator provides this information.

Obtaining a Domain Name

The first item you need for domain name service is a domain name. You can obtain an official domain name from the InterNIC. Your ISP may be willing to do this for you or to assign you a name within its domain; however, it is likely that you will have to apply for a domain name yourself. You can download the application from *ftp://rs.internic.net/templates/domain-template.txt*.

Pre-select a domain name and have your primary domain name server up and running before you attempt to register the domain name. Use **whois** as described in Chapter 13, *Internet Information Resources*, to see if the name you want is in use. Double-check with **nslookup** as described in Chapter 8, *Configuring DNS Name Service*. When you are reasonably sure the domain name is still available, start your primary name server running. If you don't want to run your own server, ask your ISP if they offer this service. If they don't, you must either find a new ISP that does, or run the service yourself.

Having the primary server up and running doesn't mean that your entire domain must be fully operational, but it does mean that a server must be running to respond to basic queries. When asked, the server should answer that it is the name server for your domain. Configure the primary server as described in Chapter 8. Test it with **nslookup**. Once you are sure that it at least answers queries about itself, register the domain name.

Submit the domain name application form via email to *hostmaster@internic.net* with a subject line containing the words "NEW DOMAIN" followed by the name of your domain. For example, assuming the completed template is stored in the file *domain.application* on a Solaris system, the following command might be used to mail it to the InterNIC for a domain named *nuts.com*:

```
% Mail hostmaster@internic.net
Subject: NEW DOMAIN nuts.com
~r domain.application
"domain.application" 49/2732
^D
EOT
```

In response to your email, you receive a reply that contains a tracking number that you use to monitor the status of your domain registration.

Use the domain name registration form to change or delete your existing domain name registration. Just fill in the form with the corrected information and mail it to *hostmaster@internic.net* with a subject line that contains either "MODIFY DOMAIN" or "REMOVE DOMAIN", as appropriate, followed by your domain name. In the very first field of the application form, item 0, ask for the type of registration action: either New ("N"), Modify ("M"), or Delete ("D"). Make sure the letter in this field matches the action indicated on the subject line when you mail in the application.

You're required to use email to submit the domain name application. The logic behind this is that if you don't have at least email access to the Internet, you don't need an Internet domain name. This helps reduce the number of frivolous domain name requests, and it automates part of the registration, further reducing the burden of handling domain name requests.

Another thing that dramatically reduces the number of frivolous domain name applications is the $100 registration fee. The registration service charges each domain $50 a year to be maintained in the registry. The initial $100 fee covers the first two years. Question 9 asks if the InterNIC should send the bill for the registration fee to you via email or postal mail. Answer with an "E" or a "P". If your "bean counters" will accept an email bill, go that way. You'll get everything finished more quickly.

The application form is largely self-explanatory, but a few items require some thought. Two things may be confusing—handles and servers. One is the request for a *NIC handle*. You have a NIC handle only if you are registered in the *NIC white pages*. The white pages (discussed in Chapter 12) is a directory of information about users, networks, hosts, and domains. A NIC handle is a record identifier for this directory. A personal NIC handle for a user entry is composed of the user's initials and perhaps a number. For example, my initials are *cwh* and my NIC handle is *cwh3*. It is unlikely that you will have a handle unless you have contacted the NIC before. If you don't have a handle, just leave it blank. The NIC will assign you one.

You're also asked for the names and addresses of your primary and secondary name servers. The servers listed must be operational and connected to the Internet.* Provide the full domain name of the primary server in response to question 7a; e.g. *almond.nuts.com.* The primary server is usually a name server located at your site, but not always. It isn't necessary to provide your own primary server; and if you aren't directly connected to the Internet, you can't. Even though you are not connected, you may still want to register your domain name with the NIC if you have email access to the Internet. This allows you to use an email address that clearly identifies your organization. In order to do this, the online service that receives your email must be able to provide your primary name service. Check with them before you fill out this form.

The secondary server should be on a separate physical network from the primary server. Putting it on a different network guarantees that other sites can look up information about your network, even if access to your network is unavailable for some reason. A large organization may have multiple independent networks, but for many sites this requirement means asking another organization to provide a secondary name server. Who do you ask?

Again, you should turn to the people who are providing your Internet access. The network that connects you to the Internet should provide secondary name servers as a service to its users. If they do not, they should be able to point you to other organizations that do provide the service. It is even possible for two organizations who are both applying for new domains to provide secondary service for each other. In other words, you provide someone with a secondary server; in return, they provide a secondary server for you.

Read the instructions that come with the domain application. The remainder of the form should be easy to fill out.

Obtaining an IN-ADDR.ARPA domain

When you obtain your Internet domain name, you should also apply for an *in-addr.arpa* domain. This special domain is sometimes called a *reverse domain.* Chapter 8 contains more information about how the *in-addr.arpa* domain is set up and used, but basically the reverse domain maps numeric IP addresses into domain names. This is the reverse of the normal process, which converts domain names to addresses. If your ISP provides your name service or your ISP assigned you an address from a block of its own addresses, you may not need to apply for an *in-addr.arpa* domain on your own. Check with your ISP *before* applying. If you do need to get a reverse domain, you can obtain the application from *ftp://rs.internic.net/templates/in-addr-template.txt.*

---

* Chapter 8 tells you how to get a name server up and running.

Choosing a Hostname

Once you have a domain name, you are responsible for assigning hostnames within that domain. You must ensure that hostnames are unique within your domain or subdomain, in the same way that host addresses must be unique within a network or subnet. But there is more to choosing a host name than just making sure the name is unique. Choosing a hostname is a surprisingly emotional issue. Many people feel very strongly about the name of their computer because they identify their computer with themselves or their work.

RFC 1178 provides excellent guidelines on how to choose a hostname. Some key suggestions from these guidelines are:

- Use real words that are short, easy to spell, and easy to remember. The point of using hostnames instead of IP addresses is that they are easier to use. If hostnames are difficult to spell and remember, they defeat their own purpose.

- Use theme names. For example, all hosts in a group could be named after human movements: fall, jump, hop, skip, walk, run, stagger, wiggle, stumble, trip, limp, lurch, hobble, etc. Theme names are often easier to choose than unrestricted names, and increase the sense of community among network users.

- Avoid using project names, personal names, acronyms, numeric names, and technical jargon. Projects and users change over time. If you name a computer after the person who is currently using it or the project it is currently assigned to, you will probably have to rename the computer in the future. Use nicknames to identify the server function of a system, e.g., *www, ftp, ns*, etc. Nicknames can easily move between systems if the server function moves. See the description of CNAME records in Chapter 8 for information on creating nicknames.

The only requirement for a hostname is that it be unique within its domain. But a well-chosen hostname can save future work and make the user happier.

Name service is the most basic network service, and it is one service that you will certainly run on your network. There are, however, other services that you should also include in your network planning process.

Other Services

Three services that are used on many networks are file servers, print servers, and mail servers. The purpose of these services and the protocols they are built on is discussed in Chapter 3. In this section we investigate what information must be passed to the users so that the client systems can be successfully configured, and how the network administrator determines that information.

File servers

At a minimum the user needs to know the hostnames of the network file servers. Using the names and the **showmount** command, the user can determine what filesystems are being offer by the servers and who is permitted to use those filesystems.* Without at least the hostname, the user would have to guess which system offered file service.

A better approach is to give users information that also includes what filesystems are being offered and who should use those filesystems. For example, if the UNIX **man** pages are made available from a central server, the users should be informed not to install the **man** pages on their local disk drives and they should be told exactly how to access the centrally supported files.

Print servers

Whether printers are shared using **lp**, **lpd**, or NFS, the basic information needed to configure the print server's clients is the same: the hostname and IP address of the print server, and the name of the printer. Printer security may also require that the user be given a username and password to access the printer.

This is the only information needed to configure the client. However, you probably will want to provide your users with additional information about the features, location and administration of shared printers.

Planning Your Mail System

TCP/IP provides the tools you need to create a reliable, flexible electronic mail system. Servers are one of the tools that improve reliability. It is possible to create a peer-to-peer email network in which every end system directly sends and receives its own mail. However, relying on every system to deliver and collect the mail requires that every system be properly administered and consistently up and running. This isn't practical, because many small systems are offline for large portions of the day. Most networks use servers so that only a few systems need to be properly configured and operational for the mail to go through.

The terminology that describes email servers is confusing because all of the server functions usually occur in one computer, and all of the terms are used interchangeably to refer to that system. In this text we differentiate between these functions, but we expect you will do all of these tasks on one UNIX system running **sendmail**. We use these terms in the following manner:

---

* See the **showmount** command in Chapter 9.

Mail server

> The mail server collects incoming mail for other computers on the network. It supports interactive logins as well as POP or IMAP so that users can read their mail as they see fit.

Mail relay

> A mail relay is a host that forwards mail between internal systems and from internal systems to remote hosts. Mail relays allow internal systems to have simple mail configurations because only the relay host needs to have software to handle special mail addressing schemes and aliases.

Mail gateway

> A mail gateway is a system that forwards email between dissimilar systems. You don't need a gateway to go from one Internet host to another because both systems use SMTP. You do need a gateway to go from SMTP to X.400 or to a proprietary mailer. In a pure TCP/IP network, this function is not needed.

The mail server is the most important component of a reliable system because it eliminates reliance on the user's system. A centrally controlled, professionally operated server collects the mail regardless of whether or not the end system is operational.

The relay host also contributes to the reliability of the email system. If mail cannot be immediately delivered by the relay host, it is queued and processed later. An end system also queues mail, but if it is shut down no attempts can be made to deliver queued mail until the system is back online. The mail server and the mail relay are operated 24 hours a day.

The design of most TCP/IP email networks is based on the following guidelines:

- Use a mail server to collect mail, and POP or IMAP to deliver the mail.

- Use a mail relay host to forward mail. Implement a simplified email address scheme on the relay host.

- Standardize on TCP/IP and SMTP. Users who insist on using a proprietary email system should be responsible for obtaining and configuring an SMTP mail gateway for that system in order to connect to your TCP/IP email network.

- Standardize on MIME for binary attachments. Avoid proprietary attachment schemes; they just cause confusion when the users of Brand X email cannot read attachments received from Brand Y.

For their client configurations, provide the users with the hostname and IP address of the mail server and the mail relay. The mail server will also require a username and password for each person.

Informing the Users

All of the configuration information that you gather or develop through the planning process must be given to the users so that they can configure their systems. You can distribute information with several techniques.

In Chapter 3 we discussed NIS, NFS, and configuration servers. All of these play a role in informing the user and in simplifying the configuration process. NIS supports several system administration databases that provide many of the basic configuration values. NFS can distribute pre-configured system files to client systems. Configuration servers, such as BOOTP and DHCP, offer every parameter needed to configure a TCP/IP system directly to the client. All of these are important, but they are not the complete solution.

The servers require that the client is configured to be a client. For NIS and NFS, the client must have a full basic configuration. Even BOOTP and DHCP require that the user know whether BOOTP or DHCP is being used so that he does not enter any incorrect values during the initial system installation. Therefore, the network administrator must directly communicate with the administrator of the end system, usually through written documentation.

Sample Planning Sheets

To communicate this information, the network administrator will often create an *installation planning sheet*—a short list of information for the system administrator. A sample planning sheet for the workstation *peanut*, based on some of the topics we have discussed, provides basic configuration details. The planning sheet lists the name, address, subnet mask, the fact that DNS is used, and the fact that RIP is used on subnet 172.16.12.0:

Hostname:
   peanut

IP address:
   172.16.12.2

Subnet mask:
   255.255.255.0

Default gateway:
   172.16.12.1 (almond.nuts.com)

Broadcast address:
   172.16.12.255

Domain name:
   nuts.com

Name servers:
> 172.16.12.1 (almond.nuts.com)
> 172.16.6.8 (pack.plant.nuts.com)

Routing protocol:
> Routing Information Protocol (RIP)

Mail server:
> 172.16.12.1 (almond.nuts.com)

Mail relay:
> 172.16.12.1 (almond.nuts.com)

Print server:
> 172.16.12.3 (pecan.nuts.com)

NFS server:
> 172.16.1.2 (filbert.nuts.com)

A similar sheet prepared for *almond* (see below) varies slightly from the planning sheet for *peanut*. The names and address are different, of course, but the real differences are caused by the fact that *almond* is a gateway. As a gateway, *almond* has more than one network interface, and each interface requires its own configuration. Each interface has its own address and can have its own name, subnet mask, and routing protocol.

Hostname:
> almond (172.16.12.1)
> mil-gw (10.104.0.19)

IP address:
> 172.16.12.1
> 10.104.0.19

Subnet mask:
> 255.255.255.0 (172.16.12.1)
> default (10.104.0.19)

Default gateway:
> none

Broadcast address:
> 172.16.12.255 (172.16.12.1)
> default (10.104.0.19)

Domain name:
> nuts.com

Name servers:
> 172.16.12.1 (almond.nuts.com)
> 172.16.6.8 (pack.plant.nuts.com)

Routing protocol:
> Routing Information Protocol (RIP) (172.16.12.1)
> Border Gateway Protocol (BGP) (10.104.0.19)

Print server:
> 172.16.12.3 (pecan.nuts.com)

NFS server:
> 172.16.1.2 (filbert.nuts.com)

We use the information from these planning sheets to configure the systems in subsequent chapters. You may, however, want to format your planning sheets differently. In this book we configure the system directly. We use the configuration commands ourselves so that we can understand and master them. In reality many basic configuration tasks are performed by a network configuration script during the initial operating system installation. You may want to format your planning sheet to be compatible with the prompts of that script. One such script is **netconfig**, which is used on Linux systems.

netconfig

During the installation of the Slackware 96 Linux operating system you are asked if you want to configure the network. If you answer "yes", **netconfig** begins. **netconfig** can be run by the superuser at any time from the shell prompt.

netconfig presents a series of screens that prompt for basic configuration information. The first two questions, hostname and domain name, are simple enough. However, the third question may cause some confusion. It asks if the system should be configured to use only the loopback interface. You may wonder why anyone would limit TCP/IP to the loopback interface. The reason is simple: the person wants to run TCP/IP but has no physical network. Students who are studying TCP/IP, perhaps on a home computer, sometimes use this so that they can work with TCP/IP without a physical network. Clearly, the users attached to your network should answer "no" to this question.

The remaining questions are straightforward. **netconfig** asks for the system's IP address, the IP address of the default gateway, and the subnet mask. It then asks if you will use a name server. If you answer "yes", it asks for the IP address of the name server.

That's it. It is easy to answer these questions using the planning sheet we developed above. But if you know what configuration questions your users will be asked and what order they will have to answer them, you can improve the planning sheet. Reorder the planning information to match the order of the questions and add answers for the yes/no questions so that the users do not get confused. Here is the *peanut* planning sheet redesigned for **netconfig**:

Enter hostname:
    peanut

Enter domain name:
    nuts.com

Do you plan to ONLY use loopback:
    No

Enter IP address:
    172.16.12.2

Enter gateway address:
    172.16.12.1

Enter netmask:
    255.255.255.0

Will you access a nameserver:
    Yes

Name Server:
    172.16.12.1

This completes your network setup.
Hold on to the remaining information for future reference.##

Broadcast address:
    172.16.12.255

Mail server:
    172.16.12.1

Mail relay:
    172.16.12.1

Print server:
    172.16.12.3

NFS server:
    172.16.1.2

Summary

Planning is the first step in configuring TCP/IP. We began this chapter by deciding whether your network will connect to the Internet and exploring how that decision impacts the rest of your planning. We also looked at the basic information needed to configure a physical network: an IP address, a subnet mask, and a broadcast address. We discussed how to plan routing, which is essential for communicating between TCP/IP networks. We outlined the basic network services, starting with domain name service, and discussed file, print, and email servers. Finally, we looked at the different ways that this planning information is communicated from the network administrator to the system administrators and users.

In the chapters that follow, we put these plans into action, starting with the configuration of the network interface in Chapter 6. First, however, we will go inside the UNIX kernel to see how TCP/IP is built into the operating system.

5

Basic Configuration

Every UNIX computer that runs TCP/IP has a technique for incorporating the basic transport and IP datagram services into its operating system. This chapter discusses two files that are fundamental to the basic configuration of TCP/IP on UNIX systems: the *kernel configuration* file and the *inetd.conf* file. Because these files are so basic to network configuration, they usually come from the manufacturer preconfigured to run TCP/IP.

We'll examine the contents of these files and the role they play in linking TCP/IP and UNIX. With this information, you should be able to modify these files for your own custom configurations.

Kernel Configuration

Kernel configuration is not really a network administration task—rather, it is a basic part of UNIX system administration, whether or not the computer is connected to a network. But TCP/IP networking, like other system functions, is integrated into the kernel.

There are two very different approaches to kernel configuration. Some systems are designed to eliminate the need to configure the kernel yourself, while others encourage you to do your own kernel configuration. Solaris 2.5.1 is an example of the former. The system comes with a generic kernel that supports all basic system services. When a Solaris system boots, it detects any new hardware added to the system. Dynamically loadable modules are used to add new features to the system. The configuration is defined in the */etc/system* file, but this file is not directly edited by the system administrator. When a new software package is added to the system, the script that installs that package makes any changes it requires to the */etc/system* file.

Linux is an example of the latter philosophy: its documentation encourages you to create your own configuration. In this text we concentrate on Linux and on FreeBSD, systems that allow you to build your own custom kernel.* Throughout this chapter, we provide examples of kernel configuration statements using these two UNIX systems. While kernel configuration involves all aspects of system configuration, we include only statements that directly affect TCP/IP configuration.

Both of the UNIX systems used in the examples come with a kernel configuration file preconfigured for TCP/IP. During the initial installation, you may need to select a preconfigured kernel that includes network support, but you probably won't need to modify the kernel configuration for networking. The kernel configuration file is normally changed only when you wish to:

- Produce a smaller, more efficient kernel by removing unneeded items
- Add a new device
- Modify a system parameter

While there is rarely any need to modify the kernel network statements, it is useful to understand what these statements do. Looking into the kernel configuration file shows how UNIX is tied to the hardware and software of the network.

CAUTION   The procedures and files used for kernel configuration vary dramatically depending on UNIX implementation. These variations make it essential that you refer to your system documentation before trying to configure the kernel on your system. Only your system documentation can provide you with the accurate, detailed instructions required to successfully complete this task.

Linux Kernel Configuration

The Linux kernel is a C program compiled and installed by **make**. The **make config** command customizes the kernel configuration and generates the files (including the Makefile) needed to compile and link the kernel. On Linux systems, the kernel source directory is */usr/src/linux*. To start the configuration process, change to the source directory and run **make config**:

```
# cd /usr/src/linux
# make config
```

The **make config** command asks many questions about your system configuration. Some of these are directly related to network configuration.

---

* The kernel configuration process of other BSD systems, such as SunOS 4.1.3, is similar to the FreeBSD example.

The first network configuration question is:

```
Networking support (CONFIG_NET) [Y/n/?]
```

Answer "yes" (y), which is the default. Networking support is necessary for all of the TCP/IP networking features that we will request later in the configuration. Even if you don't run TCP/IP, you should answer "yes" to this question. Basic network support is essential to many services.

The **make config** command asks several more general configuration questions before returning to the topic of networking. When it does, it has many networking questions to ask. The example below is an excerpt from the actual configuration of the Linux 2.0 kernel on a Slackware 96 system.*

```
Network firewalls (CONFIG_FIREWALL) [N/y/?]
Network aliasing (CONFIG_NET_ALIAS) [N/y/?]
TCP/IP networking (CONFIG_INET) [Y/n/?]
IP: forwarding/gatewaying (CONFIG_IP_FORWARD) [N/y/?]
IP: multicasting (CONFIG_IP_MULTICAST) [N/y/?]
IP: accounting (CONFIG_IP_ACCT) [N/y/?]
IP: PC/TCP compatibility mode (CONFIG_INET_PCTCP) [N/y/?]
IP: Reverse ARP (CONFIG_INET_RARP) [N/y/m/?]
IP: Disable Path MTU Discovery (normally enabled)
    (CONFIG_NO_PATH_MTU_DISCOVERY) [N/y/?]
IP: Drop source routed frames (CONFIG_IP_NOSR) [Y/n/?]
IP: Allow large windows (not recommended if <16Mb of memory)
    (CONFIG_SKB_LARGE) [Y/n/?]
Network device support (CONFIG_NETDEVICES) [Y/n/?]
Dummy net driver support (CONFIG_DUMMY) [N/y/m/?]
EQL (serial line load balancing) support (CONFIG_EQUALIZER) [N/y/m/?]
PLIP (parallel port) support (CONFIG_PLIP) [N/y/m/?]
PPP (point-to-point) support (CONFIG_PPP) [Y/m/n/?]
SLIP (serial line) support (CONFIG_SLIP) [Y/m/n/?]
 CSLIP compressed headers (CONFIG_SLIP_COMPRESSED) [Y/n/?]
 Keepalive and linefill (CONFIG_SLIP_SMART) [Y/n/?]
 Six bit SLIP encapsulation (CONFIG_SLIP_MODE_SLIP6) [N/y/?]
Radio network interfaces (CONFIG_NET_RADIO) [N/y/?]
Ethernet (10 or 100Mbit) (CONFIG_NET_ETHERNET) [Y/n/?]
3COM cards (CONFIG_NET_VENDOR_3COM) [Y/n/?]
3c501 support (CONFIG_EL1) [N/y/m/?]
3c503 support (CONFIG_EL2) [N/y/m/?]
3c509/3c579 support (CONFIG_EL3) [Y/m/n/?]
3c590 series (592/595/597) "Vortex" support (CONFIG_VORTEX) [N/y/m/?]
AMD LANCE and PCnet (AT1500 and NE2100) support (CONFIG_LANCE) [N/y/?]
Western Digital/SMC cards (CONFIG_NET_VENDOR_SMC) [N/y/?]
Other ISA cards (CONFIG_NET_ISA) [N/y/?]
EISA, VLB, PCI and on board controllers (CONFIG_NET_EISA) [N/y/?]
Pocket and portable adaptors (CONFIG_NET_POCKET) [N/y/?]
Token Ring driver support (CONFIG_TR) [N/y/?]
```

---

* The configuration questions change with every new kernel. Refer to your system's documentation for the latest information.

```
ARCnet support (CONFIG_ARCNET) [N/y/m/?]
ISDN support (CONFIG_ISDN) [N/y/m/?]
```

Each configuration option is either enabled by entering a "y" for "yes", or disabled with an "n" for "no". "m" for "module" is an alternative method for enabling some features. Features that are available as dynamically loadable modules list "m" as a possible response. If "m" is selected, the dynamically loadable module is loaded the first time a call is made to the kernel that requires the module. If "y" is selected for a feature, the code that supports that feature is compiled directly into the kernel. The default setting of each option is indicated by the uppercase letter in the square brackets at the end of the option line. For example, [Y,n] indicates an option that is enabled by default. Here, we list each option and its purpose:

CONFIG_FIREWALL

Adds the kernel support necessary to make this system a firewall. Enable this only if the Linux system will be your firewall. The full firewall installation requires additional software outside the kernel. See Chapter 12, *Network Security*, for a discussion of firewalls.*

CONFIG_NET_ALIAS

Adds the kernel support necessary for address translation. Use this feature only if you have a private internal network number and a different network address for external communications. If you do, internal addresses must be translated to valid external addresses whenever connections are made to the outside world, but it is likely that the translation will be done by your router or firewall. You should select "yes" only in the rare circumstance that the Linux box must do the translation; otherwise, select "no". See Chapter 4, *Getting Started*, for a discussion of private network numbers and address translation.

CONFIG_INET

Adds TCP/IP networking to the kernel. This is an absolute must!

CONFIG_IP_FORWARD

Determines whether or not the system forwards IP datagrams. This feature must be enabled if the Linux system is an IP router. On Linux host systems, this feature is disabled, which is the default. Select "no" unless this box is a router.

CONFIG_IP_MULTICAST

Adds multicast support to the kernel. Enable this to use multicast applications such as MBONE or Internet Talk Radio. Not sure if you need multicasting? Select "yes". You never know what applications you will add later.

---

* Building a firewall is beyond the scope of this book. See *Building Internet Firewalls*, by Brent Chapman and Elizabeth Zwicky (O'Reilly & Associates), for a full treatment of the subject.

CONFIG_IP_ACCT

Adds code to count the bytes in incoming and outgoing traffic on a per-port/pre-address basis. This could be useful for monitoring system usage, particularly in a commercial environment where usage is billed back to the originator. Additional application software would be needed to make this useful. Select "no" unless you plan to keep close tabs on usage.

CONFIG_INET_PCTCP

Handles an incompatibility problem with older versions of FTP software's PC/TCP. Use if you have clients who run the old PC/TCP software on PCs.

CONFIG_INET_RARP

Adds support for Reverse Address Resolution Protocol (RARP) to the kernel. Enable this if you plan to use RARP on your network. Not sure? Use "m" to select the loadable module that can be used when your system needs it. See Chapter 3, *Network Services*, for a description of RARP and Chapter 9 for information on configuring a RARP server.

CONFIG_NO_PATH_MTU_DISCOVERY

Removes path MTU discovery code from the kernel. (Beware of the double negative! A "y" [yes] disables MTU discovery and an "n" [no] enables it.) Select "no". Path MTU discovery is a technique that attempts to determine the smallest maximum transmission unit (MTU) along the entire path from a source to a destination. That MTU is then used for subsequent transmissions to avoid datagram fragmentation. See Chapter 1, *Overview of TCP/IP*, for a description of fragmentation.

CONFIG_IP_NOSR

Determines whether the system accepts source-routed datagrams. Source routing allows the source of the datagram to specify the routers that are used to deliver the packet. Source routes are used to force packets to travel over a specific path; for example, to test the routers in a path or to avoid a high-cost link. However, the problem with source routes is that they are used by *spoofers*. Spoofers are network intruders who pretend to be a system they are not. For example, a spoofer might pretend to be a computer on one of your enterprise subnets. By using source routing, the spoofer could cause your system to route packets off of your enterprise net that you thought were going to a local system. Enabling CONFIG_IP_NOSR makes it impossible for a spoofer to use source routes against you. Select "yes" unless you are positive that you must use source routes.

CONFIG_SKB_LARGE

Sets whether or not the system will use a large transmission window size. Large windows improve network performance at the cost of additional buffer space. Large windows can be disabled to save memory on systems with less than 16MB of RAM. See Chapter 1 for a description of the TCP transmission window.

CONFIG_NETDEVICES

Adds the general support required for network hardware devices. Always answer "yes", which is the default, to this question. It is required before configuring your Ethernet card.

CONFIG_DUMMY

Enables support for a dummy interface. An IP address can be assigned to the dummy interface even if the system has no network interface hardware. This is sometimes used by people who want to work on TCP/IP configuration even though they don't have a network connection. If you have a network, select "no".

CONFIG_EQUALIZER

Adds support for using multiple serial lines simultaneously. Using this feature, it is possible to have more than one physical PPP link established between the local host and the remote server. The system load balances between the links and attempts to treat them as a single logical network connection. This is a technique for increasing the bandwidth simply by adding additional modems and phone lines. The systems at both ends must support serial line load balancing and they must do so in exactly the same way. This option is used only when both systems are Linux systems connected by multiple serial lines. Otherwise, select "no".

CONFIG_PLIP

Adds Parallel Line IP to the kernel. PLIP is a version of SLIP that runs over the parallel printer port using a special crossover cable. This protocol is intended for transferring data between two co-located PCs, as the cable should be only 1 or 2 meters long. This has very limited applicability.

CONFIG_PPP

Adds the Point-to-Point Protocol (PPP) to the kernel. PPP is the TCP/IP standard protocol for communicating over serial lines. Select "yes" if your system will use a modem connection for TCP/IP. Chapter 6, *Configuring the Interface*, covers the configuration of this important protocol in detail.

CONFIG_SLIP

Adds the Serial Line IP (SLIP) to the kernel. SLIP is an older TCP/IP protocol once widely used for communicating over serial lines. Chapter 6 covers SLIP configuration in detail.

CONFIG_SLIP_COMPRESSED

Adds support for Van Jacobsen header compression to the kernel. Packet headers add a large amount of overhead when communicating over low-speed serial lines. Header compression greatly reduces this overhead. The systems at both ends of the serial link must use header compression for it to work. Most systems that run SLIP do use header compression.

CONFIG_SLIP_SMART

Adds support for *keepalives* to the kernel. Some servers drop a connection or timeout a route if the route or connection appears unused. Use is determined by whether or not traffic is coming in over the link. Keepalives are periodic transmissions sent for the explicit purpose of generating traffic on a link so that it is not dropped as an inactive line. The use of keepalives is discouraged. Most networks are busy enough as it is!

CONFIG_SLIP_MODE_SLIP6

Adds support for running SLIP over 6-bit serial lines. Normally a modem and line are configured for 8-bit, no-parity to run SLIP or PPP. This feature allows SLIP to be run in an environment that can not support 8-bit transmissions. This is non-standard and rarely used. The systems at both ends of the link must support this protocol for it to work.

CONFIG_NET_ETHERNET

Adds support for Ethernet hardware to the kernel. You need this for your Ethernet LAN.

The remaining questions allow you to select your network hardware. A large number of Ethernet cards are supported by Linux. In the sample, we selected the 3COM 3C509 card. The **make config** command also allows us to select ARCnet, token ring, or ISDN interfaces. Some hosts use no specific network hardware. Instead, they run SLIP or PPP over a serial port as their sole network connection. Select the hardware appropriate for your system.

After **make config** asks questions about the network configuration, it goes on to ask about several other aspects of the system configuration. Next, it tells you to do a **make dep** ; **make clean** to build the dependencies and clean up the odds and ends. When the makes are complete, you are ready to compile the kernel. The **make zImage** command builds a compressed kernel and puts it in the */usr/src/linux/i386/boot* directory.* Simply copy the new kernel file, *zImage*, to */vmlinuz* and you're ready to run.

Linux's list of network configuration options is as long lists for UNIX kernel configuration. Linux is yin to the Solaris yang. Linux permits the system administrator to configure everything, while Solaris configures everything for the administrator. BSD kernel configuration lies somewhere between these two extremes.

---

* Most Linux systems use a compressed kernel that is automatically decompressed during the system boot.

The BSD Kernel Configuration File

The BSD UNIX kernel is a C program compiled and installed by **make**. The **config** command reads the kernel configuration file and generates the files (including the Makefile) needed to compile and link the kernel. On FreeBSD systems, the kernel configuration file is located in the directory */usr/src/sys/i386/conf.**

A large kernel configuration file named *GENERIC* is delivered with the FreeBSD system. The *GENERIC* kernel file configures all of the standard devices for your system—including everything necessary for TCP/IP. No modifications are necessary for the *GENERIC* kernel to run basic TCP/IP services. The reasons for modifying the BSD kernel are the same as those discussed for the Linux kernel: to make a smaller, more efficient kernel, or to add new features.

There is no standard name for a BSD kernel configuration file. When you create a configuration file, choose any name you wish. By convention, BSD kernel configuration filenames use uppercase letters. To create a new configuration, copy *GENERIC* to the new file and then edit the newly created file. The following creates a new configuration file called *FILBERT*:

```
# cd /usr/src/sys/i386/conf
# cp GENERIC FILBERT
```

If the kernel has been modified on your system, the system administrator will have created a new configuration file in the */usr/src/sys/i386/conf* directory. The kernel configuration file contains many configuration commands that cover all aspects of the system configuration. This text discusses only those parameters that directly affect TCP/IP configuration. See the documentation that comes with the FreeBSD system for information about the other configuration commands.

TCP/IP in the BSD Kernel

For a network administrator, it is more important to understand which kernel statements are necessary to configure TCP/IP than to understand the detailed structure of each statement. Three types of statements are used to configure TCP/IP in the BSD kernel: options, pseudo-device, and device statements.

Options

The options statement tells the kernel to compile a software option into the system.

---

* */usr/src/sys* is symbolically linked to */sys*. We use */usr/src/sys* only as an example. Your system may use another directory.

The options statement that is most important to TCP/IP is:

```
options INET                    # basic networking support--mandatory
```

Every BSD-based system running TCP/IP has an **options INET** statement in its kernel configuration file. The statement produces a **–DINET** argument for the C complier, which in turn causes the IP, ICMP, TCP, UDP, and ARP modules to be compiled into the kernel. This single statement incorporates the basic transport and IP datagram services into the system. Never remove this statement from the configuration file.

There are several other options statements in addition to the required INET option. Some of these perform functions identical to features we have already seen in the Linux configuration. A few have no direct parallels in the Linux configuration.

```
options GATEWAY                 # internetwork gateway
```

The GATEWAY option determines whether the system forwards IP datagrams destined for another computer. When this option is selected, the system forwards datagrams if it has more than one network interface; i.e., the system is assumed to be a gateway. You don't need GATEWAY on a system with a single network interface. Hosts—systems with one network interface—do not forward the packets of other systems, because this would hide configuration problems on other systems on the network. If the other systems are incorrectly delivering datagrams to a host, forwarding the datagrams makes it appear as if they were correctly addressed and makes it difficult to detect the real problem. On occasion, you might even want to force a system that has multiple network interfaces not to forward datagrams by commenting **options GATEWAY** out of your configuration. This is useful for preventing a multi-homed host (a host with two network interfaces) from acting as a gateway.

```
options IPFIREWALL              # firewall
```

The IPFIREWALL option prepares the system to act as a firewall. The full firewall implementation requires application software and other tools. However, certain functions of a firewall, such as address filtering, must be implemented in the kernel. This option requests those kernel-level services. A variant of this option is IPFIREWALL_VERBOSE, which enables the same basic kernel services with enhanced error reporting. The enhanced errors can be useful for detecting intrusions, but they increase the size of the kernel.

```
options MROUTING                # Multicast routing
```

The MROUTING option adds multicast routing support to the kernel. A multicast kernel is necessary for the system to be able to interpret multicast addresses and for the system to support multicast applications like MBONE and Internet Talk Radio.

```
options IPACCT                    # ipaccounting
```

The IPACCT option adds additional code and counters that keep track of network usage, which is helpful for billing purposes.

```
options ARP_PROXYALL              # global proxy ARP
```

The ARP_PROXYALL option turns the system into a proxy ARP server. The Address Resolution Protocol (ARP) is discussed in Chapter 2, *Delivering the Data*. Proxy ARP is a variant on the standard protocol in which a server answers the ARP request for its clients. Here's how it works. Host A sends out an ARP request for the Ethernet address of host B. The proxy ARP server, C, hears the request and sends an ARP response back to A claiming that C's Ethernet address is the address of host B. A then sends traffic intended for B to C because it uses C's Ethernet address. C is therefore responsible for forwarding the traffic on to B. The proxy ARP server is usually a router and proxy ARP is used as a means of forwarding traffic between systems that cannot use normal routing for that traffic.

In Chapter 2, we saw how a system can act as a proxy ARP server for individual addresses using the **publish** option on the **arp** command. The ARP_PROXYALL kernel option creates a server for *all* addresses; not just for individual addresses configured in the ARP table.

```
options "TCP_COMPAT_42"           # emulate 4.2BSD TCP bugs
```

This option prevents connections between 4.2 and FreeBSD systems from hanging by adjusting FreeBSD to ignore mistakes made by 4.2. This parameter also disables UDP checksum calculations. The UDP checksum calculation in BSD 4.2 was incorrect, so when a host receives a UDP packet from a system running 4.2, it causes a checksum error. This parameter tells the system to ignore these errors. In addition, setting this parameter prevents the system from sending TCP Sequence Numbers that are interpreted as negative numbers by 4.2 systems. With this option, the initial sequence number will be set to zero for each connection. Forcing sequence numbers to zero is a potential security problem because it allows an intruder to guess the sequence number and to interject bogus packets into a TCP stream. For this reason, avoid using this parameter unless you must.

Pseudo-device

The second statement required by TCP/IP in all BSD configurations is a pseudo-device statement. A *pseudo-device* is a device driver not directly associated with an actual piece of hardware. The pseudo-device statement creates a header (*.h*) file that is identified by the pseudo-device name in the kernel directory. For example, the statement shown below creates the file *loop.h*:

```
pseudo-device   loop           # loopback network--mandatory
```

The loop pseudo-device is necessary to create the loopback device (lo0). This device is associated with the loopback address 127.0.0.1; it is defined as a pseudo-device because it is not really a piece of hardware.

Another pseudo-device that is used on many FreeBSD TCP/IP systems is:

```
pseudo-device   ether          # basic Ethernet support
```

This statement is necessary to support Ethernet. The ether pseudo-device is required for full support of ARP and other Ethernet specific functions. While it is possible that a system that does not have Ethernet may not require this statement, it is usually configured, and should remain in your kernel configuration.

The pseudo-terminals, or ptys, are other pseudo-devices that are universally configured:

```
pseudo-device   pty    16    # pseudo-tty's
```

This statement defines the virtual terminal devices used by remote login services such as **rlogin** and **telnet**. Pseudo-terminals are also used by many other applications, such as Emacs, that have no direct connection to TCP/IP networking. The number, 16 in the example, is the number of ptys created by the kernel. The maximum on a FreeBSD system is 64.

Other commonly configured pseudo-devices are those that support SLIP and PPP.

```
pseudo-device   sl      2    # Serial Line IP
```

This statement defines the interface for the Serial Line IP protocol. The number, 2 in the example, defines the number of SLIP pseudo-devices created by the kernel. The two devices created here would be addressed as device sl0 and sl1.

```
pseudo-device   ppp      2    # Point-to-point protocol
```

The ppp pseudo-device is the interface for the Point-to-Point Protocol. The number, 2 in the example, defines the number of PPP pseudo-devices created by the kernel. The two devices created here would be addressed as device ppp0 and ppp1. Two other pseudo-devices directly related to PPP are shown next.

```
pseudo-device   sppp         # Generic synchronous PPP
pseudo-device   tun      1   # Tunnel driver(user process ppp)
```

The sppp statement adds support for synchronous PPP data link–layer protocols. Normally, PPP runs over a dial-up line using an asynchronous link protocol. Asynchronous modems are the common modems all of us have on our home computers. Synchronous modems and synchronous link protocols are used on leased lines.

The tun pseudo-device is a tunnel driver used by user-level PPP software. *Tunneling* is when a system passes one protocol through another protocol; tun is a FreeBSD feature for doing this over PPP links. The number, 1 in the example, is the number of tunnels that will be supported by this kernel.

The last three pseudo-devices are less frequently used.

```
pseudo-device   fddi              # Generic FDDI
pseudo-device   bpfilter    4     # Berkeley packet filter
pseudo-device   disc              # Discard device
```

The fddi statement adds support for the Fiber Digital Data Interface (FDDI) to the kernel. FDDI is a local area network standard for transmitting data at 100M bps over fiber-optic cable.

The bpfilter statement adds the support necessary for capturing packets. Capturing packets is an essential part of protocol analyzers; see Chapter 11, *Troubleshooting TCP/IP*. When the bpfilter statement is included in the BSD kernel, the Ethernet interface can be placed into "promiscuous mode".* An interface in promiscuous mode passes all packets, not just those addressed to the local system, up to the software at the next layer. This feature is useful for a system administrator troubleshooting a network. But it can also be used by intruders to steal passwords and compromise security. Use the bpfilter pseudo-device only if you really need it. The number, 4 in the example, indicates the maximum number of Ethernet interfaces that can be monitored by bpfilter.

The final network pseudo-device is disc. It discards all data that it receives. This device is used only for testing.

Devices

Real hardware devices are defined using the device statement. Every host attached to a TCP/IP network requires some physical hardware for that attachment. The hardware is declared with a device statement in the kernel configuration file. There are many possible network interfaces for TCP/IP, but the most common are Ethernet interfaces.

Table 5-1 lists the Ethernet device drivers available with FreeeBSD 2.1.5.

---

* This assumes that the Ethernet hardware is capable of functioning in promiscuous mode. Not all Ethernet boards support this feature.

Table 5-1: Ethernet Cards Supported by FreeBSD

Device	Description
de0	DEC DC21040 PCI adapter
ed0	Western Digital SMC 80xx, Novell NE1000/2000, 3COM 3C503
eg0	3COM 3C505
el0	3COM 3C501
ep0	3COM 3C509
fe0	Fujitsu MB86960A/MB86965A
ie0	AT&T StarLAN 10 & EN100, 3COM 3C507, N15210
ix0	Intel EtherExpress 16
le0	DEC EtherWorks 2 and EtherWorks3
lnc0	Isolan, Novell NE2100 and NE32-VL
ze0	IBM/National Semiconductor PCMCIA adapter
zp0	3COM Etherlink III PCMICA adapter

A sample device statement shows the general format of the commands used to configure an Ethernet interface in the FreeBSD kernel:

```
device ed0 at isa? port 0x280 net irq 5 iomem 0xd8000 vector edintr
device de0
```

Note that the ed0 device statement defines the bus type (isa), the I/O base address (port 0x280), the interrupt number (irq 5) and the memory address (iomem 0xd8000). These values should match the values configured on the adapter card. All of these are standard items for configuring PC hardware.* On the other hand, the de0 device statement requires very little configuration because it configures a card attached to the PCI bus. The PCI is an intelligent bus that can determine the configuration directly from the hardware.

Ethernet is not the only TCP/IP network interface supported by FreeBSD. It supports an experimental ISDN interface as well as the DEC FDDI adapter. More widely used than these are the serial line interfaces necessary for SLIP and PPP.

```
device sio0  at isa? port "IO_COM1" tty irq 4  vector siointr
device sio1  at isa? port "IO_COM2" tty irq 3  vector siointr
device sio2  at isa? port "IO_COM3" tty irq 5  vector siointr
device sio3  at isa? port "IO_COM4" tty irq 9  vector siointr
```

The four serial interfaces, sio0 through sio3, correspond to the MS-DOS interfaces COM1 to COM4. These are needed for SLIP and PPP. Chapter 6 covers other aspects of configuring PPP and SLIP.

---

* See *Networking Personal Computers with TCP/IP*, by Craig Hunt (O'Reilly & Associates), for details about PC hardware configuration.

The device statement varies according to the interface being configured. But how do you know which hardware interfaces are installed in your system? Remember that the *GENERIC* kernel that comes with your FreeBSD system is configured for a large number of devices. A simple way to tell which hardware interfaces are installed in your system is to look at the messages displayed on the console at boot time. These messages show all of the devices, including network devices, that the kernel found during initialization. Look at the output of the **dmesg** command. It displays a copy of the console messages generated during the last boot.

The options, pseudo-device, and device statements found in the kernel configuration file tell the system to include the TCP/IP hardware and software in the kernel. The statements in your configuration may vary somewhat from those shown in the previous examples. But you have the same basic statements in your kernel configuration file. With these basic statements, FreeBSD UNIX is ready to run TCP/IP.

You will probably never change any of the variables discussed in this section. Like everything else in the kernel configuration file, they usually come correctly configured to run TCP/IP.

The Internet Daemon

The kernel configuration brings the basic transport and IP datagram services of TCP/IP into UNIX. But there is much more to the TCP/IP suite than just the basic services. How are these other protocols included in the UNIX configuration?

Some protocols are explicitly started by including them in the boot files. This technique is used, for example, to start the Routing Information Protocol (RIP) and the Domain Name Service (DNS). The daemons that service these protocols, **routed** and **named** respectively, are run from a startup file such as */etc/rc.d/rc.inet2* on a Linux system or */etc/init.d/inetsvc* and */etc/init.d/inetinit* on a Solaris system.*

Many other network daemons are not started individually. These daemons are started by a server that listens for network service requests and starts the appropriate daemon to process the request. This server is called the *internet daemon*.

The internet daemon—**inetd** (pronounced "i net d")—is started at boot time from an initialization file such as */etc/rc.d/rc.inet2*. When it is started, **inetd** reads its configuration from the */etc/inetd.conf* file. This file contains the names of the services that **inetd** listens for and starts. You can add or delete services by making changes to the *inetd.conf* file.

---

* Your system may not use these startup files, but startup files are usually located under the */etc* directory and often have names that contain *rc* or *init*.

An example of a file entry is:

```
ftp  stream  tcp  nowait  root  /usr/sbin/in.ftpd   in.ftpd
```

The fields in the *inetd.conf* entry are, from left to right:

name

> The name of a service, as listed in the */etc/services* file. In the sample entry, the value in this field is `ftp`.

type

> The type of data delivery service used, also called *socket type*. The commonly used socket types are:

> *stream*

> > The stream delivery service provided by TCP; i.e., TCP byte stream*

> *dgram*

> > The packet (datagram) delivery service provided by UDP

> *raw*

> > Direct IP datagram service

> The sample shows that FTP uses a stream socket.

protocol

> This is the name of a protocol, as given in the */etc/protocols* file. Its value is usually either "tcp" or "udp." The FTP protocol uses TCP as its transport layer protocol, so the sample entry contains `tcp` in this field.

wait-status

> The value for this field is either "wait" or "nowait." Generally, but not always, datagram type servers require "wait," and stream type servers allow "nowait." If the status is "wait," **inetd** must wait for the server to release the socket before it begins to listen for more requests on that socket. If the status is "nowait," **inetd** can immediately begin to listen for more connection requests on the socket. Servers with "nowait" status use sockets other than the connection request socket for processing; i.e., they use dynamically allocated sockets.

uid

> The uid is the username under which the server runs. This can be any valid username, but it is normally *root*. There are two common exceptions. The **finger** service often runs as the user *nobody* or *daemon* for security reasons, and the **uucp** service is sometimes run as the user *uucp* to save space in the system's accounting files.

---

* Here the reference is to TCP/IP sockets and TCP streams—not to AT&T streams I/O or BSD socket I/O.

server

> This is the full pathname of the server program started by **inetd**. Because our example is from a Solaris system, the path is */usr/sbin/in.ftpd*. On your system the path may be different.

> It is more efficient for **inetd** to provide some small services directly than it is for **inetd** to start separate servers for these functions. For these small services, the value of the server field is the keyword "internal," which means that this service is an internal **inetd** service.

arguments

> These are any command-line arguments that should be passed to the server program when it is invoked. This list always starts with `argv[0]` (the name of the program being executed). The program's manpage documents the valid command-line arguments for each program. In the example only `in.ftpd`, the server's name, is provided.

There are a few situations in which you need to modify the *inetd.conf* file. For example, you may wish to disable a service. The default configuration provides a full array of servers. Not all of them are required on every system, and for security reasons you may want to disable non-essential services on some computers. To disable a service, place a # at the beginning of its entry (which turns the line into a comment) and pass a hang-up signal to the **inetd** server. When **inetd** receives a hang-up signal, it re-reads the configuration file and the new configuration takes effect immediately.

You may also need to add new services. We'll see some examples of that in later chapters. Let's look in detail at an example of restoring a service that has been previously disabled. We'll begin by looking at the contents of an */etc/inetd.conf* file:

```
# @(#)inetd.conf 1.17 88/02/07 SMI
ftp      stream  tcp   nowait   root   /usr/sbin/in.ftpd     in.ftpd
telnet   stream  tcp   nowait   root   /usr/sbin/in.telnetd  in.telnetd
shell    stream  tcp   nowait   root   /usr/sbin/in.rshd     in.rshd
login    stream  tcp   nowait   root   /usr/sbin/in.rlogind  in.rlogind
exec     stream  tcp   nowait   root   /usr/sbin/in.rexecd   in.rexecd
finger   stream  tcp   nowait   root   /usr/sbin/in.fingerd  in.fingerd
#tftp dgram udp wait root /usr/sbin/in.tftpd in.tftpd -s /tftpboot
comsat   dgram   udp   wait     root   /usr/sbin/in.comsat   in.comsat
talk     dgram   udp   wait     root   /usr/sbin/in.talkd    in.talkd
name     dgram   udp   wait     root   /usr/sbin/in.tnamed   in.tnamed
daytime  stream  tcp   nowait   root   internal
time     stream  tcp   nowait   root   internal
echo     dgram   udp   wait     root   internal
discard  dgram   udp   wait     root   internal
time     dgram   udp   wait     root   internal
```

This part of the file shows several standard TCP/IP services. One of these, **tftp**, is commented out. The TFTP protocol is a special version of FTP that allows file transfers without username/password verification. Because of this, it is a possible security hole and is often disabled in the *inetd.conf* file.

As an example of modifying the *inetd.conf* file, we'll reconfigure the system to provide **tftp** service, which is sometimes necessary for supporting diskless devices. First, use your favorite editor to remove the comment (#) from the **tftp** entry in *inetd.conf.* (The example uses sed, everyone's favorite editor!) Then find out the process ID for **inetd** and pass it the SIGHUP signal. The following steps show how this is done on *peanut*:

```
# cd /etc
# mv inetd.conf inetd.conf.org
# cat inetd.conf.org | sed s/#tftp/tftp/ > inetd.conf
# ps -acx | grep inetd
  144 ?  I    0:12 inetd
# kill -HUP 144
```

In some situations, you may also need to modify the pathname of a server or the arguments passed to a particular server when it is invoked. For example, look again at the **tftp** entry. This line contains command-line arguments that are passed to the **tftp** server when it is started. The **−s /tftpboot** option addresses the most obvious **tftp** security hole. It prevents **tftp** users from retrieving files that are not located in the directory specified after the **−s** option. If you want to use another directory for **tftp**, you must change the *inetd.conf* file. The only command-line arguments passed to servers started by **inetd** are those defined in the *inetd.conf* file.

Security is one of the most important reasons for modifying the *inetd.conf* file. *inetd.conf* is used to implement access control through the wrapper program **tcpd**. The wrapper program replaces the server program in the server field of the *inetd.conf* entry. Then when **inetd** hears a connection request on the port, it starts **tcpd** instead of the application server. **tcpd** can then enforce extra security before it starts the application server. How to use the wrapper program for access control is covered in Chapter 12.

Summary

The basic configuration files, the kernel configuration file, the startup files, and the */etc/inetd.conf* file are necessary for installing the TCP/IP software on a UNIX system, but they require little attention from the system administrator. The kernel comes configured to run TCP/IP on most systems. Some systems, such as Solaris, are designed to eliminate kernel configuration. Others, such as Linux, encourage it as a way to produce a more efficient kernel. In either case, the only thing a network administrator needs to be aware of are the kernel configuration commands required for TCP/IP so that they are not accidentally removed from the kernel when it is rebuilt.

inetd starts essential system services. You would reconfigure only to add new services or to improve security. Security can be improved by removing unneeded services or by adding access control.

The kernel configuration defined the network interface. In Chapter 6 we configure it, calling upon the planning we did in Chapter 4.

6

Configuring the Interface

When networking protocols work only with a single kind of physical network, there is no need to identify the network interface to the software. The software knows what the interface *must* be; no configuration issues are left for the administrator. However, one important strength of TCP/IP is its flexible use of different physical networks. This flexibility adds complexity to the system administrator's task, because you must tell TCP/IP which interfaces to use, and you must define the characteristics of each interface.

Because TCP/IP is independent of the underlying physical network, IP addresses are implemented in the network software—not in the network hardware. Unlike Ethernet addresses, which are determined by the Ethernet hardware, the system administrator assigns an IP address to each network interface.

In this chapter, we use the **ifconfig** (interface configure) command to identify the network interface to TCP/IP and to assign the IP address, subnet mask, and broadcast address to the interface. We also configure a network interface to run Point-to-Point Protocol (PPP), which is the standard Network Access Layer protocol used to run TCP/IP over modem connections. Let's begin with a discussion of **ifconfig**.

The ifconfig Command

The **ifconfig** command sets, or checks, configuration values for network interfaces. Regardless of the vendor or version of UNIX, the **ifconfig** command will set the IP address, the subnet mask, and the broadcast address for each interface. Its most basic function is assigning the IP address.

Here is the **ifconfig** command that configures the Ethernet interface on *peanut*:

```
# ifconfig le0 172.16.12.2 netmask 255.255.255.0  \
broadcast 172.16.12.255
```

Many other arguments can be used with the **ifconfig** command; we discuss several of these later. But a few important arguments provide the basic information required by TCP/IP for every network interface. These are:

interface

> The name of the network interface that you want to configure for TCP/IP. In the example above, this is the Ethernet interface le0.

address

> The IP address assigned to this interface. Enter the address as either an IP address (in dotted decimal form) or as a hostname. If you use a hostname, place the hostname and its address in the */etc/hosts* file. Your system must be able to find the hostname in */etc/hosts* because **ifconfig** usually executes before DNS is running. The example uses the numeric IP address 172.16.12.2 as the **address** value.

netmask *mask*

> The subnet mask for this interface. Ignore this argument only if you're using the default mask derived from the traditional address class structure. If you are subnetting, use your subnet mask. The subnet mask chosen for our imaginary network is 255.255.255.0, so that is the value assigned to *peanut*'s le0 interface. See Chapters 2 and 4 for information on address masks and subnets.

broadcast *address*

> The broadcast address for the network. Most, but not all, systems default to the standard broadcast address, which is an IP address with all host bits set to 1. In the **ifconfig** example we explicitly set the broadcast address to 172.16.12.255 to avoid any confusion. Every system on the subnet must agree on the broadcast address.

The network administrator provides the values for the address, subnet mask, and broadcast address. The values in our example are taken directly from the planning sheet we developed in Chapter 4, *Getting Started*. But the name of the interface, the first argument on every **ifconfig** command line, must often be determined from the system's documentation.

Determining the Interface Name

In Chapter 5, *Basic Configuration*, we saw that Ethernet network interfaces come in many varieties, and that different Ethernet cards usually have different interface names. You can usually determine which interface is used on a system from the messages displayed on the console during a boot. On many systems these messages can be examined with the **dmesg** command. But even with this information, determining the name of the Ethernet interface is not always easy. The following example shows the output of the **dmesg** command on two different systems:

```
almond% dmesg | grep le0
le0 at ledma0: SBus slot f 0xc00000 sparc ipl 6
le0 is /iommu@f,e0000000/sbus@f,e0001000/ledma@f,400010/le@f,c00000

acorn> dmesg | grep eth0
eth0: smc8432 (DEC 21041 Tulip) at 0xfc80, 00:00:c0:dd:d4:da, IRQ 10
eth0: enabling 10TP port.
```

The first **dmesg** command in the example shows the messages displayed when an le0 Ethernet interface is detected during the boot of a Solaris 2.5.1 system. Nothing about these messages makes it clear that le0 is an Ethernet interface. The second **dmesg** example, which comes from a PC running Linux, provides more clues. eth0 is a more intuitive Ethernet interface name; and the Linux system displays the Ethernet address (00:00:c0:dd:d4:da) and the make and model (SMC8432) of the network adapter card. If you know what these things mean, it makes guessing the Ethernet interface name simpler.

It is not always easy to determine all available interfaces on your system by looking at the output of **dmesg**, nor by looking at device statements in the kernel configuration file. These only show you the physical hardware interfaces. In the TCP/IP protocol architecture, the Network Access Layer encompasses all functions that fall below the Internet Layer. This can include all three lower layers of the OSI Reference Model: the Physical Layer, the Data Link Layer, and the Network Layer. IP needs to know the specific interface in the Network Access Layer where packets should be passed for delivery to a particular network. This interface is not limited to a physical hardware driver. It could be a software interface into the network layer of another protocol suite. So what other methods can help you determine the network interfaces available on a system? Use the **netstat** and the **ifconfig** commands. For example, to see all network interfaces that are already configured, enter:

```
% netstat -in
```

The −i option tells **netstat** to display the status of all configured network interfaces, and the −n tells **netstat** to display its output in numeric form. The **netstat −in** command displays the following fields:

Name
> The Interface Name field shows the actual name assigned to the interface. This is the name you give to **ifconfig** to identify the interface. An asterisk (*) in this field indicates that the interface is not enabled; i.e., the interface is not "up."

Mtu

The Maximum Transmission Unit shows the longest frame (packet) that can be transmitted by this interface without fragmentation. The MTU is displayed in bytes. MTU is discussed in the section "The datagram" in Chapter 1, *Overview of TCP/IP*.

Net/Dest

The Network/Destination field shows the network or the destination host to which the interface provides access. In our Ethernet examples, this field contains a network address. The network address is derived from the IP address of the interface and the subnet mask.

This field contains a host address if the interface is configured for a point-to-point (host-specific) link. The destination address is the address of the remote host at the other end of the point-to-point link.* A point-to-point link is a direct connection between two computers. You can create a point-to-point link with the **ifconfig** command. How this is done is covered later in this chapter.

Address

The IP Address field shows the Internet address assigned to this interface.

Ipkts

The Input Packets field shows how many packets this interface has received.

Ierrs

The Input Errors field shows how many damaged packets the interface has received.

Opkts

The Output Packets field shows how many packets were sent out by this interface.

Oerrs

The Output Errors field shows how many of the packets caused an error condition.

Collis

The Collisions field shows how many Ethernet collisions were detected by this interface. Ethernet collisions are a normal condition caused by Ethernet traffic contention. This field is not applicable to non-Ethernet interfaces.

Queue

The Packets Queued field shows how many packets are in the queue, awaiting transmission via this interface. Normally this is zero.

---

* See the description of the H flag in the section "Routing Table" in Chapter 2, *Delivering the Data*.

The output of a **netstat** command shows:

```
% netstat -in
Name  Mtu   Net/Dest    Address      Ipkts Ierrs Opkts Oerrs Collis Queue
le0   1500  172.16.0.0  172.16.12.2  1547  1     1127  0     135    0
lo0   1536  127.0.0.0   127.0.0.1    133   0     133   0     0      0
```

This display shows that this workstation has only two network interfaces. In this case it is easy to identify each network interface. The lo0 interface is the loopback interface, which every TCP/IP system has. It is the same loopback device discussed in Chapter 5. le0 is a Lance Ethernet interface, also discussed in Chapter 5.

On most systems, the loopback interface is part of the default configuration, so you won't need to configure it. If you do need to configure lo0 on your system, use the following command:

```
# ifconfig lo0 127.0.0.1
```

The configuration of the Ethernet interface requires more attention. The surprising thing about the sample **netstat** display is that we haven't yet entered an **ifconfig** command for le0, and it already has an IP address! Many systems use an installation script to install UNIX. This script requests the host address, which it then uses to configure the interface.* Later we'll look at whether the user successfully set up this interface with the installation script.

The **ifconfig** command can also be used to find out what network interfaces are available on a system. The **netstat** command shows only interfaces that are configured. On some systems the **ifconfig** command can be used to show all interfaces, even those that have not yet been configured. On Solaris 2.5.1 systems, **ifconfig -a** does this; on a Linux 2.0.0 system, entering **ifconfig** without any arguments will list all of the network interfaces.

While most hosts have only one real network interface, some hosts and all gateways have multiple interfaces. Sometimes all interfaces are the same type; i.e., a gateway between two Ethernets may have two Ethernet interfaces. **netstat** on a gateway like this might display lo0, le0, and le1. Deciphering a **netstat** display with multiple interfaces of the same type is still very simple. But deciphering a system with many different types of network interfaces is more difficult. You must rely on documentation that comes with optional software to choose the correct interface. When installing new network software, always read documentation carefully.

This long discussion about determining the network interface may seem to overshadow the important **ifconfig** functions of assigning the IP address, subnet mask, and broadcast address. So let's return to these important topics.

---

* The **netconfig** command, discussed in Chapter 4, is an example of a network configuration script that runs when the operating system is installed.

Checking the Interface with ifconfig

As noted above, the UNIX installation script configures the network interface. However, this configuration may not be exactly what you want. Check the configuration of an interface with **ifconfig**. To display the current values assigned to the interface, enter **ifconfig** with an interface name and no other arguments. For example, to check interface le0:

```
% ifconfig le0
le0: flags=863<UP,BROADCAST,NOTRAILERS,RUNNING,MULTICAST> mtu 1500
        inet 172.16.12.2 netmask ffff0000 broadcast 172.16.255.255
```

When used to check the status of an interface on a Solaris 2.5.1 system, the **ifconfig** command displays two lines of output. The first line shows the interface name, the flags that define the interface's characteristics, and the Maximum Transmission Unit (MTU) of this interface. In our example the interface name is le0, and the MTU is 1500 bytes. The flags are displayed as both a numeric value and a set of keywords. The interface's flags have the numeric value 863, which corresponds to:

UP

> The interface is enabled for use.

BROADCAST

> The interface supports broadcasts, which means it is connected to a network that supports broadcasts, such as an Ethernet.

NOTRAILERS

> This interface does not support trailer encapsulation. This is an Ethernet-specific characteristic which we discuss in more detail later.

RUNNING

> This interface is operational.

MULTICAST

> This interface supports multicasting.

The second line of **ifconfig** output displays information that directly relates to TCP/IP. The keyword `inet` is followed by the Internet address assigned to this interface. Next comes the keyword `netmask`, followed by the address mask written in hexadecimal. Finally, the keyword `broadcast` and the broadcast address are displayed.

On a Linux system the **ifconfig** command displays up to six lines of information for each interface instead of the two lines displayed by the Solaris system. The additional information includes the Ethernet address, the PC IRQ and I/O Base Address, and packet statistics. The basic information is the same on both systems.

```
> ifconfig eth0
eth0   Link encap:10Mbps Ethernet  HWaddr 00:00:C0:9A:D0:DB
       inet addr:172.16.55.106  Bcast:172.16.55.255  Mask:255.255.255.0
       UP BROADCAST RUNNING MULTICAST  MTU:1500  Metric:1
       RX packets:844886 errors:0 dropped:0 overruns:0
       TX packets:7668 errors:0 dropped:0 overruns:0
       Interrupt:11 Base address:0x7c80
```

Refer to the Solaris **ifconfig le0** example at the beginning of this section. Check the information displayed in that example against the configuration plan developed in Chapter 4. You'll see that the interface needs to be reconfigured. The configuration done by the user during the UNIX installation did not provide all of the values we planned. The address (172.16.12.2) is correct, but the address mask (ffff0000 or 255.255.0.0) and the broadcast address (172.16.0.0) are incorrect. Let's look at how these values are assigned, and how to correct them.

Assigning a Subnet Mask

In order to function properly, every interface on a specific physical network segment must have the same subnet mask. For le0 on *almond* and *peanut*, the netmask value is 255.255.255.0, because both systems are attached to the same subnet. However, although *almond*'s local network interface and its external network interface are parts of the same computer, they use different netmasks because they are on different networks.

To assign a subnet mask, write the subnet mask value after the keyword "netmask" on the **ifconfig** command line. The subnet mask is usually written in the "dotted decimal" form used for IP addresses.* For example, the following command assigns the correct subnet mask to the le0 interface on *peanut*:

```
# ifconfig le0 172.16.12.2 netmask 255.255.255.0 \
broadcast 172.16.12.255
```

Putting the netmask value directly on the **ifconfig** command line is the most common, the simplest, and the best way to manually assign the subnet mask to an interface. But it is also possible to tell **ifconfig** to take the netmask value from a file instead of from the command line. Conceptually, this is similar to using a hostname in place of an IP address. The administrator can place the subnet mask value in either the *hosts* file or the *networks* file and then reference it by name. For example, the *nuts-net* administrator might add the following entry to */etc/networks*:

```
nuts-mask       255.255.255.0
```

---

* Hexadecimal notation can also be used for the subnet mask. To enter a netmask in hexadecimal form, write the value as a single hex number starting with a leading 0x. For example, the hexadecimal form of 255.255.255.0 is 0xffffff00. Choose the form that is easier for you to understand.

Once this entry has been added, you can use the name *nuts-mask* on the **ifconfig** command line, instead of the actual mask. For example:

```
# ifconfig le0 172.16.5.2 netmask nuts-mask
```

The name *nuts-mask* resolves to 255.255.255.0, which is the correct netmask value for our sample systems.

On Solaris systems, you can also use */etc/inet/netmasks* to set the subnet mask.* The */etc/inet/netmasks* file is a table of one-line entries, each containing a network address separated from a subnet mask by whitespace.† If a Solaris system on *nuts-net* (172.16.0.0) has a */etc/inet/netmasks* file that contains the entry:

```
172.16.0.0        255.255.255.0
```

then the following **ifconfig** command can be used to set the subnet mask:

```
# ifconfig le0 172.16.5.1 netmask +
```

The plus sign after the keyword `netmask` causes **ifconfig** to take the mask value from */etc/inet/netmasks*. **ifconfig** searches the file for a network address that matches the network address of the interface being configured. It then extracts the subnet mask associated with that address and applies it to the interface.

Some systems take advantage of the fact that the IP address, subnet mask, and broadcast address can be set indirectly to reduce the extent that startup files need to be customized. Reducing customization lessens the chance that a system might hang while booting because a startup file was improperly edited, and it makes it possible to pre-configure these files for all of the systems on the network. The *hosts*, *networks*, and *netmasks* files, which provide input to the **ifconfig** command, all produce NIS maps that can be centrally managed at sites using NIS.

A disadvantage of setting the **ifconfig** values indirectly is that it can make troubleshooting more cumbersome. If all values are set in the boot file, you only need to check the values there. When network configuration information is supplied indirectly, you may need to check the boot file, the *hosts* file, the *networks* file, and the *netmasks* file to find the problem. An error in any of these files could cause an incorrect configuration. To make debugging easier, many system administrators prefer to set the configuration values directly on the **ifconfig** command line.

Another disadvantage of setting the subnet mask value indirectly is that some of the files used for this are not primarily intended for this use. The *hosts* file is a particularly bad choice for storing subnet values. The *hosts* file is heavily used by other programs. Placing a subnet value in the *hosts* file might confuse one of these

---

* */etc/netmasks* is symbolically linked to */etc/inet/netmasks*.

† Use the official network address, not a subnet address.

programs. Setting the subnet value directly on the command line or from a file, such as the *netmasks* file, that is dedicated to this purpose is probably the best approach.

Setting the Broadcast Address

RFC 919, *Broadcasting Internet Datagrams*, clearly defines the format of a broadcast address as an address with all host bits set to 1. Since the broadcast address is so precisely defined, **ifconfig** should be able to compute it automatically, and you should always be able to use the default. Unfortunately, this is not the case. TCP/IP was included in BSD 4.2 before RFC 919 was an adopted standard. BSD 4.2 used a broadcast address with all host bits set to 0, and didn't allow the broadcast address to be modified during configuration. Because of this history, some releases of UNIX default to a "0-style" broadcast address for compatibility with older systems, while other releases default to the standard "1-style" broadcast address.

Avoid this confusion by defining a broadcast address for the entire network and ensuring that every device on the network explicitly sets it during configuration. Set the broadcast address in the **ifconfig** command using the keyword `broadcast` followed by the correct broadcast address. For example, the **ifconfig** command to set the broadcast address for *almond*'s le0 interface is:

```
# ifconfig le0 172.16.12.1 netmask 255.255.255.0 \
broadcast 172.16.12.255
```

Note that the broadcast address is relative to the local subnet. *almond* views this interface as connected to network 172.16.12.0; therefore, its broadcast address is 172.16.12.255. Depending on the implementation, a UNIX system could interpret the address 172.16.255.255 as host address 255 on subnet 255 of network 172.16.0.0, or as the broadcast address for *nuts-net* as a whole. In neither case would it consider 172.16.255.255 the broadcast address for subnet 172.16.12.0.

The Other Command Options

We've used **ifconfig** to set the interface address, the subnet mask, and the broadcast address. These are certainly the most important functions of **ifconfig**, but it has other functions as well. It can enable or disable trailer encapsulation, the address resolution protocol, and the interface itself. **ifconfig** also can set the routing metric used by the Routing Information Protocol and the Maximum Transmission Unit (MTU) used by the interface. We'll look at each of these functions.

Enabling and disabling the interface

The **ifconfig** command has two arguments, **up** and **down**, for enabling and disabling the network interface. The **up** argument enables the network interface and marks it ready for use. The **down** argument disables the interface so that it cannot be used for network traffic.

Use the **down** argument when interactively reconfiguring an interface. Some configuration parameters—for example, the IP address—cannot be changed unless the interface is down. First, the interface is brought down. Then, the reconfiguration is done, and the interface is brought back up. For example, the following steps change the address for an interface:

```
# ifconfig le0 down
# ifconfig le0 172.16.1.2 up
```

After these commands execute, the interface operates with the new configuration values. The **up** argument in the second **ifconfig** command is not actually required because it is the default. However, an explicit **up** is commonly used after the interface has been disabled, or when an **ifconfig** command is used in a script file to avoid problems if the default is changed in a future release.

ARP and trailers

Two options on the **ifconfig** command line, **arp** and **trailers**, are used only for Ethernet interfaces. The **trailers** option enables or disables negotiations for trailer encapsulation of IP packets. In Chapter 1, *Overview of TCP/IP*, we discussed how IP packets are sent over different physical networks by being encapsulated in the frames that those networks transmit. Trailer encapsulation is an optional technique that reduces the number of memory-to-memory copies the receiving system needs to perform.

To enable trailer encapsulation, put the keyword `trailers` on the **ifconfig** command line. When trailer encapsulation is enabled, the system requests (via the ARP protocol) that other systems also use trailer encapsulation when sending it data.

The option **–trailers** disables trailer encapsulation. Trailer encapsulation is disabled for two basic reasons. First, the I/O architecture of some systems does not derive any benefit from trailer encapsulation. If a system doesn't do memory-to-memory copies when receiving data from the network, it doesn't benefit from trailer encapsulation. Second, there are some systems that have difficulties with the negotiations for trailer encapsulation. For these reasons, many systems ignore the **trailers** argument and never use trailer encapsulation, and others allow trailer encapsulation but default to **–trailers**. Both of our sample systems, Solaris and Linux, ignore the **trailers** argument. However, some systems enable trailer encapsulation by default. Check your system documentation for the default on your system.

Chapter 2 discusses the Address Resolution Protocol (ARP), an important protocol that maps IP addresses to physical Ethernet addresses. Enable ARP with the **ifconfig** keyword `arp` and disable it with the keyword `-arp`. It is possible (though very unlikely) that a host attached to your network cannot handle ARP. This would only happen on a network using specialized equipment or developmental hardware. In these very rare circumstances, it may be necessary to disable ARP in order to interoperate with the non-standard systems. By default, **ifconfig** enables ARP. Leave ARP enabled on all your systems.

Metric

On some systems, the **ifconfig** command creates an entry in the routing table for every interface that is assigned an IP address. Each interface is the route to a network. Even if a host isn't a gateway, its interface is still its "route" to the local network. **ifconfig** determines the route's destination network by applying the interface's subnet mask to the interface's IP address. For example, the le0 interface on *almond* has an address of 172.16.12.1 and a mask of 255.255.255.0. Applying this mask to the address provides the destination network, which is 172.16.12.0. The **netstat −in** display shows the destination address:

```
% netstat -in
Name Mtu  Net/Dest    Address      Ipkts   Ierrs Opkts  Oerrs Collis Queue
le0  1500 172.16.12.0 172.16.12.1 1125826 16    569786 0     8914   0
lo0  1536 127.0.0.0   127.0.0.1    94280   0     94280  0     0      0
```

The Routing Information Protocol (RIP) is a routing protocol commonly used by UNIX. RIP does two things: it distributes routing information to other hosts, and it uses incoming routing information to build routing tables dynamically. The routes created by **ifconfig** are one source of the routing information distributed by RIP, and the **ifconfig metric** argument can be used to control how RIP uses this routing information.

RIP makes routing decisions based on the cost of a route. The route's cost is determined by a routing metric associated with the route. A routing metric is just a number. The lower the number, the lower the cost of the route. The higher the number, the higher the cost. When building a routing table, RIP favors low-cost routes over high-cost routes. Directly connected networks are given a very low cost. Therefore, the default metric is 0 for a route through an interface to a directly attached network. However, you can use the **metric** argument to supply a different routing metric for an interface.

To increase the cost of an interface to three, so that RIP prefers routes with values of 0, 1, or 2, use **metric 3** on the **ifconfig** command line:

```
# ifconfig std0 26.104.0.19 metric 3
```

Use the metric option only if there is another route to the same destination and you want to use it as the primary route. We did not use this command on *almond*, because it has only one interface connected to the outside world. But if it had a second connection, say, through a higher-speed link, then the command shown above could be used to direct traffic through the higher-performance interface.

A related **ifconfig** parameter is available on Solaris systems. RIP builds the routing table by choosing the most economical routes, and it distributes the routing table information to other hosts. The **metric** parameter controls which routes RIP selects as the lowest cost. The **private** argument, available on Solaris systems, controls the routes that RIP distributes. If **private** is specified on the **ifconfig** command line, the route created by that **ifconfig** command is not distributed by RIP. The default is **–private**, which permits the route to be distributed. The **private** parameter is not universally supported.

Additionally, not all systems make use of the **metric** argument. A Linux system doesn't create a routing table entry when it processes the **ifconfig** command. When configuring a Linux system, you add an explicit **route** command for each interface. (The **route** command is covered in the next chapter.) Linux systems ignore the **metric** argument.

Set the routing metric in a routing configuration file instead of on the **ifconfig** command line. This is the preferred method of providing routing information for newer routing software. We discuss the format of routing configuration files in the next chapter.

Maximum transmission unit

A network has a maximum transmission unit, which is the largest packet that can be transported over that physical network. On Ethernet, the maximum size is 1500 bytes, which is defined as part of the Ethernet standard. There is rarely any need to change the MTU on the **ifconfig** command line. By default, **ifconfig** chooses the optimum MTU, which is usually the largest legal MTU for a given type of network hardware. A large MTU is the default because it normally provides the best performance. However, a smaller MTU is helpful to achieve the following goals:

- To avoid fragmentation. If the traffic travels from a network with a large MTU—such as an FDDI network with an MTU of 4500 bytes—through a network with a smaller MTU like an Ethernet, the smaller MTU size may be best in order to avoid packet fragmentation. It is possible that specifying an MTU of 1500 on the interface connected to the FDDI may actually improve performance by avoiding fragmentation in the routers. This would only be done if fragmentation actually appeared to be the cause of a performance problem.

- To reduce buffer overruns or similar problems. On serial line connections it is possible to have equipment of such low performance that it cannot keep up with standard 1006-byte packets. In this case, it is possible to avoid buffer overruns or SILO overflows by using a smaller MTU. However, such solutions are temporary fixes. The real fix is to purchase the correct hardware for the application.

To change the MTU, use the **mtu** command-line argument:

```
# ifconfig fddi0 172.16.16.1 netmask 255.255.255.0 mtu 1500
```

This forces the FDDI interface on 172.16.16.1 to use an MTU of 1500 bytes.

Point-to-point

There are probably several more **ifconfig** command-line arguments available on your system. Linux has parameters to define the PC interrupt of the Ethernet hardware (**irq**) and the Ethernet hardware address (**hw**), and to enable multicasting (**multicast**) and promiscuous mode (**allmulti**). Solaris has arguments to set up or tear down the streams for an interface (**plumb/unplumb**), and to use Reverse ARP (RARP) to obtain the IP address for an interface (**auto-revarp**). But most of these parameters are not standardized between versions of UNIX.

One last feature that is available on most versions of UNIX is the ability to define point-to-point connections with the **ifconfig** command. Point-to-point connections are network links that directly connect together only two computers. Of course the computers at either end of the link could be gateways to the world, but only two computers are directly connected to the link. Examples of a point-to-point connection are two computers linked together by a leased telephone line, or two computers in an office linked together by a null modem cable.

To define a point-to-point link on a Solaris system:

```
# ifconfig zs0 172.16.62.1 172.16.62.2
```

This **ifconfig** command has two addresses immediately following the interface name. The first is the address of the local host. The second address, called the destination address, is the address of the remote host at the other end of the point-to-point link. The second address shows up as the Net/Dest value in an **netstat –ni** display.

On a Linux system, this same configuration looks slightly different:

```
> ifconfig sl0 172.16.62.1 point-to-point 172.16.62.2
```

The syntax is different but the effect is the same. This enables the interface to run in point-to-point mode and identifies the hosts at both ends of the link.

Does this set up the Point-to-Point Protocol (PPP) used for TCP/IP serial line communication? No, it does not. These **ifconfig** parameters sometimes confuse people about how to set up PPP. There is much more to configuring PPP and SLIP, which we cover in the remainder of this chapter.

Before moving on to PPP and SLIP we should note that the configuration entered on an **ifconfig** command line will not survive a system boot. For a permanent configuration, put **ifconfig** in a startup file.

Putting ifconfig in the startup files

The **ifconfig** command is normally executed at boot time by a startup file. On BSD UNIX systems, the **ifconfig** commands are usually located in */etc/rc.boot* or */etc/rc.local*. System V UNIX presents a much more complex set of startup files, but the **ifconfig** statements are usually located in a file in the */etc/init.d* directory.* On Linux systems, the startup files containing the **ifconfig** commands are usually in the */etc/rc.d* or the */etc/rc.d/init.d* directory. Use **grep** to locate the specific file that contains the **ifconfig** command:

```
> cd /etc/rc.d
> grep ifconfig *
rc.inet1:/sbin/ifconfig lo 127.0.0.1
rc.inet1:/sbin/ifconfig eth0 172.16.12.1 broadcast 172.16.12.255
    netmask 255.255.255.0
```

Because network access is important for some of the processes run by the startup files, the **ifconfig** statements execute near the beginning of the startup procedure. The simplest way to configure a network interface to suit your requirements is to edit the startup files and insert the correct **ifconfig** statements.

On our Linux system, we edit */etc/rc.d/rc.inet1* and check the two lines necessary to configure the loopback interface and the Ethernet interface. We use the *rc.inet1* file because it runs early in network startup procedure and it is the file in which the installation script placed the **ifconfig** commands. The two lines placed in the file are:

```
ifconfig lo0 127.0.0.1
ifconfig eth0 172.16.12.1 broadcast 172.16.12.255 netmask 255.255.255.0
```

Check the startup files to ensure that the interfaces on the host are properly configured at every boot.

---

* A good description of the maze of System V initialization files is provided in *Essential System Administration, Second Edition*, by Æleen Frisch (O'Reilly & Associates).

TCP/IP Over a Serial Line

TCP/IP runs over a wide variety of physical media. The media can be Ethernet cables, as in your local Ethernet, or telephone circuits, as in a wide area network. In the first half of this chapter, we used **ifconfig** to configure a local Ethernet interface. In this section, we use other commands to configure a network interface to use a telephone circuit.

Almost all data communication takes place via serial interfaces. A serial interface is just an interface that sends the data as a series of bits over a single wire, as opposed to a parallel interface that sends the data bits in parallel over several wires simultaneously. This description of a serial interface would fit almost any communications interface (including Ethernet itself), but the term is usually applied to an interface that connects to a telephone circuit via a modem or similar device. Likewise, a telephone circuit is often called a serial line.

In the TCP/IP world, serial lines are used to create wide area networks (WANs). Unfortunately, TCP/IP has not always had a standard physical layer protocol for serial lines. Because of the lack of a standard, network designers were forced to use a single brand of routers within their WANs to ensure successful physical layer communication. The growth of TCP/IP WANs led to a strong interest in standardizing serial-line communications to provide vendor independence.

Other forces that increased interest in serial line communications were the advent of small affordable systems that run TCP/IP and the advent of high-speed, dial-up modems that provide "reasonable" TCP/IP performance. When the ARPANET was formed, computers were very expensive and dial-up modems were very slow. At that time, if you could afford a computer, you could afford a leased telephone line. In recent years, however, it has become possible to own a UNIX system at home. In this new environment, there is an increasing demand for services that allow TCP/IP access over low-cost, dial-up serial lines.

These two forces—the need for standardized wide area communications and the need for dial-up TCP/IP access—have led to the creation of two serial-line protocols: Serial Line IP (SLIP) and Point-to-Point Protocol (PPP).*

The Serial Protocols

Serial Line IP was created first. It is a minimal protocol that allows isolated hosts to link via TCP/IP over the telephone network. The SLIP protocol defines a simple mechanism for framing datagrams for transmission across serial lines. SLIP sends the datagram across the serial line as a series of bytes, and it uses special

---

* Dial-up modems are usually asynchronous. Both PPP and SLIP support asynchronous, dial-up service as well as synchronous leased-line service.

characters to mark when a series of bytes should be grouped together as a datagram. SLIP defines two special characters for this purpose:

- The SLIP END character, a single byte with the decimal value 192, is the character that marks the end of a datagram. When the receiving SLIP encounters the END character, it knows that it has a complete datagram that can be sent up to IP.

- The SLIP ESC character, a single byte with the decimal value of 219, is used to "escape" the SLIP control characters. If the sending SLIP encounters a byte value equivalent to either a SLIP END character or a SLIP ESC character in the datagram it is sending, it converts that character to a sequence of two characters. The two-character sequences are ESC 220 for the END character, and ESC 221 for the ESC character itself.* When the receiving SLIP encounters these two-byte sequences, it converts them back to single-byte values. This procedure prevents the receiving SLIP from incorrectly interpreting a data byte as the end of the datagram.

SLIP is described in RFC 1055, *A Nonstandard for Transmission of IP Datagrams Over Serial Lines: SLIP*. As the name of the RFC makes clear, SLIP is not an Internet standard. The RFC does not propose a standard; it documents an existing protocol. The RFC identifies the deficiencies in SLIP, which fall into two categories:

- The SLIP protocol does not define any link control information that could be used to dynamically control the characteristics of a connection. Therefore, SLIP systems must assume certain link characteristics. Because of this limitation, SLIP can only be used when both hosts know each other's address, and only when IP datagrams are being transmitted.

- SLIP does not compensate for noisy, low-speed telephone lines. The protocol does not provide error correction or data compression.

To address SLIP's weaknesses, Point-to-Point Protocol (PPP) was developed as an Internet standard. At this writing, there are several RFCs that document Point-to-Point Protocol.† Two key documents are: RFC 1548, *The Point-to-Point Protocol (PPP)*, and RFC 1172, *The Point-to-Point Protocol (PPP) Initial Configuration Options*.

PPP addresses the weaknesses of SLIP with a three-layered protocol:

Data Link Layer Protocol
    The Data Link Layer Protocol used by PPP is a slightly modified version of High-level Data Link Control (HDLC). PPP modifies HDLC by adding a

---

* Here ESC refers to the SLIP escape character, not the ASCII escape character.

† If you want to make sure you have the very latest version of a standard, obtain the latest list of RFCs as described in Chapter 13, *Internet Information Resources*.

Protocol field that allows PPP to pass traffic for multiple Network Layer protocols. HDLC is an international standard protocol for reliably sending data over synchronous, serial communications lines. PPP also uses a proposed international standard for transmitting HDLC over asynchronous lines; so PPP can guarantee reliable delivery over any type of serial line.

Link Control Protocol

The Link Control Protocol (LCP) provides control information for the serial link. It is used to establish the connection, negotiate configuration parameters, check link quality, and close the connection. LCP was developed specifically for PPP.

Network Control protocols

The Network Control protocols are individual protocols that provide configuration and control information for the Network Layer protocols. Remember, PPP is designed to pass data for a wide variety of network protocols. NCP allows PPP to be customized to do just that. Each network protocol (DECNET, IP, OSI, etc.) has its own Network Control protocol. The Network Control protocol defined in RFCs 1331 and 1332 is the Internet Control Protocol (IPCP), which supports Internet Protocol.

Choosing a Serial Protocol

Point-to-Point Protocol (PPP) is the best TCP/IP serial protocol. PPP is preferred because it is an Internet standard, which ensures interoperability between systems from a wide variety of vendors. It has more features than SLIP, and is more robust. These benefits make PPP the best choice as a non-proprietary protocol for connecting routers over serial lines and for connecting in remote computers via dial-up lines.

However, sometimes your choice is limited. SLIP was the first widely available serial protocol for IP, and some older dial-up servers support SLIP only. PPP and SLIP do not interoperate; they are completely different protocols. So if your terminal servers only have SLIP, the remote hosts that connect through these servers must also have SLIP. Because of its installed base, SLIP will continue to be used for the foreseeable future.

So which protocol should you use? When you are designing a new serial-line service, use PPP. However, you may be forced to also support SLIP. SLIP is sometimes the only serial protocol available for a specific piece of hardware. Simply put, use PPP where you can and SLIP where you must.

Linux systems include both SLIP and PPP. However, on some other UNIX systems such as Solaris, PPP is included and SLIP is not. The only time you should consider using SLIP is when it comes as part of the operating system. Avoid downloading SLIP source code and porting it on to your system. Use PPP instead. If you have old terminal servers that support only SLIP and new computers that support only PPP, it's time to upgrade the old terminal server.

Installing PPP

The procedures for installing and configuring PPP vary from implementation to implementation.* In this section, we use the implementation of PPP included with Linux 2.0 and the supporting configuration commands that come with it. PPP is an Internet standard and most UNIX systems include support for it in the kernel as part of the standard operating system installation. Usually this does not require any action on your part. Refer to Chapter 5 for examples of how PPP is configured in the Linux kernel. The Linux system installs the PPP physical and data link layer software (the HDLC protocol) in the kernel.

Installing PPP in the kernel is only the beginning. In this section we look at how **pppd** is configured to provide PPP services on a Slackware 96 Linux system.

The PPP Daemon

Point-to-Point Protocol is implemented on the Linux system in the PPP daemon (**pppd**), which was derived from a freeware PPP implementation for BSD systems. **pppd** can be configured to run in all modes: as a client, as a server, over dial-up connections, and over dedicated connections. Clients and servers are familiar concepts from Chapter 3, *Network Services*. A dedicated connection is a direct cable connection or a leased line; neither of which need to have a telephone call placed to establish the connection. A dial-up connection is a modem link that is established by dialing a telephone number.

Configuring **pppd** for a dedicated line is the simplest configuration. A dial-up script is not needed for a leased line or direct connection. There is no point in dynamically assigning addresses because a dedicated line always connects the same two systems. Authentication is of limited use because the dedicated line physically runs between two points. There is no way for an intruder to access the link, short of "breaking and entering" or "wiretap." A single **pppd** command configures a dedicated PPP link for our Linux system. We place it in the */etc/rc.d/rc.inet1* file:

```
pppd /dev/cua3 56000 crtscts defaultroute
```

The /dev/cua3 argument selects the device to which PPP is attached. It is, of course, the same port to which the dedicated line is attached. Next, the line speed

---

* Check your system documentation to find out exactly how to configure PPP on your system.

is specified in bits per second (56000). The remainder of the command line is a series of keyword options. The **crtscts** option turns on hardware flow control. The final option, **defaultroute**, creates a default route using the remote server as the default gateway.*

PPP exchanges IP addresses during the initial link connection process. If no address is specified on the **pppd** command line, the daemon sends the address of the local host, which it learns from DNS or the host table, to the remote host. Likewise, the remote system sends its address to the local host. The addresses are then used as the source and destination addresses of the link. You can override this by specifying the addresses on the command line in the form *local-address:remote-address*. For example:

```
pppd /dev/cua3 56000 crtscts defaultroute 172.16.24.1:
```

Here we define the local address as 172.16.24.1 and leave the remote address blank. In this case **pppd** sends the address from the command line and waits for the remote server to send its address. The local address is specified on the command line when it is different from the address associated with the local hostname in the host table or the DNS server. For example, the system might have an Ethernet interface that already has an address assigned. If we want to use a different address for the PPP connection, we must specify it on the **pppd** command line; otherwise, the PPP link will be assigned the same address as the Ethernet interface.

The **pppd** command has many more options than those used in these examples.†
In fact, there are so many **pppd** command-line options, it is sometimes easier to put them in a file than it is to enter them all on the command line. **pppd** reads its options from the */etc/ppp/options* file, then the *˜/.ppprc* file, and finally from the command line. The order in which they are processed creates a hierarchy such that options on the command line can override those in the *˜/.ppprc* file, which can in turn override those in the */etc/ppp/options* file. This permits the system administrator to establish certain system-wide defaults in the */etc/ppp/options* file while still permitting the end user to customize the PPP configuration. The */etc/ppp/options* file is a convenient and flexible way to pass parameters to **pppd**.

A single **pppd** command is all that is needed to set up and configure the software for a dedicated PPP link. Dial-up connections are more challenging.

---

* If a default route already exists in the routing table, the **defaultroute** option is ignored.

† There is a full list of the **pppd** options in Appendix A, *PPP Tools*.

Dial-Up PPP

A direct connect cable can connect just two systems. When a third system is purchased, it cannot be added to the network. For that reason, most people use
expandable network technologies, such as Ethernet, for connecting systems in a
local area. Additionally, leased lines are expensive. They are primarily used by
large organizations to connect together networks of systems. For these reasons,
using PPP for dedicated network connections is less common than using it for
dial-up connections.

Several different utilities provide dial-up support for PPP. Dial-up IP (**dip**) is a popular package for simplifying the process of dialing the remote server, performing
the login, and attaching PPP to the resulting connection. We discuss **dip** in this
section because it is popular and because it comes with Slackware 96 Linux,
which is the system we have been using for our PPP examples.

One of the most important features of **dip** is a scripting language that lets you
automate all of the steps necessary to set up an operational PPP link. Appendix A
covers all of the scripting commands supported by the 3.3.7o-uri version of **dip**.
You can list the commands supported by your system by running **dip** in test mode
(–t) and then entering the **help** command:

```
> dip -t
DIP: Dialup IP Protocol Driver version 3.3.7o-uri (8 Feb 96)
Written by Fred N. van Kempen, MicroWalt Corporation.

DIP> help
DIP knows about the following commands:

        beep      bootp     break     chatkey   config
        databits  dec       default   dial      echo
        flush     get       goto      help      if
        inc       init      mode      modem     netmask
        onexit    parity    password  proxyarp  print
        psend     port      quit      reset     send
        shell     sleep     speed     stopbits  term
        timeout   wait

DIP> quit
```

These commands can configure the interface, control the execution of the script,
and process errors. Only a subset of the commands is required for a minimal
script:

```
# Ask PPP to provide the local IP address
get $local 0.0.0.0
# Select the port and set the line speed
port cua1
speed 38400
```

```
# Reset the modem and flush the terminal
reset
flush
# Dial the PPP server and wait for the CONNECT response
dial *70,301-555-1234
wait CONNECT
# Give the server 2 seconds to get ready
sleep 2
# Send a carriage-return to wake up the server
send \r
# Wait for the Login> prompt and send the username
wait ogin>
send kristin\r
# Wait for the Password> prompt and send the password
wait word>
password
# Wait for the PPP server's command-line prompt
wait >
# Send the command required by the PPP server
send ppp enabled\r
# Set the interface to PPP mode
mode PPP
# Exit the script
exit
```

The **get** command at the beginning of the script allows PPP to provide the local and remote addresses. `$local` is a script variable. There are several available script variables; all of which are covered in Appendix A. `$local` normally stores the local address, which can be set statically in the script. A PPP server, however, is capable of assigning an address to the local system dynamically. We take advantage of this capability by giving a local address of all zeros. This peculiar syntax tells **dip** to let **pppd** handle the address assignments. A **pppd** client can get addresses in three ways:

- The PPP systems can exchange their local addresses as determined from DNS. This was discussed previously for the dedicated line configuration.

- The addresses can be specified on the **pppd** command line. This was also discussed above.

- The client can allow the server to assign both addresses. This feature is most commonly used on dial-up lines. It is very popular with servers that must handle a large number of short-lived connections. A dial-up Internet Service Provider (ISP) is a good example.

The next two lines select the physical device to which the modem is connected and set the speed at which the device operates. The **port** command assumes the path */dev*, so the full device path is not used. On most PC UNIX systems the value provided to the **port** command is cua0, cua1, cua2, or cua3. These values correspond to MS-DOS ports COM1 to COM4. The **speed** command sets the maximum speed used to send data to the modem on this port. The default speed is 38400. Change it if your modem accepts data at a different speed.

The **reset** command resets the modem by sending it the Hayes modem interrupt (+++) followed by the Hayes modem reset command (ATZ). This version of **dip** uses the Hayes modem AT command set and works only with Hayes-compatible modems.* Fortunately, that includes most brands of modems. After being reset, the modem responds with a message indicating that the modem is ready to accept input. The **flush** command removes this message, and any others that might have been displayed by the modem, out of the input queue. Use **flush** to avoid the problems that can be caused by unexpected data in the queue.

The next command dials the remote server. The **dial** command sends a standard Hayes ATD **dial** command to the modem. It passes the entire string provided on the command line to the modem as part of the ATD command. The sample **dial** command generates ATD*70,301-555-1234. This causes the modem to dial *70 (which turns off call waiting), and then area code 301, exchange 555, and number 1234.† When this modem successfully connects to the remote modem, it displays the message CONNECT. The **wait** command waits for that message from the modem.

The **sleep 2** command inserts a two-second delay into the script. It is often useful to delay at the beginning of the connection to allow the remote server to initialize. Remember that the CONNECT message is displayed by the modem, not by the remote server. The remote server may have several steps to execute before it is ready to accept input. A small delay can sometimes avoid unexplained intermittent problems.

The **send** command sends a carriage return (\r) to the remote system. Once the modems are connected, anything sent from the local system goes all the way to the remote system. The **send** command can send any string. In the sample script the remote server requires a carriage return before it issues its first prompt. The carriage return is entered as \r and the newline is entered as \n.

The remote server then prompts for the username with `Login>`. The **wait ogin>** command detects this prompt and the **send kristin** command sends the username `kristin` as a response. The server then prompts for the password with `Pass-word>`. The **password** command causes the script to ask the local user to manually enter the password. It is possible to store the password in a **send** command inside

---

* If your modem doesn't use the full Hayes modem command set, avoid using **dip** commands, such as **rest** and **dial**, that generate Hayes commands. Use **send** instead. It allows you to send any string you want to the modem.

† If you have call waiting, turn it off before you attempt to make a SLIP or PPP connection. Different local telephone companies may use different codes to disable call waiting.

the script. However, this is a potential security problem if an unauthorized person gains access to the script and reads the password. The **password** command improves security.

If the password is accepted, our remote server prompts for input with the greater than (>) symbol. Many servers require a command to set the correct protocol mode. The server in our example supports several different protocols. We must tell it to use PPP by using **send** to pass it the correct command.

The script finishes with a few commands that set the correct environment on the local host. The **mode** command tells the local host to use the PPP protocol on this link. The protocol selected must match the protocol running on the remote server. Protocol values that are valid for the **dip mode** command are SLIP, CSLIP, PPP, and TERM. SLIP and CSLIP are variations of the SLIP protocol, which is discussed in the next section. TERM is terminal emulation mode. PPP is the Point-to-Point Protocol. Finally, the **exit** command ends the script, while **dip** keeps running in the background servicing the link.

This simple script does work and it should give you a good idea of the wait/send structure of a **dip** script. However, your scripts will probably be more complicated. The sample script is not robust because it does not do any error checking. If an expected response does not materialize, the sample script hangs. To address this problem, use a timeout on each **wait** command. For example, the **wait OK 10** command tells the system to wait 10 seconds for the OK response. When the OK response is detected, the **$errlvl** script variable is set to zero and the script falls through to the next command. If the OK response is not returned before the 10-second timer expires, **$errlvl** is set to a non-zero value and the script continues on to the next command. The **$errlvl** variable is combined with the **if** and **goto** commands to provide error handling in **dip** scripts. Refer to Appendix A for more details.

Once the script is created it is executed with the **dip** command. Assume that the sample script shown above was saved to a file named *start-ppp.dip*. The following command executes the script, creating a PPP link between the local system and the remote server:

```
> dip start-ppp
```

Terminate the PPP connection with the command **dip −k**. This closes the connection and kills the background **dip** process.

pppd options are not configured in the **dip** script. **dip** creates the PPP connection; it doesn't customize **pppd**. **pppd** options are stored in the */etc/ppp/options* file.

Assuming the **dip** script shown above, we might use the following **pppd** options:

```
noipdefault
ipcp-accept-local
ipcp-accept-remote
defaultroute
```

The **noipdefault** option tells the client not to look up the local address. **ipcp-accept-local** tells the client to obtain its local address from the remote server. The **ipcp-accept-remote** option tells the system to accept the remote address from the remote server. Finally, **pppd** sets the PPP link as the default route. This is the same **defaultroute** option we saw on the **pppd** command line in an earlier example. Any **pppd** option that can be invoked on the command line can be put in the */etc/ppp/options* file and thus be invoked when **pppd** is started by a **dip** script.

I use **dip** on my home computer to set up my dial PPP connection. Personally, I find **dip** simple and straightforward to use. In part, that is because I am familiar with the **dip** scripting language. You may prefer to use the **chat** command that comes with the **pppd** software package.

chat

A **chat** script is a simple "expect/send" script consisting of the strings the system expects and the strings the system sends in response. The script is organized as a list of expect/send pairs. **chat** does not really have a scripting language, but it does have some special characters that can be used to create more complex scripts. The **chat** script to perform the same dial-up and login functions as the sample **dip** script would contain:

```
'' ATZ
OK ATDT*70,301-555-1234
CONNECT \d\d\r
ogin> kristin
word> Wats?Wat?
> 'set port ppp enabled'
```

Each line in the script begins with an expected string and ends with the string sent as a response. The modem does not send a string until it receives a command. The first line on the script says, in effect, "expect nothing and send the modem a reset command." The pair of single quotes (' ') at the beginning of the line tells **chat** to expect nothing. The script then waits for the modem's OK prompt and dials the remote server. When the modem displays the CONNECT message, the script delays two seconds (\d\d) and then sends a carriage return (\r). Each \d special character causes a one-second delay. The \r special character is the carriage return. **chat** has many special characters that can be used in the expect strings and the send strings.* Finally, the script ends by sending the username, password, and remote server configuration command in response to the server's prompts.

Create the script with your favorite editor and save it in a file such as *dial-server.* Test the script using **chat** with the **−V** option, which logs the script execution through stderr:

```
% chat -V -f dial-server
```

Invoking the **chat** script is not sufficient to configure the PPP line. It must be combined with **pppd** to do the whole job. The **connect** command-line option allows you to start **pppd** and invoke a dial-up script all in one command:

```
# pppd /dev/cua1 56700 connect "chat -V -f dial-server" \
    -detach crtscts modem defaultroute
```

The **chat** command following the **connect** option is used to perform the dial-up and login. Any package capable of doing the job could be called here; it doesn't have to be **chat**.

The **pppd** command has some other options that are used when PPP is run as a dial-up client. The **modem** option causes **pppd** to monitor the carrier-detect (DCD) indicator of the modem. This indicator tells **pppd** when the connection is made and when the connection is broken. **pppd** monitors DCD to know when the remote server hangs up the line. The **−detach** option prevents **pppd** from detaching from the terminal to run as a background process. This is only necessary when running **chat** with the **−V** option. When you are done debugging the **chat** script, you can remove the **−V** option from the **chat** subcommand and the **−detach** option from the **pppd** command. An alternative is to use **−v** on the **chat** command. **−v** does not require **pppd** to remain attached to a terminal because it sends the **chat** logging information to **syslogd** instead of to stderr. We have seen all of the other options on this command line before.

PPP Daemon Security

A major benefit of PPP over SLIP is the enhanced security PPP provides. Put the following **pppd** options in the */etc/ppp/options* file to enhance security:

```
lock
auth
usehostname
domain nuts.com
```

---

* See Appendix A for more details.

The first option, **lock**, makes **pppd** use UUCP-style lock files. This prevents other applications, such as UUCP or a terminal emulator, from interfering with the PPP connection. The **auth** option requires the remote system to be authenticated before the PPP link is established. This option causes the local system to request authentication data from the remote system. It does not cause the remote system to request similar data from the local system. If the remote system administrator wants to authenticate your system before allowing a connection, she must put the **auth** keyword in the configuration of her system. The **usehostname** option requires that the hostname is used in the authentication process and prevents the user from setting an arbitrary name for the local system with the **name** option. (More on authentication in a minute.) The final option makes sure that the local hostname is fully qualified with the specified domain before it is used in any authentication procedure.

Recall that the ˜*/.ppprc* file and the **pppd** command-line options can override options set in the */etc/ppp/options* file, which could be a security problem. For this reason, several options, once configured in the */etc/ppp/options* file, cannot be overridden. That includes the options just listed.

pppd supports two authentication protocols: Challenge Handshake Authentication Protocol (CHAP) and Password Authentication Protocol (PAP). PAP is a simple password security system that is vulnerable to all of the attacks of any reusable password system. CHAP, however, is an advanced authentication system that does not use reusable passwords and that repeatedly re-authenticates the remote system.

Two files are used in the authentication process, the */etc/ppp/chap-secrets* file and the */etc/ppp/pap-secrets* file. Given the options file shown above, **pppd** first attempts to authenticate the remote system with CHAP. To do this, there must be data in the *chap-secrets* file and the remote system must respond to the CHAP challenge. If either of these conditions are not true, **pppd** attempts to authenticate the remote system with PAP. If there is no applicable entry in the *pap-secrets* file or the remote system does not respond to the PAP challenge, the PPP connection is not established. This process allows you to authenticate remote systems with CHAP (the preferred protocol), if they support it, and to fall back to PAP for systems that support only PAP. For this to work, however, you must have the correct entries in both files.

Each entry in the *chap-secrets* file contains up to four fields:

client

> The name of the computer that must answer the challenge, i.e., the computer that must be authenticated before the connection is made. This is not necessarily a client that is seeking access to a PPP server. *Client* is the term used in most of the documentation, but really this is the respondent—the system that

responds to the challenge. Both ends of a PPP link can be forced to undergo authentication. In your *chap-secrets* file you will probably have two entries for each remote system: one entry to authenticate the remote system and a corresponding entry to authenticate your system when it is challenged by the remote system.

server

The name of the system that issues the CHAP challenge, i.e., the computer that requires the authentication before the PPP link is established. This is not necessarily a PPP server. The client system can require the server to authenticate itself. *Server* is the term used in most documentation, but really this is the authenticator—the system that authenticates the response.

secret

The secret key that is used to encrypt the challenge string before it is sent back to the system that issued the challenge.

address

An address, written as a hostname or an IP address, that is acceptable for the host named in the first field. If the host listed in the first field attempts to use an address other than the address listed here, the connection is terminated even if the remote host properly encrypts the challenge response. This field is optional.

A sample *chap-secrets* file for the host *macadamia* might contain:

```
cashew      macadamia   Peopledon'tknowyou    172.16.15.3
macadamia   cashew      andtrustisajoke.      172.16.15.1
```

The first entry is used to validate *cashew*, the remote PPP server. *cashew* is being authenticated and the system performing the authentication is *macadamia*. The secret key is "Peopledon'tknowyou". The allowable address is 172.16.15.3, which is the address assigned to *cashew* in the host table. The second entry is used to validate *macadamia* when *cashew* issues the challenge. The secret key is "andtrustisajoke.". The only address *macadamia* is allowed to use is 172.16.15.1. A pair of entries, one for each end of the link, is normal. The *chap-secret* file usually contains two entries for every PPP link: one entry for validating the remote system and one entry for answering the challenge of that remote system.

Use PAP only when you must. If you deal with a system that does not support CHAP, make an entry for that system in the *pap-secrets* file. The format of *pap-secrets* entries is the same as those used in the *chap-secrets* file. A system that does not support CHAP might have the following entry in the *pap-secrets* file:

```
acorn      macadamia   Wherearethestrong?   acorn.nuts.com
macadamia  acorn       Whoarethetrusted?    macadamia.nuts.com
```

Again we have a pair of entries: one for the remote system and one for our system. We support CHAP but the remote system does not. Thus we must be able to respond using the PAP protocol in case the remote system requests authentication.

PPP authentication improves security in a dial-up environment. It is most important when you run the PPP server into which remote systems dial. In the next section, we look at PPP server configuration.

PPP Server Configuration

The PPP server is started by the */etc/ppp/ppplogin* script.* **ppplogin** is a login shell script for dial-in PPP users. Replace the login shell entry in the */etc/passwd* file with the path of **ppplogin** to start the server. A modified */etc/passwd* entry might contain:

```
craig:wJxX.iPuPzg:101:100:Craig Hunt:/tmp:/etc/ppp/ppplogin
```

The fields are exactly the same as any */etc/passwd* entry: username, password, uid, gid, gcos information, home directory, and login shell. For a remote PPP user, the home directory is */tmp* and the login shell is the full path of the **ppplogin** program. The encrypted password must be set using the **passwd** program, just as it is for any user. And the login process is the same as it is for any user. When **getty** detects incoming traffic on the serial port it invokes **login** to authenticate the user. **login** verifies the username and the password entered by the user and starts the login shell. In this case the login shell is actually a shell script that configures the PPP port and starts the PPP daemon. Our sample */etc/ppp/ppplogin* script is:

```
#!/bin/sh
mesg -n
stty -echo
exec /sbin/pppd auth passive crtscts modem
```

The first two lines demonstrate that the *ppplogin* file can contain more than just the **pppd** command. The **mesg –n** command makes sure that other users cannot write to this terminal with **talk**, **write**, or similar programs. The **stty** command turns off character echoing. On some systems, characters typed at the terminal are echoed from the remote host instead of being locally echoed by the terminal; this behavior is called *full duplex*. We don't want to echo anything back on a PPP link, so we turn full duplex off.

The key line in the script is, of course, the line that starts **pppd**. We start the daemon with several options, but one thing that is not included on the command line is the *tty* device name. In all of the previous **pppd** examples, we provided a

---

* The example is for Linux systems running **pppd**. It may be different on your system. Check your system's documentation.

device name. When it is not provided, as is this case, **pppd** uses the controlling terminal as its device and doesn't put itself in background mode. This is just what we want. We want to use the device that **login** was servicing when it invoked the *ppplogin* script.

The **auth** command-line option tells **pppd** to authenticate the remote system, which of course requires us to place an entry for that system in the *chap-secrets* or the *pap-secret* file. The **crtscts** option turns on hardware flow control, and the **modem** option tells PPP to monitor the modem's DCD indicator so that it can detect when the remote system drops the line. We have seen all of these options before. The one new option is **passive**. With **passive** set, the local system waits until it receives a valid LCP packet from the remote system, even if the remote system fails to respond to its first packet. Normally, the local system would drop the connection if the remote system fails to respond in a timely manner. This option gives the remote system time to initialize its own PPP daemon.

Creating an appropriate **ppplogin** script and defining it as a login shell in the */etc/passwd* file are all that is necessary to run **pppd** as a server.

Solaris PPP

dip and **pppd** are available for Linux, BSD, AIX, Ultrix, OSF/1, and SunOS. If you have a different operating system, you probably won't use these packages. Solaris is a good example of a system that uses a different set of commands to configure PPP.

PPP is implemented under Solaris as the Asynchronous PPP Daemon (**aspppd**). **aspppd** is configured by the */etc/asppp.cf* file. The *asppp.cf* file is divided into two sections: an `ifconfig` section and a `path` section.

```
ifconfig ipdptp0 plumb macadamia cashew up

path
    interface ipdptp0
    peer_system_name cashew
    inactivity_timeout 300
```

The **ifconfig** command configures the PPP interface (`ipdptp0`) as a point to point link with a local address of *macadamia* and a destination address of *cashew*. The **ifconfig** command does not have to define the destination address of the link. However, if you always connect to the same remote server, it will probably be defined here as the destination address. We saw all of these options in the discussion of the **ifconfig** command earlier in this chapter.

The more interesting part of this file is the `path` section, which defines the PPP environment. The **interface** statement identifies the interface used for the connection. It must be one of the PPP interfaces defined in the `ifconfig` section. In the example, only one is defined, so it must be `ipdptp0`. The **peer_system_name** statement identifies the system at the remote end of the connection, which may be the same address as the destination address from the **ifconfig** statement as it is in our example. But it doesn't have to be. It is possible to have no destination address on the **ifconfig** command and several `path` sections if you connect to several different remote hosts. The hostname on the **peer_system_name** statement is used in the dialing process as described later.

The `path` section ends with an **inactivity_timeout** statement. The command in the sample sets the timeout to 300 seconds. This is interesting because it points to a nice feature of the Solaris system. Solaris automatically dials the remote system when it detect data that needs to be delivered through that system. Further, it automatically disconnects the PPP link when it is inactive for the specified time. With this feature you can use a PPP link without manually initiating the dial program and without tying up phone lines when the link is not in use.

Like **pppd**, **aspppd** does not have a built-in dial facility. It relies on an external program to do the dialing. In the case of **aspppd**, it utilizes the dial-up facility that comes with UUCP. Here's how.

First, the serial port, the modem attached to it, and the speed at which they operate are defined in the */etc/uucp/Devices* file. For example, here we define an Automatic Call Unit (ACU is another name for a modem) attached to serial port B (cua/b) that operates at any speed defined in the *Systems* file, and that has the modem characteristics defined by the "hayes" entry in the *Dialers* file:

```
ACU cua/b - Any hayes
```

Next, the modem characteristics, such as its initialization setting and dial command, are defined in the */etc/uucp/Dialers* file. The initialization and dial commands are defined as a **chat** script using the standard expect/send format and the standard set of **chat** special characters. For example:

```
hayes =,-, "" \dA\pTE1V1X1Q0S2=255S12=255\r\c OK\r \EATDT\T\r\c CONNECT
```

The system comes with *Devices* and *Dialers* pre-configured. The pre-configured entries are probably compatible with the modem on your system. The */etc/uucp/Systems* file may be the only configuration file that you modify. In the *systems* file you need to enter the name of the remote system, select the modem you'll use, enter the telephone number, and enter a **chat** script to handle the login. For example:

```
cashew Any ACU 19200 5551234 "" \r ogin> kristin word> Wats?Watt? >
    set ppp on
```

In this one line, we identify *cashew* as the remote system, declare that we allow connections to and from that hosts at any time of the day (Any), select the ACU entry in the *Devices* file to specify the port and modem, set the line speed to 19200, send the dialer the telephone number, and define the login **chat** script.

This is not a book about UUCP, so we won't go into further details about these files. I'd suggest *Using and Managing UUCP* (by Ed Ravin, O'Reilly & Associates) for more information about UUCP and the Solaris *TCP/IP Network Administration Guide* (where did they come up with such a great name?) for more information about **aspppd**.

Installing SLIP

Installing Serial Line IP (SLIP) is very similar to installing PPP. As with PPP, support for SLIP is usually installed in the kernel—but that is only part of the configuration. The SLIP network interface also must be configured.

PPP and SLIP configuration is complicated by the fact that these serial line protocols support both dedicated and dial-up connections. For our Linux sample system, this means that two different commands are used to configure a SLIP interface depending on whether it is a dedicated or a dial-up connection. In this section we discuss both, beginning with the configuration command for dedicated connections.

slattach

The **slattach** command "attaches" the SLIP protocol to a specific serial interface. For example:

```
# slattach /dev/tty03 &
```

This command tells the SLIP protocol to use */dev/tty03* as its serial interface. The **slattach** command can optionally set some configuration parameters for the serial interface. The syntax of **slattach** on a Slackware 96 Linux system is:

```
slattach [-h | -c | -6] ttyname [baudrate]
```

The three options, −h, −c, and −6, select the type of SLIP protocol used. −h selects uncompressed SLIP with full headers. CSLIP with Van Jacobsen header compression is selected with −c. Use −6 to select six-bit SLIP. If none of these options is selected, the **slattach** command defaults to CSLIP.

The *baudrate* argument sets the interface's transmission speed. Set the speed by entering a number that corresponds to the bit rate that is used to transmit and receive data on this line, e.g., 56000. Both ends of the line must set exactly the same bit rate. This may be determined by the characteristics of the leased line, or by the hardware interfaces for a direct cable connection. Regardless, the transmission speed is a physical characteristic limited by the equipment on the line. A default transmission speed of 9600 bits per second is used if no *baudrate* value is entered on the command line.

The *ttyname* is the name of the serial interface attached to the leased line or direct cable connection. The serial interfaces are identified by the system during the boot. **dmesg** and **grep** displays the interface names on a Slackware 96 Linux system:

```
> dmesg | grep tty
tty00 at 0x03f8 (irq = 4) is a 16550A
tty01 at 0x02f8 (irq = 3) is a 16550A
tty03 at 0x02e8 (irq = 3) is a 16550A
```

This list of serial interface names is from a PC running Linux. Assume we connect the direct connection cable to tty01, which is equivalent to the MS-DOS interface COM2. In that case, use tty01 as the *ttyname* value on the **slattach** command. Notice that the **slattach** command identifies the physical serial device (*/dev/tty01*) instead of the IP network interface (*sl0*). That is because the SLIP IP interface does not exist until after **slattach** executes. The first **slattach** command creates the sl0 interface, the second creates the sl1 interface, and so on. **slattach** attaches a physical interface to the logical IP network.

Like **ifconfig**, the **slattach** command is stored in a startup file. It configures the serial interface when the system boots, and the interface remains dedicated to SLIP use unless some action is taken to detach it, i.e., the **slattach** process is killed. On a Slackware 96 Linux system the following commands might be added to the */etc/rc.d/rc.inet1* file to configure a dedicated SLIP connection:

```
slattach -c /dev/tty01 19200 &
ifconfig sl0 macadamia pointopoint cashew
route add default cashew 1
```

The **pppd** dedicated line configuration requires only one command. The **slattach** command needs an **ifconfig** command and a **route** command to complete the configuration. The **route** command is explained in Chapter 7, *Configuring Routing*.

The **slattach** command declares that the physical serial device */dev/tty01* is the SLIP network interface. In essence this creates the interface sl0. The **ifconfig** command configures the newly created SLIP interface. It sets the address of the interface to the IP address of host *macadamia*. Further, it says that the destination address of this interface is the IP address of the host *cashew* at the far end of the dedicated SLIP link. The IP addresses for both *macadamia* and *cashew* should be in the local hosts file before this **ifconfig** command is executed.

The examples in this section all use the syntax of the **slattach** command that comes with Slackware 96 Linux. SLIP commands are not standardized. The command that comes with your system will probably have a different syntax; carefully read your system's documentation so you'll know the exact syntax used on your system. For example, other versions of Linux use this syntax:

slattach [**-p** *protocol*] [**-s** *speed*] *device*

Here the various SLIP protocols are selected with the −p option. The acceptable *protocol* values are: **slip**, **cslip**, **slip6**, **cslip6**, and **adaptive**. If **adaptive** is selected, the system tries to determine which protocol is acceptable to the remote system. The −s option sets the line speed, e.g., −s **56000**. The **device** is one of the *call units* configured on the system. Examples of valid call unit device names are cua0, cua1, cua2, cua3, etc. The device names from cua0 to cua3 correspond to the MS-DOS devices COM1 to COM4. A call unit is normally associated with dial communications.

slattach expects the physical connection to the remote system to exist when **slattach** is invoked. The physical connection can be a direct connection, a leased line, or a dial line. But if a dial-up connection is used, some process, such as **cu** or **tip**, must establish the physical connection before **slattach** is invoked. As we have seen, **dip** is a command that is specifically designed to support dial-up IP connections.

Dial-Up IP

Earlier in this chapter we used **dip** to create a dial-up PPP connection. **dip** can also be used for SLIP. It is actually quite simple. A slight modification of the **dip** script used earlier creates a SLIP link. The following script connects a PC named *macadamia* to a SLIP server named *cashew*:

```
# Set the local and remote addresses
get $locip 172.16.15.1
get $rmtip 172.16.15.3
# Select the port and set the line speed
port cua1
speed 38400
# Reset the modem and flush the terminal
reset
flush
# Dial the SLIP server and wait for the CONNECT response
dial *70,301-555-1234
wait CONNECT
# Wait 2 seconds for the remote server to get ready
sleep 2
# Send a carriage-return to wake up the server
send \r
# Wait for the Login> prompt and send the username
wait ogin>
send kristin\r
# Wait for the Password> prompt and send the password
wait word>
```

```
password
# Wait for the SLIP server's command line prompt
wait >
# Send the command required by the SLIP server
send set cslip enabled\r
# Select the SLIP interface as the default route
default
# Set the interface to CSLIP mode
mode CSLIP
# Exit the script
exit
```

Modifications to a few lines from the PPP script were required to create a SLIP dial-up script. Obvious changes replace the remote server's PPP command with a SLIP command and change the **mode** command in the script to invoke SLIP instead of PPP. We also added some new lines to perform tasks for SLIP that PPP can do on its own.

The script begins by setting the local IP address and the remote IP address. $locip and $rmtip are script variables used to identify the hosts at both ends of the link, which is analogous to the **pointopoint** parameter on the **ifconfig** command that we saw in the previous section. The two **get** statements set the local interface to the address 172.16.15.1 and the destination address to 172.16.15.3. SLIP does not have a standard way within the protocol to exchange addresses. We had to add specific local and remote IP addresses to the script.

The **default** statement near the end of the script says that the SLIP connection is the local system's default route. Since SLIP is most often used to connect small isolated systems into the network, this is usually true. This statement performs the same function as the **route** command in the **slattach** example or the **defaultroute** option in the */etc/ppp/options* file.

SLIP Server Configuration

So far, we have used **dip** to establish a dial-in SLIP link to a remote server. **dip** can also provide the server side of a SLIP connection. The −i option sets **dip** to input mode, which configures the system to act as a dial-in server. An alternative, and more popular, way to invoke **dip** with the −i option is to use the **diplogin** command. **diplogin** is symbolically linked to the **dip** command and is exactly the same as specifying **dip** with the −i option. We'll use **diplogin** throughout this section.

diplogin is used as the login shell for dial-in SLIP users. The system administrator puts **diplogin** in the */etc/passwd* entry for each remote SLIP user as the user's login shell. For example:

```
craig:wJxX.iPuPzg:101:100:Craig Hunt:/tmp:/sbin/diplogin
```

login verifies the username and password, assigns the user */tmp* as a home directory and starts his login shell. In this case the shell is **diplogin**.

The **diplogin** program then tries to find an entry for the user in the */etc/diphosts* file. It searches for the username that was entered during the login process unless that username is overridden by another directly on the **diplogin** command line. For example: when the **/etc/passwd** entry shown above starts **diplogin**, the username *craig* is used to search the */etc/diphosts* file. Conversely, in the */etc/passwd* entry shown below, the username *essex* that appears after the **diplogin** command is used for the search.

```
hunt:AbxdkiThinR:102:100:Rebecca Hunt:/tmp:/sbin/diplogin essex
```

The format of entries in the */etc/diphost* file is:

user:password:remote-host:local-host:netmask:comment:protocol,mtu

user

> A username. This is the key field against which a username from the */etc/passwd* file or from an argument on the **diplogin** command line is matched.

password

> An unencrypted password, the keyword **s/key**, or null (an empty field). If an unencrypted password is entered in this field, **diplogin** prompts the user for the password. This is in addition to the standard password from the */etc/passwd* file that the user has already been required to enter. Because this second password is stored in an unencrypted format, it is not considered very secure. Sites that are big on security don't consider any reusable passwords secure enough to be meaningful, and sites that don't worry too much about security don't consider a second password necessary. For these reasons, the unencrypted password is rarely used. If this field contains the keyword **s/key**, **diplogin** invokes S/Key authentication. This requires that S/Key support is compiled into **diplogin**, and that S/Key is installed in your system. Because S/Key is a one-time password system, it's considered very secure. However, it is a headache for users and system administrators. See Chapter 12 for a full discussion of one-time passwords. If the password field is null, the authentication is left to **login** and the user is not asked for a second password.

remote-host

> The hostname or IP address of the remote host; i.e., the computer from which the user is logging in.

local-host

> The hostname or IP address of the local host; i.e., the computer on which this SLIP server is running.

netmask

The network mask for the serial interface written in dotted decimal notation, such as 255.255.0.0. If no value is provided the netmask defaults to 255.255.255.0, regardless of the class of addresses used on the network.

comment

A free-form comment field, similar to the **gcos** field in the */etc/passwd* file.

protocol,mtu

The IP protocol and the maximum transmission unit used for this connection. Possible protocol values are SLIP, CSLIP, and PPP. The MTU is any valid transmission unit specified in bytes. The largest MTU used on SLIP lines is generally 1006 bytes. However, SLIP performance is often improved by smaller packet sizes. Common choices are 512 and 256.

Assuming the two */etc/passwd* entries shown above, we might have an */etc/diphosts* file with the following entries:

```
craig::cashew:macadamia:255.255.255.240:Craig Hunt:CSLIP,512
essex::essex:macadamia::Remote client essex.nuts.com:PPP,1006
```

When the **login** authenticates the user *craig*, it starts **diplogin** as the login shell. **diplogin** finds the entry for *craig*, does not prompt for a second password, sets the local address to *macadamia* and the remote address to *cashew*, and starts a CSLIP server using an MTU of 512. However, if the user *hunt* logs into the system, **login** starts **diplogin** with the username *essex*. The */etc/diphosts* entry for *essex* starts a PPP server with a local address of *macadamia*, a remote address of *essex* and an MTU of 1006. The *essex* entry allows the netmask to default to 255.255.255.0. The servers started by **diplogin** run until the modem hangs up the connection.

Clearly **dip** is more than just a **chat** script. It provides client and server support for a variety of protocols. See Appendix A for more information about **dip**.

Troubleshooting Serial Connections

There are several layers of complexity that make PPP and SLIP connections difficult to debug. To set up PPP and SLIP, we must set up the serial port, configure the modem, configure PPP or SLIP, and configure TCP/IP. A mistake in any one of these layers can cause a problem in another layer. All of these layers can obscure the true cause of a problem. The best way to approach troubleshooting on a serial line is by debugging each layer, one layer at a time. It is usually best to troubleshoot each layer before you move on to configure the next layer.

The physical serial ports should be configured by the system during the system boot. Check the */dev* directory to make sure they are configured. On a Linux system the in-bound serial ports are */dev/ttyS0* through */dev/ttyS3* and the out-bound serial ports are */dev/cua0* through */dev/cua3*. There are many more tty* and cua* device names. However, the other devices are only associated with real physical devices if you have a multi-port serial card installed in your Linux system. Most UNIX systems use the names tty* and cua*, even if those names are just symbolic links to the real devices. Solaris 2.5.1 is a good example:

```
% ls -l /dev/tty?
lrwxrwxrwx 1 root root 6 Sep 23  1996 /dev/ttya -> term/a
lrwxrwxrwx 1 root root 6 Sep 23  1996 /dev/ttyb -> term/b
% ls -l /dev/cua/*
lrwxrwxrwx 1 root root 35 Sep 23 1996 /dev/cua/a ->
    /devices/obio/zs@0,100000:a,cu
lrwxrwxrwx 1 root root 35 Sep 23 1996 /dev/cua/b ->
    /devices/obio/zs@0,100000:b,cu
```

If the serial devices do not show up in the */dev* directory, they can be manually added with a **mknod** command. For example, the following commands create the serial devices for the first serial port on a Linux system:

```
# mknod -m 666 /dev/cua0 c 5 64
# mknod -m 666 /dev/ttyS0 c 4 64
```

However, if you need to add the serial devices manually, there may be a problem with the kernel configuration. The serial devices should be installed in your system by default during the boot.

The modem used for the connection is attached to one of the serial ports. Before attempting to build a dial-up script, make sure the modem works and that you can communicate with it through the port. Use a simple serial communications package, such as **minicom**, **kermit**, or **seyon**. First, make sure the program is configured to use your modem. It must be set to the correct port, speed, parity, number of databits, etc. Check your modem's documentation to determine these settings.

We'll use **minicom** on a Linux system for our examples. To configure **minicom**, **su** to *root* and run it with the **−s** option, which displays a configuration menu. Walk through the menu and make sure everything is properly set. One thing you might notice is that the port is set to */dev/modem*. That device name is sometimes symbolically linked to the port to which the modem is connected. If you're not sure that the link exists on your system, enter the correct port name in the **minicom** configuration, e.g., */dev/cua1*. After checking the configuration, exit the menu and use the **minicom** terminal emulator to make sure you can communicate with the modem:

```
Minicom 1.71 Copyright (c) Miquel van Smoorenburg
Press CTRL-A Z for help on special keys

AT S7=45 S0=0 L1 V1 X4 &c1 E1 Q0
OK
```

```
atz
OK
atdt555-1234
CONNECT 26400/LAPM-V
^M
Enter login> kristin
Enter user password> Wats?Watt?

    Welcome to the PPP MODEM POOL

PORT-9> set port ppp enabled
+++
OK
ath
OK
atz
OK
^A
CTRL-A Z for help | 38400 8N1 | NOR | Minicom 1.71 1995 | VT102 |
    Offline
X
```

In the sample, **minicom** displays two header lines and then sends a Hayes command (**AT**) to the modem. We didn't set this command; it was part of the default **minicom** configuration. (If it causes problems, edit it out of the configuration using the menus discussed previously.) We then reset the modem (**atz**) and dial the remote server (**atdt**). When the modems connect, we log in to the server and configure it. (The login process is different for every remote server; this is just an example.) Everything appears to be running fine, so we end the connection by getting the modem's attention (**+++**), hanging up the line (**ath**), and resetting the modem. Exit **minicom** by pressing CTRL-A followed by X. On our sample system the port and modem are working. If you cannot send simple commands to your modem, check that:

- The modem is properly connected to the port
- You have the correct cables
- The modem is powered up
- The modem is properly configured for dial-out and for echoing commands

When the modem responds to simple commands, use it to dial the remote server as we did in the example above. If the modem fails to dial the number or displays the message NO DIALTONE, check that the telephone line is connected to the correct port of the modem and to the wall jack. You may need to use an analog phone to test the telephone wall jack and you may need to replace the line between the modem and the wall to make sure that the cable is good. If the modem dials but fails to successfully connect to the remote modem, check that the local modem configuration matches the configuration required by the remote system. You must know the requirements of that remote system to successfully debug a connection. See the following list of script debugging tips for some hints on what to check. If you can successfully connect to the remote system, note everything you entered to do so, and note everything that the modem and the remote server display. Then set the remote server to PPP or SLIP mode and note how you accomplished this. You will need to duplicate all of these steps in your **dip** script.

Start with a bare-bones script, like the sample *start-ppp.dip* script, so that you can debug the basic connection before adding the complexity of error processing to the script. Run the script through **dip** using the verbose option (–v) option. This displays each line of the script as it is processed. Look for the following problems:

- The modem does not respond to the script. Check that you are using the correct device on the **port** command. Make sure that if the script contains **databits**, **parity**, **speed**, or **stopbits** commands that they are set to values compatible with your modem. Double-check that the modem is Hayes-compatible, particularly if you attempt to do modem configuration using **dip** keywords instead of using **send**.

- The modem fails to connect to the remote host. Make sure the modem is configured exactly as it was during the manual login. The modem's databits, parity, etc. need to match the configuration of the remote system. It is possible that you will need a special configuration, for example, 7-bit/even-parity, to perform the login before you can switch to the 8-bit/no-parity configuration required by PPP and SLIP. Don't forget to check that the phone number entered in the **dial** command is correct, particularly if the modem displays VOICE, RING – NO ANSWER, or BUSY when you expect to see CONNECT.

- The script hangs. It is probably waiting for a response. Make sure that the string in each **wait** command is correct. Remember that the string only needs to be a subset of the response. It is better to use the string ">" than it is to use "Port9>" if you are not sure whether the remote system always displays the same port number. Use a substring from the end of the expected response so that the script does not send to the server before the server is ready for input. Also try putting a delay into the script just before the script sends the first command to the server, e.g., **sleep 2** to delay 2 seconds. A delay is sometimes needed to allow the server to initialize the port after the modems connect.

- The remote server displays an error message. The script probably sent an incorrect value. Check the string in each **send** command. Make sure they terminate with the correct carriage-return or line-feed combination expected by the remote server.

If you have trouble with the script, try running **dip** in test mode (–t), which allows you to enter each command manually one at a time. Do this repeatedly until you are positive that you know all the commands needed to log in to the remote server. Then go back to debugging the script. You'll probably have fresh insight into the login process that will help you find the flaw in the script.

Once the script is running and the connection is successfully made, things should run smoothly. You should be able to **ping** the remote server without difficulty. If you have problems they may be in the IP interface configuration or in the default route. The script should have created the serial interface. The **netstat —ni** command shows which interfaces have been configured:

```
# netstat -ni
Name Mtu  Net/Dest     Address      Ipkts Ierrs Opkts Oerrs Collis Queue
le0  1500 172.16.15.0  172.16.15.1      1     0     4     0      0     0
lo0  1536 127.0.0.0    127.0.0.1     1712     0  1712     0      0     0
ppp0 1006 172.16.15.26 172.16.15.3      0     0     0     0      0     0
```

The interface, ppp0 in the example, has been installed. The **default** command in the script creates a default route. Use **netstat** to see the contents of the routing table:

```
# netstat -nr
Routing tables
Destination     Gateway        Flags  Refcnt  Use  Interface
127.0.0.1       127.0.0.1      UH      1      28   lo0
default         172.16.25.3    U       0      0    ppp0
172.16.15.0     172.16.15.1    U      21    1687   le0
```

The contents of routing tables are explained in detail in the next chapter. For now, just notice that interface used for the default route is ppp0, and that the default route is a route to the remote PPP server (172.16.25.3 in the example).

If the script creates the connection, the interface is installed, and the routing table contains the default route, everything should work fine. If you still have problems they may be related to other parts of the TCP/IP installation. Refer to Chapter 11, *Troubleshooting TCP/IP*, for more troubleshooting information.

Summary

TCP/IP works with a wide variety of networks. TCP/IP cannot make assumptions about the network it runs on—the network interface and its characteristics must be identified to TCP/IP. In this chapter we have looked at several examples of how to configure the physical network interface over which TCP/IP runs.

ifconfig is the most commonly used interface configuration command. It assigns the interface its IP address, sets the subnet mask, sets the broadcast address, and performs several other functions.

TCP/IP can also run over telephone lines using dial-up connections. Two protocols are available to do this: Serial Line IP (SLIP) and Point-to-Point Protocol (PPP). PPP is the preferred choice. It is an Internet standard and offers better reliability, performance, and security.

There are several steps to setting up a PPP or a SLIP connection: selecting and configuring the serial protocol, configuring the port and modem, making the dial-up connection, and completing the remote login. Some programs, such as **dip**, combine all of these steps into one program. Other programs, such as **pppd** and **chat**, separate the functions.

Configuring the network interface allows us to talk to the local network, while configuring routing allows us to talk to the world. We touched on routing in Chapter 2 and again in this chapter in our discussion of routing metrics for **ifconfig** and default routes for PPP and SLIP. In the next chapter we look at routing in much greater detail.

7

Configuring Routing

Routing is the glue that binds the Internet together. Without it, TCP/IP traffic is limited to a single physical network. Routing allows traffic from your local network to reach its destination somewhere else in the world—perhaps after passing through many intermediate networks.

The important role of routing and the complex interconnection of Internet networks make the design of routing protocols a major challenge to network software developers. Consequently, most discussions of routing concern protocol design. Very little is written about the important task of properly configuring routing protocols. However, more day-to-day problems are caused by improperly configured routers than are caused by improperly designed routing algorithms. As system administrators, we need to ensure that the routing on our systems is properly configured. This is the task we tackle in this chapter.

Common Routing Configurations

First, we must make a distinction between routing and routing protocols. All systems route data, but not all systems run routing protocols. *Routing* is the act of forwarding datagrams based on the information contained in the routing table. *Routing protocols* are programs that exchange the information used to build routing tables.

A network's routing configuration does not always require a routing protocol. In situations where the routing information does not change—for example, when there is only one possible route—the system administrator usually builds the routing table manually. Some networks have no access to any other TCP/IP networks, and therefore do not require that the system administrator build the routing table at all. The three most common routing configurations are:*

Minimal routing

A network completely isolated from all other TCP/IP networks requires only minimal routing. A minimal routing table usually is built by **ifconfig** when the network interface is configured.† If your network doesn't have direct access to other TCP/IP networks, and if you are not using subnetting, this may be the only routing table you'll require.

Static routing

A network with a limited number of gateways to other TCP/IP networks can be configured with static routing. When a network has only one gateway, a static route is the best choice. A static routing table is constructed manually by the system administrator using the **route** command. Static routing tables do not adjust to network changes, so they work best where routes do not change.

Dynamic routing

A network with more than one possible route to the same destination should use dynamic routing. A dynamic routing table is built from the information exchanged by routing protocols. The protocols are designed to distribute information that dynamically adjusts routes to reflect changing network conditions. Routing protocols handle complex routing situations more quickly and accurately than the system administrator can. Routing protocols are designed not only to switch to a backup route when the primary route becomes inoperable; they are also designed to decide which is the "best" route to a destination. On any network where there are multiple paths to the same destination, a routing protocol should be used.

Routes are built automatically by **ifconfig**, manually by the system administrator, or dynamically by routing protocols. But no matter how routes are entered, they all end up in the routing table.

The Minimal Routing Table

Let's look at the contents of the routing table constructed by **ifconfig** when *peanut*'s network interfaces were configured:

```
% netstat -rn
Routing tables
```

---

* Chapter 4, *Getting Started*, presents guidelines for choosing the correct routing configuration for your network.

† Linux is an exception. **ifconfig** does not create routing table entries on a Linux system.

```
Destination          Gateway          Flags    Refcnt Use      Interface
127.0.0.1            127.0.0.1        UH       1      132       lo0
172.16.12.0          172.16.12.2      U        26     49041     le0
```

The first entry is the loopback route to *localhost* created when lo0 was configured. The other entry is the route to network 172.16.12.0 through interface le0. Address 172.16.12.2 is not a remote gateway address. It is the address assigned to the le0 interface on *peanut*.

Look at the Flags field for each entry. Both entries have the U (up) flag set, indicating that they are ready to be used, but neither entry has the G (gateway) flag set. The G flag indicates that an external gateway is used. The G flag is not set because both of these routes are direct routes through local interfaces, not through external gateways.

The loopback route also has the H (host) flag set. This indicates that only one host can be reached through this route. The meaning of this flag becomes clear when you look at the Destination field for the loopback entry. It shows that the destination is a host address, not a network address. The loopback network address is 127.0.0.0. The destination address shown (127.0.0.1) is the address of *localhost*, an individual host. This particular host route is in most routing tables.

Although every routing table has this host-specific route, most routes lead to networks. One reason network routes are used is to reduce the size of the routing table. An organization may have only one network but hundreds of hosts. The Internet has thousands of networks but millions of hosts. A routing table with a route for every host would be unmanageable.

Our sample table contains only one network route, 172.16.12.0. Therefore, *peanut* can communicate only with hosts located on that network. The limited capability of this routing table is easily verified with the **ping** command. **ping** uses the ICMP Echo Message to force a remote host to echo a packet back to the local host. If packets can travel to and from a remote host, it indicates that the two hosts can successfully communicate.

To check the routing table on *peanut*, first **ping** another host on the local network:

```
% ping -s almond
PING almond.nuts.com: 56 data bytes
64 bytes from almond.nuts.com (172.16.12.1): icmp_seq=0. time=11. ms
64 bytes from almond.nuts.com (172.16.12.1): icmp_seq=1. time=10. ms
^C
----almond.nuts.com PING Statistics----
2 packets transmitted, 2 packets received, 0% packet loss
round-trip (ms)  min/avg/max = 10/10/11
```

ping displays a line of output for each ICMP ECHO_RESPONSE received.* When **ping** is interrupted, it displays some summary statistics. All of this indicates successful communication with *almond*. But if we check a host that is not on *nuts-net*, say a host at O'Reilly, the results are different.

```
% ping 207.25.98.2
sendto: Network is unreachable
```

Here the message "sendto: Network is unreachable" indicates that *peanut* does not know how to send data to the network that host 207.25.98.2 is on. There are only two routes in the *peanut* routing table and neither is a route to 207.25.98.0.

Even other subnets on *nuts-net* cannot be reached using this routing table. To demonstrate this, **ping** a host on another subnet. For example:

```
% ping 172.16.1.2
sendto: Network is unreachable
```

These **ping** tests show that the routing table created by **ifconfig** allows communication only with other hosts on the local network. If your network does not require access to any other TCP/IP networks, this may be all you need. However, if it does require access to other networks, you must add more routes to the routing table.

Building a Static Routing Table

As we have seen, the minimal routing table works to reach hosts only on the directly connected physical networks. To reach remote hosts, routes through external gateways must be added to the routing table. One way to do this is by constructing a static routing table with **route** commands.

Use the UNIX **route** command to add or delete entries manually in the routing table. For example, to add the route 207.25.98.0 to a Solaris system's routing table, enter:

```
# route add 207.25.98.0 172.16.12.1 1
add net 207.25.98.0: gateway almond
```

The first argument after the **route** command in this sample is the keyword **add**. The first keyword on a **route** command line is either **add** or **delete**, telling **route** either to add a new route or delete an existing one. There is no default; if neither keyword is used, **route** displays the routing table.

The next value is the destination address, which is the address reached via this route. The destination address can be specified as an IP address, a network name from the */etc/networks* file, a host name from the */etc/hosts* file, or the keyword

---

* Sun's **ping** would only display the message "almond is alive" if the −s option was not used. Some other **ping** implementations do not require the −s option.

default. Because most routes are added early in the startup process, numeric IP addresses are used more than names. This is done so that the routing configuration is not dependent on the state of the name server software. Always use the complete numeric address (all four bytes). **route** expands the address if it contains less than four bytes, and the expanded address may not be what you intended.*

If the keyword **default** is used for the destination address, **route** creates a *default route*.† The default route is used whenever there is no specific route to a destination, and it is often the only route you need. If your network has only one gateway, use a default route to direct all traffic bound for remote networks through that gateway.

Next on the **route** command line is the gateway address.‡ This is the IP address of the external gateway through which data is sent to the destination address. The address must be the address of a gateway on a directly connected network. TCP/IP routes specify the *next-hop* in the path to a remote destination. That next-hop must be directly accessible to the local host; therefore, it must be on a directly connected network.

The last argument on the command line is the routing metric. The metric argument is not used when routes are deleted, but many systems require it when a route is added. Despite being required, **route** only uses the metric to decide if this is a route through a directly attached interface or a route through an external gateway. If the metric is 0, the route is installed as a route through a local interface, and the G flag, which we saw in the **netstat −i** display, is not set. If the metric value is greater than 0, the route is installed with the G flag set, and the gateway address is assumed to be the address of an external gateway. Static routing makes no other use of the metric. Dynamic routing is required to make real use of varying metric values.

Adding Static Routes

As an example, let's configure static routing on the imaginary workstation *peanut*. Figure 7-1 shows the subnet 172.16.12.0. There are two gateways on this subnet, *almond* and *pecan. almond* is the gateway to thousands of networks on the Internet; *pecan* provides access to the other subnets on *nuts-net*. We'll use *almond* as our default gateway because it is used by thousands of routes. The smaller number of routes through *pecan* can easily be entered individually. The number of

---

* Some implementations of **route** expand "26" to 0.0.0.26, even though "26" could mean Milnet (26.0.0.0).

† The network address associated with the default route is 0.0.0.0.

‡ The syntax varies slightly between systems. Linux precedes the gateway address with the keyword **gw**. Check your system's documentation for the details.

routes through a gateway, not the amount of traffic it handles, decides which gateway to select as the default. Even if most of *peanut's* network traffic goes through *pecan* to other hosts on *nuts-net*, the default gateway should be *almond*.

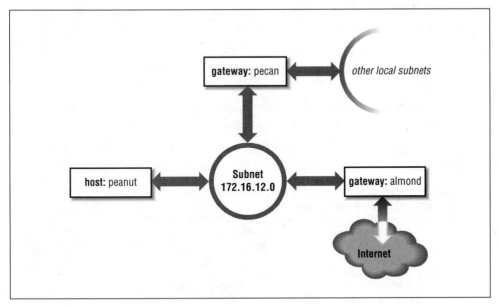

Figure 7-1: Routing on a subnet

To install the default route on *peanut*, we enter:

```
# route -n add default 172.16.12.1 1
add net default: gateway 172.16.12.1
```

The destination is **default**, and the gateway address (172.16.12.1) is *almond's* address. Now *almond* is *peanut's* default gateway. The **−n** option is not required. It just tells **route** to display numeric addresses in its informational messages. When you add **route** commands to a startup file, use the **−n** option to prevent **route** from wasting time querying name server software that may not be running.

After installing the default route, examine the routing table to make sure the route has been added:

```
% netstat -rn
Routing tables
Destination     Gateway         Flags    Refcnt Use        Interface
127.0.0.1       127.0.0.1       UH       1      132        lo0
default         172.16.12.1     UG       0      0          le0
172.16.12.0     172.16.12.2     U        26     49041      le0
```

Try **ping** again to see whether *peanut* can now communicate with remote hosts. If we're lucky,* the remote host responds and we see:

```
% ping 207.25.98.2
PING 207.25.98.2: 56 data bytes
64 bytes from ruby.ora.com (207.25.98.2): icmp_seq=0. time=110. ms
64 bytes from ruby.ora.com (207.25.98.2): icmp_seq=1. time=100. ms
^C
----207.25.98.2 PING Statistics----
2 packets transmitted, 2 packets received, 0% packet loss
round-trip (ms)  min/avg/max = 100/105/110
```

This display indicates successful communication with the remote host, which means that we now have a good route to hosts on the Internet.

However, we still haven't installed routes to the rest of *nuts-net*. If we **ping** a host on another subnet, something interesting happens:

```
% ping 172.16.1.2
PING 172.16.1.2: 56 data bytes
ICMP Host redirect from gateway almond.nuts.com (172.16.12.1)
  to pecan.nuts.com (172.16.12.3) for filbert.nuts.com (172.16.1.2)
64 bytes from filbert.nuts.com (172.16.1.2): icmp_seq=1. time=30. ms
^C
----172.16.1.2 PING Statistics----
1 packets transmitted, 1 packets received, 0% packet loss
round-trip (ms)  min/avg/max = 30/30/30
```

peanut believes that all destinations are reachable through its default route. Therefore, even data destined for the other subnets is sent to *almond*. If *peanut* sends data to *almond* that should go through *pecan, almond* sends an ICMP Redirect to *peanut* telling it to use *pecan.* (See Chapter 1, *Overview of TCP/IP*, for a description of the ICMP Redirect Message.) **ping** shows the ICMP Redirect in action. **netstat** shows the effect the redirect has on the routing table:

```
% netstat -nr
Routing tables
Destination     Gateway         Flags   Refcnt  Use        Interface
127.0.0.1       127.0.0.1       UH      1       132        lo0
172.16.12.0     172.16.12.2     U       31      686547     le0
172.16.1.2      172.16.12.3     UGHD    0       514        le0
default         172.16.12.1     UG      3       373964     le0
```

The route with the D flag set was installed by the ICMP Redirect.

Some network managers take advantage of ICMP Redirects when designing a network. All hosts are configured with a default route, even those on networks with more than one gateway. The gateways exchange routing information through

---

* It is possible that the remote host is down. If it is, **ping** receives no answer. Don't give up; try another host.

routing protocols and redirect hosts to the best gateway for a specific route. This type of routing, which is dependent on ICMP Redirects, became popular because of personal computers (PCs). Many PCs cannot run a routing protocol; some do not have a **route** command and are limited to a single default route. Clearly, ICMP Redirects are needed to support these clients. Also, this type of routing is simple to configure and well suited for implementation through a configuration server, as the same default route is used on every host. For these reasons, some network managers encourage repeated ICMP Redirects.

Other network administrators prefer to avoid ICMP Redirects and to maintain direct control over the contents of the routing table. To avoid redirects, specific routes can be installed for each subnet, using individual **route** statements:

```
# route -n add 172.16.1.0 172.16.12.3 1
add net 172.16.1.0: gateway 172.16.12.3
# route -n add 172.16.6.0 172.16.12.3 1
add net 172.16.6.0: gateway 172.16.12.3
# route -n add 172.16.3.0 172.16.12.3 1
add net 172.16.3.0: gateway 172.16.12.3
# route -n add 172.16.9.0 172.16.12.3 1
add net 172.16.9.0: gateway 172.16.12.3
```

netstat shows what the completed routing table looks like. *peanut* is directly connected only to 172.16.12.0, so all gateways in its routing table have addresses that begin with 172.16.12. The finished routing table is shown below.

```
% netstat -nr
Routing tables
Destination         Gateway           Flags     Refcnt Use Interface
127.0.0.1           127.0.0.1         UH        1      132      lo0
172.16.12.0         172.16.12.2       U         31     686547   le0
172.16.1.2          172.16.12.3       UGHD      1      514      le0
default             172.16.12.1       UG        3      373964   le0
172.16.1.0          172.16.12.3       UG        0      0        le0
172.16.6.0          172.16.12.3       UG        0      0        le0
172.16.3.0          172.16.12.3       UG        0      0        le0
172.16.9.0          172.16.12.3       UG        0      0        le0
```

The routing table we have constructed uses the default route (through *almond*) to reach external networks, and specific routes (through *pecan*) to reach other subnets within *nuts-net*. Rerunning the **ping** tests produces consistently successful results. However, if any subnets are added to the network, the routes to these new subnets must be manually added to the routing table. Additionally, if the system is rebooted, all static routing table entries are lost. Therefore, to use static routing, you must ensure that the routes are re-installed each time your system boots.

Installing static routes at startup

If you decide to use static routing, you need to make two modifications to your startup files:

1. Add the desired **route** statements to a startup file.

2. Remove any statements from the startup file that run a routing protocol.

Linux provides an interesting example, because it requires static routes to build the minimal routing table. The Linux implementation of **ifconfig** doesn't modify the routing table when a new interface is configured. The route for a new interface is explicitly added with a **route** command. These "interface routes" are stored in a startup script. On our sample Slackware Linux system, the routes are found in */etc/rc.d/rc.inet1:**

```
/sbin/route add -net 127.0.0.0
/sbin/route add -net 172.16.5.0 netmask 255.255.255.0
```

The first statement installs the route for the loopback interface. Note the abbreviated syntax of this command: it specifies a destination but no gateway. This is because Linux has a special syntax just for assigning a route to an interface. We could have written the command as:

```
/sbin/route add -net 127.0.0.0 dev lo0
```

If **dev** is not specified on the command line, the **route** command determines the correct interface from the destination address.

The second statement from the */etc/rc.d/rc.inet1* script installs the route for the Ethernet interface. This statement includes a subnet mask. If none was provided, it would default to 255.255.0.0, which is the standard for the class B address 172.16.0.0.

Installing routes for directly connected interfaces is specific to Linux. As another more general example, let's see how to add static routing to the startup script on a Solaris system. Before making changes to your real system, check your system's documentation. You may need to modify a different boot script, and the execution path of the routing daemon may be different. Only the documentation can provide the exact details you need.

On a Solaris system, edit */etc/init.d/inetinit* to add the **route** statements:

```
route -n add default 172.16.12.1 1 > /dev/console
route -n add 172.16.1.0 172.16.12.3 1 > /dev/console
route -n add 172.16.6.0 172.16.12.3 1 > /dev/console
```

---

* The actual **route** statements in *rc.inet1* use script variables. We changed these to addresses for the sake of clarity.

```
route -n add 172.16.3.0 172.16.12.3 1 > /dev/console
route -n add 172.16.9.0 172.16.12.3 1 > /dev/console
```

Next, check whether or not the script starts a routing protocol. If it does, comment out the lines that start it. You don't want a routing protocol running when you are using static routing. On our Solaris sample system, the routing software is only started if the system has more than one network interface (i.e., is a router) or the */etc/gateways* file has been created. (More on this file later.) Neither of these things is true. Therefore the routing daemon won't be run by the startup process and we don't have to do anything except add the **route** statements.

Although the startup filename may be different on your system, the procedure should be basically the same. These simple steps are all you need to set up static routing. The problem with static routing is not setting it up, but maintaining it, if you have a changeable networking environment. Routing protocols are flexible enough to handle simple and complex routing environments. That is why some startup procedures run routing protocols by default. However, most UNIX systems need only a static default route. Routing protocals are usually needed only by routers.

Interior Routing Protocols

Routing protocols are divided into two general groups: *interior* and *exterior* protocols. An interior protocol is a routing protocol used inside—interior to—an independent network system. In TCP/IP terminology, these independent network systems are called autonomous systems.* Within an autonomous system (AS), routing information is exchanged using an interior protocol chosen by the autonomous system's administration.

All interior routing protocols perform the same basic functions. They determine the "best" route to each destination, and they distribute routing information among the systems on a network. How they perform these functions, in particular, how they decide which routes are best, is what makes routing protocols different from each other. There are several interior protocols:

- The *Routing Information Protocol* (RIP) is the interior protocol most commonly used on UNIX systems. RIP is included as part of the UNIX software delivered with most systems. It is adequate for local area networks and is simple to configure.

  RIP selects the route with the lowest "hop count" (*metric*) as the best route. The RIP hop count represents the number of gateways through which data must pass to reach its destination. RIP assumes that the best route is the one

---

* Autonomous systems are described in Chapter 2, *Delivering the Data*.

that uses the fewest gateways. This approach to route choice is called a *distance-vector algorithm.*

- *Hello* is a protocol that uses delay as the deciding factor when choosing the best route. *Delay* is the length of time it takes a datagram to make the round trip between its source and destination. A Hello packet contains a time stamp indicating when it was sent. When the packet arrives at its destination, the receiving system subtracts the time stamp from the current time, to estimate how long it took the packet to arrive. Hello is not widely used. It was the interior protocol of the original 56 kbps NSFNET backbone and has had very little use otherwise.

- *Intermediate System to Intermediate System* (IS-IS) is an interior routing protocol from the OSI protocol suite. It is a *Shortest Path First* (SPF) *link-state* protocol. It was the interior routing protocol used on the T1 NSFNET backbone, and it is still used by some large service providers.

- *Open Shortest Path First* (OSPF) is another link-state protocol developed for TCP/IP. It is suitable for very large networks and provides several advantages over RIP.

Of these protocols, we will discuss RIP and OSPF in detail. OSPF is widely used on routers. RIP is widely used on UNIX systems. We will start the discussion with RIP.

Routing Information Protocol

As delivered with most UNIX systems, Routing Information Protocol (RIP) is run by the routing daemon **routed** (pronounced "route" "d"). When **routed** starts, it issues a request for routing updates and then listens for responses to its request. When a system configured to supply RIP information hears the request, it responds with an update packet based on the information in its routing table. The update packet contains the destination addresses from the routing table and the routing metric associated with each destination. Update packets are issued in response to requests, as well as periodically to keep routing information accurate.

To build the routing table, **routed** uses the information in the update packets. If the routing update contains a route to a destination that does not exist in the local routing table, the new route is added. If the update describes a route whose destination is already in the local table, the new route is used only if it has a lower cost. The cost of a route is determined by adding the cost of reaching the gateway that sent the update to the metric contained in the RIP update packet. If the total metric is less than the metric of the current route, the new route is used.

RIP also deletes routes from the routing table. It accomplishes this in two ways. First, if the gateway to a destination says the cost of the route is greater than 15, the route is deleted. Second, RIP assumes that a gateway that doesn't send updates is dead. All routes through a gateway are deleted if no updates are received from that gateway for a specified time period. In general, RIP issues routing updates every 30 seconds. In many implementations, if a gateway does not issue routing updates for 180 seconds, all routes through that gateway are deleted from the routing table.

Running RIP with routed

To run RIP using the routing daemon (**routed**),* enter the following command:

```
# routed
```

The **routed** statement is often used without any command-line arguments, but you may want to use the −q option. The −q option prevents **routed** from advertising routes. It just listens to the routes advertised by other systems. If your computer is not a gateway, you should probably use the −q option.

In the section on static routing we commented out the **routed** statement found in a startup file. If that statement is in your startup file, no other action is required to run RIP; just boot your system and RIP will run. Otherwise, add the **routed** command to your startup.

routed reads */etc/gateways* at startup and adds its information to the routing table. **routed** can build a functioning routing table simply by using the RIP updates received from the RIP suppliers. However, it is sometimes useful to supplement this information with, for example, an initial default route or information about a gateway that does not announce its routes. The */etc/gateways* file stores this additional routing information.

The most common use of the */etc/gateways* file is to define an active default route, so we'll use that as an example. This one example is sufficient because all entries in the */etc/gateways* file have the same basic format. On *peanut*, the following entry specifies *almond* as the default gateway:

```
net 0.0.0.0 gateway 172.16.12.1 metric 1 active
```

The entry starts with the keyword `net`. All entries start with the keyword `net` or the keyword `host` to indicate whether the address that follows is a network address or a host address. The destination address 0.0.0.0 is the address used for the default route. In the **route** command we used the keyword `default` to indicate this route, but in */etc/gateways* the default route is indicated by network address 0.0.0.0.

---

* On some systems the routing daemon is **in.routed**.

Next is the keyword `gateway` followed by the gateway's IP address. In this case it is the address of *almond* (172.16.12.1).

Then comes the keyword `metric` followed by a numeric metric value. The value, which is called the metric, is the cost of the route. The metric was almost meaningless when used with static routing. Now that we are running RIP, the metric is actually used to make routing decisions. The RIP metric represents the number of gateways through which data must pass to reach its final destination. But as we saw with **ifconfig**, the metric is really an arbitrary value used by the administrator to prefer one route over another. (The system administrator is free to assign any metric value.) However, it is useful to vary the metric only if you have more than one route to the same destination. With only one gateway to the Internet, the correct metric to use for *almond* is 1.

All */etc/gateways* entries end with either the keyword `passive` or the keyword `active`. "Passive" means the gateway listed in the entry is not required to provide RIP updates. Use `passive` to prevent RIP from deleting the route if no updates are expected from the gateway. A passive route is placed in the routing table and kept there as long as the system is up. In effect, it becomes a permanent static route.

The keyword `active`, on the other hand, creates a route that can be updated by RIP. An active gateway is expected to supply routing information and will be removed from the routing table if, over a period of time, it does not provide routing updates. Active routes are used to "prime the pump" during the RIP startup phase, with the expectation that the routes will be updated by RIP when the protocol is up and running.

Our sample entry ends with the keyword `active`, which means that this default route will be deleted if no routing updates are received from *almond.* Default routes are convenient; this is especially true when you use static routing. But when you use dynamic routing, default routes should be used with caution, especially if you have multiple gateways that can reach the same destination. A passive default route prevents the routing protocol from dynamically updating the route to reflect changing network conditions. Use an active default route that can be updated by the routing protocol.

RIP is easy to implement and simple to configure. Perfect! Well, not quite. RIP has three serious shortcomings:

Limited network diameter

The longest RIP route is 15 hops. A RIP router cannot maintain a complete routing table for a network that has destinations more than 15 hops away. The hop count cannot be increased because of the second shortcoming.

Slow convergence

Deleting a bad route sometimes requires the exchange of multiple routing update packets until the route's cost reaches 16. This is called "counting to infinity," because RIP keeps incrementing the route's cost until it becomes greater than the largest valid RIP metric. (In this case, 16 is infinity.) Additionally, RIP may wait 180 seconds before deleting the invalid routes. In network-speak, we say that these conditions delay the "convergence of routing"; i.e., it takes a long time for the routing table to reflect the current state of the network.

Classful routing

RIP interprets all addresses using the class rules described in Chapter 2. For RIP all addresses are class A, B, or C, which makes RIP incompatible with CIDR supernets and incapable of supporting variable-length subnets.

Nothing can be done to change the limited network diameter. A small metric is essential to reduce the impact of counting to infinity. However, limited network size is the least important of RIP's shortcomings. The real work of improving RIP concentrates on the other two problems, slow convergence and classful routing.

Features have been added to RIP to address slow convergence. Before discussing them we must understand how the "count-to-infinity" problem occurs. Figure 7-2 illustrates a network where a counting-to-infinity problem might happen.

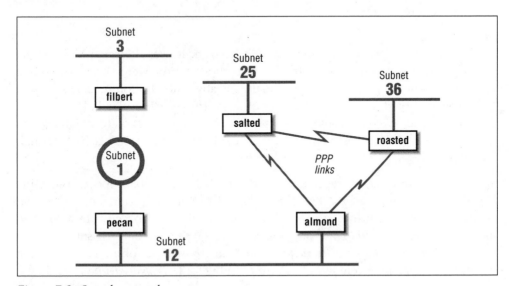

Figure 7-2: Sample network

Figure 7-2 shows that *almond* reaches subnet 3 through *pecan* and then through *filbert*. Subnet 3 is 2 hops away from *almond* and 1 hop away from *pecan*.

Therefore *pecan* advertises a cost of 1 for subnet 3 and *almond* advertises a cost of 2, and traffic continues to be routed through *pecan*. That is, until something goes wrong. If *filbert* crashes, *pecan* waits for an update from *filbert* for 180 seconds. While waiting, *pecan* continues to send updates to *almond* that keep the route to subnet 3 in *almond's* routing table. When *pecan's* timer finally expires, it removes all routes through *filbert* from its routing table, including the route to subnet 3. It then receives an update from *almond* advertising that *almond* is 2 hops away from subnet 3. *pecan* installs this route and announces that it is 3 hops away from subnet 3. *almond* receives this update, installs the route, and announces that it is 4 hops away from subnet 3. Things continue on in this manner until the cost of the route to subnet 3 reaches 16 in both routing tables. If the update interval is 30 seconds, this could take a long time!

Split horizon and *poison reverse* are two features that attempt to avoid counting to infinity. Here's how:

Split horizon

> With this feature, a router does not advertise routes on the link from which those routes were obtained. This would solve the count-to-infinity problem described above. Using the split horizon rule, *almond* would not announce the route to subnet 3 on subnet 12 because it learned that route from the updates it received from *pecan* on subnet 12. While this feature works for the example described above, it does not work for all count-to-infinity configurations. (More on this later.)

Poison reverse

> This feature is an enhancement of split horizon. It uses the same idea: "Don't advertise routes on the link from which those routes were obtained." But it adds a positive action to that essentially negative rule. Poison reverse says that a router should advertise an infinite distance for routes on this link. With poison reverse, *almond* would advertise subnet 3 with a cost of 16 to all systems on subnet 12. The cost of 16 means that subnet 3 cannot be reached through *almond*.

Split horizon and poison reverse solve the problem described above. But what happens if *almond* crashes? Refer to Figure 7-2. With split horizon, *salted* and *roasted* do not advertise to *almond* the route to subnet 12 because they learned the route from *almond*. They do, however, advertise the route to subnet 12 to each other. When *almond* goes down, *salted* and *roasted* perform their own count to infinity before they remove the route to subnet 12. *Triggered updates* address this problem.

Triggered updates are a big help. Instead of waiting the normal 30-second update interval, a triggered update is sent immediately. Therefore, when an upstream router crashes or a local link goes down, immediately after the router updates its local routing table, it sends the changes to its neighbors. Without triggered updates, counting to infinity can take almost 8 minutes! With triggered updates, neighbors are informed in a few seconds. Triggered updates also use network bandwidth efficiently. They don't include the full routing table; they include only the routes that have changed.

Triggered updates take positive action to eliminate bad routes. Using triggered updates, a router advertises the routes deleted from its routing table with a infinite cost to force downstream routers to also remove them. Again, look at Figure 7-2. If *almond* crashes, *roasted* and *salted* wait 180 seconds and remove the routes to subnets 1, 3, and 12 from their routing tables. They then send each other triggered updates with a metric of 16 for subnets 1, 3, and 12. Thus they tell each other that they cannot reach these networks and no count to infinity occurs. Split horizon, poison reverse, and triggered updates go a long way to eliminating counting to infinity.

It is the final shortcoming—the fact that RIP is incompatible with CIDR supernets and variable-length subnets—that caused the RIP protocol to be moved to "historical" status in 1996. RIP is not compatible with current and future plans for the TCP/IP protocol stack. A new version of RIP had to be created to address this final problem.

RIP Version 2

RIP Version 2 (RIP-2), defined in RFC 1723, is a new version of RIP. It is not a completely new protocol. It simply defines extensions to the RIP packet format. RIP-2 adds a network mask and a next hop address to the destination address and metric found in the original RIP packet.

The network mask frees the RIP-2 router from the limitation of interpreting addresses based on strict address class rules. The mask is applied to the destination address to determine how the address should be interpreted. Using the mask, RIP-2 routers support variable-length subnets and CIDR supernets.

The next hop address is the IP address of the gateway that handles the route. If the address is 0.0.0.0, the source of the update packet is the gateway for the route. The next hop route permits a RIP-2 supplier to provide routing information about gateways that do not speak RIP-2. Its function is similar to an ICMP Redirect, pointing to the best gateway for a route and eliminating extra routing hops.

RIP-2 adds other new features to RIP. It transmits updates via the multicast address 224.0.0.9 to reduce the load on systems that are not capable of processing a RIP-2 packet. RIP-2 also introduces a packet authentication scheme to reduce the possibility of accepting erroneous updates from misconfigured systems.

Despite these changes, RIP-2 is compatible with RIP. The original RIP specification allowed for future versions of RIP. RIP has a version number in the packet header, and it had several empty fields for extending the packet. The new values used by RIP-2 did not require any changes to the structure of the packet. The new values are simply placed in the empty fields that the original protocol reserved for future use. Properly implemented RIP routers can receive RIP-2 packets and extract the data that they need from the packet without becoming confused by the new data.

Split horizon, poison reverse, triggered updates, and RIP-2 eliminate most of the problems with the original RIP protocol. But RIP-2 is still a distance vector protocol. There are other, newer routing technologies that are considered superior for large networks. In particular, *link-state* routing protocols are favored because they provide rapid routing convergence and reduce the possibility of routing loops.

Open Shortest Path First

Open Shortest Path First (OSPF), defined by RFC 2178, is a *link-state* protocol. As such, it is very different from RIP. A router running RIP shares information about the entire network with its neighbors. Conversely, a router running OSPF shares information about its neighbors with the entire network. The "entire network" means, at most, a single autonomous system. RIP doesn't try to learn about the entire Internet, and OSPF doesn't try to advertise to the entire Internet. That's not their job. These are interior routing protocols; and so their job is to construct the routing inside of an autonomous system. OSPF further refines this task by defining a hierarchy of routing areas within an autonomous system:

Areas
> An *area* is an arbitrary collection of interconnected networks, hosts and routers. Areas exchange routing information with other areas within the autonomous system through *area border routers.*

Backbone
> A *backbone* is a special area that interconnects all of the other areas within an autonomous system. Every area must connect to the backbone, because the backbone is responsible for distributing routing information between the areas.

Stub area
> A *stub area* has only one area border router, which means that there is only one route out of the area. In this case, the area border router does not need to advertise external routes to the other routers within the stub area. It can simply advertise itself as the default route.

Only a large autonomous system needs to be subdivided into areas. The sample network shown in Figure 7-2 is small and would not need to be divided. We can, however, use it as an example to illustrate the different areas. We could divide this autonomous system into any areas we wish. Assume we divide it into three areas: area 1 contains subnet 3; area 2 contains subnet 1 and subnet 12; and area 3 contains subnet 25, subnet 36, and the PPP links. Furthermore, we could define area 1 as a stub area because *filbert* is that area's only area border router. We also could define area 2 as the backbone area because it interconnects the other two areas and all routing information between areas 1 and 3 must be distributed by area 2. Area 2 contains two area border routers, *almond* and *filbert*, and one interior router, *pecan*. Area 3 contains three routers: *almond*, *roasted*, and *salted*.

Clearly OSPF provides lots of flexibility for subdividing an autonomous system. But why is it necessary? One problem for a link-state protocol is the large quantity of data that can be collected in the *link-state database* and the amount of time it can take to calculate the routes from that data. A look at the protocol shows why this is true.

Every OSPF router builds a *directed graph* of the entire network using the Dijkstra Shortest Path First (SPF) algorithm. A directed graph is a map of the network from the perspective of the router, that is, the root of the graph is the router. The graph is built from the link-state database, which includes information about every router on the network and all the neighbors of every router. The link-state database for the autonomous system in Figure 7-2 contains 5 routers and 10 neighbors: *filbert* has 1 neighbor, *pecan*; *pecan* has 2 neighbors, *filbert* and *almond*; *almond* has 3 neighbors, *pecan*, *salted*, and *roasted*; *salted* has 2 neighbors, *almond* and *roasted*; and *roasted* has 2 neighbors, *salted* and *almond*. Figure 7-3 shows the graph of this autonomous system from the perspective of *filbert*. The Dijkstra algorithm builds the map in this manner:

1. Install the local system as the root of the map with a cost of 0.

2. Locate the neighbors of the system just installed and add them to the map. The cost of reaching the neighbors is calculated as the sum of the cost to reach the system just installed plus the cost it advertises for reaching each neighbor. For example: assume that *almond* advertises a cost of 20 for *salted* and that the cost of reaching *almond* is 15. Then the cost for *salted* in *filbert*'s map is 35.

3. Walk through the map and select the lowest-cost path for each destination. For example, when *salted* is added to the map, its neighbors include *roasted*. The path to *roasted* through *salted* is temporarily added to the map. In this third phase of the algorithm, the cost of reaching *roasted* through *almond* is compared to the cost of reaching it through *salted*. The lowest-cost path is selected. Figure 7-3 shows the deleted paths in dotted lines. Steps 2 and 3 of the algorithm are repeated for every system in the link-state database.

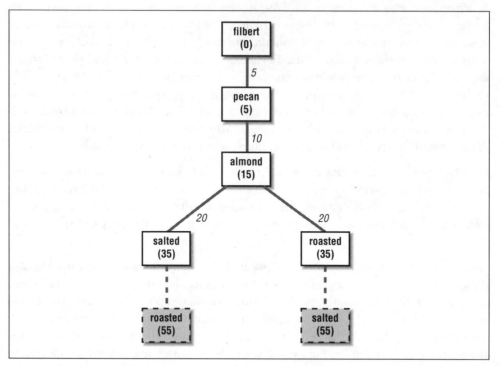

Figure 7-3: A network graph

The information in the link-state database is gathered and distributed in a simple and efficient manner. An OSPF router discovers its neighbors through the use of Hello packets.* It sends Hello packets and listens for Hello packets from adjacent routers. The Hello packet identifies the local router and lists the adjacent routers from which it has received packets. When a router receives a Hello packet that lists it as an adjacent router, it knows it has found a neighbor. It knows this because it can hear packets from that neighbor and, because the neighbor lists it as an adjacent router, the neighbor must be able to hear packets from it. The newly discovered neighbor is added to the local system's neighbor list.

The OSPF router then advertises all of its neighbors. It does this by *flooding* a Link-State Advertisement (LSA) to the entire network. The LSA contains the address of every neighbor and the cost of reaching that neighbor from the local system. Flooding means that the router sends the LSA out of every interface and that every router that receives the LSA sends it out of every interface except the one from which it was received. To avoid flooding duplicate LSAs, the routers store a copy of the LSAs they receive and discard duplicates.

---

* Don't confuse Hello packets with the Hello protocol. These are OSPF Hello packets.

Figure 7-2 provides an example. When OSPF starts on *pecan* it sends a Hello packet on subnet 1 and one on subnet 12. *filbert* and *almond* hear the Hello and respond with Hello packets that list *pecan* as an adjacent router. *pecan* hears their Hello packets and adds them to its neighbor list. *pecan* then creates an LSA that lists *filbert* and *almond* as neighbors with appropriate cost assigned to each. For instance, *pecan* might assign a cost of 5 to *filbert* and a cost of 10 to *almond*. *pecan* then floods the LSA on subnet 1 and subnet 12. *filbert* hears the LSA and floods it on subnet 3. *almond* receives the LSA and floods it on both of its PPP links. *salted* floods the LSA on the link toward *roasted*, and *roasted* floods it on the same link to *salted*. When *salted* and *roasted* received the second copy of the LSA, they discarded it, because it duplicated one that they have already received from *almond*. In this manner, every router in the entire network receives every other router's link-state advertisement.

OSPF routers track the state of their neighbors by listening for Hello packets. Hello packets are issued by all routers on a periodic basis. When a router stops issuing packets, it or the link it is attached to is assumed to be down. Its neighbors update their LSA and flood them through the network. The new LSAs are included into the link-state database on every router on the network and every router recalculates their network map based on this new information. Clearly, limiting the number of routers by limiting the size of the network reduces the burden of recalculating the map. For many networks the entire autonomous system is small enough. For others, dividing the autonomous system into areas improves efficiency.

Another feature of OSPF that improves efficiency is the *designated router*. The designated router is one router on the network that treats all other routers on the network as its neighbors, while all other routers treat only the designated router as their neighbor. This helps reduce the size of the link-state database and thus improves the speed of the shortest-path-first calculation. Assume a broadcast network with 5 routers. Five routers each with 4 neighbors produce a link-state database with 20 entries. But if one of those routers is the designated router, then that router has 4 neighbors and all other routers have only 1 neighbor, for a total of 8 link-state database entries. While there is no need for a designated router on such a small network, the larger the network, the more dramatic the gains. For example, a broadcast network with 25 routers has a link-state database of 50 entries when a designated router is used, versus a database of 600 entries without one.

OSPF provides the router with an end-to-end view of the route between two systems instead of the limited next-hop view provided by RIP. Flooding quickly disseminates routing information throughout the network. Limiting the size of the link-state database through areas and designated routers speeds the SPF calculation. Taken altogether, OSPF is an efficient link-state routing protocol.

OSPF also offers additional features. It provides password authentication to ensure that the update comes from a valid router. Currently OSPF uses an eight-character, clear-text password. Work is underway to add a Message Digest 5 (MD5) crypto-checksum for stronger authentication.

OSPF also supports *equal-cost multi-path routing*. This mouthful means that OSPF routers can maintain more than one path to a single destination. Given the proper conditions, this feature can be used for load balancing across multiple network links. However, most systems are not designed to take advantage of this feature. Refer to your router's documentation to see if it supports load balancing across equal-cost OSPF routes.

With all of these features, OSPF is the preferred TCP/IP interior routing protocol for dedicated routers.

Exterior Routing Protocols

Exterior routing protocols are used to exchange routing information between autonomous systems. The routing information passed between autonomous systems is called *reachability information*. Reachability information is simply information about which networks can be reached through a specific autonomous system.

RFC 1771 defines Border Gateway Protocol, the leading exterior routing protocol, and provides the following description of the routing function of an autonomous system:

> The classic definition of an Autonomous System is a set of routers under a single technical administration, using an interior gateway protocol and common metrics to route packets within the AS, and using an exterior gateway protocol to route packets to other ASs. . . .
> The administration of an AS appears to other ASs to have a single coherent interior routing plan and presents a consistent picture of what networks are reachable through it. From the standpoint of exterior routing, an AS can be viewed as monolithic . . .

Moving routing information into and out of these monoliths is the function of exterior routing protocols. Exterior routing protocols are also called exterior gateway protocols. Don't confuse *an* exterior gateway protocol with *the* Exterior Gateway Protocol (EGP). EGP is not a generic term; it is a particular exterior routing protocol, and an old one at that.

Exterior Gateway Protocol

A gateway running EGP announces that it can reach networks that are part of its autonomous system. It does not announce that it can reach networks outside its autonomous system. For example, the exterior gateway for our imaginary autonomous system *nuts-as* can reach the entire Internet through its external connection, but only one network is contained in its autonomous system. Therefore, it would only announce one network (172.16.0.0) if it ran EGP.

Before sending routing information, the systems first exchange EGP *Hello* and *I-Heard-You* (I-H-U) messages. These messages establish a dialog between two EGP gateways. Computers communicating via EGP are called *EGP neighbors*, and the exchange of Hello and I-H-U messages is called *acquiring a neighbor.*

Once a neighbor is acquired, routing information is requested via a *poll*. The neighbor responds by sending a packet of reachability information called an *update*. The local system includes the routes from the update into its local routing table. If the neighbor fails to respond to three consecutive polls, the system assumes that the neighbor is down and removes the neighbor's routes from its table. If the system receives a poll from its EGP neighbor, it responds with its own update packet.

Unlike the interior protocols discussed above, EGP does not attempt to choose the "best" route. EGP updates contain distance-vector information, but EGP does not evaluate this information. The routing metrics from different autonomous systems are not directly comparable. Each AS may use different criteria for developing these values. Therefore, EGP leaves the choice of a "best" route to someone else.

When EGP was designed, the network relied upon a group of trusted core gateways to process and distribute the routes received from all of the autonomous systems. These core gateways were expected to have the information necessary to choose the best external routes. EGP reachability information was passed into the core gateways, where the information was combined and passed back out to the autonomous systems.

A routing structure that depends on a centrally controlled group of gateways does not scale well and is therefore inadequate for the rapidly growing Internet. As the number of autonomous systems and networks connected to the Internet grew, it became difficult for the core gateways to keep up with the expanding workload. This is one reason why the Internet moved to a more distributed architecture that places a share of the burden of processing routes on each autonomous system. Another reason is that no central authority controls the commercialized Internet. The Internet is composed of many equal networks. In a distributed architecture, the autonomous systems require routing protocols, both interior and exterior, that can make intelligent routing choices. Because of this, EGP is no longer popular.

Border Gateway Protocol

Border Gateway Protocol (BGP) is the leading exterior routing protocol of the Internet. It is based on the OSI *InterDomain Routing Protocol* (IDRP). BGP supports *policy-based routing*, which uses non-technical reasons (for example, political, organizational, or security considerations) to make routing decisions. Thus BGP enhances an autonomous system's ability to choose between routes and to implement routing policies without relying on a central routing authority. This feature is important in the absence of core gateways to perform these tasks.

Routing policies are not part of the BGP protocol. Policies are provided externally as configuration information. As described in Chapter 2, the National Science Foundation provides Routing Arbiters (RAs) at the Network Access Points (NAPs) where large Internet Service Providers (ISPs) interconnect. The RAs can be queried for routing policy information. Most ISPs also develop private policies based on the bilateral agreements they have with other ISPs. BGP can be used to implement these policies by controlling the routes it announces to others and the routes it accepts from others. In the **gated** section of this chapter we discuss the **import** command and the **export** command, which control what routes are accepted (import) and what routes are announced (export). The network administrator enforces the routing policy through configuring the router.

BGP is implemented on top of TCP, which provides BGP with a reliable delivery service. BGP uses well-known TCP port 179. It acquires its neighbors through the standard TCP three-way handshake. BGP neighbors are called *peers*. Once connected, BGP peers exchange OPEN messages to negotiate session parameters, such as the version of BGP that is to be used.

The UPDATE message lists the destinations that can be reached through a specific path and the attributes of the path. BGP is a *path vector protocol*. It is called a path vector protocol because it provides the entire end-to-end path of a route in the form of a sequence of autonomous system numbers. Having the complete AS path eliminates the possibility of routing loops and count-to-infinity problems. A BGP UPDATE contains a single path vector and all of the destinations reachable through that path. Multiple UPDATE packets may be sent to build a routing table.

BGP peers send each other complete routing table updates when the connection is first established. After that, only changes are sent. If there are no changes, just a small (19-byte) KEEPALIVE message is sent to indicate that the peer and the link are still operational. BGP is very efficient in its use of network bandwidth and system resources.

By far the most important thing to remember about exterior protocols is that most systems never run them. Exterior protocols are only required when an AS must exchange routing information with another AS. Most routers within an AS run an interior protocol such as OSPF. Only those gateways that connect the AS to another AS need to run an exterior routing protocol. Your network is probably an independent part of an AS run by someone else. Internet Service Providers are good examples of autonomous systems made up of many independent networks. Unless you provide a similar level of service, you probably don't need to run an exterior routing protocol.

Choosing a Routing Protocol

Although there are many routing protocols, choosing one is usually easy. Most of the interior routing protocols mentioned above were developed to handle the special routing problems of very large networks. Some of the protocols have only been used by large national and regional networks. For local area networks, RIP is still the most common choice. For larger networks, OSPF is the choice.

If you must run an exterior routing protocol, the protocol that you use is often not a matter of choice. For two autonomous systems to exchange routing information, they must use the same exterior protocol. If the other AS is already in operation, its administrators have probably decided which protocol to use, and you will be expected to conform to their choice. Most often this choice is BGP.

The type of equipment affects the choice of protocols. Routers support a wide range of protocols, though individual vendors may have a preferred protocol. Hosts don't usually run routing protocols at all, and most UNIX systems are delivered with only RIP. Allowing host systems to participate in dynamic routing could limit your choices. **gated**, however, gives you the option to run many different routing protocols on a UNIX system. While the performance of hardware designed specifically to be a router is generally better, **gated** gives you the option of using a UNIX system as a router.

In the following sections we discuss the Gateway Routing Daemon (**gated**) software that combines interior and exterior routing protocols into one software package. We look at examples of running RIP, RIPv2, OSPF, and BGP with **gated**.

Gateway Routing Daemon

Routing software development for general purpose UNIX systems is limited. Most sites use UNIX systems only for simple routing tasks for which RIP is usually adequate. Large and complex routing applications, which require advanced routing protocols, are handled by dedicated router hardware that is optimized specifically for routing. Many of the advanced routing protocols are only available for UNIX systems in **gated**. **gated** combines several different routing protocols in a single software package.

Additionally, **gated** provides other features that are usually only associated with dedicated routers:

- Systems can run more than one routing protocol. **gated** combines the routing information learned from different protocols, and selects the "best" routes.

- Routes learned through an interior routing protocol can be announced via an exterior routing protocol, which allows the reachability information announced externally to adjust dynamically to changing interior routes.

- Routing policies can be implemented to control what routes are accepted and what routes are advertised.

- All protocols are configured from a single file (*/etc/gated.conf*) using a single consistent syntax for the configuration commands.

- **gated** is constantly being upgraded. Using **gated** ensures that you're running the most up-to-date routing software.

gated's Preference Value

There are two sides to every routing protocol implementation. One side, the external side, exchanges routing information with remote systems. The other side, the internal side, uses the information received from the remote systems to update the routing table. For example, when OSPF exchanges Hello packets to discover a neighbor, it is an external protocol function. When OSPF adds a route to the routing table, it is an internal function.

The external protocol functions implemented in **gated** are the same as those in other implementations of the protocols. However, the internal side of **gated** is unique for UNIX systems. Internally, **gated** processes routing information from different routing protocols, each of which has its own metric for determining the best route, and combines that information to update the routing table. Before **gated** was written, if a UNIX system ran multiple routing protocols each would write routes into the routing table without knowledge of the other's action. The route found in the table was the last one written—not necessarily the best route.

With multiple routing protocols and multiple network interfaces, it is possible for a system to receive routes to the same destination from different protocols. **gated** compares these routes and attempts to select the best one. However, the metrics used by different protocols are not directly comparable. Each routing protocol has its own metric. It might be a hop count, the delay on the route, or an arbitrary value set by the administrator. **gated** needs more than that protocol's metric to select the best route. It uses its own value to prefer routes from one protocol or interface over another. This value is called *preference*.

Preference values help **gated** combine routing information from several different sources into a single routing table. Table 7-1 lists the sources from which **gated** receives routes, and the default preference given to each source. Preference values range from 0 to 255, with the lowest number indicating the most preferred route. From this table you can see that **gated** prefers a route learned from OSPF over the same route learned from BGP.

Table 7-1: Default Preference Values

Route Type	Default Preference
direct route	0
OSPF	10
Internally generated default	20
ICMP redirect	30
static route	60
Hello protocol	90
RIP	100
OSPF ASE routes	150
BGP	170
EGP	200

Preference can be set in several different configuration statements. It can be used to prefer routes from one network interface over another, from one protocol over another, or from one remote gateway over another. Preference values are not transmitted or modified by the protocols. Preference is used only in the configuration file. In the next section we'll look at the **gated** configuration file (*/etc/gated.conf*) and the configuration commands it contains.

Configuring gated

gated is available from *http://www.gated.org*. Appendix B, *A gated Reference*, provides information about downloading and compiling the software. In this section, we use **gated** release 3.5.5, the version of **gated** that is currently available without restrictions. There are other, newer versions of **gated** available to members of the Gated Consortium. If you plan to build products based on **gated** or you plan to do research on routing protocols using **gated**, you should join the consortium. For the purposes of this book, release 3.5.5 is fine.

gated reads its configuration from the */etc/gated.conf* file. The configuration commands in the file resemble C code. All statements end with a semicolon, and associated statements are grouped together by curly braces. This structure makes it simple to see what parts of the configuration are associated with each other, which is important when multiple protocols are configured in the same file. In addition to structure in the language, the */etc/gated.conf* file also has a structure.

The different configuration statements, and the order in which these statements must appear, divide *gated.conf* into sections: *option statements, interface statements, definition statements, protocol statements, static statements, control statements*, and *aggregate statements*. Entering a statement out of order causes an error when parsing the file.

Two other types of statements do not fall into any of these categories. They are *directive statements* and *trace statements*. These can occur anywhere in the *gated.conf* file and do not directly relate to the configuration of any protocol. These statements provide instructions to the parser, and instructions to control tracing from within the configuration file.

The **gated** configuration commands are summarized in Table 7-2. The table lists each command by name, identifies the statement type, and provides a very short synopsis of each command's function. The entire command language is covered in detail in Appendix B, *A gated Reference*.

Table 7-2: gated Configuration Statements

Statement	Type	Function
%directory	directive	Sets the directory for include files
%include	directive	Includes a file into *gated.conf*
traceoptions	trace	Specifies which events are traced
options	option	Defines gated options
interfaces	interface	Defines interface options
autonomoussystem	definition	Defines the AS number
routerid	definition	Defines the originating router for BGP or OSPF
martians	definition	Defines invalid destination addresses
snmp	protocol	Enables reporting to SNMP
rip	protocol	Enables RIP
hello	protocol	Enables Hello protocol
isis	protocol	Enables ISIS protocol
kernel	protocol	Configures kernel interface options
ospf	protocol	Enables OSPF protocol
redirect	protocol	Removes routes installed by ICMP
egp	protocol	Enables EGP
bgp	protocol	Enables BGP
icmp	protocol	Configures the processing of general ICMP packets
static	static	Defines static routes
import	control	Defines what routes are accepted
export	control	Defines what routes are advertised
aggregate	aggregate	Controls route aggregation
generate	aggregate	Controls creation of a default route

Just from this brief description, you can see that the **gated** configuration language has many commands. The language provides configuration control for several different protocols and additional commands to configure the added features of **gated** itself. All of this can be confusing.

To avoid confusion, don't try to understand the details of everything offered by **gated**. Your routing environment will not use all of these protocols and features. Even if you are providing the gateway at the border between two anonymous systems, you will probably only run two routing protocols: one interior protocol and one exterior protocol. Only those commands that relate to your actual configuration need to be included in your configuration file. As you read this section, skip the things you don't need. For example, if you don't use the BGP protocol, don't study the **bgp** statement. When you do need more details about a specific statement, look it up in Appendix B. With this in mind, let's look at some sample configurations.

Sample gated.conf Configurations

The details in Appendix B may make **gated** configuration appear more complex than it is. **gated**'s rich command language can be confusing, as can its support for multiple protocols and the fact that it often provides a few ways to do the same thing. But some realistic examples will show that individual configurations do not need to be complex.

The basis for the sample configurations is the network in Figure 7-4. We have installed a new router that provides our backbone with direct access to the Internet, and we have decided to install new routing protocols. We'll configure a host to listen to RIP-2 updates, an interior gateway to run RIP-2 and OSPF, and an exterior gateway to run OSPF and BGP.

Gateway *cashew* interconnects subnet 172.16.9.0 and subnet 172.16.1.0. To hosts on subnet 9, it advertises itself as the default gateway, because it is the gateway to the outside world. It uses RIP-2 to advertise routes on subnet 9. On subnet 1, gateway *cashew* advertises itself as the gateway to subnet 9 using OSPF.

Gateway *brazil* provides subnet 1 with access to the Internet through autonomous system 164. Because gateway *brazil* provides access to the Internet, it announces itself as the default gateway to the other systems on subnet 1 using OSPF. To the external autonomous system, it uses BGP to announce itself as the path to the internal networks it learns about through OSPF.

Let's look at the routing configuration of host *macadamia*, gateway *cashew*, and gateway *brazil*.

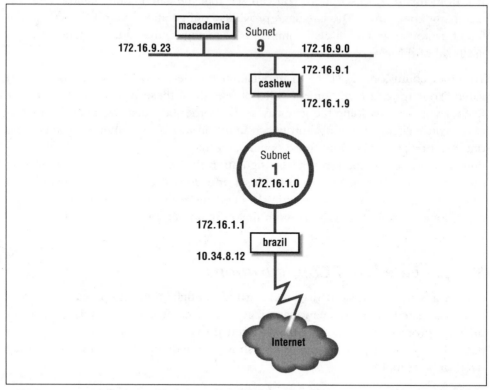

Figure 7-4: Sample routing topology

A host configuration

The host routing configuration is very simple. The **rip yes** statement enables RIP, and that's all that is really required to run RIP. That basic configuration should work for any system that runs RIP. The additional clauses enclosed in curly braces modify the basic RIP configuration. We use a few clauses to create a more interesting example. Here is the RIP-2 configuration for host *macadamia*:

```
#
#   enable rip, don't broadcast updates,
#   listen for RIP-2 updates on the multicast address,
#   check that the updates are authentic.
#
rip yes {
        nobroadcast ;
        interface 172.16.9.23
            version 2
            multicast
            authentication simple "REAL^stuff" ;

} ;
```

This sample file shows the basic structure of *gated.conf* configuration statements. Lines beginning with a sharp sign (#) are comments.* All statements end with semicolons. Clauses associated with a configuration statement can span multiple lines and are enclosed in curly braces ({}). In the example, the `nobroadcast` and `interface` clauses apply directly to the rip statement. The `version`, `multicast`, and `authentication` keywords are part of the interface clause.

The keyword `nobroadcast` prevents the host from broadcasting its own RIP updates. The default is `nobroadcast` when the system has one network interface and `broadcast` when it has more than one. The `nobroadcast` keyword performs the same function as the **-q** command-line option does for **routed**. However, **gated** can do much more than **routed**, as the next clause shows.

The `interface` clause defines interface parameters for RIP. The parameters associated with this clause say that RIP-2 updates will be received via the RIP-2 multicast address on interface 172.16.9.23, and that authentic updates will contain the password `REAL^stuff`. For RIP-2, `simple` authentication is a clear-text password up to 16 bytes long. This is not intended to protect the system from malicious actions; it is only intended to protect the routers from a configuration accident. If a user mistakenly sets his system up as a RIP supplier, he is very unlikely to accidently enter the correct password into his configuration. Stronger authentication will soon be available in the form of a Message Digest 5 (MD5) cryptographic checksum by specifying `md5` in the authentication clause.

Interior gateway configurations

Gateway configurations are more complicated than the simple host configuration shown above. Gateways always have multiple interfaces and occasionally run multiple routing protocols. Our first sample configuration is for the interior gateway between subnet 9 and the central backbone, subnet 1. It uses RIP-2 on subnet 9 to announce routes to the UNIX hosts. It uses OSPF on subnet 1 to exchange routes with the other gateways. Here's the configuration of gateway *cashew*:

```
#  Don't time-out subnet 9
interfaces {
    interface 172.16.9.1 passive ;
} ;
# Define the OSPF router id
routerid 172.16.1.9 ;
# Enable RIP-2; announce OSPF routes to
# subnet 9 with a cost of 5.
rip yes {
    broadcast ;
    defaultmetric 5 ;
```

---

* Comments can also be enclosed between a * and a *\.

```
      interface 172.16.9.1
            version 2
            multicast
            authentication simple "REAL^stuff" ;
    } ;
    # Enable OSPF; subnet 1 is the backbone area;
    # use password authentication.
    ospf yes {
        backbone {
            authtype simple ;
            interface 172.16.1.9 {
                priority 5 ;
                authkey "It'sREAL" ;
                } ;
            } ;
    } ;
```

The `interfaces` statement defines routing characteristics for the network interfaces. The keyword `passive` in the interface clause is used here, just as we have
seen it used before, to create a permanent static route that will not be removed
from the routing table. In this case, the permanent route is through a directly
attached network interface. Normally when **gated** thinks an interface is malfunctioning, it increases the cost of the interface by giving it a high-cost preference
value (120) to reduce the probability of a gateway routing data through a non-
operational interface. **gated** determines that an interface is malfunctioning when it
does not receive routing updates on that interface. We don't want **gated** to down-
grade the 172.16.9.1 interface, even if it does think the interface is malfunctioning,
because our router is the only path to subnet 9. That's why this configuration
includes the clause `interface 172.16.9.1 passive`.

The `routerid` statement defines the router identifier for OSPF. Unless it is explicitly defined in the configuration file, **gated** uses the address of the first interface it
encounters as the default router identifier address. Here we specify the address of
the interface that actually speaks OSPF as the OSPF router identifier.

In the previous example we discussed all the clauses on the **rip** statement except
one—the `defaultmetric` clause. The `defaultmetric` clause defines the RIP
metric used to advertise routes learned from other routing protocols. This gateway
runs both OSPF and RIP-2. We wish to advertise the routes learned via OSPF to
our RIP clients, and to do that, a metric is required. We choose a RIP cost of 5. If
the `defaultmetric` clause is not used, routes learned from OSPF are not advertised to the RIP clients.* This statement is required for our configuration.

The `ospf yes` statement enables OSPF. The first clause associated with this statement is `backbone`. It states that the router is part of the OSPF backbone area.

---

* This is not strictly true. The routes are advertised with a cost of 16, meaning that the destinations are
unreachable.

Every `ospf yes` statement must have at least one associated area clause. It can define a specific area, e.g., `area 2`, but at least one router must be in the backbone area. While the OSPF backbone is area 0, it cannot be specified as `area 0`; it must be specified with the keyword `backbone`. In our sample configuration, subnet 1 is the backbone and all routers attached to it are in the backbone area. It is possible for a single router to attach to multiple areas with a different set of configuration parameters for each area. Notice how the nested curly braces group the clauses together. The remaining clauses in the configuration file are directly associated with the backbone area clause.

The `authtype simple ;` clause says that simple, password-based authentication is used in the backbone area. Two choices, `simple` and `none`, are available for authtype in GateD 3.5.5. `none` means no authentication is used. `simple` means that the correct eight-character password must be used or the update will be rejected. Password authentication is used only to protect against accidents. It is not intended to protect against malicious actions. Stronger authentication based on MD5 is being developed.

The interface that connects this router to the backbone area is defined by the interface clause. It has two associated subclauses. The `authkey "It'sREAL" ;` clause defines the password used for simple authentication by this interface. The `priority 5 ;` clause defines the priority used by this router when the backbone is electing a designated router. The higher the priority number, the less likely a router will be elected as the designated router. Use `priority` to steer the election toward the most capable routers.

Exterior gateway configuration

The configuration for gateway *brazil* is the most complex because it runs both OSPF and BGP. The configuration file for gateway *brazil* is:

```
# Defines our AS number for BGP
autonomoussystem 249;

# Defines the OSPF router id
routerid 172.16.1.1;

# Disable RIP
rip no;

# Enable BGP
bgp yes {
   preference 50 ;
   group type external peeras 164 {
        peer 10.6.0.103 ;
        peer 10.20.0.72 ;
        };
};
```

```
# Enable OSPF; subnet 1 is the backbone area;
# use password authentication.
ospf yes {
     backbone {
          authtype simple ;
          interface 172.16.1.1 {
               priority 10 ;
               authkey "It'sREAL" ;
               } ;
          } ;
};

# Announce routes learned from OSPF and route
# to directly connected network via BGP to AS 164
export proto bgp as 164 {
     proto direct ;
     proto ospf ;
};

# Announce routes learned via BGP from
# AS number 164 to our OSPF area.
export proto ospfase type 2  {
     proto bgp as 164  {
          all ;
          };
};
```

This configuration enables both BGP and OSPF, and sets certain protocol-specific parameters. BGP needs to know the AS number, which is 249 for *nuts-net*. OSPF needs to know the router identifier address. We set it to the address of the router interface that runs OSPF. The AS number and the router identifier are defined early in the configuration because `autonomoussystem` and `routerid` are definition statements, and therefore must occur before the first protocol statement. Refer back to Table 7-2 for the various statement types.

The first protocol statement is the one that turns RIP off. We don't want to run RIP and the default for **gated** is to turn RIP on. Therefore we explicitly disable RIP with the `rip no ;` statement.

BGP is enabled by the `egp yes` statement, which also defines a few additional BGP parameters. The `preference 50 ;` clause tells **gated** to set the preference for routes received via BGP to 50. The default for these routes is 170. By changing the preference to 50, we make the routes highly favored. Setting a preference value of 50 allows BGP routes to override static routes, though they will not override routes learned from OSPF. This is solely for the purpose of illustration. You probably don't want to make an external route highly preferred. See Table 7-1 for the list of default preferences.

The `group` clause sets parameters for all of the BGP peers in the group. The clause defines the type of BGP connection being created. The example is a classic external routing protocol connection, and the external autonomous system we are connecting to is AS number 164. **gated** can create five different types of BGP sessions, but only one, `type external`, is used to directly communicate with an external autonomous system. The other four group types are used for internal BGP (IBGP).* IBGP is simply an acronym used for BGP when it is used to move routing information around inside of an autonomous system. In our example we use it to move routing information between autonomous systems.

The BGP neighbors from which updates are accepted are indicated by the peer clauses. Each peer is a member of the group. Everything related to the group, such as the AS number, applies to every system in the group. To accept updates from any system, use `allow` in place of the list of peers.

The OSPF protocol is enabled by the **ospf yes** statement. The configuration of OSPF on this router is the same as it is for other routers in the backbone area. The only parameter that has been changed from the previous example is the priority number. Because this route has a particularly heavy load, we have decided to make it slightly less preferred for the designated router election.

The export statements control the routes that **gated** advertises to other routers. The first export statement directs **gated** to use BGP (`proto bgp`) to advertise to autonomous system 164 (`as 164`) any directly connected networks (`proto direct`) and any routes learned from OSPF (`proto ospf`). Notice that the AS number specified in this statement is not the AS number of *nuts-net*. It is the autonomous system number of the external system. The first line of the export statement defines to whom we are advertising. The proto clauses located within the curly braces define what we are advertising.

The second export statement announces the routes learned from the external autonomous system. The routes are received via BGP and are advertised via OSPF. Because these are routes from an external autonomous system, they are advertised as *autonomous system external* (ASE) routes. That's why the export statement specifies `ospfase` as the protocol through which the routes are announced. The `type 2` parameter defines the type of external routes that are being advertised. There are two types supported by **gated**. Type 2 routes are those learned from an exterior gateway protocol that does not provide a routing metric comparable to the OSPF metric. These routes are advertised with the cost of reaching the border router. In this case, the routes are advertised with the OSPF cost of reaching gateway *brazil*. Type 1 routes are those learned from an external protocol that does provide a metric directly comparable to the OSPF metric. In that case, the metric from the external protocol is added to the cost of reaching the border router when routes are advertised.

---

* See Appendix B for information on all group types.

The source of the routes advertised in the second export statement is the BGP connection (`proto bgp`) to autonomous system 164 (`as 164`). The proto clause is qualified with an optional *route filter*. A route filter is used to select the routes from a specific source. The filter can list networks with associated netmasks to select an individual destination. In the example, the keyword `all` is used to select all routes received via BGP, which is, in fact, the default.

All of the routes received from an external autonomous system could produce a very large routing table. Individual routes are useful when you have multiple border routers that can reach the outside world. However, if you have only one border router, a default route may be all that is needed. To export a default route, insert an `options gendefault ;` statement in the beginning of the configuration file.* This tells **gated** to generate a default route when the system peers with a BGP neighbor. Next, replace the second export statement in the sample file with the following export statement:

```
# Announce a default route when peering
# with a BGP neighbor.
export proto ospfase type 2   {
     proto default ;
};
```

This export statement tells **gated** to advertise the border router as the default gateway, but only when it has an active connection to the external system.

These few examples show that *gated.conf* files are usually small and easy to read. Use **gated** if you need to run a routing protocol on your computer. It allows you to use the same software and the same configuration language on all of your hosts, interior gateways, and exterior gateways.

Testing the Configuration

Test the configuration file before you try to use it. The **gated** configuration syntax is complex and it is easy to make a mistake. Create your new configuration in a test file; test the new configuration; then move the test configuration to */etc/gated.conf*. Here's how.

Assume that a configuration file called *test.conf* has already been created. It is tested using −f and −c on the command line:

```
% gated -c -f test.conf trace.test
```

The −f option tells **gated** to read the configuration from the named file instead of from */etc/gated.conf*. In the sample it reads the configuration from *test.conf*. The −c option tells **gated** to read the configuration file and check for syntax errors.

---

* The `generate` statement is an alternative way to create a default route. See Appendix B for details.

When **gated** finishes reading the file, it terminates; it does not modify the routing table. The −c option turns on tracing, so specify a trace file or the trace data will be displayed on your terminal. In the sample we specified *trace.test* as the trace file. The −c option also produces a snapshot of the state of **gated** after reading the configuration file and writes the snapshot to */usr/tmp/gated_dump*. You don't need to be superuser or to terminate the active **gated** process to run **gated** when the −c option is used.

The dump and the trace file (*trace.test*) can then be examined for errors and other information. When you're confident that the configuration is correct, become superuser and move your new configuration (*test.conf*) to */etc/gated.conf*.

An alternative command for testing the configuration file is **gdc**, though it must be run by the root user. It includes features for checking and installing a new configuration. **gdc** uses three different configuration files. The current configuration is */etc/gated.conf*. The previous configuration is stored in */etc/gated.conf−*. The "next" configuration is stored in */etc/gated.conf+*, which is normally the configuration that needs to be tested. Here's how **gdc** tests a configuration:

```
# cp test.conf /etc/gated.conf+
# gdc checknew
configuration file /etc/gated.conf+ checks out okay
# gdc newconf
# gdc restart
gated not currently running
gdc: /etc/gated was started
```

In this sample the test configuration was copied to */etc/gated.conf+* and tested with the **gdc checknew** command. If syntax problems are found in the file, a warning message is displayed and the detailed error messages are written to */usr/tmp/gated_parse*. There were no syntax errors in the example so we make the test file the current configuration with the **gdc newconf** command. This command moves the current configuration to *gated.conf−* and moves the new configuration (*gated.conf+*) to the current configuration. The **gdc restart** command terminates **gated** if it is currently running—it was not in the example—and starts a new copy of **gated** using the new configuration.

Running gated at startup

As with any routing software, **gated** should be included in your startup file. Some systems come with the code to start **gated** included in the startup file. If your system doesn't, you'll need to add it. If you already have code in your startup file that runs **routed**, replace it with code to run **gated**. **gated** and **routed** should not be running at the same time.

Our imaginary gateway, *almond*, is a Solaris system with code in the
/etc/init.d/inetinit file that starts **routed**. We comment out those lines, and add
these lines:

```
if [ -f /usr/sbin/gated -a -f /etc/gated.conf ]; then
     /usr/sbin/gated;      echo -n 'gated' > /dev/console
fi
```

This code assumes that **gated** is installed in */usr/sbin* and that the configuration file
is named */etc/gated.conf.* The code checks that **gated** is present, and that the configuration file */etc/gated.conf* exists. If both files are found, **gated** begins.

The code checks for a configuration file because **gated** usually runs with one. If
gated is started without a configuration file, it checks the routing table for a default
route. If it doesn't find one, it starts RIP; otherwise, it just uses the default route.
Create an */etc/gated.conf* file even if you only want to run RIP. The configuration
file documents your routing configuration and protects you if the default configuration of **gated** changes in the future.

Summary

Routing is the glue that binds networks together to build internets. Without it, networks cannot communicate with each other. Configuring routing is an important
task for the network administrator.

Minimal routing is required to communicate through the network interface to the
directly attached network. These routes can be seen in the routing table where
they show up as entries that do not have the G (gateway) flag set. On most systems, minimal routes are created but the **ifconfig** command when an interface is
installed. On Linux systems the route through the interface must be explicitly
installed with a **route** command.

The **route** command is used to build a static routing table. Static routing is routing
that is manually maintained by the network administrator. Routes are added to or
removed from the routing table with the **route** command. The most common use
for static routing is to install a default route.

Dynamic routing uses routing protocols to select the best routes and to update the
routing table. Their are many different dynamic routing protocols. The one that is
available on most UNIX systems is *Routing Information Protocol* (RIP). RIP is run
by **routed**. **routed** builds the routing table from information received on the network and from information read from */etc/gateway*.

gated is a software package that provides several more routing protocols for UNIX
systems, including advanced protocols such as *Open Shortest Path First* (OSPF) and

Border Gateway Protocol (BGP). **gated** is configured through the */etc/gated.conf* file. The **gated** configuration commands are covered in Appendix B.

This is the last chapter on how to create the physical network connection. Once routing is installed, the system is capable of basic communication. In the next chapter, we begin the discussion of the various applications and services that are necessary to make the network truly useful.

8

Configuring DNS Name Service

Congratulations! You have installed TCP/IP in the kernel, configured the network interface, and configured routing. At this point, you have completed all of the configuration tasks required to run TCP/IP on a UNIX system. While none of the remaining tasks are *required* for TCP/IP software to operate, they are necessary for making the network more friendly and useful. In the next two chapters, we look at how to configure basic TCP/IP network services. Perhaps the most important of these is name service.

Strictly speaking, name service is not necessary for computers to communicate. It is, as the name implies, a service—specifically, a service intended to make the network more user-friendly. Computers are perfectly happy with IP addresses, but people prefer names. The importance of name service is indicated by the amount of coverage it has in this book. Chapter 3, *Network Services*, discusses *why* name service is needed; this chapter covers *how* it is configured, and Appendix C, *A named Reference*, covers the *details* of the nameserver configuration commands. This chapter provides sufficient information to show you how to configure BIND 4 software to run on your system.* But if you want to know more about why something is done, don't hesitate to refer to Chapter 3 and Appendix C.

BIND: UNIX Name Service

In UNIX, DNS is implemented by the *Berkeley Internet Name Domain* (BIND) software. BIND is a client/server software system. The client side of BIND is called the *resolver*. It generates the queries for domain name information that are sent to the

---

* BIND 4 is the version of domain name software used on most UNIX systems. Another version of DNS software—BIND 8—is also available. BIND 8 uses a different configuration file syntax. We use BIND 4 because it's the most widely used and comes with both Slackware 96 Linux and Solaris 2.5.1.

server. The DNS server software answers the resolvers' queries. The server side of BIND is a daemon called **named** (pronounced "name" "d").

This chapter covers three basic BIND configuration tasks:

- Configuring the BIND resolver
- Configuring the BIND nameserver (**named**)
- Constructing the nameserver database files, called the *zone files*

The term *zone* is often used interchangeably with the word *domain*, but here we make a distinction between these terms. We use zone to refer to the domain database file, while the term domain is used in more general contexts. In this book, a domain is part of the domain hierarchy identified by a domain name. A zone is a collection of domain information contained in a domain database file. The file that contains the domain information is called a zone file.

RFC 1033, the *Domain Administrators Operations Guide*, defines the basic set of standard records used to construct zone files. Many RFCs propose new DNS records that are not widely implemented. In this chapter and in Appendix C we stick to the basic resource records that you are most likely to use. We'll use these records to construct the zone files used in this chapter. But how, or even if, you need to construct zone files on your system is controlled by the type of BIND configuration you decide to use.

BIND Configurations

BIND configurations are described by the type of service the software is configured to provide. The four levels of service that can be defined in a BIND configuration are resolver-only systems, caching-only servers, primary servers, and secondary servers.

The resolver is the code that asks nameservers for domain information. On UNIX systems, it is implemented as a library, rather than a separate client program. Some systems, called resolver-only systems, use only the resolver; they don't run a nameserver. Resolver-only systems are very easy to configure: you just need to set up the */etc/resolv.conf* file.

The three other BIND configurations all require that the local system run the **named** server software. They are:

Primary
> The primary nameserver is the authoritative source for all information about a specific domain. It loads the domain information from a locally maintained disk file that is built by the domain administrator. This file (the zone file) contains the most accurate information about a piece of the domain hierarchy

over which this server has authority. The primary server is a master server, because it can answer any query about its domain with full authority.*

Configuring a primary server requires creating a complete set of configuration files: zone files for the regular domain and the reverse domain, the boot file, the cache file, and the loopback file. No other configuration requires creating this complete set of files.

Secondary

A secondary server transfers a complete set of domain information from the primary server. The zone file is transferred from the primary server and stored on the secondary server as a local disk file. This transfer is aptly called a *zone file transfer*. A secondary server keeps a complete copy of all domain information, and can answer queries about that domain with authority. Therefore, a secondary server is also considered a master server.

Configuring a secondary server does not require creating local zone files, because the zone files are downloaded from the primary server. However, the other files (a boot file, a cache file, and a loopback file) are required.

Caching-only

A caching-only server runs the nameserver software, but keeps no nameserver database files. It learns the answer to every nameserver query from some remote server. Once it learns an answer, the server caches the answer and uses it to answer future queries for the same information. All nameservers use cached information in this manner, but a caching-only server depends on this technique for all of its nameserver information. It is not considered an authoritative (or master) server, because all of the information it provides is second-hand.

Only a boot file and a cache file are required for a caching-only configuration. But the most common configuration also includes a loopback file. This is probably the most common nameserver configuration, and apart from the resolver-only configuration, it is the easiest to configure.

A server may be any one of these configurations or, as is often the case, it may combine elements of more than one type of configuration. However, all systems run the resolver, so let's begin by examining the configuration of the client side of the DNS software.

---

* The terms *master server* and *authoritative server* are used interchangeably.

Configuring the Resolver

The resolver is configured in the */etc/resolv.conf* file. The resolver is not a separate and distinct process; it is a library of routines called by network processes. The *resolv.conf* file is read when a process using the resolver starts, and is cached for the life of that process. If the configuration file is not found, the resolver attempts to connect to the **named** server running on the local host. While this may work, I don't recommend it. By allowing the resolver configuration to default, you give up control over your system and become vunerable to variations in the techniques used by different systems to determine the default configuration. For these reasons, the resolver configuration file should be created on every system running BIND.

The Resolver Configuration File

The configuration file clearly documents the resolver configuration. It allows you to identify up to three nameservers, two of which provide backup if the first server doesn't respond. It defines the default domain and various other processing options. The *resolv.conf* file is an important part of configuring name service.

resolv.conf is a simple, human-readable file. There are system-specific variations in the commands used in the file, but the entries supported by most systems are:

nameserver *address*

> The **nameserver** entries identify, by IP address, the servers that the resolver is to query for domain information. The nameservers are queried in the order that they appear in the file. If no response is received from a server, the next server in the list is tried until the maximum number of servers are tried.* If no **nameserver** entries are contained in the *resolv.conf* file or no *resolv.conf* file exists, all nameserver queries are sent to the local host. However, if there is a *resolv.conf* file and it contains **nameserver** entries, the local host is *not* queried unless one entry points to the local host. Specify the local host with its official IP address, not with the loopback address and not with 0.0.0.0. The official address avoids problems seen on some versions of UNIX. A resolver-only configuration never contains a **nameserver** entry that points to the local host.

domain *name*

> The **domain** entry defines the default domain name. The resolver appends the default domain name to any hostname that does not contain a dot.† It then uses the expanded hostname in the query it sends to the name server. For

---

* Three is the maximum number of servers tried by most BIND implementations.

† This is the most common way that default domain names are used, but it is not the only way. See the section "Domain Names" in Chapter 3 for more details.

example, if the hostname *almond* (which does not contain a dot) is received by the resolver, the default domain name is appended to *almond* to construct the query. If the value for `name` in the **domain** entry is `nuts.com`, the resolver queries for *almond.nuts.com*. If the environment variable LOCALDO-MAIN is set, it overrides the **domain** entry and the value of LOCALDOMAIN is used to expand hostname.

search `domain` ...

The **search** entry defines a series of domains that are searched when a hostname does not contain a dot. Assume the entry **search essex.nuts.com butler.nuts.com**. A query for the hostname *roaster* is first tried as *roaster.essex.nuts.com*. If that fails to provide a successful match, the resolver queries for *roaster.butler.nuts.com*. If that query fails, no other attempts are made to resolve the hostname. This is different from the action of the **domain** entry. Assume the entry **domain butler.nuts.com**. Now a query for *roaster* is first tried as *roaster.butler.nuts.com* and then as *roaster.nuts.com* if the first query fails. When a **search** statement is used, only the domains explicitly mentioned on the command line are searched. When a **domain** statement is used, the default domain and its parents are searched. A parent domain must be at least two fields long to be searched. The resolver would not search for *roaster.com*. Use either a **search** statement or a **domain** statement. Never use both in the same configuration. If the environment variable LOCALDOMAIN is set, it overrides the **search** entry.

sortlist `network` ...

Addresses from the networks listed on the **sortlist** command are preferred over other addresses. If the resolver receives multiple addresses in response to a query about a multi-homed host or a router, it reorders the addresses so that an address from a network listed in the **sortlist** statement is placed in front of the other addresses. Normally addresses are returned to the application by the resolver in the order that they are received. The only exception to this is that, by default, addresses on a shared network are preferred over other addresses. So if the computer running the resolver is connected to network 172.16.0.0 and one of the addresses returned in a multiple address response is from that network, the address from 172.16.0.0 is placed in front of the other addresses.

The **sortlist** command is rarely used. To be of any use, it requires that a remote host has multiple addresses for the same name; that the path to one of those addresses is clearly superior to the others; and that you know enough about the remote configuration to know which address is preferable.

options `option` ...

The **options** entry is used to select optional settings for the resolver. At this writing there are two valid keywords for `option`: debug to turn on debugging; and `ndots:`*n* to set the number of dots in a hostname used to determine whether or not the default domain needs to be applied. The default is 1. Therefore a hostname with one dot in it does not have the default domain appended before it is passed to the nameserver. If `options` `ndots:2` is specified, a hostname with one dot in it has the default domain added before the query is sent out, but an address with two or more dots does not have the default domain added.

The most common *resolv.conf* configuration defines the default domain name, the local host as the first nameserver, and two backup nameservers. An example of this configuration is:

```
# Domain name resolver configuration file
#
domain nuts.com
# try yourself first
nameserver 172.16.12.2
# try almond next
nameserver 172.16.12.1
# finally try filbert
nameserver 172.16.1.2
```

The example is based on our imaginary network, so the default domain name is *nuts.com*. The configuration is for *peanut* and it specifies itself as the first name-server. The backup servers are *almond* and *filbert*. The configuration does not contain a sort list or any options, as these are infrequently used. This is an example of an average resolver configuration.

A resolver-only configuration

The resolver-only configuration is very simple. It is identical to the average configuration shown above except that it does not contain a **nameserver** entry for the local system. A sample *resolv.conf* file for a resolver-only system is shown below:

```
# Domain name resolver configuration file
#
domain nuts.com
# try almond
nameserver 172.16.12.1
# next try filbert
nameserver 172.16.1.2
```

The configuration tells the resolver to pass all queries to *almond*; if that fails, try *filbert*. Queries are never resolved locally. This simple *resolv.conf* file is all that is required for a resolver-only configuration.

Configuring named

While the resolver configuration requires, at most, one configuration file, several files are used to configure **named**. The complete set of **named** configuration files are:

named.boot
Sets general **named** parameters and points to the sources of domain database information used by this server. These sources can be local disk files or remote servers.

named.ca
Points to the root domain servers

named.local
Used to locally resolve the loopback address

named.hosts
The zone file that maps hostnames to IP addresses

named.rev
The zone file for the reverse domain that maps IP addresses to hostnames

The filenames shown here are generic names. We use them to make it easier to discuss the files in this text. The files can have any names you wish. Use the file-names *named.boot* and *named.local* for the boot file and the loopback address file. Use the name *named.ca* or one of the well-known alternatives, *named.root* and *root.ca*, for the file that lists the root servers. However, don't use the names *named.hosts* and *named.rev* for your zone files. Use descriptive names. In the following sections, we'll look at how each of these files is used, starting with *named.boot*.

The named.boot File

The *named.boot* file points **named** to sources of DNS information. Some of these sources are local files; others are remote servers. You only need to create the files referenced in the primary and cache statements. We'll look at an example of each type of file you may need to create.

Table 8-1 summarizes the *named.boot* configuration statements used in this chapter. It provides just enough information to help you understand the examples. Not all of the *named.boot* configuration commands are used in the examples, and you probably won't use all of the commands in your configuration. The commands are designed to cover the full spectrum of configurations, even the configurations of root servers. If you want more details about all of the *named.boot* configuration statements, Appendix C contains a full explanation of each command.

Table 8-1: named.boot Configuration Commands

Command	Function
directory	Defines a directory for all subsequent file references
primary	Declares this server as primary for the specified zone
secondary	Declares this server as secondary for the specified zone
cache	Points to the cache file
forwarders	Lists servers to which queries are forwarded
options	Enables optional BIND processing
xfrnets	Limits zone transfers to specific addresses

The way in which you configure the *named.boot* file controls whether the name-server acts as a primary server, a secondary server, or a caching-only server. The best way to understand these different configurations is to look at sample **named.boot** files. The next sections show examples of each type of configuration.

Configuring a caching-only nameserver

A caching-only server configuration is simple. A *named.boot* file and a *named.ca* file are all that you need, though the *named.local* file is usually also used. The most common *named.boot* file for a caching-only server is:

```
;
;   a caching-only server configuration
;
primary         0.0.127.IN-ADDR.ARPA    /etc/named.local
cache           .                       /etc/named.ca
```

The only line in this sample file required for a caching-only configuration is the **cache** statement. It tells **named** to maintain a cache of nameserver responses, and to initialize the cache with the list of root servers found in the file *named.ca*. The name of the file containing the root server list can be any name you wish, but *root.cache*, *named.root*, and *named.ca* are often used. The presence of a cache statement does not make this a caching-only configuration; a cache statement is used in every server configuration. It is the absence of primary and secondary statements that makes this a caching-only configuration.

However, there is one primary statement that is an exception to this rule. You'll see it in our sample *named.boot* file, and in almost every caching-only configuration. It defines the local server as the primary server for its own loopback domain, and it says that the information for the loopback domain is stored in the file *named.local*. The loopback domain is an *in-addr.arpa* domain* that maps the

---

* See Chapter 4, *Getting Started*, for a description of *in-addr.arpa* domains.

address 127.0.0.1 to the name *localhost*. The idea of resolving your own loopback address makes sense to most people, so most *named.boot* files contain this entry.

These primary and cache statements are the only statements used in most caching-only server configurations, but other statements can be added. A **forwarders** statement, and even an **options** statement are sometimes used. The **forwarders** statement causes the caching-only server to send all of the queries that it cannot resolve from its own cache to specific servers. For example:

```
forwarders 172.16.12.1 172.16.1.2
```

This statement forwards every query that cannot be answered from the local cache to 172.16.12.1 and 172.16.1.2. The **forwarders** command builds a rich DNS cache on selected servers located on the local network. This reduces the number of times that queries must be sent out on the wide area network, which is particularly useful if you have limited bandwidth to the wide area network or if you are charged for usage.

When network access to the outside world is severely limited, use the following statement to force the local server to always use the forwarder.

```
options forward-only
```

With this statement in the configuration file, the local server will not attempt to resolve a query itself even if it cannot get an answer to that query from the forwarders.

Adding **forwarders** or **options** statements does not change this from being a caching-only server configuration. Only the addition of primary and secondary commands will do that.

Primary and secondary server configurations

The imaginary *nuts.com* domain is the basis for our sample primary and secondary server configurations. Here is the *named.boot* file to define *almond* as the primary server for the *nuts.com* domain:

```
;
;   nuts.com primary nameserver boot file.
;
directory                               /etc
primary    nuts.com                     named.hosts
primary    16.172.IN-ADDR.ARPA          named.rev
primary    0.0.127.IN-ADDR.ARPA         named.local
cache      .                            named.ca
```

The **directory** statement saves keystrokes on the subsequent filenames. It tells **named** that all relative filenames (i.e., filenames that don't begin with a /), no matter where they occur in the **named** configuration, are relative to the directory */etc*.

The first primary statement declares that this is the primary server for the *nuts.com* domain, and that the data for that domain is loaded from the file *named.hosts*. In our examples, we'll use the filename *named.hosts* as the zone filename, but you should choose a more descriptive filename. For example, a better name for the *nuts.com* zone file is *nuts.com.hosts*.

The second primary statement points to the file that maps IP addresses from 172.16.0.0 to hostnames. This statement says that the local server is the primary server for the reverse domain *16.172.in-addr.arpa*, and that the data for that domain is loaded from the file *named.rev*. Again, the filename *named.rev* is just an example; use descriptive names in your actual configuration.

The format of a primary statement is the keyword `primary`, the domain name, and the name of the zone file from which the domain information is read. All primary statements have this simple format.

The final two statements in the sample configuration are the primary statement for the loopback domain and the cache statement. These statements are discussed earlier in the section about caching-only configurations. They have the same function in every configuration and are found in almost every configuration.

A secondary server's configuration differs from a primary's by using **secondary** instead of **primary** statements. Secondary statements point to remote servers as the source of the domain information instead of local disk files. Secondary statements begin with the keyword `secondary`, followed by the name of the domain, the address of one or more authoritative servers for that domain, and finally the name of a local file where information received from the remote server will be stored. The following *named.boot* file configures *filbert* as a secondary server for the *nuts.com* domain:

```
;
;   nuts.com secondary nameserver boot file.
;
directory                                           /etc
secondary    nuts.com             172.16.12.1      nuts.com.hosts
secondary    16.172.IN-ADDR.ARPA  172.16.12.1      172.16.rev
primary      0.0.127.IN-ADDR.ARPA                  named.local
cache        .                                     named.ca
```

The first secondary statement makes this a secondary server for the *nuts.com* domain. The statement tells **named** to download the data for the *nuts.com* domain from the server at IP address 172.16.12.1, and to store that data in the file */etc/nuts.com.hosts*. If the *nuts.com.hosts* file does not exist, **named** creates it, gets the zone data from the remote server, and writes the data in the newly created file. If the file does exist, **named** checks with the remote server to see if the remote server's data is different from the data in the file. If the data has changed, **named** downloads the updated data and overwrites the file contents with the new data. If the data has not changed, **named** loads the contents of the disk file and doesn't bother with a zone transfer.* Keeping a copy of the database on a local disk file makes it unnecessary to transfer the zone file every time the local host is rebooted. It's only necessary to transfer the zone when the data changes.

The next line in this configuration says that the local server is also a secondary server for the reverse domain *16.172.in-addr.arpa*, and that the data for that domain should also be downloaded from 172.16.12.1. The reverse domain data is stored locally in a file named *172.16.rev*, following the same rules discussed previously for creating and overwriting *nuts.com.hosts*.

Standard Resource Records

The configuration commands discussed above and listed in Table 8-1 are used only in the *named.boot* file. All other files used to configure **named** (*named.hosts*, *named.rev*, *named.local*, and *named.ca*) store domain database information. These files all have the same basic format and use the same type of database records. They use standard resource records, called RRs. These are defined in RFC 1033, the *Domain Administrators Operations Guide*, and other RFCs. Table 8-2 summarizes all of the standard resource records used in this chapter. These records are covered in detail in Appendix C.

Table 8-2: Standard Resource Records

Resource Record Text Name	Record Type	Function
Start of Authority	SOA	Marks the beginning of a zone's data, and defines parameters that affect the entire zone.
Nameserver	NS	Identifies a domain's nameserver.
Address	A	Converts a hostname to an address.
Pointer	PTR	Converts an address to a hostname.
Mail Exchange	MX	Identifies where to deliver mail for a given domain name.
Canonical Name	CNAME	Defines an alias hostname.
Host Information	HINFO	Describes a host's hardware and OS.
Well-Known Service	WKS	Advertises network services.
Text	TXT	Stores arbitrary text strings.

The resource record syntax is described in Appendix C, but a little understanding of the structure of these records is necessary to read the sample configuration files used in this chapter.

---

* Appendix C (in the SOA record section) discusses how **named** determines if data has been updated.

The format of DNS resource records is:

[*name*] [*ttl*] IN *type data*

name

> This is the name of the domain object the resource record references. It can be an individual host or an entire domain. The string entered for the *name* field is relative to the current domain unless it ends with a dot. If the name field is blank, the record applies to the domain object that was named last. For example, if the A record for *peanut* is followed by an MX record with a blank *name* field, both the A record and the MX record apply to *peanut*.

ttl

> Time-to-live defines the length of time, in seconds, that the information in this resource record should be kept in a remote system's cache. Usually this field is left blank and the default *ttl*, set for the entire zone in the SOA record, is used.*

IN Identifies the record as an Internet DNS resource record. There are other classes of records, but they are rarely used. Curious? See Appendix C for the other, non-Internet, classes.

type

> Identifies the kind of resource record. Table 8-2 lists the record types under the heading "Record Type." Specify one of these values in the *type* field.

data

> The information specific to this type of resource record. For example, in an A record this is the field that contains the actual IP address.

In the following sections we look at each of the remaining configuration files. As you look at the files, remember that all of the records in these files are standard resource records that follow the format described above.

The Cache Initialization File

The cache statement in *named.boot* points to a cache initialization file. Each server that maintains a cache has such a file. It contains the information needed to begin building a cache of domain data when the nameserver starts. The root domain is indicated on the cache statement by a single dot, and the *named.ca* file contains the names and addresses of the root servers.

The *named.ca* file is sometimes called a "hints" file, because it contains hints **named** uses to initialize the cache. The hints it contains are the names and

---

* See the section on SOA records in Appendix C.

addresses of the root servers. It is used to help the local server locate a root server during startup. Once a root server is found, an authoritative list of root servers is downloaded from that server. The hints are not referred to again until the local server is forced to restart. The information in the *named.ca* file is not referred to often, but it is critical for booting a **named** server.

The basic *named.ca* file contains NS records that name the root servers, and A records that provide the addresses of the root servers. A sample *named.ca* file is shown below:

```
;
.                          3600000  IN  NS   A.ROOT-SERVERS.NET.
A.ROOT-SERVERS.NET.        3600000  IN  A    198.41.0.4
;
.                          3600000      NS   B.ROOT-SERVERS.NET.
B.ROOT-SERVERS.NET.        3600000  IN  A    128.9.0.107
;
.                          3600000      NS   C.ROOT-SERVERS.NET.
C.ROOT-SERVERS.NET.        3600000  IN  A    192.33.4.12
;
.                          3600000      NS   D.ROOT-SERVERS.NET.
D.ROOT-SERVERS.NET.        3600000  IN  A    128.8.10.90
;
.                          3600000      NS   E.ROOT-SERVERS.NET.
E.ROOT-SERVERS.NET.        3600000  IN  A    192.203.230.10
;
.                          3600000      NS   F.ROOT-SERVERS.NET.
F.ROOT-SERVERS.NET.        3600000  IN  A    192.5.5.241
;
.                          3600000      NS   G.ROOT-SERVERS.NET.
G.ROOT-SERVERS.NET.        3600000  IN  A    192.112.36.4
;
.                          3600000      NS   H.ROOT-SERVERS.NET.
H.ROOT-SERVERS.NET.        3600000  IN  A    128.63.2.53
;
.                          3600000      NS   I.ROOT-SERVERS.NET.
I.ROOT-SERVERS.NET.        3600000  IN  A    192.36.148.17
```

This file contains only nameserver and address records. Each NS record identifies a nameserver for the root (.) domain. The associated A record gives the address of each root server. The ttl value for all of these records is 3600000—a very large value that is approximately 42 days.

Create the *named.ca* file by downloading the file *domain/named.root* from *rs.internic.net* (198.41.0.7) via anonymous **ftp**. The file stored at the InterNIC is in the correct format for a UNIX system. The example below shows the superuser downloading the *named.root* file directly into the local system's *named.ca* file. The file doesn't even need to be edited: it is ready to run.

```
# ftp rs.internic.net
Connected to rs.internic.net.
Name (rs.internic.net:craig): anonymous
331 Guest login ok, send your email address as password.
Password: craig@nuts.com
230 Guest login ok, access restrictions apply.
Remote system type is UNIX.
Using binary mode to transfer files.
ftp> get domain/named.root named.ca
200 PORT command successful.
150 Opening data connection for domain/named.root (2119 bytes).
226 Transfer complete.
2119 bytes received in 0.137 secs (15 Kbytes/sec)
ftp> quit
221 Goodbye.
```

Download the *named.root* file every few months to keep accurate root server information in your cache. A bogus root server entry could cause problems with your local server. The data given above is correct as of publication, but could change at any time.

If your system is not connected to the Internet, it won't be able to communicate with the root servers. Initializing your cache file with the servers listed above would be useless. In this case, initialize your cache with entries that point to the major nameservers on your local network. Those servers must also be configured to answer queries for the "root" domain. However, this root domain contains only NS records pointing to the domain servers on your local network. For example: assume that *nuts.com* is not connected to the Internet and that *almond* and *pecan* are going to act as root servers for this isolated domain. Both servers declare they are primary for the root domain in their *named.boot* files. They load the root from a zone file that contains NS records and A records, stating that they are authoritative for the root and delegating the *nuts.com* and *16.172.in-addr.arpa* domains to the local nameservers that service those domains. (How domains are delegated is covered later in the chapter.) Details of this type of configuration are provided in *DNS and BIND* by Liu and Albitz (O'Reilly & Associates).

The named.local File

The *named.local* file is used to convert the address 127.0.0.1 (the "loopback address") into the name *localhost*. It's the zone file for the reverse domain 0.0.127.IN-ADDR.ARPA. Because all systems use 127.0.0.1 as the "loopback" address, this file is virtually identical on every server. Here's a sample *named.local* file:

```
@           IN   SOA     almond.nuts.com. jan.almond.nuts.com. (
                 1                       ; serial
```

```
                         360000              ; refresh every 100 hours
                         3600                ; retry after 1 hour
                         3600000             ; expire after 1000 hours
                         360000              ; default ttl is 100 hours
                         )
              IN   NS    almond.nuts.com.
     0        IN   PTR   loopback.
     1        IN   PTR   localhost.
```

Neither the NS record nor the first PTR record is required. The first PTR record maps the network 127.0.0.0 to the name *loopback*, which is an alternative to mapping the network name in the */etc/networks* file. Only the SOA record and the second PTR record are needed. The required PTR record is the same on every host: host address 1 on network 127.0.0 is mapped to the name *localhost*.

The SOA record's data fields and the NS record that contains the computer's hostname vary from system to system. The sample SOA record identifies *almond.nuts.com.* as the server originating this zone, and the email address *jan.almond.nuts.com.* as the point of contact for any questions about the zone. (Note that in an SOA record the email address is written with a dot separating the recipient's name from the hostname: *jan* is the user and *almond.nuts.com* is the host.) Many systems do not include the NS record; but when it is used, it contains the computer's hostname. Change these three data fields and you can use this identical file on any host.

The files discussed so far, *named.boot, named.ca,* and *named.local,* are the only files required to configure caching-only servers and secondary servers. Most of your servers will use only these files, and the files used will contain almost identical information on every server.

The simplest way to create these three files is to copy a sample file and modify it for your system. Most systems come with sample files. If your system doesn't, sample configuration files are available in the *conf/master* directory* of the *bind.tar.gz* file. This compressed **tar** file can be obtained via anonymous **ftp** from the *isc/bind/src* directory on *ftp.isc.org.* The *named.local* file shown above was derived from the *named.local* sample that comes with BIND.

The remaining **named** configuration files, *named.hosts* and *named.rev,* are more complex, but the relative number of systems that require these files is small. Only the primary server needs all of the configuration files, and there should be only one primary server per zone.

---

* The sample *named.ca* file in this directory is called *root.cache.*

The Reverse Domain File

The *named.rev* file is very similar in structure to the *named.local* file. Both of these files translate IP addresses into hostnames, so both files contain PTR records.

The *named.rev* file in our example is the zone file for the *16.172.in-addr.arpa* domain. The domain administrator creates this file on *almond*, and every other host that needs this information gets it from there.

```
;
;          Address to hostname mappings.
;
@         IN     SOA     almond.nuts.com. jan.almond.nuts.com. (
                                 10099    ;   Serial
                                 43200    ;   Refresh
                                 3600     ;   Retry
                                 3600000  ;   Expire
                                 2592000 ) ; Minimum
                 IN     NS      almond.nuts.com.
                 IN     NS      filbert.nuts.com.
                 IN     NS      foo.army.mil.
1.12             IN     PTR     almond.nuts.com.
2.12             IN     PTR     peanut.nuts.com.
3.12             IN     PTR     pecan.nuts.com.
4.12             IN     PTR     walnut.nuts.com.
2.1              IN     PTR     filbert.nuts.com.
6                IN     NS      salt.plant.nuts.com.
                 IN     NS      pecan.nuts.com.
```

Like all zone files, the *named.rev* file begins with an SOA record. The @ in the name field of the SOA record references the current domain. In this case it is the domain defined by the primary statement in our sample *named.boot* file:

```
primary   16.172.IN-ADDR.ARPA           named.rev
```

The @ in the SOA record allows the primary statement to define the zone file domain. This same SOA record is used on every zone; it always references the correct domain name because it references the domain defined for that particular zone file in *named.boot*. Change the hostname (*almond.nuts.com.*) and the manager's mail address (*jan.almond.nuts.com.*), and use this SOA record in any of your zone files.

The NS records that follow the SOA record define the nameservers for the domain. Generally the nameservers are listed immediately after the SOA, before any other record has the chance to modify the domain name. Recall that a blank name field means that the last domain name is still in force. The SOA's domain reference is still in force because the following NS records have blank name fields.

PTR records dominate the *named.rev* file because they are used to translate addresses to hostnames. The PTR records in our example provide address-to-name conversions for hosts 12.1, 12.2, 12.3, 12.4, and 2.1 on network 172.16. Because they don't end in dots, the values in the name fields of these PTR records are relative to the current domain. For example, the value 3.12 is interpreted as *3.12.16.172.in-addr.arpa*. The host name in the data field of the PTR record is fully qualified to prevent it from being relative to the current domain name. Using the information in this PTR, **named** will translate *3.12.16.172.in-addr.arpa* into *pecan.nuts.com*.

The last two lines of this file are additional NS records. As with any domain, subdomains can be created in an *in-addr.arpa* domain. This is what the last two NS records do. These NS records point to *pecan* and *salt* as nameservers for the subdomain *6.16.172.in-addr.arpa*. Any query for information in the *6.16.172.in-addr.arpa* subdomain is referred to them. NS records that point to the servers for a subdomain must be placed in the higher-level domain before you can use that subdomain.

Subdomains in the *in-addr.arpa* domain are not as common or as useful as subdomains in the host namespace. Domain names and IP addresses are not the same thing, and do not have the same structure. When an IP address is turned into an *in-addr.arpa* domain name, the four bytes of the address are treated as four distinct pieces. In reality, the IP address is 32 contiguous bits. Subnets divide up the IP address space and subnet masks are bit-oriented, which does not limit them to byte boundaries. *in-addr.arpa* subdomains divide up the domain name space and can only occur at a full byte boundary because each byte of the address is treated as a distinct "name."

The named.hosts File

The *named.hosts* file contains most of the domain information. This file converts hostnames to IP addresses, so A records predominate; but it also contains MX, CNAME, and other records. The *named.hosts* file, like the *named.rev* file, is only created on the primary server. All others servers get this information from the primary server.

```
;
;       Addresses and other host information.
;
@       IN      SOA     almond.nuts.com. jan.almond.nuts.com. (
                                10118           ; Serial
                                43200           ; Refresh
                                3600            ; Retry
                                3600000         ; Expire
                                2592000 )       ; Minimum
;       Define the nameservers and the mail servers
                IN      NS      almond.nuts.com.
                IN      NS      filbert.nuts.com.
```

```
                          IN      NS      foo.army.mil.
                          IN      MX      10 almond.nuts.com.
                          IN      MX      20 pecan.nuts.com.
    ;
    ;         Define localhost
    ;
    localhost             IN      A       127.0.0.1
    ;
    ;         Define the hosts in this zone
    ;
    almond                IN      A       172.16.12.1
                          IN      MX      5 almond.nuts.com.
    loghost               IN      CNAME   almond.nuts.com.
    peanut                IN      A       172.16.12.2
                          IN      MX      5 almond.nuts.com.
    goober                IN      CNAME   peanut.nuts.com.
    pecan                 IN      A       172.16.12.3
    walnut                IN      A       172.16.12.4
    filbert               IN      A       172.16.1.2
    ;         host table has BOTH host and gateway entries for 10.104.0.19
    mil-gw                IN      A       10.104.0.19
    ;
    ;     Glue records for servers within this domain
    ;
    pack.plant            IN      A       172.16.18.15
    acorn.sales           IN      A       172.16.6.1
    ;
    ;         Define sub-domains
    ;
    plant                 IN      NS      pack.plant.nuts.com.
                          IN      NS      pecan.nuts.com.
    sales                 IN      NS      acorn.sales.nuts.com.
                          IN      NS      pack.plant.nuts.com.
```

Like the *named.rev* file, the *named.hosts* file begins with an SOA record and a few
NS records that define the domain and its servers, but the *named.hosts* file contains a wider variety of resource records than a *named.rev* file does. We'll look at
each of these records in the order in which they occur in the sample file, so that
you can follow along using the sample file as your reference.

The first MX record identifies a mail server for the entire domain. This record says
that *almond* is the mail server for *nuts.com* with a preference of 10. Mail
addressed to *user@nuts.com* is redirected to *almond* for delivery. Of course for
almond to successfully deliver the mail, it must be properly configured as a mail
server. The MX record is only part of the story. We look at configuring **sendmail** in
Chapter 10, *sendmail.*

The second MX record identifies *pecan* as a mail server for *nuts.com* with a preference of 20. Preference numbers let you define alternate mail servers. The lower
the preference number, the more desirable the server. Therefore, our two sample
MX records say "send mail for the *nuts.com* domain to *almond* first; if *almond* is

unavailable, try sending the mail to *pecan*." Rather than relying on a single mail server, preference numbers allow you to create backup servers. If the main mail server is unreachable, the domain's mail is sent to one of the backups instead.

These sample MX records redirect mail addressed to *nuts.com*, but mail addressed to *user@walnut.nuts.com* will still be sent directly to *walnut.nuts.com*—not to *almond* or *pecan*. This configuration allows simplified mail addressing in the form *user@nuts.com* for those who want to take advantage of it, but it continues to allow direct mail delivery to individual hosts for those who wish to take advantage of that.

The first A record in this example defines the address for *localhost*. This is the opposite of the PTR entry in the *named.local* file. It allows users within the *nuts.com* domain to enter the name *localhost* and have it resolved to the address 127.0.0.1 by the local nameserver.

The next A record defines the IP address for *almond*. (Note that the records that relate to a single host are grouped together, which is the most common structure used in zone files.) The A record is followed by an MX record and a CNAME record that both relate to *almond*. The *almond* MX record points back to the host itself, and the CNAME record defines an alias for the host name.

This host-specific MX record is provided as a courtesy to remote mailers. Some mailer implementations look for an MX record first, and then query for the host's address. Providing an MX record saves these mailers one additional nameserver query.

peanut's A record is also followed by an MX record and a CNAME record. However, *peanut*'s MX record serves a different purpose. It directs all mail addressed to *user@peanut.nuts.com* to *almond*. This MX record is required because the MX records at the beginning of the zone file redirect mail only if it is addressed to *user@nuts.com*. If you also want to redirect mail addressed to *peanut*, you need a "peanut-specific" MX record.

The name field of the CNAME record contains an alias for the official hostname. The official name, called the canonical name, is provided in the data field of the record. Because of these records, *almond* can be referred to by the name *loghost*, and *peanut* can be referred to as *goober*. The *loghost* alias is a generic hostname used to direct **syslogd** output to *almond*.* Hostname aliases should *not* be used in other resource records.† For example, don't use an alias as the name of a mail server in an MX record. Use *only* the "canonical" (official) name that's defined in an A record.

---

* See Chapter 3 for a further discussion of generic hostnames.

† See Appendix C for additional information about using CNAME records in the *named.hosts* file.

Your *named.hosts* file will be much larger than the sample file we've discussed, but it will contain essentially the same records. If you know the names and addresses of the hosts in your domain, you have most of the information necessary to create the **named** configuration.

Starting named

After you construct the *named.boot* file and the required zone files, start **named**. **named** is usually started at boot time from a startup script, but it can be started at the command prompt:

```
# named
```

The first time you run it, watch for error messages. **named** logs errors to the *messages* file.* Once **named** is running to your satisfaction, use **nslookup** to query the nameserver to make sure it is providing the correct information.

Using nslookup

nslookup is a debugging tool provided as part of the BIND software package. It allows anyone to directly query a nameserver and retrieve any of the information known to the DNS system. It is helpful for determining if the server is running correctly and is properly configured, or for querying for information provided by remote servers.

The **nslookup** program is used to resolve queries either interactively or directly from the command line. Below is a command-line example of using **nslookup** to query for the IP address of a host:

```
% nslookup almond.nuts.com
Server:  peanut.nuts.com
Address:  172.16.12.2

Name:    almond.nuts.com
Address:  172.16.12.1
```

Here, a user asks **nslookup** to provide the address of *almond.nuts.com*. **nslookup** displays the name and address of the server used to resolve the query, and then it displays the answer to the query. This is useful, but **nslookup** is more often used interactively.

The real power of **nslookup** is seen in interactive mode. To enter interactive mode, type **nslookup** on the command line without any arguments. Terminate an interac-

---

* This file if found at */usr/adm/messages* on both our Linux and Solaris sample systems but it might be located somewhere else on your system. Check your system's documentation.

tive session by entering CTRL-D (^D) or the **exit** command at the **nslookup** prompt. Redone in an interactive session, the previous query shown is:

```
% nslookup
Default Server:  peanut.nuts.com
Address:  172.16.12.2

> almond.nuts.com
Server:  peanut.nuts.com
Address:  172.16.12.2

Name:     almond.nuts.com
Address:  172.16.12.1

> ^D
```

By default, **nslookup** queries for A records, but you can use the **set type** command to change the query to another resource record type, or to the special query type "ANY." ANY is used to retrieve all available resource records for the specified host.

The following example checks MX records for *almond* and *peanut*. Note that once the query type is set to MX, it stays MX. It doesn't revert to the default A-type query. Another **set type** command is required to reset the query type.

```
% nslookup
Default Server:  peanut.nuts.com
Address:  172.16.12.2

> set type=MX
> almond.nuts.com
Server:  peanut.nuts.com
Address:  172.16.12.2

almond.nuts.com    preference = 5, mail exchanger = almond.nuts.com
almond.nuts.com    inet address = 172.16.12.1

> peanut.nuts.com
Server:  peanut.nuts.com
Address:  172.16.12.2

peanut.nuts.com    preference = 5, mail exchanger = almond.nuts.com
peanut.nuts.com    inet address = 172.16.12.2
> exit
```

You can use the **server** command to control the server used to resolve queries. This is particularly useful for going directly to an authoritative server to check some information. The following example does just that. In fact, this example contains several interesting commands:

- First we **set type=NS** and get the NS records for the *zoo.edu* domain.

- From the information returned by this query, we select a server and use the **server** command to direct **nslookup** to use that server.

- Next, using the **set domain** command, we set the default domain to *zoo.edu*. **nslookup** uses this default domain name to expand the hostnames in its queries, in the same way that the resolver uses the default domain name defined in *resolv.conf.*

- We reset the query type to ANY. If the query type is not reset, **nslookup** still queries for NS records.

- Finally, we query for information about the host *tiger.zoo.edu*. Because the default domain is set to *zoo.edu*, we simply enter *tiger* at the prompt.

```
% nslookup
Default Server:  peanut.nuts.com
Address:  172.16.12.2

> set type=NS
> zoo.edu
Server:  peanut.nuts.com
Address:  172.16.12.2

Non-authoritative answer:
zoo.edu nameserver = NOC.ZOO.EDU
zoo.edu nameserver = NI.ZOO.EDU
zoo.edu nameserver = NAMESERVER.AGENCY.GOV
Authoritative answers can be found from:
NOC.ZOO.EDU      inet address = 172.28.2.200
NI.ZOO.EDU       inet address = 172.28.2.240
NAMESERVER.AGENCY.GOV inet address = 172.21.18.31
> server NOC.ZOO.EDU
Default Server:  NOC.ZOO.EDU
Address:  172.28.2.200

> set domain=zoo.edu
> set type=any
> tiger
Server:  NOC.ZOO.EDU
Address:  172.28.2.200

tiger.zoo.edu    inet address = 172.28.172.8
tiger.zoo.edu    preference = 10, mail exchanger = tiger.ZOO.EDU
tiger.zoo.edu    CPU=ALPHA OS=UNIX
tiger.zoo.edu    inet address = 172.28.172.8, protocol = 6
        7 21 23 25 79
tiger.ZOO.EDU    inet address = 172.28.172.8
> exit
```

The final example shows how to download an entire domain from an authoritative server and examine it on your local system. The **ls** command requests a zone transfer and displays the contents of the zone it receives.* If the zone file is more than a few lines long, redirect the output to a file, and use the **view** command to examine the contents of the file. (**view** sorts a file and displays it using the UNIX **more** command.) The combination of **ls** and **view** are helpful when tracking down a remote hostname. In the example that follows, the **ls** command retrieves the *big.com* zone and stores the information in *temp.file*. Then **view** is used to examine *temp.file*.

```
peanut% nslookup
Default Server:  peanut.nuts.com
Address:  172.16.12.2

> server minerals.big.com
Default Server:  minerals.big.com
Address:  192.168.20.1

> ls big.com > temp.file
[minerals.big.com]
########
Received 406 records.
> view temp.file
 acmite                 192.168.20.28
 adamite                192.168.20.29
 adelite                192.168.20.11
 agate                  192.168.20.30
 alabaster              192.168.20.31
 albite                 192.168.20.32
 allanite               192.168.20.20
 altaite                192.168.20.33
 alum                   192.168.20.35
 aluminum               192.168.20.8
 amaranth               192.168.20.85
 amethyst               192.168.20.36
 andorite               192.168.20.37
 apatite                192.168.20.38
 beryl                  192.168.20.23
--More-- q
> exit
```

These examples show that **nslookup** allows you to:

* Query for any specific type of standard resource record.

* Directly query the authoritative servers for a domain.

* Get the entire contents of a domain into a file so you can view it.

---

* For security reasons, many nameservers do not respond to the **ls** command. See the **xfrnets** command in Appendix C for information on how to limit access to zone transfers.

Use **nslookup**'s **help** command to see its other features. Turn on debugging (with **set debug**) and examine the additional information this provides. As you play with this tool, you'll find many helpful features.

Summary

Domain Name Service (DNS) is an important user service that should be used on every system connected to the Internet. UNIX implementations of DNS are based on the Berkeley Internet Name Domain (BIND) software. BIND provides both a DNS client and a DNS server.

The BIND client issues name queries and is implemented as library routines. It is called the *resolver*. The resolver is configured in the *resolv.conf* file. All systems run the resolver.

The BIND server answers name queries and it runs as a daemon. It is called **named**. **named** is configured by the *named.boot* file, which defines where the server gets the domain database information and the type of server being configured. The server types are primary, secondary and caching servers. Because all servers are caching servers, a single configurtaion often encompasses more than one server type.

The original domain database source files are found on the primary server. The domain database file is called a zone file. The zone file is constructed from standard resources records (RR) that are defined in RFCs. The RRs share a common structure and are used to define all DNS database information.

The DNS server can be tested using **nslookup**. This test tool is included with the BIND release.

In this chapter we have seen how to configure and test domain name service. In the next chapter we configure several other services.

9

Configuring Network Servers

Now our attention turns to configuring network servers. As with name service, these servers are not strictly required for the network to operate, but they provide services that are central to the network's purpose.

There are many network services—many more than can be covered in this chapter. We concentrate on servers that provide "computer-to-computer" services.* The services covered in this chapter are:

- The Network File System (NFS)
- The Line Printer Daemon (LPD)
- The Network Information Service (NIS)
- The Bootstrap Protocol (BOOTP)
- Dynamic Host Configuration Protocol (DHCP)
- The Post Office Protocol (POP)

We begin with NFS, which is the server that provides file sharing on UNIX networks.

The Network File System

The Network File System (NFS) allows directories and files to be shared across a network. It was originally developed by Sun Microsystems, but is now supported by virtually all UNIX implementations and many non-UNIX operating systems. Through NFS, users and programs can access files located on remote systems as if

---

* Notably absent is **sendmail**. It requires so much discussion, it has its own chapter (Chapter 10)!

they were local files. In a perfect NFS environment, the user neither knows nor cares where files are actually stored.

NFS has several benefits:

- It reduces local disk storage requirements because a network can store a single copy of a directory, while the directory continues to be fully accessible to everyone on the network.

- NFS simplifies central support tasks—files can be updated centrally, yet available throughout the network.

- NFS allows users to use familiar UNIX commands to manipulate remote files instead of learning new commands. There is no need to use **ftp** or **rcp** to copy a file between hosts on the network; **cp** works fine.

There are two sides to NFS—a client side and a server side. The client is the system that uses the remote directories as if they were part of its local filesystem. The server is the system that makes the directories available for use. Attaching a remote directory to the local filesystem (a client function) is called *mounting* a directory. Offering a directory for remote access (a server function) is called *sharing* a directory.* Frequently, a system runs both the client and the server NFS software. In this section we'll look at how to configure a system to share and mount directories using NFS.

If you're responsible for an NFS server for a large site, you should take care in planning and implementing the NFS environment. The discussion in this chapter tells how NFS is configured to run on a client and a server, but you may want more details to design an optimal NFS environment. For a comprehensive treatment, see *Managing NFS and NIS*, by Hal Stern (O'Reilly & Associates).

NFS Daemons

The Network File System is run by several daemons, some performing client functions and some performing server functions. Before we discuss the NFS configuration, let's look at the function of the daemons that run NFS:

nfsd [*nservers*]

The NFS daemon, **nfsd**, runs on NFS servers. This daemon services the client's NFS requests. The *nservers* option is available on Solaris systems. It specifies how many daemons should be started.

mountd

The NFS mount daemon, **mountd**, processes the clients' mount requests. NFS servers run the mount daemon.

---

* An older term for this function is *exporting*. Many systems still refer to file sharing as exporting.

lockd

> The lock daemon, **lockd**, handles file lock requests. Both clients and servers run the lock daemon. Clients request file locks, and servers grant them.

statd

> The network status monitor daemon, **statd**, is required by **lockd** to provide monitoring services. In particular, it allows locks to be reset properly after a crash. Both clients and servers run **statd**.

The daemons necessary to run NFS are started from boot scripts. On a Solaris system, two scripts located in the */etc/init.d* directory, *nfs.client* and *nfs.server*, handle this job. The *nfs.client* script starts the **statd** and **lockd** programs.* NFS server systems run those two daemons, plus the NFS server daemon, **nfsd**, and the mount server daemon, **mountd**. On Solaris systems, the *nfs.server* script starts **mountd** and 16 copies of **nfsd**.

Each system has its own technique for starting these daemons. If some of the daemons aren't starting, make sure your startup scripts are correct.

Sharing Filesystems

The first step in configuring a server is deciding which filesystems will be shared, and what restrictions will be placed on them. Only filesystems that provide a benefit to the client should be shared. Before you share a filesystem, think about what purpose it will serve. Some common reasons for sharing filesystems are:

- To provide disk space to diskless clients
- To prevent unnecessary duplication of the same data on multiple systems
- To provide centrally supported programs and data
- To share data among users in a group

Once you've selected the filesystems you'll share, you must configuring them for sharing using the appropriate commands for your system. In the following sections we emphasize the way this is done on Solaris systems. It is very different on Linux systems. Check your system's documentation to find out exactly how it implements NFS file sharing.

The share command

On Solaris systems, directories are shared using the **share** command.

---

* On your system, the prefix "rpc." may be used on the daemon names. For example, the Slackware Linux system uses the filename *rpc.nfsd* for the NFS daemon. Check your system's documentation.

A simplified syntax for the **share** command is:

```
share -F nfs [-o options] pathname
```

where *pathname* is the path of the directory the server is offering to share with its clients, and *options* are the access controls for that directory. The commonly used options are:

rw The **rw** option grants read and write access to the shared filesystem. It can be specified in the form **rw=***host*:*host* . . . to identify the individual hosts that are granted this access. When used in this way, only the hosts identified in the list are given access to the filesystem. If the colon-separated list of hostnames is not provided with the **rw** option, all hosts are given read/write access to the filesystem. In fact, if no options are specified at all, the **share** command defaults to giving all clients read/write access. This default is acceptable if your systems are on an isolated network, but if they are on a connected network, this could open up a security hole. It is the best practice to restrict access to those hosts that you really trust.

ro This option limits access to read-only. It also can be specified with a colon-separated host list, e.g., **ro=***host*:*host* . . . . When the host list is included, only the hosts on the list have access and that access is limited to read-only.

root=*host*

This option allows the *root* user on the specified host to have root access to the shared filesystem. Normally, the root user on a remote system is mapped to the userid *nobody* and given only normal user privileges. Granting root access is a big security risk.

The **rw** and **ro** options can be combined to grant different levels of access to different clients. For example:

```
share -F nfs -o rw=almond:pecan ro  /usr/man
share -F nfs -o rw=peanut:almond:pecan:walnut  /export/home/research
```

The first **share** command grants read and write access to *almond* and *pecan* and read-only access to all other clients. On the other hand, the second **share** command grants read/write access to *peanut*, *almond*, *pecan*, and *walnut*, and no access of any kind to any other client.

The **share** command does not survive a boot. Put the **share** commands in the */etc/dfs/dfstab* file to make sure that the filesystems continue to be offered to your clients even if the system reboots. Here is a sample *dfstab* file containing our two **share** commands:

```
% cat /etc/dfs/dfstab
#   place share(1M) commands here for automatic execution
#   on entering init state 3.
```

```
#
#    share [-F fstype] [ -o options] [-d "<text>"] <pathname> [resource]
#    .e.g,
#    share  -F nfs  -o rw=engineering  -d "home dirs"  /export/home2
share -F nfs -o rw=almond:pecan ro  /usr/man
share -F nfs -o rw=peanut:almond:pecan:walnut  /export/home/research
```

The **share** command, the *dfstab* file, and even the terminology "share" are Solaris-specific. Most UNIX systems say that they are exporting files, instead of sharing files, when they are offering files to NFS clients. Furthermore, they do not use the **share** command or the *dfstab* file; instead, they offer filesystems through the */etc/exports* file. Linux is an example of such a system.

The /etc/exports file

The */etc/exports* file is the NFS server configuration file for Linux systems. It controls which files and directories are shared (exported), which hosts can access them, and what kinds of access are allowed. A sample */etc/exports* file might contain these entries:

```
/usr/man        almond(rw) pecan(rw)  (ro)
/usr/local      (ro)
/home/research  peanut(rw) almond(rw) pecan(rw) walnut(rw)
```

This sample file says that:

- */usr/man* can be mounted by any client, but it can be written to only by *almond* and *pecan*. Other clients have read-only access.

- */usr/local* can be mounted by any client, with read-only access.

- */home/research* can be mounted only by the hosts *peanut, almond, pecan,* and *walnut*. These four hosts have read-write access.

The options used in each of the entries in the */etc/exports* file determine what kinds of access are allowed. The information derived from the sample file is based on the options specified on each line in the file. The general format of the entries is as follows:

```
directory [host(option)]...
```

directory names the directory or file that is available for export. The *host* is the name of the client granted access to the exported directory while the *option* specifies the type of access being granted. The options used in the sample file are:

ro   Read-only prevents NFS clients from writing to this directory. Attempts by clients to write to a read-only directory fail with the message: "Read-only filesystem" or "Permission denied." If **ro** is specified without a client hostname, all clients are granted read-only access.

rw Read-write permits clients to read and write to this directory. When specified without hostname, as simply (**rw**), all clients are granted read-write access. If a hostname is specified, only the named host is given read-write permission.

Mounting Remote Filesystems

You need some basic information before you can decide which NFS directories to mount on your system. You need to know which servers are connected to your network, and which directories are available from those servers. A directory cannot be mounted unless it is first exported by a server.

Your network administrator is a good source for this information. The administrator can tell you what systems are providing NFS service, what directories they are exporting, and what these directories contain. If you are the administrator of an NFS server, you should develop this type of information for your users. See Chapter 4, *Getting Started*.

On Solaris systems you can also obtain information about the shared directories directly from the servers by using the **showmount** command. The NFS servers are usually the same centrally supported systems that provide other services such as mail and domain name service. Select a likely server and query it with the command **showmount −e** *hostname*. In response to this command, the server lists the directories that it exports and the conditions applied to their export.

For example, a **showmount −e** query to *filbert* produces the following output:

```
% showmount -e filbert
export list for filbert:
/usr/man               (everyone)
/home/research         peanut,almond,walnut,pecan
/usr/local             (everyone)
```

The export list shows the NFS directories exported by *filbert*, as well as who is allowed to access those directories. From this list, *peanut*'s administrator may decide to mount any of the directories offered by *filbert*. Our imaginary administrator decides to:

1. Mount */usr/man* from *filbert* instead of maintaining the **man** pages locally.

2. Mount */home/research* to more easily share files with other systems in the research group.

3. Mount the centrally maintained programs in */usr/local*.

These selections represent some of the most common motivations for mounting NFS directories. These are to:

- Save disk space

- Share files with other systems

- Maintain common files centrally

The amount to which you use NFS is a personal choice. Some people prefer the greater personal control you get from keeping files locally, while others prefer the convenience offered by NFS. Your site may have guidelines for how NFS should be used, which directories should be mounted, and which files should be centrally maintained. Check with your network administrator if you're unsure about how NFS is used at your site.

The mount command

A client must mount a shared directory before using it. "Mounting" the directory attaches it to the client's filesystem hierarchy. Only directories offered by the servers can be mounted, but any part of the offered directory, such as a subdirectory or a file, can be mounted.

NFS directories are mounted using the **mount** command. The general structure of the **mount** command is:

```
mount hostname:remote-directory local-directory
```

The *hostname* identifies an NFS server, and the *remote-directory* identifies all or part of a directory offered by that server. The **mount** command attaches that remote directory to the client's filesystem using the directory name provided for *local-directory*. The client's local directory, called the mount point, must be created before **mount** is executed. Once the mount is completed, files located in the remote directory can be accessed through the local directory exactly as if they were local files.

For example, assume that *filbert.nuts.com* is an NFS server and that it shares the files shown in the section above. Further assume that the administrator of *peanut* wants to access the */home/research* directory. The administrator simply creates a local */home/research* directory, and mounts the remote */home/research* directory offered by *filbert* on this newly created mount point.

```
# mkdir /home/research
# mount filbert:/home/research /home/research
```

Once a remote directory is mounted, it stays attached to the local file system until it is explicitly dismounted or the local system reboots. To dismount a directory, use the **umount** command. On the **umount** command line, specify either the local or remote name of the directory that is to be dismounted. For example, the administrator of *peanut* can dismount the remote *filbert:/home/research* filesystem from the local */home/research* mount point, with either:

```
# umount /home/research
```

or:

```
# umount filbert:/home/research
```

Booting also dismounts NFS directories. Because systems frequently wish to mount the same filesystems every time they boot, UNIX provides a system for automatically remounting after a boot.

The vfstab and fstab files

UNIX systems use the information provided in a special table to remount all types of filesystems, including NFS directories, after a system reboot. The table is a critical part of providing users consistent access to software and files, so care should be taken whenever it is modified. Two different files with two different formats are used for this purpose by the different flavors of UNIX. Linux and BSD systems use the */etc/fstab* file and Solaris, our System V example, uses the */etc/vfstab* file.

The format of the NFS entries in the Solaris *vfstab* file is:

```
filesystem - mountpoint nfs - yes options
```

The various fields in the entry must appear in the order shown above and they must be separated by whitespace. The items in bold (both dashes and the words **nfs** and **yes**) are keywords that must appear exactly as shown above. *filesystem* is the name of the directory offered by the server. *mountpoint* is the pathname of the local mount point, and *options* are the mount options discussed below. A sample NFS *vfstab* entry is:

```
filbert:/home/research - /home/research nfs - yes rw,soft
```

This entry mounts the NFS filesystem *filbert:/home/research* on the local mount point */home/research*. The filesystem is mounted with the **rw** and **soft** options set. The mount options available on Solaris systems are:

rw If permitted, mount the filesystem read/write. If the filesystem is restricted by the server to read-only, a warning is issued and the filesystem is mounted read-only.

ro Mount the filesystem read-only.

remount

   If the filesystem is already mounted read-only, remount the filesystem as read/write.

soft

> If the server fails to respond, return an error and don't retry the request.

hard

> If the server fails to respond, retry until it does respond. This is the default.

bg Do the retries in background mode.

fg Do the retries in foreground mode.

intr

> Allow a keyboard interrupt to kill a process that is hung waiting for the server to respond. Hard-mounted filesystems can become hung because the client retries forever, even if the server is down. This is a default.

nointr

> Don't allow keyboard interrupts. In general, this is a bad idea.

nosuid

> Do not allow an executable stored on the mounted filesystem to run **setuid**. This improves security but may limit utility.

On the Solaris system, the NFS filesystems defined in the *vfstab* file are mounted by a **mountall** command located in a startup file. On the Linux system, the startup file contains a **mount** command with the **−a** flag set, which causes Linux to mount all filesystems listed in *fstab*. The format of NFS entries in the */etc/fstab* file is:

```
filesystem  mountpoint  nfs  options
```

The fields must appear in the order shown and must be separated by whitespace. The keyword **nfs** is required for NFS filesystems. `filesystem` is the name of the directory being mounted. `mountpoint` is the pathname of the local mount point. `options` are any of the Linux mount options listed in Table 9-1.

Table 9-1: Linux Mount Options

Option	Purpose
async	Use asynchronous file I/O.
auto	Mount when −a option is used.
dev	Allow character and block special devices on the filesystem.
exec	Permit execution of files from the filesystem.
noauto	Don't mount with the −a option.
nodev	Don't allow character and block special devices on the filesystem.
noexec	Don't allow execution of files from the filesystem.
nosuid	Don't allow programs stored on the filesystem to run **setuid** or **setgid**.
nouser	Only root can mount the filesystem.
remount	Remount a mounted filesystem with new options.

Table 9-1: *Linux Mount Options (continued)*

Option	Purpose
ro	Mount the filesystem read-only.
rw	Mount the filesystem read-write.
suid	Allow programs to run **setuid** or **setgid**.
sync	Use synchronous filesystem I/O.
user	Permit ordinary users to mount the filesystem.
soft	Allow the access to time out if the server doesn't respond.
timeo=*time*	The length of *time* before an access times out. Must be used with **soft**.

A **grep** of *fstab* shows sample NFS entries.*

```
% grep nfs /etc/fstab
filbert:/usr/spool/mail    /usr/spool/mail    nfs rw    0 0
filbert:/usr/man           /usr/man           nfs rw    0 0
filbert:/home/research     /home/research     nfs rw    0 0
```

The **grep** shows that there are three NFS filesystems contained in the */etc/fstab* file. The **mount −a** command in the boot script remounts these three directories every time the system boots.

The *vfstab* and *fstab* files are the most common methods used for mounting filesystems at boot time. There is another technique that automatically mounts NFS filesystems, but only when they are actually needed. It is called *automounter*.

NFS Automounter

Automounter is a feature available in some NFS implementations. The best example of automounter is the implementation that comes with Solaris, which is the implementation we use in this section.

The automounter configuration files are called *maps*. Three basic map types are used to define the automounter filesystem (autofs).

These map types are:

Master map

> The configuration file read by **automount**. It lists all of the other maps that are used to define the autofs filesystem.

Direct map

> A configuration file that lists the mount points, pathnames, and options of filesystems that are to be mounted by the automounter daemon (**automountd**).

---

* **grep** is used because the *fstab* file contains other information not related to NFS.

Indirect map

A configuration file that contains pathnames and "relative" mount points. The mount points are relative to a directory path declared in the master map. How indirect maps are used will become clear in the examples.

On Solaris systems the automounter daemon (**automountd**) and the **automount** command are started by the */etc/init.d/autofs* script. The script is run with the **start** option to start automounter, i.e., **autofs start**. It is run with the **stop** option to shut down automounter. **automount** and **automountd** are two distinct, separate programs. **automountd** runs as a daemon and dynamically mounts filesystems when they are needed. **automount** processes the *auto_master* file to determine the filesystems that can be dynamically mounted.

To use automounter, first configure the */etc/auto_master* file. Entries in the *auto_master* file have this format:

```
mount-point     map-name        options
```

The Solaris system comes with a default *auto_master* file preconfigured. Customize the file for your configuration. Comment out the +auto_master entry. It is only used if you run NIS+ and your servers offer a centrally maintained *auto_master map*. Also ignore the /xfn entry. It does not apply to systems that use DNS. Add an entry for your direct map. In the example it is called auto_direct. Here is */etc/auto_master* after our modifications:

```
# Master map for automounter
#
#+auto_master
#/xfn           -xfn
/net            -hosts          -nosuid
/home           auto_home
/-              auto_direct
```

All lines that begin with a sharp sign (#) are comments, including the +auto_master and /xfn lines we commented out. The first real entry in the file specifies that the shared filesystems offered by every NFS server listed in the */etc/hosts* file are automatically mounted under the */net* directory. A sub-directory is created for each server under */net* using the server's hostname. For example: assume that *filbert* is listed in the *hosts* file and that it exports the */usr/local* directory. This **net** entry automatically makes that remote directory available on the local host as */net/filbert/usr/local*.

The second entry automatically mounts the home directories listed in the */etc/auto_home* map under the */home* directory. A default */etc/auto_home* file is provided with the Solaris system. Comment out the +auto_home entry found in the default file. It is used only if you run NIS+ and your servers offer a centrally maintained *auto_home* map. Add entries for individual user home directories or for all home directories from specific servers. Here is a modified *auto_home* map:

```
# Home directory map for automounter
#
#+auto_home
craig           almond:/export/home/craig
*               pecan:/export/home/&
```

The first entry mounts the */export/home/craig* filesystem shared by *almond* on the local mount point */home/craig*. The *auto_home* map is an indirect map, so the mount point specified in the map (`craig`) is relative to the */home* mount point defined in the *auto_master* map. The second entry mounts every home directory found in the */export/home* filesystem offered by *pecan* to a "like-named" mount point on the local host. For example: assume that *pecan* has two home directories, */export/home/daniel* and */export/home/kristin*. Automounter makes them both available on the local host as */home/daniel* and */home/kristin*. The asterisk (*) and the ampersand (&) are wildcard characters used specifically for this purpose in autofs maps.

That's it for the *auto_home* map. Refer back to the *auto_master* map. The third and final entry in the */etc/auto_master* file is:

```
/-              auto_direct
```

We added this entry for our direct map. The special mount point /- means that the map name refers to a direct map. Therefore the real mount points are found in the direct map file. We named our direct map file */etc/auto_direct*. There is no default direct map file. You must create it from scratch. The file we created is:

```
# Direct map for automounter
#
/home/research  -rw       filbert:/home/research
/usr/man        -ro,soft  pecan,almond,filbert:/usr/share/man
```

The format of entries in a direct map file is:

```
mount-point     options   remote filesystem
```

Our sample file contains two typical entries. The first entry mounts the remote filesystem */home/research* offered by the server *filbert* on the local mount point */home/research*. It is mounted read-write. The second entry mounts the **man** pages read-only with a "soft" timeout.* Note that three servers are specified for the **man** pages in a comma-separated list. If a server is unavailable or fails to respond within the soft timeout period, the client asks the next server in the list. This is one of the nice features of automounter.

---

* See the description of NFS mount options earlier in this chapter.

Automounter has four key features: the −hosts map, wildcarding, automounting, and multiple servers. The −hosts map makes every exported filesystem from every server listed in the */etc/hosts* file available to the local user. The wildcard characters make it very easy to mount every directory from a remote server to a like-named directory on the local system. Automounting goes hand-in-glove with these two features because only the filesystems that are actually used are mounted. While −hosts and wildcards make a very large number of filesystems available to the local host, automounting limits the filesystems that are actually mounted to those that are needed. The last feature, multiple servers, improves the reliability of NFS by removing the dependence on a single server.

NFS Authentication Server

The *PC NFS Authentication and Print Server* (**pcnfsd**) is needed to support non-UNIX clients on an NFS network. The print services of this daemon are covered in the next section. The authentication services are the services needed by NFS.

The reason NFS needs an authentication server for some clients springs from the difference between *trusted host* security and *password authenticated* security. Trusted host security is discussed in Chapter 12, *Network Security*. Essentially, it works this way: we trust that a remote host has already authenticated its users, and we grant those users equivalent access to our local host. This is more or less how NFS treats its clients. The Solaris **share** command grants NFS access to hosts. A user is allowed to access files through NFS using standard UNIX *user*, *group*, and *world* file permissions based on the *userid* (UID) and *groupid* (GID) provided by the trusted host. Remember, unless a **share** command option is used to restrict access, all hosts are trusted to access the shared filesystem.

The trusted host model does not work for non-UNIX clients for a couple of reasons. First, some systems do not perform local user authentication; for example, anyone who sits at the keyboard of a DOS PC has complete access to the system. Second, some systems do not employ user or group IDs and do not have any values that can be mapped to the UNIX user or group file permissions. At best, an unauthenticated user can be granted world permissions.* We need a server that authenticates usernames and passwords and assigns UIDs and GIDs to the authenticated users. That's what the PC NFS authentication server does.

The authentication server can run on any system on the network. It is not necessary to run it on the NFS server, but that is the most common configuration. The PC NFS authentication server is not included in the software of all UNIX systems. It is included with our Linux system but not with our Solaris system. If it doesn't

---

* Users who have not been authenticated are assigned the user ID *nobody* and given world permissions.

come with your UNIX system, don't worry; the source code for **pcnfsd** is available from many anonymous FTP servers on the Internet. Download the source code. Compile the software with **make.*** If **pcnfsd** compiles without errors, copy the daemon into a system directory such as */usr/etc*. Then add code to start **pcnfsd** from a boot script. On a Slackware Linux system, simply uncomment the lines in the */etc/rc.d/rc.inet2* file that start **rpc.nfsd**.

Normally starting a daemon from **inetd** is an alternative to starting it from a boot script. However, Sun cautions against starting **pcnfsd** from **inetd** because the slow startup of this daemon can cause time-out errors.

Once the **pcnfsd** daemon is installed and running, the server authenticates usernames and passwords for its clients. Here's how. When the user asks to mount a remote filesystem, the client software prompts him for a username and password. It sends them to the authentication server. The server validates them against its */etc/passwd* file. A user that can successfully login to the server is consider to be a valid NFS user. The server sends the client the UID and GID that are assigned to the user in the *passwd* file. The client uses them for NFS access.

The authentication server must have an entry in the */etc/passwd* file for every user who needs NFS access. It is common for a large UNIX server, such as the mail server that has an account for every mail user, to be used as the authentication server.

NFS print services

NFS-based print services are easy to understand and simple to configure. The NFS server exports a printer spool directory to its clients, and the clients copy print files into that directory. **pcnfsd** sends files deposited in the directory to printers accessible to the server. Any printer defined by the server can be used.

To add NFS print service to an NFS server, first install **pcnfsd**. Next, make a print spool directory on the server for the print clients. Add the spool directory to the shared filesystems in the */etc/dfs/dfstab* file or */etc/exports* file, as appropriate for your system.

Finally tell **pcnfsd** what directory to use for spooling print jobs. Use the *spool* command in the */etc/pcnfsd.conf* configuration file to define the directory name on most systems. On others, for example our Linux system, define the directory on the **pcnfsd** command line. See the **pcnfsd** manpage for details.

Finished! Running **pcnfsd** and exporting the printer spool directory are all that is required to configure an NFS print server, assuming that the printers are already

---

* See *Networking Personal Computers with TCP/IP* by Craig Hunt (O'Reilly & Associates) for a full example of downloading, compiling, and installing **pcnfsd**.

properly configured. Check the printers by logging directly into the print server and issuing an **lpr** command for each printer you wish to test. See the following section on **lpr** and **lpd** if a printer is not properly configured.

Line Printer Daemon

The *Line Printer Daemon* (**lpd**) provides printer services for local and remote users. **lpd** manages the printer spool area and the print queues. **lpd** is started at boot time from a startup script. It is generally included in the startup of Linux and BSD systems by default, so you might not need to add it to your startup script. For example, it is started by the */etc/rc.d/rc.inet2* script on a Slackware Linux system.

The printcap File

When **lpd** starts, it reads the */etc/printcap* file to find out about the printers available for its use. The *printcap* file defines the printers and their characteristics. Configuring a *printcap* file is the scariest part of setting up a UNIX print server. It scares system administrators because the parser that reads the file is very finicky, and the syntax of the parameters in the file is terse and arcane. Most parser problems can be avoided by following these rules:

- Start each entry with a printer name that begins in the first column. No whitespace should precede the first printer name. Multiple printer names can be used if they are separated by pipe characters (|). One entry must have the printer name *lp*. If you have more than one printer on the server, assign *lp* to the "default" printer.

- Continue printer entries across multiple lines by escaping the newline character at the end of the line with a backslash (\), and by beginning the following line with a tab. Take care that no blank space comes after the backslash. The character after the backslash must be the newline character.

- Every field, other than the printer name, begins and ends with a colon. The character before the backslash on a continued line is a colon and the first character after the tab on the continuation line is a colon.

- Begin comments with a sharp sign (#).

The configuration parameters used in a *printcap* file describe the characteristics of the printer. These characteristics are called "capabilities" in the *printcap* documentation, but really they are the printer characteristics that **lpd** needs to know in order to communicate with the printer. Parameters are identified by names that are two characters long and are usually assigned a value. The syntax of the parameters varies slightly depending on the type of value they are assigned. Parameters come in three different flavors:

Boolean

> All *printcap* Boolean values default to "false." Specifying a Boolean enables its function. Booleans are specified simply by entering the two-character parameter name in the file. For example, :**rs**: enables security for remote users.

Numeric

> Some parameters are assigned numeric values. For example, :**br#9600**: sets the baud rate for a serial printer.

String

> Some parameters use string values. For example, :**rp=laser**: defines the name of a remote printer.

A glance at the manpage shows that there are many *printcap* parameters. Thankfully, you'll never need to use most of them. Most printer definitions are fairly simple, and most *printcap* files are small. Writing a *printcap* from scratch is often unnecessary. Ask the other system administrators on the newsgroup for your system. You'll be surprised how often others have already solved the problem and how willing they are to help.

Print servers usually have only one or two directly attached printers; any other printers defined in the *printcap* are probably remote printers. Most, if not all, of the printers defined in a client's *printcap* are remote printers.

```
#
# Remote LaserWriter
#
lw:\
        :lf=/var/adm/lpd-errs:\
        :lp=:rm=pecan:rp=lw:\
        :sd=/var/spool/lpd-lw:
```

The *lw* printer in this sample *printcap* file is a remote printer. The remote machine to which the printer is attached is defined by the :**rm=pecan**: parameter and the name of the remote printer on that machine is defined by the :**rp=lw**: parameter. The **lf** parameter points to the log file used to log status and error messages. Multiple printers can use the same log file. The final parameter, **sd**, defines the spool directory. Each printer has its own unique spool directory. Defining the remote printer in the client's *printcap* file is all that is needed to configure an LPD client.

LPD security

The line printer daemon uses trusted host security, and it can use the same security file (*hosts.equiv*) as the **r** commands.* All of the users on a host listed in the server's *hosts.equiv* file are permitted to use the server's printers. To restrict access

---

* See Chapter 12 for more information about the **r** commands and trusted host security.

to only those remote users who have accounts on the server, include the :**rs**: Boolean in the printer description in the *printcap* file. When :**rs**: is specified, only users who are logged into "like-named" accounts on a trusted host are granted access to the printer. This parameter is applied on a printer-by-printer basis, so it is possible to restrict access to a special printer while permitting broader access to the other printers on the system.

A problem with using the *hosts.equiv* file for printer access is that the file also grants "password-free" login access. It is common to want to share a printer without wanting to grant any other access to the print server. To accommodate this, **lpd** also uses the */etc/hosts.lpd* file for security. A trusted host defined in that file is given access only to printers, and the :**rs**: parameter works with this host just as it does with a host defined in the *hosts.equiv* file.

The syntax of the *hosts.lpd* file is exactly the same as the syntax of the *hosts.equiv* file. A *hosts.lpd* file might contain:

```
brazil
acorn
```

This example shows a file that restricts printer access to the users who are logged into *brazil* and *acorn*.

Using LPD

Print jobs are sent to the line printer daemon using the *Line Printer Remote* (**lpr**) program. The **lpr** program creates a control file and sends it and the print file to **lpd**. There are many possible **lpr** command-line arguments, but in general the command simply identifies the printer and the file to be printed, as in:

```
% lpr -Plj ch09
```

This command sends a file called *ch09* to a printer called *lj*. The printer can be local or remote. It doesn't matter as long as the printer is defined in the *printcap* file and therefore known to **lpd**.

The client software provides commands to allow the user to check the status of the print job. Table 9-2 lists these commands, their syntax, and their meaning.

Table 9-2: Line Printer Commands

Command	Usage
lpc restart [*printer*]	Starts a new printer daemon.
lpc status [*printer*]	Displays printer and queue status.
lpq −P*printer* [*user*] [*job*]	Lists the jobs in the printer's queue.
lprm −P*printer job*	Removes a print job from the queue.

In this syntax *printer* is the name of the printer as defined in the */etc/printcap* file, *user* is the username of the owner of a print job, and *job* is the job number associated with the print job while it is waiting in the queue. The keyword **all** can be used in place of a printer name in any **lpc** command to refer to all printers.

While **lpc** is primarily for the system administrator, the **status** and **restart** commands can be used by anyone. All of the commands shown in Table 9-2 are available to users.

The **lpq** command displays a list of jobs queued for a printer. Command-line arguments permit the user to select which printer queue is displayed and to limit the display from that queue to a specific user's jobs or even to a specific job. Here's an example of displaying the queue for the printer *laser*:

```
% lpq -Plaser
Rank    Owner      Job  Files                           Total Size
1st     tyler      405  ...                              5876 bytes
2nd     daniel     401  ...                             12118 bytes
3rd     daniel     404  ...                             12118 bytes
```

A queued print job can be removed by the owner of the job with the **lprm** command. Assume that *daniel* wants to remove print job number 404 shown in the example above. He enters the following command:

```
% lprm -Plaser 404
dfA404acorn dequeued
cfA404acorn dequeued
```

Along with the **r** commands, **lpd** and **lpr** were among the first commands created for UNIX to exploit the power of TCP/IP networking. Managing printers is primarily a system administration task. Only those aspects of LPD related to remote printing and network security are covered here.

Solaris Line Printer Service

The Solaris system uses the Line Printer (LP) print service that is used by most System V UNIX systems. LP offers the same type of service as LPD.

The LP configuration files are located in the */etc/lp* directory. These files perform the same basic function as the */etc/printcap* file does for LPD. However, the */etc/lp* files are not directly edited by the system administrator. On a Solaris system, printers are configured through administrative commands or through the Printer Manager window of the **admintool**. Figure 9-1 shows the Printer Manager window. Clients select *Add*, the *Access to Printer* from the Add Printer sub-menu of the Edit menu, and enter the name of the remote printer and its server in the window that appears. Servers share printers simply by selecting *Add Local Printer* in the same menu and configuring a local printer. By default, Solaris shares all local printers.

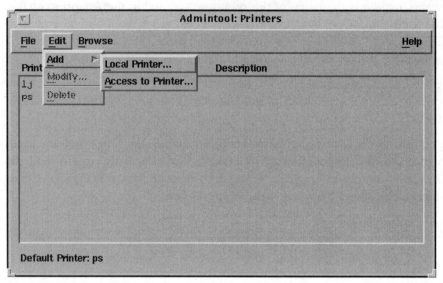

Figure 9-1: Printer Manager

Remote printer access is controlled by the */etc/lp/Systems* file. It comes pre-configured with the following entry:

```
+:x:-:s5:-:n:10:-:-:Allow all connections
```

As the comment at its end makes clear, this entry grants all remote systems access to the local printers. The first field defines the name of the host being granted access. When a plus (+) is used in this field, it means all hosts.

The fields in an */etc/lp/Systems* entry are separated by colons (:). The field containing an x and all of the fields containing a dash (-) can be ignored. These fields are unused.

The fourth field identifies the type of operating system used on the remote client. It contains either s5 for System V computers that use LP to print jobs, or bsd for BSD systems that use LPD.

The n in the sixth field indicates that this "connection" should never be timed out and removed from the system. A timeout period in minutes could be entered in this field, but this is not usually done. Keep the connection available as long as the local server is up. The 10 is a related value. It indicates that if a connection to a remote system fails, it should be retried after 10 minutes. This is a good value. It is long enough to give the remote system a chance to restart after a crash. Both n and 10 are the defaults and don't usually need to be changed.

Don't directly edit the */etc/lp/Systems* file. Modify it with the **lpsystem** command. To remove a system from the *Systems* file, use **lpsystem** with the −r *hostname* command-line argument, where *hostname* is the value in the first field of the entry you wish to delete. For example, to remove the plus sign (+) entry from the default */etc/lp/Systems* file, type:

```
# lpsystem -r +
```

To add an entry to the *Systems* file, use the **lpsystem** command without the **−r** option. For example, to add a BSD system named *macadamia*, enter:

```
# lpsystem -t bsd -y "Linux PC in room 820" macadamia
```

The command adds the following entry to the *Systems* file:

```
macadamia:x:-:bsd:-:n:10:-:-:Linux PC in room 820
```

The **−t** command-line option defines the operating system type. The **−y** option defines the comment; *macadamia* is, of course, the hostname. We accepted the default values for the timeout and the retry intervals. These could have been modified from the command line using the **−T** *timeout* and the **−R** *retry* options. See the manpage for **lpsystem** for more information.

All UNIX systems provide some technique for sharing printers. The network administrator's task is to ensure that the printers are accessible via the network and that they are properly secured.

Network Information Service

The *Network Information Service* (NIS)* is an administrative database that provides central control and automatic dissemination of important administrative files. NIS converts several standard UNIX files into databases that can be queried over the network. The databases are called *NIS maps*. Some maps are created from files that you're familiar with from system administration, such as the password file (*/etc/passwd*) and the groups file (*/etc/group*). Others are derived from files related to network administration:

/etc/ethers
> Creates the NIS maps *ethers.byaddr* and *ethers.byname*. The */etc/ethers* file is used by RARP (see Chapter 2, *Delivering the Data*).

/etc/hosts
> Produces the maps *hosts.byname* and *hosts.byaddr* (see Chapter 3, *Network Services*).

---

* NIS was formerly called the "Yellow Pages," or *yp*. Although the name has changed, the abbreviation *yp* is still used.

/etc/networks

Produces the maps *networks.byname* and *networks.byaddr* (see Chapter 3).

/etc/protocols

Creates the two maps *protocols.byname* and *protocols.byaddr* (see Chapter 2).

/etc/services

Produces a single map called *services.byname* (see Chapter 2).

/etc/aliases

Defines electronic mail aliases and produces the maps *mail.aliases* and *mail.byaddr* (see Chapter 10, *sendmail*).

Check the maps available on your server with the **ypcat −x** command. This command produced the same map list on both our Solaris and Linux sample systems. Your server may display a longer list. Here is the list from my Solaris system:

```
% ypcat -x
Use "passwd"    for map  "passwd.byname"
Use "group"     for map  "group.byname"
Use "networks"  for map  "networks.byaddr"
Use "hosts"     for map  "hosts.byname"
Use "protocols" for map  "protocols.bynumber"
Use "services"  for map  "services.byname"
Use "aliases"   for map  "mail.aliases"
Use "ethers"    for map  "ethers.byname"
```

The advantage of using NIS is that these important administrative files can be maintained on a central server, and yet completely accessible to every workstation on the network. All of the maps are stored on a master server that runs the NIS server process **ypserv**. The maps are queried remotely by client systems. Clients run **ypbind** to locate the server.

The NIS server and its clients are a *NIS domain*—a term NIS shares with DNS. The NIS domain is identified by a NIS domain name. The only requirement for the name is that different NIS domains accessible through the same local network must have different names. Although NIS domains and DNS domains are distinct entities, Sun recommends using the DNS domain name as the NIS domain name to simplify administration and reduce confusion.

NIS uses its domain name to create a directory within */var/yp* where the NIS maps are stored. For example, the DNS domain of our imaginary network is *nuts.com*, so we also use this as our NIS domain name. NIS creates a directory named */var/yp/nuts.com* and stores the NIS maps in it.

While the NIS protocols and commands were originally defined by Sun Microsystems, the service is now widely implemented. To illustrate this, the majority of examples in this section come from Linux—not from Solaris. The syntax of the commands is very similar from system to system.

The command **domainname** checks or sets the NIS domain name. The superuser can make *nuts.com* the NIS domain name by entering:

```
# domainname nuts.com
```

The NIS domain name is normally configured at startup by placing the **domainname** command in one of the startup files. On Linux and Solaris systems, the value for the NIS domain name is taken from the */etc/defaultdomain* file. This file is used as input to a **domainname** command in one of the startup files. As shown below, *defaultdomain* contains only the name of the NIS domain.

```
% cat /etc/defaultdomain
nuts.com
```

Initialize the NIS server and build the initial maps with **make**. The */var/yp/Makefile* contains the instructions needed to build the maps. As noted above, it creates a directory using the NIS domain name. The Makefile reads the files in the */etc* directory and places maps created from them in the new directory. To initialize a Linux system as a NIS server:

```
# domainname nuts.com
# cd /var/yp
# make
make[1]: Entering directory '/var/yp/nuts.com'
Updating hosts.byname...
Updating hosts.byaddr...
Updating networks.byaddr...
Updating networks.byname...
Updating protocols.bynumber...
Updating protocols.byname...
Updating rpc.byname...
Updating rpc.bynumber...
Updating services.byname...
Updating passwd.byname...
Updating passwd.byuid...
Updating group.byname...
Updating group.bygid...
Updating netid.byname...
make[1]: Leaving directory '/var/yp/nuts.com'
```

After initializing the maps, start the NIS server process **ypserv** and the NIS binder process **ypbind**.

```
# ypserv
# ypbind
```

Our system is now running as both a NIS server and a NIS client. A quick test with **ypwhich** shows that we are bound to the correct server. **ypcat** or **ypmatch** test that we can retrieve data from the server.

```
# ypwhich
localhost
# ypcat hosts
172.16.55.105              cow cow.nuts.com
172.16.55.106              pig pig.nuts.com
172.16.26.36              island.nuts.com island
127.0.0.1                localhost
```

The clients need only to define the correct domain name and to run the binder software **ypbind**:

```
# domainname nuts.com
# ypbind
```

Most NIS clients use **ypbind** to locate the server. Using the NIS domain name, **ypbind** broadcasts a request for a server for that domain. The first server that responds is the server to which the client "binds." The theory is that the server that responds quickest is the server with the least workload. Generally this works well. However, it is possible for the client to bind to an inappropriate system, e.g., a system that was accidentally configured to run **ypserv** or one that was maliciously configured to be a false server. Because of this possibility, some systems allow you to explicitly configure the server to which the client will bind. Linux provides the */etc/yp.conf* file for this purpose. The syntax of the entries in different versions of this file varies, so see your system documentation before attempting to use it.

Place the NIS domain name in the */etc/defaultdomain* file and the **ypserv** and **ypbind** commands in a startup file so that the NIS setup will survive the boot. These commands may already be in your startup file. On our Linux client all we needed to do was uncomment the appropriate lines in */etc/rc.d/rc.inet2*. On the Linux NIS server it was a little more complicated. In addition to uncommenting the lines for **domainname** and **ypbind** we added lines to start **ypserv**.

NIS is a possible alternative to DNS but most systems use both NIS and DNS. Hostnames can be converted to IP addresses by DNS, NIS, and the host file. The order in which the various sources are queried is defined in the *nsswitch.conf* file.

The nsswitch.conf file

The Name Service Switch file (*nsswitch.conf*) defines the order in which the sources of information are searched. Despite its name, it applies to more than just name service. All of the databases handled by NIS are covered by the *nsswitch.conf* file, as shown in this example:

```
hosts:      dns  nis  files
networks:   nis  [NOTFOUND=return]  files
services:   nis  files
protocols:  nis  files
```

The first entry in the file says that a hostname lookup is first passed to DNS for resolution; if DNS fails to find a match, the lookup is then passed to NIS and finally looked up in the *hosts* file. The second entry says that network names are looked up through NIS. The [NOTFOUND=return] string says to use the *networks* file only if NIS fails to respond, that is, if NIS is down. In this case, if NIS answers that it cannot find the requested network name, terminate the search. The last two entries search for services port and protocol numbers through NIS and then in the files in the */etc* directory.

NIS+

Before leaving the topic of NIS, we should say a word about NIS+. It is just a short discussion, because I do not use NIS+ and I do not know much about it.

NIS+ replaces NIS on Sun systems. It is not a new version of NIS, but a completely new software product that provides all of the functionality of NIS and some new features. The new features are:

- Improved security. NIS does not authenticate servers, as we noted in the **ypbind** discussion above, or clients. NIS+ provides authentication of users with a secure DES-encrypted authentication scheme. NIS+ also provides various levels of access so that different users have authority to look at different levels of data. NIS can only provide the same access to everyone in the NIS domain.

- A hierarchical, decentralized architecture. NIS+, like DNS, is a distributed, hierarchical database system. This allows for a very large namespace. It also allows distributed management of the information structure while maintaining consistent access to the data. NIS is a flat structure. All information about a NIS domain comes from a single master server and NIS domains are not interrelated.

- Enhanced data structures. NIS converts ASCII files into simple keyed files that the NIS+ documentation calls "two-column maps." NIS+ builds multicolumn database *tables*. Tables can be searched in a variety of ways to retrieve information about an entry. In addition, NIS+ tables can be linked together to provide related information about an entry.

Clearly NIS+ has some excellent new features and advantages over NIS. So why don't I use it? Good question! The hierarchical architecture and enhanced data structures are important if you have a very large network and lots of data in your namespace. However, many sites evolved using NIS on local subnets and do not see the need to move the entire enterprise under NIS+. Improved security seems like a real winner, but sites with low security requirements don't see the need for additional security and sites with high security requirements may already be behind a firewall that blocks external NIS queries. Additionally, NIS+ is not available for as many operating systems as NIS. Taken together, these reasons have slowed the move to NIS+.

To learn more about NIS+ and how to install it on your system, read the *NIS+ Transition Guide*, the *Name Service Configuration Guide*, and the *Name Service Administration Guide*. All of these are available from Sun as part of the Solaris System and Network Administration manual set.

NIS and NIS+ provide a wide range of system configuration information to their clients. However, they cannot provide all of the information needed to configure a TCP/IP system. In the next two sections, we look at configuration servers that can do the entire job.

A BOOTP Server

A UNIX system becomes a BOOTP server when it runs the BOOTP daemon (**bootpd**). Some systems, such as Linux, include the daemon with the operating system. Other systems, like Solaris, do not. Even systems that provide **bootpd** as part of the system software do not run the daemon by default.

There are two ways to run the BOOTP daemon: it can be started at boot time from a startup script or it can be started by the *Internet daemon*, **inetd**. If the server has a large number of clients that are frequently rebooted, run **bootpd** from a startup file. Starting **bootpd** in this manner reduces the amount of "startup" overhead because the daemon is only started once. Possible lines for starting **bootpd** from the *rc.inet2* file on a Slackware Linux system are:

```
if [ -f /usr/sbin/bootpd -a -f /etc/bootptab ]; then
    echo -n " bootpd"
    /usr/sbin/bootpd -s
fi
```

The code checks to make sure that the daemon and its configuration file are available. **bootpd** is then started with the **-s** switch. This switch tells **bootpd** to continue running and listening to the bootps port, and not to time out even if there is no activity on that port. The disadvantage of starting **bootpd** in this manner is that it continues to use system resources even when it is not needed. The preferred way to start **bootpd** is from **inetd**. To start it from **inetd** on a Slackware 96 Linux system, uncomment the **bootps** entry in the *inetd.conf* file and correct the path and daemon name.* The completed *inetd.conf* entry is:

```
bootps     dgram     udp wait root /usr/sbin/bootpd     bootpd
```

---

* The Slackware 96 *inetd.conf* file attempts to start **in.bootpd** instead of **bootpd**, which is the actual name of the daemon on that system. I'm sure this will be corrected in later releases of Slackware.

This entry tells **inetd** to listen to UDP port 67 identified as bootps in the */etc/services* file and, if it hears data on that port, to run */usr/sbin/bootpd* as user *root*. Once the line is added to the *inetd.conf* file, send a SIGHUP to **inetd** to force it to read the new configuration, as in this example:

```
# ps -acx | grep inetd
  93 ?  S    0:00 inetd
# kill -HUP 93
```

If your systems does not include BOOTP software, don't panic: **bootpd** is available from the Internet. The same software found in the Linux system can be downloaded in the *bootp-DD2.4.3.tar* file. Download and untar the source code. **su** to *root* and compile the server software with **make**. The Makefile has entry points for several different UNIX architectures. (For our sample Solaris system, we use the *sunos5gcc* entry point.) If the software compiles without errors do a **make install** to install the executable daemon in the */usr/sbin* directory. Do a **make install**.man to install the manpages in */usr/local/man.*

You should define all network services, including BOOTP, in the */etc/services* file. Add the following lines to your */etc/service* file when **bootpd** is installed:

```
    bootps          67/udp                      # bootp server
    bootpc          68/udp                      # bootp client
```

Finally, make sure that you include **bootpd** in the */etc/inetd.conf* file as shown earlier in this section. Once it is included and **inetd** is reloaded with a SIGHUP signal, you are ready to run.

Installing the daemon is only the beginning. The real challenge of managing a BOOTP server is providing the configuration information that clients need. The package found on Linux systems and in the *bootp-DD2.4.3.tar* file is the BOOTP daemon from Carnegie Mellon University (CMU). It has its own unique configuration commands. Other BOOTP server implementations use other configuration commands. However, the type of information provided by BOOTP is the same regardless of the implementation.

The CMU server reads its configuration from the */etc/bootptab* file. The syntax used in this file is very similar to the syntax of the */etc/termcap* and the */etc/printcap* files. Each **bootpd** configuration parameter is two characters long and is separated from the other parameters by a colon. The general format of a *bootptab* entry is:

```
hostname:pa=value:pa=value:pa=value...
```

Where *hostname* is the hostname of the client, *pa* is the two character parameter name, and *value* is the value assigned to that parameter for this client.

Newline characters separate each client's entry. If an entry spans multiple lines, the newline character at the end of each line must be escaped with a backslash (\).

Comments in the *bootptab* file begin with a sharp sign (#). Table 9-3 contains a list of the *bootptab* configuration parameters.

Table 9-3: bootptab Configuration Parameters

Parameter	Description	Example
bf	Bootfile	:bf=null
bs	Bootfile size	:bs=22050
cs	Cookie servers list	:cs=172.16.3.7
df	Dump file	:df=/var/tmp/bootp_db.dump
dn	Domain name	:dn=nuts.com
ds	Domain name servers list	:ds=172.16.35.5
ef	Vendor extension file	:ef=/usr/local/xyz.extensions
gw	Gateways list	:gw=128.2.13.1
ha	Hardware address	:ha=7FF8100000AF
hd	Bootfile directory	:hd=/usr/boot
hn	Send hostname boolean	:hn
ht	Hardware type	:ht=ethernet
im	Impress servers list	:im=172.16.8.12
ip	Host IP address	:ip=172.16.11.1
lg	Log servers list	:lg=172.16.12.1
lp	LPR servers list	:lp=172.16.6.6
ns	IEN-116 name servers list	:ns=172.16.12.6
nt	Network Time Protocol server list	:nt=172.16.50.30
ra	Reply address list	:ra=172.16.12.255
rl	Resource location servers	:rl=172.16.99.35
sa	TFTP server	:sa=172.16.12.1
sm	Subnet mask	:sm=255.255.255.0
sw	Swap server	:sw=172.16.12.56
T*n*	Vendor extension *n*	:T132="12345927AD3B"
tc	Template continuation	:tc=default1
td	Secure TFTP directory	:td=/tftpboot
to	Time offset	:to=18000
ts	Time servers list	:ts=172.16.12.1
vm	Vendor magic cookie selector	:vm=auto
yd	NIS domain name	:yd=nuts
ys	NIS server	:ys=172.16.12.1

Every parameter in Table 9-3 that has the word "list" in its description accepts a list of whitespace-separated values. For example, the name server list is defined using the *ds* parameter in this format: **:ds=172.16.12.1 172.16.7.3:**. One parameter in the table, *hn*, is a Boolean. If it is specified, the server sends the *hostname* from the *bootptab* entry to the client. As a Boolean *hn* does not take any values, but all the other parameters do.

Use these parameters to configure TCP/IP for each client on your network. The following sample *bootptab* file defines the domain name, name servers, the default routers, the Ethernet addresses, the hostnames, the IP addresses, the print servers, and the subnet masks for three different systems. (Don't worry about the details yet; each command will be explained later.)

```
#  /etc/bootptab file for nuts.com
acorn:\
        :hd=/usr/boot:bf=null:\
        :ds=172.16.12.1 172.16.3.5:\
        :sm=255.255.255.0:\
        :lp=172.16.12.1:\
        :gw=172.16.3.25:\
        :ht=1:ha=0080c7aaa804:\
        :dn=nuts.com:hn:ip=172.16.3.4:
peanut:\
        :hd=/usr/boot:bf=null:\
        :ds=172.16.12.1 172.16.3.5:\
        :sm=255.255.255.0:\
        :lp=172.16.12.1:\
        :gw=172.16.12.1:\
        :ht=1:ha=0800200159C3:\
        :dn=nuts.com:hn:ip=172.16.12.2:
hickory:\
        :hd=/usr/boot:bf=null:\
        :ds=172.16.12.1 172.16.3.5:\
        :sm=255.255.255.0:\
        :lp=172.16.12.1:\
        :gw=172.16.3.25:\
        :ht=1:ha=0000c0a15e10:\
        :dn=nuts.com:hn:ip=172.16.3.16
```

Notice that much of the information is repetitive. All of the clients use the same domain name, name servers, subnet masks, and print servers. Systems on the same subnets also use the same default routers. It is possible to define repetitive information in templates that are then referenced in individual client configurations. The following example uses a global template that defines the domain name, name servers, subnet mask, and print servers. The template is then referenced in each of the subsequent configurations by using the **tc** parameter.

```
#  /etc/bootptab file for nuts.com
defaults:\
        :hd=/usr/boot:\
        :dn=nuts.com:ds=172.16.12.1 172.16.3.5:\
        :sm=255.255.255.0:\
        :lp=172.16.12.1:\
        :hn:
acorn:\
        :tc=defaults:\
        :bf=null:\
        :gw=172.16.3.25:\
```

```
        :ht=1:ha=0080c7aaa804:\
        :ip=172.16.3.4:
peanut:\
        :tc=defaults:\
        :bf=null:\
        :gw=172.16.12.1:\
        :ht=1:ha=0800200159C3:\
        :ip=172.16.12.2:
hickory:\
        :tc=defaults:\
        :bf=null:\
        :gw=172.16.3.25:\
        :ht=1:ha=0000c0a15e10:\
        :ip=172.16.3.16:
```

The first entry, *defaults*, is the template. The remaining entries are client entries. The template defines information used by all of the hosts and the specific client entries define information unique to those hosts. Looking at the template and at one of the host entries shows a full configuration. First, let's examine the meaning of each parameter in the *defaults* template:

defaults: \

> The name by which this template is referenced is *defaults*. A template can be assigned any name as long as it doesn't conflict with any hostname in the *bootptab* file.

:hd=/usr/boot: \

> The first line of the *defaults* template defines the boot directory (*hd*). BOOTP clients can be diskless systems that boot from the server. The value provided by **hd** is used by a diskless system to retrieve the boot image. This directory is not used by our clients, but could be needed if a terminal server, router, or other diskless device was added to the network.

:dn=nuts.com:ds=172.16.12.1 172.16.3.5: \

> This line defines the domain name and the addresses of the domain name servers. The **dn** parameter defines the domain name as *nuts.com*. The **ds** parameter defines the IP addresses of the name servers used on this network.

:sm=255.255.255.0: \

> The **sm** parameter defines this network's subnet mask.

:lp=172.16.12.1: \

> This parameter defines the IP address of an **lpr** server that is available to every system on the network.

:hn:

> The **hn** parameter tells the server to send the hostname to the client. When this parameter is incorporated in the *peanut* entry as part of this template, the server sends the name *peanut* to the client. When it is incorporated in the

entry for *acorn*, the name *acorn* is sent. Because this is the last line in the *defaults* template, it does not end with a backslash.

Now let's look at the parameters in a client entry:

acorn: \
The hostname associated with this client entry is *acorn*.

:tc=defaults: \
This **tc** parameter tells **bootpd** to incorporate all of the information defined in the *defaults* template into this client entry. To use multiple templates in a client entry, include multiple **tc** parameters. Exclude an individual parameter from a template by specifying the parameter preceded by an at-sign (@). For example, to exclude the **lpr** server parameter provided by the *defaults* template from inclusion in the *acorn* configuration, we could have added :@lp: to the *acorn* entry.

:bf=null: \
The **bf** parameter defines the name of the boot file for diskless systems. In the sample, the parameter intentionally points to a file that does not exist because the client has a disk and we want it to boot from its local disk. When a client has its own disk, a value is not required in this field. However, in this case, the value is commonly set to "null" to ensure that if the client accidently has a boot file value in its BOOTREQUEST packet, the value will be overwritten by the server.

:gw=172.16.3.25: \
The default gateway for this subnet is 172.16.3.25.

:ht=1:ha=0080c7aaa804: \
The **ht** parameter identifies the type of hardware used for the client's network interface. The hardware type is identified by a number or by a keyword. There are several possible values but only two are meaningful: **ht** will be either 1 for Ethernet or 6 for Token Ring. See the *bootptab* manpage if you're interested in the other, rarely used, values.

The **ha** parameter defines the physical hardware address associated with the client's network interface. The example shows an Ethernet address. The type of address provided must be consistent with the hardware type defined by the **ht** parameter. These two parameters always appear together in a *bootptab* file.

:ip=172.16.3.4: \
The IP address for this client is 172.16.3.4.

With only three clients in the example, the benefit of using templates may not be immediately clear. The benefits of saving time, reducing typing, and avoiding errors are clearer when a large number of systems are involved.

It is possible to configure a BOOTP server to handle a very large number of clients. However, if a large number of clients rely on a single boot server and all of the clients attempt to boot at one time, the server can be overwhelmed. This might happen in the case of a power outage. There are two mitigating fators: Because most clients cache the configuration provided by the server in a local disk file, they are not completely dependent on the server; and the BOOTP protocol includes back-off algorithms that avoid contention problems. Still, it is possible for an overloaded server to cause a significant delay when booting its clients. One way to avoid problems is to have several boot servers. One server for each subnet is a good design because it eliminates the need to pass BOOTP information through a router, which requires a special configuration.

BOOTP gateway

Normally a BOOTREQUEST packet is not forwarded between networks because it is transmitted from the client using the limited broadcast address— 255.255.255.255. According to the RFCs, the limited broadcast address should not be forwarded, though it is possible to configure some routers to do so. The CMU BOOTP software provides a BOOTP gateway program that eliminates the need to create a special router configuration and allows you to put the configuration server on a different subnet from the BOOTP clients. The BOOTP gateway is **bootpgw**.

If your system includes BOOTP software, you may already have **bootpgw**. Linux includes **bootpgw**. If your system doesn't have it, it will when you download and install the *bootp-2.4.3.tar* file.

bootpgw is run as an alternative to **bootpd**. Both of these programs listen to the same port. The *inetd.conf* entry for **bootpgw** is:

```
bootps dgram udp wait root /usr/sbin/bootpgw bootpgw 172.16.12.1
```

inetd listens to the bootps port and starts the **bootpgw** program when data is received on that port. (Adding the bootps port to */etc/services* is covered above in the **bootpd** installation.) When **bootpgw** starts, it reads the hostname or address of the BOOTP server from the command line. In the example, the remote BOOTP server is 172.16.12.1. If the data received on the bootps port is a BOOTREQUEST packet, **bootpgw** retransmits the BOOTREQUEST as a unicast packet addressed directly to the remote configuration server.

At least one system on each subnet must run either **bootpd** or **bootpgw** to either reply to BOOTREQUEST packets or to forward them to a system that will. It is not possible to run both **bootpd** and **bootpgw** on one system and there is no reason to try. If the subnet has a local BOOTP server up and running, there is no need to forward BOOTREQUEST packets to another network. Use **bootpgw** on very small subnets that do not justify a local configuration server. On all other subnets, use a local BOOTP server.

BOOTP extensions

As described in Chapter 3, Dynamic Host Configuration Protocol (DHCP) is based on the Bootstrap Protocol (BOOTP). As you might expect, the DHCP enhancements are included in the **bootp-2.4.3.tar** file. Set the **–DDYNAMIC** option in the Makefile to compile the DHCP extensions into **bootpd**. The DHCP extensions add the following */etc/bootptab* configuration parameters:

:T254=*number*
> The *number* of addresses that can be dynamically assigned, written in hex.

:T253=*mode*
> The *mode* in which dynamic addresses are written into the updated *bootptab* file. If the mode is 0, addresses are written as IP addresses. If the mode is 1, addresses must be written as hostnames. If a hostname can't be found for a dynamically assigned address, the address assignment is not made when the mode is set to 1. If the mode is 2, the dynamic address is written to the *bootptab* file as a hostname if there is a valid hostname for the address. If there is not, the IP address is used. Mode 2 is the default and usually should not be changed.

:T250=*string*
> The *string* contains any additional configuration settings that should be provided to the DHCP clients in the form of *bootptab* parameters.

:dl=*time*
> The amount of *time* that the client can keep the address. The client must renew its request for the address before the amount of time specified with the **dl** parameter has elapsed. If the client does not renew its lease on the address, the server is free to assign the address to another client. If the **dl** parameter is not used, the address is permanently assigned.

To use these parameters in the *bootptab* file, create a special entry in the file that begins with the string **.dynamic–***n*. *n* in this string is a number from 1 to 32767. An example should make this clear. Assume that we want to automatically assign the addresses from 172.16.12.64 to 172.16.12.192, and that we want to manually assign the other addresses. We might enter the following in the *bootptab* file:

```
.dynamic-1:ip=172.16.12.64:T254=0x80:T250="gw=172.16.12.1:ds=172.16.12.3"
```

This defines a dynamic address group starting at 172.16.12.64. The group contains 128 (80 hex) available addresses. Tell clients assigned an address from this group to use 172.16.12.3 as a name server and to use 172.16.12.1 as a gateway.

When **bootpd** receives an address request from a client it creates an entry for the client using the information defined above, and physically appends that new entry to the end of the *bootptab* file. The first client request adds the following entry to the end of the *bootptab* file:

```
172.16.12.64:ha=0080c7aaa804:gw=172.16.12.1:ds=172.16.12.3
```

To assign the client a hostname instead of just an IP address, add hostnames to the domain server database for all of the addresses in the address group.

These extensions help **bootpd** provide services to DHCP clients. There are also software packages available that have been designed from the beginning to be DHCP servers.

DHCP

Dynamic Host Configuration Protocol provides three important features:

Backward compatibility
A DHCP server can support BOOTP clients. Properly configured, a DHCP server can support all of your clients.

Full configurations
A DHCP server provides a complete set of TCP/IP configuration parameters. (See Appendix D, *A dhcpd Reference*, for a full list.) The network administrator can handle the entire configuration for her users.

Dynamic address assignments
A DHCP server can provide permanent addresses manually, permanent addresses automatically, and temporary addresses dynamically. The network administrator can tailor the type of address to the needs of the network and the client system.

In this section we configure a DHCP server that supports BOOTP clients, performs dynamic address allocation, and provides a wide range of configuration parameters for its clients.

Several implementations of DHCP are available for UNIX systems. Some are commercial packages and some run on a specific version of UNIX. We use the Internet Software Consortium (ISC) Dynamic Host Configuration Protocol Daemon (**dhcpd**). It is freely available over the Internet and runs on a wide variety of UNIX systems, including both our Linux and Solaris sample systems. (See Appendix D for information on downloading and compiling **dhcpd**.) If you use different DHCP server software, it will have different configuration commands, but it probably performs the same basic functions.

dhcpd.conf

dhcpd reads its configuration from the */etc/dhcpd.conf* file. The configuration file contains the instructions that tell the server what subnets and hosts it services, and what configuration information it should provide them. *dhcpd.conf* is an ASCII text file that I find more readable than the *bootptab* file. The easiest way to learn about the *dhcpd.conf* file is to look at a sample.

```
# Define global values that apply to all systems.

default-lease-time 86400;
max-lease-time 604800;
get-lease-hostnames true;
option subnet-mask 255.255.255.0;
option domain-name "nuts.com";
option domain-name-servers 172.16.12.1, 172.16.3.5;
option lpr-servers 172.16.12.1;
option interface-mtu 1500;

# Identify the subnet served, the options related
# to the subnet, and the range of addresses that
# are available for dynamic allocation.

subnet 172.16.3.0 netmask 255.255.255.0 {
    option routers 172.16.3.25;
    option broadcast-address 172.16.3.255;
    range 172.16.3.50 172.16.3.250;
}

subnet 172.16.12.0 netmask 255.255.255.0 {
    option routers 172.16.12.1;
    option broadcast-address 172.16.12.255;
    range 172.16.12.64 172.16.12.192;
    range 172.16.12.200 172.16.12.250;
}

# Identify each BOOTP client with a host statement

group {
    use-host-decl-names true;
    host acorn {
        hardware ethernet 00:80:c7:aa:a8:04;
        fixed-address 172.16.3.4;
    }
    host peanut {
        hardware ethernet 08:80:20:01:59:c3;
        fixed-address 172.16.12.2;
    }
    host hickory {
        hardware ethernet 00:00:c0:a1:5e:10;
        fixed-address 172.16.3.16;
    }
}
```

This sample configuration file is similar to the example used above for *bootptab*. It defines a server that is connecting to, and serving, two separate subnets. It assigns IP addresses dynamically to the DHCP clients on each subnet and supports a few BOOTP clients. All of the lines that begin with a sharp sign (#) are comments. The first real configuration line defines a parameter for the server.

We begin the *dhcpd.conf* file with a set of parameters and options that apply to all of the subnets and clients served. The first three lines are parameters, which provide direction to the server. All three of the sample parameters define some aspect of how **dhcpd** should handle dynamic address assignments.

default-lease-time

> Tells the server how many seconds long a default address lease should be. The client can request that the address be leased for a specific period of time. If it does, it is assigned the address for that period of time, given some restrictions. Frequently, clients do not request a specific lifetime for an address lease. When that happens, the default-lease-time is used. In the example, the default lease is set to one day (86400 seconds).

max-lease-time

> Sets the upper limit for how long an address can be leased. Regardless of the length of time requested by the client, this is the longest address lease that **dhcpd** will grant. The life of the lease is specified in seconds. In the example, it is one week.

get-lease-hostname

> Directs **dhcpd** to provide a hostname to each client that is assigned a dynamic address. Further, the hostname is to be obtained from DNS. This parameter is a Boolean. If it is set to false, which is the default, the client receives an address but no hostname. Looking up the hostname for every possible dynamic address adds substantial time to the startup. Set this to "false". Only set this to true if the server handles a very small number of dynamic addresses.

We will use a few more parameters in this configuration. All of the parameters are documented in Appendix D, *A dhcpd Reference*.

The next four lines are options. The options all start with the keyword `option`. The keyword is followed by the name of the option and the value assigned to the option. Options define configuration values that are used by the client.

The meaning of the sample options is easy to deduce. The option names are very descriptive. We are providing the clients with the subnet mask, domain name, domain server addresses, and print server address. These values parallel those in the *bootptab* example shown earlier in this chapter.

DHCP, however, can do more than BOOTP. For sake of illustration we also define the maximum transmission unit (MTU). The sample `interface-mtu` option tells the client that the MTU is 1500 bytes. In this case the option is not needed because 1500 bytes is the default for Ethernet. However, it illustrates the point that DHCP can provide a very complete set of configuration information.

The subnet statements define the networks that **dhcpd** will serve. The identity of each network is determined from the address and the address mask, both of which are required by the subnet statement. **dhcpd** provides configuration services only to clients that are attached to one of these networks. There must be a subnet statement for every subnet to which the server physically connects—even if some subnets do not contain any clients. **dhcpd** requires the subnet information to complete its startup.

The options and parameters defined in a subnet statement apply only to the subnet and its clients. The meaning of the sample options is clear. They tell the clients what router to use and what broadcast address to use. The **range** parameter is more interesting, as it goes to the heart of one of DHCP's key features.

The **range** parameter defines the scope of addresses that are available for dynamic address allocation. It always occurs in association with a subnet statement, and the range of addresses must fall within the address space of the subnet. The scope of the **range** parameter is defined by the two addresses it contains. The first address is the lowest address that can be automatically assigned and the second address is the highest address that can be assigned. The first **range** parameter in the example identifies a contiguous group of addresses from 172.16.3.50 to 172.16.3.250 that are available for dynamic assignment. Notice that the second subnet statement has two **range** parameters. This creates two separate groups of dynamic addresses. The reason for this might be that some addresses were already manually assigned before the DHCP server was installed. Regardless of the reason, the point is that we define a noncontiguous dynamic address space with multiple **range** statements.

If a **range** parameter is defined in a subnet statement, any DHCP client on the subnet that requests an address is granted one as long as addresses are available. If a **range** parameter is not defined, dynamic addressing is not enabled.

To provide automatic address assignment for BOOTP clients, add the dynamic-bootp argument to the **range** parameter. For example:

```
range dynamic-bootp 172.16.8.10 172.16.8.50;
```

By default, BOOTP clients are assigned permanent addresses. It is possible to override this default behavior with either the **dynamic-bootp-lease-cutoff** or the **dynamic-bootp-lease-length** parameter. However, BOOTP clients do not understand address leases and they do not know that they should renew an address.

Therefore the **dynamic-bootp-lease-cutoff** and the **dynamic-bootp-lease-length** parameters are only used in special circumstances. If you're interested in these parameters, see Appendix D.

Each BOOTP client should have an associated host statement that is used to assign the client configuration parameters and options. It can be used to manually assign the client a permanent, fixed address. The sample configuration file ends with three host statements: one for *acorn*, one for *peanut*, and one for *hickory*. Each host statement contains a hardware parameter that defines the type of network hardware (ethernet) and the physical network address (e.g., 08:80:20:01:59:c3) used by the client. The hardware parameter is required in host statements for BOOTP clients. The Ethernet address is used by **dhcpd** to identify the BOOTP client. DHCP clients can also have associated host statements. For DHCP clients, the hardware parameter is optional because a DHCP client can be identified by the **dhcp-client-identifier** option. However, it is simpler for a DHCP client connected via Ethernet to be identified by its Ethernet address.

A wide variety of parameters and options can be defined in the host statement. For example, adding to each host statement an option similar to the following one assigns each client a hostname:

```
option host-name acorn;
```

It is often easier, however, to define options and parameters at a higher level. Global options apply to all systems. Subnet options apply to every client on the subnet, but the options defined inside of a **host** statement only apply to a single host. The **host-name** option shown above would need to be repeated with a different hostname in every host statement. An easier way to define a parameter or option for a group of hosts is to use a **group** statement.

A **group** statement groups together any other statements. The sole purpose of the **group** statement is to apply parameters and options to all members of the group. That is exactly what we do in the example. The **group** statement in the sample configuration groups all of the host statements together. The **use-host-decl-names** parameter in the **group** statement applies to every host in the group. This particular parameter tells **dhcpd** to assign each client the hostname that is declared on the host statement associated with that client, which makes the hostname option unnecessary for this configuration.

Given the sample *dhcpd.conf* file shown earlier, when **dhcpd** receives a BOOTREQUEST packet from a client with the Ethernet address 08:80:20:01:59:c3, it sends that client:

- The address 172.16.12.2

- The hostname *peanut*

- The default router address 172.16.12.1

- The broadcast address 172.16.12.255

- The subnet mask 255.255.255.0

- The domain name *nuts.com*

- The domain name server addresses 172.16.12.1 and 172.16.3.5

- The print server address 172.16.12.1

- The MTU for an Ethernet interface

The client receives all global values, all subnet values and all host values that are appropriate. Clearly DHCP can provide a complete configuration.

Your DHCP configuration, though larger in the number of systems supported, probably is simpler than the example. Some commands appear in the sample primarily for the purpose of illustration. The biggest difference is that most sites do not serve more than one subnet with a single configuration server. Servers are normally placed on each subnet. This reduces the burden on the server, particularly the burden that can be caused by a network-wide power outage. It eliminates the need to move boot packets through routers. Also, the fact that addresses are assigned at the subnet level makes placing the system that does that assignment at the subnet level seem somehow more logical. In the next section we look at how to keep distributed servers updated.

Managing Distributed Servers

Large networks have multiple servers. As noted earlier, the servers are often distributed around the network with a server on every subnet. This improves booting efficiency, but it conflicts with the goal of central configuration control. The more servers, the more dispersed the control, and the more likely that a configuration error will occur. Implementing distributed servers requires a technique for maintaining central control and coordinating configuration information among the servers. TCP/IP offers several techniques for doing this.

Any file transfer protocol can be used to move configuration data, or any other kind of data, from a central system to a group of distributed systems. Either FTP or TFTP will work, but both of these protocols present difficulties when used in this way. FTP and TFTP are *interactive* protocols; both require multiple commands to retrieve a file, making them difficult to script. Additionally, FTP requires password authentication before it grants access to a file and most security experts frown on storing passwords inside of scripts. For these reasons we don't concentrate on using these protocols to distribute the configuration file. Besides, if you know how to use FTP (and you should!), you know how to use it to send a configuration file.

Another possibility is to use *Network File System* (NFS) to distribute the information. NFS allows files on the server to be used by clients as if they are local files. It is a powerful tool, but it does have limitations when used to distribute configuration information to boot servers. The same power outage that affects the distributed servers can cause the central server to crash. The distributed servers and their clients can be delayed in booting waiting for the central server to come back online. Sharing a single copy of the configuration file conflicts with the effort to distribute boot services because it puts too much reliance on the central server.

One way to avoid this problem is for the distributed servers to periodically copy the configuration file from the mounted filesystem to a local disk. This is very simple to script, but it creates the possibility that the servers will be "out of sync" at certain times—the distributed servers copy the configuration file on a periodic schedule without knowing if, in the interim, the master file has been updated. Of course, it is possible for all of the remote servers to export filesystems that the central server mounts. It is then possible for the central server to copy the configuration file directly to the remote filesystems whenever the master file is updated. However, there are easier ways to do this.

The UNIX r-commands **rcp** and **rdist** provide the most popular methods for distributing the configuration file.

Remote copy (**rcp**) is simply a file transfer protocol. It has two advantages over FTP for this particular application: it is easy to script and it does not require a password. **rcp** is easy to script because only a single line is needed to complete a transfer. An example of transferring the file *bootptab* from the master server to a remote server named *pistachio.nuts.com* is:

```
# rcp /etc/bootptab pistachio.nuts.com:/etc/bootptab
```

For every remote server that the file is sent to, add a line like the one shown above to the procedure that updates the master configuration file.

rcp is only one choice for distributing the central configuration file. **rdist**, while a little harder to use, is often a better choice because it has several features that make it particularly well suited for this application.

rdist

The *Remote File Distribution Program* (**rdist**) is designed to maintain identical copies of files on multiple hosts. A single **rdist** command can distribute several different files to many different hosts. It does this by following the instructions stored in an **rdist** configuration files called a *Distfile*.

The function of a *Distfile* is similar to that of the Makefile used by the **make** command, and it has a similar syntax and structure. Now, don't panic! It's not that bad. The initial configuration of an **rdist** command is more difficult than the straightrward syntax of an **rcp** command, but the **rdist** command provides much more control and is much easier to maintain in the long run.

A *Distfile* is composed of *macros* and *primitives*. Macros can be assigned a single value or a list of values. If a list of values is used, the list is enclosed in parentheses, e.g., *macro = (value value)*. Once assigned a value, the macro is referenced using the syntax ${*macro*}, where *macro* is the name of the macro. The other components of a *Distfile*, the primitives, are explained in Table 9-4.*

Table 9-4: rdist Primitives

Primitive	Description
install	Recursively updates files and directories.
notify *address*	Sends error/status mail messages to *address*.
except *file*	Omits *file* from the update.
except_pat *pattern*	Omits filenames that match the pattern.
special "*command*"	Executes *command* after each file update.

The simplest way to understand how the primitives and macros are combined to make a functioning *Distfile* is to look at a sample. The following configuration file distributes the current version of **bootpd** and the latest *bootptab* configuration file to the remote boot servers *pecan*, *pistachio*, and *cashew*:

```
HOSTS = ( pecan root@cashew pistachio )
FILES = ( /usr/etc/bootpd /etc/bootptab )

${FILES} -> ${HOSTS}
        install ;
        notify craig@almond.nuts.com
```

Let's look at each line of the file:

HOSTS = (pecan root@cashew pistachio)
This line defines HOSTS, a macro that contains the hostname of each of the remote servers. Notice the entry for *cashew*. It tells **rdist** to login as *root* on *cashew* to perform the update. On *pecan* and *pistachio*, **rdist** will run under the same username it has on the local host.

FILES = (/usr/etc/bootpd /etc/bootptab)
This macro, FILES, defines the two files that will be sent.

---

* For more details, see the **rdist** manpage.

${FILES} -> ${HOSTS}

The -> symbol has a special meaning to **rdist**. It tells **rdist** to copy the files named at the left of the symbol to the hosts named at the right. In this case FILES is a macro that contains the file names */usr/etc/bootpd* and */etc/bootptab*, and HOSTS is a macro that contains the hostnames *pecan, cashew,* and *pistachio.* Therefore this command tells *rdist* to copy two files to three different hosts. Any primitives that follow apply to this file-to-host mapping.

install ;

The *install* primitive explicitly tells **rdist** to copy the specified files to the specified hosts if the corresponding file is out-of-date on the remote host. A file is considered "out-of-date" if the creation date or the size is not the same as the master file. The semicolon at the end of this line indicates that another primitive follows.

notify craig@almond.nuts.com

Status and error messages are to be mailed to *craig@almond.nuts.com.*

Additional files and hosts can be easily added to this file. In the long run most people find **rdist** the simplest way to distribute multiple files to multiple hosts.

One final note: the configuration file does not have to be called *Distfile.* Any file name can be specified on the **rdist** command line using the **–f** option. For example, the *Distfile* shown above could be saved under the name *bootp.dist* and invoked with the following command:

```
% rdist -f bootp.dist
```

Mail Servers

In this section we configure a system to act as a post office server. A post office server, or mailbox server, is a computer that holds mail for a client computer until the client is ready to download it for the mail reader. This service is essential to support mobile users and to support small systems that are frequently offline and thus not able to receive mail in real time. We look at two techniques for creating a mailbox server: *Post Office Protocol* (POP), which is the most popular protocol for this purpose, and *Internet Message Access Protocol* (IMAP), which is growing in popularity. We start with POP.

POP Server

A UNIX host turns into a POP mail server when it runs a POP daemon. Check your system's documentation to see if a POP daemon is included in the system software. If it isn't clear from the documentation, check the *inetd.conf* file, or try the simple **telnet** test from Chapter 4, *Getting Started.* If the server responds to the

telnet test, not only is the daemon available on your system, it is installed and ready to run.

```
% telnet localhost 110
Trying 127.0.0.1 ...
Connected to localhost.
Escape character is '^]'.
+OK POP3 almond Server (Version 1.004) ready
quit
+OK POP3 almond Server (Version 1.004) shutdown
Connection closed by foreign host.
```

This example is from a Linux system, which comes with POP3 ready to run. The Solaris system, on the other hand, does not ship with POP2 or POP3. Don't worry if your system doesn't include this software. POP3 software is available from several sites on the Internet where it is stored in both the *popper17.tar* and the *pop3d.tar* files. I have used them both and they both work fine.

If you don't have POP3 on your system, download the source code. Extract it using the UNIX **tar** command. *pop3d.tar* creates a directory called *pop3d* under the current directory, but *popper17.tar* does not. If you decide to use popper, create a new directory before extracting it with **tar**. Edit the Makefile to configure it for your system and do a **make** to compile the POP3 daemon. If it compiles without errors, install the daemon in a system directory.

Most network daemons are started by the Internet daemon, **inetd**. POP3 is no exception. Start POP3 from **inetd** by placing the following in the *inetd.conf* file:

```
pop3    stream tcp    nowait root    /etc/pop3d          pop3d
```

This entry assumes you are using **pop3d**, that you placed the executable in the */etc* directory, and that the port for this daemon is identified in the */etc/services* file by the name **pop3**. If these things aren't true, adjust the entry accordingly.

Make sure that POP3 is actually defined in */etc/services*. If it isn't, add the following line to that file:

```
pop3        110/tcp             # Post Office Version 3
```

Once the lines are added to the *services* file and the *inetd.conf* file, send a SIGHUP to **inetd** to force it to read the new configuration, as in this example:

```
# ps -ef | grep inetd
  root 109   1  0   Jun 09 ?   0:01 /usr/sbin/inetd -s
# kill -HUP 109
```

Now that POP3 is installed, rerun the test using **telnet localhost pop3**. If the POP3 daemon answers, you're in business. All users who have a valid user account on the system are now able to download mail via POP3 or read the mail directly on the server.

IMAP Server

Internet Message Access Protocol (IMAP) is an alternative to POP. It provides the same basic service as POP and adds features to support mailbox synchronization. Mailbox synchronization is the ability to read mail on a client or directly on the server while keeping the mailboxes on both systems completely up-to-date. On an average POP server, the entire contents of the mailbox are moved to the client and either deleted from the server or retained as if never read. Deletion of individual messages on the client is not reflected on the server because all of the messages are treated as a single unit that is either deleted or retained after the initial transfer of data to the client. IMAP provides the ability to manipulate individual messages on either the client or the server and to have those changes reflected in the mailboxes of both systems.

IMAP is not a new protocol—it is about as old as POP3. Nor is IMAP completely standardized. There have been four distinct versions of IMAP: IMAP, IMAP2, IMAP3, and the current version IMAP4. New RFCs about IMAP are still being issued. There are currently more than 10. The fear that IMAP is still in flux and that it is difficult to implement has discouraged some vendors, so it is not as widely implemented as POP. This is changing, however. The growing importance of email as a means of communicating, even when people are out of the office, increases the need for a mailbox that can be read and maintained from anywhere. The number of IMAP implementations is rising. Sun sells one for Solaris, another comes with Slackware 96 Linux in the */usr/sbin/imapd* file, and IMAP source code can be obtained via anonymous FTP from *ftp.cac.washington.edu*. We use the University of Washington source code to update IMAP on our Linux system for the examples in this section.

Download */mail/imap.tar.Z* from *ftp.cac.washington.edu* as a binary image. Uncompress and untar the file. This creates a directory containing the source code and Makefile needed to build IMAP.* Read the Makefile carefully. It supports many versions of UNIX. If you find yours listed in the Makefile, use the three-character operating system type listed there. For our Linux system we entered:

```
# make lnx
```

If it compiles without error, as it does on our Linux system, it produces three daemons: **ipop2d**, **ipop3d**, and **imapd**. We are familiar with installing POP2 and POP3. The new one is **imapd**. Install it in */etc/services*:

```
imap        143/tcp       # IMAP version 4
```

---

* The name of the directory tells you the current release level of the software. At this writing it is imap-4.1.BETA.

Also add it to */etc/inetd*:

```
imap  stream  tcp  nowait  root  /usr/sbin/imapd  imapd
```

Now basic IMAP service is available to every user with an account on the server.

A nice feature of the University of Washington package is that it provides implementations of POP2 and POP3 as well as IMAP. This is important because most email clients run POP3.* The IMAP server can only be accessed by an IMAP client. Installing POP2 and POP3 along with IMAP gives you the chance to evaluate IMAP and to provide it for your adventurous users while still supporting the majority of users.

POP and IMAP are mail access servers. There is a great deal more to configuring a complete email system, as we will see in the next chapter.

Summary

This chapter covers several important TCP/IP network services.

Network File System (NFS) is the leading TCP/IP file-sharing protocol. It allows server systems to share directories with clients that are then used by the clients as if they were local disk drives. NFS uses trusted hosts and UNIX UIDs and GIDs for authentication and authorization. **pcnfsd** provides password-based user authentication and NFS-based printer sharing for non-UNIX clients.

NFS-based printer sharing is not the only type of printer sharing available on a TCP/IP network. It is also possible to use the *Line Printer Daemon* (LPD). This software is originally from BSD UNIX but is widely available. The **lpd** program reads the printer definitions from the *printcap* file.

Network Information Service (NIS) is a server that distributes several system administrations databases. It allows central control of and automatic distribution of important system configuration information.

Bootstrap Protocol provides a wide range of configuration values to its client. Each implementation of BOOTP has a different configuration file and command syntax. The CMU BOOTP server stores configuration parameters in the */etc/bootptab* file and uses a syntax very similar to the */etc/printcap* syntax.

Dynamic Host Configuration Protocol (DHCP) extends BOOTP to provide the full set of configuration parameters defined in the *Requirements for Internet Hosts* RFC. It also provides for *dynamic address* allocation, which allows a network to make maximum use of a limited set of addresses.

---

* The pine mail client supports IMAP.

Large networks use distributed boot servers to avoid overloading a single server and to avoid sending boot parameters through IP routers. The configuration files on distributed boot servers are kept synchronized through file transfer, NFS file sharing, or the *Remote File Distribution Program* (**rdist**).

Post Office Protocol (POP) and *Internet Message Access Protocol* (IMAP) servers allow email to be stored on the mail server until the user is ready to read it. In the next chapter, we take a closer look at configuring an electronic mail system as we explore **sendmail**.

10

sendmail

Users have a love-hate relationship with email; they love to use it, and hate when it doesn't work. It's the system administrator's job to make sure it does work. That is the job we tackle in this chapter.

sendmail is not the only mail transport program. MMDF (Multichannel Memorandum Distribution Facility) predates sendmail and is still used today. There are also variations of basic sendmail, such as IDA sendmail, that are widely used. But plain sendmail is the most widely used mail transport program, and it's the one we cover.

This entire chapter is devoted to sendmail, and an entire book is easily devoted to the subject.* In part this is because of email's importance, but it is also because sendmail has a complex configuration.

The variety of programs and protocols used for email complicates configuration and support. SMTP sends email over TCP/IP networks. Another program sends mail between users on the same system. Still another sends mail between systems on UUCP networks. Each of these mail systems—SMTP, UUCP, and local mail— has its own delivery program and its own mail addressing scheme. All of this can cause confusion for mail users and for system administrators.

---

* See *sendmail*, by Costales and Allman (O'Reilly & Associates), for a book-length treatment of sendmail.

sendmail's Function

sendmail eliminates some of the confusion caused by multiple mail delivery programs. It does this by routing mail for the user to the proper delivery program based on the email address. It accepts mail from a user's mail program, interprets the mail address, rewrites the address into the proper form for the delivery program, and routes the mail to the correct delivery program. sendmail insulates the end user from these details. If the mail is properly addressed, sendmail will see that it is properly passed on for delivery. Likewise, for incoming mail, sendmail interprets the address and either delivers the mail to a user's mail program or forwards it to another system.

Figure 10-1 illustrates sendmail's special role in routing mail between the various mail programs found on UNIX systems.

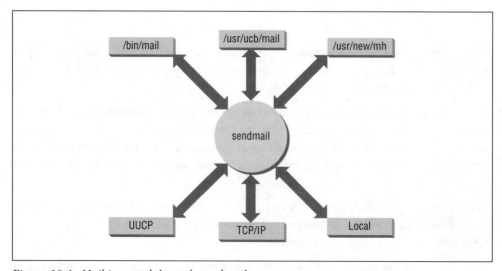

Figure 10-1: Mail is routed through sendmail

In addition to routing mail between user programs and delivery programs, sendmail:

- Receives and delivers SMTP (internet) mail
- Provides system-wide mail aliases, which allow mailing lists

Configuring a system to perform all of these functions properly is a complex task. In this chapter we discuss each of these functions, look at how they are configured, and examine ways to simplify the task. First, we'll see how sendmail is run to receive SMTP mail. Then we'll see how mail aliases are used, and how sendmail is configured to route mail based on the mail's address.

Running sendmail as a Daemon

To receive SMTP mail from the network, run sendmail as a daemon during system startup. The sendmail daemon listens to TCP port 25 and processes incoming mail. In most cases the code to start sendmail is already in one of your boot scripts. If it isn't, add it. The following code is from the Slackware Linux */etc/rc.d/rc.M* startup script:

```
# Start the sendmail daemon:
if [ -x /usr/sbin/sendmail ]; then
  echo "Starting sendmail daemon (/usr/sbin/sendmail -bd -q 15m)..."
  /usr/sbin/sendmail -bd -q 15m
fi
```

First, this code checks for the existence of the sendmail program. If the program is found, the code displays a startup message on the console and runs sendmail with two command-line options. One option, the **–q** option, tells sendmail how often to process the mail queue. In the sample code, the queue is processed every 15 minutes (**–q15m**), which is a good setting to process the queue frequently. Don't set this time too low. Processing the queue too often can cause problems if the queue grows very large, due to a delivery problem such as a network outage. For the average desktop system, every hour (**–q1h**) or half hour (**–q30m**) is an adequate setting.

The other option relates directly to receiving SMTP mail. The option (**–bd**) tells sendmail to run as a daemon and to listen to TCP port 25 for incoming mail. Use this option if you want your system to accept incoming TCP/IP mail.

The Linux example is a simple one. Some systems have a more complex startup script. Solaris 2.5, which dedicates the entire */etc/init.d/sendmail* script to starting sendmail, is a notable example. The mail queue directory holds mail that has not yet been delivered. It is possible that the system went down while the mail queue was being processed. Versions of sendmail prior to sendmail V8, such as the version that comes with Solaris 2.5, create lock files when processing the queue. Therefore lock files may have been left behind inadvertently and should be removed during the boot. Solaris checks for the existence of the mail queue directory and removes any lock files found there. If a mail queue directory doesn't exist, it creates one. The additional code found in some startup scripts is not required when running sendmail V8. All you really need is the sendmail command with the **–bd** option.

sendmail Aliases

It is almost impossible to exaggerate the importance of mail aliases. Without them, a sendmail system could not act as a central mail server. Mail aliases provide for:

- Alternate names (nicknames) for individual users
- Forwarding of mail to other hosts
- Mailing lists

sendmail mail aliases are defined in the *aliases* file.* The basic format of entries in the *aliases* file is:

```
alias: recipient [, recipient,...]
```

`alias` is the name to which the mail is addressed, and `recipient` is the name to which the mail is delivered. `recipient` can be a username, the name of another alias, or a full email address containing both a username and a hostname. Including a hostname allows mail to be forwarded to a remote host. Additionally, there can be multiple recipients for a single alias. Mail addressed to that alias is delivered to all of the recipients, thus creating a mailing list.

Aliases that define nicknames for individual users can be used to handle frequently misspelled names. You can also use aliases to deliver mail addressed to special names, such as *postmaster* or *root*, to the real users that do those jobs. Aliases can also be used to implement simplified mail addressing, especially when used in conjunction with MX records.† This *aliases* file from *almond* shows all of these uses:

```
# special names
postmaster: clark
root: norman
# accept firstname.lastname@nuts.com
rebecca.hunt: becky@peanut
jessie.mccafferty: jessie@walnut
anthony.resnick: anthony@pecan
andy.wright: andy@filbert
# a mailing list
admin: kathy, david@peanut, sara@pecan, becky@peanut, craig,
       anna@peanut, jane@peanut, christy@filbert
owner-admin: admin-request
admin-request: craig
```

The first two aliases are special names. Using these aliases, mail addressed to *postmaster* is delivered to the local user *clark*, and mail addressed to *root* is delivered to *norman*.

---

* The location of the file is defined in the "Options" section of the sendmail configuration file.

† Chapter 8, *Configuring DNS Name Service*, discusses MX records.

The second set of aliases is in the form of *firstname* and *lastname*. The first alias in this group is *rebecca.hunt*. Mail addressed to *rebecca.hunt* is forwarded from *almond* and delivered to *becky@peanut*. Combine this alias with an MX record that names *almond* as the mail server for *nuts.com*, and mail addressed to *rebecca.hunt@nuts.com* is delivered to *becky@peanut.nuts.com*. This type of addressing scheme allows each user to advertise a consistent mailing address that does not change just because the user's account moves to another host. Additionally, if a remote user knows that this *firstname.lastname* addressing scheme is used at *nuts.com*, he can address mail to Rebecca Hunt as *rebecca.hunt@nuts.com* without knowing her real email address.

The last two aliases are for a mailing list. The alias *admin* defines the list itself. If mail is sent to *admin*, a copy of the mail is sent to each of the recipients (*kathy*, *david*, *sara*, *becky*, *craig*, *anna*, *jane*, and *christy*). Note that the mailing list continues across multiple lines. A line that starts with a blank or a tab is a continuation line.

The *owner-admin* alias is a special form used by sendmail. The format of this special alias is **owner-***listname* where *listname* is the name of a mailing list. The person specified on this alias line is responsible for the list identified by *listname*. If sendmail has problems delivering mail to any of the recipients in the *admin* list, an error message is sent to *owner-admin*. The *owner-admin* alias points to *admin-request* as the person responsible for maintaining the mailing list *admin*. Aliases in the form of *listname*-**request** are commonly used for administrative requests, such as subscribing to a list, for manually maintained mailing lists. Notice that we point an alias to another alias, which is perfectly legal. The *admin-request* alias resolves to *craig*.

sendmail does not use the *aliases* file directly. The *aliases* file must first be processed by the **newaliases** command. **newaliases** is equivalent to **sendmail** with the **−bi** option, which causes sendmail to build the aliases database. **newaliases** creates the database files that are used by sendmail when it is searching for aliases. Invoke **newaliases** after updating the *aliases* file to make sure that sendmail is able to use the new aliases.*

Personal mail forwarding

In addition to the mail forwarding provided by *aliases*, sendmail allows individual users to define their own forwarding. The user defines her personal forwarding in the *.forward* file in her home directory. sendmail checks for this file after using the *aliases* file and before making final delivery to the user. If the *.forward* file exists,

---

* If the D option is used (see Appendix E, *A sendmail Reference*), sendmail automatically rebuilds the aliases database—even if **newaliases** is not run.

sendmail delivers the mail as directed by that file. For example, say that user *kathy* has a *.forward* file in her home directory that contains *kathy@podunk.edu*. The mail that sendmail would normally deliver to the local user *kathy* is forwarded to *kathy's* account at *podunk.edu*.

Use the *.forward* file for temporary forwarding. Modifying *aliases* and rebuilding the database takes more effort than modifying a *.forward* file, particularly if the forwarding change will be short-lived. Additionally, the *.forward* file puts the user in charge of his own mail forwarding.

Mail aliases and mail forwarding are handled by the *aliases* file and the *.forward* file. Everything else about the sendmail configuration is handled in the *sendmail.cf* file.

The sendmail.cf File

The sendmail configuration file is *sendmail.cf*.* It contains most of the sendmail configuration, including the information required to route mail between the user mail programs and the mail delivery programs. The *sendmail.cf* file has three main functions:

- It defines the sendmail environment.

- It rewrites addresses into the appropriate syntax for the receiving mailer.

- It maps addresses into the instructions necessary to deliver the mail.

Several commands are necessary to perform all of these functions. Macro definitions and option commands define the environment. Rewrite rules rewrite email addresses. Mailer definitions define the instructions necessary to deliver the mail. The terse syntax of these commands makes most system administrators reluctant to read a *sendmail.cf* file, let alone write one! Fortunately, you can avoid writing your own *sendmail.cf* file, and we'll show you how.

Locating a Sample sendmail.cf File

There is rarely any good reason to write a *sendmail.cf* file from scratch. Locate an existing file with a configuration similar to your system's and modify it. That's how you configure sendmail, and that's what we discuss in this section.

Sample configuration files are delivered with most systems' software. Some system administrators use the configuration file that comes with the system and make small modifications to it to handle site-specific configuration requirements. We cover this approach to sendmail configuration later in this chapter.

---

* The default location for the configuration file is the */etc* directory, but it is often placed in other directories, such as */etc/mail* and */usr/lib*.

Other system administrators prefer to use the latest version of sendmail. They download the *sendmail.tar* file and use the **m4** source files it contains to build a *sendmail.cf* file. The samples that come with your system are adequate only if you also use the sendmail executable that comes with your system. If you update sendmail, use the **m4** source files that are compatible with the updated version of sendmail.

The **tar** file can be downloaded via anonymous **ftp** from *ftp.sendmail.org*.* Login and change to the *pub/sendmail* directory. This displays a list of the available versions of sendmail. See Appendix E, *A sendmail Reference*, for an example of downloading and installing the sendmail distribution.

The sendmail *cf/cf* directory contains several sample configuration files. Several of these are generic files preconfigured for different operating systems. The *cf/cf* directory on my system contains generic configurations for BSD, Solaris, SunOS, HP Unix, Ultrix, OSF1, and Next Step. The directory also contains a few prototype files designed to be easily modified and used for other operating systems. We will modify the *tcpproto.mc* file, which is for systems that have direct TCP/IP network connections and no direct UUCP connections, to run on our Linux system.

Building a sendmail.cf with m4 macros

The prototype files that come with the sendmail **tar** are not "ready to run." They must be edited and then processed by the **m4** macro processor to produce the actual configuration files. For example, the *tcpproto.mc* file contains the following macros:

```
divert(0)dnl
VERSIONID('@(#)tcpproto.mc    8.5 (Berkeley) 3/23/96')
OSTYPE(unknown)
FEATURE(nouucp)
MAILER(local)
MAILER(smtp)
```

These macros are not sendmail commands; they are input for the **m4** macro processor. The few lines shown above are the important lines in the *tcpproto.mc* file. They are preceded by a section of comments, not shown here, that is discarded by **m4** because it follows a **divert(−1) command**, which diverts the output to the "bit bucket." This section of the file begins with a divert(0) command that means these commands should be processed and that the results should be directed to standard output.†

---

* Even if your UNIX system comes with its own version of sendmail, obtain the **tar** file for the useful documentation it contains, e.g., the *Sendmail Installation and Operation Guide*, by Eric Allman.

† The **dnl** option is used to prevent excessive blank lines from appearing in the output file. It affects the appearance, but not the function, of the output file. **dnl** can appear at the end of any macro command.

The VERSIONID macro is used for version control. Usually the value passed in the macro call is a version number in RCS (Release Control System) or SCCS (Source Code Control System) format. This macro is optional and we just ignore it.

The OSTYPE macro defines operating system–specific information for the *sendmail.cf* file. The *cf/ostype* directory contains more than 30 pre-defined operating system macro files. The OSTYPE macro is required and the value passed in the OSTYPE macro call must match the name of one of the files in the directory. Examples of values are: `bsd4.4`, `solaris2`, and `linux`.

The FEATURE macro defines optional features to be included in the *sendmail.cf* file. The *nouucp* feature in the sample shown above says that no special UUCP address processing is to be included in the output file. Recall that in the previous section we identified *tcpproto.mc* as the prototype file for systems that have no UUCP connections. Another prototype file would have different FEATURE values.

The prototype file ends with the mailer macros. These must be the last macros in the input file. The sample shown above specifies the local mailer macro, which adds the local mailer and the prog mailer to the output, and the smtp mailer macro, which adds mailers for SMTP, Extended SMTP, 8-bit SMTP and relayed mail. All of these mailers are described later in this chapter.

To create a sample *sendmail.cf* for a Linux system from the *tcpproto.mc* prototype file, copy the prototype file to a work file. Edit the work file by changing the OSTYPE line from `unknown` to `linux` to specify the correct operating system. In the example we use **sed** to change `unknown` to `linux`. We store the result in a file we call *linux.mc*:

```
# sed 's/unknown/linux/' < tcpproto.mc > linux.mc
```

Then enter the **m4** command:

```
# m4 ../m4/cf.m4 linux.mc > sendmail.cf
```

The *sendmail.cf* file output by the **m4** command is in the correct format to be read by the sendmail program.* In fact, the output file produced above is almost identical to the sample *linux.smtp.cf* configuration file delivered with Linux.

OSTYPE is not the only thing in the macro file that can be modified to create a custom configuration. There are a large number of configuration options, all of which are explained in Appendix E. As an example we modify a few options to create a custom configuration that converts *user@host* email addresses originating from our computer into *firstname.lastname@domain*. To do this, we create two new configuration files: a macro file with specific values for the domain that we

---

* New syntax and functions in the latest version of the *sendmail.cf* file may not be supported by older versions of the sendmail program.

name *nuts.com.m4* and a modified macro control file, *linux.mc*, that calls the new *nuts.com.m4* file.

We create the new macro file *nuts.com.m4* and place it in the *cf/domain* directory. The new file contains the following:

```
MASQUERADE_AS(nuts.com)
FEATURE(masquerade_envelope)
FEATURE(genericstable)
```

These lines say that we want to hide the real hostname and display the name *nuts.com* in its place in outbound email addresses. Also, we want to do this on "envelope" addresses as well as message header addresses. The last line says that we will use the generic address conversion database, which converts login user-names to any value we wish. We must build the database by creating a text file with the data we want and processing that file through the **makemap** command that comes with sendmail V8.

The format of the database can be very simple:

```
dan Dan.Scribner@nuts.com
tyler Tyler.McCafferty@nuts.com
pat Pat.Stover@nuts.com
willy Bill.Wright@nuts.com
craig Craig.Hunt@nuts.com
```

Each line in the file has two fields: the first field is the key, which is the login name, and the second field is an email address containing the user's real first and last names separated by a dot. Fields are separated by spaces. Using this database, a query for **dan** will return the value **Dan.Scribner@nuts.com**. A small database such as this one can be easily built by hand. On a system with a large number of existing user accounts, you may want to automate this process by extracting the user's login name, and first and last names from the */etc/passwd* file. The gcos field of the */etc/passwd* file often contains the user's real name.* Once the data is in a text file convert it to a database with the **makemap** command. The **makemap** command is included in the sendmail V8 **tar** file. It requires the ndbm library. The syntax of the **makemap** command is:

> **makemap** *type name*

makemap reads the standard input and writes the database out to a file it creates using the value provided by *name* as the filename. The *type* field identifies the database type. The most commonly supported database types for sendmail V8 are

---

* See Appendix E for a sample script that builds the realnames database from */etc/passwd*.

dbm, btree, and hash.* All of these types can be made with the **makemap** command.

Assume that the data shown above has been put in a file named *realnames*. The following command converts that file to a database:

```
# makemap hash genericstable < realnames
```

makemap reads the text file and produces a database file called *genericstable*. The database maps login names to real names, e.g., the key `willy` returns the value `Bill.Wright@nuts.com`.

Now that we have created the database, we create a new sendmail configuration file to use it. All of the **m4** macros related to using the database are in the *nuts.com.m4* file. We need to include that file in the configuration. To do that, add a DOMAIN(`nuts.com`) line to the macro control file (*linux.mc*) and then process the *linux.mc* through **m4**. The following **grep** command shows what the macros in the file look like after the change:

```
# grep '^[A-Z]' linux.mc
VERSIONID('@(#)tcpproto.mc     8.5 (Berkeley) 3/23/96')
OSTYPE(linux)
DOMAIN(nuts.com)
FEATURE(nouucp)
MAILER(local)
MAILER(smtp)
# m4 ../m4/cf.m4 linux.mc > sendmail.cf
```

Use the prototype *mc* files as the starting point of your configuration if you install sendmail from the **tar** file. To use the latest version of sendmail you must build a compatible *sendmail.cf* file using the **m4** macros. Don't attempt to use an old *sendmail.cf* file with a new version of sendmail. You'll just cause yourself grief. As you can see from the sample above, **m4** configuration files are very short and can be constructed from only a few macros. Use **m4** to build a fresh configuration every time you upgrade sendmail.

Conversely, you should not use a *sendmail.cf* file created from the prototype files found in the sendmail distribution with an old version of sendmail. Features in these files require that you run a compatible version of sendmail, which means it is necessary to recompile sendmail to use the new configuration file.† This is not something every system administrator will choose to do, because some systems don't have the correct libraries; others don't even have a C compiler! If you choose

---

* On Sun OS and Solaris systems, NIS maps and NIS+ tables are built with standard commands that come with those operating systems. The syntax for using those maps within sendmail is different (see Table 10-4). *Networking Personal Computers with TCP/IP*, by Craig Hunt (O'Reilly & Associates) provides an example of using a NIS map inside of sendmail.

† See Appendix E for information about compiling sendmail.

not to recompile sendmail, you can use the sample *sendmail.cf* file provided with your system as a starting point. However, if you have major changes planned for your configuration, it is probably easier to recompile sendmail and build a new configuration with **m4** than it is to make major changes directly to the *sendmail.cf.*

In the next part of this chapter, we use one of the sample *sendmail.cf* files provided with Linux. The specific file we start with is *linux.smtp.cf* found in the */usr/src/sendmail* directory on the Slackware 96 version of Linux. All of the things that we discuss in the remainder of the chapter apply equally well to *sendmail.cf* files that are produced by **m4**. The structure of a *sendmail.cf* file, the commands that it contains, and the tools used to debug it are universal.

General sendmail.cf Structure

Many *sendmail.cf* files have more or less the same structure because most are descendants of a few original files. Therefore, the files provided with your system probably are similar to the ones used in our examples. Some systems use a different structure, but the functions of the sections described here will be found somewhere in most *sendmail.cf* files.

The Linux file, *linux.smtp.cf,* is our example of *sendmail.cf* file structure. The section labels from the sample file are used here to provide an overview of the *sendmail.cf* structure. These sections will be described in greater detail when we modify a sample configuration. The sections are:

Local Information
Defines the information that is specific to the individual host. In the *linux.smtp.cf* file, Local Information defines the host name, the names of any mail relay hosts, and the mail domain. It also contains the name that sendmail uses to identify itself when it returns error messages, the message that sendmail displays during an SMTP login, and the version number of the *sendmail.cf* file. (Increase the version number each time you modify the configuration.) This section is usually customized during configuration.

Options
Defines the sendmail options. This section usually requires no modifications.

Message Precedence
Defines the various message precedence values used by sendmail. This section is not modified.

Trusted Users
Defines the users who are trusted to override the sender address when they are sending mail. This section is not modified. Adding users to this list is a potential security problem.

Format of Headers

Defines the format of the headers that sendmail inserts into mail. This section is not modified.

Rewriting Rules

Defines the rules used to rewrite mail addresses. Rewriting Rules contains the general rules called by sendmail or other rewrite rules. This section is not modified during the initial sendmail configuration. Rewrite rules are usually only modified to correct a problem or to add a new service.

Mailers

Defines the instructions used by sendmail to invoke the mail delivery programs. The specific rewrite rules associated with each individual mailer are also defined in this section. The mailer definitions are usually not modified. However, the rewrite rules associated with the mailers are sometimes modified to correct a problem or to add a new service.

The section labels in the sample file delivered with your system are probably different from these. However, the structure of your sample file is probably similar to the structure discussed above in these ways:

- The information that is customized for each host is probably at the beginning of the file.

- Similar types of commands, e.g., option commands, header commands, etc., are usually grouped together.

- The bulk of the file consists of rewrite rules.

- The last part of the file probably contains mailer definitions intermixed with the rewrite rules that are associated with the individual mailers.

Look at the comments in your *sendmail.cf* file. Sometimes these comments provide valuable insight into the file structure and the things that are necessary to configure a system.

It's important to realize how little of *sendmail.cf* needs to be modified for a typical system. If you pick the right sample file to work from, you may only need to modify a few lines in the first section. From this perspective, sendmail configuration appears to be a trivial task. So why are system administrators intimidated by it? In large part it is because of the difficult syntax of the *sendmail.cf* configuration language.

sendmail Configuration

Every time sendmail starts up, it reads *sendmail.cf*. For this reason, the syntax of the *sendmail.cf* commands is designed to be easy for sendmail to parse—not necessarily easy for humans to read. As a consequence, sendmail commands are very terse, even by UNIX standards.

The configuration command is not separated from its variable or value by any spaces. This "run together" format makes the commands hard to read. Figure 10-2 illustrates the format of a command. In the figure, a **define macro** command assigns the value *nuts.com* to the macro D.

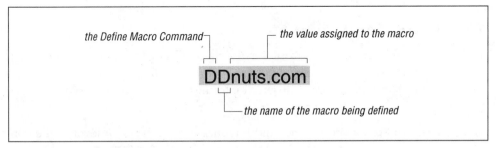

Figure 10-2: A sendmail.cf configuration command

Starting with version 8 of sendmail, variable names are no longer restricted to a single character. Long variable names, enclosed in braces, are now acceptable. For example, the define macro shown in Figure 10-2 could be written:

```
D{Domain}nuts.com
```

However, a quick check of the *sendmail.cf* delivered with my Linux system shows that not a single long variable name was used. The traditional, short variable names are still the most common. This terse syntax can be very hard to decipher, but it helps to remember that the first character on the line is always the command. From this single character you can determine what the command is and therefore its structure. Table 10-1 lists the *sendmail.cf* commands and their syntax.

Table 10-1: sendmail Configuration Commands

Command	Syntax	Meaning
Version Level	V*level*[/*vendor*]	Specify version level.
Define Macro	D*xvalue*	Set macro *x* to *value*.
Define Class	C*cword1*[*word2*]...	Set class *c* to *word1 word2* ....
Define Class	F*cfile*	Load class *c* from *file*.
Set Option	O*option=value*	Set *option* to *value*.

Table 10-1: sendmail Configuration Commands (continued)

Command	Syntax	Meaning
Trusted Users	T*user1*[*user2 . . .*]	Trusted users are *user1 user2 . . . .*
Set Precedence	P*name=number*	Set *name* to precedence *number.*
Define Mailer	M*name*, {*field=value*}	Define mailer *name.*
Define Header	H[?*mflag*?]*name:format*	Set header format.
Set Ruleset	S*n*	Start ruleset number *n.*
Define Rule	R*lhs rhs comment*	Rewrite *lhs* patterns to *rhs* format.
Key File	K*name type* [*argument*]	Define database *name.*

The following sections describe each configuration command in more detail.

The Version Level Command

The version level command is an optional command not found in all *sendmail.cf* files. You don't add a **V** command to the *sendmail.cf* file or change one if it is already there. The **V** command is inserted into the configuration file when it is first built from **m4** macros or by the vendor.

The *level* number on the **V** command line indicates the version level of the configuration syntax. V1 is the oldest configuration syntax and V7 is the version supported by sendmail V8.8.5. Every level in between adds some feature extensions. The *vendor* part of the **V** command identifies if any vendor specific syntax is supported. The default *vendor* value for the sendmail distribution is "Berkeley".

The **V** command tells the sendmail executable the level of syntax and commands required to support this configuration. If the sendmail program cannot support the requested commands and syntax, it displays the following error message:

```
# /usr/lib/sendmail -Ctest.cf
test.cf: line 63: Bad V line: Only V1/sun syntax is supported in
    this release
```

The error message shown above indicates that this sendmail program supports level 1 configuration files with Sun syntax extensions.* The example was produced on a Solaris 2.5.1 running the sendmail program that came with the operating system. In the example we attempted to read a *sendmail.cf* that was created by the **m4** macros that came with sendmail 8.8.5. The syntax and functions needed by the *sendmail.cf* file are not available in the sendmail program. To use this configuration file, we would have to compile a newer version of the sendmail program. See Appendix E for an example of compiling sendmail.

---

* See Table 10-4 for Sun-specific syntax.

You will never change the values on a **V** command. You might, however, need to customize some **D** commands.

The Define Macro Command

The define macro command (**D**) defines a macro and stores a value in it. Once the macro is defined, it is used to provide the stored value to other *sendmail.cf* commands and directly to sendmail itself. This allows sendmail configurations to be shared by many systems, simply by modifying a few system-specific macros.

A macro name can be any single ASCII character or, as of sendmail V8, a word enclosed in curly braces. User-created macros use uppercase letters as names. sendmail's own internal macros use lowercase letters and special characters as names. This does not mean that you won't be called upon to define a value for a macro with a lowercase name. A few of these internal macros are sometimes defined in the *sendmail.cf* file. Table 10-2 provides a complete list of sendmail's internal macros.[*]

Table 10-2: sendmail's Internal Macros

Name	Function
a	Origination date in RFC 822 format
b	Current date in RFC 822 format
c	Hop count
d	Date in UNIX (ctime) format
e	SMTP entry message
f	Sender "from" address
g	Sender address relative to the recipient
h	Recipient host
i	Queue id
j	Fully qualified domain name (host plus domain)
k	UUCP node name
l	Format of the UNIX from line
m	Name of this domain (domain only)
n	Name of the daemon (for error messages)
o	Set of "operators" in addresses[a]
p	Sendmail's pid
q	Default format of sender address[a]
r	Protocol used
s	Sender's hostname
t	Numeric representation of the current time
u	Recipient user

---

[*] See the *Sendmail Installation and Operation Guide* for more details on each internal macro.

Table 10-2: sendmail's Internal Macros (continued)

Name	Function
v	Version number of sendmail
w	Hostname of this site (host only)
x	Full name of the sender
z	Home directory of the recipient
-	Validated sender address

a. Obsolete in sendmail V8.

To retrieve the value stored in a macro, reference it as **$x**, where *x* is the macro name. Macros are expanded when the *sendmail.cf* file is read. A special syntax, **$&x**, is used to expand macros when they are referenced. The **$&x** syntax is only used with certain internal macros that change at runtime.

The code below defines the macros R, M, and Q. After this code executes, $R returns *almond*, $M returns *nuts.com*, and $Q returns *almond.nuts.com*. This sample code defines Q as containing the value of R ($R), plus a literal dot, plus the value of M ($M).

```
DRalmond
DMnuts.com
DQ$R.$M
```

If you customize your *sendmail.cf* file, it will probably be necessary to modify some macro definitions. The macros that usually require modification define site-specific information, such as hostnames and domain names.

Conditionals

A macro definition can contain a conditional. Here's a conditional:

```
DX$g$?x ($x)$.
```

The D is the define macro command; X is the macro being defined; and $g says to use the value stored in macro g. But what does "$?x ($x)$." mean? The construct $?x is a conditional. It tests whether macro x has a value set. If the macro has been set, the text following the conditional is interpreted. The $. construct ends the conditional.

Given this, the assignment of macro X is interpreted as follows: X is assigned the value of g; and if x is set, it is also assigned a literal blank, a literal left parenthesis, the value of x, and a literal right parenthesis.

So if g contains *chunt@nuts.com* and x contains *Craig Hunt*, X will contain:

```
chunt@nuts.com (Craig Hunt)
```

The conditional can be used with an "else" construct, which is $ | . The full syntax of the conditional is:

```
$?x text1 $| text2 $.
```

This is interpreted as:

- if ($?) *x* is set;
- use *text1*;
- else ($|);
- use *text2*;
- end if ($.).

The Define Class Command

Two commands, **C** and **F**, define sendmail classes. A class is similar to an array of values. Classes are used for anything with multiple values that are handled in the same way, such as multiple names for the local host or a list of **uucp** hostnames. Classes allow sendmail to compare against a list of values, instead of against a single value. Special pattern matching symbols are used with classes. The **$=** symbol matches any value in a class, and the **$~** symbol matches any value not in a class. (More on pattern matching later.)

Like macros, classes usually have single-character names, and user-created classes use uppercase letters for names. Class values can be defined on a single line, on multiple lines, or loaded from a file. For example, class w is used to define all of the hostnames by which the local host is known. To assign class w the values *goober* and *pea*, you can enter the values on a single line:

```
Cwgoober pea
```

Or you can enter the values on multiple lines:

```
Cwgoober
Cwpea
```

You can also use the **F** command to load the class values from a file. The **F** command reads a file and stores the words found there in a class variable. For example, to define class w and assign it all of the strings found in */etc/sendmail.cw*, use:

```
Fw/etc/sendmail.cw
```

You may need to modify a few class definitions when creating your *sendmail.cf* file. Frequently information relating to **uucp**, to alias hostnames, and to special domains for mail routing is defined in class statements. If your system has a **uucp** connection as well as a TCP/IP connection, pay particular attention to the class definitions. But in any case, check the class definitions carefully and make sure they apply to your configuration.

Here we **grep** the Linux sample configuration file for lines beginning with **C** or **F**:

```
% grep '^[CF]' linux.smtp.cf
Cwlocalhost
CP.
CO @ %
C..
CE root
```

This **grep** shows that *linux.smtp.cf* defines classes w, P, O, ., and E. w contains the host's alias hostnames. P holds pseudo-domains used for mail routing. O stores operators that cannot be part of a valid username. The class . (dot) is primarily of interest because it shows that variable names do not have to be alphabetic characters. E lists the usernames that should always be associated with the local host's fully qualified domain name, even if simplified email addresses are being used for all other users. (More on simplified addresses later.) In our sample file, the variables are all assigned default values.

Remember that your system will be different. The uppercase letters used for some of these class names mean that they are user-created classes. These same class names may be used for other purposes on your system, and are only presented here as an example. Carefully read the comments in your *sendmail.cf* file for guidance as to how classes and macros are used in your configuration.

The class names that are lowercase letters or special characters are reserved for internal sendmail use. All internal classes defined in sendmail versions after 8.8 are shown in Appendix E. Most of these can be ignored. Only class w, which defines all of the hostnames the system will accept as its own, is commonly modified in the *sendmail.cf* file.

The Set Option Command

The set option commands (O) command is used to define the sendmail environment. Use the **O** command to set values appropriate for your installation. The value assigned to an option is a string, an integer, a Boolean, or a time interval, as appropriate for the individual option. All options define values used directly by sendmail.

There are no user-created options. The meaning of each sendmail option is defined within sendmail itself. Appendix E lists the meaning and use of each option, and there are plenty of them.

A few sample options from the *linux.smtp.cf* file are shown below. The **AliasFile** option defines the name of the sendmail *aliases* file as */etc/aliases*. If you want to put the *aliases* file elsewhere, change this option. The **TempFileMode** option defines the default file mode as 0600 for temporary files created by sendmail in */var/spool/mqueue*. The **Timeout.queuereturn** option sets the timeout interval for undeliverable mail, here set to five days (5d). These options show the kind of general configuration parameters set by the **option** command.

```
# location of alias file
O AliasFile=/etc/aliases
# temporary file mode
O TempFileMode=0600
# default timeout interval
O Timeout.queuereturn=5d
```

The syntax of the option command shown in this example and in Table 10-1 was introduced in sendmail version 8.7.5. Prior to that the option command used a syntax more like the other sendmail commands. The old syntax is: O*ovalue*, where O is the command, *o* is the single character option name, and *value* is the value assigned to the option. The options shown in the previous discussion, if written in the old syntax, would be:

```
# location of alias file
OA/etc/aliases
# temporary file mode
OF0600
# default timeout interval
OT5d
```

Appendix E contains a full listing of the old options as well as the new options.

Most of the options defined in a sample file don't require modification. People change options settings because they want to change the sendmail environment, not because they have to. The options in your configuration file are almost certainly correct for your system.

Defining Trusted Users

The **T** command defines a list of users who are trusted to override the sender address using the mailer −f flag.* Normally the trusted users are defined as *root*, *uucp*, and *daemon*. Trusted users can be specified as a list of usernames on a single command line, or on multiple command lines. The users must be valid usernames from the */etc/passwd* file.

---

* Mailer flags are listed in Appendix E.

The most commonly defined trusted users are:

```
Troot
Tdaemon
Tuucp
```

Most sites do not need to modify this list.

Defining Mail Precedence

Precedence is one of the factors used by sendmail to assign priority to messages entering its queue. The **P** command defines the message precedence values available to sendmail users. The higher the precedence number, the greater the precedence of the message. The default precedence of a message is 0. Negative precedence numbers indicate especially low-priority mail. Error messages are not generated for mail with a negative precedence number, making low priorities attractive for mass mailings. Some commonly used precedence values are:

```
Pfirst-class=0
Pspecial-delivery=100
Plist=-30
Pbulk=-60
Pjunk=-100
```

To specify the precedence he desires, a user adds a Precedence header to his message. He uses the text name from the **P** command in the Precedence header to set the specific precedence of the message. Given the precedence definitions shown above, a user who wanted to avoid receiving error messages for a large mailing could select a message precedence of −60 by including the following header line in his mail:

```
Precedence: bulk
```

The five precedence values shown above are probably more than you'll ever need.

Defining Mail Headers

The **H** command defines the format of header lines that sendmail inserts into messages. The format of the header command is the **H** command, optional header flags enclosed in question marks, a header name, a colon, and a header template. The header template is a combination of literals and macros that are included in the header line. Macros in the header template are expanded before the header is inserted in a message. The same conditional syntax used in macro definitions can be used in header templates, and it functions in exactly the same way: it allows you to test whether a macro is set and to use another value if it is not set.

The header flags often arouse more questions than they merit. The function of the flags is very simple. The header flags control whether or not the header is inserted into mail bound for a specific mailer. If no flags are specified, the header is used for all mailers. If a flag is specified, the header is used only for a mailer that has the same flag set in the mailer's definition. (Mailer flags are listed in Appendix E.) Header flags only control header *insertion*. If a header is received in the input, it is passed to the output, regardless of the flag settings.

Some sample header definitions from the *linux.smtp.cf* sample file are:

```
H?P?Return-Path: $g
H?D?Date: $a
H?F?From: $?x$x <$g>$|$g$.
H?x?Full-Name: $x
HSubject:
H?M?Message-Id: <$t.$i@$j>
```

The headers provided in your system's *sendmail.cf* are sufficient for most installations. It's unlikely you'll ever need to change them.

Defining Mailers

The **M** commands define the mail delivery programs used by sendmail. The syntax of the command is:

```
Mname, {field=value}
```

name is an arbitrary name used internally by sendmail to refer to this mailer. The name doesn't matter as long as it is used consistently within the *sendmail.cf* file to refer to this mailer. For example, the mailer used to deliver SMTP mail within the local domain might be called *smtp* on one system, and it might be called *ether* on another system. The function of both mailers is the same, only the names are different.

There are a few exceptions to this freedom of choice. The mailer that delivers local mail to users on the same machine must be called *local,* and a mailer named *local* must be defined in the *sendmail.cf* file. Three other special mailer names are:

prog
    Delivers mail to programs.

file
    Sends mail to files.

include
    Directs mail to `:include:` lists.

Of these, only the *prog* mailer must be defined in the *sendmail.cf* file. The other two are defined internally by sendmail.

The mailer name is followed by a comma-separated list of *field=value* pairs that define the characteristics of the mailer. Table 10-3 shows the single character *field* identifiers and the contents of the *value* field associated with each of them. Most mailers don't require all of these fields.

Table 10-3: Mailer Definition Fields

Field	Meaning	Contents	Example
P	Path	Path of the mailer	P=/bin/mail
F	Flags	sendmail flags for this mailer	F=lsDFMe
S	Sender	Rulesets for sender addresses	S=10
R	Recipient	Rulesets for recipient addresses	R=20
A	Argv	The mailer's argument vector	A=sh -c $u
E	Eol	End-of-line string for the mailer	E=\r\n
M	Maxsize	Maximum message length	M=100000
L	Linelimit	Maximum line length	L=990
D	Directory	*prog* mailer's execution directory	D=$z:/
U	Userid	User and group ID used to run mailer	U=uucp:wheel
N	Nice	**nice** value used to run mailer	N=10
C	Charset	Content-type for 8-bit MIME characters	C=iso8859-1
T	Type	Type information for MIME errors	T=dns/rfc822/smtp

The Path (P) fields contain either the path to the mail delivery program or the literal string [IPC]. Mailer definitions that specify P=[IPC] use sendmail to deliver mail via SMTP.* The path to a mail delivery program varies from system to system depending on where the systems store the programs. Make sure you know where the programs are stored before you modify the Path field. If you use a sample configuration from another computer, such as the samples we use in this chapter, make sure that the mailer paths are valid for your system.

The Flags (F) field contains the sendmail flags used for this mailer. These are the mailer flags referenced earlier in this chapter under "Defining Mail Headers," but mailer flags do more than just control header insertion. There are a large number of flags. Appendix E describes all of them and their functions.

The Sender (S) and the Recipient (R) fields identify the rulesets used to rewrite the sender and recipient addresses for this mailer. Each ruleset is identified by its number. We'll have more to say about rulesets later in this chapter, and we will refer to the S and R values when troubleshooting the sendmail configuration.

The Argv (A) field defines the argument vector passed to the mailer. It contains, among other things, macro expansions that provide the recipient username (which

---

* Sun systems use [TCP] as well as [IPC].

is **$u**),* the recipient hostname (**$h**), and the sender's from address (**$f**). These macros are expanded before the argument vector is passed to the mailer.

The End-of-line (E) field defines the characters used to mark the end of a line. A carriage return and a line feed (CRLF) is the default for SMTP mailers.

Maxsize (M) defines, in bytes, the longest message that this mailer will handle. This field is used most frequently in definitions of UUCP mailers.

Linelimit (L) defines, in bytes, the maximum length of a line that can be contained in a message handled by this mailer. This mailer field was introduced in sendmail V8. Previous versions of sendmail limited lines to 80 characters because this was the limit for SMTP mail before MIME mail was introduced.

The Directory (D) field specifies the working directory for the *prog* mailer. More than one directory can be specified for the directory field by separating the directory paths with colons. The example in Table 10-3 tells *prog* to use the recipient's home directory, which is the value returned by the internal macro **$z**. If that directory is not available, it should use the root (/) directory.

Specify the default user and the group ID used to execute the mailer with the Userid (U) field. The example **U=uucp:wheel** says that the mailer should be run under the user ID *uucp* and the group ID *wheel*. If no value is specified for the Userid field, the value defined by the **DefaultUser** option is used.

Use Nice (N) to change the **nice** value for the execution of the mailer. This allows you to change the scheduling priority of the mailer. This is rarely used. If you're interested, see the **nice** manpage for appropriate values.

The last two fields are used only for MIME mail. Charset (C) defines the character set used in the Content-type header when an 8-bit message is converted to MIME. If Charset is not defined, the value defined in the **DefaultCharset** option is used. If that option is not defined, *unknown-8bit* is used as the default value.

The Type (T) field defines the type information used in MIME error messages. MIME-type information defines the mailer transfer agent type, the mail address type, and the error code type. The default is *dns/rfc822/smtp*.

Some common mailer definitions

The following mailer definitions are from *linux.smtp.cf*:

```
Mlocal, P=/usr/bin/procmail, F=lsDFMAw5:/|@ShP, S=10/30, R=20/40,
        T=DNS/RFC822/X-Unix, A=procmail -a $h -d $u
 Mprog, P=/bin/sh, F=lsDFMoeu, S=10/30, R=20/40, D=$z:/,
        T=X-Unix, A=sh -c $u
```

---

* In the *prog* mailer definition, **$u** actually passes a program name in the argument vector.

```
Msmtp,  P=[IPC], F=mDFMuX,  S=11/31, R=21, E=\r\n, L=990,
       T=DNS/RFC822/SMTP, A=IPC $h
Mesmtp, P=[IPC], F=mDFMuXa, S=11/31, R=21, E=\r\n, L=990,
        T=DNS/RFC822/SMTP, A=IPC $h
Msmtp8, P=[IPC], F=mDFMuX8, S=11/31, R=21, E=\r\n, L=990,
       T=DNS/RFC822/SMTP, A=IPC $h
Mrelay, P=[IPC], F=mDFMuXa8, S=11/31, R=61, E=\r\n, L=2040,
        T=DNS/RFC822/SMTP, A=IPC $h
```

This example contains the following mailer definitions:

- A definition for local mail delivery, always called *local*. This definition is required by sendmail.

- A definition for delivering mail to programs, always called *prog*. This definition is found in most configurations.

- A definition for TCP/IP mail delivery, here called *smtp*.

- A definition for an Extended SMTP mailer, here called *esmtp*.

- A definition for an SMTP mailer that handles unencoded 8-bit data, here called *smtp8*.

- A definition for a mailer that relays TCP/IP mail through an external mail relay host, here called *relay*.

A close examination of the fields in one of these mailer entries, for example the entry for the *smtp* mailer, shows the following:

Msmtp

A mailer, arbitrarily named *smtp*, is being defined.

P=[IPC]

The path to the program used for this mailer is [IPC], which means deliver of this mail is handled internally by sendmail.

F=mDFMuX

The sendmail flags for this mailer say that this mailer can send to multiple recipients at once; that Date, From, and Message-Id headers are needed; that uppercase should be preserved in hostnames and user names; and that lines beginning with a dot have an extra dot prepended. Refer to Appendix E for more details.

S=11/31

The sender address in the mail "envelope" is processed through ruleset 11 and the sender address in the message is processed through ruleset 31. More on this later.

R=21

All recipient addresses are processed through ruleset 21.

E=\r\n

> Lines are terminated with a carriage return and a line feed.

L=990

> This mailer will handle lines up to 990 bytes long.

T=DNS/RFC822/SMTP

> The MIME-type information for this mailer says that DNS is used for host-names, RFC 822 email addresses are used, and SMTP error codes are used.

A=IPC $h

> The meaning of each option in an argument vector is exactly as defined on the manpage for the command; see the *local* mailer as an example. In the case of the *smtp* mailer, however, the argument refers to an internal *sendmail* process. The macro **$h** is expanded to provide the recipient host (**$h**) address.

Despite this long discussion, don't worry about mailer definitions. The sample configuration file that comes with your operating system contains the correct mailer definitions to run sendmail in a TCP/IP network environment. You shouldn't need to modify any mailer definitions.

Rewriting the Mail Address

Rewrite rules are the heart of the *sendmail.cf* file. Rulesets are groups of individual rewrite rules used to parse email addresses from user mail programs and rewrite them into the form required by the mail delivery programs. Each rewrite rule is defined by an **R** command. The syntax of the **R** command is:

```
Rpattern     transformation     comment
```

The fields in an **R** command are separated by tab characters. The comment field is ignored by the system, but good comments are vital if you want to have any hope of understanding what's going on. The pattern and transformation fields are the heart of this command.

Pattern Matching

Rewrite rules match the input address against the pattern, and if a match is found, rewrite the address in a new format using the rules defined in the transformation. A rewrite rule may process the same address several times because, after being rewritten, the address is again compared against the pattern. If it still matches, it is rewritten again. The cycle of pattern matching and rewriting continues until the address no longer matches the pattern.

The pattern is defined using macros, classes, literals, and special metasymbols. The macros, classes, and literals provide the values against which the input is compared, and the metasymbols define the rules used in matching the pattern. Table 10-4 shows the metasymbols used for pattern matching.

Table 10-4: Pattern Matching Symbols

Symbol	Meaning
$@	Match exactly zero tokens.
$*	Match zero or more tokens.
$+	Match one or more tokens.
$-	Match exactly one token.
$=$x$	Match any token in class x.
$~$x$	Match any token not in class x.
$$x$	Match all tokens in macro x.
$%$x$	Match any token in the NIS map named in macro x.[a]
$!$x$	Match any token not in the NIS map named in macro x.[a]
$%y	Match any token in the NIS hosts.byname map.[a]

a. This symbol is specific to Sun operating systems.

All of the metasymbols request a match for some number of tokens. A token is a string of characters in an email address delimited by an operator. The operators are the characters defined in the **OperatorChars** option.* Operators are also counted as tokens when an address is parsed. For example:

```
becky@peanut.nuts.com
```

This email address contains seven tokens: becky, @, peanut, ., nuts, ., and com. This address would match the pattern:

```
$-@$+
```

The address matches the pattern because:

- It has exactly one token before the @ that matches the requirement of the **$-** symbol.

- It has an @ that matches the pattern's literal @.

- It has one or more tokens after the @ that match the requirement of the **$+** symbol.

Many addresses, *hostmaster@rs.internic.net*, *craigh@ora.com*, etc., match this pattern, but other addresses do not. For example, *rebecca.hunt@nuts.com* does not match because it has three tokens: rebecca, ., and hunt, before the @. Therefore, it fails to meet the requirement of exactly one token specified by the **$-** symbol.

---

* On older systems, they are defined in the *o* macro. See Appendix E.

Using the metasymbols, macros, and literals, patterns can be constructed to match any type of email address.

When an address matches a pattern, the strings from the address that match the metasymbols are assigned to *indefinite tokens*. The matching strings are called indefinite tokens because they may contain more than one token value. The indefinite tokens are identified numerically according to the relative position in the pattern of the metasymbol that the string matched. In other words, the indefinite token produced by the match of the first metasymbol is called $1; the match of the second symbol is called $2; the third is $3; and so on. When the address *becky@peanut.nuts.com* matched the pattern **$-@$+**, two indefinite tokens were created. The first is identified as $1 and contains the single token, *becky*, that matched the **$-** symbol. The second indefinite token is $2 and contains the five tokens—peanut, ., nuts, ., and com—that matched the **$+** symbol. The indefinite tokens created by the pattern matching can then be referenced by name ($1, $2, etc.) when rewriting the address.

A few of the symbols in Table 10-4 are used only in special cases. The **$@** symbol is normally used by itself to test for an empty, or null, address. The symbols that test against NIS maps, can only be used on Sun systems that run the sendmail program that Sun provides with the operating system. We'll see in the next section that systems running sendmail V8 can use NIS maps, but only for transformation—not for pattern matching.

Transforming the Address

The transformation field, from the righthand side of the rewrite rule, defines the format used for rewriting the address. It is defined with the same things used to define the pattern: literals, macros, and special metasymbols. Literals in the transformation are written into the new address exactly as shown. Macros are expanded and then written. The metasymbols perform special functions. The transformation metasymbols and their functions are shown in Table 10-5.

Table 10-5: Transformation Metasymbols

Symbol	Meaning
$*n*	Substitute indefinite token *n*.
$[*name*$]	Substitute the canonical form of *name*.
$(*map key* $@*argument* $:*default*$)	Substitute a value from database *map* indexed by *key*.
$>*n*	Call ruleset *n*.
$@	Terminate ruleset.
$:	Terminate rewrite rule.

The $n symbol, where n is a number, is used for the indefinite token substitution discussed above. The indefinite token is expanded and written to the "new" address. Indefinite token substitution is essential for flexible address rewriting. Without it, values could not be easily moved from the input address to the rewritten address. The following example demonstrates this.

Addresses are always processed by several rewrite rules. No one rule tries to do everything. Assume the input address *mccafferty@peanut* has been through some preliminary processing and now is:

```
kathy.mccafferty<@peanut>
```

Assume the current rewrite rule is:

```
R$+<@$->      $1<@$2.$D>    user@host -> user@host.domain
```

The address matches the pattern because it contains one or more tokens before the literal <@, exactly one token after the <@, and then the literal >. The pattern match produces two indefinite tokens that are used in the transformation to rewrite the address.

The transformation contains the indefinite token $1, a literal <@, indefinite token $2, a literal dot (.), the macro D, and the literal >. After the pattern matching, $1 contains *kathy.mccafferty* and $2 contains *peanut*. Assume that the macro D was defined elsewhere in the *sendmail.cf* file as *nuts.com*. In this case the input address is rewritten as:

```
kathy.mccafferty<@peanut.nuts.com>
```

Figure 10-3 illustrates this specific address rewrite. It shows the tokens derived from the input address, and how those tokens are matched against the pattern. It also shows the indefinite tokens produced by the pattern matching, and how the indefinite tokens, and other values from the transformation, are used to produce the rewritten address. After rewriting, the address is again compared to the pattern. This time it fails to match the pattern because it no longer contains exactly one token between the literal <@ and the literal >. So, no further processing is done by this rewrite rule and the address is passed to the next rule in line. Rules in a ruleset are processed sequentially, though a few metasymbols can be used to modify this flow.

The $>n symbol calls ruleset n and passes the address defined by the remainder of the transformation to ruleset n for processing. For example:

```
$>9 $1 % $2
```

This transformation calls ruleset 9 ($>9), and passes the contents of $1, a literal %, and the contents of $2 to ruleset 9 for processing. When ruleset 9 finishes processing, it returns a rewritten address to the calling rule. The returned email address is

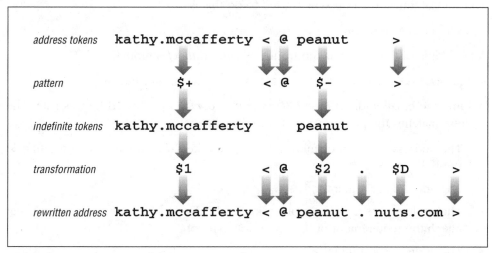

Figure 10-3: Rewriting an address

then compared again to the pattern in the calling rule. If it still matches, ruleset 9 is called again.

The recursion built into rewrite rules creates the possibility for infinite loops. sendmail does its best to detect possible loops, but you should take responsibility for writing rules that don't loop. The $@ and the $: symbols are used to control processing and to prevent loops. If the transformation begins with the $@ symbol, the entire ruleset is terminated and the remainder of the transformation is the value returned by the ruleset. If the transformation begins with the $: symbol, the individual rule is executed only once. Use $: to prevent recursion and to prevent loops when calling other rulesets. Use $@ to exit a ruleset at a specific rule.

The $[*name*$] symbol converts a host's nickname or its IP address to its canonical name by passing the value *name* to the name server for resolution. For example, using the *nuts.com* name servers, $[goober$] returns *peanut.nuts.com* and $[[172.16.12.1]$] returns *almond.nuts.com*.

In the same way that a hostname or address is used to look up a canonical name in the name server database, the $(*map key*$) syntax uses the *key* to retrieve information from the database identified by *map*. This is a more generalized database retrieval syntax than is the one that returns canonical hostnames, and it is more complex to use. Before we get into the details of setting up and using databases from within sendmail, let's finish describing the rest of the syntax of rewrite rules.

There is a special rewrite rule syntax that is used in ruleset 0. Ruleset 0 defines the triple (*mailer, host, user*) that specifies the mail delivery program, the recipient host, and the recipient user.

The special transformation syntax used to do this is:

```
$#mailer$@host$:user
```

An example of this syntax taken from the *linux.smtp.cf* sample file is:

```
R$*<@$*>$*      $#smtp$@$2$:$1<@$2>$3      user@host.domain
```

Assume the email address *david<@filbert.nuts.com>* is processed by this rule. The address matches the pattern $*<@$+>$* because:

- The address has zero or more tokens (the token *david*) that match the first $* symbol.

- The address has a literal <@.

- The address has zero or more tokens (the five tokens *filbert.nuts.com*) that match the requirement of the second $* symbol.

- The address has a literal >.

- The address has zero or more, in this case zero, tokens that match the requirement of the last $* symbol.

This pattern match produces two indefinite tokens. Indefinite token $1 contains *david* and $2 contains *filbert.nuts.com*. No other matches occurred, so $3 is null. These indefinite tokens are used to rewrite the address into the following triple:

```
$#smtp$@filbert.nuts.com$:david<@filbert.nuts.com>
```

The components of this triple are:

$#smtp
: *smtp* is the internal name of the mailer that delivers the message.

$@filbert.nuts.com
: *filbert.nuts.com* is the recipient host.

$:david<@filbert.nuts.com>
: *david<@filbert.nuts.com>* is the recipient user.

There is one special variant of this syntax, also used only in ruleset 0, that passes error messages to the user:

```
$#error$@comment$:message
```

The **comment** field is ignored by sendmail. **message** is the text of an error message returned to the user, for example:

```
R<@$+>     $#error$@5.1.1$:"user address required"
```

This rule returns the message "user address required" if the address matches the pattern.

Transforming with a database

External databases can be used to transform addresses in rewrite rules. The database is included in the transformation part of a rule by using the following syntax:

```
$(map key [$@argument...] [$:default] $)
```

map is the name assigned to the database within the *sendmail.cf* file. The name assigned to *map* is not limited by the rules that govern macro names. Like mailer names, map names are only used inside of the *sendmail.cf* file and can be any name you choose. Select a simple descriptive name, such as "users" or "mailboxes." The map name is assigned with a **K** command. (More on the **K** command in a moment.)

key is the value used to index into the database. The value returned from the database for this key is used to rewrite the input address. If no value is returned, the input address is not changed unless a *default* value is provided.

An *argument* is an additional value passed to the database procedure along with the key. Multiple arguments can be used, but each argument must start with $@. The argument can be used by the database procedure to modify the value it returns to sendmail. It is referenced inside the database as %*n*, where *n* is a digit that indicates the order in which the argument appears in the rewrite rule—%1, %2, and so on—when multiple arguments are used. (Argument %0 is the *key*.)

An example will make the use of arguments clear. Assume the following input address:

```
tom.martin<@sugar>
```

Further, assume the following database with the internal sendmail name of "relays":

```
oil     %1<@relay.fats.com>
sugar   %1<@relay.calories.com>
salt    %1<@server.sodium.org>
```

Finally, assume the following rewrite rule:

```
R$+<@$->    $(relays $2 $@ $1 $:$1<@$2> $)
```

The input address *tom.martin<@sugar>* matches the pattern because it has one or more tokens (tom.martin) before the literal <@ and exactly one token (sugar) after it. The pattern matching creates two indefinite tokens and passes them to the transformation. The transformation calls the database (relays) and passes it token $2 (sugar) as the key and token $1 (tom.martin) as the argument. If the key is not found in the database the default ($1<@$2>) is used. In this case, the key is found in the database. The database program uses the key to retrieve

"%1@relay.calories.com", expands the %1 argument, and returns "tom.martin@relay.calories.com" to sendmail, which uses the returned value to replace the input address.

Before a database can be used within sendmail, it must be defined. This is done with the **K** command. The syntax of the **K** command is:

```
Kname type [arguments]
```

name is the name used to reference this database within sendmail. In the example above, the *name* is "relays".

type is the class of database. The *type* specified in the **K** command must match the database support complied into your sendmail. Most sendmail programs do not support all database types, but a few basic types are widely supported. Common types are dbm, hash, btree, and nis. There are many more, all of which are described in Appendix E.

arguments are optional. Generally, the only argument is the path of the database file. Occasionally the arguments include flags that are interpreted by the database program. The full list of K command flags that can be passed in the argument field are listed in Appendix E.

To define the "relays" database file used in the example above, we might enter the following command in the *sendmail.cf* file:

```
Krelays dbm /usr/local/relays
```

The name *relays* is simply a name you chose because it is descriptive. The database type *dbm* is a type supported by your version of sendmail and was used by you when you built the database file. Finally, the argument */usr/local/relays* is the location of the database file you created.

Don't worry if you're confused about how to build and use database files within sendmail. We will revisit this topic later in the chapter and the examples will make the practical use of database files clear.

The Set Ruleset Command

Rulesets are groups of associated rewrite rules that can be referenced by a number. The **S** command marks the beginning of a ruleset and identifies it with a number. In the **S***n* command syntax, *n* is the number that identifies the ruleset. Numbers in the range of 0 to 99 are used.

Rulesets can be thought of as subroutines, or functions, designed to process email addresses. They are called from mailer definitions, from individual rewrite rules, or directly by sendmail. Six rulesets have special functions and are called directly by sendmail. These are:

- Ruleset 3 is the first ruleset applied to addresses. It converts an address to the canonical form: *local-part@host.domain*.

  In specific circumstances the *@host.domain* part is added by sendmail after ruleset 3 terminates. This happens only if the mail has been received from a mailer with the C flag set.* In our sample configuration file, none of the mailers use this flag. If the C flag is set, the sender's *@host.domain* is added to all addresses that have only a *local-part*. This processing is done after ruleset 3 and before rulesets 1 and 2. (This function is represented in Figure 10-4 by the box marked "D.")

- Ruleset 0 is applied to the addresses used to deliver the mail. Ruleset 0 is applied after ruleset 3, and only to the recipient addresses actually used for mail delivery. It resolves the address to the triple (*mailer, host, user*) composed of the name of the mailer that will deliver the mail, the recipient hostname, and the recipient username.

- Ruleset 1 is applied to all sender addresses in the message.

- Ruleset 2 is applied to all recipient addresses in the message.

- Ruleset 4 is applied to all addresses in the message and is used to translate internal address formats into external address formats.

- Ruleset 5 is applied to local addresses after sendmail processes the address against the aliases file. Ruleset 5 is only applied to local addresses that do not have an alias.

Figure 10-4 shows the flow of the message and addresses through these rulesets. The D box does not symbolize a ruleset. It is the internal sendmail process described above. The S and R symbols do stand for rulesets. They have numeric names just like all normal rulesets, but the numbers are not fixed as is the case with rulesets 0, 1, 2, 3, 4, and 5. The S and R ruleset numbers are defined in the S and R fields of the mailer definition. Each mailer may specify its own S and R rulesets for mailer-specific cleanup of the sender and recipient addresses just before the message is delivered. There are, of course, many more rulesets in most *sendmail.cf* files. The other rulesets provide additional address processing and are called by existing rulesets using the $>*n* construct.† The rulesets provided in any sample *sendmail.cf* file will be adequate for delivering SMTP mail. It's unlikely you'll have to add to these rulesets, unless you want to add new features to your mailer.

---

* See Appendix E for the full set of mailer flags.

† See Table 10-5.

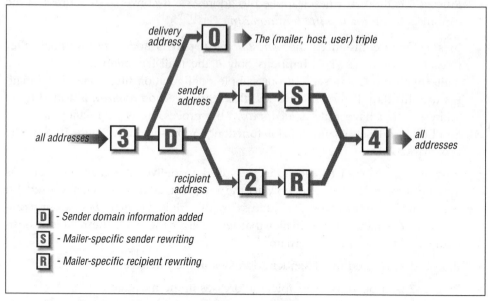

Figure 10-4: Sequence of rulesets

Modifying a sendmail.cf File

In this section we put into practice everything we discussed about sample configuration files—their structure and the commands used to build them. We'll modify the prototype configuration file, *linux.smtp.cf,* for use on *peanut.nuts.com.* We've chosen to modify this file because its configuration is closest to the configuration we need for *peanut.nuts.com. peanut* is a Linux workstation on a TCP/IP Ethernet, and it uses SMTP mail and domain name service (DNS).

The following sections are titled according to the sections of the file, and they describe the modifications we'll make to the file, section by section. Remember that other *sendmail.cf* files will probably use different section titles, but the basic information provided in the configuration will be the same.

Modifying Local Information

The first line in the local information section of the *sendmail.cf* file defines class w.* Class w is the full set of host names for which this system accepts mail. Use the class w command to add hostnames to this set. sendmail initializes this class to the value in macro w (**$w**), which is the hostname of this computer. On most systems that is enough; sendmail is able to correctly identify most of the other

---

* The full text of the local information section is shown in Appendix E.

hostnames for which it should accept mail by querying DNS. The w class needs only to identify systems that expect this host to accept mail for them and that do not have CNAME or MX entries in the DNS that point to this host. You'll need to add a hostname to class w, or an MX record to DNS, if you see the following mail error:

```
mil-gw.nuts.com. config error: mail loops back to me (MX problem?)
```

In our sample, we accept the **Cw** command as written, and let sendmail define the value for w internally. This is the most common method for desktop systems like *peanut*. On the system *almond*, which is also known by the name *mil-gw*, we would add values to class w as follows:

```
Cwlocalhost mil-gw mil-gw.nuts.com
```

Now mail addressed to *user@mil-gw.nuts.com* would be accepted by *almond* and not rejected as being addressed to the wrong host.

Some mail servers might need to be configured to accept mail for many different hostnames. In that case you may want to load class w from a file containing all of the hostnames. Do that with the **F** command.

No modification is necessary for the **j** macro definition because, on this system, sendmail obtains a fully qualified domain name for the **j** macro from DNS. On some systems this is the case; on other systems sendmail obtains the hostname without the domain extension. If **j** doesn't contain the full name, initialize *j* with the hostname (**$w**) and the domain name. In the sample file we would do this by "uncommenting" the **Dj** command and editing the domain string to be *nuts.com*. However, there is no need to do this because **j** has the correct value.

To test if **j** is set to the correct value on your system, run sendmail with the **–bt** option and the debug level set to 0.4. In response to this, sendmail displays several lines of information, including the value of **j**. In the example below, sendmail displays the value *peanut.nuts.com* for **j**. If it displayed only *peanut*, we would edit *sendmail.cf* to correct the value for **j**.

```
# sendmail -bt -d0.4
Version 8.8.5
 Compiled with: LOG MATCHGECOS MIME8TO7 NAMED_BIND NDBM
                NETINET NETUNIX NEWDB SCANF USERDB XDEBUG
canonical name: peanut.nuts.com
 UUCP nodename: peanut
        a.k.a.: peanut.nuts.com
        a.k.a.: [172.16.12.2]

============ SYSTEM IDENTITY (after readcf) ============
      (short domain name) $w = peanut
  (canonical domain name) $j = peanut.nuts.com
```

```
              (subdomain name) $m = nuts.com
                  (node name) $k = peanut
=========================================================

ADDRESS TEST MODE (ruleset 3 NOT automatically invoked)
Enter <ruleset> <address>
> ^D
```

The next line in the local information section defines class P. In our sample configuration file, class P stores the names of some special mail routing domains. These pseudo-domain names allow us to address users who are not on the Internet with Internet style email addresses. For example, mail can be addressed using the normal UUCP "bang" syntax, e.g., *ora!los!craig*, or it can be addressed in a pseudo-Internet format, e.g., *craig@los.ora.uucp*. These mail routing domains simplify the address that the user enters, and route the mail to the correct mail relay host. However, pseudo-domains are rarely needed because most mailers now support standard Internet-style addresses. The class P definition in *linux.smtp.cf* does not require any modification. The only value assigned as a pseudo-domain is a dot (.), which is used in this *sendmail.cf* file to identify canonical domain names.

The configuration file has macro definitions for several mail relays. None of these are assigned a value in our sample file. You only need a relay host if your system cannot deliver the mail because it lacks capability or connectivity. UNIX systems do not lack capability, but a firewall might limit connectivity. Some sites use a mail relay so that only one systems needs a full *sendmail.cf* configuration. The other hosts at the site simply forward their mail to the smart host for delivery. If this is the configuration policy of your site, enter the name of the mail relay as the "smart" relay. For example:

```
DSrelay.nuts.com
```

We don't enter anything in any of the relay settings on *peanut*. This desktop system will handle all its own mail. Hey, that's why we run UNIX!

The local information section in the sample file also includes four key file definitions. Three of these **K** commands are commented out, and all four of them can be ignored. The one key file definition that is not commented out defines the *dequote* database, which is an internal sendmail database used to remove quotes from within email addresses. The *user* key file, which is commented out, is also an internal database. It is used to check if a username exists. The last two databases exist only if you create them. The *domaintable* is used to rewrite domain names and the *mailertable* database is used to send mail addressed to a specific domain through a particular mailer to a specific remote host.

The version number doesn't *require* modification—but it's a good idea to keep track of the changes you make to your sendmail configuration, and this is the place to do it. Each time you modify the configuration, change the version number by adding your own revision number. At the same time, enter a comment in the file describing the changes you made. Usually, this is the last change made to the files so the comments reflect all changes. For example, the original version number section in the *linux.smtp.cf* file is:

```
######################
#   Version Number    #
######################

DZ8.7.3
```

After we have finished all of our modifications, it will contain:

```
######################
#   Version Number    #
######################
#  R1.0 - modified for peanut by Craig
#       - cleaned up the comments in the local info section
#  R1.1 - modified macro M to use nuts.com instead of the
#          hostname in outgoing mail
#  R2.0 - added rule a to S11 & S31 to rewrite to first.last format

DZ8.7.3R2.0
```

Finally, we need to understand the purpose of a few other classes and macros found in this section. The M macro is used to rewrite the sender host address. Define a value for M to hide the name of the local host in outbound mail. Classes E and M are both related to macro M. Class E defines the usernames for which the hostname is not rewritten even if the M macro is defined. For example, *root@peanut.nuts.com* is not rewritten to *root@nuts.com* even if M is defined as DMnuts.com. Class M is defines other hostnames, not just the local hostname, that should be rewritten to the value of macro M. This is used on mail servers that might need to rewrite sender addresses for their clients. For example:

```
# who I masquerade as (null for no masquerading) (see also $=M)
DMnuts.com

# class M: domains that should be converted to $M
CMacorn.nuts.com brazil.nuts.com filbert.nuts.com
```

Given the macro M and class M definitions shown above. This host would rewrite mail from *user@brazil.nuts.com* or *user@acorn.nuts.com* to *user@nuts.com*. *peanut* is not a server so we won't use class M. But we will use macro M later in the configuration.

We spent lots of time looking at the local information section because almost everything you will need to do to configure a system can be done here. We will quickly discuss the other section before getting into the really challenging task of working with rewrite rules.

Modifying Options

The section, "Options," defines the sendmail environment. For example, some of the options specify the file paths used by sendmail, as in these lines from the *linux.smtp.cf* file:

```
# location of alias file
O AliasFile=/etc/aliases
# location of help file
O HelpFile=/usr/lib/sendmail.hf
# status file
O StatusFile=/etc/sendmail.st
# queue directory
O QueueDirectory=/var/spool/mqueue
```

If these paths are correct for your system, don't modify them. On *peanut* we want to keep the files just where they are, which is generally the case when you use a *sendmail.cf* file that was designed for your operating system. In fact, you will probably not need to change any of the options if you use a configuration file designed for your operating system. If you're really curious about sendmail options, see Appendix E.

The next few sections of the *linux.smtp.cf* file define the messages' precedences, the trusted users, and the headers. None of these sections are modified. Following these sections are the rewrite rules and the mailers. This material is the bulk of the file and the heart of the configuration. The sample configuration file is designed to allow SMTP mail delivery on a Linux system running DNS, so we assume no modifications are required. We want to test the configuration before copying it into *sendmail.cf*. We'll save it in a temporary configuration file, *test.cf*, and use the troubleshooting features of sendmail to test it.

Testing sendmail.cf

sendmail provides powerful tools for configuration testing and debugging. These test tools are invoked on the sendmail command line using some of the many sendmail command-line arguments. Appendix E lists all of the command-line arguments; Table 10-6 summarizes those that relate to testing and debugging.

Table 10-6: sendmail Arguments for Testing and Debugging

Argument	Function
−t	Send to everyone listed in To:, Cc:, and Bcc:.
−bt	Run in test mode.
−bv	Verify addresses; don't collect or deliver mail.
−bp	Print the mail queue.
−C*file*	Use *file* as the configuration file.

Table 10-6: sendmail Arguments for Testing and Debugging (continued)

Argument	Function
−d*level*	Set debugging level.
−O*option*=*value*	Set *option* to the specified *value*.
−e	Defines how errors are returned.
−v	Run in verbose mode.

Some command-line arguments are used to verify address processing and to gain confidence in the new configuration. Once you think your configuration will work, choose friends at various sites and send them mail. Use the −C argument to read the test configuration file and the −v argument to display the details of the mail delivery. −v displays the complete SMTP exchange between the two hosts.

By observing if your mailer properly connects to the remote mailer and formats the addresses correctly, you'll get a good idea of how the configuration is working. The following example is a test from *peanut* using the *test.cf* configuration file we just created:

```
peanut# /usr/lib/sendmail -Ctest.cf -t -v
To: craigh@ora.com
From: craig
Subject: Sendmail Test
Ignore this test.
^D
craigh@ora.com... Connecting to ora.com. via smtp...
220-ruby.ora.com Sendmail 8.6.13/8.6.11 ready at Sat, 16 Nov 1996
220 ESMTP spoken here
>>> EHLO peanut.nuts.com
250-ruby.ora.com Hello craig@peanut.nuts.com [172.16.12.2], pleased
      to meet you
250-EXPN
250-SIZE
250 HELP
>>> MAIL From:<craig@peanut.nuts.com> SIZE=64
250 <craig@peanut.nuts.com>... Sender ok
>>> RCPT To:<craigh@ora.com>
250 <craigh@ora.com>... Recipient ok
>>> DATA
354 Enter mail, end with "." on a line by itself
>>> .
250 SAA27399 Message accepted for delivery
craigh@ora.com... Sent (SAA27399 Message accepted for delivery)
Closing connection to ora.com.
>>> QUIT
221 ruby.ora.com closing connection
```

We entered everything before the CTRL-D (^D). Everything after the ^D was displayed by sendmail. Figure 10-5 highlights some of the important information in this display, and notes the sendmail macros that relate to the highlighted material.

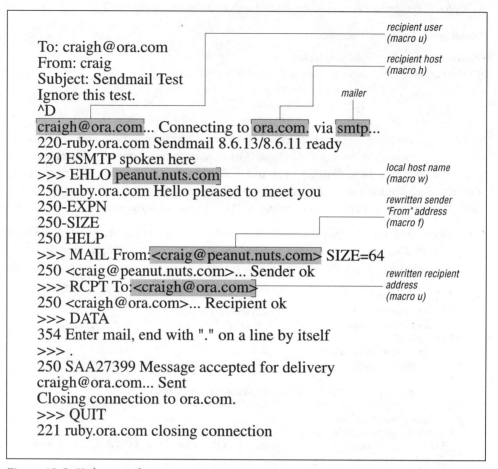

Figure 10-5: Verbose mail output

This test successfully transfers mail to a remote Internet site. The sendmail output shows that *peanut* sent the mail to *ora.com* via the *smtp* mail delivery program. The sendmail greeting shows that the remote host handling this SMTP connection is *ruby.ora.com*. Therefore, *ruby* must be the mail server for the *ora.com* domain; i.e., the MX record for *ora.com* points to *ruby.ora.com*.

The ESMTP and EHLO messages indicate that both *peanut* and *ruby* use Extended Simple Mail Transfer Protocol (ESMTP).

Everything worked just fine! We could quit right now and use this configuration. But like most computer people, we cannot stop ourselves from tinkering in order to make things "better."

The From: address, *craig@peanut.nuts.com*, is clearly a valid address but it is not quite what we want. What we want is to have people address us as *firstname.lastname@domain*—not as *user@host.domain*, which is exactly the configuration we created earlier in this chapter with a few lines of **m4** code. We will create the same configuration here to provide an example of how to use the various troubleshooting tools that come with sendmail. However, if you really want to make major sendmail configuration changes, you should use **m4** to build your configuration.

Most changes to *sendmail.cf* are small and are made near the beginning of the file in the Local Information section. Looking closely at that section provides the clues we need to solve part of our configuration problem.

Without knowing what "masquerading" means, the comments for class E, class M, and macro M lead us to guess that the value set for macro M will be used to rewrite the hostname.* In particular, the comment "names that should be exposed as from this host, even if we masquerade" led me to believe that masquerading hides the hostname. Based on this guess, we set a value for macro M as follows:

```
# who I masquerade as (null for no masquerading) (see also $=M)
DMnuts.com
```

Are we sure that setting a value for the M macro will hide the hostname? No, but changing the value in *test.cf* and running another test will do no harm. Running the test program with the test configuration has no affect on the running sendmail daemon that was started by the **sendmail −bd −q1h** command in the boot script. Only an instantiation of sendmail with the **−Ctest.cf** argument will use the *test.cf* test configuration.

Testing Rewrite Rules

In the initial test, the From: address went into sendmail as *craig*, and it came out as *craig@peanut.nuts.com*. Obviously it has been rewritten. This time we test whether the change we made to the macro M in the configuration files modifies the rewrite process by directly testing the rewrite rulesets. First, we need to find out what rules were used to rewrite this address. To get more information, we run sendmail with the **−bt** option.

When sendmail is invoked with the **−bt** option, it prompts for input using the greater than symbol (>). At the prompt, enter one of the test commands shown in Table 10-7.

---

* In the **m4** source file we configured masquerading with the **MASQUERADE_AS(nuts.com)** command.

Table 10-7: sendmail Testing Commands

Command	Function
ruleset[,*ruleset*]... *address*	Process *address* through *ruleset*(s).
.D*mvalue*	Assign *value* to macro *m*.
.C*cvalue*	Add *value* to class *c*.
=S*ruleset*	Display the rules in *ruleset*.
=M	Display the mailer definitions.
−d*value*	Set the debug flag to *value*.
$*m*	Display the value of macro *m*.
$=*c*	Display the contents of class *c*.
/mx *host*	Display the MX records for *host*.
/parse *address*	Return the mailer/host/user triple for *address*.
/try *mailer address*	Process *address* for *mailer*.
/tryflags *flags*	Set the address processed by /parse or /try to **H** (Header), **E** (Envelope), **S** (Sender), or **R** (Recipient).
/canon *hostname*	Canonify *hostname*.
/map *mapname key*	Display the value for *key* found in *mapname*.

The most basic test is a ruleset number followed by an email address. The address is the test data, and the ruleset number is the ruleset to be tested. The address is easy to select; it is the one that was improperly rewritten. But how do you know which ruleset to specify?

Use Figure 10-4 to determine which rulesets to enter. Ruleset 3 is applied to all addresses. It is followed by different rulesets depending on whether the address is a delivery address, a sender address, or a recipient address. Furthermore, the rulesets used for sender and recipient addresses vary depending on the mailer that is used to deliver the mail. All addresses are then processed by ruleset 4.

There are two variables in determining the rulesets used to process an address: the type of address and the mailer through which it is processed. The three address types are delivery address, recipient address, and sender address. You know the address type because you select the address being tested. In our test mail we were concerned about the sender address. Which mailer is used is determined by the delivery address. To find out which mailer delivered the test mail, run sendmail with the −bv argument and the delivery address:

```
# sendmail -bv craigh@ora.com
craigh@ora.com... deliverable: mailer smtp, host ora.com.,
    user craigh@ora.com
```

Knowing the mailer, we can use sendmail with the −bt option to process the sender From: address. There are two types of sender addresses: the sender address in the "envelope" and the sender address in the message header. The message header address is the one on the **From:** line sent with the message during the SMTP DATA transfer. You probably see it in the mail headers when you view the message with your mail reader. The "envelope" address is the address used during the SMTP protocol interactions. sendmail allows us to view the processing of both of these addresses:

```
# /usr/lib/sendmail -bt -Ctest.cf
ADDRESS TEST MODE (ruleset 3 NOT automatically invoked)
Enter <ruleset> <address>
> /tryflags HS
> /try smtp craig
Trying header sender address craig for mailer smtp
rewrite: ruleset  3    input: craig
rewrite: ruleset 96    input: craig
rewrite: ruleset 96 returns: craig
rewrite: ruleset  3 returns: craig
rewrite: ruleset  1    input: craig
rewrite: ruleset  1 returns: craig
rewrite: ruleset 31    input: craig
rewrite: ruleset 51    input: craig
rewrite: ruleset 51 returns: craig
rewrite: ruleset 61    input: craig
rewrite: ruleset 61 returns: craig < @ *LOCAL* >
rewrite: ruleset 93    input: craig < @ *LOCAL* >
rewrite: ruleset 93 returns: craig < @ nuts . com . >
rewrite: ruleset 31 returns: craig < @ nuts . com . >
rewrite: ruleset  4    input: craig < @ nuts . com . >
rewrite: ruleset  4 returns: craig @ nuts . com
Rcode = 0, addr = craig@nuts.com
> /tryflags ES
> /try smtp craig
Trying envelope sender address craig for mailer smtp
rewrite: ruleset  3    input: craig
rewrite: ruleset 96    input: craig
rewrite: ruleset 96 returns: craig
rewrite: ruleset  3 returns: craig
rewrite: ruleset  1    input: craig
rewrite: ruleset  1 returns: craig
rewrite: ruleset 11    input: craig
rewrite: ruleset 51    input: craig
rewrite: ruleset 51 returns: craig
rewrite: ruleset 61    input: craig
rewrite: ruleset 61 returns: craig < @ *LOCAL* >
rewrite: ruleset 94    input: craig < @ *LOCAL* >
rewrite: ruleset 94 returns: craig < @ peanut . nuts . com . >
rewrite: ruleset 11 returns: craig < @ peanut . nuts . com . >
rewrite: ruleset  4    input: craig < @ peanut . nuts . com . >
rewrite: ruleset  4 returns: craig @ peanut . nuts . com
Rcode = 0, addr = craig@peanut.nuts.com
> ^D
```

The **/tryflags** command defines the type of address to be processed by a **/try** or a **/parse** command. Four flags are available for the **/tryflags** command: S for sender,

R for recipient, **H** for header, and **E** for envelope. By combining two of these flags, the first **/tryflags** command says we will process a header sender (HS) address. The **/try** command tells sendmail to process the address through a specific mailer. In the example, we process the email address *craig* through the mailer *smtp*. First, we process it as the header sender address, and then as the envelope sender address. From this test, we can tell that the value that we entered in the **M** macro is used to rewrite the sender address in the message header but it is not used to rewrite the sender address in the envelope.

Unfortunately, older versions of sendmail, such as the version that comes with Solaris 2.5.1, don't support **/try** and **/tryflags**. Testing these older systems requires a little more effort. Knowing the mailer is still the key to determining the rulesets called to process the sender `From:` address. A **grep** of the *test.cf* file displays the rulesets that the *smtp* mailer uses for sender addresses.

```
% grep ^Msmtp /etc/sendmail.cf
Msmtp,      P=[IPC], F=mDFMuX, S=11/31, R=21, E=\r\n, L=990,
Msmtp8,     P=[IPC], F=mDFMuX8, S=11/31, R=21, E=\r\n, L=990,
```

Again, refer to Figure 10-4 It shows that the sender address goes through ruleset 3, ruleset 1, the ruleset specified by **S**, and ruleset 4. The mailer definition for *smtp* in our sample configuration defines two rulesets for S—11 and 31.* The first ruleset is used for rewriting the sender address in the "envelope" and the second is used to rewrite the sender address in the message header.

Based on the information in Figure 10-4 and in the S field of the *smtp* mailer, we know that the rulesets that process the message header sender address are 3, 1, 31 and 4. So we run sendmail with the **–bt** option and enter **3,1,31,4 craig** at the command prompt. This command processes the sender address through each of these rulesets in succession. We also know that the envelope sender address is processed by rulesets 3, 1, 11, and 4. To test that, we enter **3,1,11,4 craig**.

The results of these tests are exactly the same as those shown in the example above. The value of the M macro rewrites the hostname in the message sender address just as we wanted. The hostname in the envelope sender address is not rewritten. Usually this is acceptable. However, we want to create exactly the same configuration as in the **m4** example. The **FEATURE(masquerade_envelope)** command used in the **m4** example causes the envelope sender address to be rewritten. Therefore, we want this configuration to also rewrite it.

The only difference between how the message and envelope addresses are processed is that one goes through ruleset 31 and the other goes through ruleset 11. The tests show that both rulesets call ruleset 51 and then ruleset 61. They diverge

---

* Many versions of sendmail define only one ruleset each for S and R.

at that point because ruleset 31 calls ruleset 93 and ruleset 11 calls ruleset 94. The tests also show that ruleset 93 provides the address rewrite that we want for the message sender address, while the envelope sender address is not processed in the manner we desire by ruleset 94. The *test.cf* code for rulesets 94, 11, and 31 is shown below:

```
###############################################################
###  Ruleset 94 -- convert envelope names to masquerade form    ###
###############################################################
S94
#R$+                       $@ $>93 $1
R$* < @ *LOCAL* > $*       $: $1 < @ $j . > $2


#
# , envelope sender rewriting
#
S11
R$+               $: $>51 $1         sender/recipient common
R$* :; <@>        $@                 list:; special case
R$*               $: $>61 $1         qualify unqual'ed names
R$+               $: $>94 $1         do masquerading


#
#   header sender and masquerading header recipient rewriting
#
S31
R$+               $: $>51 $1         sender/recipient common
R:; <@>           $@                 list:; special case
R$* <@> $*        $@ $1 <@> $2       pass null host through
R< @ $* > $*      $@ < @ $1 > $2     pass route-addr through
R$*               $: $>61 $1         qualify unqual'ed names
R$+               $: $>93 $1         do masquerading
```

Clearly, ruleset 94 does not do what we want and ruleset 93 does. A quick inspection of ruleset 94 shows that it does not contain a single reference to macro M. Yet the comment on the line in ruleset 11 that calls it indicates that ruleset 94 should "do masquerading." The first line of ruleset 94 calls ruleset 93, but it is commented out. Our solution is to uncomment the first line of ruleset 94 so that it now calls ruleset 93, which is the ruleset that really does the masquerade processing.

Debugging a *sendmail.cf* file is more of an art than a science. Deciding to edit the first line of ruleset 94 to call ruleset 93 is little more than a hunch. The only way to verify the hunch is through testing. We run **sendmail –bt –Ctest.cf** again to test the addresses *craig*, *craig@peanut*, and *craig@localhost* through rulesets 3, 1, 11, and 4. All tests run successfully, rewriting the various input addresses into *craig@nuts.com*. We then retest by sending mail via **sendmail –v –t –Ctest.cf**. Only when all of these tests run successfully do we really believe in our hunch and move on to the next task, which is to rewrite the user part of the email address into the user's first and last names.

Using Key Files in sendmail

The last feature we added to the **m4** source file was **FEATURE(genericstable)**, which adds a database process to the configuration that we use to convert the user portion of the email address from the user's login name to the user's first and last names. To do the same thing here, create a text file of login names and first and last names and build a database with **makemap.**[*]

```
# cat realnames
dan Dan.Scribner
tyler Tyler.McCafferty
pat Pat.Stover
willy Bill.Wright
craig Craig.Hunt
# makemap dbm realnames < realnames
```

Once the database is created, define it for sendmail. Use the **K** command to do this. To use the database that we have just built, insert the following lines into the Local Information section of the *sendmail.cf* file:

```
# define a database to map login names to firstname.lastname
Krealnames dbm /etc/realnames
```

The **K** command defines *realnames* as the internal sendmail name of this database. Further, it identifies that this is a database of type *dbm* and that the path to the database is */etc/realnames*. sendmail adds the correct filename extensions to the pathname depending on the type of the database, so you don't need to worry about it.

Finally, we add a new rule that uses the database to rewrite addresses. We add it to ruleset 11 and ruleset 31 immediately after the lines in those rulesets that call ruleset 93. This way, our new rule gets the address as soon as ruleset 93 finishes processing it.

```
# when masquerading convert login name to firstname.lastname
R$-<@$M.>$*     $:$(realnames $1 $)<@$2.>$3     user=>first.last
```

This rule is designed to process the output of ruleset 93, which rewrites the hostname portion of the address. Addresses that meet the criteria to have the hostname part rewritten are also the addresses for which we want to rewrite the user part. Look at the output of ruleset 93 from the earlier test. That address, *craig<@nuts.com.>*, matches the pattern **$-<@$M.>$***. The address has exactly one token (*craig*) before the literal **<@**, followed by the value of M (*nuts.com*), the literal **.>** and zero tokens.

---

[*] See the **m4** section for more information about **makemap.**

The transformation part of this rule takes the first token ($1) from the input address and uses it as the key to the *realnames* database, as indicated by the $:$(realnames $1 $) syntax. For the sample address *craig<@nuts.com>*, $1 is *craig*. When used as an index into the database *realnames* shown at the beginning of this section, it returns *Craig.Hunt*. This returned value is prepended to the literal <@, the value of indefinite token $2, the literal .>, and the value of $3, as indicated by the <@$2.>$3 part of the transformation. The effect of this new rule is to convert the username to the user's real first and last names.

After adding the new rule to rulesets 11 and 31, a test yields the following results:

```
# sendmail -bt -Ctest.cf
ADDRESS TEST MODE (ruleset 3 NOT automatically invoked)
Enter <ruleset> <address>
> 3,1,11,4 craig
rewrite: ruleset  3    input: craig
rewrite: ruleset 96    input: craig
rewrite: ruleset 96 returns: craig
rewrite: ruleset  3 returns: craig
rewrite: ruleset  1    input: craig
rewrite: ruleset  1 returns: craig
rewrite: ruleset 11    input: craig
rewrite: ruleset 51    input: craig
rewrite: ruleset 51 returns: craig
rewrite: ruleset 61    input: craig
rewrite: ruleset 61 returns: craig < @ *LOCAL* >
rewrite: ruleset 93    input: craig < @ *LOCAL* >
rewrite: ruleset 93 returns: craig < @ nuts . com . >
rewrite: ruleset 11 returns: Craig . Hunt < @ nuts . com . >
rewrite: ruleset  4    input: Craig . Hunt < @ nuts . com . >
rewrite: ruleset  4 returns: Craig . Hunt @ nuts . com
> 3,1,31,4 craig
rewrite: ruleset  3    input: craig
rewrite: ruleset 96    input: craig
rewrite: ruleset 96 returns: craig
rewrite: ruleset  3 returns: craig
rewrite: ruleset  1    input: craig
rewrite: ruleset  1 returns: craig
rewrite: ruleset 31    input: craig
rewrite: ruleset 51    input: craig
rewrite: ruleset 51 returns: craig
rewrite: ruleset 61    input: craig
rewrite: ruleset 61 returns: craig < @ *LOCAL* >
rewrite: ruleset 93    input: craig < @ *LOCAL* >
rewrite: ruleset 93 returns: craig < @ nuts . com . >
rewrite: ruleset 31 returns: Craig . Hunt < @ nuts . com . >
rewrite: ruleset  4    input: Craig . Hunt < @ nuts . com . >
rewrite: ruleset  4 returns: Craig . Hunt @ nuts . com
> ^D
```

If the tests do not give the results you want, make sure that you have correctly entered the new rewrite rules and that you have correctly built the database. If sendmail complains that it can't lock the database file, you need to download a more recent release of sendmail V8. The following error message could also be displayed:

```
test.cf: line 116: readcf: map realnames: class dbm not available
```

This indicates that your system does not support dbm databases. Change the database type on the **K** command line to hash and rerun **sendmail –bt**. If it complains again, try it with btree. When you find a type of database that your sendmail likes, rerun **makemap** using that database type. If your sendmail doesn't support any database type, see Appendix E for information on re-compiling sendmail with database support.

Note that all of the changes made directly to the *sendmail.cf* file in the second half of this chapter (masquerading the sender address, masquerading the envelope address and converting usernames) were handled by just three lines in the **m4** source file. These examples were used to demonstrate how to use the sendmail test tools. If you really need to make a new, custom configuration, use **m4**. It is easiest to maintain and enhance the sendmail configuration through the **m4** source file.

Summary

sendmail sends and receives SMTP mail, processes mail aliases, and interfaces between user mail agents and mail delivery agents. sendmail is started as a daemon at boot time to process incoming SMTP mail. sendmail aliases are defined in the */etc/aliases* file. The rules for interfacing between user agents and mail delivery agents can be complex. sendmail uses the *sendmail.cf* file to define these rules.

Configuring the *sendmail.cf* file is the most difficult part of setting up a sendmail server. The file uses a very terse command syntax that is hard to read. Sample *sendmail.cf* files are available to simplify this task. Most systems come with a sample file and others are available with the sendmail V8 software distribution. The sendmail V.8 sample files must first be processed by the **m4** macro processor. Once the proper sample file is available very little of it needs to be changed. Almost all of the changes needed to complete the configuration occur at the beginning of the file and are used to define information about the local system, such as the hostname and the name of the mail relay host. sendmail provides an interactive testing tool that is used to check the configuration before it is installed.

This chapter concludes our study of TCP/IP servers configuration, our last configuration task. In the next chapter we begin to look at the ongoing tasks that are part of running a network once it has been installed and configured. We begin this discussion with troubleshooting.

11

Troubleshooting TCP/IP

Network administration tasks fall into two very different categories: configuration and troubleshooting. Configuration tasks prepare for the expected; they require detailed knowledge of command syntax, but are usually simple and predictable. Once a system is properly configured, there is rarely any reason to change it. The configuration process is repeated each time a new operating system release is installed, but with very few changes.

In contrast, network troubleshooting deals with the unexpected. Troubleshooting frequently requires knowledge that is conceptual rather than detailed. Network problems are usually unique and sometimes difficult to resolve. Troubleshooting is an important part of maintaining a stable, reliable network service.

In this chapter, we discuss the tools you will use to ensure that the network is in good running condition. However, good tools are not enough. No troubleshooting tool is effective if applied haphazardly. Effective troubleshooting requires a methodical approach to the problem, and a basic understanding of how the network works. We'll start our discussion by looking at ways to approach a network problem.

Approaching a Problem

To approach a problem properly, you need a basic understanding of TCP/IP. The first few chapters of this book discuss the basics of TCP/IP and provide enough background information to troubleshoot most network problems. Knowledge of how TCP/IP routes data through the network, between individual hosts, and between the layers in the protocol stack, is important for understanding a network problem. But detailed knowledge of each protocol usually isn't necessary. When you need these details, look them up in a definitive reference—don't try to recall them from memory.

Not all TCP/IP problems are alike, and not all problems can be approached in the same manner. But the key to solving any problem is understanding what the problem is. This is not as easy as it may seem. The "surface" problem is sometimes misleading, and the "real" problem is frequently obscured by many layers of software. Once you understand the true nature of the problem, the solution to the problem is often obvious.

First, gather detailed information about exactly what's happening. When a user reports a problem, talk to her. Find out which application failed. What is the remote host's name and IP address? What is the user's hostname and address? What error message was displayed? If possible, verify the problem by having the user run the application while you talk her through it. If possible, duplicate the problem on your own system.

Testing from the user's system, and other systems, find out:

- Does the problem occur in other applications on the user's host, or is only one application having trouble? If only one application is involved, the application may be misconfigured or disabled on the remote host. Because of security concerns, many systems disable some services.

- Does the problem occur with only one remote host, all remote hosts, or only certain "groups" of remote hosts? If only one remote host is involved, the problem could easily be with that host. If all remote hosts are involved, the problem is probably with the user's system (particularly if no other hosts on your local network are experiencing the same problem). If only hosts on certain subnets or external networks are involved, the problem may be related to routing.

- Does the problem occur on other local systems? Make sure you check other systems on the same subnet. If the problem only occurs on the user's host, concentrate testing on that system. If the problem affects every system on a subnet, concentrate on the router for that subnet.

Once you know the symptoms of the problem, visualize each protocol and device that handles the data. Visualizing the problem will help you avoid oversimplification, and keep you from assuming that you know the cause even before you start testing. Using your TCP/IP knowledge, narrow your attack to the most likely causes of the problem, but keep an open mind.

Troubleshooting Hints

Below we offer several useful troubleshooting hints. They are not part of a troubleshooting methodology—just good ideas to keep in mind.

- Approach problems methodically. Allow the information gathered from each test to guide your testing. Don't jump on a hunch into another test scenario without ensuring that you can pick up your original scenario where you left off.

- Work carefully through the problem, dividing it into manageable pieces. Test each piece before moving on to the next. For example, when testing a network connection, test each part of the network until you find the problem.

- Keep good records of the tests you have completed and their results. Keep a historical record of the problem in case it reappears.

- Keep an open mind. Don't assume too much about the cause of the problem. Some people believe their network is always at fault, while others assume the remote end is always the problem. Some are so sure they know the cause of a problem that they ignore the evidence of the tests. Don't fall into these traps. Test each possibility and base your actions on the evidence of the tests.

- Be aware of security barriers. Security firewalls sometimes block **ping**, **traceroute**, and even ICMP error messages. If problems seem to cluster around a specific remote site, find out if they have a firewall.

- Pay attention to error messages. Error messages are often vague, but they frequently contain important hints for solving the problem.

- Duplicate the reported problem yourself. Don't rely too heavily on the user's problem report. The user has probably only seen this problem from the application level. If necessary, obtain the user's data files to duplicate the problem. Even if you cannot duplicate the problem, log the details of the reported problem for your records.

- Most problems are caused by human error. You can prevent some of these errors by providing information and training on network configuration and usage.

- Keep your users informed. This reduces the number of duplicated trouble reports, and the duplication of effort when several system administrators work on the same problem without knowing others are already working on it. If you're lucky, someone may have seen the problem before and have a helpful suggestion about how to resolve it.

- Don't speculate about the cause of the problem while talking to the user. Save your speculations for discussions with your networking colleagues. Your speculations may be accepted by the user as gospel, and become rumors. These rumors can cause users to avoid using legitimate network services and may undermine confidence in your network. Users want solutions to their problems; they're not interested in speculative techno-babble.

- Stick to a few simple troubleshooting tools. For most TCP/IP software problems, the tools discussed in this chapter are sufficient. Just learning how to use a new tool is often more time-consuming than solving the problem with an old familiar tool.

- Thoroughly test the problem at your end of the network before locating the owner of the remote system to coordinate testing with him. The greatest difficulty of network troubleshooting is that you do not always control the systems at both ends of the network. In many cases, you may not even know who does control the remote system.* The more information you have about your end, the simpler the job will be when you have to contact the remote administrator.

- Don't neglect the obvious. A loose or damaged cable is always a possible problem. Check plugs, connectors, cables, and switches. Small things can cause big problems.

Diagnostic Tools

Because most problems have a simple cause, developing a clear idea of the problem often provides the solution. Unfortunately, this is not always true, so in this section we begin to discuss the tools that can help you attack the most intractable problems. Many diagnostic tools are available, ranging from commercial systems with specialized hardware and software that may cost thousands of dollars, to free software that is available from the Internet. Many software tools are provided with your UNIX system. You should also keep some hardware tools handy.

To maintain the network's equipment and wiring you need some simple hand tools. A pair of needle-nose pliers and a few screwdrivers may be sufficient, but you may also need specialized tools. For example, attaching RJ45 connectors to Unshielded Twisted Pair (UTP) cable requires special crimping tools. It is usually easiest to buy a ready-made network maintenance toolkit from your cable vendor.

---

* Chapter 13 explains how to find out who is responsible for a remote network

A full-featured cable tester is also useful. Modern cable testers are small hand-held units with a keypad and LCD display that test both thinnet or UTP cable. Tests are selected from the keyboard and results are displayed on the LCD screen. It is not necessary to interpret the results because the unit does that for you and displays the error condition in a simple text message. For example, a cable test might produce the message "Short at 74 feet." This tells you that the cable is shorted 74 feet away from the tester. What could be simpler? The proper test tools make it easier to locate, and therefore fix, cable problems.

A laptop computer can be a most useful piece of test equipment when properly configured. Install TCP/IP software on the laptop. Take it to the location where the user reports a network problem. Disconnect the Ethernet cable from the back of the user's system and attach it to the laptop. Configure the laptop with an appropriate address for the user's subnet and reboot it. Then **ping** various systems on the network and attach to one of the user's servers. If everything works, the fault is probably in the user's computer. The user trusts this test because it demonstrates something she does every day. She will have more confidence in the laptop than an unidentifiable piece of test equipment displaying the message "No faults found." If the test fails, the fault is probably in the network equipment or wiring. That's the time to bring out the cable tester.

Another advantage of using a laptop as a piece of test equipment is its inherent versatility. It runs a wide variety of test, diagnostic, and management software. Install UNIX on the laptop and run the software discussed in the rest of this chapter from your desktop or your laptop.

This book emphasizes free or "built-in" software diagnostic tools that run on UNIX systems. The software tools used in this chapter, and many more, are described in RFC 1470, *FYI on a Network Management Tool Catalog: Tools for Monitoring and Debugging TCP/IP Internets and Interconnected Devices*. A catchy title, and a very useful RFC! The tools listed in that catalog and discussed in this book are:

ifconfig
> Provides information about the basic configuration of the interface. It is useful for detecting bad IP addresses, incorrect subnet masks, and improper broadcast addresses. Chapter 6, *Configuring the Interface*, covers **ifconfig** in detail. This tool is provided with the UNIX operating system.

arp
> Provides information about Ethernet/IP address translation. It can be used to detect systems on the local network that are configured with the wrong IP address. **arp** is covered in this chapter, and is used in an example in Chapter 2, *Delivering the Data*. **arp** is delivered as part of UNIX.

netstat

> Provides a variety of information. It is commonly used to display detailed statistics about each network interface, network sockets, and the network routing table. **netstat** is used repeatedly in this book, most extensively in Chapters 2, 6, and 7. **netstat** is delivered as part of UNIX.

ping

> Indicates whether a remote host can be reached. **ping** also displays statistics about packet loss and delivery time. **ping** is discussed in Chapter 1 and used in Chapter 7. **ping** also comes as part of UNIX.

nslookup

> Provides information about the DNS name service. **nslookup** is covered in detail in Chapter 8, *Configuring DNS Name Service*. It comes as part of the BIND software package.

dig

> Also provides information about name service, and is similar to **nslookup**.

ripquery

> Provides information about the contents of the RIP update packets being sent or received by your system. It is provided as part of the **gated** software package, but it does not require that you run **gated**. It will work with any system running RIP.

traceroute

> Prints information about each routing hop that packets take going from your system to a remote system.

snoop

> Analyzes the individual packets exchanged between hosts on a network. **snoop** is a TCP/IP protocol analyzer that examines the contents of packets, including their headers. It is most useful for analyzing protocol problems. **tcp-dump** is a tool similar to **snoop** that is available via anonymous FTP from the Internet.

This chapter discusses each of these tools, even those covered earlier in the text. We start with **ping**, which is used in more troubleshooting situations than any other diagnostic tool.

Testing Basic Connectivity

The **ping** command tests whether a remote host can be reached from your computer. This simple function is extremely useful for testing the network connection, independent of the application in which the original problem was detected. **ping** allows you to determine whether further testing should be directed toward the network connection (the lower layers) or the application (the upper layers). If **ping** shows that packets can travel to the remote system and back, the user's problem is probably in the upper layers. If packets can't make the round trip, lower protocol layers are probably at fault.

Frequently a user reports a network problem by stating that he can't **telnet** (or **ftp**, or send email, or whatever) to some remote host. He then immediately qualifies this statement with the announcement that it worked before. In cases like this, where the ability to connect to the remote host is in question, **ping** is a very useful tool.

Using the hostname provided by the user, **ping** the remote host. If your **ping** is successful, have the user **ping** the host. If the user's **ping** is also successful, concentrate your further analysis on the specific application that the user is having trouble with. Perhaps the user is attempting to **telnet** to a host that only provides anonymous **ftp**. Perhaps the host was down when the user tried his application. Have the user try it again, while you watch or listen to every detail of what he is doing. If he is doing everything right and the application still fails, detailed analysis of the application with **snoop** and coordination with the remote system administrator may be needed.

If your **ping** is successful and the user's **ping** fails, concentrate testing on the user's system configuration, and on those things that are different about the user's path to the remote host, when compared to your path to the remote host.

If your **ping** fails, or the user's **ping** fails, pay close attention to any error messages. The error messages displayed by **ping** are helpful guides for planning further testing. The details of the messages may vary from implementation to implementation, but there are only a few basic types of errors:

Unknown host

> The remote host's name cannot be resolved by name service into an IP address. The name servers could be at fault (either your local server or the remote system's server), the name could be incorrect, or something could be wrong with the network between your system and the remote server. If you know the remote host's IP address, try to **ping** that. If you can reach the host using its IP address, the problem is with name service. Use **nslookup** or **dig** to test the local and remote servers, and to check the accuracy of the host name the user gave you.

Network unreachable

> The local system does not have a route to the remote system. If the numeric IP address was used on the **ping** command line, re-enter the **ping** command using the hostname. This eliminates the possibility that the IP address was entered incorrectly, or that you were given the wrong address. If a routing

protocol is being used, make sure it is running and check the routing table with **netstat**. If RIP is being used, **ripquery** will check the contents of the RIP updates being received. If a static default route is being used, re-install it. If everything seems fine on the host, check its default gateway for routing problems.

No answer

The remote system did not respond. Most network utilities have some version of this message. Some **ping** implementations print the message "100% packet loss." **telnet** prints the message "Connection timed out" and **sendmail** returns the error "cannot connect." All of these errors mean the same thing. The local system has a route to the remote system, but it receives no response from the remote system to any of the packets it sends.

There are many possible causes of this problem. The remote host may be down. Either the local or the remote host may be configured incorrectly. A gateway or circuit between the local host and the remote host may be down. The remote host may have routing problems. Only additional testing can isolate the cause of the problem. Carefully check the local configuration using **netstat** and **ifconfig**. Check the route to the remote system with **traceroute**. Contact the administrator of the remote system and report the problem.

All of the tools mentioned here will be discussed later in this chapter. However, before leaving **ping**, let's look more closely at the command and the statistics it displays.

The ping Command

The basic format of the **ping** command on a Solaris system is:*

ping *host* [*packetsize*] [*count*]

host

The hostname or IP address of the remote host being tested. Use the hostname or address provided by the user in the trouble report.

packetsize

Defines the size in bytes of the test packets. This field is required only if the *count* field is going to be used. Use the default *packetsize* of 56 bytes.

count

The number of packets to be sent in the test. Use the *count* field, and set the value low. Otherwise, the **ping** command may continue to send test packets

---

* Check your system's documentation. **ping** varies slightly from system to system. On Linux, the format shown above would be: **ping** [–c *count*] [–s *packetsize*] *host*

until you interrupt it, usually by pressing CTRL-C (^C). Sending excessive numbers of test packets is not a good use of network bandwidth and system resources. Usually five packets are sufficient for a test.

To check that *ns.uu.net* can be reached from *almond*, we send five 56-byte packets with the following command:

```
% ping -s ns.uu.net 56 5
PING ns.uu.net: 56 data bytes
64 bytes from ns.uu.net (137.39.1.3): icmp_seq=0. time=32.8 ms
64 bytes from ns.uu.net (137.39.1.3): icmp_seq=1. time=15.3 ms
64 bytes from ns.uu.net (137.39.1.3): icmp_seq=2. time=13.1 ms
64 bytes from ns.uu.net (137.39.1.3): icmp_seq=3. time=32.4 ms
64 bytes from ns.uu.net (137.39.1.3): icmp_seq=4. time=28.1 ms

----ns.uu.net PING Statistics----
5 packets transmitted, 5 packets received, 0% packet loss
round-trip (ms), min/avg/max = 13.1/24.3/32.8
```

The −s option is included because *almond* is a Solaris workstation, and we want packet-by-packet statistics. Without the −s option, Sun's **ping** command only prints a summary line saying "ns.uu.net is alive." Other **ping** implementations do not require the −s option; they display the statistics by default.

This test shows an extremely good wide area network link to *ns.uu.net* with no packet loss and a fast response. The round-trip between *peanut* and *ns.uu.net* took an average of only 24.3 milliseconds. A small packet loss, and a round-trip time an order of magnitude higher, would not be abnormal for a connection made across a wide area network. The statistics displayed by the **ping** command can indicate low-level network problems. The key statistics are:

- The sequence in which the packets are arriving, as shown by the ICMP sequence number (`icmp_seq`) displayed for each packet.

- How long it takes a packet to make the round trip, displayed in milliseconds after the string `time=`.

- The percentage of packets lost, displayed in a summary line at the end of the **ping** output.

If the packet loss is high, the response time is very slow, or packets are arriving out of order, there could be a network hardware problem. If you see these conditions when communicating over great distances on a wide area network, there is nothing to worry about. TCP/IP was designed to deal with unreliable networks, and some wide area networks suffer a lot of packet loss. But if these problems are seen on a local area network, they indicate trouble.

On a local network cable segment, the round-trip time should be near 0, there should be little or no packet loss, and the packets should arrive in order. If these things are not true, there is a problem with the network hardware. On an Ethernet the problem could be improper cable termination, a bad cable segment, or a bad piece of "active" hardware, such as a hub, switch, or transceiver. Check the cable with a cable tester as described earlier. Good hubs and switches often have built-in diagnostic software that can be checked. Cheap hubs and transceivers may require the "brute force" method of disconnecting individual pieces of hardware until the problem goes away.

The results of a simple **ping** test, even if the **ping** is successful, can help you direct further testing toward the most likely causes of the problem. But other diagnostic tools are needed to examine the problem more closely and find the underlying cause.

Troubleshooting Network Access

The "no answer" and "cannot connect" errors indicate a problem in the lower layers of the network protocols. If the preliminary tests point to this type of problem, concentrate your testing on routing and on the network interface. Use the **ifconfig**, **netstat**, and **arp** commands to test the Network Access Layer.

Troubleshooting with the ifconfig Command

ifconfig checks the network interface configuration. Use this command to verify the user's configuration if the user's system has been recently configured, or if the user's system cannot reach the remote host while other systems on the same network can.

When **ifconfig** is entered with an interface name and no other arguments, it displays the current values assigned to that interface. For example, checking interface le0 on a Solaris system gives this report:

```
% ifconfig le0
le0: flags=863<UP,BROADCAST,NOTRAILERS,RUNNING,MULTICAST> mtu 1500
        inet 172.16.55.105 netmask ffffff00 broadcast 172.16.55.255
```

The **ifconfig** command displays two lines of output. The first line of the display shows the interface's name and its characteristics. Check for these characteristics:

UP The interface is enabled for use. If the interface is "down," have the system's superuser bring the interface "up" with the **ifconfig** command (e.g., **ifconfig le0 up**). If the interface won't come up, replace the interface cable and try again. If it still fails, have the interface hardware checked.

RUNNING

This interface is operational. If the interface is not "running," the driver for this interface may not be properly installed. The system administrator should review all of the steps necessary to install this interface, looking for errors or missed steps.

The second line of **ifconfig** output shows the IP address, the subnet mask (written in hexadecimal), and the broadcast address. Check these three fields to make sure the network interface is properly configured.

Two common interface configuration problems are misconfigured subnet masks and incorrect IP addresses. A bad subnet mask is indicated when the host can reach other hosts on its local subnet and remote hosts on distant networks, but it cannot reach hosts on other local subnets. **ifconfig** quickly reveals if a bad subnet mask is set.

An incorrectly set IP address can be a subtle problem. If the network part of the address is incorrect, every **ping** will fail with the "no answer" error. In this case, using **ifconfig** will reveal the incorrect address. However, if the host part of the address is wrong, the problem can be more difficult to detect. A small system, such as a PC that only connects out to other systems and never accepts incoming connections, can run for a long time with the wrong address without its user noticing the problem. Additionally, the system that suffers the ill effects may not be the one that is misconfigured. It is possible for someone to accidentally use your IP address on his system, and for his mistake to cause your system intermittent communications problems. An example of this problem is discussed later. This type of configuration error cannot be discovered by **ifconfig**, because the error is on a remote host. The **arp** command is used for this type of problem.

Troubleshooting with the arp Command

The **arp** command is used to analyze problems with IP to Ethernet address translation. The **arp** command has three useful options for troubleshooting:

–a   Display all ARP entries in the table.

–d *hostname*
    Delete an entry from the ARP table.

–s *hostname ether-address*
    Add a new entry to the table.

With these three options you can view the contents of the ARP table, delete a problem entry, and install a corrected entry. The ability to install a corrected entry is useful in "buying time" while you look for the permanent fix.

Use **arp** if you suspect that incorrect entries are getting into the address resolution table. One clear indication of problems with the ARP table is a report that the "wrong" host responded to some command, like **ftp** or **telnet**. Intermittent problems that affect only certain hosts can also indicate that the ARP table has been corrupted. ARP table problems are usually caused by two systems using the same IP address. The problems appear intermittent, because the entry that appears in the table is the address of the host that responded quickest to the last ARP request. Sometimes the "correct" host responds first, and sometimes the "wrong" host responds first.

If you suspect that two systems are using the same IP address, display the address resolution table with the **arp −a** command. Here's an example from a Solaris system:*

```
% arp -a
Net to Media Table
Device   IP Address                Mask          Flags   Phys Addr
------   --------------------      ---------------  -----   ---------------
le0      peanut.nuts.com           255.255.255.255          08:00:20:05:21:33
le0      pecan.nuts.com            255.255.255.255          00:00:0c:e0:80:b1
le0      almond.nuts.com           255.255.255.255  SP      08:00:20:22:fd:51
le0      BASE-ADDRESS.MCAST.NET 240.0.0.0          SM      01:00:5e:00:00:00
```

It is easiest to verify that the IP and Ethernet address pairs are correct if you have a record of each host's correct Ethernet address. For this reason you should record each host's Ethernet and IP address when it is added to your network. If you have such a record, you'll quickly see if anything is wrong with the table.

If you don't have this type of record, the first three bytes of the Ethernet address can help you to detect a problem. The first three bytes of the address identify the equipment manufacturer. A list of these identifying prefixes is found in the *Assigned Numbers* RFC, in the section entitled "Ethernet Vendor Address Components." This information is also available at *ftp://ftp.isi.edu/in-notes/iana/-assignments/ethernet-numbers*.

From the vendor prefixes we see that two of the ARP entries displayed in our example are Sun systems (8:0:20). If *pecan* is also supposed to be a Sun, the 0:0:0c Cisco prefix indicates that a Cisco router has been mistakenly configured with *pecan*'s IP address.

If neither checking a record of correct assignments nor checking the manufacturer prefix helps you identify the source of the errant ARP, try using **telnet** to connect to the IP address shown in the ARP entry. If the device supports **telnet**, the login banner might help you identify the incorrectly configured host.

---

* The format in which the ARP table is displayed may vary slightly between systems.

ARP problem case study

A user called in asking if the server was down, and reported the following problem. The user's workstation, called *cashew*, appeared to "lock up" for minutes at a time when certain commands were used, while other commands worked with no problems. The network commands that involved the NIS name server all caused the lock-up problem, but some unrelated commands also caused the problem. The user reported seeing the error message:

```
NFS getattr failed for server almond: RPC: Timed out
```

The server *almond* was providing *cashew* with NIS and NFS services. The commands that failed on *cashew* were commands that required NIS service, or that were stored in the centrally maintained */usr/local* directory exported from *almond*. The commands that ran correctly were installed locally on the user's workstation. No one else reported a problem with the server, and we were able to **ping** *cashew* from *almond* and get good responses.

We had the user check the */usr/adm/messages* file for recent error messages, and she discovered this:

```
Mar  6 13:38:23 cashew vmunix: duplicate IP address!!
        sent from ethernet address: 0:0:c0:4:38:1a
```

This message indicates that the workstation detected another host on the Ethernet responding to its IP address. The "imposter" used the Ethernet address 0:0:c0:4:38:1a in its ARP response. The correct Ethernet address for *cashew* is 8:0:20:e:12:37.

We checked *almond*'s ARP table and found that it had the incorrect ARP entry for *cashew*. We deleted the bad *cashew* entry with the **arp –d** command, and installed the correct entry with the **–s** option, as shown below:

```
# arp -d cashew
cashew (172.16.180.130) deleted
# arp -s cashew 8:0:20:e:12:37
```

ARP entries received via the ARP protocol are temporary. The values are held in the table for a finite lifetime and are deleted when that lifetime expires. New values are then obtained via the ARP protocol. Therefore, if some remote interfaces change, the local table adjusts and communications continue. Usually this is a good idea, but if someone is using the wrong IP address, that bad address can keep reappearing in the ARP table even if it is deleted. However, manually entered values are permanent; they stay in the table and can only be deleted manually. This allowed us to install a correct entry in the table, without worrying about it being overwritten by a bad address.

This quick fix resolved *cashew's* immediate problem, but we still needed to find the culprit. We checked the */etc/ethers* file to see if we had an entry for Ethernet address 0:0:c0:4:38:1a, but we didn't. From the first three bytes of this address, 0:0:c0, we knew that the device was a Western Digital card. Since our network has only UNIX workstations and PCs, we assumed the Western Digital card was installed in a PC. We also guessed that the problem address was recently installed because the user had never had the problem before. We sent out an urgent announcement to all users asking if anyone had recently installed a new PC, reconfigured a PC, or installed TCP/IP software on a PC. We got one response. When we checked his system, we found out that he had entered the address 172.16.180.130 when he should have entered 172.16.180.138. The address was corrected and the problem did not recur.

Nothing fancy was needed to solve this problem. Once we checked the error messages, we knew what the problem was and how to solve it. Involving the entire network user community allowed us to quickly locate the problem system and to avoid a room-to-room search for the PC. Reluctance to involve users and make them part of the solution is one of the costliest, and most common, mistakes made by network administrators.

Checking the Interface with netstat

If the preliminary tests lead you to suspect that the connection to the local area network is unreliable, the **netstat −i** command can provide useful information. The example below shows the output from the **netstat −i** command:

```
% netstat -i
Name Mtu  Net/Dest Address     Ipkts  Ierrs Opkts  Oerrs Collis Queue
le0  1500 nuts.com almond      442697 2     633424 2     50679  0
lo0  1536 loopback localhost   53040  0     53040  0     0      0
```

The line for the loopback interface, lo0, can be ignored. Only the line for the real network interface is significant, and only the last five fields on that line provide significant troubleshooting information.

Let's look at the last field first. There should be no packets queued (Queue) that cannot be transmitted. If the interface is up and running, and the system cannot deliver packets to the network, suspect a bad drop cable or a bad interface. Replace the cable and see if the problem goes away. If it doesn't, call the vendor for interface hardware repairs.

The input errors (Ierrs) and the output errors (Oerrs) should be close to 0. Regardless of how much traffic has passed through this interface, 100 errors in either of these fields is high. High output errors could indicate a saturated local network or a bad physical connection between the host and the network. High input errors could indicate that the network is saturated, the local host is overloaded, or there is a physical network problem. Tools, such as **ping** statistics or a cable tester, can help you determine if it is a physical network problem. Evaluating the collision rate can help you determine if the local Ethernet is saturated.

A high value in the collision field (Collis) is normal, but if the percentage of output packets that result in a collision is too high, it indicates that the network is saturated. Collision rates greater than 5% bear watching. If high collision rates are seen consistently, and are seen among a broad sampling of systems on the network, you may need to subdivide the network to reduce traffic load.

Collision rates are a percentage of output packets. Don't use the total number of packets sent and received; use the values in the Opkts and Collis fields when determining the collision rate. For example, the output in the **netstat** sample above shows 50679 collisions out of 633424 outgoing packets. That's a collision rate of 8%. This sample network could be overworked; check the statistics on other hosts on this network. If the other systems also show a high collision rate, consider subdividing this network.

Subdividing an Ethernet

To reduce the collision rate, you must reduce the amount of traffic on the network segment. A simple way to do this is to create multiple segments out of the single segment. Each new segment will have fewer hosts and, therefore, less traffic. We'll see, however, that it's not quite this simple.

The most effective way to subdivide an Ethernet is to install an Ethernet switch. Each port on the switch is essentially a separate Ethernet. So a 16-port switch gives you 16 Ethernets to work with when balancing the load. On most switches the ports can be used in a variety of ways (see Figure 11-1). Lightly used systems can be attached to a hub that is then attached to one of the switch ports to allow the systems to share a single segment. Servers and demanding systems can be given dedicated ports so that they don't need to share a segment with anyone. Additionally, some switches provide a few Fast Ethernet 100 Mbps ports. These are called asymmetric switches because different ports operate at different speeds. Use the Fast Ethernet ports to connect heavily used servers. If you're buying a new switch, buy a 10/100 switch with auto-sensing ports. This allows every port to be used at either 100 Mbps or at 10 Mbps, which give you the maximum configuration flexibility.

Figure 11-1 shows an 8-port 10/100 Ethernet switch. Ports 1 and 2 are wired to Ethernet hubs. A few systems are connected to each hub. When new systems are added they are distributed evenly among the hubs to prevent any one segment from becoming overloaded. Additional hubs can be added to the available switch ports for future expansion. Port 4 attaches a demanding system with its own private segment. Port 6 operates at 100 Mbps and attaches a heavily used server. A port can be reserved for a future 100 Mbps connection to a second 10/100 Ethernet switch for even more expansion.

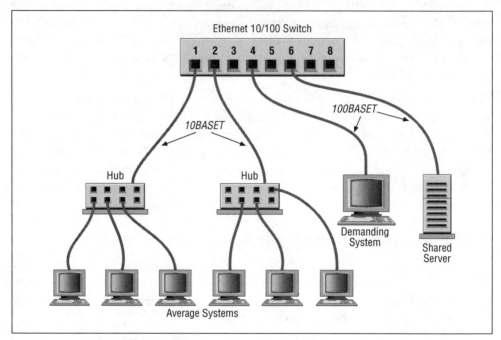

Figure 11-1: Subdividing an Ethernet with switches

Before allocating the ports on your switch, evaluate what services are in demand, and who talks to whom. Then develop a plan that reduces the amount of traffic flowing over any segment. For example, if the demanding system on Port 4 uses lots of bandwidth because it is constantly talking to one of the systems on Port 1, all of the systems on Port 1 will suffer because of this traffic. The computer that the demanding system communicates with should be moved to one of the vacant ports or to the same port (4) as the demanding system. Use your switch to the greatest advantage by balancing the load.

Should you segment an old coaxial cable Ethernet by cutting the cable and joining it back together through a router or a bridge? No. If you have an old network that is finally reaching saturation, it is time to install a new network built on a more robust technology. A *shared media* network, a network where everyone is on the same cable (in this example, a coaxial cable Ethernet) is an accident waiting to happen. Design a network that a user cannot bring down by merely disconnecting his system, or even by accidentally cutting a wire in his office. Use *Unshielded Twisted Pair* (UTP) cable, ideally Category 5 cable, to create a 10BaseT Ethernet or

100BaseT Fast Ethernet that wires equipment located in the user's office to a hub securely stored in a wire closet. The network components in the user's office should be sufficiently isolated from the network so that damage to those components does not damage the entire network. The new network will solve your collision problem and reduce the amount of hardware troubleshooting you are called upon to do.

Network hardware problems

Some of the tests discussed in this section can show a network hardware problem. If a hardware problem is indicated, contact the people responsible for the hardware. If the problem appears to be in a leased telephone line, contact the telephone company. If the problem appears to be in a wide area network, contact the management of that network. Don't sit on a problem expecting it to go away. It could easily get worse.

If the problem is in your local area network, you will have to handle it yourself. Some tools, such as the cable tester described above, can help. But frequently the only way to approach a hardware problem is by brute force—disconnecting pieces of hardware until you find the one causing the problem. It is most convenient to do this at the switch or hub. If you identify a device causing the problem, repair or replace it. Remember that the problem can be the cable itself, rather than any particular device.

Checking Routing

The "network unreachable" error message clearly indicates a routing problem. If the problem is in the local host's routing table, it is easy to detect and resolve. First, use **netstat −nr** and **grep** to see whether or not a valid route to your destination is installed in the routing table. This example checks for a specific route to network 128.8.0.0:

```
% netstat -nr | grep '128\.8\.0'
128.8.0.0    26.20.0.16    UG    0    37    std0
```

This same test, run on a system that did not have this route in its routing table, would return no response at all. For example, a user reports that the "network is down" because he cannot **ftp** to *sunsite.unc.edu*, and a **ping** test returns the following results:

```
% ping -s sunsite.unc.edu 56 2
PING sunsite.unc.edu: 56 data bytes
sendto: Network is unreachable
ping: wrote sunsite.unc.edu 64 chars, ret=-1
sendto: Network is unreachable
ping: wrote sunsite.unc.edu 64 chars, ret=-1
```

```
----sunsite.unc.edu PING Statistics----
2 packets transmitted, 0 packets received, 100% packet loss
```

Based on the "network unreachable" error message, check the user's routing table. In our example, we're looking for a route to *sunsite.unc.edu.* The IP address* of sunsite.unc.edu is 152.2.254.81, which is a class B address. Remember that routes are network-oriented. So we check for a route to network 152.2.0.0:

```
% netstat -nr | grep '152\.2\.0\.0'
%
```

This test shows that there is no *specific* route to 152.2.0.0. If a route was found, **grep** would display it. Since there's no specific route to the destination, remember to look for a default route. This example shows a successful check for a default route:

```
% netstat -nr | grep def
default        172.16.12.1    UG    0    101277    le0
```

If **netstat** shows the correct specific route, or a valid default route, the problem is not in the routing table. In that case, use **traceroute**, as described later in this chapter, to trace the route all the way to its destination.

If **netstat** doesn't return the expected route, it's a local routing problem. There are two ways to approach local routing problems, depending on whether the system uses static or dynamic routing. If you're using static routing, install the missing route using the **route add** command. Remember, most systems that use static routing rely on a default route, so the missing route could be the default route. Make sure that the startup files add the needed route to the table whenever the system reboots. See Chapter 7, *Configuring Routing*, for details about the **route add** command.

If you're using dynamic routing, make sure that the routing program is running. For example, the command below makes sure that **gated** is running:

```
% ps `cat /etc/gated.pid`
  PID TT STAT  TIME COMMAND
27711 ? S   304:59 gated -tep /etc/log/gated.log
```

If the correct routing daemon is not running, restart it and specify tracing. Tracing allows you to check for problems that might be causing the daemon to terminate abnormally.

---

* Use **nslookup** to find the IP address if you don't know it. **nslookup** is discussed later in this chapter.

Checking RIP Updates

If the routing daemon is running and the local system receives routing updates via Routing Information Protocol (RIP), use **ripquery** to check the updates received from your RIP suppliers. For example, to check the RIP updates being received from *almond* and *pecan*, the *peanut* administrator enters the following command:

```
% ripquery -1 -n -r almond pecan
44 bytes from almond.nuts.com(172.16.12.1):
        0.0.0.0, metric 3
        10.0.0.0, metric 0
264 bytes from pecan.nuts.com(172.16.12.3):
        172.16.5.0, metric 2
        172.16.3.0, metric 2
             .
             .
             .
        172.16.12.0, metric 2
        172.16.13.0, metric 2
```

After an initial line identifying the gateway, **ripquery** shows the contents of the incoming RIP packets, one line per route. The first line of the report above indicates that **ripquery** received a response from *almond*. That line is followed by two lines for the two routes advertised by *almond*. *almond* advertises the default route (destination 0.0.0.0) with a metric of 3, and its direct route to Milnet (destination 10.0.0.0) with a metric of 0. Next, **ripquery** shows the routes advertised by *pecan*. These are the routes to the other *nuts-net* subnets.

The three **ripquery** options used in this example are:

−1 Sends the query as a RIP version 1 packet. By default, queries are sent as RIP version 2 packets. Older systems may only support RIP version 1.

−n Causes **ripquery** to display all output in numeric form. **ripquery** attempts to resolve all IP addresses to names if the **−n** option is not specified. It's a good idea to use the **−n** option; it produces a cleaner display, and you don't waste time resolving names.

−r Directs **ripquery** to use the RIP REQUEST command, instead of the RIP POLL command, to query the RIP supplier. RIP POLL is not universally supported. You are more likely to get a successful response if you specify **−r** on the **ripquery** command line.

The routes returned in these updates should be the routes you expect. If they are not, or if no routes are returned, check the configuration of the RIP suppliers. Routing configuration problems cause RIP suppliers to advertise routes that they shouldn't, or to fail to advertise the routes that they should. You can detect these problems only by applying your knowledge of your network configuration. You must know what is right to detect what is wrong. Don't expect to see error messages or strange garbled routes. For example, assume that in the previous test *pecan* returned the following update:

```
264 bytes from pecan.nuts.com(172.16.12.3):
        0.0.0.0, metric 2
        172.16.3.0, metric 2
                .
                .
                .
        172.16.12.0, metric 2
        172.16.13.0, metric 2
```

This update shows that *pecan* is advertising itself as a default gateway with a lower cost (2 versus 3) than *almond.* This would cause every host on this subnet to use *pecan* as its default gateway. If this is not what you wanted, the routing configuration of *pecan* should be corrected.*

Tracing Routes

If the local routing table and RIP suppliers are correct, the problem may be occurring some distance away from the local host. Remote routing problems can cause the "no answer" error message, as well as the "network unreachable" error message. But the "network unreachable" message does not always signify a routing problem. It can mean that the remote network cannot be reached because something is down between the local host and the remote destination. **traceroute** is the program that can help you locate these problems.

traceroute traces the route of UDP packets from the local host to a remote host. It prints the name (if it can be determined) and IP address of each gateway along the route to the remote host.

traceroute uses two techniques, small *ttl* (time-to-live) values and an invalid port number, to trace packets to their destination. **traceroute** sends out UDP packets with small ttl values to detect the intermediate gateways. The ttl values start at 1 and increase in increments of 1 for each group of three UDP packets sent. When a gateway receives a packet, it decrements the ttl. If the ttl is then 0, the packet is not forwarded and an ICMP "Time Exceeded" message is returned to the source of the packet. **traceroute** displays one line of output for each gateway from which it receives a "Time Exceeded" message. Figure 11-2 shows a sample of the single line of output that is displayed for a gateway, and it shows the meaning of each field in the line. When the destination host receives a packet from **traceroute**, it returns an ICMP "Unreachable Port" message. This happens because **traceroute** intentionally uses an invalid port number (33434) to force this error. When **traceroute** receives the "Unreachable Port" message, it knows that it has reached

---

* Correct routing configuration is discussed in Chapter 7.

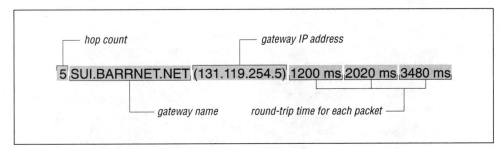

Figure 11-2: traceroute output

the destination host, and it terminates the trace. So, **traceroute** is able to develop a list of the gateways, starting at one hop away and increasing one hop at a time until the remote host is reached. Figure 11-3 illustrates the flow of packets tracing to a host three hops away. The following shows a **traceroute** to *ds.internic.net* from a Linux system hanging off BBN PlaNET. **traceroute** sends out three packets at each ttl value. If no response is received to a packet, **traceroute** prints an asterisk (*). If a response is received, **traceroute** displays the name and address of the gateway that responded, and the packet's round-trip time in milliseconds.

```
% traceroute ds.internic.net
traceroute to ds.internic.net (198.49.45.10), 30 hops max, 40 byte packets
 1  gw-55.nuts.com (172.16.55.200)  0.95 ms  0.91 ms  0.91 ms
 2  172.16.230.254 (172.16.230.254)  1.51 ms  1.33 ms  1.29 ms
 3  gw225.nuts.com (172.16.2.252)  4.13 ms  1.94 ms  2.20 ms
 4  192.221.253.2 (192.221.253.2)  52.90 ms  81.19 ms  58.09 ms
 5  washdc1-br2.bbnplanet.net (4.0.36.17)  6.5 ms  5.8 ms  5.88 ms
 6  nyc1-br1.bbnplanet.net (4.0.1.114)  13.24 ms  12.71 ms  12.96 ms
 7  nyc1-br2.bbnplanet.net (4.0.1.178)  14.64 ms  13.32 ms  12.21 ms
 8  cambridge1-br1.bbnplanet.net (4.0.2.86)  28.84 ms  27.78 ms  23.56 ms
 9  cambridge1-cr14.bbnplanet.net (199.94.205.14) 19.9 ms  24.7 ms 22.3 ms
10  attbcstoll.bbnplanet.net (206.34.99.38)  34.31 ms  36.63 ms  32.21 ms
11  ds0.internic.net (198.49.45.10)  33.19 ms  33.34 ms *
```

This trace shows that 10 intermediate gateways are involved, that packets are making the trip, and that round-trip travel time for packets from this host to *ds.internic.net* is about 33 ms.

Variations and bugs in the implementation of ICMP on different types of gateways, and the unpredictable nature of the path a datagram can take through a network, can cause some odd displays. For this reason, you shouldn't examine the output of **traceroute** too closely. The most important things in the **traceroute** output are:

- Did the packet get to its remote destination?

- If not, where did it stop?

In the code below we show another trace of the path to *ds.internic.net*. This time the trace does not go all the way through to the InterNIC.

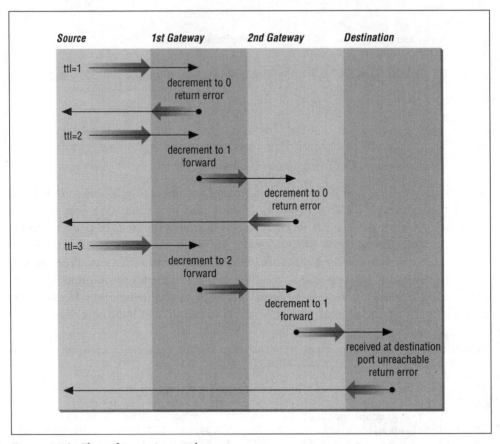

Figure 11-3: Flow of traceroute packets

```
% traceroute ds.internic.net
traceroute to ds.internic.net (198.49.45.10), 30 hops max,
     40 byte packets
 1  gw-55.nuts.com (172.16.55.200)  0.959 ms  0.917 ms  0.913 ms
 2  172.16.230.254 (172.16.230.254)  1.518 ms  1.337 ms  1.296 ms
 3  gw225.nuts.com (172.16.2.252)  4.137 ms  1.945 ms  2.209 ms
 4  192.221.253.2 (192.221.253.2)  52.903 ms  81.19 ms  58.097 ms
 5  washdc1-br2.bbnplanet.net (4.0.36.17)  6.5 ms  5.8 ms  5.888 ms
 6  nyc1-br1.bbnplanet.net (4.0.1.114)  13.244 ms  12.717 ms  12.968 ms
 7  nyc1-br2.bbnplanet.net (4.0.1.178)  14.649 ms  13.323 ms  12.212 ms
 8  cambridge1-br1.bbnplanet.net (4.0.2.86)  28.842 ms  27.784 ms
     23.561 ms
 9  * * *
10  * * *
     .
     .
     .
29  * * *
30  * * *
```

When **traceroute** fails to get packets through to the remote end system, the trace trails off, displaying a series of three asterisks at each hop count until the count reaches 30. If this happens, contact the administrator of the remote host you're trying to reach, and the administrator of the last gateway displayed in the trace. Describe the problem to them; they may be able to help.* In our example, the last gateway that responded to our packets was *cambridge1-br1.bbnplanet.net.* We would contact this system administrator, and the administrator of *ds.internic.net.*

Checking Name Service

Name server problems are indicated when the "unknown host" error message is returned by the user's application. Name server problems can usually be diagnosed with **nslookup** or **dig**. **nslookup** is discussed in detail in Chapter 8. **dig** is an alternative tool with similar functionality that is discussed in this chapter. Before looking at **dig**, let's take another look at **nslookup** and see how it is used to troubleshoot name service.

Three features of **nslookup** covered in Chapter 8 are particularly important for troubleshooting remote name server problems. These features are its ability to:

- Locate the authoritative servers for the remote domain using the NS query
- Obtain all records about the remote host using the ANY query
- Browse all entries in the remote zone using **nslookup**'s **ls** and **view** commands

When troubleshooting a remote server problem, directly query the authoritative servers returned by the NS query. Don't rely on information returned by non-authoritative servers. If the problems that have been reported are intermittent, query all of the authoritative servers in turn and compare their answers. Intermittent name server problems are sometimes caused by the remote servers returning different answers to the same query.

The ANY query returns all records about a host, thus giving the broadest range of troubleshooting information. Simply knowing what information is (and isn't) available can solve a lot of problems. For example, if the query returns an MX record but no A record, it is easy to understand why the user couldn't **telnet** to that host! Many hosts are accessible to mail that are not accessible by other network services. In this case, the user is confused and is trying to use the remote host in an inappropriate manner.

If you are unable to locate any information about the hostname that the user gave you, perhaps the hostname is incorrect. Given that the hostname you have is

---

* Chapter 13, *Internet Information Resources*, explains how to find out who is responsible for a specific computer.

wrong, looking for the correct name is like trying to find a needle in a haystack. However, **nslookup** can help. Use **nslookup**'s **ls** command to dump the remote zone file, and redirect the listing to a file. Then use **nslookup**'s **view** command to browse through the file, looking for names similar to the one the user supplied. Many problems are caused by a mistaken hostname.

All of the **nslookup** features and commands mentioned here are used in Chapter 8. However, some examples using these commands to solve real name server problems will be helpful. The three examples that follow are based on actual trouble reports.*

Some systems work, others don't

A user reported that she could resolve a certain hostname from her workstation, but could not resolve the same hostname from the central system. However, the central system could resolve other hostnames. We ran several tests and found that we could resolve the hostname on some systems and not on others. There seemed to be no predictable pattern to the failure. So we used **nslookup** to check the remote servers.

```
% nslookup
Default Server:  almond.nuts.com
Address:  172.16.12.1

> set type=NS
> foo.edu.
Server:  almond.nuts.com
Address:  172.16.12.1

foo.edu          nameserver = gerbil.foo.edu
foo.edu          nameserver = red.big.com
foo.edu          nameserver = shrew.foo.edu
gerbil.foo.edu   inet address = 198.97.99.2
red.big.com   inet address = 184.6.16.2
shrew.foo.edu    inet address = 198.97.99.1
> set type=ANY
> server gerbil.foo.edu
Default Server:  gerbil.foo.edu
Address:  198.97.99.2

> hamster.foo.edu
Server:  gerbil.foo.edu
Address:  198.97.99.2

hamster.foo.edu          inet address = 198.97.99.8
> server red.big.com
Default Server:  red.big.com
```

---

* The host and server names are fictitious, but the problems were real.

```
Address:  184.6.16.2
> hamster.foo.edu
Server:  red.big.com
Address:  184.6.16.2

*** red.big.com can't find hamster.foo.edu: Non-existent domain
```

This sample **nslookup** session contains several steps. The first step is to locate the authoritative servers for the host name in question (*hamster.foo.edu*). We set the query type to NS to get the name server records, and query for the domain (*foo.edu*) in which the hostname is found. This returns three names of authoritative servers: *gerbil.foo.edu*, *red.big.com*, and *shrew.foo.edu*.

Next, we set the query type to ANY to look for any records related to the hostname in question. Then we set the server to the first server in the list, *gerbil.foo.edu*, and query for *hamster.foo.edu*. This returns an address record. So server *gerbil.foo.edu* works fine. We repeat the test using *red.big.com* as the server, and it fails. No records are returned.

The next step is to get SOA records from each server and see if they are the same:

```
> set type=SOA
> foo.edu.
Server:  red.big.com
Address:  184.6.16.2

foo.edu          origin = gerbil.foo.edu
       mail addr = amanda.gerbil.foo.edu
       serial=10164, refresh=43200, retry=3600, expire=3600000,
       min=2592000
> server gerbil.foo.edu
Default Server:  gerbil.foo.edu
Address:  198.97.99.2

> foo.edu.
Server:  gerbil.foo.edu
Address:  198.97.99.2

foo.edu          origin = gerbil.foo.edu
       mail addr = amanda.gerbil.foo.edu
       serial=10164, refresh=43200, retry=3600, expire=3600000,
       min=2592000

> exit
```

If the SOA records have different serial numbers, perhaps the zone file, and therefore the hostname, has not yet been downloaded to the secondary server. If the serial numbers are the same and the data is different, as in this case, there is a definite problem. Contact the remote domain administrator and notify her of the problem. The administrator's mailing address is shown in the "mail addr" field of the SOA record. In our example, we would send mail to *amanda@gerbil.foo.edu* reporting the problem.

The data is here and the server can't find it!

This problem was reported by the administrator of one of our secondary name servers. The administrator reported that his server could not resolve a certain hostname in a domain for which his server was a secondary server. The primary server was, however, able to resolve the name. The administrator dumped his cache (more on dumping the server cache in the next section), and he could see in the dump that his server had the correct entry for the host. But his server still would not resolve that hostname to an IP address!

The problem was replicated on several other secondary servers. The primary server would resolve the name; the secondary servers wouldn't. All servers had the same SOA serial number, and a dump of the cache on each server showed that they all had the correct address records for the hostname in question. So why wouldn't they resolve the hostname to an address?

Visualizing the difference between the way primary and secondary servers load their data made us suspicious of the zone file transfer. Primary servers load the data directly from local disk files. Secondary servers transfer the data from the primary server via a zone file transfer. Perhaps the zone files were getting corrupted. We displayed the zone file on one of the secondary servers, and it showed the following data:

```
% cat /usr/etc/sales.nuts.com.hosts
PCpma       IN      A           172.16.64.159
            IN      HINFO       "pc" "n3/800salesnutscom"
PCrkc       IN      A           172.16.64.155
            IN      HINFO       "pc" "n3/800salesnutscom"
PCafc       IN      A           172.16.64.189
            IN      HINFO       "pc" "n3/800salesnutscom"
accu        IN      A           172.16.65.27
cmgds1      IN      A           172.16.130.40
cmg         IN      A           172.16.130.30
PCgns       IN      A           172.16.64.167
            IN      HINFO       "pc" "(3/800salesnutscom"
gw          IN      A           172.16.65.254
zephyr      IN      A           172.16.64.188
            IN      HINFO       "Sun" "sparcstation"
ejw         IN      A           172.16.65.17
PCecp       IN      A           172.16.64.193
            IN      HINFO       "pc" "n^Lsparcstationstcom"
```

Notice the odd display in the last field of the HINFO statement for each PC.* This data might have been corrupted in the transfer or it might be bad on the primary server. We used **nslookup** to check that.

```
% nslookup
Default Server:  almond.nuts.com
Address:  172.16.12.1

> server acorn.sales.nuts.com
Default Server:  acorn.sales.nuts.com
Address:  172.16.6.1

> set query=HINFO
> PCwlg.sales.nuts.com
Server:  acorn.sales.nuts.com
Address:  172.16.6.1

PCwlg.sales.nuts.com      CPU=pc  OS=ov
packet size error (0xf7fff590 != 0xf7fff528)
> exit
```

In this **nslookup** example, we set the server to *acorn.sales.nuts.com*, which is the primary server for *sales.nuts.com*. Next we queried for the HINFO record for one of the hosts that appeared to have a corrupted record. The "packet size error" message clearly indicates that **nslookup** was even having trouble retrieving the HINFO record directly from the primary server. We contacted the administrator of the primary server and told him about the problem, pointing out the records that appeared to be in error. He discovered that he had forgotten to put an operating system entry on some of the HINFO records. He corrected this, and it fixed the problem.

Cache corruption

The problem described above was caused by having the name server cache corrupted by bad data. Cache corruption can occur even if your system is not a secondary server. Sometimes the root server entries in the cache become corrupted. Dumping the cache can help diagnose these types of problems.

For example, a user reported intermittent name server failures. She had no trouble with any hostnames within the local domain, or with some names outside the local domain, but names in several different remote domains would not resolve. **nslookup** tests produced no solid clues, so the name server cache was dumped and examined for problems. The root server entries were corrupted, so **named** was reloaded to clear the cache and reread the *named.ca* file. Here's how it was done.

---

* See Appendix D, *A dhcpd Reference*, for a detailed description of the HINFO statement.

The SIGINT signal causes **named** to dump the name server cache to the file */var/tmp/named_dump.db*. The following command passes **named** this signal:

```
# kill -INT `cat /etc/named.pid`
```

The process ID of **named** can be obtained from */etc/named.pid*, as in the example above, because **named** writes its process ID in that file during startup.*

Once SIGINT causes **named** to snapshot its cache to the file, we can then examine the first part of the file to see if the names and addresses of the root servers are correct. For example:

```
# head -10 /var/tmp/named_dump.db
; Dumped at Wed Sep 18 08:45:58 1991
; --- Cache & Data ---
$ORIGIN .
.          80805   IN      SOA     NS.NIC.DDN.MIL. HOSTMASTER.NIC.DDN.MIL.
                ( 910909 10800 900 604800 86400 )
           479912  IN      NS      NS.NIC.DDN.MIL.
           479912  IN      NS      AOS.BRL.MIL.
           479912  IN      NS      A.ISI.EDU.
           479912  IN      NS      C.NYSER.NET.
           479912  IN      NS      TERP.UMD.EDU.
```

The cache shown above is clean. If intermittent name server problems lead you to suspect a cache corruption problem, examine the cache and check the names and addresses of all the root servers. The following symptoms might indicate a problem with the root server cache:

- Incorrect root server names. The section on */etc/named.ca* in Chapter 8 explains how you can locate the correct root server names. The easiest way to do this is to get the file *domain/named.root* from the InterNIC.

- No address or an incorrect address for any of the servers. Again, the correct addresses are in *domain/named.root*.

- A name other than root (.) in the name field of the first root server NS record, or the wildcard character (*) occurring in the name field of a root or top-level name server. The structure of NS records is described in Appendix D.

A "bad cache" with multiple errors might look like this:

```
# head -10 /var/tmp/named_dump.db
; Dumped at Wed Sep 18 08:45:58 1991
; --- Cache & Data ---
$ORIGIN .
arpa  80805   IN      SOA     SRI-NIC.ARPA. HOSTMASTER.SRI-NIC.ARPA.
              ( 910909 10800 900 604800 86400 )
        479912  IN      NS      NS.NIC.DDN.MIL.
```

---

* On our Linux system the process ID is written to */var/run/named.pid*.

```
        479912  IN   NS   AOS.BRL.MIL.
        479912  IN   NS   A.ISI.EDU.
        479912  IN   NS   C.NYSER.NET.
        479912  IN   NS   TERP.UMD.EDU.
  *     479912  IN   NS   NS.FOO.MIL.
```

This contrived example has three glaring errors. The "arpa" entry in the first field of the SOA record is invalid, and is the most infamous form of cache corruption. The last NS record is also invalid. NS.FOO.MIL. is not a valid root server, and an asterisk (*) in the first field of a root server record is not normal.

If you see problems like these, force **named** to reload its cache with the SIGHUP signal as shown below:

```
# kill -HUP `cat /etc/named.pid`
```

This clears the cache and reloads the valid root server entries from your *named.ca* file.

If you know which system is corrupting your cache, instruct your system to ignore updates from the culprit by using the **bogusns** statement in the */etc/named.boot* file. The **bogusns** statement lists the IP addresses of name servers whose information cannot be trusted. For example, in the previous section we described a problem where *acorn.sales.nuts.com* (172.16.16.1) was causing cache corruption with improperly formatted HINFO records. The following entry in the *named.boot* file blocks queries to *acorn.sales.nuts.com* and thus blocks the cache corruption:

```
bogusns 172.16.16.1
```

The **bogusns** entry is only a temporary measure. It is designed to keep things running while the remote domain administrator has a chance to diagnose and repair the problem. Once the remote system is fixed, remove the **bogusns** entry from *named.boot.*

dig: An Alternative to nslookup

An alternative to **nslookup** for making name service queries is **dig**. **dig** queries are usually entered as single-line commands, while **nslookup** is usually run as an interactive session. But the **dig** command performs essentially the same function as **nslookup**. Which you use is mostly a matter of personal choice. They both work well.

As an example, we'll use **dig** to ask the root server *terp.umd.edu* for the NS records for the *mit.edu* domain. To do this, enter the following command:

```
% dig @terp.umd.edu mit.edu ns
```

In this example, *@terp.umd.edu* is the server that is being queried. The server can be identified by name or IP address. If you're troubleshooting a problem in a remote domain, specify an authoritative server for that domain. In this example we're asking for the names of servers for a top-level domain (*mit.edu*), so we ask a root server.

If you don't specify a server explicitly, **dig** uses the local name server, or the name server defined in the */etc/resolv.conf* file. (Chapter 8 describes *resolv.conf.*) Optionally, you can set the environment variable LOCALRES to the name of an alternate *resolv.conf* file. This alternate file will then be used in place of */etc/resolv.conf* for **dig** queries. Setting the LOCALRES variable will only affect **dig**. Other programs that use name service will continue to use */etc/resolv.conf.*

The last item on our sample command line is *ns*. This is the query type. A query type is a value that requests a specific type of DNS information. It is similar to the value used in **nslookup**'s **set type** command. Table 11-1 shows the possible **dig** query types and their meanings.

Table 11-1: dig Query Types

Query Type	DNS Record Requested
a	Address records
any	Any type of record
mx	Mail Exchange records
ns	Name Server records
soa	Start of Authority records
hinfo	Host Info records
axfr	All records in the zone
txt	Text records

Notice that the function of **nslookup**'s **ls** command is performed by the **dig** query type **axfr**.

dig also has an option that is useful for locating a hostname when you have only an IP address. If you only have the IP address of a host, you may want to find out the hostname because numeric addresses are more prone to typos. Having the hostname can reduce the user's problems. The *in-addr.arpa* domain converts addresses to hostnames, and **dig** provides a simple way to enter *in-addr.arpa* domain queries. Using the **−x** option, you can query for a number to name conversion without having to manually reverse the numbers and add "in-addr.arpa." For example, to query for the hostname of IP address 18.72.0.3, simply enter:

```
% dig -x 18.72.0.3

; <<>> DiG 2.1 <<>> -x
;; res options: init recurs defnam dnsrch
;; got answer:
;; ->>HEADER<<- opcode: QUERY, status: NOERROR, id: 6
;; flags: qr aa rd ra; Ques: 1, Ans: 1, Auth: 0, Addit: 0
```

```
;; QUESTIONS:
;;      3.0.72.18.in-addr.arpa, type = ANY, class = IN

;; ANSWERS:
3.0.72.18.in-addr.arpa. 21600    PTR    BITSY.MIT.EDU.

;; Total query time: 74 msec
;; FROM: peanut to SERVER: default -- 172.16.12.1
;; WHEN: Sat Jul 12 11:12:55 1997
;; MSG SIZE  sent: 40  rcvd: 67
```

The answer to our query is BITSY.MIT.EDU, but **dig** displays lots of other output. The first five lines and the last four lines provide information and statistics about the query. For our purposes, the only important information is the answer.*

Analyzing Protocol Problems

Problems caused by bad TCP/IP configurations are much more common than problems caused by bad TCP/IP protocol implementations. Most of the problems you encounter will succumb to analysis using the simple tools we have already discussed. But on occasion, you may need to analyze the protocol interaction between two systems. In the worst case, you may need to analyze the packets in the data stream bit by bit. Protocol analyzers help you do this.

snoop is the tool we'll use. It is provided with the Solaris operating system.† Although we use **snoop** in all of our examples, the concepts introduced in this section should be applicable to the analyzer that you use, because most protocol analyzers function in basically the same way. Protocol analyzers allow you to select, or filter, the packets you want to examine, and to examine those packets byte by byte. We'll discuss both of these functions.

Protocol analyzers watch all the packets on the network. Therefore, you only need *one* system that runs analyzer software on the affected part of the network. One Solaris system with **snoop** can monitor the network traffic and tell you what the other hosts are (or aren't) doing. This, of course, assumes a shared media network. If you use an Ethernet switch, only the traffic on an individual segment can be seen. Some switches provide a monitor port. For others you may need to take your monitor to the location of the problem.

---

* To see a single-line answer to this query, pipe **dig**'s output to **grep**; e.g., **dig –x 18.72.0.3 | grep PTR**.

† If you don't use Solaris, try **tcpdump**. It is available via anonymous FTP on the Internet and is similar to **snoop**.

Packet Filters

snoop reads all the packets on an Ethernet. It does this by placing the Ethernet interface into *promiscuous mode*. Normally, an Ethernet interface only passes packets up to the higher layer protocols that are destined for the local host. In promiscuous mode, all packets are accepted and passed to the higher layer. This allows **snoop** to view all packets and to select packets for analysis, based on a filter you define. Filters can be defined to capture packets from, or to, specific hosts, protocols, and ports, or combinations of all these. As an example, let's look at a very simple **snoop** filter. The following **snoop** command displays all packets sent between the hosts *almond* and *peanut*:

```
# snoop host almond and host peanut
Using device /dev/le (promiscuous mode)
peanut.nuts.com -> almond.nuts.com ICMP Echo request
almond.nuts.com -> peanut.nuts.com ICMP Echo reply
peanut.nuts.com -> almond.nuts.com RLOGIN C port=1023
almond.nuts.com -> peanut.nuts.com RLOGIN R port=1023
^C
```

The filter "host almond and host peanut" selects only those packets that are from *peanut* to *almond*, or from *almond* to *peanut*. The filter is constructed from a set of primitives, and associated hostnames, protocol names, and port numbers. The primitives can be modified and combined with the operators **and**, **or**, and **not**. The filter may be omitted; this causes **snoop** to display all packets from the network.

Table 11-2 shows the primitives used to build **snoop** filters. There are a few additional primitives and some variations that perform the same functions, but these are the essential primitive. See the **snoop** manpage for additional details.

Table 11-2: Expression Primitives

Primitive	Matches Packets
dst host | **net** | **port** *destination*	To *destination* host, net, or port
src host | **net** | **port** *source*	From *source* host, net, or port
host *destination*	To or from *destination* host
net *destination*	To or from *destination* network
port *destination*	To or from *destination* port
ether *address*	To or from Ethernet *address*
protocol	Of *protocol* type (**icmp**, **udp**, or **tcp**)

Using these primitives with the operators **and** and **or**, complex filters can be constructed. However, filters are usually simple. Capturing the traffic between two hosts is probably the most common filter. You may further limit the data captured to a specific protocol, but often you're not sure which protocol will reveal the problem. Just because the user sees the problem in **ftp** or **telnet** does not mean that is where the problem actually occurs. Analysis must often start by capturing all packets, and can only be narrowed after test evidence points to some specific problem.

Modifying analyzer output

The example in the previous section shows that **snoop** displays a single line of summary information for each packet received. All lines show the source and destination addresses, and the protocol being used (ICMP and RLOGIN in the example). The lines that summarize the ICMP packets identify the packet types (Echo request and Echo reply in the example). The lines that summarize the application protocol packets display the source port and the first 20 characters of the packet data.

This summary information is sufficient to gain insight into how packets flow between two hosts and into potential problems. However, troubleshooting protocol problems requires more detailed information about each packet. **snoop** has options that give you control over what information is displayed. To display the data contained in a packet, use the **−x** option. It causes the entire contents of the packet to be dumped in hex and ASCII. In most cases, you don't need to see the entire packet; usually, the headers are sufficient to troubleshoot a protocol problem. The **−v** option displays the headers in a well-formatted and very detailed manner. Because of the large number of lines displayed for each packet, only use **−v** when you need it.

The following example shows an ICMP Echo Request packet displayed with the **−v** option. The same type of packet was summarized in the first line of the previous example.

```
# snoop -v host almond and host macadamia
Using device /dev/le (promiscuous mode)
ETHER:   ----- Ether Header -----
ETHER:
ETHER:   Packet 3 arrived at 16:56:57.90
ETHER:   Packet size = 98 bytes
ETHER:   Destination = 8:0:20:22:fd:51, Sun
ETHER:   Source      = 0:0:c0:9a:d0:db, Western Digital
ETHER:   Ethertype = 0800 (IP)
ETHER:
IP:   ----- IP Header -----
IP:
IP:   Version = 4
IP:   Header length = 20 bytes
IP:   Type of service = 0x00
IP:        xxx. .... = 0 (precedence)
IP:        ...0 .... = normal delay
IP:        .... 0... = normal throughput
IP:        .... .0.. = normal reliability
IP:   Total length = 84 bytes
IP:   Identification = 3049
```

```
IP:    Flags = 0x0
IP:          .0.. .... = may fragment
IP:          ..0. .... = last fragment
IP:    Fragment offset = 0 bytes
IP:    Time to live = 64 seconds/hops
IP:    Protocol = 1 (ICMP)
IP:    Header checksum = fde0
IP:    Source address = 172.16.55.106, macadamia.nuts.com
IP:    Destination address = 172.16.12.1, almond.nuts.com
IP:    No options
IP:
ICMP:  ----- ICMP Header -----
ICMP:
ICMP:  Type = 8 (Echo request)
ICMP:  Code = 0
ICMP:  Checksum = ac54
ICMP:
```

The detailed formatting done by **snoop** maps the bytes received from the network to the header structure. Look at the description of the various header fields in Chapter 1, *Overview of TCP/IP*, and Appendix F, *Selected TCP/IP Headers*, for more information.

Protocol Case Study

This example is an actual case that was solved by protocol analysis. The problem was reported as an occasional **ftp** failure with the error message:

```
netout: Option not supported by protocol
421 Service not available, remote server has closed connection
```

Only one user reported the problem, and it occurred only when transferring large files from a workstation to the central computer, via our FDDI backbone network.

We obtained the user's data file and were able to duplicate the problem from other workstations, but only when we transferred the file to the same central system via the backbone network. Figure 11-4 graphically summarizes the tests we ran to duplicate the problem.

We notified all users of the problem. In response, we received reports that others had also experienced it, but again only when transferring to the central system, and only when transferring via the backbone. They had not reported it, because they rarely saw it. But the additional reports gave us some evidence that the problem did not relate to any recent network changes.

Because the problem had been duplicated on other systems, it probably was not a configuration problem on the user's system. The **ftp** failure could also be avoided if the backbone routers and the central system did not interact. So we concentrated our attention on those systems. We checked the routing tables and ARP

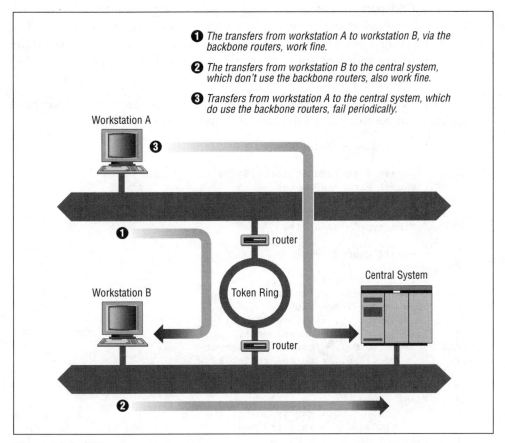

Figure 11-4: FTP test summary

tables, and ran **ping** tests on the central system and the routers. No problems were observed.

Based on this preliminary analysis, the **ftp** failure appeared to be a possible protocol interaction problem between a certain brand of routers and a central computer. We made that assessment because the transfer routinely failed when these two brands of systems were involved, but never failed in any other circumstance. If the router or the central system were misconfigured, they should fail when transferring data to other hosts. If the problem was an intermittent physical problem, it should occur randomly regardless of the hosts involved. Instead, this problem occurred predictably, and only between two specific brands of computers. Perhaps there was something incompatible in the way these two systems implemented TCP/IP.

Therefore, we used **snoop** to capture the TCP/IP headers during several **ftp** test runs. Reviewing the dumps showed that all transfers that failed with the "netout" error message had an ICMP Parameter Error packet near the end of the session, usually about 50 packets before the final close. No successful transfer had this ICMP packet. Note that the error did *not* occur in the last packet in the data stream, as you might expect. It is common for an error to be detected, and for the data stream to continue for some time before the connection is actually shut down. Don't assume that an error will always be at the end of a data stream.

Here are the headers from the key packets. First, the IP header of the packet from the backbone router that caused the central system to send the error:

```
ETHER:  ----- Ether Header -----
ETHER:
ETHER:  Packet 1 arrived at 16:56:36.39
ETHER:  Packet size = 60 bytes
ETHER:  Destination = 8:0:25:30:6:51, CDC
ETHER:  Source      = 0:0:93:e0:a0:bf, Proteon
ETHER:  Ethertype = 0800 (IP)
ETHER:
IP:     ----- IP Header -----
IP:
IP:     Version = 4
IP:     Header length = 20 bytes
IP:     Type of service = 0x00
IP:           xxx. .... = 0 (precedence)
IP:           ...0 .... = normal delay
IP:           .... 0... = normal throughput
IP:           .... .0.. = normal reliability
IP:     Total length = 552 bytes
IP:     Identification = 8a22
IP:     Flags = 0x0
IP:           .0.. .... = may fragment
IP:           ..0. .... = last fragment
IP:     Fragment offset = 0 bytes
IP:     Time to live = 57 seconds/hops
IP:     Protocol = 6 (TCP)
IP:     Header checksum = ffff
IP:     Source address = 172.16.55.106, fs.nuts.com
IP:     Destination address = 172.16.51.252, bnos.nuts.com
IP:     No options
IP:
```

And this is the ICMP Parameter Error packet sent from the central system in response to that packet:

```
ETHER:  ----- Ether Header -----
ETHER:
ETHER:  Packet 3 arrived at 16:56:57.90
ETHER:  Packet size = 98 bytes
ETHER:  Destination = 0:0:93:e0:a0:bf, Proteon
ETHER:  Source      = 8:0:25:30:6:51, CDC
ETHER:  Ethertype = 0800 (IP)
ETHER:
IP:     ----- IP Header -----
IP:
```

```
IP:     Version = 4
IP:     Header length = 20 bytes
IP:     Type of service = 0x00
IP:         xxx. .... = 0 (precedence)
IP:         ...0 .... = normal delay
IP:         .... 0... = normal throughput
IP:         .... .0.. = normal reliability
IP:     Total length = 56 bytes
IP:     Identification = 000c
IP:     Flags = 0x0
IP:         .0.. .... = may fragment
IP:         ..0. .... = last fragment
IP:     Fragment offset = 0 bytes
IP:     Time to live = 59 seconds/hops
IP:     Protocol = 1 (ICMP)
IP:     Header checksum = 8a0b
IP:     Source address = 172.16.51.252, bnos.nuts.com
IP:     Destination address = 172.16.55.106, fs.nuts.com
IP:     No options
IP:
ICMP:   ----- ICMP Header -----
ICMP:
ICMP:   Type = 12 (Parameter problem)
ICMP:   Code = 0
ICMP:   Checksum = 0d9f
ICMP:   Pointer = 10
```

Each packet header is broken out bit-by-bit and mapped to the appropriate TCP/IP header fields. From this detailed analysis of each packet, we see that the router issued an IP Header Checksum of 0xffff, and that the central system objected to this checksum. We know that the central system objected to the checksum because it returned an ICMP Parameter Error with a Pointer of 10. The Parameter Error indicates that there is something wrong with the data the system has just received, and the Pointer identifies the specific data that the system thinks is in error. The tenth byte of the router's IP header is the IP Header Checksum. The data field of the ICMP error message returns the header that it believes is in error. When we displayed that data we noticed that when the central system returned the header, the checksum field was "corrected" to 0000. Clearly the central system disagreed with the router's checksum calculation.

Occasional checksum errors will occur. They can be caused by transmission problems, and are intended to detect these types of problems. Every protocol suite has a mechanism for recovering from checksum errors. So how should they be handled in TCP/IP?

To determine the correct protocol action in this situation, we turned to the authoritative sources—the RFCs. RFC 791, *Internet Protocol*, provided information about the checksum calculation, but the best source for this particular problem was RFC 1122, *Requirements for Internet Hosts—Communication Layers*, by R. Braden. This

RFC provided two specific references that define the action to be taken. These excerpts are from page 29 of RFC 1122:

> In the following, the action specified in certain cases is to "silently discard" a received datagram. This means that the datagram will be discarded without further processing and that the host will not send any ICMP error message (see Section 3.2.2) as a result . . . .
>
> . . .
>
> A host MUST verify the IP header checksum on every received datagram and silently discard every datagram that has a bad checksum.

Therefore, when a system receives a packet with a bad checksum, it is not supposed to do anything with it. The packet should be discarded, and the system should wait for the next packet to arrive. The system should not respond with an error message. A system cannot respond to a bad IP header checksum, because it cannot really know where the packet came from. If the header checksum is in doubt, how do you know if the addresses in the header are correct? And if you don't know for sure where the packet came from, how can you respond to it?

IP relies on the upper-layer protocols to recover from these problems. If TCP is used (as it was in this case), the sending TCP eventually notices that the recipient has never acknowledged the segment, and it sends the segment again. If UDP is used, the sending application is responsible for recovering from the error. In neither case does recovery rely on an error message returned from the recipient.

Therefore, for an incorrect checksum, the central system should have simply discarded the bad packet. The vendor was informed of this problem and, much to their credit, they sent us a fix for the software within two weeks. Not only that, the fix worked perfectly!

Not all problems are resolved so cleanly. But the technique of analysis is the same no matter what the problem.

Simple Network Management Protocol

Troubleshooting is necessary to recover from problems, but the ultimate goal of the network administrator is to avoid problems. That is also the goal of network management software. The network management software used on TCP/IP networks is based on the *Simple Network Management Protocol* (SNMP).

SNMP is a client/server protocol. In SNMP terminology, it is described as a *manager/agent protocol*. The *agent* (the server) runs on the device being managed, which is called the *Managed Network Entity*. The agent monitors the status of the device and reports that status to the manager.

The *manager* (the client) runs on the *Network Management Station* (NMS). The NMS collects information from all of the different devices that are being managed, consolidates it, and presents it to the network administrator. This design places all of the data manipulation tools and most of the human interaction on the NMS. Concentrating the bulk of the work on the manager means that the agent software is small and easy to implement. Correspondingly, most TCP/IP network equipment comes with an SNMP management agent.

SNMP is a request/response protocol. UDP port 161 is its well-known port. SNMP uses UDP as its transport protocol because it has no need for the overhead of TCP. "Reliability" is not required because each request generates a response. If the SNMP application does not receive a response, it simply re-issues the request. "Sequencing" is not needed because each request and each response travels as a single datagram.

The request and response messages that SNMP sends in the datagrams are called *Protocol Data Units* (PDU). The five PDUs used by SNMP are listed in Table 11-3. These message types allow the manager to request management information, and when appropriate, to modify that information. The messages also allow the agent to respond to manager requests and to notify the manager of unusual situations.

Table 11-3: SNMP Protocol Data Units

PDU	Use
GetRequest	Manager requests an update.
GetNextRequest	Manager requests the next entry in a table.
GetResponse	Agent answers a manager request.
SetRequest	Manager modifies data on the managed device.
Trap	Agent alerts manager of an unusual event.

The NMS periodically requests the status of each managed device (GetRequest) and each agent responds with the status of its device (GetResponse). Making periodic requests is called *polling*. Polling reduces the burden on the agent because the NMS decides when polls are needed, and the agent simply responds. Polling also reduces the burden on the network because the polls originate from a single system at a predictable rate. The shortcoming of polling is that it does not allow for real-time updates. If a problem occurs on a managed device, the manager does not find out until the agent is polled. To handle this, SNMP uses a modified polling system called *trap-directed polling*.

A *trap* is an interrupt signaled by a predefined event. When a trap event occurs, the SNMP agent does not wait for the manager to poll; instead it immediately sends information to the manager. Traps allow the agent to inform the manager of unusual events while allowing the manager to maintain control of polling. SNMP traps are sent on UDP port 162. The manager sends polls on port 161 and listens for traps on port 162. Table 11-4 lists the trap events defined in the RFCs.

Table 11-4: Generic Traps Defined in the RFCs

Trap	Meaning
coldStart	Agent restarted; possible configuration changes
warmStart	Agent reinitialized without configuration changes
enterpriseSpecific	An event significant to this hardware or software
authenticationFailure	Agent received an unauthenticated message
linkDown	Agent detected a network link failure
linkUp	Agent detected a network link coming up
egpNeighborLoss	The device's EGP neighbor is down

The last three entries in this table show the roots of SNMP in *Simple Gateway Management Protocol* (SGMP), which was a tool for tracking the status of network routers. Routers are generally the only devices that have multiple network links to keep track of and are the only devices that run *Exterior Gateway Protocol* (EGP).* These traps are not significant for most systems.

The most important trap may be the **enterpriseSpecific** trap. The events that signal this trap are defined differently by every vendor's SNMP agent software. Therefore it is possible for the trap to be tuned to events that are significant for that system. SNMP uses the term "enterprise" to refer to something that is privately defined by a vendor or organization as opposed to something that is globally defined by an RFC.

SNMP has twice as much jargon as the rest of networking—and that's saying something! Managed Network Entity, NMS, PDU, trap, polling, enterprise—that's just the beginning! We also need to mention (below) what SMI is, what a MIB is, and what ANS.1 is used for. Why this bewildering array of acronyms and buzzwords? I think there are two main reasons:

- Network management covers a wide range of different devices, from repeaters to mainframe computers. A "vendor-neutral" language is needed to define terms for the manufacturers of all of this different equipment.

- SNMP is based on the *Common Management Information Protocol* (CMIP) that was created by the *International Standards Organization* (ISO). Formal international standards always spend a lot of time defining terms because it is important to make terms clear when they are used by people from many different cultures who speak many different languages.

---

* EGP is covered in Chapter 7.

Now that you know why you have to suffer through all of this jargon, let's define a few more important terms.

The *Structure of Management Information* (SMI) defines how data should be presented in an SNMP environment. The SMI is documented in RFC 1155 and RFC 1065, *Structure and Identification of Management Information for TCP/IP-based Internets*. The SMI defines how managed objects are named, the syntax in which they are defined, and how they are encoded for transmission over the network. The SMI is based on previous ISO work.

Each managed object is given a globally unique name called an *object identifier*. The object identifier is part of a hierarchical name space that is managed by the ISO. The hierarchical name structure is used, just like it is in DNS, to guarantee that each name is globally unique. In an object identifier, each level of the hierarchy is identified by a number.

Objects are defined just as formally as they are named. The syntax used to define managed objects is *Abstract Syntax Notation One (ASN.1)*. ASN.1 is ISO Standard 8824, *Specification of Abstract Syntax Notation One (ASN.1)*. It is a very formal set of language rules for defining data. It makes the data definition independent of incompatibilities between systems and character sets. ASN.1 also includes a set of rules for encoding data for transfer over a network. These rules are defined in ISO Standard 8825, *Specification of Basic Encoding Rules for Abstract Syntax Notation One (ASN.1)*. The *Basic Encoding Rules* (BER) define that bit 8 of an octet is sent first, that 2's complement is used for signed integers, and other nitty-gritty details of data transmission.

Every object managed by SNMP has a unique object identifier defined by the ASN.1 syntax and encoding defined by BER. When all of these unique objects are grouped together, they are called the *Management Information Base* (MIB). The MIB refers to all information that is managed by SNMP. However, we usually refer to "a MIB" or "the MIBs" (plural), meaning the individual databases of management information formally defined by an RFC or privately defined by a vendor.

MIBI and MIBII are standards defined by RFCs. MIBII is a superset of MIBI, and is the standard MIB for monitoring TCP/IP. It provides such information as the number of packets transmitted into and out of an interface, and the number of errors that occurred sending and receiving those packets—useful information for spotting usage trends and potential trouble spots. Every agent supports MIBI or MIBII.

Some systems also provide a private MIB in addition to the standard MIBII. Private MIBs add to the monitoring capability by providing system-specific information. Most UNIX systems do not provide private MIBs. Private MIBs are most common on network hardware like routers, hubs, and switches.

No matter what MIBs are provided by the agents, it is the monitoring software that displays the information for the system administrator. A private MIB won't do you any good unless your network monitoring software also supports that MIB. For this reason, most administrators prefer to purchase a monitor from the vendor that supplies the bulk of their network equipment. Another possibility is to select a monitor that includes a *MIB compiler*, which gives you the most flexibility. A MIB compiler reads in the ASN.1 description of a MIB and adds the MIB to the monitor. A MIB compiler makes the monitor *extensible* because if you can get the ASN.1 source from the network equipment vendor, you can add the vendor's private MIB to your monitor.

MIB compilers are only part of the advanced features offered by some monitors. Some of the features offered are:

Network maps
> Some monitors automatically draw a map of the network. Colors are used to indicate the state (up, down, etc.) of the devices on the network. At a glance, the network manager sees the overall state of the network.

Tabular data displays
> Data displayed in tables or rendered into charts is used to make comparisons between different devices. Some monitors output data that can then be read into a standard spreadsheet or graphing program.

Filters
> Filters sift the data coming in from the agents in order to detect certain conditions.

Alarms
> Alarms indicate when "thresholds" are exceeded or special events occur. For example, you may want an alarm to trigger when your server exceeds some specified number of transmit errors.

Don't be put off by the jargon. All of this detail is necessary to formally define a network management scheme that is independent of the managed systems, but you don't need to memorize it. You need to know that a MIB is a collection of management information, that an NMS is the network management station, and that an agent runs in each managed device in order to make intelligent decisions when selecting an SNMP monitor. This information provides that necessary background. The features available in network monitors vary widely; so does the price. Select an SNMP monitor that is suitable for the complexity of your network and the size of your budget.

Summary

Every network will have problems. This chapter discusses the tools and techniques that can help you recover from these problems, and the planning and monitoring that can help avoid them. A solution is sometimes obvious if you can just gain enough information about the problem. UNIX provides several built-in software tools that can help you gather information about system configuration, addressing, routing, name service and other vital network components. Gather your tools and learn how to use them before a breakdown occurs.

In the next chapter, we talk about another task that is important to the maintenance of a reliable network: keeping your network secure.

12

Network Security

Hosts attached to a network—particularly the worldwide Internet—are exposed to a wider range of security threats than are unconnected hosts. Network security reduces the risks of connecting to a network. But by nature, network access and computer security work at cross-purposes. A network is a data highway designed to increase access to computer systems, while security is designed to control access. Providing network security is a balancing act between open access and security.

The highway analogy is very appropriate. Like a highway, the network provides equal access for all—welcome visitors as well as unwelcome intruders. At home, you provide security for your possessions by locking your house, not by blocking the streets. Likewise, network security generally means providing adequate security on individual host computers, not providing security directly on the network.

In very small towns, where people know each other, doors are often left unlocked. But in big cities, doors have deadbolts and chains. In the last decade, the Internet has grown from a small town of a few thousand users to a big city of millions of users. Just as the anonymity of a big city turns neighbors into strangers, the growth of the Internet has reduced the level of trust between network neighbors. The ever-increasing need for computer security is an unfortunate side effect. Growth, however, is not all bad. In the same way that a big city offers more choices and more services, the expanded network provides increased services. For most of us, security consciousness is a small price to pay for network access.

Network break-ins have increased as the network has grown and become more impersonal, but it is easy to exaggerate the extent of these security breaches. Over-reacting to the threat of break-ins may hinder the way you use the network. Don't make the cure worse than the disease. The best advice about network security is to use common sense. RFC 1244, *Site Security Handbook*, by Holbrook, Reynold, et al., states this principle very well:

> Common sense is the most appropriate tool that can be used to establish your security policy. Elaborate security schemes and mechanisms are impressive, and they do have their place, yet there is little point in investing money and time on an elaborate implementation scheme if the simple controls are forgotten.

This chapter emphasizes the simple controls that can be used to increase your network's security. A reasonable approach to security, based on the level of security required by your system, is the most cost-effective—both in terms of actual expense and in terms of productivity.

Security Planning

One of the most important network security tasks, and probably one of the least enjoyable, is developing a network security policy. Most computer people want a technical solution to every problem. We want to find a program that "fixes" the network security problem. Few of us want to write a paper on network security policies and procedures. However, a well-thought-out security plan will help you decide what needs to be protected, how much you are willing to invest in protecting it, and who will be responsible for carrying out the steps to protect it.

Assessing the Threat

The first step toward developing an effective network security plan is to assess the threat that connection presents to your systems. RFC 1244 identifies three distinct types of security threats usually associated with network connectivity:

Unauthorized access
> A break-in by an unauthorized person.

Disclosure of information
> Any problem that causes the disclosure of valuable or sensitive information to people who should not have access to the information.

Denial of service
> Any problem that makes it difficult or impossible for the system to continue to perform productive work.

Assess these threats in relation to the number of users who would be affected, as well as to the sensitivity of the information that might be compromised. For some organizations, break-ins are an embarrassment that can undermine the confidence that others have in the organization. Intruders tend to target government and academic organizations that will be embarrassed by the break-in. But for most organizations, unauthorized access is not a major problem unless it involves one of the other threats: disclosure of information or denial of service.

Assessing the threat of information disclosure depends on the type of information that could be compromised. While no system with highly classified information should ever be directly connected to the Internet, systems with other types of sensitive information might be connected without undue hazard. In most cases, files such as personnel and medical records, corporate plans, and credit reports can be adequately protected by standard UNIX file security procedures. However, if the risk of liability in case of disclosure is great, the host may choose not to be connected to the Internet.

Denial of service can be a severe problem if it impacts many users or a major mission of your organization. Some systems can be connected to the network with little concern. The benefit of connecting individual workstations and small servers to the Internet generally outweighs the chance of having service interrupted for the individuals and small groups served by these systems. Other systems may be vital to the survival of your organization. The threat of losing the services of a mission-critical system must be evaluated seriously before connecting such a system to the network.

In his class on computer security, Brent Chapman classifies information security threats into three categories: threats to the secrecy, availability, and integrity of data. Secrecy is the need to prevent the disclosure of sensitive information. Availability means that you want information and information processing resources available when they are needed; a denial-of-service attack disrupts availability. The need for the integrity of information is equally obvious, but its link to computer security is more subtle. Once someone has gained unauthorized access to a system, the integrity of the information on that system is in doubt. Furthermore, some intruders just want to compromise the integrity of data. We are all familiar with cases where intruders gain access to a Web server and change the data on the server in order to embarrass the organization that runs the Web site. Thinking about the impact network threats have on your data can make it easier to assess the threat.

Network threats are not, of course, the only threats to computer security, or the only reasons for denial of service. Natural disasters and internal threats (threats from people who have legitimate access to a system) are also serious. Network security has had a lot of publicity, so it's a fashionable thing to worry about; but more computer time has probably been lost because of fires than has ever been lost because of network security problems. Similarly, more data has probably been improperly disclosed by authorized users than by unauthorized break-ins. This book naturally emphasizes network security, but network security is only part of a larger security plan that includes physical security and disaster recovery plans.

Many traditional (non-network) security threats are handled, in part, by physical security. Don't forget to provide an adequate level of physical security for your network equipment and cables. Again, the investment in physical security should be based on your realistic assessment of the threat.

Distributed Control

One approach to network security is to distribute responsibility for, and control over, segments of a large network to small groups within the organization. This approach involves a large number of people in security, and runs counter to the school of thought that seeks to increase security by centralizing control. However, distributing responsibility and control to small groups can create an environment of small networks composed of trusted hosts. Using the analogy of small towns and big cities, it is similar to creating a neighborhood watch to reduce risks by giving people connection with their neighbors, mutual responsibility for one another, and control over their own fates.

Additionally, distributing security responsibilities formally recognizes one of the realities of network security—most security actions take place on individual systems. The managers of these systems must know that they are responsible for security, and that their contribution to network security is recognized and appreciated. If people are expected to do a job, they must be empowered to do it.

Use subnets to distribute control

Subnets are a possible tool for distributing network control. A subnet administrator should be appointed when a subnet is created. She is then responsible for the security of the network and for assigning IP addresses to the devices connected to the networks. Assigning IP addresses gives the subnet administrator some control over who connects to the subnet. It also helps to ensure that she knows each system connected and who is responsible for that system. When the subnet administrator gives a system an IP address, she also delegates certain security responsibilities to the system's administrator. Likewise, when the system administrator grants a user an account, the user takes on certain security responsibilities.

The hierarchy of responsibility flows from the network administrator, to the subnet administrator, to the system administrator, and finally to the user. At each point in this hierarchy the individuals are given responsibilities and the power to carry them out. To support this structure, it is important for users to know what they are responsible for and how to carry out that responsibility. The network security policy described in the next section provides this information.

Use mailing lists to distribute information

If your site adopts distributed control, you must develop a system for disseminating security information to each group. Mailing lists for each administrative level can be used for this purpose. The network administrator receives security information from outside authorities, filters out irrelevant material, and forwards the relevant material to the subnet administrators. Subnet administrators forward the relevant parts to their system administrators, who in turn forward what they consider important to the individual users. The filtering of information at each level ensures that individuals get the information they need, without receiving too much. If too much unnecessary material is distributed, users begin to ignore everything they receive.

At the top of this information structure is the information that the network administrator receives from outside authorities. In order to receive this, the network administrator should join the appropriate mailing lists and newsgroups and browse the appropriate Web sites. A few places to start looking for computer security information are the following:

Your UNIX Vendor
> Many vendors have their own security information mailing lists.

Security Newsgroups
> The *comp.security* newsgroups—*comp.security.unix*, *comp.security.firewalls*, *comp.security.announce*, and *comp.security.misc*—contain some useful information. Like most newsgroups, they contain lots of unimportant and uninteresting material. But they also contain an occasional gem.

FIRST Mailing List
> The Forum of Incident Response and Security Teams (FIRST) is a worldwide organization of computer security response teams. FIRST provides a public mailing list, *first-info@first.org*, for computer security information. To subscribe to this list, send email to *first-majordomo@first.org* that contains the line:
>
> **subscribe first-info** *YOUR-EMAIL-ADDRESS*
>
> where *YOUR-EMAIL-ADDRESS* is literally your email address.

NIST Computer Security Alerts
> The National Institute of Standards and Technology's Computer Security Division maintains a Web site with pointers to security-related Web pages all over the world. As a single source for security alerts from several different organizations, the site *http://csrc.nist.gov/secalert/* can't be beat.

Computer Emergency Response Team (CERT) Advisories
> The CERT advisories provide information about known security problems, and the fixes to these problems. You can retrieve these advisories from

ftp://info.cert.org/pub/cert_advisories. The CERT Web site is also worth a visit: *http://www.cert.org.*

DDN Security Bulletins

These bulletins are very similar in content to the CERT advisories, though DDN bulletins do occasionally add information. DDN bulletins and CERT advisories deal primarily with network security threats. DDN bulletins can be viewed online with your Web browser at *http://nic.ddn.mil/SCC/bulletins.html.*

Risks Forum

The risks forum discusses the full range of computer security risks. The forum is available on the Web at *http://catless.ncl.ac.uk/Risks.*

Computer Virus Information

The VIRUS-L list deals primarily with computer viruses—a threat usually associated with PCs. You can retrieve the VIRUS-L archive from *ftp://ftp.infospace.com/pub/virus-l.* An equally important document, at *http://ciac.llnl.gov/ciac/CIACHoaxes.html,* provides information about computer virus hoaxes. False rumors about computer viruses can waste as much time as tracking down real viruses.

Writing a Security Policy

Security is largely a "people problem." People, not computers, are responsible for implementing security procedures, and people are responsible when security is breached. Therefore, network security is ineffective unless people know their responsibilities. It is important to write a security policy that clearly states what is expected and who it is expected from. A network security policy should define:

The network user's security responsibilities

The policy may require users to change their passwords at certain intervals, to use passwords that meet certain guidelines, or to perform certain checks to see if their accounts have been accessed by someone else. Whatever is expected from users, it is important that it be clearly defined.

The system administrator's security responsibilities

The policy may require that every host use specific security measures, login banner messages, and monitoring and accounting procedures. It might list applications that should not be run on any host attached to the network.

The proper use of network resources

Define who can use network resources, what things they can do, and what things they should not do. If your organization takes the position that email, files, and histories of computer activity are subject to security monitoring, tell the users very clearly that this is the policy.

The actions taken when a security problem is detected

What should be done when a security problem is detected? Who should be notified? It is easy to overlook things during a crisis, so you should have a detailed list of the exact steps that a system administrator, or user, should take when a security breach has been detected. This could be as simple as telling the users to "touch nothing, and call the network security officer." But even these simple actions should be in the policy so that they are readily available.

Connecting to the Internet brings with it certain security responsibilities. RFC 1281, *A Guideline for the Secure Operation of the Internet*, provides guidance for users and network administrators on how to use the Internet in a secure and responsible manner. Reading this RFC will provide insight into the information that should be in your security policy.

A great deal of thought is necessary to produce a complete network security policy. The outline shown above describes the contents of a network policy document, but if you are personally responsible for writing a policy, you may want more detailed guidance. I also recommend that you read RFC 1244. It is a very good guide for developing a security plan.

Security planning (assessing the threat, assigning security responsibilities, and writing a security policy) is the basic building block of network security, but a plan must be implemented before it can have any effect. In the remainder of this chapter, we'll turn our attention to implementing basic security procedures.

User Authentication

Good passwords are one of the simplest parts of good network security. Passwords are used to log in to systems that use password authentication. Popular mythology says that network security breaches are caused by sophisticated security crackers who discover software security holes to break into computer systems. In reality, many intruders enter systems simply by guessing or stealing passwords, or by exploiting well-known security problems in outdated software. Later in this chapter we look at guidelines for keeping software up-to-date, and at ways to prevent a thief from stealing your password. First, let's see what we can do to prevent it from being guessed.

These are a few things that make it easy to guess passwords:

- Accounts that use the account name as the password. Accounts with this type of trivial password are called *joe accounts*.

- Guest or demonstration accounts that require no password, or use a well-publicized password.

- System accounts with default passwords.

- User who tell their passwords to others.

Guessing these kinds of passwords requires no skill, just lots of spare time! Changing your password frequently is a deterrent to password guessing. However, if you choose good passwords, don't change them so often that it is hard to remember them. Many security experts recommend that passwords should be changed about every 3 to 6 months.

A more sophisticated form of password guessing is *dictionary guessing*. Dictionary guessing uses a program that encrypts each word in a dictionary (e.g., */usr/dict/words*) and compares each encrypted word to the encrypted password in the */etc/passwd* file. Dictionary guessing is not limited to words from a dictionary. Things known about you (your name, initials, telephone number, etc.) are also run through the guessing program when trying to guess the password for your account. Because of dictionary guessing, you must protect the */etc/passwd* file.

Some systems provide a *shadow password file* to hide the encrypted passwords from potential intruders. If your system has a shadow password facility, use it. Hiding encrypted passwords greatly reduces the risk of password guessing.

The Shadow Password File

Shadow password files have restricted permissions that prevent them from being read by intruders. The encrypted password is stored only in the shadow password file, */etc/shadow*, and not in the */etc/passwd* file. The *passwd* file is maintained as a world-readable file because it contains information that various programs use. The *shadow* file can only be read by root and it does not duplicate the information in the *passwd* file. It only contains passwords and the information needed to manage them. The format of a *shadow* file entry on a Solaris system is:

username:password:lastchg:min:max:warn:inactive:expire:flag

username is the login username. *password* is the encrypted password or one of the keyword values NP and *LK*. *lastchg* is the date that the password was last changed, written as the number of days from January 1, 1970 to the date of the change. *min* is the minimum number of days that must elapse before the password can be changed. *max* is the maximum number of days the user can keep the password before it must be changed. *warn* is the number of days before the password expires that the user is warned. *inactive* is the number of days the account can be inactive before it is locked. *expire* is the date on which the account will be closed. *flag* is unused.

The encrypted password appears only in this file. Every password field in the */etc/passwd* file contains an **x**, which tells the system to look in the *shadow* file for the real password. Every password field in the */etc/shadow* file contains either an encrypted password, NP, or *LK*. If it contains the keyword NP, it means that there is no password because this is not a login account. System accounts, such as *daemon* or *uucp*, are not login accounts, so they have NP in the password field. *LK* in the password field means that this account has been locked and is therefore disabled from any further use.

While the most important purpose of the *shadow* file is to protect the password, the additional fields in the shadow entry provide other useful security services. One of these is *password aging*. A password aging mechanism defines a lifetime for each password. When a password reaches the end of its lifetime, the password aging mechanism notifies the user to change the password. If it is not changed within some specified period, the password is removed from the system and the user is blocked from using his account.

The lastchg, max, and warn fields all play a role in password aging. They allow the system to know when the password was changed and how long it should be kept, as well as when the user should be warned about his impending doom. Another nice feature of the shadow file is the min field. This is a more subtle aspect of password aging. It prevents the user from changing her favorite password to a dummy password and then immediately back to her favorite. When the password is changed it must be used for the number of days defined by min before it can be changed again. This reduces one of the common tricks used to avoid really changing passwords.

The inactive and expire fields help eliminate unused accounts. Here "inactivity" is determined by the number of days the account continues with an expired password. Once the password expires, the user is given some number of days to log in and set a new password. If the user does not log in before the specified number of days has elapsed, the account is locked and the user cannot log in.

The expire field lets you a create user account that has a specified "life." When the date stored in the expire field is reached, the user account is disabled even if it is still active. The expiration date is stored as the number of days since January 1, 1970.

On a Solaris system the */etc/shadow* file is not edited directly. It is modified by using the "users" sub-window of the **admintool** or special options on the **passwd** command line. This window is shown in Figure 12-1. The username, password, min, max, warn, inactive, and expire fields are clearly shown.

The **passwd** command on Solaris systems has −n *min*, −w *warn*, and −x *max* options to set the min, max, and warn fields in the */etc/shadow* file. Only the root user can invoke these options.

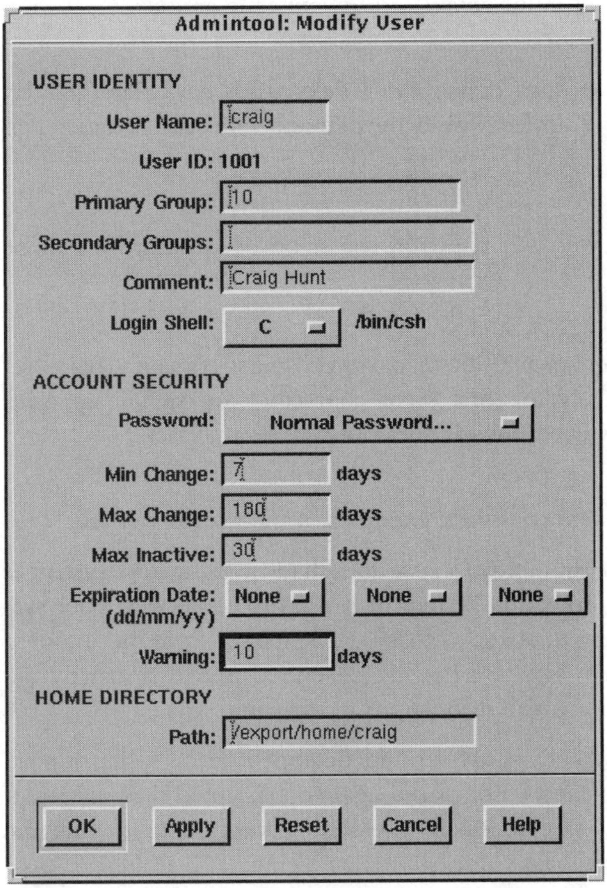

Figure 12-1: Admintool password maintenance

Here root sets the maximum life of Tyler's password to 180 days:

```
# passwd -x 180 tyler
```

The Solaris system permits the system administrator to set default values for all of these options so that they do not have to be set every time a user is added through the **admintool** or the **passwd** command line. The default values are set in the */etc/default/passwd* file.

```
% cat /etc/default/passwd
#ident  "@(#)passwd.dfl 1.3     92/07/14 SMI"
MAXWEEKS=
MINWEEKS=
PASSLENGTH=6
```

The default values that can be set in the */etc/default/passwd* file are:

MAXWEEKS

> The maximum life of a password defined in weeks—not days. The 180-day period used in the example above would be defined with this parameter as MAXWEEKS=26.

MINWEEKS

> The minimum number of weeks a password must be used before it can be changed.

PASSLENGTH

> The minimum number of characters that a password must contain. This is set to 6 in the sample file. Only the first eight characters are significant on a Solaris system. Setting the value above 8 does not change that fact.

WARNWEEKS

> The number of weeks before a password expires that the user is warned.

This section uses Solaris as an example because the shadow password system is provided as part of the Solaris operating system. If it doesn't come with your system, you may be able to download shadow password software from the Internet. It is available for Linux systems. The *shadow* file described above is exactly the same format used on Linux systems and it functions in the same way.

No intruder can take the encrypted password and decrypt it back to its original form, but encrypted passwords can be compared against encrypted dictionaries. If bad passwords are used, they can be easily guessed. Take care to protect the */etc/passwd* file and choose good passwords.

Choosing a Password

A good password is an essential part of security. We usually think of the password used for login; however, one-time passwords and encryption keys are needed. For all of these purposes you want to choose a good password. Choosing a good password boils down to this, don't choose a password that can be guessed using the techniques described above. Some guidelines for choosing a good password are:

- Don't use your login name.
- Don't use the name of anyone or anything.
- Don't use any English, or foreign language, word or abbreviation.
- Don't use any personal information associated with the owner of the account. For example, don't use initials, phone number, social security number, job title, organizational unit, etc.

- Don't use keyboard sequences, e.g., qwerty.

- Don't use any of the above spelled backwards, or in caps, or otherwise disguised.

- Don't use an all-numeric password.

- Don't use a sample password, no matter how good, that you've gotten from a book that discusses computer security.

- *Do* use a mixture of numbers, special characters, and mixed-case letters.

- *Do* use at least six characters.

- *Do* use a seemingly random selection of letters and numbers.

Common suggestions for constructing seemingly random passwords are:

1. Use the first letter of each word from a line in a book, song, or poem. For example: "People don't know you and trust is a joke."* would produce Pd'ky&tiaj.

2. Use the output from a random password generator. Select a random string that can be pronounced and is easy to remember. For example, the random string "adazac" can be pronounced a-da-zac, and you can remember it by thinking of it as "A-to-Z." Add uppercase letters to create your own emphasis, e.g., aDAzac.†

3. Use two short words connected by punctuation, e.g., wRen%Rug.

4. Use numbers and letters to create an imaginary vanity license plate password, e.g., 2hot4U?.

A common theme of these suggestions is that the password should be easy to remember. Avoid passwords that must be written down to be remembered. If unreliable people gain access to your office and find the password you have written down, the security of your system will be compromised.

However, don't assume that you will not be able to remember a random password. It may be difficult the first few times you use the password, but any password that is used often enough is easy to remember. If you have an account on a system that you rarely use, you may have trouble remembering a random password. But in that case, the best solution is to get rid of the account. Unused and under-utilized accounts are prime targets for intruders. They like to attack unused accounts because there is no user to notice changes to the files or strange *Last login:* messages. Remove all unused accounts from your systems.

---

* Toad the Wet Sprocket, "Walk on the Ocean."

† A VMS-system password generator created this password.

How do you ensure that the guidance for creating new passwords is followed? The most important step is to make sure that every user knows these suggestions and the importance of following them. Cover this topic in your network security plan, and periodically reinforce it through newsletter articles and online system bulletins.

It is also possible to use programs that force users to follow specific password selection guidelines. The Web page *http://csrc.nist.gov/tools/tools.htm* lists several programs that do exactly that.

One-Time Passwords

Sometimes good passwords are not enough. Passwords are transmitted across the network as clear text. Intruders use protocol-analyzer software to spy on network traffic and steal passwords. If a thief steals your password, it does not matter how good the password was.

The thief can be on any network that handles your TCP/IP packets. If you log in through your local network you have to worry only about local snoops. But if you log in over the Internet you must worry about unseen listeners from any number of unknown networks.

The **rlogin** command is not vulnerable to this type of attack. **rlogin** does not send the password over the network, because user authentication is done only on the local host. The remote host accepts the user because it trusts the local host. However, trust should be extended only to UNIX hosts on your local network that you really do trust. Never extend trust to remote systems. It is too easy for an intruder to pretend that he is logged into a trusted system by stealing the trusted system's IP address, or by corrupting DNS so that it gives his system's address in response to the trusted system's name. **rlogin** does not help when you must log in from a remote site or an untrusted system. Use one-time passwords for remote logins. Because a one-time password can be used only once, a thief who steals the password cannot use it.

Naturally, one-time passwords systems are a hassle. You must carry a list of one-time passwords, or something that can generate them, with you any time you want to log in. If you forget the password list, you cannot log in. However, this may not be as big a problem as it seems. You usually log in from your office where your primary login host is probably on your desktop or your local area network. When you log in to your desktop system from its keyboard, the password does not traverse the network, so you can use a reusable password. And **rlogin** can be used between UNIX hosts on a local area network. One-time passwords are only needed for the occasions when you log in from a remote location or an untrusted host. For this reason, some one-time password systems are designed to allow reusable passwords when they are appropriate.

There are several one-time password systems. Some use specialized hardware such as "smart cards." OPIE is a free software system that requires no special hardware.

OPIE

One-time Passwords In Everything (OPIE) is free software from the U.S. Naval Research Laboratory (NRL) that modifies a UNIX system to use one-time passwords. OPIE is directly derived from SKey, which is a one-time password system created by Bell Communications Research (Bellcore).

Download OPIE from *ftp://ftp.nrl.navy.mil/pub/security/opie/opie-2.3.tar.gz*. It is a binary file. **gunzip** the file and extract it using **tar**. The directory this produces contains the source files, Makefiles, and scripts necessary to compile and install OPIE.

OPIE comes with **configure**, an auto-configuration script that detects your system's configuration and modifies the Makefile accordingly. It does a good job, but you still should manually edit the Makefile to make sure it is correct. For example: my Linux system uses the Washington University FTP daemon **wu.ftpd**. OPIE replaces **login**, **su**, and **ftpd** with its own version of these programs. On my Linux system, **configure** did not find **ftpd** and I did not notice the problem when I checked the Makefile. **make** ran without errors but **make install** failed during the install of the OPIE FTP daemon. The Makefile was easily corrected and the rerun of **make install** was successful.

The effects of OPIE are evident as soon as the install completes. Run **su** and you're prompted with `root's response:` instead of `Password:`. **login** prompts with `Response or Password:` instead of just `Password:`. The `response` requested by these programs is the OPIE equivalent of a password. Programs that prompt with `Response or Password` accept either the OPIE response or the traditional password from the */etc/passwd* file. This feature permits users to migrate gracefully from traditional passwords to OPIE. It also allows local console logins with re-usable passwords while permitting remote logins with one-time passwords. The best of both worlds—convenient local logins without creating separate local and remote login accounts!

To use OPIE you must first select a secret password that is used to generate the one-time password list, and then you must run the program that generates the list. To select a secret password, run **opiepassword** as shown below:

```
$ opiepasswd -c
Updating kristin:
Reminder  -  Only use this method from the console; NEVER from remote.
```

```
If you are using telnet, xterm, or a dial-in, type ^C now or exit with
no password. Then run opiepasswd without the -c parameter.
Using MD5 to compute responses.
Enter old secret pass phrase: 3J5Wd6PaWP
Enter new secret pass phrase: 9WA11WSfW95/NT
Again new secret pass phrase: 9WA11WSfW95/NT
```

The example above shows the user *kristin* updating her secret password. She runs
opiepasswd from the computer's console, as indicated by the **−c** command option.
Running **opiepasswd** from the console is the most secure. If it is not run from the
console, you must have a copy of the **opiekey** software with you to generate the
correct responses needed to enter your old and new secret passwords because
clear-text passwords are only accepted from the console. Kristin is prompted to
enter her old password and to select a new one. OPIE passwords must be at least
10 characters long. Since the new password is long enough, **opiepasswd** accepts it
and displays the following two lines:

```
ID kristin OPIE key is 499 be93564
CITE JAN GORY BELA GET ABED
```

These lines tell Kristin the information she needs to generate OPIE login responses
and the first response she will need to log in to the system. The one-time password needed for Kristin's next login response is the second line of this display: a
group of six short, uppercase character strings. The first line of the display contains the initial sequence number (499) and the seed (be93564) she needs, along
with her secret password, to generate OPIE login responses. The software used to
generate those responses is **opiekey**.

opiekey takes the login sequence number, the user's seed, and the user's secret
password as input and outputs the correct one-time password. If you have **opiekey**
software on the system from which you are initiating the login, you can produce
one-time passwords one at a time. If, however, you will not have access to
opiekey when you are away from your login host, you can use the **−n** option to
request several passwords. Write the passwords down, put them in your wallet,
and you're ready to go!* In the following example we request five (**−n 5**)
responses from **opiekey**:

```
$ opiekey -n 5 495 wi01309
Using MD5 algorithm to compute response.
Reminder: Don't use  opiekey  from  telnet   or dial-in sessions.
Enter secret pass phrase: UUaX26CPaU
491: HOST VET FOWL SEEK IOWA YAP
492: JOB ARTS WERE FEAT TILE IBIS
```

---

* Security experts will cringe when they read this suggestion. Writing down passwords is a "no-no."
Frankly, I think the people who steal wallets are more interested in my money and credit cards than in
the password to my system. But you should consider this suggestion in light of the level of protection
that your system needs.

```
493: TRUE BRED JOEL USER HALT EBEN
494: HOOD WED MOLT PAN FED RUBY
495: SUB YAW BILE GLEE OWE NOR
```

First **opiekey** tells us that it is using the MD5 algorithm to produce the responses, which is the default for OPIE. For compatibility with older Skey or OPIE implementations, force **opiekey** to use the MD4 algorithm by using the −4 command-line option. **opiekey** prompts for your secret password. This is the password you defined with the **opiepasswd** command. It then prints out the number of responses requested and lists them in sequence number order. The login sequence numbers in the example are 495 to 491. When the sequence number gets down to 10, rerun **opiepasswd** and select a new secret password. Selecting a new secret password resets the sequence number to 499. The OPIE login prompt displays a sequence number and you must provide the response that goes with that sequence number. For example:

```
login: tyler
otp-md5 492 wi01309
Response or Password: JOB ARTS WERE FEAT TILE IBIS
```

At the `login:` prompt Tyler enters her username. The system then displays a single line that tells her that one-time passwords are being generated with the MD5 algorithm (otp-md5), that this is login sequence number 492, and that the seed used for her one-time passwords is wi01309. She looks up the response for login number 492 and enters the six short strings. She then marks that response off her list because it cannot be used again to log into the system. A response from the list must be used any time she is not sitting at the console of her system. Reusable passwords can be used only at the console.

Secure the r Commands

Some applications use their own security mechanisms. Make sure that the security for these applications is configured properly. In particular, check the UNIX **r** commands, which are a set of UNIX networking applications comparable to **ftp** and **telnet**. Care must be taken to ensure that the **r** commands don't compromise system security. Improperly configured **r** commands can open access to your computer facilities to virtually everyone in the world.

In place of password authentication, the **r** commands use a security system based on trusted hosts and users. Trusted users on trusted hosts are allowed to access the local system without providing a password. Trusted hosts are also called "equivalent hosts" because the system assumes that users given access to a trusted host should be given equivalent access to the local host. The system assumes that user accounts with the same name on both hosts are "owned" by the same user. For example, a user logged in as *becky* on a trusted system is granted the same access as a user logged in as *becky* on the local system.

This authentication system requires databases that define the trusted hosts and the trusted users. The databases used to configure the **r** commands are */etc/hosts.equiv* and *.rhosts*.

The */etc/hosts.equiv* file defines the hosts and users that are granted "trusted" **r** command access to your system. This file can also define hosts and users that are explicitly denied trusted access. Not having trusted access doesn't mean that the user is denied access; it just means that he is required to supply a password.

The basic format of entries in the */etc/hosts.equiv* file is:

```
[+ | -][hostname] [+ | -][username]
```

The *hostname* is the name of a "trusted" host, which may optionally be preceded by a plus (+) sign. The plus sign has no real significance, except when used alone. A + sign without a hostname following it is a wildcard character that means "any host."

If a host is granted equivalence, users logged into that host are allowed access to like-named user accounts on your system without providing a password. (This is one good reason for administrators to observe uniform rules in handing out login names.) The optional *username* is the name of a user on the trusted host who is granted access to all user accounts. If *username* is specified, that user is not limited to like-named accounts, but is given access to all user accounts without being required to provide a password.*

The *hostname* may also be preceded by a minus sign (–). This explicitly says that the host is *not* an equivalent system. Users from that host must always supply a password when they use an **r** command to interact with your system. A *username* can also be preceded with a minus sign. This says that, whatever else may be true about that host, the user is "not trusted" and must always supply a password.

The following examples show how entries in the *hosts.equiv* file are interpreted:

peanut
> Allows password-free access from any user on *peanut* to a like-named user account on your local system.

–peanut
> Denies password-free access from any user on *peanut* to accounts on your system.

peanut –david
> Denies password-free access to the user *david*, if he attempts to access your system from *peanut*.

---

* The *root* account is not included.

peanut +becky

>   Allows the user *becky* to access any account (except *root*) on your system, without supplying a password, if she logs in from *peanut.*

+ becky

>   Allows the user *becky* to access any account (except *root*) on your system without supplying a password, no matter what host she logs in from.

This last entry is an example of something that should never be used in your configuration. Don't use a standalone plus sign (+) in place of a hostname. It allows access from any host anywhere, and can open up a big security hole. For example, if the entry shown above was in your *hosts.equiv* file, an intruder could create an account named *becky* on his system and gain access to every account on your system. Check the */etc/hosts.equiv* and *~/.rhosts* files, and */etc/hosts.lpd*, to make sure that none of them contain a plus-sign (+) entry. Remember to check the *.rhosts* file in every user's home directory.

A simple typographical error could give you a standalone plus sign. For example, consider the entry:

```
+ peanut becky
```

The system administrator probably meant "give *becky* password-free access to all accounts when she logs in from *peanut.*" However, with an extraneous space after the + sign, it means "allow users named *peanut* and *becky* password-free access from any host in the world." Don't use a plus sign in front of a hostname, and always use care when working with the */etc/hosts.equiv* file to avoid security problems.

When configuring the */etc/hosts.equiv* file, grant trusted access only to the systems and users you actually trust. Don't grant trusted access to every system attached to your local network. It is best only to trust hosts from your local network when you know the person responsible for that host, and when you know that the host is not available for public use. Don't grant trusted access by default—have some reason for conferring trusted status. Never grant trust to remotely located systems. It is too easy for an intruder to corrupt routing or DNS in order to fool your system when you grant trust to a remote system. Also, never begin your *hosts.equiv* file with a minus sign (−) as the first character. (This confuses some systems, causing them to improperly grant access.) Always err on the side of caution when creating a *hosts.equiv* file. Adding trusted hosts as they are requested is much easier than recovering from a malicious intruder.

The *.rhosts* file grants or denies password-free **r** command access to a specific user's account. It is placed in the user's home directory and contains entries that define the trusted hosts and users. Entries in the *.rhosts* file use the same format as entries in the *hosts.equiv* file, and function in almost the same way. The difference is the scope of access granted by entries in these two files. In the *.rhosts* file, the entries grant or deny access to a single user account; the entries in *hosts.equiv* control access to an entire system.

This functional difference can be shown in a simple example. Assume the following entry:

```
pecan anthony
```

In *almond's hosts.equiv* file, this entry means that the user *anthony* on *pecan* can access any account on *almond* without entering a password. In an *.rhosts* file in the home directory of user *resnick*, the exact same entry allows *anthony* to **rlogin** from *pecan* as *resnick* without entering a password, but it does not grant password-free access to any other accounts on *almond*.

Individuals use the *.rhosts* file to establish equivalence among the different accounts they own. The entry shown above would probably only be made if *anthony* and *resnick* are the same person. For example, I have accounts on several different systems. Sometimes my username is *hunt*, and sometimes it is *craig*. It would be nice if I had the same account name everywhere, but that is not always possible; the names *craig* and *hunt* are used by two other people on my local network. I want to be able to **rlogin** to my workstation from any host that I have an account on, but I don't want mistaken logins from the other *craig* and the other *hunt*. The *.rhosts* file gives me a way to control this problem.

For example, assume my username on *almond* is *craig*, but my username on *filbert* is *hunt*. Another user on *filbert* is *craig*. To allow myself password-free access to my *almond* account from *filbert*, and to make sure that the other user doesn't have password-free access, I put the following *.rhosts* file in my home directory:

```
filbert hunt
filbert -craig
```

Normally the *hosts.equiv* file is searched first, followed by the user's *.rhosts* file, if it exists. The first explicit match determines whether or not password-free access is allowed. Therefore, the *.rhosts* file cannot override the *hosts.equiv* file. The exception to this is root user access. When a root user attempts to access a system via the **r** commands, the *hosts.equiv* file is not checked, only *.rhosts* in the root user's home directory is consulted. This allows root access to be more tightly controlled. If the *hosts.equiv* file was used for root access, entries that grant trusted access to hosts would give root users on those hosts root privileges. You can add trusted hosts to *hosts.equiv* without granting remote root users root access to your system.

If security is particularly important at your site, you should remember that the user can provide access with the *.rhosts* file even when the *hosts.equiv* file doesn't exist. The only way to prevent users from doing this is to periodically check for and remove the *.rhosts* files. As long as you have the **r** commands on your system, it is possible for a user to accidentally compromise the security of your system.

Secure Shell

The **r** commands, also called the remote shell, pose a security threat. You cannot use these commands to provide secure remote access, even if you use all the techniques given in the previous section. At best, only trusted local systems can be given access via the **r** commands. The reason for this is that the **r** commands grant trust based on a belief that the IP address uniquely identifies the correct computer. Normally it does. But an intruder can corrupt DNS to provide the wrong IP address or corrupt routing to deliver to the wrong network and thus undermine the authentication scheme used by the **r** commands.

An alternative to the remote shell is the secure shell (SSH). SSH replaces the standard **r** commands with secure commands that include encryption and authentication. SSH uses a strong authentication scheme to ensure that the trusted host really is the host it claims to be. SSH provides a number of public key encryption schemes to ensure that every packet in the stream of packets is from the source it claims to be from. SSH is secure and easy to use.

The secure shell is available via the Internet at *http://www.cs.hut.fi/ssh*. The Web site also provides information about the secure shell. Download and compile SSH. Use the **configure** command that comes with the SSH source code to detect the configuration of your system and build the correct Makefile. Then **make** and install the components of SSH. The key components are:

sshd

> The Secure Shell daemon handles incoming SSH connections. **sshd** should be started at boot time from one of the boot scripts. Don't start **sshd** from *inetd.conf*. **sshd** generates an encryption key every time it starts. This can cause it to be slow to start, which makes it unsuitable for *inetd.conf*. A system serving SSH connections must run **sshd**.

ssh

> The Secure Shell user command. **ssh** command replaces **rsh** and **rlogin**. It is used to securely pass a command to a remote system or to securely log in to a remote system. This command creates the outgoing connections that are handled by the remote Secure Shell daemon. A client system that wants to use a SSH connection must have the **ssh** command.

scp

> Secure copy (**scp**) is the Secure Shell version of **rcp**.

ssh-keygen

Generates the public and private encryption keys used to secure the transmission for the Secure Shell.

When an **ssh** client connects to a **sshd** server, they exchange public keys. The systems compare the keys they receive to the known keys that they have stored in the */etc/ssh_known_hosts* file and in the *.ssh/known_hosts* file in the user's host directory.* If the key is not found or has changed, the user is asked to verify that the new key should be accepted:

```
> ssh pecan
Host key not found from the list of known hosts.
Are you sure you want to continue connecting (yes/no)? yes
Host 'pecan' added to the list of known hosts.
craig's password: Watts.Watt.
Last login: Thu Sep 25 15:01:32 1997 from peanut
Linux 2.0.0.
/usr/X11/bin/xauth:  creating new authority file /home/craig/.Xauthority
```

If the key is found in one of the files or is accepted by the user, the client uses it to encrypt a randomly generated session key. The session key is then sent to the server and both systems use the key to encrypt the remainder of the SSH session.

The client is authenticated if it is listed in the *hosts.equiv* file, the *shost.equiv* file, the user's *.rhosts* file, or the by the **r** commands and the format of the *shost.equiv* and the *.shosts* files is the same as their **r** command equivalents. Notice that in the sample above the user is prompted for a password. If the client is not listed in one of the files, password authentication is used. There is no need to worry about password thieves, because SSH encrypts the password before it is sent across the link.

Users can employ a public key challenge/response protocol for authentication. First generate your public and private encryption keys:

```
> ssh-keygen
Initializing random number generator...
Generating p:  ....................................++ (distance 616)
Generating q:  ...................++ (distance 244)
Computing the keys...
Testing the keys...
Key generation complete.
Enter file in which to save the key (/home/craig/.ssh/identity):
Enter passphrase: Pdky&tiaj.
Enter the same passphrase again: Pdky&tiaj.
Your identification has been saved in /home/craig/.ssh/identity.
Your public key is:
```

---

* The system administrator can initialize the *ssh_known_hosts* file by running **make-ssh-known-hosts**, which gets the key from every host within a selected domain.

```
1024 35 158564823484025855320901702005057103023948197170850159592181522
craig@pecan
Your public key has been saved in /home/craig/.ssh/identity.pub
```

The **ssh-keygen** command creates your keys. Enter a password, called a "passphrase" here, that is at least 10 characters long. Use the rules described above to pick a good passphrase that is easy to remember. If you forget the passphrase, no one will be able to recover it for you.

Once you have created your keys on the client system, copy the public key to your account on the server. The public key is stored in your home directory on the client in *.ssh/identity.pub*. Copy it to *.ssh/authorized_keys* in your home directory on the server. Now when you log in using **ssh**, you are prompted for the passphrase:

```
> ssh pecan
Enter passphrase for RSA key 'craig@pecan': Pdky&tiaj.
Last login: Thu Sep 25 17:11:51 1997
Linux 2.0.0.
```

To improve system security, the **r** commands should be disabled after SSH is installed. Comment **rshd**, **rlogind**, **rexcd**, and **rexd** out of the *inetd.conf* file to disable inbound connections to the **r** commands. To ensure that SSH is used for outbound connections, replace **rlogin** and **rsh** with **ssh**. To do this, store copies of the original **rlogin** and **rsh** in a safe place, re-run **configure** with the special options shown below, and run **make install**:

```
# whereis rlogin
/usr/bin/rlogin
# whereis rsh
/usr/bin/rsh
# cp /usr/bin/rlogin /usr/lib/rlogin
# cp /usr/bin/rsh /usr/lib/rsh
# ./configure --with-rsh=/usr/bin --program-transform-name='s/^s/r/'
# make install
```

The example assumes that the path to the original **rlogin** and **rsh** commands is */usr/bin*. Use whatever is correct for your system.

After replacing the **rlogin** and **rsh**, you can still log in to systems that don't support SSH. You will, however, be warned that it is not a secure connection:

```
> rlogin cow
Secure connection to cow refused; reverting to insecure method.
Using rsh.  WARNING: Connection will not be encrypted.
Last login: Wed Sep 24 22:15:28 from peanut
Sun Microsystems Inc.   SunOS 5.5.1     Generic May 1996
You have new mail.
```

SSH is an excellent way to have secure communications between systems across the Internet. However, it does require that both systems have SSH installed. When you control both ends of the link, this is not a problem. But there are times when you must log in from a system that is not under your control. For those occasions, one-time passwords, as provided by OPIE, are still essential.

Application Security

Having good user authentication is an important security measure. However, using good user authentication isn't the only thing that you can do to improve the security of your computer and your network. Many break-ins occur when bugs in applications are exploited or when applications are misconfigured. In this section we'll look at some things you can do to improve application security.

Remove Unnecessary Software

Any software that allows an incoming connection from a remote site has the potential of being exploited by an intruder. Some security experts recommend you remove every daemon from the */etc/inetd.conf* file that you don't absolutely need. (Configuring the *inetd.conf* files is discussed in Chapter 6, *Configuring the Interface*, with explicit examples of removing **tftp** from service.)

Server systems may require several daemons, but most desktop systems require very few, if any. Removing the daemons from *inetd.conf* only prevents in-bound connections. It does not prevent out-bound connections. A user can still initiate a **telnet** to a remote site even after the **telnet** daemon is removed from her system's *inetd.conf*. A simple approach used by some people is to start by removing everything from *inetd.conf* and then add back to the file only those daemons that you decide you really need.

Keep Software Updated

Vendors frequently release new versions of network software for the express purpose of improving network security. Use the latest version of the network software offered by your vendor. Track the security alerts, CERT advisories, and bulletins to know what programs are particularly important to keep updated.

Even programs that are installed to improve security can have bugs that compromise security. The shadow password software for Linux is an example. You must use *shadow-960129.tar* or later, or risk compromising your system. If you fail to keep the software on your system up-to-date you open a big security hole for intruders. Intruders don't discover new problems; they exploit well-known problems. Keep track of the known security problems so you can keep your system up-to-date.

Stay informed about the latest information about all fixes for your system. The computer security advisories are a good way to do this. Contact your vendor and find out what services they provide for distributing security fixes. Make sure that the vendor knows that security is important to you.

Security Monitoring

A key element of effective network security is security monitoring. Good security is an ongoing process, and following the security guidelines discussed above is just the beginning. You must also monitor the systems to detect unauthorized user activity, and to locate and close security holes. Over time a system will change—active accounts become inactive; file permissions are changed. You need to detect and fix these problems as they arise.

Know Your System

Network security is monitored by examining the files and logs of individual systems on the network. To detect unusual activity on a system, you must know what activity is normal. What processes are normally running? Who is usually logged in? Who commonly logs in after hours? You need to know this, and more, about your system in order to develop a "feel" for how things should be. Some common UNIX commands—**ps** and **who**—can help you learn what normal activity is for your system.

The **ps** command displays the status of currently running processes. Run **ps** regularly to gain a clear picture of what processes run on the system at different times of the day, and who runs them. The Linux **ps −au** command and the **ps −ef** Solaris command display the user and the command that initiated each process. This should be sufficient information to learn who runs what, and when they run it. If you notice something unusual, investigate it. Make sure you understand how your system is being used.

The **who** command provides information about who is currently logged into your system. It displays who is logged in, what device they are using, when they logged in and, if applicable, what remote host they logged in from. (The **w** command, a variation of **who** available on some systems, also displays the currently active process started by each user.) The **who** command helps you learn who is usually logged in, as well as what remote hosts they normally log in from. Investigate any variations from the norm.

If any of these routine checks gives you reason to suspect a security problem, examine the system for unusual or modified files, for files that you know should be there but aren't, and for unusual login activity. This close examination of the system can also be made using everyday UNIX commands. Not every command or

file we discuss will be available on every system. But every system will have some
tools that help you keep a close eye on how your system is being used.

Looking for Trouble

Intruders often leave behind files or shell scripts to help them re-enter the system
or gain root access. Use the **ls −a | grep** ´^\.´ command to check for files with
names that begin with a dot (.). Intruders particularly favor names such as *.mail,
.xx,* ... (dot, dot, dot), .. (dot, dot, space), or ..*^G* (dot, dot, control-G).

If any files with names like these are found, suspect a break-in. (Remember that
one directory named **.** and one directory named **..** are in every directory except
the root directory.) Examine the contents of any suspicious files and follow your
normal incident-reporting procedures.

You should also examine certain key files if you suspect a security problem:

/etc/inetd.conf
> Check the names of the programs started from the */etc/inetd.conf* file. In par-
> ticular, make sure that it does not start any shell programs (e.g., */bin/csh*). Also
> check the programs that are started by **inetd** to make sure the programs have
> not been modified. */etc/inetd.conf* should not be world-writable.

r command security files
> Check */etc/hosts.equiv, /etc/hosts.lpd*, and the *.rhosts* file in each user's home
> directory to make sure they have not been improperly modified. In particular,
> look for any plus-sign (+) entries, and any entries for hosts outside of your
> local trusted network. These files should not be world-writable.

/etc/passwd
> Make sure that the */etc/passwd* file has not been modified. Look for new user-
> names, and changes to the UID or GID of any account. */etc/passwd* should not
> be world-writable.

*Files run by **cron** or **at***
> Check all of the files run by **cron** or **at**, looking for new files or unexplained
> changes. Sometimes intruders use procedures run by **cron** or **at** to re-admit
> themselves to the system, even after they have been kicked off.

Executable files
> Check all executable files, binaries, and shell files to make sure they have not
> been modified by the intruder. The master checklist, mentioned in the previ-
> ous section, is helpful for this. Executable files should not be world-writable.

If you find or even suspect a problem, follow your reporting procedure and let
people know about the problem. This is particularly important if you are con-

nected to a local area network. A problem on your system could spread to other systems on the network.

Checking files

The **find** command is a powerful tool for detecting potential filesystem security problems because it can search the entire filesystem for files based on file permissions. Intruders often leave behind setuid programs to grant themselves root access. The following command searches for these files, recursively, starting from the root directory:

```
# find / -user root -perm -4000 -print
```

This **find** command starts searching at the root (/) for files owned by the user root (**-user root**) that have the setuid permission bit set (**-perm -4000**). All matches found are displayed at the terminal (**-print**). If any filenames are displayed by **find**, closely examine the individual files to make sure that these permissions are correct. As a general rule, shell scripts should not have setuid permission.

You can use the **find** command to check for other problems that might open security holes for intruders. The other common problems that **find** checks for are world-writable files (**–perm –2**), setgid files (**–perm –2000**), and unowned files (**–nouser –o –nogroup**). World-writable and setgid files should be checked to make sure that these permissions are appropriate. As a general rule, files with names beginning with a dot (**.**) should not be world-writable, and setgid permission, like setuid, should be avoided for shell scripts.

The process of scanning the filesystem can be automated with the Tripwire program. Tripwire is available from Purdue University at *ftp://coast.cs.purdue.edu/pub/tools/unix/Tripwire*. This package not only scans the filesystem for problems, it computes digital signatures to ensure that if any files are changed, the changes will be detected.

Checking login activity

Strange login activity, at odd times of the day or from unfamiliar locations, can indicate attempts by intruders to gain access to your system. We have already used the **who** command to check who is currently logged into the system. To check who has logged into the system in the past, use the **last** command.

The **last** command displays the contents of the *wtmp* file.* It is useful for learning normal login patterns and detecting abnormal login activity. The *wtmp* file keeps a historical record of who logged into the system, when they logged in, what remote site they logged in from, and when they logged out.

---

* This file is frequently stored in */usr/adm* or */etc*.

Figure 12-2 shows a single line of **last** command output. The figure highlights the fields that show the user who logged in, the device, the remote location from which the login originated (if applicable), the day, the date, the time logged in, the time logged out (if applicable), and the elapsed time.

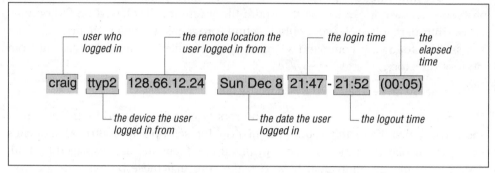

Figure 12-2: Last command output

Simply typing **last** produces a large amount of output because every login stored in *wtmp* is displayed. To limit the output, specify a username or tty device on the command line. This limits the display to entries for the specified username or terminal. It is also useful to use **grep** to search **last**'s output for certain conditions. For example, the command below checks for logins that occur on Saturday or Sunday:

```
% last | grep 'S[au]' | more
craig       console                    Sun Dec 15 10:33    still logged in
reboot      ~                          Sat Dec 14 18:12
shutdown    ~                 .        Sat Dec 14 18:14
craig       ttyp3    modems.nuts.com   Sat Dec 14 17:11 - 17:43  (00:32)
craig       ttyp2    172.16.12.24      Sun Dec  8 21:47 - 21:52  (00:05)
            .
            .
--More--
```

The next example searches for root logins not originating from the console. If you didn't know who made the two logins reported in this example, be suspicious:

```
% last root | grep -v console
root        ttyp3    peanut.nuts.com   Tue Oct 29 13:12 - down   (00:03)
root        ftp      almond.nuts.com   Tue Sep 10 16:37 - 16:38  (00:00)
```

While the **last** command is a major source of information about previous login activity, it is not the only source. On some systems, the *messages* file records logins to the root account and failed logins.* Failed logins and root logins at odd times or from odd places are suspicious. The following **grep** command checks */usr/adm/messages* for root login activity on a Linux system:

---

* Some systems, such as Solaris, don't log **su** activity and root logins in the *messages* file.

```
% grep -i login /usr/adm/messages
Nov 23 10:39:10 peanut login: ROOT LOGIN ON tty1
Nov 23 11:11:50 peanut login: 2 LOGIN FAILURES ON tty1, craig
Nov 23 11:25:11 peanut login: 2 LOGIN FAILURES ON tty1, root
Nov 23 11:25:16 peanut login: ROOT LOGIN ON tty1
Nov 23 11:28:15 peanut login: ROOT LOGIN ON tty1
Nov 24 22:31:40 peanut login: 2 LOGIN FAILURES ON tty1, craig
Nov 27 19:47:52 peanut login: 2 LOGIN FAILURES ON tty1, craig
Nov 29 11:10:36 peanut login: 2 LOGIN FAILURES ON tty1, craig
Dec  1 19:41:50 peanut login: 2 LOGIN FAILURES ON tty1, craig
Dec  9 22:05:27 peanut login: ROOT LOGIN ON tty1
```

Report any security problems that you detect, or even suspect. Don't be embarrassed to report a problem because it might turn out to be a false alarm. Don't keep quiet because you might get "blamed" for the security breach. Your silence will only help the intruder.

Automated Monitoring

Manually monitoring your system is time-consuming and prone to errors and omissions. Fortunately, several automated monitoring tools are available. The Web site *http://ciac.llnl.gov/ciac/ToolsUnixSysMon.html* lists many of them. Tripwire (mentioned earlier), Tiger, COPS, and SATAN are all popular monitoring tools. COPS and SATAN are described below.

COPS

COPS (Computer Oracle Password and Security) is a collection of programs that automate many of the computer monitoring procedures discussed in the previous sections. As with any monitoring system, COPS detects potential problems; it does not correct them. COPS does not replace personal monitoring by the system administrator, but it does provide additional tools to help the administrator perform monitoring tasks.

The tools in the COPS package check:

- Permissions for files, directories, and devices
- Contents of */etc/passwd* and */etc/group* files
- Contents of */etc/hosts.equiv* and ˜/.rhosts files
- Changes in SUID status

After completing these checks, COPS mails a report of the results to the system administrator.

COPS can be obtained at *ftp://coast.cs.purdue.edu/pub/tools/unix*. The **tar** file contains the source code and instructions for building COPS. Once COPS is built, edit the COPS shell file so that the variable SECURE points to the directory that contains the COPS programs, and the variable SECURE_USERS contains the email address of the person who should receive the COPS report. By default, the report is not mailed to anyone; it is written to a file. To force the report to be mailed to the SECURE_USERS, edit the COPS shell script by changing the MMAIL variable to MMAIL=YES.

The great advantage of COPS is that it is simple. COPS removes the hassles from security monitoring, making it more likely that these tasks will be performed. To run COPS, simply enter:

```
% cops
```

cops uses the system's hostname to create a directory within the directory defined by the SECURE variable. It writes the security report in this new directory in a file named after the current date. The format of the report's filename is *year_month_day*. For example, on *peanut* the home directory for the COPS programs is */usr/local/cops*. If the current date is January 24, 1997, running the **cops** program creates the directory */usr/local/cops/peanut* and writes the report into that directory with the file name *1997_Jan_24*. Here's a sample report:

```
peanut:/usr/local/cops/peanut> cat 1997_Jan_24
ATTENTION:
Security Report for Fri Jan 24 16:21:21 EST 1997
from host peanut

**** root.chk ****
**** dev.chk ****
Warning! NFS file system /home/craig exported with no restrictions!
**** is_able.chk ****
Warning! /usr/spool/uucp is _World_ writable!
Warning! /etc/securetty is _World_ readable!
**** rc.chk ****
**** cron.chk ****
**** group.chk ****
**** home.chk ****
Warning! User uucp's home directory /var/spool/uucppublic is mode 01777!
Warning! User nobody's home directory /dev/null is not a directory!
        (mode 020666)
Warning! User guest's home directory /dev/null is not a directory!
        (mode 020666)
**** passwd.chk ****
Warning! Password file, line 15, uid > 8 chars
        postmaster:*:14:12:postmaster:/var/spool/mail:/bin/bash
**** user.chk ****
**** misc.chk ****
**** ftp.chk ****
ftp-Warning! Incorrect permissions on "ls" in /home/ftp/bin!
ftp-Warning! Incorrect permissions on "passwd" in /home/ftp/etc!
ftp-Warning! Incorrect permissions on "group" in /home/ftp/etc!
```

```
**** pass.chk ****
**** kuang ****
**** bug.chk ****
```

Look at each line in the report you receive. Some lines might indicate real problems, such as the first warning line in our sample report that indicates */home/craig* is exported via NFS without proper access control. Other lines might indicate conditions that are not problems for your system. In our example, we decide to leave */etc/securetty* with world-read permission. Read the file *docs/warnings* for an explanation of each warning message. Evaluate each line of the report and correct anything that needs correcting. Rerun COPS and examine the new report. It should report only the problems that you are willing to accept.

Once you're satisfied with your system's security, schedule COPS to run at regular intervals. New problems can be introduced into your system over time. It's better to have the COPS discover the problem than to have the "robbers" discover it!

SATAN

Another tool for testing the security of your system is the *Security Administrator's Tool for Analyzing Networks* (SATAN). SATAN's introduction was met by near hysteria in the popular press, largely because of the tool's name. Despite its name, SATAN is just another security tool.

SATAN does have some unique features. While COPS is intended for use on an individual system, SATAN is designed to test entire networks of systems. This is both a feature and a problem. If you are the administrator of your network, running SATAN allows you to check all of the systems on the network from one central system. If, however, you are responsible for only one system and you use SATAN to probe the other systems on your network, you will irritate all of the other system administrators on the network who will view the SATAN probes as attempted break-ins. Use SATAN only to test systems on your own network that you have officially recognized authority over.

Another feature of SATAN is that it uses your system's Web browser as the interface for viewing the security reports it generates. This is helpful if you have a large network of systems. The browser's ability to link together related documents allows SATAN to organize various hierarchies of security information. Use the browser to search for the most critical errors, the most troublesome subnets, or the most vulnerable hosts. The screenshot in Figure 12-3 shows a display of hosts listed in sequence from the one with the most security errors to the one with the least. Clicking on a hostname provides a specific report of the errors on that host.

The information in Figure 12-3 comes from the *foo.org* database provided in the SATAN documentation set. Download the binary file *satan.doc.tar.Z* from *ftp://ftp.win.tue.nl/pub/security/unix*. Uncompress and untar the file and follow the

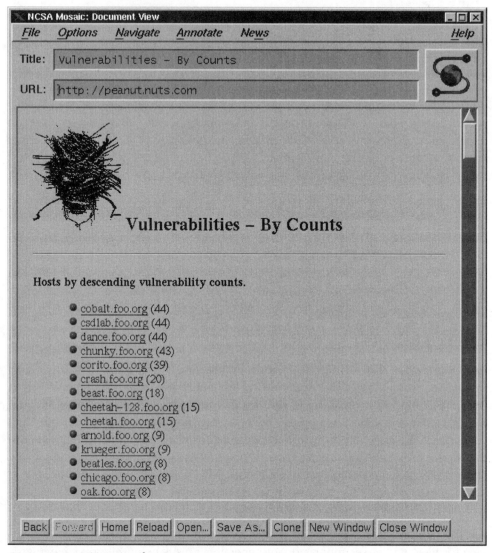

Figure 12-3: SATAN interface

simple instructions in the README file to build the documentation system. You can then play with SATAN without the danger of accidentally probing any of the systems on your network. If you like what you see, you can download the full product from the same location by getting the binary file *satan.tar.Z*.

For many sites, well-informed users and administrators, good password security, and good system monitoring provide adequate network security. But for some security-conscious sites, more may be desired. That "more" is usually some technique for limiting access between systems connected to the network, or for limiting access to the data the network carries. In the remainder of this chapter we look at various security techniques that limit access.

Access Control

Access control is a technique for limiting access. Routers and hosts that use access control check the address of a host requesting a service against an *access control list*. If the list says that the remote host is permitted to use the requested service, the access is granted. If the list says that the remote host is not permitted to access the service, the access is denied. Access control does not bypass any normal security checks. It adds a check to validate the source of a service request, and retains all of the normal checks to validate the user.

Access control systems are common in terminal servers and routers. For example, Cisco routers have an access control facility. Access control software is also available for UNIX hosts. Two such packages are **xinetd** and the *TCP wrappers* program. Clearly, there are a variety of ways to implement access controls. In this section we use TCP wrappers ("wrapper").

wrapper

The wrapper package performs two basic functions: it logs requests for Internet services, and provides an access control mechanism for UNIX systems. Logging requests for specific network services is a useful monitoring function, especially if you are looking for possible intruders. If this were all it did, wrapper would be a useful package. But the real power of wrapper is its ability to control access to network services.

The wrapper software is available through the *http://csrc.nist.gov/tools/tools.htm* Web page. The wrapper *tar* file contains the C source code and Makefile necessary to build the wrapper daemon **tcpd**.

Make **tcpd** and then install it in the same directory as the other network daemons. Edit */etc/inetd.conf* and replace the path to each network service daemon that you wish to place under access control with the path to **tcpd**. The only field in the */etc/inetd.conf* entry affected by **tcpd** is the sixth field, which contains the path to the network daemon.

For example, assume that the entry for the **finger** daemon in */etc/inetd.conf* on our Solaris system is:

```
finger  stream  tcp  nowait  nobody  /usr/etc/in.fingerd  in.fingerd
```

The value in the sixth field is */usr/etc/in.fingerd*. To monitor access to the **finger** daemon, replace this value with */usr/etc/tcpd*, as in the following entry:

```
finger   stream tcp nowait nobody /usr/etc/tcpd   in.fingerd
```

Now when **inetd** receives a request for **fingerd**, it starts **tcpd** instead. **tcpd** then logs the **fingerd** request, checks the access control information, and, if permitted, starts the real **finger** daemon to handle the request.

Make a similar change for every service you want to place under access control. Good candidates for access control are **ftpd**, **tftpd**, **telnetd**, **rshd**, **rlogind**, **rexecd**, and **fingerd**. Obviously, **tcpd** cannot control access for daemons that are not started by **inetd**, such as **sendmail** and NFS.

Using the wrapper on our Slackware 96 Linux system is even easier. There is no need to download and install the **tcpd** software. It comes as an integral part of the Linux release. You don't even have to edit the */etc/inetd.conf* file because the sixth field of the entries in that file already point to the **tcpd** program, as shown below:

```
finger   stream tcp nowait nobody /usr/sbin/tcpd   in.fingerd -w
```

tcpd access control files

The information **tcpd** uses to control access is in two files, */etc/hosts.allow* and */etc/hosts.deny*. Each file's function is obvious from its name. *hosts.allow* contains the list of hosts that are allowed to access the network's services, and *hosts.deny* contains the list of hosts that are denied access. If the files are not found, **tcpd** permits every host to have access and simply logs the access request. Therefore, if you only want to monitor access, don't create these two files.

If the files are found, **tcpd** checks the *hosts.allow* file first, followed by the *hosts.deny* file. It stops as soon as it finds a match for the host and the service in question. Therefore, access granted by *hosts.allow* cannot be overridden by *hosts.deny*.

The format of entries in both files is the same:

service-list : *host-list* [: *shell-command*]

The *service-list* is a list of network services, separated by commas. These are the services to which access is being granted (*hosts.allow*) or denied (*hosts.deny*). Each service is identified by the process name used in the seventh field of the */etc/inetd.conf* entry. This is simply the name that immediately follows the path to **tcpd** in *inetd.conf*. (See Chapter 5, *Basic Configuration*, for a description of the arguments field in the */etc/inetd.conf* entry.)

Again, let's use **finger** as an example. We changed its *inetd.conf* entry to read:

```
finger   stream tcp nowait nobody /usr/etc/tcpd   in.fingerd
```

Therefore, we would use **in.fingerd** as the service name in a *hosts.allow* or *hosts.deny* file.

The *host-list* is a comma-separated list of hostnames, domain names, Internet addresses, or network numbers. The systems listed in the host-list are granted access (*hosts.allow*) or denied access (*hosts.deny*) to the services specified in the service-list. A hostname or an Internet address matches an individual host. For example, *peanut* is a hostname and 172.16.12.2 is an Internet address. Both match a particular host. A domain name matches every host within that domain; e.g., *.nuts.com* matches *almond.nuts.com, peanut.nuts.com, pecan.nuts.com,* and any other hosts in the domain. When specified in a **tcpd** access control list, domain names always start with a dot (.). A network number matches every IP address within that network's address space. For example, 172.16. matches 172.16.12.1, 172.16.12.2, 172.16.5.1, and any other address that begins with 172.16. Network addresses in a **tcpd** access control list always end with a dot (.).

A completed *hosts.allow* entry that grants FTP and telnet access to all hosts in the *nuts.com* domain is shown below:

```
ftpd,telnetd : .nuts.com
```

Two special keywords can be used in *hosts.allow* and *hosts.deny* entries. The keyword `ALL` can be used in the service-list to match all network services, and in the host-list to match all hostnames and addresses. The second keyword, `LOCAL`, can be used only in the host-list. It matches all local hostnames. **tcpd** considers a hostname "local" if it contains no embedded dots. Therefore, the hostname *peanut* would match on `LOCAL`, but the hostname *peanut.nuts.com* would not match. The following entry affects all services and all local hosts:

```
ALL : LOCAL
```

The final field that can be used in these entries is the optional shell-command field. The shell command specified in this field will execute whenever a match occurs. The command is executed in addition to the normal functions of the access list match. In other words, if a match occurs for an entry that has an optional shell command, **tcpd** logs the access, grants or denies access to the service, and then passes the shell command to the shell for execution.

A more complete example of how **tcpd** is used will help you understand these entries. First, assume that you wish to allow every host in your local domain (*nuts.com*) to have access to all services on your system, but you want to deny access to every service to all other hosts. Make an entry in */etc/hosts.allow* to permit access to everything by everyone in the local domain:

```
ALL : LOCAL, .nuts.com
```

The keyword **ALL** in the services-list indicates that this rule applies to all network services. The colon (:) separates the services-list from the host-list. The keyword **LOCAL** indicates that all local hostnames without a domain extension are acceptable, and that the *nuts.com* domain name extensions are also acceptable. To prevent access from everyone else, make an entry in the */etc/hosts.deny* file:

```
ALL : ALL
```

Every system that does not match the entry in */etc/hosts.allow* is passed on to */etc/hosts.deny*. Here the entry denies access to everyone, regardless of what service they are asking for. Remember, even with **ALL** in the services-list field, only services started by **inetd**, and only those services whose entries in *inetd.conf* have been edited to invoke **tcpd**, are affected. This does not provide security for any other service.

Encryption

Encryption is a technique for limiting access to the data carried on the network. Encryption encodes the data in a form that can be read only by systems that have the "key" to the encoding scheme. The original text, called the "clear text," is encrypted using an encryption device (hardware or software) and an encryption key. This produces encoded text, which is called the cipher. To recreate the "clear text," the cipher must be decrypted using the same type of encryption device and an appropriate key.

Largely because of spy novels and World War II movies, encryption is one of the first things that people think of when they think of security. However, encryption is not always applicable to network security. Encrypting data for transmission across a network requires that the same encryption equipment, or software, be used at both ends of the data exchange. Unless you control both ends of the network and can ensure that the same encryption device is available, it is difficult to use end-to-end data encryption. For this reason, encryption is most commonly used to exchange data in individual applications where the software at both ends of the network is defined by a single vendor. For example, a Web server and a Web browser from the same vendor use the same encryption. Encrypting all types of data is limited to places where the entire system is under the control of a single authority, such as military networks, private networks, individual systems, or when the individuals at both ends of the communication can reach personal agreement on the encryption technique and key.

What is needed to make encryption truly useful in a global network are universally recognized encryption standards and a trusted infrastructure to support those standards. *Public-key encryption* is the technology that will make encryption an important security technology for an open global network like the Internet. Public-key systems encode the clear-text with a key that is widely known and publicly available, but the cipher can only be decoded back to clear-text with a secret key. This means that Dan can look up Kristin's public key in a trusted database and use it to encode a message to her that no one else can read. Even though everyone on the Internet has access to the public key, only Kristin can decrypt the message using her secret key. Kristin can then look up Dan's public key to encrypt her reply. This encrypted communication takes place without Dan or Kristin ever divulging their secret keys. However, to ensure that the keys have not been tampered with, public-key cryptography requires a trusted system for distributing public keys. And because the encrypting key is available to everyone, it requires a digital signature system to authenticate that a message is really from whom it purports to be from.

Government and industry are working on the standards and infrastructure for public-key cryptography. The type of encryption used in the examples in this section is symmetric encryption. It requires that the same encryption technique and the same secret key is used for both encrypting and decrypting the message. It does not rely on public keys, digital signatures, or a widely accepted infrastructure, but its usefulness is limited. Truly effective public-key cryptography must wait for the creation of a trusted public-key infrastructure.

When is symmetric encryption useful?

Before using encryption, decide why you want to encrypt the data, whether the data should be protected with encryption, and whether the data should even be stored on a networked computer system.

A few valid reasons for encrypting data are:

- To prevent casual browsers from viewing sensitive data files

- To prevent accidental disclosure of sensitive data

- To prevent privileged users (e.g., system administrators) from viewing private data files

- To complicate matters for intruders who attempt to search through a system's files

Encryption is not a substitute for good computer security. Encryption can protect sensitive or personal information from casual snooping, but it should never be the sole means of protecting critical information. Encryption systems can be broken, and encrypted data can be deleted or corrupted just like any other data. So don't let encryption lull you into a false sense of security. Some information is so sensitive or critical that it should not be stored on a networked computer system, even if it is encrypted. Encryption is only a small part of a complete security system. To find out more about file encryption, see *PGP: Pretty Good Privacy*, by Simson Garfinkel (O'Reilly & Associates). It provides a book-length treatment of PGP, an encryption program used for files and electronic mail.

Firewalls

A firewall system is a popular way to provide network security. The term "firewall" implies protection from danger, and just as the firewall in your car protects the passengers' compartment from the car's engine, a firewall computer system protects your network from the outside world. A firewall computer provides strict access control between your systems and the outside world.

The concept of a firewall is quite simple. A firewall is a choke point through which all traffic between a secured network and an unsecured network must pass. In practice, it is usually a choke point between an enterprise network and the Internet. Creating a single point through which all traffic must pass allows the traffic to be more easily monitored and controlled and allows security expertise to be concentrated on that single point.

Firewalls are implemented in many ways. In fact, there are so many different types of firewalls, the term is almost meaningless. When someone tells you they have a firewall you really can't know exactly what they mean. Covering all of the different types of firewall architectures requires an entire book—see *Building Internet Firewalls* (O'Reilly & Associates). Here we cover the screened subnet architecture (probably the most popular firewall architecture), and the multi-homed host architecture, which is essentially a firewall-in-a-box.

The most common firewall architecture contains at least four hardware components: an exterior router, a secure server (called a Bastion Host), an exposed network (called a Perimeter Network), and an interior router. Each hardware component provides part of the complete security scheme. Figure 12-4 illustrates this architecture.

The exterior router is the only connection between the enterprise network and the outside world. This router is configured to do a minimal level of access control. It checks to make sure that no packet coming from the external world has a source address that matches the internal network. If our network number is 172.16, the exterior router discards any packets it receives on its exterior interface that contain the source address 172.16. That source address should only be received by the router on its interior interface. Security people call this type of access control *packet filtering*. In some ways it is similar to the packet filtering we did in Chapter 11 because packets are "filtered out" based on IP header information.

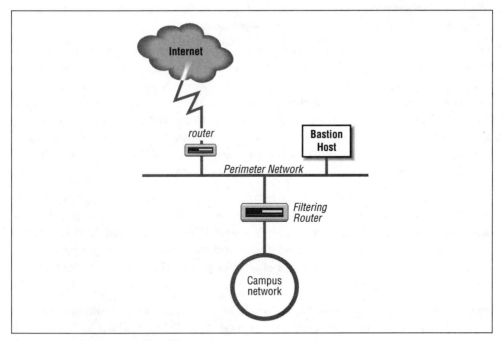

Figure 12-4: Screened subnet firewall

The interior router does the bulk of the access control work. It filters packets not only on address but also on protocol and port numbers to control the services that are accessible to and from the interior network. What services are blocked by this router are up to you. If you plan to use a firewall, the services that will be allowed and those that will be denied should be defined in your security policy document. Almost every service can be a threat. These threats must be evaluated in light of your security needs. Services that are intended only for internal users (NIS, NFS, X-Windows, etc.) are almost always blocked. Services that allow writing to internal systems (the **r** commands, telnet, FTP, SMTP, etc.) are usually blocked. Services that provide information about internal systems (DNS, fingerd, etc.) are usually blocked. This doesn't leave much running! That is where the bastion host and perimeter network come in.

The bastion host is a secure server. It provides an interconnection point between the enterprise network and the outside world for the restricted services. Some of the services that are restricted by the interior gateway may be essential for a useful network. Those essential services are provided through the bastion host in a secure manner. The bastion host provides some services directly, such as DNS, SMTP mail services, and anonymous FTP. Other services are provided as *proxy services*. When the bastion host acts as a proxy server, internal clients connect to the outside through the bastion hosts and external systems respond back to the internal clients through the host. The bastion host can therefore control the traffic flowing into and out of the site to any extent desired.

There can be more than one secure server, and there often is. The perimeter network connects the servers together and connects the exterior router to the interior router. The systems on the perimeter network are much more exposed to security threats than are the systems on the interior network. This is as it must be. After all, the secure servers are needed to provide service to the outside world as well as to the internal network. Isolating the systems that must be exposed on a separate network lessens the chance that a compromise of one of those systems will lead directly to the compromise of an internal system.

The multi-homed host architecture attempts to duplicate all of these firewall functions in a single box. It works by replacing an IP router with a multi-homed host that does not forward packets at the IP layer.* The multi-homed host effectively severs the connection between the interior and exterior networks. To provide the interior network with some level of network connectivity, it performs similar functions to the bastion hosts.

Figure 12-5 shows a comparison between an IP router and a multi-homed host firewall. A router handles packets up through the IP layer. The router forwards each packet based on the packet's destination address, and the route to that destination indicated in the routing table. A host, on the other hand, does not forward packets. The multi-homed host processes packets through the Application Layer, which provides it with complete control over how packets are handled.†

This definition of a firewall—as a device completely distinct from an IP router—is not universally accepted. Some people refer to routers with special security features as firewalls, but this is really just a matter of semantics. In this book, routers with special security features are called "secure routers" or "secure gateways." Firewalls, while they may include routers, do more than just filter packets.

Functions of the firewall

An intruder cannot mount a direct attack on any of the systems behind a firewall. Packets destined for hosts behind the firewall are simply delivered to the firewall. The intruder must instead mount an attack directly against the firewall machine. Because the firewall machine can be the target of break-in attacks, it employs very strict security guidelines. But because there is only one firewall versus many machines on the local network, it is easier to enforce strict security on the firewall.

---

* The role that IP routers, also called gateways, play in gluing the Internet together is covered extensively in earlier chapters.

† See the GATEWAY option in Chapter 5, *Basic Configuration*, for information on how to prevent a multi-homed host from forwarding packets.

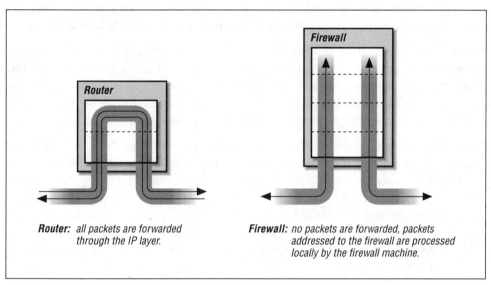

Router: all packets are forwarded through the IP layer.

Firewall: no packets are forwarded, packets addressed to the firewall are processed locally by the firewall machine.

Figure 12-5: Firewalls versus routers

The disadvantage of a firewall system is obvious. In the same manner that it restricts access from the outside into the local network, it restricts access from the local network to the outside world. To minimize the inconvenience caused by the firewall, the system must do many more things than a router does. Some firewalls provide:

- DNS name service for the outside world
- Email forwarding
- Proxy services

Only the minimal services truly needed to communicate with external systems should be provided on a firewall system. Other common network services (NIS, NFS, **rsh**, **rcp**, **finger**, etc.) should generally not be provided. Services are limited to decrease the number of holes through which an intruder can gain access. On firewall systems, security is more important than service.

The biggest problems for the firewall machine are **ftp** service and remote terminal service. To maintain a high level of security, user accounts are discouraged on the firewall machine; however, user data must pass through the firewall system for **ftp** and remote terminal services. This problem can be handled by creating special user accounts for **ftp** and **telnet** that are shared by all internal users. But group accounts are generally viewed as security problems. A better solution is to provide proxy services on the firewall. To do this you need to run a proxy server on the firewall and proxy clients on your internal system. Most commercial client software includes support for proxy services. Many packages are compatible with SOCKS, a freely available proxy service package that can be downloaded from the Internet.

Because to be effective a firewall must be constructed with great care, and because there are many configuration variables for setting up a firewall machine, vendors offer special firewall software. Some vendors sell special-purpose machines designed specifically for use as firewall systems. Before setting up your own firewall, investigate the options available from your hardware vendor.

The details of setting up a firewall system are beyond the scope of this book. Before you proceed, I recommend you read *Building Internet Firewalls* and *Firewalls and Internet Security*, listed in the bibliography at the end of this chapter. Unless you have skilled UNIX systems administrators with adequate free time, a do-it-yourself firewall installation is a mistake. Hire a company that specializes in firewall design and installation. If your information is valuable enough to protect with a firewall, it must be valuable enough to protect with a professionally installed firewall.

Firewall systems are useful to many sites, but for some others they are not appropriate. The restrictions they place on individual users are not acceptable to some organizations, and these restrictions can drive independent-minded users to find other ways to handle their communications needs. Think seriously about your real security needs before selecting a solution.

Routing control

A firewall system works by controlling routing between the protected system and the rest of the world. A carefully modified static routing table can be used to provide a similar type of protection between internal systems on an enterprise network.

As we discussed in the chapters on routing and troubleshooting, it is necessary for your system to have a routing table entry for every network with which it will communicate. This can be either an explicit route for an individual network, or a default route for all networks. Without the proper routes, your system cannot communicate with remote networks, and the remote networks cannot communicate with your system. Regardless of how the remote site sets up its routing, it cannot communicate with your host if your host does not have a route back to the remote site. Because of this, you can control which remote sites are able to communicate with your system by controlling the contents of the routing table.

For example, assume that the *nuts.com* personnel department is on subnet 172.16.9.0, and that the router for their subnet is 172.16.9.1. They want to talk only to other hosts on their subnet and to a management system named *hick-*

ory.nuts.com (172.16.18.7). To implement this policy with the routing table, each host administrator on the personnel subnet:

1. Makes sure that no routing protocol is running, and that none is started automatically at boot time.

2. Disables source routing.

3. Makes sure that there is no default route in the routing table, and that a default route is not added automatically at boot time.

4. Adds a host-specific route to 172.16.18.7 (*hickory.nuts.com*), and makes sure that this static route is added each time the system boots.

Using **netstat** to display this limited routing table on host 172.16.9.14 shows the following:

```
# netstat -nr
Routing tables
Destination     Gateway         Flags     Refcnt Use    Interface
127.0.0.1       127.0.0.1       UH        2      7126   lo0
172.16.18.7     172.16.9.1      UGH       1      1285   le0
172.16.9.0      172.16.9.14     U         30     89456  le0
```

The display shows the loopback route, a route to the local subnet (172.16.9.0), and a host route to *hickory.nuts.com* (172.16.18.7). There are no other routes, so there are no other locations with which this host can communicate. Therefore, if an intruder launched an attack against this system, he would receive no response.

This security technique is less restrictive than an internal firewall, because it affects only the systems that contain the data or processes that are being protected. This technique is easy to implement and does not require special equipment or software. However, it is also much less secure than a firewall. If any of these systems is successfully attacked, all of the systems could be compromised. Each system being protected this way must be properly configured, while one firewall can protect a group of systems. This works only when there are a small number of systems and they are all under the control of a single network administrator. In a few situations, this is a possible alternative to an internal firewall..

Words to the Wise

I am not a security expert; I am a network administrator. In my view, good security is good system administration and vice versa. Most of this chapter is just common-sense advice. It is probably sufficient for most circumstances, but certainly not for all.

Make sure you know whether there is an existing security policy that applies to your network or system. If there are policies, regulations, or laws governing your situation, make sure to obey them. Never do anything to undermine the security system established for your site.

No system is completely secure. No matter what you do, you will have problems. Realize this and prepare for it. Prepare a disaster recovery plan and do everything necessary, so that when the worst does happen, you can recover from it with the minimum possible disruption.

A good listing of available security publications can be found at *http://csrc.nist.gov/secpub*. If you want to read more about security, I recommend the following:

- RFC 1244, *Site Security Handbook*, P. Holbrook, J. Reynold, et al., July 1991.

- RFC 1281, *Guidelines for the Secure Operation of the Internet*, R. Pethia, S. Crocker, and B. Fraser, November 1991.

- *Practical UNIX and Internet Security*, Simson Garfinkel and Gene Spafford, O'Reilly & Associates, 1996.

- *Building Internet Firewalls*, Brent Chapman and Elizabeth Zwicky, O'Reilly & Associates, 1995.

- *Computer Security Basics*, Deborah Russell and G. T. Gangemi, Sr., O'Reilly & Associates, 1991.

- *Firewalls and Internet Security*, William Cheswick and Steven Bellovin, Addison-Wesley, 1994.

Summary

Network access and computer security work at cross-purposes. Attaching a computer to a network increases the security risks for that computer. Evaluate your security needs to determine what must be protected and how vigorously it must be protected. Develop a written site security policy that defines your procedures and documents the security duties and responsibilities of employees at all levels.

Network security is essentially good system security. Good user authentication, effective system monitoring, and well-trained system administrators provide the best security. Tools are available to help with these tasks. SSH, OPIE, Tripwire, COPS, SATAN, TCP Wrapper, encryption, and firewalls are all tools that can help.

Like troubleshooting, network security is an ongoing process. In the final chapter, we discuss another ongoing process—learning. Now we look at ways you can keep abreast of the most current information in network administration.

13

Internet Information Resources

Now that our network is configured, debugged, and secure, how will we use it? Increasingly, a network serves not merely as a delivery link between two hosts, but as a path to information resources. Information servers, file repositories, databases, and information directories are available throughout the Internet. But, with millions of devices connected to the Internet, finding these services can be a daunting task.

This chapter explores various ways to avail yourself of this storehouse of information. We look at how information is retrieved from network servers, some tools that make it easier to locate that information, and how to configure your system as an anonymous FTP server.

The World Wide Web

The primary method used to retrieve network information is the World Wide Web. The Web is an interlinked network of hypertext servers based on the *Hypertext Transfer Protocol* (HTTP) that runs on top of TCP/IP. The Web is accessed via a *browser*, a program that provides a consistent graphical interface to the user. All of the popular UNIX browsers—Netscape, Mosaic, Arena, etc.—are modeled after the original Mosaic browser developed at the National Center for Supercomputer Applications (NCSA). Therefore, they share a common look and feel.

Most UNIX systems do not ship with a built-in browser; you need to download one from the Internet. The Netscape browser is available at the URL *http://www.netscape.com*. It can be downloaded, evaluated, and then purchased. (It's nice to be able to try before you buy!) The Mosaic browser is available free of charge at *ftp://ftp.ncsa.edu/Web/Mosaic/Unix/binaries*. They both work well and in an almost identical manner. However, Netscape is the most popular browser and has an active development team.

Obtaining information from hypertext Web pages is the most common use for a browser. Use yours to keep up with the most current network information. Figure 13-1 shows a network administrator checking the security alerts at the Computer Security Resource Clearinghouse at the National Institute of Standards and Technology.

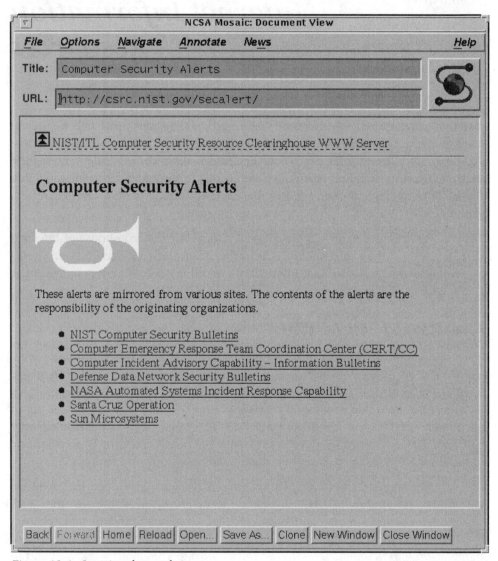

Figure 13-1: Security alerts website

The URL field near the top of the sample screen is the location of the Web page we are reading. On some other browsers this field is labeled "Location" or "Netsite," but in all cases it performs the same function: it holds the path to the information resource. In the example the location is *http://csrc.nist.gov/secalert/*. "URL" stands for *universal resource locator*. It is a standard way of defining a network resource and it has a specific structure:

>   *service://server/path/file*

In the sample URL, *http* is the service; *csrc.nist.gov* is the server; and *secalerts* is the path to the resource contained on that server. This tells the browser to locate a host with the domain name *csrc.nist.gov*, and to ask it for the hypertext information located in the *secalerts* path. Hypertext is not the only type of information that can be retrieved by a browser. The browser is intended to provide a consistent interface to various types of network resources. HTTP is only one of the services that can be specified in a URL.

A Web browser can be used to view local hypertext files. This is how the **gated** documentation is delivered. Figure 13-2 shows a network administrator reading the **gated** documentation. The URL in Figure 13-2 is *file://localhost/usr/doc/-config_guide/config.html*. The service is *file*, which means that the resource is to be read via the standard filesystem. The server is the local host (*localhost*). The path is */usr/doc/config_gated*, and the file is *config.html*.

Another browser service that is often used by a network administrator is FTP. Figure 13-3 shows a network administrator using a browser to download software. The URL in Figure 13-2 is *ftp://ftp.ncsa.edu/Web/Mosaic/Unix/binaries/2.6*. FTP is the service used to access the resource, which in this case is a binary file. The server is *ftp.ncsa.edu*, which is the anonymous FTP server at the National Center for Super Computing Applications. The path is */Web/Mosaic/Unix/binaries/2.6* and the file is any of the files listed on the screen.

Reading important announcements and documentation and downloading files are probably the most common uses a network administrator has for a Web browser. There are, however, many other things that can be done with a browser and a huge number of resources available on the network. A detailed discussion of browsers and the Web is beyond the scope of this book. See *The Whole Internet User's Guide and Catalog*, by Ed Krol (O'Reilly & Associates), for a full treatment of these subjects.

The browser provides a consistent interface to a variety of network services. But it is not the only way, or necessarily the best way, to access all of these services. In particular, it may not be the fastest or most efficient way to download a file. Figure 13-2 shows a file being downloaded from an anonymous FTP server. An alternative is to invoke **ftp** directly from the command-line interface.

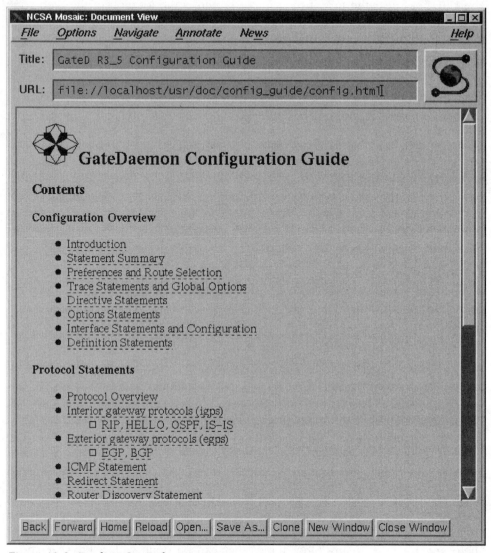

Figure 13-2: Reading GateD documentation

Anonymous FTP

Anonymous FTP is mentioned throughout this book as a technique for retrieving publicly available files and programs from the many FTP servers around the Internet. Anonymous FTP is simply an **ftp** session in which you log into the remote server using the username *anonymous* and, by convention, your email address as

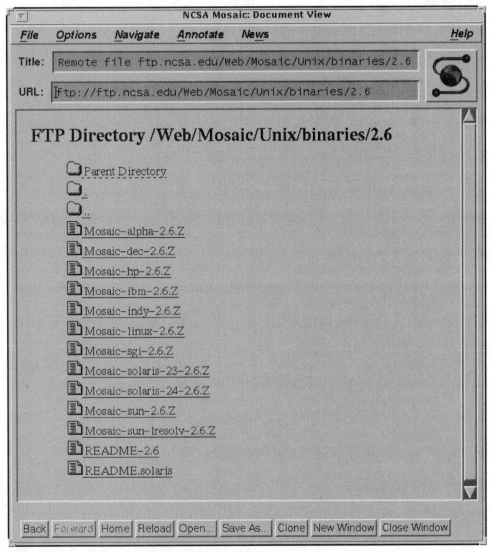

Figure 13-3: Browser FTP interface

the password.* The anonymous FTP example below should make this simple process clear:

```
% ftp ftp.ncsa.edu
Connected to ftp.ncsa.uiuc.edu.
220 FTP server Wed May 21 1997 ready.
Name (ftp.ncsa.edu:kathy): anonymous
```

---

* Some FTP servers request your real username as a password.

```
331 Guest login ok, use email address as password.
Password:
ftp> cd /Web/Mosaic/Unix/binaries/2.6
250 CWD command successful.
ftp> binary
200 Type set to I.
ftp> get Mosaic-hp-2.6.Z Mosaic.Z
200 PORT command successful.
150 Opening BINARY mode data connection for Mosaic-hp-2.6.Z.
226 Transfer complete.
local: Mosaic.Z remote: Mosaic-hp-2.6.Z
809343 bytes received in 3.5 seconds (2.3e+02 Kbytes/s)
ftp> quit
221 Goodbye.
```

In this example, the user logs into the server *ftp.ncsa.edu* using the username *anonymous* and the password *kathy@nuts.com*, which is her email address. With anonymous FTP, she can log in even though she doesn't have an account on *ftp.ncsa.edu*. Of course what she can do is restricted, but she can retrieve certain files from the system, and that's just what she does. She changes to the */Web/Mosaic/Unix/binaries/2.6* directory and gets the compressed file *Mosaic-hp-2.6.Z*. The file is retrieved in binary mode.

Creating an FTP Server

Using the anonymous FTP service offered by a remote server is very simple. However, setting up an anonymous FTP service on your own system is a little more complicated. Here are the steps to set up an anonymous FTP server:

1. Add user *ftp* to the */etc/passwd* file.

2. Create an *ftp* home directory owned by user *ftp* that cannot be written to by anyone.

3. Create a *bin* directory under the *ftp* home directory that is owned by *root*, and that cannot be written to by anyone. The **ls** program should be placed in this directory and changed to mode 111 (execute-only).

4. Create an *etc* directory in the *ftp* home directory that is owned by *root*, and that cannot be written to by anyone. Create special *passwd* and *group* files in this directory, and change the mode of both files to 444 (read-only).

5. Create a *pub* directory in the *ftp* home directory that is owned by *root* and is only writable by *root*, i.e., mode 644. Don't allow remote users to store files on your server, unless it is absolutely necessary and your system is on a private, non-connected network. If you must allow users to store files on the server, change the ownership of this directory to *ftp* and the mode to 666 (read and write). This should be the only directory where anonymous FTP users can store files.

The following examples show each of these steps. First, create the *ftp* home directory and the required subdirectories. In our example, we create the *ftp* directory under the */usr* directory.

```
# mkdir /usr/ftp
# cd /usr/ftp
# mkdir bin
# mkdir etc
# mkdir pub
```

Then copy ls to */usr/ftp/bin*, and set the correct permissions.

```
# cp /bin/ls /usr/ftp/bin
# chmod 111 /usr/ftp/bin/ls
```

Create a group that will be used only by anonymous FTP, a group that has no other members. In our example we create a group called *anonymous*. An entry for this new group is added to the */etc/group* file, and a file named */usr/ftp/etc/group* is created that contains only this single entry.

```
anonymous:*:15:
```

Create a user named *ftp* by placing an entry for that user in the file */etc/passwd*. Also create a file named */usr/ftp/etc/passwd* that contains only the *ftp* entry. Here's the entry we used in both files:

```
ftp:*:15:15:Anonymous ftp:/usr/ftp:
```

These examples use a GID of 15 and a UID of 15. These are only examples; pick a UID and GID that aren't used for anything else on your system.

A **cat** of the newly created */usr/ftp/etc/passwd* and */usr/ftp/etc/group* files shows the following:

```
% cat /usr/ftp/etc/passwd
ftp:*:15:15:Anonymous ftp:/usr/ftp:
% cat /usr/ftp/etc/group
anonymous:*:15:
```

After the edits are complete, set both files to mode 444:

```
# chmod 444 /usr/ftp/etc/passwd
# chmod 444 /usr/ftp/etc/group
```

Set the correct ownership and mode for each of the directories. The ownership of */usr/ftp/pub*, */usr/ftp/bin*, and */usr/ftp/etc* do not need to be changed because the directories were created by *root*.

```
# cd /usr/ftp
# chmod 644 pub
# chmod 555 bin
# chmod 555 etc
```

```
# cd ..
# chown ftp ftp
# chmod 555 ftp
```

If you must allow users to write their own files in the *pub* directory, make the following changes:*

```
# chown ftp pub
# chmod 666 pub
```

For most UNIX systems, the installation is complete. But if you have a Sun OS 4.x system, a few more steps are necessary. The dynamic linking used by Sun OS requires that the *ftp* home directory contains:

1. The runtime loader

2. The shared C library

3. */dev/zero*

These Sun-specific steps are shown in the following examples. First, create the directory */usr/ftp/usr/lib*, then copy the files *ld.so* and *libc.so.** into the new directory, and set the file permissions:

```
# cd /usr/ftp
# mkdir usr
# mkdir usr/lib
# cp /usr/lib/ld.so usr/lib
# cp /usr/lib/libc.so.* usr/lib
# chmod 555 libc.so.*
# chmod 555 usr/lib
# chmod 555 usr
```

Next, create the *ftp/dev* directory, and run **mknod** to create *dev/zero*:

```
# cd /usr/ftp
# mkdir dev
# cd dev
# mknod zero c 3 12
# cd ..
# chmod 555 dev
```

Now you can copy the files you wish to make publicly available into */usr/ftp/pub*. To prevent these files from being overwritten by remote users, set the mode to 644 and make sure the files are not owned by user *ftp*.

Once you complete the configuration steps necessary for your system, test it thoroughly before announcing the service. Make sure that your server provides the anonymous FTP service you want, without providing additional "services" that you

---

* This opens a large security hole. Allow users to write their own files to the anonymous FTP server only if you must.

don't want (such as allowing anonymous users access to files outside of the *ftp* home directory). Anonymous FTP is a potential security risk. If you offer this service at all, limit the number of systems at your site that provide it (one is usually enough), and take care to ensure that the installation is done properly.

Finding Files

Anonymous FTP requires detailed knowledge from the user. To retrieve a file, you must know the FTP server and the directory where the file is located. When the network was small, this was not a major problem. There were a limited number of important FTP servers, and they were well stocked with files. You could always **ftp** to a major server and search through some directories using **ftp**'s **ls** command. This old approach is not compatible with a large and expanding Internet for two reasons:

- There are now thousands of major anonymous FTP servers. Knowing them all is difficult.

- There are now millions of Internet users. They cannot all rely on a few well-known servers. The servers would quickly be overwhelmed with **ftp** requests.

archie is an application designed to help with this problem. It provides a database of information about anonymous FTP sites and the files they contain.

archie

archie expands the usefulness of anonymous FTP by helping you locate the file, program, or other information that you need. **archie** uses information servers that maintain databases containing information about hundreds of FTP servers, and thousands of files and programs throughout the Internet.

archie's primary database is a listing of files and the servers from which the files can be retrieved. In the simplest sense, you tell **archie** which file you're looking for, and **archie** tells you which FTP servers the file is available from.

archie can be used in four different ways: interactively, through electronic mail, via a Web browser, or from an **archie** client. To use **archie** interactively, **telnet** to one of the **archie** servers.* Log in using the username *archie* and no password. At the `archie>` prompt, type **help** to get a full set of interactive **archie** commands.

There are many interactive **archie** commands, but the basic function of locating a program that is accessible via anonymous FTP can be reduced to two commands.

---

* The list of publicly accessible servers is available at *http://www.bunyip.com/products/archie/-world/servers.html*.

prog *pattern*

Display all files in the database with names that match the specified *pattern*.

mail *address*

Mail the output of the last command to *address*, which is normally your own email address.

The following example uses both of these commands to interactively search for *gated-R3_5_5.tar*, and then mail the results of the search to *craig@peanut.nuts.com*.

```
% telnet archie.internic.net
Trying 198.49.45.10...
Connected to archie.ds.internic.net.
Escape character is '^]'.
UNIX(r) System V Release 4.0 (ds0)

login: archie

# Bunyip Information Systems, Inc., 1993, 1994, 1995

archie> prog gated-R3_5_5.tar
# Search type: sub.
# Your queue position: 1
# Estimated time for completion: 5 seconds.
working... O

Host ftp.zcu.cz    (147.228.206.16)
Last updated 11:32 27 Jun 1997

  Location: /pub/security/merit/gated
    FILE -r--r--r-- 1460773 bytes Jan 1997 gated-R3_5_5.tar.gz

archie> mail craig@peanut.nuts.com
archie> quit
```

The **archie** output provides all of the information you need to initiate an anonymous FTP transfer:

- The name of the server (*ftp.zcu.cz* in our example)

- The directory on the server that contains the file (*/pub/security/merit/gated* in our example)

- The full name of the file (*gated-R3_5_5.tar.gz* in our example)

You can also use **archie** by sending email to *archie* at any one of the **archie** servers; for example, *archie@archie.internic.net*. The text of the mail message must contain a valid **archie** email command. To get a complete list of **archie** email commands, send mail containing the *help* command to one of the servers. In the example below, the email help file is requested from *archie.internic.net*.

```
% mail archie@archie.internic.net
Subject:
help
^D
EOT
```

While these two methods of accessing **archie** work fine, the best way to use **archie** is through a Web browser. Many Web servers provide an **archie** interface. *http://pubweb.nexor.co/uk/public/archie/servers.html* lists several of these gateways. The server used in Figure 13-4 is *http://archie.bunyip.com/archie.html*. Enter the name of the program you want to locate in the `Search for:` box and press the `Search` button. Your browser displays the search results with links directly to the file you're seeking. For example, assume we rerun the search for *gated-R3_5_5.tar.gz* using the *http://archie.bunyip.com/archie.html* Web page. The server returns a list of eight matches, the first of which is the anonymous FTP server at *ftp.zcu.cz*. The filename *gated-R3_5_5.tar.gz* that is displayed next to the FTP server is a link. Clicking on the link transfers the file from *ftp.zcu.cz* to your system. Search and retrieval all in one interface!

While the Web browser provides the easiest interface to **archie**, some people prefer to run an **archie** client on their local system. Using an **archie** client reduces the load on the servers and improves responsiveness for the user. If you believe you'll access **archie** very frequently, it might be worth setting up an **archie** client.

archie client software

archie client software is available via anonymous FTP from the *ftp.bunyip.com* server. The software is stored in the *pub/archie/clients* directory. The README file in this directory provides a short description of each type of client. There are at least three different client software packages for UNIX: an X windows client and two command-line clients, one written in C and the other written in Perl. Check the **archie** servers for the latest developments in client software.

This section uses the command-line **archie** client written in C as an example. The C code and the instruction to **make** the client are all contained in the *c-archie-1.4.1.tar.gz* file from *ftp.bunyip.com*. Once the client has been made and installed, it is invoked using the command:

```
% archie [options] string
```

The `string` is the name of the file that you are asking **archie** to find. It can be the exact filename, a substring of the name, or a regular expression.

The *options* control how the *string* is interpreted. The **−e** option searches for a filename that exactly matches the string; the **−s** option matches on any record that contains the string as any part of the filename; and the **−r** option interprets the string as a UNIX regular expression when looking for matches.

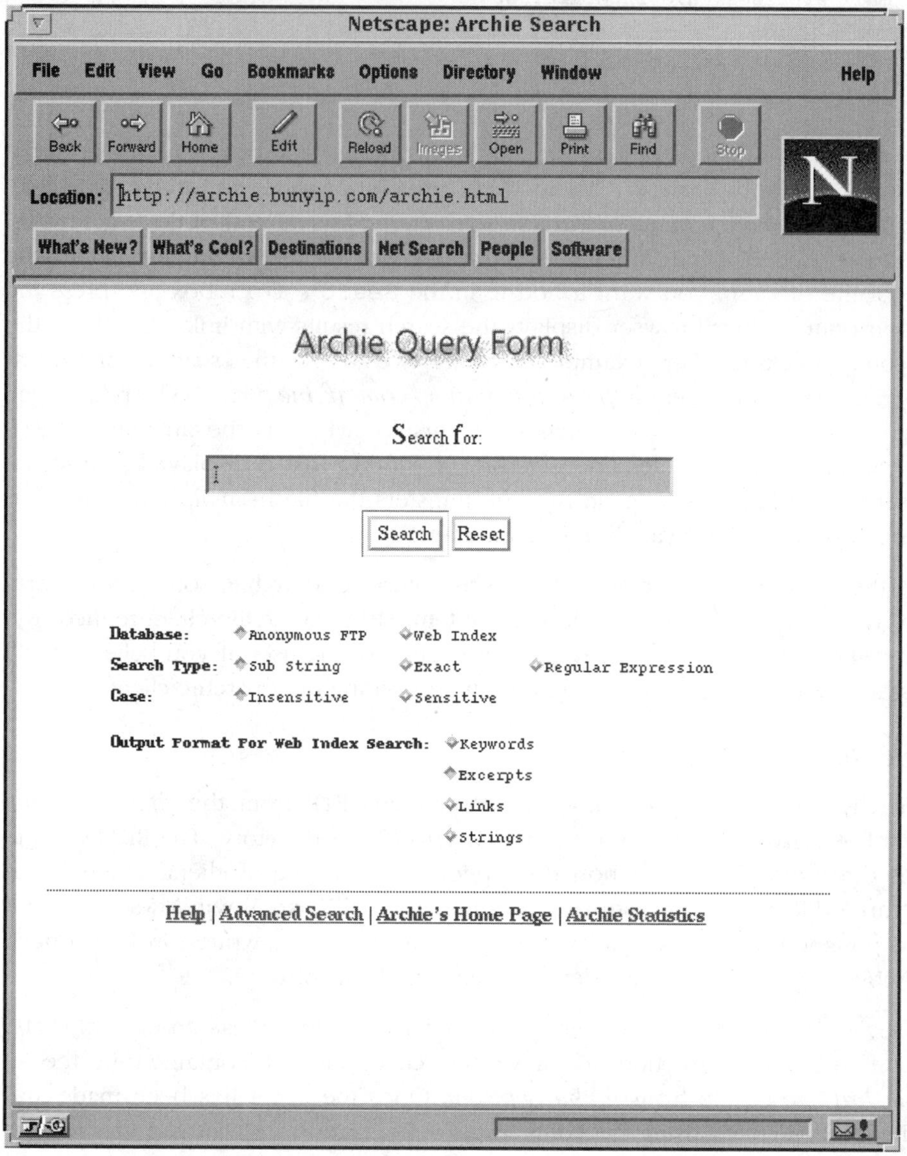

Figure 13-4: Archie Web interface

The following example uses the **archie** client to search for sites from which the **ppp** software can be retrieved. The search uses a regular expression that will match any compressed **tar** file with a name that starts with **ppp**.

```
% archie -r '^ppp.*\.tar\.Z' > ppp.locations
```

Our example stores **archie**'s output in the file *ppp.locations*. You can then examine *ppp.locations* to find the closest FTP server that has the latest version of the **ppp** tar file. Redirecting the output to a file is usually a good idea because **archie** often produces a lot of output. By default, the **archie** client will return as many as 95 matches to the search. To limit the number of matches returned, use the option −m*n*, where *n* is the maximum number of matches **archie** should return. For example, −m5 limits the search to five matches.

The **archie** database is frequently out-of-date or dominated by obscure FTP servers that have poor connectivity. This limits its utility. But sometimes **archie** is the only place you have to start your search for a file.

Retrieving RFCs

Throughout this book, we have referred to many RFCs. These are the Internet documents used for everything from general information to the definitions of the TCP/IP protocols standards. As a network administrator, there are several important RFCs that you'll want to read. In this section we describe how you can obtain them.

RFCs are available via the World Wide Web at *http://www.internic.net*. Follow the links from that home page through the directory services to the IETF RFC page. The page allows you to search the RFCs for keywords or to load the RFC index. The index is particularly useful if you know the number of the RFC you want. Figure 13-5 shows a network administrator scrolling through the index looking for RFC 1122.

In another example the network administrator does not know which RFCs contain the information she is looking for, but she knows what she wants. The administrator is trying to find out more about the SMTP service extensions that have been proposed for Extended SMTP. Figure 13-6 shows the four RFCs displayed as a result of her query.

The Web provides the most popular and best method for browsing through RFCs. However, if you know what you want, anonymous FTP can be a faster way to retrieve a specific document. RFCs are stored at *ds.internic.net* in the *rfc* directory. It stores the RFCs with filenames in the form *rfcnnnn.txt* or *rfcnnnn.ps*, where *nnnn* is the RFC number and *txt* or *ps* indicates whether the RFC is ASCII text or PostScript. To retrieve RFC 1122, **ftp** to *ds.internic.net* and enter **get rfc/rfc1122.txt** at the `ftp>` prompt. This is generally a very quick way to get an RFC, if you know what you want.

To help you find out which RFC you do want, get the *rfc-index.txt* file. It is a complete index of all RFCs by RFC number, and it's available from *ds.internic.net* in the *rfc* directory. You'll only need to get a new RFC index occasionally. Most of

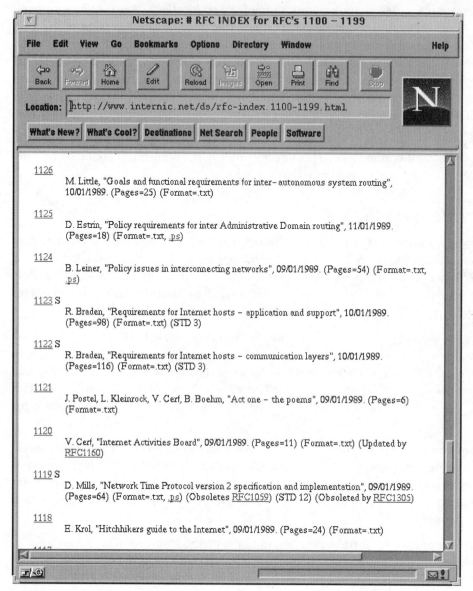

Figure 13-5: The RFC index

the time, the RFC you're looking for has been in publication for some time and is already listed in the index. Retrieve the RFC index and store it on your system. Then search it for references to the RFCs you're interested in.

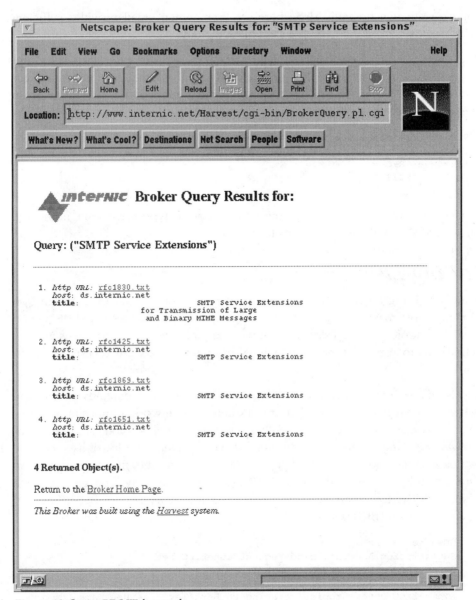

Figure 13-6: An RFC Web search

Retrieving RFCs by mail

While anonymous FTP is the fastest way and the Web is the best way to get an RFC, they are not the only ways. You can also obtain RFCs through electronic mail. Electronic mail is available to many users who are denied direct access to Internet services because they are on a non-connected network or are sitting behind a restrictive firewall. Also, there are times when email provides sufficient service because you don't need the document quickly.

Retrieve RFCs through email by sending mail to *rfc-info@isi.edu*. Leave the "Subject:" line blank. Request the RFC in the body of the email text with the lines `Retrieve: RFC` and `Doc-ID: RFCnnnn`, where *nnnn* is the RFC number. In this example, we request RFC 1258.

```
% mail rfc-info@isi.edu
Subject:
Retrieve: RFC
Doc-ID: RFC1258
^D
```

The technique works very well. In the time it took to type these paragraphs, the requested RFC was already in my mailbox.

Mailing Lists

Mailing lists bring together people with similar interests to exchange information and ideas. Most mailing lists run under usage guidelines that restricted discussion to a specific topic. Mailing lists are often used as places to report problems and get solutions, or to receive announcements. Some mailing lists are digests of newsgroups.

There is an enormous number of mailing lists. The *list-of-lists* contains information about many of the mailing lists that are of interest to network administrators.* Use a Web browser to search for mailing lists that interest you at *http://catalog.com/vivian/interest-group-search.html*. If you prefer, the list-of-lists can be downloaded via anonymous FTP from *nisc.sri.com* in the file *netinfo/interest-groups.txt* and searched with standard UNIX tools. Either way, you get the same information. The following example is the list-of-lists entry for the Berkeley Internet Name Domain (BIND) software mailing list:

```
BIND@uunet.uu.net
   Subscription Address: bind-request@uunet.uu.net
   Owner: BIND-REQUEST@UUNET.UU.NET
   Description:
    This list covers topics relating to Berkeley Internet Name Domain
    (BIND) domain software.
```

The entry has four sections: the address of the mailing list, the address to which subscription requests are sent, the address of the owner, and a description of the list.

---

* Despite its large size, not every network administration mailing list is contained in the *interest-groups.txt* file. You hear about some lists by word of mouth.

When you find a list you wish to join, don't send mail directly to the list asking to be enrolled. Instead, send the enrollment request to the subscription address, which identifies the person or process that maintains the list. If the list is manually maintained, as in the BIND example above, send your enrollment request to *list-name*-**request**@*host* where *list-name* is the actual name of the list, and is followed by the literal string **–request**. The **–request** extension is widely used as the address for administrative requests, such as being added to or dropped from a list, when lists are manually maintained. For example, to join the BIND mailing list, send your enrollment request to *bind-request@uunet.uu.net*. All other correspondence is sent directly to *bind@uunet.uu.net*.

Many mailing lists automate list management with programs like majordomo and LISTSERV. You can tell the type of server being used by looking at the subscription address in the list-of-lists. The user portion of that address will be either "majordomo" or "LISTSERV," depending on the server being used. To subscribe to a majordomo list, send email to the subscription address and type the following in the body of the message:

> subscribe *list-address your-address*

where *list-address* is the address of the email list, and *your-address* is your email address.

To subscribe to a LISTSERV mailing list, send email to the subscription address with the following in the message body:

> subscribe *list your-name*

where *list* is the name of the list, not necessarily its address, as that name appears in the first line of its list-of-lists entry. *your-name* is your first and last name. This is not your email address. LISTSERV takes your email address from the email headers.

Newsgroups

A mailing list is one way of distributing announcements and exchanging questions and answers, but it is not the most efficient way. A mail message is sent to every person on the list. It is sent immediately, and it must be stored on the local system until it is read. Thus, if there are 100 people on a list, 100 messages are sent over the network and stored at 100 receiving systems. Network news provides a more efficient method for distributing this kind of information. The information is stored around the network on, for most sites, one or two news servers. Therefore, instead of moving mail messages to every individual on your network who wants to discuss the Linux operating system, news articles about Linux are stored at one location where they can be read when the user is ready. Not only does this reduce the network load, it reduces the number of redundant copies that are stored on local disk files.

Network news is delivered over TCP/IP networks using the *Network News Transfer Protocol* (NNTP). NNTP is included as part of the TCP/IP protocol stack on most UNIX systems and requires no special configuration. The only thing you need to know to get started is the name of your closest network news server. Ask your ISP. Most ISPs provide network news as part of their basic service.

NNTP is a simple command/response protocol. The NNTP server listens to port 119:

```
% telnet news.nuts.com 119
Trying 172.16.16.19...
Connected to news.nuts.com.
Escape character is '^]'.
200 news.nuts.com ready (posting ok).
quit
205
Connection closed by foreign host.
```

A **help** command sent to this server would have produced a list of 23 NNTP commands. Luckily this is not how you read network news. You use a *newsreader*.

UNIX systems often include a news reader. Our sample Linux system includes several different readers: **nn**, **rn**, **tin**, and **trn**. Your system may have anyone one of these or another newsreader. See the appropriate manpage for specific instructions on using a particular reader.

Regardless of the reader you have, they all have certain things in common. They all provide a way to subscribe to a news group, read articles from the group, and post your own articles to the group. In this **trn** example from our Linux system, the titles of the first 26 articles in the *comp.os.linux.announce* group are listed. To read an article, the user scrolls down to select the article and presses Enter. All readers provide a similar interface.

```
comp.os.linux.announce          50 articles (moderated)

    a root       1  Ringconnect
    b Clark      1  NTLUG Meeting
    d Dave       1  Caldera
    e Martin     1  Linux Users Group Meeting
    f Evan       1  COMDEX Canada
    g Jimn       1  Salt Lake Linux Users Group
    i Tyde       1  San Fransisco Linux users' group
    j Andy       1  Worcester Linux Users' Group
    l Bob        1  MELUG meeting
    o Olaf       1  IP tunnel
    r Norbert    1  Index files
    s Albert     1  Client-/Server-Backup
```

```
t Michael    1  Parallel programming
u Oz         1  FTP client
v Ted        1  Important notice
w Kamran     1  DIPC available
x Ken        1  Web site
y Cindy      1  CD-ROM available now!
z Bishop     1  C program documentation tool

-- Select threads (date order) -- Top 38% [>Z] --
```

Our sample Solaris system doesn't include any news readers mentioned above. But it doesn't matter. News is supported in the Netscape Navigator Web browser. Selecting Netscape News from the Windows menu in the Netscape browser opens a news reader. Figure 13-7 shows us reading news from *comp.os.linux*. There are many, many newsgroups. Most of the newsgroups that are of interest to a network administrator are found in the *comp* category. *comp.os* contains sub-groups for various operating systems. *comp.unix* lists groups for various flavors of UNIX. *comp.networks* and *comp.internet* provide information about networks and the Internet. *comp.security* and *comp.virus* provide security information.

There is a tremendous amount of dross in most news groups. But if you need a question answered or information on a specific topic, they can be invaluable.

The White Pages

archie helps you locate important programs. The Web helps you retrieve important documents. **whois** helps you locate important people. One of the most important pieces of information in a network is who is in charge at the other end. In Chapter 11, *Troubleshooting TCP/IP*, we pointed out that it is important to know who is responsible for the other end of the link when troubleshooting a network problem. **whois** is a tool that helps you find this out.

whois obtains the requested information from the Internet white pages. The white pages is a database of information about responsible people that is maintained by the InterNIC. When you request an official network number or domain name, you are asked to provide your *NIC handle*, which is the index of your personal record in the white pages database. If you don't have a handle, the InterNIC assigns you one and automatically registers you in the white pages. Because of this, everyone who is responsible for an official network or domain has an entry in the white pages, and that entry can be retrieved by anyone who needs to contact them.

Many UNIX systems provide a **whois** command to query the InterNIC white pages. The general form of this command is:

```
% whois [-h server] name
```

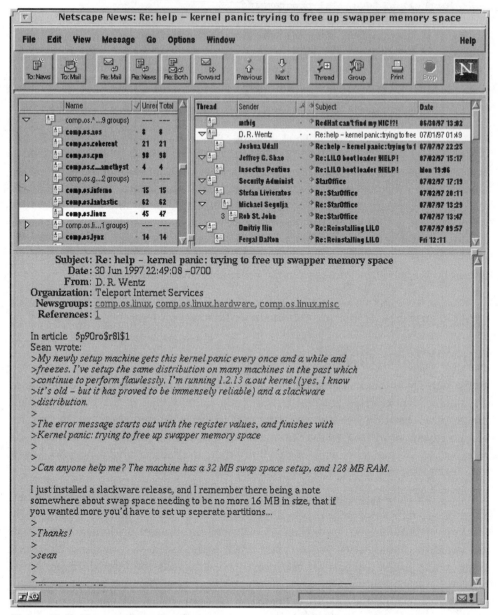

Figure 13-7: Netscape news interface

The *name* field is the information to be searched for in the white pages database. The *server* field is the name of a system containing the white pages. Use *rs.internic.net* to locate responsible people, which is the default on most systems.

In the following example, we search for an entry for *Craig Hunt*. An individual's name is entered in the white pages as: *last-name, first-name initial*. So we ask to search for *Hunt, Craig*.*

```
% whois 'Hunt, Craig'
[rs.internic.net]
Hunt, Craig (CH999)    info@foo.bar      +1 (123) 555 6789
Hunt, Craig W. (CWH3) Hunt@ENH.NIST.GOV    (301) 975-3827

To single out one record, look it up with "!xxx", where xxx is the
handle, shown in parenthesis following the name, which comes first.

The InterNIC Registration Services Host contains ONLY Internet
Information (Networks, ASN's, Domains, and POC's).
Please use the whois server at nic.ddn.mil for MILNET Information.
```

If multiple matches are returned, as in this case, follow with a query for the individual's NIC handle to get the full information display. To query for the NIC handle, which is the field enclosed in parentheses directly following the username, simply enter the handle on the **whois** command line. The message at the end of the sample output implies that handles are entered as !xxx. This is not true. The UNIX **whois** command does not require the ! syntax. For example, to get more details about CWH3, enter:

```
%  whois cwh3
[rs.internic.net]
Hunt, Craig W. (CWH3)           Hunt@ENH.NIST.GOV
   National Institute of Standards and Technology
   Computer Systems and Communications Division
   Technology Building, Room A151
   Gaithersburg, MD 20899
   (301) 975-3827 (FTS) 879-3827

   Record last updated on 03-Dec-90.
   Database last updated on 15-Jul-97 04:35:06.
```

User information is generally only useful if you know exactly who you want to send email to and you don't know his or her address. The white pages database contains several other kinds of records, a few of which are very helpful for locating the people responsible for networks, domains, and hosts throughout the Internet. These record types are:

Domain

Provides detailed contact information for the people responsible for the specified domain.

---

* **whois hunt** would return several matches. Be as specific as possible to reduce the number of matches.

Network

Provides detailed information for the contacts for the specified network.

Host

Provides general information about the specified host. This record type is not as useful as the others.

These record types can be used in the **whois** query to speed processing and limit the amount of output. All of the record types shown above can be abbreviated to their first two letters.

A sample query for the domain *ora.com* produces the following results:

```
% whois 'do ora.com'
O'Reilly & Associates (ORA-DOM1)
   101 Morris Street
   Sebastopol, CA 95472

   Domain Name: ORA.COM

   Administrative Contact, Technical Contact, Zone Contact:
      Pearce, Eric  (EP86)  eap@ORA.COM
      707-829-0515 x221
   Billing Contact:
      Johnston, Rick  (RJ724)  rick@ORA.COM
      707-829-0515 x331

   Record last updated on 28-Jan-97.
   Record created on 14-Jun-89.
   Database last updated on 15-Jul-97 04:35:06 EDT.

   Domain servers in listed order:

   NS.ORA.COM                  207.25.97.8
   NS.SONGLINE.COM             204.148.41.1
```

The query displays the name, address, and telephone number of the contacts for the domain, as well as a list of hosts providing authoritative name service for the domain.

To query the host record for a specific host, in this case one of the name servers listed above, simply query the desired hostname. For example, to find out more about *ns.songline.com*, enter:

```
% whois 'host ns.songline.com'
[No name] (NS2441-HST)

   Hostname: NS.SONGLINE.COM
   Address: 204.148.41.1
   System: Sun Sparc20 running Solaris 2.4
```

```
        Record last updated on 21-Aug-95.
        Database last updated on 15-Jul-97 04:35:06 EDT.
```

This query displays the hostname, IP address, and the system type: essentially the same information we could get from DNS.

A much more interesting query is for the point of contact for a specific network. To find out, enter a **whois** query with the network number. In our example, the IP address of one of the servers is 207.25.97.8. This is a class C address, so the network number is 207.25.97.0. The query is constructed as shown in the example below:

```
% whois 'net 207.25.97.0'
ANS CO+RE Systems, Inc. (NETBLK-ANS-C-BLOCK4)
    100 Clearbrook Rd
    Elmsford, NY 10523

    Netname: ANS-C-BLOCK4
    Netblock: 207.24.0.0 - 207.27.255.255
    Maintainer: ANS

    Coordinator:
        Vaidya, Vijay   (VV38)   vijay@ANS.NET
        914-789-5360
    Alternate Contact:
        ANS Hostmaster   (AH-ORG)   hostmaster@ANS.NET
        (800)456-6300   fax: (914)789-5310


    Domain System inverse mapping provided by:

    NS.ANS.NET                   192.103.63.100
    NIS.ANS.NET                  147.225.1.2

    Record last updated on 02-Sep-96.
    Database last updated on 15-Jul-97 04:35:06 EDT.
```

This query could also be done by network name, ANS-C-BLOCK4 in our example, but frequently you won't know the network name until you get the response from your query. In addition to the network name and number, this query tells you who is responsible for this network, and what name servers provide *in-addr.arpa* domain service for this network.

With the information from these queries, we could contact the domain administrator and the network administrator. From these key contacts, we could learn about the administrators of individual systems in their domain or on their network. This information could put us directly in touch with the other system administrator we need to talk to when debugging a network problem.

Not all systems have a local **whois** command. If your system doesn't, **telnet** to *rs.internic.net* and enter **whois** at the command-line prompt. You'll then be prompted with *Whois:*. At this prompt enter any name you wish to search for, or enter *help* for more information.

Summary

There is a wealth of information available through the network. Much of the available material provides information about TCP/IP and networking. The RFCs are, of course, a great source of information, but many RFCs are not written for beginners. It can be difficult determining which RFCs to read first. To help you make that decision, some RFCs that provide general information are identified as FYIs (For Your Information). The FYIs can be obtained from *http://www.internic.net* in the same manner as the RFCs.

In addition, you can find many books and papers about networking. My favorite reference to Internet information resources is *The Whole Internet User's Guide & Catalog*, by Ed Krol (O'Reilly & Associates). Not only does it explain how to use the information retrieval tools introduced in this chapter, it provides a well-organized catalog of many of the information sources available on the network.

As you explore these information sources, you'll see that there is much more to the network than can ever be covered in one book. This book has been your launching pad—helping you connect your system to the network. Now that your system is up and running, use it as a tool to expand your information horizons.

In this appendix:
- *Dial-Up IP*
- *The PPP Daemon*
- *chat*

A

PPP Tools

This appendix is a reference for **dip**, **pppd**, and **chat**. These tools are used to create dial-up IP connection for the *Point to Point Protocol* (PPP). **dip** and **chat** are both scripting languages. Creating a script that initializes the modem, dials the remote server, logs in, and configures the remote server is the biggest task in configuring a PPP connection. Chapter 6, *Configuring the Interface*, provides examples and tutorial information about all three of the programs covered here. This appendix provides a reference to the programs.

Dial-Up IP

dip is a scripting tool designed specifically for creating SLIP and PPP connections.*
The syntax of the **dip** command is:

>   dip [*options*] [*scriptfile*]

The **dip** command is invoked with either an option set or a script file specified, or with both. When *scriptfile* is specified, **dip** executes the commands contained in the script file to create a point-to-point connection. Examples of scripts and **dip** are shown in Chapter 6. The *options* valid with script files are:

−v Runs **dip** in verbose mode. In this mode, **dip** echos each line of the script file as it is executed, and displays enhanced status messages.

−m *mtu*
   Sets the Maximum Transmission Unit (MTU) to the number of bytes specified by *mtu*. The default MTU is 296 bytes.

---

* *Serial Line IP* (SLIP) predates PPP. Today most serial connections are PPP, which is what this appendix emphasizes.

−p *proto*

> Selects the serial line protocol. Possible values for *proto* are: SLIP, CSLIP, PPP, or TERM.

The other **dip** command line options are:

−k Kills the last **dip** process you started. You can only kill a process you own, unless of course you're *root*.

−l *device*

> Identifies that the process to be killed is the one that has locked the specified *device*. This option is only valid when used with the −k option.

−i [*username*]

> Runs **dip** as a login shell to provide a PPP or SLIP server. The **diplogin** command is equivalent to **dip** −i. These two forms of the command are used interchangeably, but **diplogin** is the most common form. **diplogin** is placed in the login shell field of the */etc/passwd* file entry for each PPP client. From there it is run by **login**. The username from the */etc/passwd* file is used to retrieve additional configuration information from */etc/diphosts*. If the optional *username* is specified with the **diplogin** command, that username is used to retrieve the information from the */etc/diphosts* file. Chapter 6 provides a tutorial and examples of running **diplogin** to create a PPP server, and of using the */etc/diphosts* file.

−a Prompts for the username and password. The −a option is valid only when used with the −i option. The **diplogini** command is equivalent to **dip** −i −a. **diplogini** is used as a login shell in the */etc/passwd* file where it is run by **login**.

−t Runs **dip** in test mode, which allows you to input individual script language commands directly from the keyboard. The −t option is frequently used in combination with −v so that the result of each command can be better observed. As shown in Chapter 6, this option is used to debug a **dip** script.

diplogin and **diplogini** are used only on servers and are not used with a script file. The script file is used on the PPP clients when **dip** is configured to dial into a remote server. The script file contains the instructions used to do this.

The dip Script File

The script file is made up of comments, labels, variables, and commands. Any line that begins with a sharp sign (#) is a comment. A label is a line that contains only a string ending in a colon. Labels are used to divide the script into separate procedures. For example, the section of the script that dials the remote host might begin with the label:

```
Dial-in:
```

A variable stores a value. A variable name is a string that begins with a dollar sign ($). You might, for example, create a variable to hold a loop counter and give it the name **$loopcntr**. It is possible to create your own variables, but this is rarely done. The variables that are used in most scripts are the special variables defined by **dip**. Table A-1 lists the special variables and the value that each holds.

Table A-1: dip Special Variables

Variable	Value Stored
$errlvl	The return code of the last command
$locip	The IP address of the local host
$local	The fully qualified domain name of the local host
$rmtip	The IP address of the remote host
$remote	The fully qualified domain name of the remote host
$mtu	The Maximum Transmission Unit in bytes
$modem	The modem type; currently this must be HAYES
$port	The name of the serial device, e.g., cua0
$speed	The transmission speed of the port

The final component of the script file is the command list. There are many script commands. Because this appendix is a reference, we cover them all. However, most scripts are built using only a few of these commands. See the sample scripts in Chapter 6 and at the end of this section for realistic **dip** scripts. The complete list of script commands is:

beep [n]

Tells the system to beep the user. Repeat *n* times.

bootp

Tells the system to use the BOOTP protocol to obtain the local and remote IP addresses. This command applies only to SLIP. PPP has its own protocol for assigning addresses; SLIP does not. Usually SLIP addresses are statically set inside the script. However, some SLIP servers have evolved techniques for dynamic address assignment. The most common method is for the server to display the address as clear text immediately after the connection is made. Use the **get $locip remote** command to retrieve the address from this type of SLIP server. Other SLIP servers require you to send them a command before they will display the address. Put the required server command in the script and follow it with the **get** command. Finally, a few SLIP servers use BOOTP to distribute addresses. Use the **bootp** command in your script to enable BOOTP when it is required by your SLIP server.

break

Sends a BREAK. Some remote servers may require a BREAK as an attention character.

chatkey *keyword code*

Maps a modem response *keyword* to a numeric *code*. The predefined mappings are:

0	OK
1	CONNECT
2	ERROR
3	BUSY
4	NO CARRIER
5	NO DIALTONE

config [interface | routing] [pre | up | down | post] *arguments . . .*

Modifies interface characteristics (**interface**) or the routing table (**routing**) either before (**pre**) the link comes up, when it is **up**, when it goes **down**, or after (**post**) the link is shutdown. For example:

```
config up routing add canary gw ibis
```

adds a route to *canary* using *ibis* as the gateway when the link is up. Allowing users to modify the routing table or interface characteristics is very dangerous. The **config** command is disabled in the DIP code and requires re-compilation to be enabled.

databits 7 | 8

Sets the number of data bits to 7 or 8. 8 bits is recommended for PPP and SLIP links.

dec *$variable* [*value*]

Decrements *$variable* by *value*. The default value is 1.

default

Sets the PPP connection as the default route.

dial *phonenumber* [*timeout*]

Dials the *phonenumber*. If the remote modem does not answer within *timeout* seconds, the connection aborts. **$errlvl** is set to a numeric value based on the keyword returned by the local modem. Set **chatkey** for the keyword to numeric mappings.

echo on | off

Enables or disables the display of modem commands.

exit [*n*]

Exits the script, optionally returning the number *n* as the exit status.

flush

Clears the input buffer.

get *$variable* [ask | remote [*timeout*]] *value*

Sets *$variable* to *value*, unless **ask** or **remote** is specified. When **ask** is specified, the user is prompted for the value. When **remote** is specified, the value is read from the remote machine, optionally waiting *timeout* seconds for the remote system to respond.

goto *label*

Jumps to the section of the script identified by *label*.

help

Lists the **dip** script commands.

if *expr* goto *label*

A conditional statement that jumps to the section of the script identified by *label* if the *expression* evaluates to true. The expression must compare a variable to a constant using one of these operators: == (equal), != (not equal), < (less than), > (greater than), <= (less than or equal to), >= (greater than or equal to).

inc *$variable* [*value*]

Increments *$variable* by *value*. The default value is 1.

init *command*

Sets the command string used to initialize the modem. The default is ATE0 Q0 V1 X1.

mode SLIP | CSLIP | PPP | TERM

Selects the serial protocol. The default is SLIP.

modem *type*

Sets the modem type. Ignore this command. The only legal value is HAYES, and that is the default.

netmask *mask*

Sets the subnet mask.

parity E | O | N

Sets the parity to even (**E**), odd (**O**), or no (**N**). No parity (**N**)is recommended for SLIP and PPP links.

password

Prompts the user for the password.

proxyarp

Installs a proxy ARP entry for the remote system in the local host's ARP table.

print *$variable*

Displays the contents of *$variable*.

psend *command*

Executes *command* through the default shell passing the output to the serial device. The command runs using the user's real UID.

port *device*

Identifies the serial device, such as cua0, that attaches the modem.

quit

Exits the script with a nonzero exit status, aborting the connection.

reset

Resets the modem.

send *string*

Passes *string* to the serial device.

shell *command*

Executes *command* through the default shell. The command runs using the user's real UID.

skey [*timeout*]

Waits for an S/Key challenge from the remote terminal server, prompts the user for the secret key, and generates and sends the response. Waits *timeout* seconds for the challenge. If the timer expires, **$errlvl** is set to 1; otherwise, it is set to 0. S/Key must be compiled into **dip**.

sleep *time*

Delays *time* seconds.

speed *bits-per-second*

Sets the port speed. The default is 38400.

stopbits 1 | 2

Sets the number of stop bits to 1 or 2.

term

Enables terminal mode. In terminal mode, keyboard input is passed directly to the serial device.

timeout *time*

> Sets the *time* in seconds that the line is allowed to remain inactive. When this timer expires, the link is closed.

wait *text* [*timeout*]

> Waits *timeout* seconds for the *text* string to arrive from the remote system. If *timeout* is not specified, the script will wait forever.

In the next section we put some of these commands to work in a realistic script.

A sample dip script

This script is based on the PPP sample from Chapter 6. Labels and error detection have been added to create a more robust script.

```
# Select configuration settings
setup:
# Ask PPP to provide the addresses
get $local 0.0.0.0
# Select the port
port cua1
# Set the port speed
speed 57600
# Create a loop counter
get $loopcntr 0

# Dial the remote server
dialin:
# Reset the modem and clear the input buffer
reset
flush
# Dial the PPP server and check the modem response
dial *70,301-555-1234
# If BUSY, dial again
if $errlvl == 3 goto redial
# If some other error, abort
if $errlvl != 1 goto dial-error
# Otherwise rest loop counter
get $loopcntr 0
# Give the server 2 seconds to get ready
sleep 2

# Login to the remote server
login:
# Send a carriage-return to wake up the server
send \r
# Wait for the Username> prompt and send the username
wait name> 20
if $errlvl != 0 goto try-again
send kristin\r
# Wait for the Password> prompt and send the password
wait word> 10
```

```
if $errlvl != 0 goto server-failure
password
# Wait for the PPP server's command line prompt
wait > 20
if $errlvl != 0 goto server-failure
# Send the command required by the PPP server
send ppp enabled\r

# Success! We're on-line
connected:
# Set the interface to PPP mode
mode PPP
# Exit the script
exit

# Error processing routines

# Try dialing 3 times.  Wait 5 seconds between attempts
redial:
inc $loopcntr
if $loopcntr > 3 goto busy-failure
sleep 5
goto dialin

# Try a second carriage return
try-again:
inc $loopcntr
if $loopcntr > 1 goto server-failure
goto login


dial-error:
print Dial up of $remote failed.
quit

server-failure:
print $remote failed to respond.
quit

busy-failure:
print $remote is busy.  Try again later.
quit
```

This script provides a realistic example of the commands used in most scripts. However, you may encounter a particularly tough scripting problem. If you do, the abundance of scripting commands available with **dip** should be able to handle it. If **dip** can't do the job, try **expect**. See *Exploring Expect* by Don Libes (O'Reilly & Associates) for a full description of the **expect** scripting language.

The PPP Daemon

The PPP Daemon (**pppd**) is a freely available implementation of the Point-to-Point Protocol (PPP) that runs on many UNIX systems. Examples of configuring and using **pppd** are covered in Chapter 6. The syntax of the **pppd** command is:

> **pppd** [*device*] [*speed*] [*options*]

device is the name of the serial port over which the PPP protocol operates and *speed* is the transmission speed of that port in bits per second. The complexity of this command comes not from these simple parameters but from the large number of *options* that it supports. There are so many options, in fact, that they are often stored in a file. There are three options files that can be used with **pppd**: the */etc/ppp/options* file, which is used to set system-wide **pppd** options; the ˜/.*ppprc* file, which is used by an individual to set personal **pppd** options, and the */etc/ppp/options*.device file, which sets options for a serial device, e.g., */etc/ppp/options.cua0* sets options for cua0. The order of precedence for options is that those specified in the */etc/ppp/options*.device file are the highest priority, followed by those defined on the command line, then those in the ˜/.*ppprc* file, and, finally, those defined in the */etc/ppp/options* file. Some options that relate to system security, once defined in the */etc/ppp/options* file, cannot be overridden by the user through the command line or the ˜/.*ppprc* file. The system administrator can override any option set by the user by setting the option in the */etc/ppp/options*.device file.

The following list contains all of the **pppd** options except those that do not relate to TCP/IP:

local_IP_address:remote_IP_address
> Defines static local and remote IP addresses. Either address may be omitted. For example: 172.16.25.3: defines only the local address, while :172.16.25.12 defines only the remote address. The default local address is the IP address associated with the local system's hostname.

−ac
> Disables Address/Control compression negotiation.

−all
> Disables all LCP and IPCP negotiations.

−am
> Disables **asyncmap** negotiation. Sends all control characters as two-character escape sequences.

asyncmap *map*

Defines the ASCII control characters that must be sent as two-character escape sequences. The first 32 ASCII characters are control characters. *map* is a 32-bit hex number with each bit representing a control character. Bit 0 (00000001) represents the character 0x00; bit 31 (80000000) represents the character 0x1f. If a bit is on in *map*, the character represented by that bit must be sent as an escape sequence. If no **asyncmap** option is specified, all control characters are sent as escape sequences. The **asyncmap** option can also be written in the form −**as** *map*.

auth

Requires the use of an authentication protocol. See Chapter 6 for a discussion of the authentication protocols CHAP and PAP.

bsdcomp *receive,transmit*

Enables the BSD-Compress scheme to compress packets. The maximum length code word used to compress packets accepted by this host is *receive* bits long. The maximum code word length used to compress packets sent by this host is *transmit* bits long. Acceptable code word length is 9 to 15 bits. Disable compression when receiving or transmitting by placing a 0 in *receive* or *transmit*, respectively.

−bsdcomp

Disables BSD-Compress compression.

+chap

Requires the use of the *Challenge Handshake Authentication Protocol* (CHAP).

−chap

Disables the use of CHAP. This is a bad idea.

chap-interval *n*

Tells system to use CHAP to reauthenticate the remote system every *n* seconds.

chap-max-challenge *n*

Tells system to send the CHAP challenge to the remote system a maximum of *n* times until the remote system responds. The default is 10.

chap-restart *n*

Tells system to wait *n* seconds before retransmitting a CHAP challenges when the remote system fails to respond. The default is 3 seconds.

connect *script*

> Invokes a *script* to create the serial connection. Any scripting language can be used, but **chat** is the most common. See Chapter 6 for an example of using **connect** to invoke an inline **chat** script.

crtscts

> Enables hardware flow control (RTS/CTS).

−crtscts

> Disables hardware flow control (RTS/CTS).

debug

> Logs all control packets sent or received using **syslogd** with facility *daemon* and level *debug*. The **debug** option can also be written as **−d**.

defaultroute

> Defines the PPP link as the default route. The route is removed when the connection is closed.

−defaultroute

> Prevents users from creating a default route using the **defaultroute** option.

−detach

> Prevents **pppd** from running as a background process. See the example in Chapter 6.

disconnect *script*

> Invokes a *script* to gracefully shut down the serial connection. Any scripting language can be used, but **chat** is the most common.

domain *name*

> Defines the name of the local domain. Use this if **hostname** does not return a fully qualified name for the local system.

escape *x,x, . . .*

> Specifies characters that should be transmitted as two-character escape sequences. The characters are specified in a comma-separated list of hex numbers. Any character except 0x20 − 0x3f and 0x5e can be escaped.

file *file*

> Defines another options file, where *file* is the name of the new file. Options are normally read for */etc/ppp/options*, ~*/.ppprc*, the command line, and */etc/ppp/options*.device. See the description of these files earlier in this section.

−ip

> Disables IP address negotiation. When used, the remote IP address must be explicitly defined by a **pppd** option.

+ip-protocol

Enables the IPCP and IP protocols, which is the default.

−ip-protocol

Disables the IPCP and IP protocols. This should never be used on a TCP/IP network. It is for pure IPX networks.

ipcp-accept-local

Tells system to use the local IP address provided by the remote server even if it is defined locally.

ipcp-accept-remote

Tells system to use the remote IP address provided by the remote server even if it is defined locally.

ipcp-max-configure *n*

Tells system to send the IPCP configure-request packet a maximum of *n* times. The default is 10.

ipcp-max-failure *n*

Tells system to accept up to *n* IPCP configure-NAKs before sending a configure-reject. The default is 10.

ipcp-max-terminate *n*

Tells system to send no more than *n* IPCP terminate-request packets without receiving an acknowledgment. The default is 3.

ipcp-restart *n*

Tells system to wait *n* seconds before resending an IPCP configure-request packet. The default is 3.

ipparam *string*

Passes *string* to the ip-up and ip-down scripts. */etc/ppp/ip-up* is a shell script executed by **pppd** when the link comes up. */etc/ppp/ip-down* is a shell script executed by **pppd** when the link is brought down.

kdebug *n*

Enables kernel-level debugging. *n* is 1 to print general debugging messages, 2 to print received packets, and 4 to print transmitted packets.

lcp-echo-failure *n*

Tells system to terminate the connection if no reply is received to *n* LCP echo-requests. Normally echo-requests are not used for this purpose because "link down" conditions are determined by the modem hardware.

lcp-echo-interval *n*

Tells system to wait *n* seconds before sending another LCP echo-request when the remote system fails to reply.

lcp-max-configure *n*

Tells system to send the LCP configure-request packet a maximum of *n* times. The default is 10.

lcp-max-failure *n*

Tells system to accept up to *n* LCP configure-NAKs before sending a configure-reject. The default is 10.

lcp-max-terminate *n*

Tells system to send no more than *n* LCP terminate-request transmissions without receiving an acknowledgment. The default is 3.

lcp-restart *n*

Tells system to wait *n* seconds before resending a LCP configure-request packet. The default is 3.

local

Tells system to ignore the DCD (Data Carrier Detect) and DTR (Data Terminal Ready) modem control lines.

lock

Tells system to use a UUCP-style lock file to ensure that **pppd** has exclusive access to the serial device.

login

Tells system to use the */etc/passwd* file to authenticate PAP users. Records the login in the *wtmp* file.

modem

Tells system to use the DCD (Data Carrier Detect) and DTR (Data Terminal Ready) modem control lines; wait for the DCD signal before opening the serial device; and drop the DTR signal when terminating a connection.

−mn

Disables magic number negotiation.

mru *n*

Sets the Maximum Receive Unit (MRU) to *n* bytes. MRU is used to tell the remote system the maximum packet size the local system can accept. The minimum is 128. The default is 1500.

−mru

Disables Maximum Receive Unit (MRU) negotiation.

mtu *n*

Sets the Maximum Transmission Unit (MTU) to *n* bytes. MTU defines the maximum length of a packet that can be sent. The smaller of the local MTU and the remote MRU is used to define the maximum packet length.

name *name*

> Tells system to use *name* as the name of the local system for authentication purposes.

netmask *mask*

> Defines the subnet mask.

noipdefault

> Instructs system not to use **hostname** to determine the local IP address. The address must be obtained from the remote system or explicitly set by an option.

+pap

> Requires the use of the *Password Authentication Protocol* (PAP).

−pap

> Disables the use of PAP.

papcrypt

> Instructs system not to accept passwords that are identical to those in the */etc/ppp/pap-secrets* file because the ones in the file are encrypted. Therefore the transmitted password should not match an entry in the *pap-secrets* file until it is also encrypted.

pap-max-authreq *n*

> Tells system to transmit no more than *n* PAP authenticate-requests if the remote system does not respond. The default is 10.

pap-restart *n*

> Tells system to wait *n* seconds before retransmitting a PAP authenticate-request. The default is 3 seconds.

pap-timeout *n*

> Tells system to wait no more than *n* seconds for the remote system to authenticate itself. When *n* is 0, there is no time limit.

passive

> Tells system to wait for a Link Control Protocol (LCP) packet from the remote system even if that system does not reply to the initial LCP packet sent by the local system. Without this option the local system aborts the connection when it does not receive a reply. The **passive** option can also be written as −p.

−pc

> Disables protocol field compression negotiation. By default, protocol field compression is not used. Setting this option means that even if the remote end requests it, it will not be used.

persist

Tells system to reopen the connection if it was terminated by a SIGHUP signal.

pred1comp

Tells system to ask the remote system to use Predictor-1 compression.

−pred1comp

Tells system not to use Predictor-1 compression.

proxyarp

Tells system to enable proxy ARP. This adds a proxy ARP entry for the remote system to the local system's ARP table.

−proxyarp

Disables the **proxyarp** option, preventing users from creating proxy ARP entries with *pppd*.

remotename *name*

Tells system to use *name* as the remote system's name for authentication purposes.

silent

Tells system to wait for an LCP packet from the remote system. Do not send the first LCP packet.

usehostname

Disables the **name** option, forcing the local hostname to be used for authentication purposes.

user *username*

Tells system to use *username* for PAP authentication when challenged by a remote host.

−vj

Disables Van Jacobson header compression.

−vjccomp

Disables the connection-ID compression option in Van Jacobson header compression.

vj-max-slots *n*

Tells system to use *n* connection slots for Van Jacobson header compression. *n* must be a number from 2 to 16.

Several of the options listed above concern PPP security. One of the strengths of PPP is its security. The *Challenge Handshake Authentication Protocol* (CHAP) is the preferred PPP security protocol. The *Password Authentication Protocol* (PAP) is less secure and only provided for compatibility with less capable systems. The usernames, IP addresses, and secret keys used for these protocols are defined in the */etc/ppp/chap-secrets* file and the */etc/ppp/pap-secrets* file. Chapter 6 shows the format of these files and describes their use.

It is very important that the directory */etc/ppp* and the files in that directory not be world- or group-writable. Modifications to the *chap-secrets*, *pap-secrets*, or *options* files could compromise system security. In addition, the script files */etc/ppp/ip-up* and */etc/ppp/ip-down* may run with root privilege. If **pppd** finds a file with the name *ip-up* in the */etc/ppp* directory, it executes it as soon as the PPP connection is established. The *ip-up* script is used to modify the routing table, process the **sendmail** queue, or do other tasks that depend on the presences of the network connection. The *ip-down* script is executed by **pppd** after the PPP connection is closed and is used to terminate processes that depend on the link. Clearly these scripts and the */etc/ppp* directory must be protected.

Signal processing

pppd handles the following signals:

SIGUSR1

> This signal toggles debugging on or off. The first SIGUSR1 signal received by **pppd** turns on debugging and begins logging diagnostic messages through **syslogd** with facility set to *daemon* and level set to *debug*. The second SIGUSR1 signal turns off debugging and closes the log file. See the **debug** option described above.

SIGUSR2

> This signal causes **pppd** to renegotiate compression. It has limited applicability because it is only needed to restart compression after a fatal error has occurred. Most people close the PPP connection and open a new one after a fatal error.

SIGHUP

> This signal closes the PPP connection, returns the serial device to its normal operating mode, and terminates **pppd**. If the **persist** option is specified, **pppd** opens an new connection instead of terminating.

SIGINT

> This signal, or the SIGTERM signal, closes the PPP connection, returns the serial device to its normal operating mode, and terminates **pppd**. The **persist** option has no effect.

chat

chat is a general-purpose scripting language that is used to control the modem, dial the remote server, and perform the remote system login. **chat** is less powerful than **dip** but is widely used. The "expect/send" structure of a **chat** script is the fundamental structure used in most scripting languages.

A **chat** script is composed of expect/send pairs. These pairs consist of the string expected from the remote system, separated by whitespace from the response that is sent to the remote host when the expected string is received. If no string is expected from the remote system, two quotes (**""**) or two apostrophes (**''**) are used to "expect nothing." A simple **chat** script is:

```
"" \r name> jane word> TOga!toGA
```

The script expects nothing (**""**) until it sends the remote system a carriage return (**\r**). Then the script expects the remote system to send the string **name>**, which is part of the system's **Username>** prompt. In response to this prompt, the script sends the username **jane**. Finally the script waits for part of the **Password>** prompt and responds with **TOga!toGA**. A script this simple can be defined directly on the **chat** command line:

```
% chat -v -t30 "" \r name> jane word> TOga!toGA
```

This command runs **chat** in verbose mode, sets the length of time the script waits for an expected string to 30 seconds, and then executes the simple login script described above.

The syntax of the **chat** command is:

chat [*options*] [*script*]

The **chat** command options are:

−v   Runs the **chat** script in verbose mode. Verbose mode logs informational messages via **syslogd**.

−V   Runs the **chat** script in stderr verbose mode. The stderr verbose mode displays informational messages on the stderr device. See Chapter 6 for an example of this being used with **pppd**.

−t *timeout*
   Sets the maximum time to wait for an expected string. If the expected string is not received in *timeout* seconds, the reply string is not sent and the script terminates—unless an alternate send is defined. If defined, the alternate send (more about this later) is sent and the remote system is given one more *timeout* period to respond. If this fails, the script is terminated with a nonzero error code. By default, the timeout period is 45 seconds.

–f *scriptfile*

> Reads the **chat** script from the *scriptfile* instead of from the command line. Multiple lines of expect/send pairs are permitted in the file.

–r *reportfile*

> Writes the output generated by REPORT strings to the *reportfile*. By default, REPORT strings are written to stderr. The REPORT keyword is covered below.

In order to make the scripts more useful and robust, **chat** provides special keywords, escape sequences, and alternate send/expect pairs that can be used in the script. First let's look at the five **chat** keywords.

Two keywords transmit special signals to the remote system. The keyword EOT sends the End of Transmission character. On UNIX systems this is usually the End of File character, which is a CTRL-D. The BREAK keyword sends a line break to the remote system. The three remaining keywords define processing characteristics for the script itself.

The TIMEOUT keyword defines the amount of time to wait for an expected string. Because it is defined inside the script, the timeout value can be changed for each expected string. For example, assume you want to allow the remote server 30 seconds to display the initial Username> prompt but only 5 seconds to display Password> once the username has been sent. Enter this script command:

```
TIMEOUT 30 name> karen TIMEOUT 5 word> beach%PARTY
```

The ABORT keyword and the REPORT keyword are similar. They both define strings that, when received, cause a special action to take place. The ABORT keyword defines strings that cause the script to abort if they are received when the system is expecting the string CONNECT from the modem. The REPORT keyword defines substrings that determine what messages received on the serial port should be written to stderr or the report file. A sample **chat** script file illustrates both of these keywords:

```
REPORT CONNECT
ABORT BUSY
ABORT 'NO CARRIER'
ABORT 'RING - NO ANSWER'
"" ATDT5551234
CONNECT \r
name> karen
word> beach%PARTY
```

The first line says that any message received by the script that contains the word CONNECT will be logged. If the **–r** command-line option was used when **chat** was started, the message is logged in the file defined by that option. Otherwise the message is displayed on stderr. The point of this command is to display the modem's connect message to the user. For example: the complete message might be CONNECT 28,800 LAPM/V, which tells the user the link speed and the transmission protocol used by the modems. The CONNECT message means success. The next three lines of the script begin with the keyword ABORT and define the modem messages that mean failure. If the modem responds with BUSY, NO CARRIER, or RING – NO ANSWER, the script aborts.

The last four lines are the basic expect/send pairs we have seen repeatedly in this section. We expect nothing (`""`) and send the dial command to the modem (ATDT). We expect CONNECT from the modem and send a carriage return (`\r`) to the remote server. We expect `Username>` from the remote server and send `karen`. Finally, we expect `Password>` from the server and send `beach%PARTY`.

chat extends the standard expect/send pair with an alternate send and an alternate expect to improve robustness. You may define an alternate send string and an alternate expect value to be used when the script times out waiting for the primary expected value. The alternate send and the alternate expect are indicated in the script by preceding them with dashes. For example:

```
gin:-BREAK-gin: becca
```

In this sample we wait for the string `gin:` and send the string `becca`. The first string and the last string compose the standard expect/send pair. The alternate send/expect is only used if the timer expires and the expected `gin:` string has not been received. When this occurs, the script sends a line break, restarts the timer, and waits for `gin:` again, because that is what our alternate send/expect pair (`-BREAK-gin:`) tells the script to do. Note that unlike the standard expect/send pair, in the send/expect pair a value is transmitted before a string is expected, i.e., the send comes before the expect. Another example more in keeping with our other script examples is:

```
name>--name> karen
```

Here the script expects the **name>** string. If it is not received, the script sends an empty line, which is simply a carriage return, and again waits for the **name>** string. This action is dictated by the alternate send/expect pair, `--name>`. The pair begins with a dash that signals the start of the send string, but the next character is the second dash that marks the beginning of the alternate expect string. There is no send string. It is this "empty string" that causes the script to send a single return character. This example is more common than the BREAK example shown above, though a little harder to explain.

The carriage return character is not the only special character that can be sent from a **chat** script. **chat** provides several escape sequences for sending and receiving special characters. Table A-2 lists these.

Table A-2: chat Escape Sequences

Escape Sequence	Meaning
\b	The backspace character.
\c	Send without the terminating return character.
\d	Delay sending for one second.
\K	Send a BREAK.
\n	Send a newline character.
\N	Send a null character.
\p	Delay sending 1/10th of a second.
\q	Send the string but don't log it.
\r	The carriage return.
\s	The space character.
\t	The tab character.
\\	The backslash character.
ddd	The ASCII character with the octal value ddd.
^*C*	A control character.

All of the escape sequences start with a backslash (\) except for the sequence used to enter a control character. Control characters are entered as a caret (^) followed by an uppercase letter. For example control X is entered as ^X. The escape sequences that are described in Table A-2 with the words "send" or "sending" can only be used in a send string; all others can be used in either a send or expect string. Several escape sequences are used in the following example:

```
    "" \d\d^G\p^G\p\p^GWake\sUp!\nSleepy\sHead!
```

Expect nothing (""). Wait two seconds (\d\d). Send three ASCII BELL characters, which is CTRL-G on the keyboard, at intervals of 1/10 of a second (^G\p^G\p\p^G). Send the string Wake Up!. Go to a new line (\n) and send the string Sleepy Head!.

B

A gated Reference

This appendix covers the syntax of the **gated** command and the **gated** configuration language. As a reference to the **gated** configuration language, this appendix stands on its own. But to fully understand how to configure **gated**, use this reference in conjunction with the sample configuration files in Chapter 7, *Configuring Routing*.

gated is constantly being improved. As it is upgraded, the command language changes. Refer to the latest manpages for the most recent information about **gated**.

The gated Command

The syntax of the **gated** command is:

> gated [–c] [–C] [–n] [–N] [–t *trace_options*] [–f *config_file*]
> [*trace_file*]

The –c and –n command-line options debug the routing configuration file without impacting the network or the kernel routing table. Frequently, these debugging options are used with a test configuration identified by the –f *config_file* option:

–c Tells **gated** to read the configuration file and check for syntax errors. When **gated** finishes reading the configuration file, it produces a snapshot of its status and then terminates. It writes the snapshot to */usr/tmp/gated_dump*. Running **gated** with the –c option does not require superuser privilege, and it is not necessary to terminate the active **gated** process.

−C Checks the configuration file for syntax errors. **gated** exits with a status 1 if there are errors and 0 if there are none. Because this provides exit status, it is useful for script files.

−n Tells **gated** not to update the kernel routing table. This is used to test the routing configuration with real routing data without interfering with system operation.

−f *config_ file*

Tells **gated** to read the configuration from *config_ file* instead of from the default configuration file, */etc/gated.conf.* Used in conjunction with the **−c** option, **−f** checks a new configuration without interfering with the currently running **gated** configuration.

The **−N** command-line option prevents **gated** from running in background mode as a daemon. This option is used when **gated** is started from *inittab.* By default, **gated** runs as a daemon.

The command-line arguments *trace_options* and *trace_ file* are used for protocol tracing. The *trace_ file* argument names the file to which the trace output is written. If a file is not specified, the trace is written to the standard output. Tracing usually produces a large amount of output.

The command-line options used for tracing are:

−t This option turns on tracing. If **−t** is specified with no *trace_options*, **gated** defaults to **general** tracing, which traces normal protocol interactions and routing table changes. **gated** always logs protocol errors even if no tracing is specified. You can define several different *trace_options*, all of which are described later in this appendix. A few *trace_options* (**detail**, **send**, **recv**) cannot be specifed on the **gated** command line. Two others are most useful when they are defined on the command line:

symbols

Traces the symbols read from the kernel, which is primarily of interest to developers debugging the interaction of **gated** and the kernel.

iflist

Traces the list of interfaces read from the kernel. Use this to determine what interfaces are detected by the kernel interface scan.

The advantage of placing a trace option on the command line is that it can trace activities that happen before the configuration file is processed. For the two options listed above, this is an essential advantage. For other options it is not very important. Most trace options are specified in the configuration file. See the **traceoptions** command later in this appendix for more details.

Signal Processing

gated processes the following signals:

SIGHUP

Tells **gated** to reread the configuration file. The new configuration replaces the one that **gated** is currently running. SIGHUP loads the new configuration file without interrupting **gated** service. SIGHUP is available for quick configuration changes.

At most sites, the routing configuration changes infrequently. The few times you need to change to a new configuration, terminate **gated** and rerun it with the new configuration. This is a more accurate test of how things will run at the next boot.

SIGINT

Tells **gated** to snapshot its current state to the file */usr/tmp/gated_dump*.

SIGTERM

Tells **gated** to shut down gracefully. All protocols are shut down following the rules of that protocol. For example, EGP sends a CEASE message and waits for it to be confirmed. SIGTERM removes from the kernel routing table all routes learned via the exterior routing protocols. If you need to preserve those routes while **gated** is out of operation, use SIGKILL.

SIGKILL

Tells **gated** to terminate immediately and dump core. Routes are not removed from the routing table, and no graceful shutdown is attempted.

SIGUSR1

Tells **gated** to toggle tracing. If no trace flags are set, SIGUSR1 has no effect. But if tracing is enabled, the first SIGUSR1 causes **gated** to toggle off tracing and to close the trace file. The next SIGUSR1 turns tracing back on and opens the trace file. When the trace file is closed, it can be moved or removed without interfering with the operation of **gated**. Use this to periodically empty out the trace file to prevent it from becoming too large.

SIGUSR2

Tell **gated** to check for changes in the status of the network interfaces.

The following is an example of **gated** signal handling. First, the SIGUSR1 signal is passed to the **gated** process using the process ID obtained from the *gated.pid* file (*/var/run/gated.pid* in this case).

```
# kill -USR1 `cat /var/run/gated.pid`
```

Next, the old trace file (*/usr/tmp/gated.log* in this case) is removed, and **gated** is passed another SIGUSR1 signal.

```
# rm /usr/tmp/gated.log
# kill -USR1 `cat /etc/gated.pid`
```

After receiving the second signal, **gated** opens a fresh trace file (still named */usr/tmp/gated.log*). An **ls** shows that the new file has been created.

```
# ls -l /usr/tmp/gated.log
-rw-rw-r--  1 root              105 Jul  6 16:41 /usr/tmp/gated.log
```

The gated Configuration Language

The **gated** configuration language is a highly structured language similar to C in appearance. Comments either begin with a #, or they begin with /* and end with */. **gated** configuration statements end with a semicolon, and groups of associated statements are enclosed in curly braces. The language structure is familiar to most UNIX system administrators, and the structure makes it easy to see what parts of the configuration are associated with each other. This is important when multiple protocols are configured in the same file.

The configuration language is composed of nine types of statements. Two statement types, *directive statements* and *trace statements*, can occur anywhere in the *gated.conf* file and do not directly relate to the configuration of any protocol. These statements provide instructions to the parser and control tracing from within the configuration file. The other seven statement types are *options statements*, *interface statements*, *definition statements*, *protocol statements*, *static statements*, *control statements*, and *aggregate statements*. These statements must appear in the configuration file in the correct order, starting with options statements and ending with aggregate statements. Entering a statement out of order causes an error when parsing the file.

The remainder of this appendix provides a description of all commands in the **gated** configuration language, organized by statement type.

Directive Statements

Directive statements provide direction to the **gated** command language parser about "include" files. An include file is an external file whose contents are parsed into the configuration as if it were part of the original *gated.conf* file. Include files can contain references to other include files, and these references can be nested up to 10 levels deep.

The two directive statements are:

%include *filename*

> Identifies an include file. The contents of the file are "included" in the *gated.conf* file at the point in the *gated.conf* file where the **%include** directive

is encountered. *filename* is any valid UNIX filename. If *filename* is not fully qualified, i.e., does not begin with a /, it is considered to be relative to the directory defined in the **%directory** directive.

%directory *pathname*

Defines the directory where the include files are stored. When it is used, **gated** looks in the directory identified by *pathname* for any include file that does not have a fully qualified filename.

Unless you have a very complex routing configuration, avoid using include files. In a complex environment, segmenting a large configuration into smaller, more easily understood segments can be helpful, but most **gated** configurations are very small. One of the great advantages of **gated** is that it combines the configuration of several different routing protocols into a single file. If that file is small and easy to read, segmenting the file unnecessarily complicates things.

Trace Statements

Trace statements allow you to control the trace file and its contents from within the *gated.conf* file. The trace statement is:

traceoptions ["*trace_file*" [replace] [size *bytes*[k | m] files *n*]] [nostamp]
    trace_options [except *trace_options*] ;

Its components are as follows:

trace_file

Identifies the file that receives the trace output. It has exactly the same function as the *trace_file* argument on the **gated** command line.

replace

Replaces the existing trace file. If you do not use this keyword, the trace output is appended to the current contents of the file.

size *bytes*[k | m] [files *n*]

Limits the trace file to a maximum size of *bytes*. The optional **k** or **m** indicates thousands (**k**) or millions (**m**) of bytes. Thus 1000000 and 10m are equivalent entries. The size of the trace file cannot be less than 10k bytes. *n* defines the maximum number of trace files that should be saved. When the trace file reaches the maximum size, it is saved as *trace_file*.0, *trace_file*.1, *trace_file*.2 up to *trace_file.n*. The next save then overwrites *trace_file*.0. The value for *n* must be at least 2.

nostamp

Specifies that trace lines should not begin with a timestamp. Timestamping each line of trace data is the default.

`trace_options`

> Define the events to be traced by **gated**. Each trace option is specified by a keyword name. The available trace options are:

none

> Turns off all tracing.

all Turns on all types of global tracing.

general

> Turns on both **normal** and **route** tracing.

state

> Traces state machine transitions for protocols such as OSPF and BGP. The RFCs describe these protocols using *finite state machine* (FSM) diagrams or tables. The protocols transition from one state to another based on the occurrence of certain events. For example, the state might change from *idle* to *connect* when a *connection open* event occurs. This is a highly specialized trace flag, useful only to those who have a thorough understanding of the protocols involved. Use this option within the protocol statement to trace a specific protocol's transitions.

normal

> Traces normal protocols interactions. Errors are always traced.

policy

> Traces the application of routing policies. Use this to check that you have properly configured your routing policy.

task

> Traces system-level processing.

timer

> Traces the various timers used by a protocol or peer.

route

> Traces routing table changes. Use this to check that routes are properly installed by the protocol.

detail

> Traces the contents of the packets exchanged by the router. Must be specified before **send** or **recv**.

send

> Limits the **detail** trace to packets sent by this router.

recv

> Limits the **detail** trace to packets received by this router. Without these two options, all packets are traced when **detail** is specified.

symbols

> Traces the symbols read from the kernel at startup. See the **−t** command-line argument.

iflist

> Traces the kernel interface list. See the **−t** command-line argument.

parse

> Traces the lexical analyzer and parser.

adv

> Traces the allocation and release of blocks.

except *trace_options*

> Disables specific trace options. Must be used in conjunction with *trace_options* that enable a wide variety of tracing. For example: `traceoptions all except state` turns on all traces except for finite state machine tracing.

gated provides the flexibility for you to choose where you want to control tracing—on the command line or in the configuration file. By and large, the same trace options can be set on the **gated** command line or in the configuration file. **detail, send** and **recv** can be set only in the configuration file.

Two others, **symbols** and **iflist**, are primarily used on the command line. Refer to the section on the **gated** command line for a description of setting trace options with **−t**.

Some trace options are only useful for protocol developers and other experts. For most of us, **general**, which enables **normal** and **route** tracing, is an appropriate level of information for debugging routing problems. Occasionally **policy** is useful for testing a routing policy. Most of the time, however, no tracing is needed.

Options Statements

Options statements define parameters that direct **gated** to do special internal processing. Options statements appear before any other configuration statements in the *gated.conf* file.

The options statement syntax is:

> options
> [nosend]
> [noresolv]
> [gendefault [preference *preference*] [gateway *gateway*]]
> [syslog [upto] *log_level*]
> [mark *time*]
> ;

An options statement can contain:

nosend

> Instructs system not to send any packets. This option tests **gated** without actu-
> ally sending out routing information. Use for RIP and HELLO. It is not yet
> implemented for BGP and is not useful for OSPF.

noresolv

> Instructs system not to use the Domain Name System (DNS) to resolve host-
> names and addresses. DNS failures can cause **gated** to deadlock during
> startup. Use this to prevent deadlock.

gendefault [preference *preference*] [gateway *gateway*]

> Generates a default route, with a preference of 20, when **gated** peers with an
> EGP or BGP neighbor. If **gateway** is not defined, the gateway in the generated
> route is the system itself; the default route is not installed in the kernel table;
> and it is used only to advertise this system as a default gateway. If **gateway** is
> specified, the default route is installed in the kernel table with the specified
> router as the next hop. This option can be overridden with the **nogendefault**
> option.

syslog [upto] *log_level*

> Tells system to use the setlogmask facility to control **gated** logging. See the set-
> logmask(3) manpage if this facility is available on your system.

mark *time*

> Sends a periodic timestamp message to the trace file. *time* defines how fre-
> quently the timestamp should be issued. Use this to determine if gated is **run-
> ning**.

Interface Statements

An interface statement defines configuration options for the network interfaces.
The *interface_list* identifies the interfaces affected by the configuration
options. The interfaces in the list are identified by interface name (e.g., le0), by
hostname, by IP address, or by the keyword **all**. The keyword **all** refers to every

interface on the system. The interface name can refer to a single interface or a group of interfaces. For example, an interface name of eth0 refers to the interface eth0, whereas the name le refers to all installed interfaces that start with the letters le (which might include le0, le1, and le2). A hostname can be used if it resolves to only one address.

Most system administrators prefer to use the IP address to identify an interface. After all, IP addresses are inherently a part of TCP/IP, and it's TCP/IP routing that this file configures.

Additionally, remote systems know this interface by its IP address, not its interface name. Finally, DNS may provide more than one address for a hostname, and future UNIX operating systems may allow more than one address per interface. IP addresses are safest.

gated supports four types of interfaces: loopback, broadcast, point-to-point, and non-broadcast multi-access (NBMA). All of these are discussed in the text of this book except for NBMA. It is a multi-access interface, but the underlying network is not capable of broadcast. Examples are frame relay and X.25.

gated ignores any interface in the list that has an invalid local, remote, or broadcast address, or an invalid subnet mask. **gated** also ignores a point-to-point interface that has the same local and remote addresses. **gated** assumes that interfaces that are not marked UP by the kernel do not exist.

The syntax of the interfaces statement is:

```
interfaces {
    options
        [strictinterfaces]
        [scaninterval time] ;
    interface interface_list
        [preference preference]
        [down preference preference]
        [passive]
        [simplex]
        [reject]
        [blackhole] ;
    define address
        [broadcast address] | [pointtopoint address]
        [netmask mask]
        [multicast] ;
} ;
```

The configuration options defined before the interface list are global options. The global options are:

strictinterfaces
> Generates a fatal error if an interface is referenced in the configuration file that is not found when **gated** scans the kernel at startup and is not listed in a **define** statement. (See the **define** option later in this section.) Normally a warning message is issued and **gated** continues running.

scaninterval *time*
> Specifies how often **gated** scans the kernel interface list for changes. The default is every 15 seconds on most systems, and 60 seconds on systems that pass interface status changes through the routing socket, e.g., BSD 4.4. Note that **gated** also scans the interface list on receipt of a SIGUSR2.

The **interface** command defines the *interface_list* and all of the options that affect the specified interfaces. Options available on this statement are:

preference *preference*
> Sets the preference for this interface. The value *preference* is a number between 0 and 255. **gated** prefers routes through interfaces with low preference numbers. The default preference for all directly attached network interfaces is 0.

down preference *preference*
> Sets the preference used when **gated** believes an interface is not functioning properly. The default is 120.

passive
> Prevents **gated** from downgrading the preference of the interface when it is not functioning properly. **gated** assumes that an interface is down when it stops receiving routing information through that interface. **gated** only performs this check if the interface is actively participating in a routing protocol.

simplex
> Specifies that **gated** should not use packets generated by this system as an indication that the interface is functioning properly. Only packets from remote systems are used to indicate that the interface is operating.

reject | blackhole
> Either of these keywords identifies the interface as the "blackhole interface" used to install rejected routes in the kernel. (See the control statements for more about rejected routes.) This is available only on BSD systems that have installed a reject/blackhole pseudo-interface.

The **define** *address* command lists interfaces that might not be present when **gated** scans the kernel interface list at startup. It overrides the **strictinterfaces** option for the interface defined by *address*. Possible options for the **define** command are:

broadcast *address*
> Defines the broadcast address.

pointopoint *address*
> Defines the local address for a point-to-point interface. (See Chapter 6 for a discussion of point-to-point interfaces.) When this option is used, the address on the **define** statement specifies the address of the remote host, and the address specified after the **pointopoint** keyword defines the local address. Don't use both **broadcast** and **pointopoint** in the same **define**.

netmask *mask*
> Defines the subnet mask.

multicast
> Specifies that the interface supports multicasting.

Definition Statements

Definition statements are general configuration statements that relate to more than one protocol. Definition statements must appear before any protocol statements in *gated.conf*. The three definition statements are:

autonomoussystem *asn* [loops *n*] ;
> Defines the autonomous system number (*asn*) used by BGP or EGP. The **loops** number defines the number of times this autonomous system may appear in an AS path for path vector protocols, such as BGP. The default value for *n* is 1.

routerid *address* ;
> Defines the router identifier used by BGP and OSPF. Use the address of your primary OSPF or BGP interface. By default, **gated** uses the address of the first interface it encounters.

martians {
> host *address* [allow];
> *address* [mask *mask* | masklen *number*] [allow] ;
> default [allow] ; } ;

Changes the list of addresses about which all routing information is ignored. Sometimes a misconfigured system sends out obviously invalid destination addresses. These invalid addresses, called martians, are rejected by the routing software. This command allows changes to the list of martian addresses. A martian address can be specified as a host address by using the **host** keyword before the address, or as a network address by simply specifying the address.

An address mask can be defined for a network address. The mask can be defined in dotted decimal notation using the **mask** keyword or as a numeric prefix length using the **masklen** keyword. The address masks `mask 255.255.0.0` and `masklen 16` are equivalent. If no address mask is specified, the natural mask is used.

Specifying an address in the **martians** statement adds the address to the martians list. The **allow** keyword is used to remove an address from the martians list. When an address is removed from the martians list, it then becomes a valid address for routing.

gated contains a standard martian list of addresses that are known to be invalid. This is the default martian list. The option **default allow** removes all of the standard entries from the martians list and permits unrestricted routing. Don't do this if you're on a connected network.

Here is a sample of each definition statement:

```
autonomoussystem 249 ;
routerid 172.16.12.2 ;
martians {
        host 0.0.0.26 ;
        192.168.0.0 masklen 16 allow ;
} ;
```

The statements in the sample perform the following functions:

- The **autonomoussystem** statement tells **gated** to use AS number 249 for its BGP or EGP packets.

- The **routerid** statement tells **gated** to use 172.16.12.2 as the router identifier for OSPF and BGP.

- The **martians** statement prevents routes to 0.0.0.26 from being included in the table, but it allows routes to the private IP addresses in the range 192.168.0.0 to 192.168.255.255.

Protocol Statements

Protocol statements enable or disable protocols and set protocol options. The protocol statements occur after the definition statements and before the static statements. There are many protocol statements and more may be added at any time. There are statements for the various interior and exterior routing protocols, and for other things that are not really routing protocols.

In this section we begin with the interior protocols, move on to the exterior protocols, and finish with the special "protocols."

The ospf Statement

```
ospf yes | no | on | off [{
   defaults {
      preference preference ;
      cost cost ;
      tag [as] tag ;
      type 1 | 2 ; } ;
   exportlimit routes ;
   exportinterval time ;
   traceoptions trace_options ;
   monitorauthkey password ;
   backbone | area number {
      authtype 0 | 1 | none | simple ;
      stub [cost cost] ;
      networks {
         address [mask mask  /masklen number] [restrict] ;
         host address [restrict] ; } ;
      stubhosts {
         address cost cost ; } ;
      interface interface_list [nonbroadcast] [cost cost] {
         pollinterval time ;
         routers {
            address [eligible] ; } ;
            interface_parameters } ;
      virtuallink neighborid router_id transitarea area {
            interface_parameters } ;
   } ; } ] ;
```

The **ospf** statement enables or disables the Open Shortest Path First (OSPF) routing protocol. By default, OSPF is disabled. It is enabled by specifying **yes** or **on** (it doesn't matter which you use) and it is disabled with **no** or **off**.

NOTE   For the sake of brevity, this text explains only the first occurrence of any *gated.conf* parameter if it is used the same way in subsequent commands. Only differences between commands are explained. For example, **yes | no | on | off** is not explained again, because it is always used in the same way to enable or disable a protocol.

The **ospf** statement has many configuration parameters:

defaults

Defines the defaults used when importing OSPF routes from an external autonomous system and announcing those routes to other OSPF routers. The link-state advertisement (LSA) used to announce these routes is called an ASE (autonomous system external) because it contains routes from external autonomous systems. See the description of OSFP in Chapter 7.

preference *preference*

Defines the preference of OSPF ASE routes. The default is 150.

cost *cost*

Defines the cost used when advertising a non-OSPF route in an ASE. The default is 1.

tag [as] *tag*

Defines the OSPF ASE tag value. The tag is not used by the OSPF protocol, but may be used by an export policy to filter routes. (See the **export** statement later in this appendix.) When the **as** keyword is specified, the tag field may contain AS path information.

type 1 | 2

Defines the type of ASE used. The default is type 1. Type 1 contains routes learned from an external protocol that provides a metric directly comparable to the OSPF metric. The metric is added to the cost of reaching the border router when routes are advertised. A type 2 ASE contains routes learned from an exterior gateway protocol that does not provide a routing metric comparable to the OSPF metric. These routes are advertised with the cost of reaching the border router. See Chapter 7.

exportlimit *routes*

Defines the maximum number of ASE LSAs that will be flooded at one time. The default is 100.

exportinterval *time*

Defines how frequently ASE link-state advertisements are flooded to the network. The default is once per second.

traceoptions *trace_options*

Defines the tracing used to debug OSPF. In addition to the standard trace flags, OSPF supports:

lsabuild

Traces construction of link-state advertisements (LSA).

spf Traces the Shortest Path First (SPF) calculations.

hello

> Traces the OSPF HELLO packets.

dd Traces the OSPF Database Description packets.

request

> Traces the OSPF Link-State Request packets.

lsu Traces the OSPF Link-State Update packets.

ack

> Traces OSPF Link-State Ack packets.

monitorauthkey *password*

> Defines the password used for **ospf_monitor** queries. By default these queries are not authenticated. If **monitorauthkey** is specified, incoming queries must contain the specified password.

backbone | area *number*

> Defines the OSPF area of which this router is a member. Every router must belong to an area. If more than one area is configured, at least one must be the backbone. The backbone is defined using the **backbone** keyword. All other areas are defined by the **area** keyword and the number of the area, e.g., `area 1`. See Chapter 7 for a discussion of OSPF areas. Several configuration parameters are associated with each area:

> **authtype 0 | 1 | none | simple**
>
> > Specifies the authentication scheme used in this area. The authentication schemes can be defined by **none** or **0** for no authentication, or **simple** or **1** for password authentication. Each system in an area must use this same authentication scheme.

> **stub** [cost *cost*]
>
> > Specifies that this is a stub area. A stub area is one in which there are no ASE routes. If a cost is specified, it is used to advertise a default route into the stub area.

> **networks**
>
> > Defines the range of networks contained within this area. The specified ranges are advertised into other areas as summary network LSAs and not as inter-area routes. If **restrict** is specified, the summary network LSAs are not advertised. The entries in the networks list are either specified as host addresses by using the **host** keyword before the address, or as a network address by simply specifying the address. An address mask can be defined for a network address. The mask can be defined in dotted decimal

notation using the **mask** keyword or as a numeric prefix length using the **masklen** keyword. The address masks `mask 255.255.0.0` and `masklen 16` are equivalent. If no address mask is specified, the natural mask is used. This option can reduce the amount of routing information propagated between areas.

stubhosts

Lists the directly attached hosts, and their costs, that should be advertised as reachable from this router. List point-to-point interfaces here.

interface *interface_list* [nobroadcast] [cost *cost*]

Defines the interfaces used by OSPF. If the keyword **nobroadcast** is specified, the interface connects to a non-broadcast multi-access (NBMA) network. If **nobroadcast** is not used, the interface connects to a broadcast or a point-to-point network. Specify the cost of the interface with the **cost** keyword, e.g., `cost 5`. The default cost is 1.

Two options are specific to NBMA interfaces:

pollinterval *time*

Defines the time interval at which OSPF HELLO packets are sent to neighbors.

routers

Lists all neighbors by address. The **eligible** keyword indicates if the neighbor can become a designated router.

Point-to-point interfaces have one additional parameter:

nomulticast

Forces **gated** to unicast OSPF packets over this interface. By default, OSPF packets to neighbors on point-to-point interfaces are sent via the IP multicast mechanism. Use this option if the remote neighbor does not support multicasting.

All interfaces—NBMA, point-to-point, and broadcast—can use these parameters:

enable | disable ;

Enables or disables the interface.

retransmitinterval *time* ;

Defines the number of seconds between link-state advertisement retransmissions.

transitdelay *time* ;

Defines the estimated number of seconds required to transmit a link-state update over this interface. It must be greater than 0.

priority *priority* ;
> Defines this system's priority for the designated router election. *priority* is a number from 0 to 255. The router with the highest priority becomes the designated router. A router whose priority is 0 is ineligible to become the designated router. See Chapter 7 for a discussion of desginated routers.

hellointerval *time* ;
> Defines the number of seconds between transmissions of HELLO packets.

routerdeadinterval *time* ;
> Defines the timeout before a neighbor is declared down. *time* is the maximum number of seconds this router will wait for a neighbor's Hello packet.

authkey *key* ;
> Defines a key used to authenticate OSPF packets. The *key* is specified as one to eight decimal digits separated by periods, a one- to eight-byte hexadecimal string preceded by 0x, or a one- to eight-character string in double quotes.

virtuallink neighborid *router_id* transitarea *area*
> Defines a virtual link for the backbone area. The *router_id* is the router identifier of the remote router at the other end of the virtual link. The transit area must be one of the other areas configured on this system. All standard interface parameters defined above may be specified on a virtual link.

The rip Statement

rip yes | no | on | off [{
   broadcast ;
   nobroadcast ;
   nocheckzero ;
   preference *preference* ;
   defaultmetric *metric* ;
   query authentication [none | [simple | md5 *password*]] ;
   interface *interface_list*
      [noripin] | [ripin]
      [noripout] | [ripout]
      [metricin *metric*]
      [metricout *metric*]
      [version 1 | 2 [multicast | broadcast]]

    [[secondary] authentication [none | [simple | md5 *password*]] ;
trustedgateways *gateway_list* ;
sourcegateways *gateway_list* ;
traceoptions *trace_options* ; }] ;

The **rip** statement enables or disables RIP. By default RIP is enabled. The **rip** statement options are:

broadcast

Forces **gated** to broadcast RIP update packets even if the system has only one network interface. By default, RIP updates are not broadcast if the system has only one network interface and are broadcast if it has more than one network interface; i.e., hosts do not broadcast updates and routers do.

nobroadcast

Forces **gated** to not broadcast RIP update packets even if the system has more than one network interface. If a **sourcegateways** clause is present, routes are still unicast directly to that gateway. See **sourcegateways** later in this section.

nocheckzero

Specifies that **gated** should not reject incoming version 1 RIP packets where the reserved fields are 0. Rejecting those packets is standard practice.

preference *preference* ;

Sets the **gated** preference for routes learned from RIP. The default preference for these routes is 100.

defaultmetric *metric* ;

Defines the metric used when advertising routes via RIP that were learned from other protocols. The default *metric* is 16, which to RIP indicates an unusable route. This means that by default, routes learned from other protocols are not advertised as valid routes by RIP. Set a lower value only if you want all routes learned from other protocols advertised at that metric.

query authentication [none | [simple | md5 *key*]] ;

Specifies the authentication used for non-router query packets. The default is **none**. If **simple** is specified, the *key* is a 16-byte password. If **md5** is specified, the *key* is a 16-byte value used with the packet contents to generate a Message Digest 5 cryptographic checksum.

interface *interface_list*

Identifies the interfaces over which RIP runs and defines the configuration parameters of those interfaces. The *interface_list* can contain interface names, hostnames, IP addresses, or the keyword **all**. Possible parameters are:

noripin

Tells system to ignore RIP packets received on this interface. The default is to listen to RIP packets on all non-loopback interfaces.

ripin

Tells system to listen to RIP packets received on this interface. This is the default.

noripout

Tells system not to send RIP packets out this interface. The default is to send RIP on all broadcast and non-broadcast interfaces when in broadcast mode. See the **nobroadcast** option defined earlier in this list.

ripout

Tells system to send RIP packets out this interface. This is the default.

metricin `metric`

Specifies the RIP metric used for routes received on this interface. The default is the kernel interface metric plus 1, which is the default RIP hop count. If this metric is specified it is used as the absolute value, and is not added to the kernel metric.

metricout

Specifies the RIP metric added to routes sent out this interface. The default is 0. This option can only increase the metric.

version 1 | 2 [multicast | broadcast]

Identifies the version of RIP used for updates sent out this interface. Available versions are RIP 1 and RIP 2. RIP 1 is the default. If RIP 2 is specified and IP multicast is supported, full version 2 packets are sent via multicast. If multicast is not available, version 1–compatible version 2 packets are sent via broadcast. The keyword **multicast**, the default, specifies this behavior. The keyword **broadcast** specifies that RIP version 1–compatible version 2 packets should be broadcast on this interface, even if IP multicast is available. Neither keyword is used with version 1.

[secondary] authentication [none | simple | md5 `key`**]**

Defines the RIP version 2 authentication used on this interface. The default authentication type is **none**. If **simple** is specified, the `key` is a 16-byte password. If **md5** is specified, the `key` is a 16-byte value used with the packet contents to generate a Message Digest 5 cryptographic checksum. If **secondary** is specified, this defines the secondary authentication. Packets are always sent using the primary authentication technique. The secondary authentication type is defined only for incoming packets. Inbound packets are checked against both the primary and secondary authentication method before being discarded as invalid.

trustedgateways *gateway_list* ;

> Defines the list of gateways from which RIP accepts updates. The *gateway_list* is simply a list of hostnames or IP addresses. By default, all gateways on the shared network are trusted to supply routing information. But if the **trustedgateways** statement is used, only updates from the gateways in the list are accepted.

sourcegateways *gateway_list* ;

> Defines a list of gateways to which RIP sends packets directly. By default, RIP packets are broadcast or multicast to several systems on the shared network— but if this statement is used, RIP unicasts packets directly to the listed gateways.

traceoptions *trace_options*

> Defines tracing for RIP. RIP supports most of the standard tracing options and these packet-tracing options:

packets

> Traces all RIP packets.

request

> Traces the RIP information request packets, such as REQUEST, POLL, and POLLENTRY.

response

> Traces all RIP RESPONSE packets.

other

> Traces any other type of RIP packet.

The hello Statement

hello yes | no | on | off [{
    broadcast ;
    nobroadcast ;
    preference *preference* ;
    defaultmetric *metric* ;
    interface *interface_list*
            [nohelloin] | [helloin]
            [nohelloout] | [helloout]
            [metricin *metric*]
            [metricout *metric*] ;
    trustedgateways *gateway_list* ;
    sourcegateways *gateway_list* ;
    traceoptions *trace_options* ; }] ;

This statement enables or disables Hello. By default, Hello is disabled. The default metric is 30000 (30 seconds is the highest possible Hello metric) and the default preference is 90. Unless the preference values are altered, routes learned from Hello are preferred over those learned from RIP.

The **hello** statement has basically the same options as the **rip** statement. The only command differences are the keywords **nohelloin** and **nohelloout**, but they perform the same function for Hello as **noripin** and **noripout** do for RIP.

The **hello** statement supports most of the standard trace options. In addition, the option **packets** can be specified to trace all HELLO packets.

The isis Statement

isis yes | no | dual | ip | iso {
    level 1 | 2 ;
    traceoptions *isis_traceoptions* ;
    systemid *6_digit_hexstring* ;
    area *hexstring* ;
    set *isis_parm value* ; ...
    circuit *string*
      metric level 1 | 2 *metric*
      priority level 1 | 2 *priority* ; } ;

The **isis** statement enables the IS-IS protocol. By default, it is disabled. The **dual** keyword enables IS-IS for both ISO and IP addressing. The **ip** keyword enables it for IP addressing and **iso** enables it for ISO addressing. The options that may appear in the **isis** statement are:

level

    Indicates whether the router, called an *intermediate system* (IS) in OSI terminology, is a Level 1 (intra-area) or Level 2 (inter-area) IS. Default is Level 1.

traceoptions

    Defines the IS-IS trace options. These are different from other **gated** trace options. The **isis_traceoptions** are:

all Traces everything.

iih Traces ISIS HELLO packets.

lanadj

    Traces LAN adjacency updates.

p2padj

    Traces point-to-point adjacency updates.

lspdb

Traces signatures in the LSP database.

lspcontent

Traces contents of the LSP database.

lspinput

Traces input processing of the LSPs.

flooding

Traces flooding of the LSPs.

buildlsp

Traces creation of the LSPs.

csnp

Traces processing of the CSNPs.

psnp

Traces processing of the PSNPs.

route

Traces route changes.

update

Traces routing updates.

paths

Traces paths calculated by the Shortest Path First (SPF) algorithm.

spf Traces the operation of the Shortest Path First (SPF) algorithm.

events

Traces protocol events.

systemid

Defines the IS-IS system ID. If no system identifier is specified, the system ID portion of the first circuit's NSAP address is used.

area

Adds area addresses to those configured automatically from the circuits. IS-IS area addresses are automatically configured based on the real circuits over which IS-IS runs.

circuit

Defines the circuits used by IS-IS. Circuits normally are UNIX interfaces, and *string* is an interface name. The circuit options are:

metric

Defines the Level 1 and Level 2 metrics for each circuit. *metric* is a numeric value in the range 1 to 63. The default value is 63.

priority

> Defines the value used by IS-IS when electing a designated router. Routers with high priority values are preferred for the designated router. *priority* is a numeric value between 0 and 127. If no priority is specified, a random value is selected.

See *A Guide to Gated Integrated IS-IS*, by Steve Heimlich, for information on IS-IS configuration. The document is included in the **gated** distribution.

The bgp Statement

bgp yes | no | on | off [{
    preference *preference* ;
    defaultmetric *metric* ;
    traceoptions *trace_options* ;
    group type external peeras *as_number*
        | internal peeras *as_number*
        | igp peeras *as_number* proto *proto*
        | routing peeras *as_number* proto *proto* interface *interface_list*
        | test peeras *as_number* {
      allow {
          address mask *mask* | masklen *number*
          all
          host *address* } ;
      peer *address*
        [metricout *metric*]
        [localas *as_number*]
        [nogendefault]
        [gateway *address*]
        [preference *preference*]
        [preference2 *preference*]
        [lcladdr *address*]
        [holdtime *time*]
        [version *number*]
        [passive]
        [sendbuffer *number*]
        [recvbuffer *number*]
        [indelay *time*]
        [outdelay *time*]
        [keep all | none]
        [analretentive]
        [noauthcheck]
        [noaggregatorid]

[keepalivesalways]
[v3asloopokay]
[nov4asloop]
[logupdown]
[ttl *ttl*]
[traceoptions *trace_options*] ; } ; }] ;

This statement enables or disables BGP. By default, BGP is disabled. The default preference is 170. By default, BGP does not advertise a metric. Unlike the RIP metric, the BGP metric does not play a primary role in determining the best route. The BGP metric is simply an arbitrary 16-bit value that can be used as one criterion for choosing a route. The **defaultmetric** statement can be used to define a metric that BGP will use when advertising routes.

Trace options can be specified for all of BGP or for individual BGP peers. BGP supports most of the standard trace options as well as the following:

packets

Traces all BGP packets.

open

Traces BGP OPEN packets.

update

Traces BGP UPDATE packets.

keepalive

Traces BGP KEEPALIVE packets.

BGP peers must be members of a group. The group statement declares the group, defines which peers are members of the group, and defines the group "type." Multiple group statements may be specified, but each must have a unique combination of type and autonomous system number. There are four possible group types:

group type external peeras *as_number*

Specifies that BGP will run as a classic exterior gateway protocol. The peers listed in this group are members of an external autonomous system. Full policy checking is applied to all incoming and outgoing routes.

group type internal peeras *as_number*

Specifies that BGP will be used to distribute routes to an internal group that has no traditional interior gateway protocol. Routes received from external BGP peers are readvertised to this group with the received metric.

group type igp peeras *as_number* **proto** *proto*

Specifies that BGP will be used to distribute path attributes to an internal group that runs an interior gateway protocol. BGP advertises the AS path, path origin, and transitive optional attributes if the path attributes are provided by the IGP's tag mechanism. `proto` is the name of the interior gateway protocol, e.g., `proto ospf`.

group type routing peeras `as_number` **proto** `proto` **interface** `interface_list`
Specifies that BGP will be used internally to carry external routes, while an interior gateway protocol is used to carry only internal routes. Normally the routes learned by BGP from external autonomous systems are written in the routing table, where they are picked up and distributed by an interior protocol to the local autonomous sytem. For this type of group, BGP distributes the external routes itself and the interior protocol is limited to distributing only those routes that are interior to the local autonomous system. `proto` is the name of the interior protocol.

group type test peeras `as_number`
Specifies that the members of this group are test peers. All routing information exchanged by test peers is discarded.

A **group** clause contains **peer** subclauses. Any number of **peer** subclauses may belong to a group. Peers are specified explicitly with a **peer** statement, or implicitly with the **allow** statement.

allow
Any peer whose address is contained in the specified address range is a member of the group. The keyword **all** matches all possible addresses. The keyword **host** precedes an individual host address. The address and mask pairs define a range of addresses. Network masks can be defined with the keyword **mask** and an address mask written in dotted decimal notation or with the keyword **masklen** and the prefix length written as a decimal number. All parameters for these peers must be defined in the **group** clause.

peer `address`
The peer identified by `address` is a member of the group.

The BGP **peer** subclause allows the following parameters, which can also be specified on the **group** clause. If placed on the **group** clause, the parameters affect all peers in the group. The available options are:

metricout `metric`
Defines the primary metric for routes sent to the peer, which overrides the default metric, a metric specified on the group and any metric specified by export policy.

localas `as_number`
Defines the local system's autonomous system number (asn). The default is to use the asn defined in the **autonomoussystem** statement.

nogendefault

Prevents **gated** from generating a default route when BGP peers with this neighbor, even if **gendefault** is set in the **options** directive statement.

gateway *address*

Identifies the next-hop gateway through which packets for this peer are routed. Use this only if the neighbor does not share a network with the local system. This option is rarely needed.

preference *preference*

Defines the preference used for routes learned from this peer, which permits **gated** to prefer routes from one peer, or group of peers, over another.

preference2 *preference*

Defines the "second" preference. In the case of a preference tie, the second preference is used to break the tie. The default value is 0.

lcladdr *address*

Defines the address of the local interface used to communicate with this neighbor.

holdtime *time*

Defines the number of seconds the peer should wait for a keepalive, update, or notification message before closing the connection. The value is sent to the peer in the Hold Time field of the BGP Open message. The value must be either 0 (no keepalives will be sent) or at least 3.

version *version*

Identifies the version of the BGP protocol to use with this peer. By default, the version is negotiated when the connection is opened. Currently supported versions are 2, 3, and 4.

passive

Specifies that **gated** should wait for the peer to issue an OPEN. By default, **gated** periodically sends OPEN messages until the peer responds.

sendbuffer *buffer_size*

recvbuffer *buffer_size*

Defines the size of the send and receive buffers. The default is 65535 bytes, which is the maximum. These parameters are not used on normally functioning systems.

indelay *time*

outdelay *time*

Implements "route dampening." **indelay** defines the number of seconds a route must be stable before it is accepted. **outdelay** is the number of seconds a route must be present in the **gated** routing database before it is exported to this peer. The default value for each is 0, meaning that these features are disabled. Use this only if the routing table is fluctuating so rapidly it is unstable.

keep all

Tells system to retain routes learned from this peer even if the routes' AS paths contain our local AS number. Normally routes that contain the local AS number are discarded as potential routing loops.

analretentive

Tells system to issue warning messages for events, such as duplicate routes, that are normally "silently ignored."

noauthcheck

Instructs system not to verify that incoming packets have an authentication field of all 1s. Use this to interoperate with an implementation that uses the authentication field.

noaggregatorid

Sets the routerid in the aggregator attribute to 0. By default, it is set to the router identifier. Use this to prevent this router from creating aggregate routes with AS paths that differ from other routers in the AS.

keepalivesalways

Instructs system to send a keepalive even when an update could have correctly substituted for one. Used for interoperability with some routers.

v3asloopokay

Allows advertisement of a route with a loop in the AS path, i.e., with an AS appearing more than once in the path, to version 3 external peers.

nov4asloop

Prevents a route with a loop in the AS path from being advertised to version 4 external peers. Used to avoid passing such routes to a peer that incorrectly forwards them to version 3 neighbors.

logupdown

Logs every time a BGP peer enters or leaves the ESTABLISHED state.

ttl *ttl*

Defines the IP ttl for local neighbors. By default it is set to 1. Use this option if the local neighbor discards packets sent with a ttl of 1. Not all UNIX kernels allow the ttl to be specified for TCP connections.

The BGP trace options are covered previously.

The egp Statement

```
egp yes | no | on | off [ {
    preference preference ;
    defaultmetric metric ;
    packetsize maxpacketsize ;
    traceoptions trace_options ;
    group [peeras as_number] [localas as_number] [maxup number] {
      neighbor address
        [metricout metric]
        [preference preference]
        [preference2 preference]
        [ttl ttl]
        [nogendefault]
        [importdefault]
        [exportdefault]
        [gateway address]
        [lcladdr address]
        [sourcenet network]
        [minhello | p1 interval]
        [minpoll | p2 interval]
        [traceoptions trace_options] ; } ; }] ;
```

This statement enables or disables EGP. By default, EGP is disabled. The default metric for announcing routes via EGP is 255, and the default preference for routes learned from EGP is 200.

The **packetsize** argument defines the size of the largest EGP packet that will be sent or accepted. *maxpacketsize* is the size in bytes. The default is 8192 bytes. If **gated** receives a packet larger than *maxpacketsize* it is discarded, but *maxpacketsize* is increased to the size of the larger packet so that future packets won't have to be discarded.

The **traceoptions** statement defines the tracing for EGP. Tracing can be specified for the EGP protocol or for an individual EGP neighbor. The EGP trace options are:

packets
    Traces all EGP packets.

hello
    Traces EGP HELLO/I-HEARD-U packets.

acquire
    Traces EGP ACQUIRE/CEASE packets.

update

Traces EGP POLL/UPDATE packets.

The **egp** statement has two clauses: the `group` clause and the `neighbor` clause. EGP neighbors must be part of a group, and all of the neighbors in a group must be members of the same autonomous system. Use the `group` clause to define parameters for a group of EGP neighbors. Values set in a `group` clause apply to all neighbor clauses in the group. There can be multiple `group` clauses. The following parameters are set by the `group` clause:

peeras

Identifies the autonomous system number of the autonomous system to which the members of the group belong. If not specified, this number is learned from the neighbors.

localas

Defines the local system's autonomous system number. The default is to use the asn defined in the **autonomoussystem** statement.

maxup

Defines the number of EGP neighbors **gated** is to acquire. The default is to acquire all listed neighbors.

The `neighbor` clause defines one EGP neighbor. The only part of the clause that is required is the **address** argument, which is the host name or IP address of the neighbor. All other parameters are optional. All of these optional parameters can also be specified in the `group` clause if you want to apply the parameter to all neighbors. The `neighbor` clause parameters are:

metricout *metric*

Used for all routes sent to this neighbor. This value overrides the **defaultmetric** value set in the **egp** statement, but only for this specific neighbor.

preference *preference*

Defines the preference used for routes learned from this neighbor, which permits **gated** to prefer routes from one neighbor, or group of neighbors, over another.

preference2 *preference*

Defines the "second" preference. In the case of a preference tie, the second preference is used to break the tie. The default value is 0.

ttl *ttl*

Defines the IP ttl for local neighbors. By default, it is set to 1. Use this option if the local neighbor discards packets sent with a ttl of 1.

nogendefault

> Prevents **gated** from generating a default route when EGP peers with this neighbor, even if **gendefault** is set in the **options** directive statement.

importdefault

> Tells system to accept the default route if it is included in this neighbor's EGP update. By default, it is ignored.

exportdefault

> Tells system to send the default route in EGP updates to this EGP neighbor. Normally a default route is not included in an EGP update.

gateway *address*

> Identifies the next-hop gateway through which packets for this neighbor are routed. Use this only if the neighbor does not share a network with the local system. This option is rarely needed.

lcladdr *address*

> Defines the address of the local interface used to communicate with the neighbor.

sourcenet *network*

> Changes the network queried in EGP POLL packets. By default, this is the shared network. However, if the neighbor does not share a network with your system, the neighbor's network address should be specified here. This parameter is normally not needed. Do not use it if you share a network with the EGP neighbor.

minhello | **p1** *time*

> Sets the interval between the transmission of EGP HELLO packets.* The default Hello interval is 30 seconds. If the neighbor fails to respond to three HELLO packets, the system stops trying to acquire the neighbor. Setting a larger interval gives the neighbor a better chance to respond. The interval can be defined as seconds, minutes:seconds, or hours:minutes:seconds. For example, a 3-minute interval could be specified as 180 (seconds), 3:00 (minutes), or 0:3:00 (no hours and 3 minutes). The keyword **p1** can be used instead of the keyword **minhello**.

minpoll | **p2** *time*

> Sets the time interval between sending polls to the neighbor. The default is 120 seconds. If three polls are sent without a response, the neighbor is declared "down" and all routes learned from that neighbor are removed from the routing table. This can cause the routing table to be very unstable if a

---

* Don't confuse this with the Hello protocol. Refer to the discussion of HELLO and I-H-U packets in Chapter 7.

neighbor becomes congested and can't respond to rapid polls. A longer polling interval provides a more stable, but less responsive, routing table. Again the interval is defined as seconds, minutes:seconds, or hours:minutes:seconds.

The snmp Statement

snmp yes | no | on | off [{
   port *port* ;
   debug ;
   traceoptions *trace_options* ; }] ;

This command controls whether **gated** informs the SNMP management software of its status. SNMP is not a routing protocol and is not started by this command. You must run SNMP software independently. This statement only controls whether **gated** keeps the management software apprised of its status. The default is on, so **gated** does inform SNMP of its status.

The snmp statement supports three options:

port *port*
> This option changes the SNMP port used by **gated**. By default, the SNMP daemon listens to port 199.

debug
> Enables debugging of **gated**'s SNMP code. By default, it is disabled. This option is used by code developers.

traceoptions *trace_options*
> Traces the interactions between **gated** and the SNMP daemon. The **detail**, **send**, and **recv** options are not supported. Instead, the **snmp** statement uses these options:
>
> **receive**
>> Traces all requests received from the SNMP daemon.
>
> **register**
>> Traces SNMP requests to register variables.
>
> **resolve**
>> Traces SNMP requests to resolve variable names.
>
> **trap**
>> Traces SNMP trap requests.

The redirect Statement

redirect yes | no | on | off [{
    preference `preference` ;
    interface `interface_list` [noredirects | redirects] ;
    trustedgateways `gateway_list` ;
    traceoptions `trace_options` ; }] ;

This statement controls whether ICMP redirects are allowed to modify the kernel routing table. It does not prevent a system from sending redirects, only from listening to them. If **no** or **off** is specified, **gated** attempts to remove the effects of ICMP redirects from the kernel routing table whenever the redirects are detected. Remember that ICMP is part of IP; therefore, the redirects may be installed in the kernel table before they are seen by **gated**. If you disable redirects, **gated** actively removes the redirected routes from the routing table. By default, ICMP redirects are enabled on hosts that quietly listen to interior routing protocols and disabled on gateways that actively participate in interior routing protocols.

The default preference of a route learned from a redirect is 30, which can be changed with the **preference** option. The **interface** statement controls how redirects are handled on an interface-by-interface basis. Redirects are ignored if **noredirects** is specified and are permitted if **redirects**, which is the default, is specified. The **trustedgateways** statement enables redirects on a gateway-by-gateway basis. By default, redirects are accepted from all routers on the local network. If the **trustedgateways** statement is used, only redirects received from a gateway listed in the `gateway_list` are accepted. The gateway_list is simply a list of hostnames or addresses. The `trace_options` defined on the **traceoptions** statement are the standard **gated** trace options.

The icmp Statement

icmp {
    traceoptions `trace_options` ; }

On some systems, **gated** listens to all ICMP messages but only processes the ICMP redirect packets. That processing is controlled by the redirect statement. In the future, more functionality may be added. At present the **icmp** statement is used only to enable tracing of ICMP messages. The tracing options supported by the **icmp** statement are:

packets

  Traces all ICMP packets.

redirect

  Traces ICMP REDIRECT packets.

routerdiscovery

> Traces ICMP ROUTER DISCOVERY packets.

info

> Traces ICMP informational packets.

error

> Traces ICMP error packets.

The routerdiscovery Statement

The Router Discovery Protocol informs hosts of the routers that are available on the network. It provides an alternative to static routes, routing protocols, and ICMP redirects for hosts that simply need to know the address of their default router. The Router Discovery Protocol is implemented as a server running on the router and a client running on the host. Both the server (router) software and the client (host) software are provided by **gated**.

First let's look at the server configuration statement:

routerdiscovery server yes | **no** | **on** | **off** [{
   traceoptions *trace_options* ;
   interface *interface_list*
     [**minadvinterval** *time*]
     [**maxadvinterval** *time*]
     [**lifetime** *time*] ;
   address *interface_list*
     [**advertise** | **ignore**]
     [**broadcast** | **multicast**]
     [**ineligible** | **preference** *preference*] ; }] ;

The **routerdiscovery** statement for both the client and server support tracing. The **state** trace flag can be used to trace finite state machine transitions. Router discovery packet tracing, however, is not done here. It is enabled via the ICMP statement.

The `interface` clause defines the physical interfaces and the parameters that apply to them. Only physical interfaces can be defined in the interface clause. Addresses are specified in the address clauses shown below. The interface parameters are:

maxadvinterval *time*

> Defines the maximum time interval between sending router advertisements. It must be more than 4 seconds and less than 30:00 minutes. The default is 10:00 minutes (600 seconds).

minadvinterval *time*

> Defines the minimum time interval between sending router advertisements. It must be no less than 3 seconds and no greater than **maxadvinterval**. The default is 0.75 × maxadvinterval.

lifetime *time*

> Defines how long clients should consider the addresses in a router advertisement valid. It must be greater than **maxadvinterval** and no more than 2:30:00 (two hours, thirty minutes). The default is 3 × maxadvinterval.

The address clause defines the IP addresses used and the parameters that apply to them. The address clause parameters are:

advertise | ignore

> **advertise** specifies that the address should be included in router advertisements, which is the default. **ignore** specifies that the address should not be included in router advertisements.

broadcast | multicast

> **broadcast** specifies that the address should be included in a broadcast router advertisement because some systems on the network do not support multicasting. This is the default if the router does not support multicasting.
>
> **multicast** specifies that the address should only be included in a multicast router advertisement. If the system does not support multicasting, the address is not advertised.

ineligible | preference *preference*

> Defines the preference of the address as a default router. *preference* is a 32-bit signed integer. The higher values mean the address is more preferable. Note that this is not **gated** preference. This is a value transmitted as part of the Router Discovery Protocol.
>
> The keyword **ineligible** assigns a preference of hex 80000000 that means the address is not eligible to be the default router. Hosts use ineligible addresses to verify ICMP redirects.

For **routerdiscovery** to work, the hosts must have the **routerdiscovery** client software. It is part of **gated** and is configured by the **routerdiscovery** client statement.

The routerdiscovery client statement

routerdiscovery client yes | no | on | off [{
    traceoptions *trace_options* ;
    preference *preference* ;
    interface *interface_list*
        [enable | disable]

> [broadcast | multicast]
> [quiet | solicit] ; }] ;

The client uses the same trace options as the server. Other options are different, however. The full list of client options is:

preference *preference* ;

> Defines the preference of default routes learned from **routerdiscovery**. The default is 55. Unlike the server statement, this is **gated** preference.

interface *interface_list*

> Defines the interfaces used by **routerdiscovery**.

enable | disable

> Enables or disables **routerdiscovery** on the interface. **enable** is the default.

broadcast | multicast

> Specifies whether router solicitations should be broadcast or multicast on the interface. By default, router solicitations are multicast if it is supported; otherwise, router solicitations are broadcast. If the **multicast** keyword is specified and multicast is not available, the router solicitations are not sent. Generally, if these options are not specified, **gated** will do the right thing.

quiet | solicit

> Specifies whether router solicitations are sent on this interface. **solicit**, which is the default, sends router solicitations. **quiet** listens to Router Advertisements but does not send router solicitations.

The kernel Statement

kernel {
  options
     [nochange]
     [noflushatexit]
     [remnantholdtime *time*] ;
  routes *number* ;
  flash
     [limit *number*]
     [type **interface** | interior | all] ;
  background
     [limit *number*]
     [priority **flash** | higher | lower] ;
  traceoptions *trace_options* ; } ;

The **kernel** statement defines the interactions between **gated** and the kernel.

options

Defines three possible configuration options. These are:

nochange

Limits **gated** to deletes and adds. Use on early versions of the routing socket code that have a malfunctioning change operation.

noflushatexit

Prevents route deletions at shutdown. Normally shutdown processing deletes routes that do not have a "retain" indication. Use to speed startup on systems with thousands of routes.

remnantholddimte *time*

Defines the length of time routes read from the kernel forwarding table at startup are retained. The default is 3 minutes or as soon as they are over-ridden. *time* can be a value between 0 and 15 minutes. A 0 value causes the routes to be deleted immediately.

routes *number*

Defines the maximum number of routes **gated** will install in the kernel. By default there is no limit to the number of routes in the kernel forwarding table.

flash

Tunes the parameters used for flash updates. When routes change, the process of notifying the kernel is called a "flash update."

limit *number*

Sets the maximum number of routes processed during one flash update. The default is 20. A value of −1 causes all route changes to be processed. Large updates can slow the processing of "time critical" protocols. 20 is a good default.

type interface | interior | all

Specifies the type of routes processed during a flash update. By default, only interface routes are installed during a flash update. **interior** specifies that interior routes are also installed, and **all** specifies that interior and exterior routes should be processed. Specifying `flash limit -1 all` causes all routes to be installed during the flash update, which mimics the behavior of previous versions of **gated**.

background

Tunes the parameters used for background processing. Since only interface routes are normally installed during a flash update, most routes are processed in batches in the background.

limit *number*

Sets the number of routes processed in one batch. The default is 120.

priority flash | higher | lower

Sets the priority for processing batch updates. The default is **lower**, which means that batch updates are processed at a lower priority than flash updates. To process kernel updates at the same priority as flash updates, specify flash.

Many tracing options work for the kernel interface because, in many cases, it is handled as a routing protocol. The command-line trace, **symbols** and **iflist**, provide information about the kernel. The kernel statement trace options are:

remnants

Traces routes read from the kernel when **gated** starts.

request

Traces **gated** kernel Add/Delete/Change operations.

The remaining trace options only apply to systems that use the routing socket to exchange routing information with the kernel.

info

Traces informational messages received from the routing socket.

routes

Traces routes exchanged with the kernel.

redirect

Traces redirect messages received from the kernel.

interface

Traces interface status messages received from the kernel.

other

Traces any other messages received from the kernel.

static Statements

static statements define the static routes used by **gated**. A single **static** statement can specify several routes. The **static** statements occur after protocol statements and before control statements in the *gated.conf* file. To **gated**, static routes are any routes defined with **static** statements. However, unlike the routes in a static routing table, these routes can be overridden by routes with better preference values.

The structure of a **static** statement is:

static {
  [default] | [[host] *address* [mask *mask* | masklen *n*]] gateway *gateways*
    [interface *interface_list*]
    [preference *preference*]

```
    [retain]
    [reject]
    [blackhole]
    [noinstall] ;
address [mask mask  |  masklen n] interface interface
    [preference preference]
    [retain]
    [reject]
    [blackhole]
    [noinstall] ; } ;
```

The **static** statement has two different clauses. The one with the keyword **gateway** is the one you'll use. This clause contains information similar to that provided by the **route** command. A static route is defined as a destination address reached though a gateway. The format of this clause is:

[default] | [[host] *address* [mask *mask* | masklen *number*]] **gateway** *gateways*
Defines a static route through one or more gateways. The destination is defined by the keyword **default** (for the default route) or by a destination address. The destination address can be preceded by the keyword **host**, if it is a host address, or followed by an address mask. The address mask can be defined with the keyword **mask** and a dotted decimal address mask, or by the keyword **masklen** and a numeric prefix length. The listed gateways must be on a directly attached network. Possible configuration parameters are:

interface *interface_list*
When specified, gateways in the *gateway_list* must be directly reachable through one of these interfaces.

preference *preference*
Sets the **gated** preference for this static route. The default is 60.

retain
Prevents this static route from being removed during a graceful shutdown. Normally only interface routes are retained in the kernel forwarding table. Use this to provide some routing when **gated** is not running.

reject
Installs this route as a "reject route." Packets sent to a reject route are dropped and an "unreachable" message is sent back to the source. Not all kernels support reject routes.

blackhole
Installs this route as a "blackhole route." A blackhole route is the same as a reject route except the "unreachable" message is not sent.

noinstall
>   Instructs system to advertise this route via routing protocols but not to install it in the kernel forwarding table.

The other **static** statement clause uses the keyword **interface** instead of the keyword **gateway**. Use this clause only if you have a single physical network with more than one network address—a rare occurrence. **ifconfig** normally creates only one destination for each interface. This special form of the static statement adds additional destinations to the interface.

address [mask *mask* | masklen *number*] **interface** *interface*

The **preference, retain, reject, blackhole,** and **noinstall** options are the same as described above.

The default preference of a static route is 60, which prefers static routes over several other routing sources. If you want other types of routes to override static routes, use the **preference** argument on the **static** statement to increase the preference number. (Remember that high preference values mean less-preferred routes.)

The following example defines a static default route through the gateway 172.16.12.1. The preference is set to 125 so that routes learned from RIP are preferred over this static route:

```
static {
        default gateway 128.66.12.1 preference 125 ;
    } ;
```

Control Statements

The control statements define your routing policy. Often when administrators hear the terms "routing policy" or "policy-based routing," they assume that this is something done inside the routing protocol.

In reality, a routing policy is defined outside of the routing protocol in the configuration file. The policy defines what routes are accepted and what routes are advertsied. **gated** does this with two control statements: **import** and **export**. The **import** statement defines which routes are accepted and from what sources those routes are accepted. The **export** statement defines which routes are advertised based on the source of the routes and the protocol used to advertise them.

The **import** and **export** statements use **gated** preference, routing metrics, routing filters, and AS paths to define routing policy. Preference and metrics are controlled by these keywords:

restrict

Says that the routes are not to be imported, in the case of the import command, or exported in the case of the export command. This keyword blocks the use of a specific route.

preference *preference*

Defines the preference value used when comparing this route to other routes. Preference is used when installing routes; not when advertising routes.

metric *metric*

Specifies the metric used when advertising a route.

Route filters match routes by destination address. Among other places, route filters are used on martians and **import** and **export** statements. A route matches the most specific filter that applies. Specifying more than one filter with the same destination, mask, and modifiers generates an error. Import and export route filters can be specified in the following ways:*

address [mask *mask* | masklen *number*] [exact | refines]

Defines a range of addresses using an address and an address mask. The address mask can be defined with the keyword **mask** and a mask written in dotted decimal notation or with the keyword **masklen** and a numeric prefix length. If no mask is defined the natural mask of the network is used. Two options can be used:

exact

Matches a network, but no subnets or hosts of that network.

refines

Matches subnets and/or hosts of a network, but not the network itself.

all   Matches every possible address.

default

Matches only the default route.

host *address*

Matches an individual host address.

---

* Route filters may include additional parameters. On **import** statements they include a preference, and on **export** statements a metric. "Preference" and "metric" are described previously.

A routing filter that matches everything on network number 192.168.12.0 and the individual host 10.104.19.12 contains:

```
192.168.12.0 masklen 24 ;
host 10.104.19.12 ;
```

When no route filtering is specified in an **import** or **export** statement, all routes from the specfied source will match that statement. If any filters are specified, only routes that match the specified filters are imported or exported.

Border Gateway Protocol (BGP) is designed to support policy-based routing. A key feature of BGP is that it is a path-vector protocol. Import and export statements allow you to use the AS path vector to enforce your routing policy.

An AS path lists the autonomous systems end-to-end for a route, and provides an indication of the completeness of the path. Each autonomous system that a route passes through prepends its AS number to the beginning of the AS path.

The "origin" of the path indicates its completeness. An origin of **igp** indicates the route was learned from an interior routing protocol and is most likely complete. An origin of **egp** indicates the route was learned from an exterior routing protocol that does not support AS paths (EGP for example) and the path is most likely not complete.

When the path information is definitely not complete, an origin of **incomplete** is used. All of these origins can be specified in the **import** and **export** statements, and therefore used in your routing policy. The keyword **any** is used when the policy applies to all origins.

The AS path can also be used in the control statements by defining an AS path regular expression.* The AS path regular expression provides a pattern-matching syntax used to filter routes based on the autonomous system numbers in the AS paths associated with those routes.

An AS path regular expression is a regular expression composed of autonomous system numbers and special operators. Table B-1 lists the AS path operators. The AS path operator operates on an AS path term, which is an autonomous system number, a dot (.), which matches any autonomous system number, or a parentheses-enclosed subexpression.

---

* AS path regular expressions are defined in RFC 1164.

Table B-1: AS Path Operators

Symbol	Meaning
{m,n}	At least m and at most n repetitions.
{m}	Exactly m repetitions.
{m,}	m or more repetitions.
*	0 or more repetitions.
+	1 or more repetitions.
?	0 or 1 repetition.
aspath_term | aspath_term	Matches either the AS term on the left, or the AS term on the right.

A simple AS path regular expression might be:

```
import proto bgp aspath 164+ origin any restrict ;
```

This restricts all routes that have one or more occurrences of autonomous system number 164 in their path vector.

The import Statement

The format of an **import** statement varies depending on the source protocol. The format of the **import** statements for the exterior gateway protocols is:

import proto bgp | egp autonomoussystem *as_number*
    [restrict] |
    [[preference *preference*] {
    route_filter [restrict | (preference *preference*)]] ; } ;

import proto bgp aspath *aspath_regexp*
    origin any | igp | egp | incomplete
    [restrict] |
    [[preference *preference*] {
    route_filter [restrict | (preference *preference*)]] ; } ;

BGP and EGP importation may be controlled by autonomous system number. BGP also can control importation using AS path regular expressions. Routes that are rejected by the routing policy are stored in the routing table with a negative preference. A negative preference prevents a route from being installed in the forwarding table or exported to other protocols. Handling rejected routes in this manner alleviates the need to break and re-establish a session if routing policy changes during a reconfiguration.

The format of the import statements for the RIP, HELLO, and redirect protocols is:

import proto rip | hello | redirect
    [interface *interface_list* | **gateway** *gateway_list*]
    [restrict] |
    [[preference *preference*] {
    route_filter [restrict | (**preference** *preference*)]] ; } ;

This statement controls what routes are imported based on the source protocol, interface and gateway. The order of precedence is from the most general (protocol) to the most specific (gateway). Unlike BGP and EGP, these protocols do not save routes that were rejected because these protocols have short update intervals.

The **preference** option is not used with RIP or HELLO. RIP and HELLO don't use preference to choose between routes of the same protocol. They use the protocol metrics.

The format of the **import** statement for the OSPF protocol is:

import proto ospfase [**tag** *ospf_tag*] [restrict] |
    [[preference *preference*] {
    route_filter [restrict | (**preference** *preference*)]] ; } ;

Due to the nature of OSPF, only the importation of ASE routes can be controlled. Furthermore, it is only possible to restrict the importation of OSPF ASE routes when functioning as an AS border router. This requires you to specify an **export ospfase** statement in addition to the **import ospfase** statement. Specify an empty **export** statement to control importation of ASEs when no ASEs are being exported. (See the following section, "The export Statement.") If a tag is specified, the **import** statement only applies to routes with the tag. OSPF ASE routes that are rejected by policy are stored in the table with a negative preference.

OSPF routes are imported into the **gated** routing table with a preference of 10. Preference is not used to choose between OSPF ASE routes. OSPF costs are used for that purpose.

The export Statement

The syntax of the **export** statement is similar to the syntax of the **import** statement and the meaning of many of the parameters is identical. An important difference between the two statements is that while route importation is controlled by source information, route exportation is controlled by both source and destination. Thus **export** statements define where the routes will be sent and where they originated. The destination of the route advertisement is defined by the `proto` clause at the beginning of the **export** statement. The source of the routes is defined in the export list.

Each export statement varies slightly for each protocol. To advertise routes via EGP and BGP, use this syntax:

export proto bgp | **egp as** *as_number*
    [restrict] |
    [[metric *metric*] {
    export_list ; }] ;

Routes are exported via EGP and BGP to the specified autonomous system. **restrict** blocks exports to the AS. Valid BGP or EGP metrics can be specified. If no export list is defined, only the direct routes of the attached interfaces are exported. If an export list is used, it must explicitly specify everything that should be exported.

To advertise routes via RIP and HELLO, use this syntax:

export proto rip | **hello**
    [**interface** *interface_list* | **gateway** *gateway_list*]
    [restrict] |
    [[metric *metric*] {
    export_list ; }] ;

Routes exported by RIP and HELLO are sent via the specified protocol and can be sent through a specifc interface or to a specific gateway. Set *metric* if you plan to export static or internally generated default routes. The **metric** option is only used when exporting non-RIP routes via RIP or non-HELLO routes via HELLO.

If no export list is specified, RIP exports direct routes and RIP routes, and HELLO exports direct routes and HELLO routes. If an export list is used it must explicitly specify everything that should be exported.

To advertise routes via OSPF, use this syntax:

export proto osfpase [**type** 1 | 2] [**tag** *ospf_tag*]
    [restrict] |
    [[metric *metric*] {
    export_list ; }] ;

Only OSPF ASE routes can be exported by **gated**. There are two types of OSPF ASE routes, type 1 and type 2. They are described in Chapter 7 and earlier in this appendix. The default type is specified in the **ospf protocol** statement, but it can be overridden here. The *ospf_tag* is an arbitrary 32-bit number used to filter routing information. The default tag value is specified in the **ospf protocol** statement but it can be overridden here.

The source of the routes advertised by a protocol is defined by the export list. Each of the commands listed above contains an export list option. Just like those commands, the export list syntax varies depending on the source protocol of the routes. The commands described above define the protocols that are used to advertise the routes. The export lists shown below describe the protocols from which the routes are obtained. The biggest confusion caused by the export list syntax is that it is almost identical to the syntax shown above. In both cases we define protocols, autonomous systems, interfaces, gateways, and so on. In the first case we are defining the protocols, interfaces, etc., to which routes are sent, and in this case we define the protocols, interfaces, etc., from which routes are recieved.

To export routes learned from BGP and EGP, use this export list syntax:

export proto bgp | egp autonomoussystem *as_number*
    [restrict] |
    [[metric *metric*] {
    route_filter [restrict | metric *metric*] ; }] ;

This defines routes learned via BGP or EGP from a specific autonomous system. Routes can be restricted, or have a metric applied, based on matching the source AS number or the route filter.

When BGP is configured, **gated** assigns all routes an AS path. For interior routes, the AS path specifies **igp** as the origin and no autonomous systems in the AS path (the current AS is added when the route is exported). For EGP routes, the AS path specifies **egp** as the origin and the source AS as the AS path. For BGP routes, the AS path learned from BGP is used. If you run BGP, the export of all routes may be controlled by the AS path using this syntax:

proto *proto* | **all**
    aspath *aspath_regexp* **origin any** | **igp** | **egp** | **incomplete**
    [restrict] |
    [[metric *metric*] {
    route_filter [restrict | metric *metric*] ; }] ;

The source of the routes can be any one protocol (*proto*) or all (**all**) protocols. The importation of routes can be controlled by matching their AS paths against the AS path regular expression (*aspath_regexp*) or by matching their addresses against the *route_filter*. Route filters and AS path regular expressions are explained above.

To export routes learned from RIP and HELLO, use this export list syntax:

proto rip | **hello**
    [**interface** *interface_list* | **gateway** *gateway_list*]
    [restrict] |
    [[metric *metric*] {
    route_filter [restrict | metric *metric*] ; }] ;

The export of RIP and HELLO routes may be controlled by protocol, source interface, source gateway, or route filter.

To export routes learned from OSPF, use this export list syntax:

proto ospf | ospfase
    [restrict] |
    [[metric *metric*] {
    route_filter [restrict | metric *metric*] ; }] ;

The export of OSPF and OSPF ASE routes may be controlled by protocol and route filter. Exporting OSPF routes can also be controlled by *tag* using the syntax shown below:

proto proto | all tag *tag*
    [restrict] |
    [[metric *metric*] {
    route_filter [restrict | metric *metric*] ; }] ;

OSPF and RIP version 2 provide a tag field. For all other protocols, the tag is always 0. Routes may be selected based on the contents of the tag field.

There are other sources of routes that are not true routing protocols, and export lists can be defined for these sources. The two export lists for these sources are:

proto direct | static | kernel
    [interface *interface_list*]
    [restrict] |
    [[metric *metric*] {
    route_filter [restrict | metric *metric*] ; }] ;

The export of these routes can be controlled based on the source "protocol" and the source interface. The "protocols" in this case are routes to direct interfaces, static routes, or routes learned from the kernel.

proto default | aggregate
    [restrict] |
    [[metric *metric*] {
    route_filter [restrict | metric *metric*] ; }] ;

The export of these routes may only be controlled based on source "protocol." **default** refers to routes created by the **gendefault** option. **aggregate** refers to routes created by the aggregate statements, the topic of the next section.

The Aggregate Statements

Route aggregation is used by regional and national networks to reduce the number of routes advertised. With careful planning, large network providers can announce a few aggregate routes instead of hundreds of client network routes. Enabling aggregation is the main reason that CIDR blocks are allocated as contiguous address blocks.

Most of us don't have hundreds of routes to advertise. But we may have a classless address composed of a few class C address and we may need to tell **gated** how to handle it. Older versions of **gated** automatically generated an aggregate route to a natural network using the old Class A, B, and C concept; i.e., interface address 192.168.16.1 created a route to 192.168.16.0. With the advent of classless interdomain routing, this can be the wrong thing to do. **gated** does not aggregate routes unless it is explicitly configured with the aggregate statement:

aggregate default | address [mask *mask* | masklen *number*]
   [preference *preference*] [brief] {
  proto *proto*
     [as *as_number* | tag *tag* | aspath *aspath_regexp*]
     [restrict] |
     [[preference *preference*] {
     route_filter [restrict | (preference *preference*)]] ; } ;

Several options are available for the aggregate statement:

preference *preference;*
> Defines the preference of the resulting aggregate route. The default is 130.

brief
> Specifies that the AS path of the agregate route should be the longest common AS path. The default is to build an AS path consisting of all contributing AS paths.

proto *proto*
> Only aggregate routes learned from the specified protocol. The value of *proto* may be any currently configured protocol. This includes the "protocols" **direct**, **static**, and **kernel**, discussed in the previous section; **all** for all possible protocols; and **aggregate** for other route aggregations.

as *as_number*
> Only aggregate routes learned from the specified autonomous system.

tag *tag*
> Only aggregate routes with the specified tag.

aspath *aspath_regexp*
>   Only aggregate routes that match the specified AS path.

restrict
>   Indicates routes that are not to be aggregated.

Routes that match the route filters may contribute to the aggregate route. A route may only contribute to an aggregate route that is more general than itself. Any given route may only contribute to one aggregate route, but an aggregate route may contribute to a more general aggregate.

A slight variation of aggregation is the generation of a route based on the existence of certain conditions. The most common usage for this is to create a default based on the presence of a route from a peer on a neighboring backbone. This is done with the **generate** statement.

generate default | address [mask *mask* | masklen *number*]
>   [preference *preference*] {
>   proto *proto*
>   >   [as *as_number* | tag *tag* | aspath *aspath_regexp*]
>   >   [restrict] |
>   >   [[preference *preference*] {
>   >   *route_filter* [restrict | preference *preference*]] ;
>   } ; } ;

The **generate** statement uses many of the same options as the **aggregate** statement. These options are described earlier in this appendix.

A named Reference

This appendix provides detailed information about **named** syntax and the commands and files used to configure it. This is primarily a reference to use in conjunction with the tutorial information in Chapter 8, *Configuring DNS Name Service*. This information is useful to any domain administrator.

The named Command

The server side of DNS is run by the name server daemon, **named**. The syntax of the **named** command is:*

> named [–d *level*] [–p *port*[/*localport*]] [[–b] *bootfile*] [[–q] [[–r]

The three options used on the **named** command line are:

–d *level*

Logs debugging information in the file */usr/tmp/named.run*. The argument *level* is a number from 1 to 9. A higher *level* number increases the detail of the information logged, but even when *level* is set to 1, the *named.run* file grows very rapidly. Whenever you use debugging, keep an eye on the size of the *named.run* file and use SIGUSR2 to close and remove the file if it gets too large. Signal handling is covered in the next section.

It is not necessary to turn on debugging with the **–d** option to receive error messages from **named**. **named** displays error messages on the console and stores them in the *messages*, even if debugging is not specified. The **–d** option provides *additional* debugging information.

---

* Sun systems use **in.named** instead of **named**.

–p *port[/localport]*

Defines the UDP/TCP port used by **named.** *port* is the port number used to connect to the remote name server. *localport* is the number of the port on which the local name server daemon listens for connections. If the **–p** option is not specified, the standard port (53) is used. Since port 53 is a well-known port, changing the port number makes the name server inaccessible to standard software packages. Therefore, **–p** is only used for testing.

–b *bootfile*

Specifies the file **named** uses as its configuration file. By default the configuration file is */etc/named.boot,* but the **–b** option allows the administrator to choose another configuration file. Note that the **–b** is optional. As long as the filename used for *bootfile* doesn't start with a dash, the **–b** flag is not required. Any filename written on the **named** command line is assumed to be the boot file.

–q Logs all incoming queries. **named** must be compiled with the QRYLOG option set to enable this type of logging.

–r Turns off recursion. With this option set, the server will only provide answers for zones for which it is an authoritative server. It will not pursue the query through other servers or zones.

Signal Processing

named handles the following signals:

SIGHUP

Causes **named** to reread the *named.boot* file and reload the name server database. **named** then continues to run with the new configuration. This signal is particularly useful for forcing secondary servers to reload a database from the primary server. Normally the databases are downloaded from the primary server on a periodic basis. Using SIGHUP causes the reload to occur immediately.

SIGINT

Causes **named** to dump its cache to */usr/tmp/named_dump.db.* The dump file contains all of the domain information that the local name server knows. The file begins with the root servers, and marks off every domain under the root that the local server knows anything about. If you examine this file, you'll see that it shows a complete picture of the information the server has learned.

SIGUSR1

Turns on debugging; each subsequent SIGUSR1 signal increases the level of debugging. Debugging information is written to */usr/tmp/named.run* just as it is when the −**d** option is used on the **named** command line. Debugging does not have to be enabled with the −**d** option for the SIGUSR1 signal to work. SIGUSR1 allows debugging to be turned on when a problem is suspected, without stopping **named** and restarting it with the −**d** option.

SIGUSR2

Turns off debugging and closes */usr/tmp/named.run*. After issuing SIGUSR2, you can examine *named.run* or remove it if it is getting too large.

Optionally, some other signals can be handled by **named**. These additional signals require **named** to be compiled with the appropriate options to support the signals:

SIGABRT

Writes statistics data to */var/tmp/named.stats*. **named** must be compiled with −DSTATS for this signal to work.

SIGSYS

Writes profiling data into the */var/tmp* directory. **named** must be compiled with profiling to support this signal.

SIGTERM

Writes back the primary and secondary database files. This is used to save data modified by dynamic updates before the system is shut down. **named** must be compiled with dynamic updating enabled.

SIGWINCH

Toggles logging of all incoming queries via **syslogd**. **named** must be compiled with QRYLOG option to support this.

named.boot Configuration Commands

The */etc/named.boot* file defines the name server configuration and tells **named** where to obtain the name server database information. *named.boot* contains the following types of records:

directory *directory-path*

Defines a default directory used for all subsequent file references anywhere in the **named** configuration. If **named** is forced to dump memory, the memory dump is stored in this directory.

primary *domain-name file-name*

Declares the local name server as the primary master server for the domain specified by *domain-name*. As a primary server, the system loads the name server database from the local disk file specified by *name* in the *file-name* field.

secondary *domain-name* *server-address-list* *file-name*

> Makes the local server a secondary master server for the domain identified by *domain-name*. The *server-address-list* contains the IP address of at least one other master server for this domain. Multiple addresses can be provided in the list, but at least the primary server's address should be provided. The local server will try each server in the list until it successfully loads the name server database. The local server transfers the entire domain database and stores all of the data it receives in a local file identified by *file-name*. After completing the transfer, the local server answers all queries for information about the domain with complete authority.

cache . *file-name*

> The **cache** command points to the file used to initialize the name server cache with a list of root servers. This command starts with the keyword **cache**, followed by the name of the root domain (.), and ends with the name of the file that contains the root server list. This file can have any name you wish, but it is usually called *named.ca*, *named.root*, or *root.cache*. The **cache** command is included in every *named.boot* file. **named** needs the list of root servers as a starting point from which to locate all other DNS domains.

forwarders *server-address* *server-address* . . .

> The **forwarders** command provides **named** with a list of servers to try if it can't resolve a query from its own cache. In the syntax shown, *server-address* is the IP address of a server on your network that can perform a recursive name server query for the local host. (A recursive query* means that the remote server pursues the answer to the query, even if it does not have the answer itself, and returns the answer to the originator.) The servers listed on the **forwarders** command line (the servers are also called "forwarders") are tried in order until one responds to the query. The listed servers develop an extensive cache that benefits every host that uses them. Because of this, their use is often recommended. If you plan to use **forwarders**, your network administrator should define the list of forwarders for your network. The forwarders only develop a rich cache if they are used by several hosts.

slave

> The **slave** command forces the local server to use only the servers listed on the forwarders command line. The slave command can only be used if a **forwarders** command is also present in the *named.boot* file. A server that has a **slave** command in its *named.boot* file is called a *slave server*. A slave server does not attempt to contact the authoritative servers for a domain, even if the forwarding servers do not respond to its query. Regardless of the

---

* Chapter 3, *Network Services*, discusses recursive and nonrecursive name server queries.

circumstances, a slave server queries only the forwarders. The **slave** command is used when limited network access makes the forwarders the only servers that can be reached by the local host. The **slave** command is not used on systems that have full Internet access because it limits their flexibility.

sortlist *network network* . . .

The **sortlist** command causes **named** to prefer addresses from the listed networks over addresses from other networks. Normally, DNS sorts the addresses in a response only if the host issuing the query and the name server share a network. In that case, the shared network is the preferred network.

xfrnets *address[&mask]* . . .

The **xfrnets** command limits zone transfers to hosts with the specified *address*. The *address* is written in dotted decimal notation and is intepreted as a network address. The optional mask field is used to change the interpretation of the *address*. When a bit is on in the mask field, that bit is significant for determining which hosts will be allowed to receive a zone file transfer. For example, **xfrnets 172.16.0.0** allows every host on network 172.16 to do zone file transfers, while **xfrnets 172.16.12.3&255.255.255.255** limits zone file transfers to the single host 172.16.12.3.

For security reasons, many sites do not want to let everyone list all of the hostnames in their domain. **xfrnets** limits the ability to retrieve your entire domain to specific, trusted hosts. **tcplist** is an alternative form of this command maintained for compatibility with older server implementations.

include *file*

The **include** command includes the contents of *file* at the location that the command appears in the boot file. This command can be used for very large configurations that are maintained by different people.

bogusns *address address* . . .

The **bogusns** command prevents queries from being sent to the name server specified by *address*. *address* must be an IP address, not a domain name. This command is used to avoid cache contamination when you know that a remote name server is providing incorrect informatiom. **bogusns** is only a temporary fix placed in the boot file until the remote domain administrator has a chance to fix the real problem.

limit *name value*

The **limit** command changes BIND's internal quotas. *value* is a number that specifies the new quota setting. **k**, **m**, or **g**, for kilobytes, megabytes, and gigabytes, respectively, can be appended to the new quota value number as appropriate. *name* is the name of the quota being set. There are four possible values for *name*: **datasize** sets the process data size quota;* **transfers-in** sets the number of named transfer subprocesses that BIND may spawn at any one time; **transfers-per-ns** sets the maximum number of simultaneous zone transfers allowed to any one remote nameserver. There can be multiple limit commands in a boot file—one for each quota that is being set.

options *option option . . .*

The **options** command enables optional features of BIND. The *option* keywords are Booleans. Specifying an *option* on the command line turns on the optional behavior. By default, the optional features are turned off. Valid *option* values are: **query-log**—logs all queries via syslogd, which produces a very large amount of log data. **forward-only**—all queries are to be sent to the forwarders; this is exactly the same as the **slave** command, though this syntax is now preferred over the **slave** syntax. **fake-iquery**—the nameserver responds to inverse queries with a fake reply rather than an error; used if you have some clients that cannot properly handle the error. **no-recursion**—the name server answers a query for data only in a zone for which it is authoritative; all other queries are answered with a referral to another server. **no-fetch-glue**—the nameserver does not fetch missing glue records for a query response; the resulting response could be incomplete; it is used with **no-recursion** to limit cache growth and reduce the chance of cache corruption.

check-names *source action*

The **check-names** command tells the name server to check host names against the standards for hostnames defined in RFC 952, and to check non-hostname responses to make sure that they contain nothing but printable characters. The *source* is the source of the hostname or string data that is being checked. The *source* can be **primary** for the primary zone file; **secondary** for the secondary zone file, or **response** for the message received during recursive search. The *action* tells the name server what to do when an error is detected: **fail** (reject the data; do not load, cache, or forward it); **warn** (send an error message to the system log); or **ignore** (process the data as if no error occurred). Multiple **check-names** commands can appear in a boot file; one for each source of data. The action for each source can be different.

max-fetch *value*

The **max-fetch** command performs exactly the same function as the **limit transfers-in** command described previously. The **limit** command is now the preferred syntax.

---

* This is a kernel quota and therefore can be set only on systems that provide a kernel call to implement this.

At this writing, an experimental *named.boot* command is supported in some configurations:

stub *domain-name server-address-list file-name*

This command declares that this is a "stub" server for the domain specified by *domain-name*. The stub information is loaded from a server specified in the *server-address-list* and is stored in the file identified by *file-name*. The format of the **stub** command is the same as the **secondary** command and the functions of the fields in the command are the same. However, the **stub** command has very limited applicability. It is only used on a primary host that is not secondary for its subordinate domains. In that limited case, it is used to ensure that the primary host has the correct NS records for its subordinate domains.

There is a *named.boot* command that is no longer widely supported. You'll occasionally encounter descriptions of it in material written about name service, and for that reason it's discussed here. But don't use it in your configurations. It is:

domain *name*

This command functions in exactly the same way as the domain command used in the *resolv.conf* file. It is an obsolete command and may not be available in future releases of BIND. You don't need this command because the default domain name is easily defined in *resolv.conf.*

Zone File Records

Two types of entries are used to construct a zone file: *control entries* that simplify constructing the file, and *standard resource records* that define the domain data contained in the zone file. While there are several types of standard resource records, there are only two control statements. These are:

$INCLUDE *filename*

Identifies a file that contains data to be included in the zone file. The data in the included file must be valid control entries or standard resource records. $INCLUDE allows a large zone file to be divided into smaller, more manageable units.

The *filename* specified on the command line is relative to the directory named on the directory statement in the *named.boot* file. For example: if the *named.boot* file for *almond* contains a **directory /etc** statement, and a zone file on *almond* contains an **$INCLUDE sales.hosts** statement, then the file */etc/sales.hosts* would be included in that zone file. If you don't want the filename to be relative to that directory, specify a fully qualified name, such as */usr/dns/sales.hosts.*

$ORIGIN *domainname*

Changes the default domain name used by subsequent records in the zone file. Use this command to put more than one domain in a zone file. For example, an **$ORIGIN sales** statement in the *nuts.com* zone file sets the domain name to *sales.nuts.com*. All subsequent resource records would be relative to this new domain.

The **named** software uses **$ORIGIN** statements to organize its own information. Dumping the **named** database, with the SIGINT signal, produces a single file containing all the information that the server knows. This file, *named_dump.db*, contains many **$ORIGIN** entries used to place all of the domains that **named** knows about into a single file.

These two control entries are helpful for organizing and controlling the data in a zone file, but all of the actual database information comes from standard resource records. All of the files pointed to by *named.boot* contribute to the DNS database, so all of these files are constructed from standard resource records.

Standard Resource Records

The format of standard resource records, sometimes called RRs, is defined in RFC 1033, the *Domain Administrators Operations Guide*. The format is:

[*name*] [*ttl*] *class type data*

The individual fields in the standard resource record are:

name

This is the name of the object affected by this resource record. The named object can be as specific as an individual host, or as general as an entire domain. The string entered for *name* is relative to the current domain unless a fully qualified domain name is used.* Certain *name* values have special meaning. These are:

A blank name field denotes the current named object. The current name stays in force until a new name value is encountered in the name field. This permits multiple RRs to be applied to a single object without having to repeat the object's name for each record.

.. Two dots in the name field refer to the root domain. However, a single dot (the actual name of the root) also refers to the root domain, and is more commonly used.

---

* The FQDN must be specified all the way to the root; i.e., it must end with a dot.

@ A single at-sign (@) in the name field refers to the current origin. The origin is a domain name derived by the system from the current domain name or explicitly set by the system administrator using the **$ORIGIN** command.

* An asterisk in the name field is a wildcard character. It stands for a name composed of any string. It can be combined with a domain name or used alone. Used alone, an asterisk in the named field means that the resource record applies to objects with names composed of any string of characters plus the name of the current domain. Used with a domain name, the asterisk is relative to that domain. For example, *.bitnet. in the name field means any string plus the string .bitnet.

ttl
Time-to-live defines the length of time in seconds that the information in this resource record should be kept in the cache. *ttl* is specified as a numeric value up to eight characters in length. If no value is set for *ttl*, it defaults to the value defined for the entire zone file in the minimum field of the SOA record.

class
This field defines the address class of the resource record. The Internet address class is IN. All resource records used by Internet DNS have IN in this field, but it is possible for a zone file to hold non-Internet information. For example, information used by the Hesiod server, a name server developed at MIT, is identified by HS in the class field, and chaosnet information is identified by a CH in the class field. All resource records used in this book have an address class of IN.

type
This field indicates the type of data this record provides. For example, the A type RR provides the address of the host identified in the name field. All of the standard resource record types are discussed in this appendix.

data
This field contains the information specific to the resource record. The format and content of the data field vary according to the resource record type. The data field is the meat of the RR. For example, in an A record, the data field contains the IP address.

In addition to the special characters that have meaning in the name field, zone file records use these other special characters:

; The semicolon is the comment character. Use the semicolon to indicate that the remaining data on the line is a comment.

(   )

Parentheses are the continuation characters. Use parentheses to continue data beyond a single line. After an opening parenthesis, all data on subsequent lines is considered part of the current line until a closing parenthesis.

\x The backslash is an escape character. A non-numeric character following a backslash (\) is taken literally and any special meaning that the character may ordinarily have is ignored. For example, \; means a semicolon—not a comment.

\ddd

The backslash can also be followed by three decimal numbers. When the escape character is used in this manner the decimal numbers are interpreted as an absolute byte value. For example, \255 means the byte value 11111111.

The same general resource record format is used for each of the resource records in a zone file. Each resource record is described below.

Start of Authority record

The Start of Authority (SOA) record marks the beginning of a zone, and is usually the first record in a zone file. All of the records that follow are part of the zone declared by the SOA. Each zone has only one SOA record; the next SOA record encountered marks the beginning of another zone. Because a zone file is normally associated with a single zone, it normally contains only one SOA record.

The format of the SOA record is:

```
[zone][ttl] IN SOA origin contact (
      serial
              refresh
              retry
              expire
              minimum
      )
```

The components of the SOA record are:

zone

This is the name of the zone. Usually the SOA name field contains an at-sign (@). When used in an SOA record, the at-sign refers back to the domain name declared in the *named.boot* primary statement that points to this zone file.

ttl

Time-to-live is left blank on the SOA record.

IN   The address class is IN for all Internet RRs.

SOA

SOA is the resource record type. All the information that follows this is part of the data field and is specific to the SOA record.

origin

This is the hostname of the primary master server for this domain. It is normally written as a fully qualified domain name. For example, *almond* is the master server for *nuts.com*, so this field contains *almond.nuts.com.* in the SOA record for *nuts.com*.

contact

The email address of the person responsible for this domain is entered in this field. The address is modified slightly. The at-sign (@) that usually appears in an Internet email address is replaced by a dot. Therefore, if *david@almond.nuts.com* is the mailing address of the administrator of the *nuts.com* domain, the *nuts.com* SOA record contains *david.almond.nuts.com.* in the contact field.

serial

This is the version number of the zone file. It is an eight-digit numeric field usually entered as a simple number, e.g., 117. However, the composition of the number is up to the administrator. Some choose a format that shows the date the zone was updated, e.g., 92031100. Regardless of the format, the important thing is that the serial number must increase every time the data in the zone file is modified.

The serial field is extremely important. It is used by the secondary master servers to determine if the zone file has been updated. To make this determination, a secondary server requests the SOA record from the primary server and compares the serial number of the data it has stored to the serial number received from the primary server. If the serial number has increased, the secondary server requests a full zone transfer. Otherwise it assumes that it has the most current zone data. You must increment the serial number each time you update the zone data. If you don't, the new data will not be disseminated to the secondary servers.

refresh

This specifies the length of time that the secondary server should wait before checking with the primary server to see if the zone has been updated. Every *refresh* seconds, the secondary server checks the SOA serial number to see if the zone file needs to be reloaded. Secondary servers check the serial numbers of their zones whenever they restart or receive a SIGHUP signal. But it is important to keep the secondary server's database current with the primary server, so **named** does not rely on these unpredictable events. The `refresh` interval provides a predictable cycle for reloading the zone that is controlled by the domain administrator.

The value used in `refresh` is a number, up to eight digits long, that is the maximum number of seconds that the primary and secondary servers' databases can be out of sync. A low `refresh` value keeps the data on the servers closely synchronized, but a very low `refresh` value is not usually required. A value set lower than needed places an unnecessary burden on the network and the secondary servers. The value used in `refresh` should reflect the reality of how often your domain database is updated.

Most sites' domain databases are very stable. Systems are added periodically, but not generally on an hourly basis. When you are adding a new system, you can assign the hostname and address of that system before the system is operational. You can then install this information in the name server database before it is actually needed, ensuring that it is disseminated to the secondary servers long before it has to be used.

If extensive changes are planned, the `refresh` time can be temporarily reduced while the changes are underway. Therefore, you can normally set `refresh` time high, reducing load on the network and servers. Two (43200 seconds) to four (21600 seconds) times a day for `refresh` is adequate for many sites.

The process of retrieving the SOA record, evaluating the serial number and, if necessary, downloading the zone file is called a *zone refresh*. Thus the name *refresh* is used for this value.

`retry`

This defines how long secondary servers should wait before trying again if the primary server fails to respond to a request for a zone refresh. `retry` is specified in seconds and can be up to eight digits long.

You should not set the `retry` value too low. If a primary server fails to respond, the server or the network could be down. Quickly retrying a down system gains nothing and costs network resources. A secondary server that backs up a large number of zones can have problems when *retry* values are short. If the secondary server cannot reach the primary servers for several of its zones, it can become stuck in a retry loop.* Avoid problems; use an hour (3600) or a half hour (1800) for the *retry* value.

---

* The server may alternate between periods when it fails to respond and when it resolves queries, or it may display the error "too many open files."

expire

This defines how long the zone's data should be retained by the secondary servers without receiving a zone refresh. The value is specified in seconds and is up to eight digits long. If after *expire* seconds the secondary server has been unable to refresh this zone, it should discard all of the data.

expire is normally a very large value. 3600000 seconds (about 42 days) is commonly used. This says that if there has been no answer from the primary server to refresh requests repeated every *retry* seconds for the last 42 days, discard the data. 42 days is a good value.

minimum

This is the value used as the default ttl in all resource records where an explicit ttl value is not provided. This is a number, up to eight digits long, that specifies how many seconds resource records from this zone should be held in a remote host's cache.

Make this a large value. Most of the records in a zone remain unchanged for long periods of time. Hosts are added to a zone, but hostnames (if they are well chosen) and addresses are not frequently changed. Forcing remote servers to query again for data that has not changed, just because it had a short ttl, is a waste of resources. If you plan to change a record, put a short ttl on that record; don't set the entire zone to a short ttl by setting a low minimum. Use a short minimum only if the entire database is being replaced. Use at least a week (604800) for normal operation.

A sample SOA record for the *nuts.com* domain is:

```
@    IN  SOA   almond.nuts.com. david.almond.nuts.com. (
                92031101            ; serial
                43200              ; refresh twice a day
                3600               ; retry every hour
                3600000            ; expire after 1000 hours
                2419200            ; default ttl is one month
                )
```

Notice the serial number in this SOA. The serial number is in the format *yymmddvv*—where *yy* is the year, *mm* is the month, *dd* is the day, and *vv* is the version written that day. This type of serial number allows the administrator to track what day the zone was updated. Adding the version number allows for multiple updates in a single day. This zone file was created March 11, 1992, and it is the first update that day.

This SOA record also says that *almond* is the primary server for this zone and that the person responsible for this zone can be reached at the email address *david@almond.nuts.com*. The SOA tells the secondary servers to check the zone for changes twice a day and to retry every hour if they don't get an answer. If they retry a thousand times and never get an answer, they should discard the data for this zone. Finally, if an RR in this zone does not have an explicit *ttl*, it will default to 1 month.

Name server record

Name server (NS) resource records identify the authoritative servers for a zone. These records are the pointers that link the domain hierarchy together. NS records in the top-level domains point to the servers for the second-level domains, which in turn contain NS records that point to the servers for their subdomains. Name server records pointing to the servers for subordinate domains are required for these domains to be accessible. Without NS records, the servers for a domain would be unknown.

The format of the NS RR is:

[*domain*] [*ttl*] IN NS *server*

domain
> The name of the domain for which the host specified in the server field is an authoritative name server.

ttl
> Time-to-live is usually blank.

IN The address class is IN.

NS The name server resource record type is NS.

server
> The hostname of a computer that provides authoritative name service for this domain.

> Usually domains have at least one server that is located outside of the local domain. The server name cannot be specified relative to the local domain; it must be specified as a fully qualified domain name. To be consistent, many administrators use fully qualified names for all servers, even though it is not necessary for servers within the local domain.

Address record

The majority of the resource records in a *named.hosts* zone file* are address records. Address records are used to convert hostnames to IP addresses, which is the most common use of the DNS database.

---

* Chapter 8 describes the various **named** configuration files.

The address RR contains the following:

[*host*] [*ttl*] **IN A** *address*

host

> The name of the host whose address is provided in the data field of this record. Most often the hostname is written relative to the current domain.

ttl

> Time-to-live is usually blank.

IN The address class is IN.

A The address resource record type is A.

address

> The IP address of the host is written here in dotted decimal form, e.g., 128.66.12.2.

A *glue record* is a special type of address record. Most address records refer to hosts within the zone, but sometimes an address record needs to refer to a host in another zone. This is done to provide the address of a name server for a subordinate domain. Recall that the NS record for a subdomain server identifies the server by name. An address is needed to communicate with that server, so an A record must also be provided. The address record, combined with the name server record, links the domains together—thus the term "glue record."

Mail exchanger record

The mail exchanger (MX) record redirects mail to a mail server. It can redirect mail for an individual computer or an entire domain. MX records are extremely useful for domains that contain some systems that don't run mail software. Mail addressed to those systems can be redirected to computers that do run mail software. MX records are also used to simplify mail addressing by redirecting mail to servers that understand the simplified addresses.

The format of the MX RR is:

[*name*] [*ttl*] **IN MX** *preference host*

name

> The name of a host or domain to which the mail is addressed. Think of this as the value that occurs after the @ in a mailing address. Mail addressed to this name is sent to the mail server specified by the MX record's host field.

ttl

> Time-to-live is usually blank.

IN The address class is IN.

MX

The Mail Exchanger resource record type is MX.

preference

A host or domain may have more than one MX record associated with it. The preference field specifies the order in which the mail servers are tried. Servers with low preference numbers are tried first, so the most preferred server has a preference of 0. Preference values are usually assigned in increments of 5 or 10, so that new servers can be inserted between existing servers without editing the old MX records.

host

The name of the mail server to which mail is delivered when it is addressed to the host or domain identified in the name field.

Here is how MX records work. If a remote system understands how to use MX records and has mail to send to a host, it requests the host's MX records. DNS returns all of the MX records for the specified host. The remote server chooses the MX with the lowest preference value and attempts to deliver the mail to that server. If it cannot connect to that server, it will try each of the remaining servers in preference order until it can deliver the mail. If no MX records are returned by DNS, the remote server delivers the mail directly to the host to which the mail is addressed. MX records only define how to redirect mail. The remote system and the mail server perform all of the processing that actually delivers the mail.

Because the remote system will first try to use an MX record, many domain administrators include MX records for every host in the zone. Many of these MX records point right back to the host to which the mail is addressed, e.g., an MX for *almond* with a host field of *almond.nuts.com*. These records are used to reduce the processing load of the remote computer. A nice gesture!

An important use for MX records is to allow mail to non-Internet sites to be delivered using Internet-style addressing. MX records do this by redirecting the mail to computers that know how to deliver the mail to non-Internet networks. For example, sites using **uucp** can register an Internet domain name with UUNET. UUNET uses MX records to redirect Internet mail addressed to these non-connected sites to *uunet.uu.net*, which delivers the mail to its final destination via **uucp**.

Here are some MX examples. All of these examples are for the imaginary domain *nuts.com*. In the first example, mail addressed to *hazel.nuts.com* is redirected to *almond.nuts.com* with this MX record:

```
hazel        IN    MX    10 almond
```

The second example is an MX record used to simplify mail addressing. People can send mail to any user in this domain without knowing the specific computer that the user reads his mail on. Mail addressed to *user@nuts.com* is redirected by this MX record to *almond*, which is a mail server that knows how to deliver mail to every individual user in the domain.

```
nuts.com.   IN    MX    10 almond.nuts.com.
```

The last example is an MX record that redirects mail addressed to any *host* within the domain to a central mail server. Mail addressed to any host, *pecan.nuts.com*, *acorn.nuts.com*, or *anything.nuts.com*, is redirected to *almond*. This is the most common use of the wildcard character (*).

```
*.nuts.com.   IN    MX    10 almond.nuts.com.
```

In these examples, the *preference* is 10 so that a mail server with a lower preference number can be added to the zone without changing the existing MX record. Also notice that the host names in the first example are specified relative to the *nuts.com* domain, but the other names are not relative because they end in a dot. All of these names *could* have been entered as relative names, because they all are hosts in the *nuts.com* domain. Fully qualified names were used only to vary the examples. Finally, the wildcard MX record applies only to hosts that do not have a specific MX record. If the specific record for *hazel* is in the same configuration as the wildcard record, the wildcard MX does not apply to *hazel*.

Canonical Name record

The Canonical Name (CNAME) resource record defines an alias for the official name of a host. The CNAME record provides a facility similar to nicknames in the host table. The facility provides alternate host names for the convenience of users, and generic hostnames used by applications (such as *loghost* used by **syslogd**).

The CNAME record is frequently used to ease the transition from an old hostname to a new hostname. While it is best to avoid hostname changes by carefully choosing hostnames in the first place, not all changes can be avoided. When you do make a name change, it can take a long time before it becomes completely effective, particularly if the host name is embedded in a mailing list run at a remote site. To reduce problems for the remote site, use a CNAME record until they can make the change.

The format of the CNAME record is:

nickname [*ttl*] **IN CNAME** *host*

nickname
> This hostname is an alias for the official hostname defined in the *host* field. The *nickname* can be any valid hostname.

ttl

Time-to-live is usually blank.

IN The address class is IN.

CNAME

The Canonical Name resource record type is CNAME.

host

The canonical name of the host is provided here. This hostname must be the official hostname; it cannot be an alias.

One important thing to remember about the CNAME record is that all other resource records must be associated with the official hostname and not with the nickname. This means that the CNAME record should not be placed between a host and the list of RRs associated with that host. The example below shows a correctly placed CNAME record:

```
peanut      IN    A        128.66.12.2
            IN    MX       5 peanut.nuts.com.
            IN    HINFO    SUN-3/60 "SUN OS 4.0"
            IN    WKS      129.6.16.2 TCP ftp telnet smtp domain
            IN    WKS      128.66.12.2 UDP domain
goober      IN    CNAME    peanut.nuts.com.
```

In this example, the hostname *peanut* stays in force for the MX, HINFO, and WKS records because they all have blank name fields. The CNAME record changes the name field value to *goober*, which is a nickname for *peanut*. Any RRs with blank name fields following this CNAME record would associate themselves with the nickname *goober*, which is illegal. An improper CNAME placement is:

```
peanut      IN    A        128.66.12.2
goober      IN    CNAME    peanut.nuts.com.
            IN    MX       5 peanut.nuts.com.
            IN    HINFO    SUN-3/60 "SUN OS 4.0"
            IN    WKS      128.66.12.2 TCP ftp telnet smtp domain
            IN    WKS      128.66.12.2 UDP domain
```

This improperly placed CNAME record causes **named** to display the error message "goober.nuts.com has CNAME and other data (illegal)." Check */usr/adm/messages* for **named** error messages to ensure that you have not misplaced any CNAME records.

Domain Name Pointer record

The Domain Name Pointer (PTR) resource records are used to convert numeric IP addresses to hostnames. This is the opposite of what is done by the address record that converts hostnames to addresses. PTR records are used to construct the *in-addr.arpa* reverse domain files.

Many administrators ignore the reverse domains, because things appear to run fine without them. Don't ignore them. Keep these zones up-to-date. Several programs use the reverse domains to map IP addresses to hostnames when preparing status displays. A good example is the **netstat** command. Some service providers—*ftp.uu.net* is the best example—use the reverse domains to track who is using their service. If they cannot map your IP address back to a hostname, they reject your connection.

The format of the PTR record is:

name [*ttl*] **IN PTR** *host*

name

> The *name* specified here is actually a number. The number is defined relative to the current *in-addr.arpa* domain. Names in an *in-addr.arpa* domain are IP addresses specified in reverse order. If the current domain is *66.128.in-addr.arpa*, then the name field for *peanut* (128.66.12.2) is 2.12. These digits (2.12) are added to the current domain (*66.128.in-addr.arpa*) to make the name *2.12.66.128.in-addr.arpa*. Chapter 4, *Getting Started*, discusses the unique structure of *in-addr.arpa* domain names.

ttl

> Time-to-live is usually blank.

IN The address class is IN.

PTR

> The Domain Name Pointer resource record type is PTR.

host

> This is the fully qualified domain name of the computer whose address is specified in the name field. The host must be specified as a fully qualified name because the name cannot be relative to the current *in-addr.arpa* domain.

There are many examples of PTR records in the sample *named.rev* file shown in Chapter 8.

Host Information record

The Host Information (HINFO) resource record provides a short description of the hardware and operating system used by a specific host. The hardware and software are described using standard terminology defined in the *Assigned Numbers* RFC in the sections on *Machine Names* (hardware) and *System Names* (software). There are a large number of hardware and software designators listed in the RFC. Most name use the same general format. Names with embedded blanks must be enclosed in quotes, so some names have a dash (–) where you might expect a blank. A machine name is usually the manufacturer's name in uppercase letters separated from the model number by a dash; e.g., IBM–PC/AT or SUN–3/60. The system name is usually the manufacturer's operating system name written in uppercase letters; e.g., DOS or "SUN OS 4.0." Naturally the rapid changes in the computer market constantly make the data in the *Assigned Numbers* RFC out-of-date. Because of this, many administrators make up their own values for machine names and system names.

The format of the HINFO record is:

[*host*] [*ttl*] **IN HINFO** *hardware software*

host

> The hostname of the computer whose hardware and software is described in the data section of this resource record.

ttl

> Time-to-live is usually blank.

IN The address class is IN.

HINFO

> HINFO is the resource record type. All of the information that follows is part of the HINFO data field.

hardware

> This field identifies the hardware used by this host. It contains the machine name defined in the *Assigned Numbers* RFC. This field must be enclosed in quotes if it contains any blanks. A single blank space separates the hardware field from the software field that follows it.

software

> This field identifies the operating system software this host runs. It contains the system name defined for this operating system in the *Assigned Numbers* RFC. Use quotes if the system name contains any blanks.

No widely used application makes use of the HINFO record; the record just provides information. Some security-conscious sites discourage its use. They fear that this additional information helps intruders narrow their attacks to the specific hardware and operating system that they wish to crack.

Well-Known Services record

The Well-Known Services (WKS) resource record names the network services supported by the specified host. The official protocol names and services names used on the WKS record are defined in the *Assigned Numbers* RFC. The simplest way to list the names of the well-known services is to **cat** the */etc/services* file on your system. Each host can have no more than two WKS records; one record for TCP and one for UDP. Because several services are usually listed on the WKS record, each record may extend through multiple lines.

The format of the WKS record is:

[*host*] [*ttl*] IN WKS *address protocol services*

host

> The hostname of the computer that provides the advertised services.

ttl

> Time-to-live is usually blank.

IN   The address class is IN.

WKS

> The resource record type is WKS. All of the information that follows is variable information for the WKS record.

address

> The IP address of the host written in dotted decimal format, e.g., 128.66.12.2.

protocol

> The transport level protocol through which the service communicates—either TCP or UDP.

services

> The list of services provided by this host. As few or as many services as you choose may be advertised, but the names used to advertise the services must be the names found in the */etc/services* file. Items in the list of services are separated by spaces. Parentheses are used to continue the list beyond a single line.

There are no widely used applications that make use of this record. It is only used to provide general information about the system. Again, security-conscious sites may not wish to advertise all of their services. Some protocols, such as **tftp** and **finger**, are prime targets for intruders.

Text record

The Text (TXT) resource record holds string data. The text data can be in any format. There are no standard TCP/IP applications for processing TXT records. These records are used to provide free-form information about the named object. Some sites create local processes for TXT records and define a local format for the information. For example, a TXT record could hold the Ethernet address of a host at one site and a room number at another site.

The format of the TXT record is:

[*name*] [*ttl*] **IN TXT** *string*

name
> The name of the domain object with which the string data is associated.

ttl
> Time-to-live is usually blank.

IN The address class is IN.

TXT
> The resource record type is TXT.

string
> The *string* field contains text data enclosed in quotation marks.

A dhcpd Reference

This appendix covers the syntax of the **dhcpd** command and the *dhcpd.conf* configuration file. It is a reference to the Internet Software Consortium (ISC) Dynamic Host Configuration Protocol (DHCP) server, ISC **dhcpd**. To fully understand how to configure and use **dhcpd** in realistic network environments, see the tutorial and sample configuration files in Chapter 9, *Configuring Network Servers*.

dhcpd is under development. The information in this appendix is based on Beta Release 5 Patch Level 16. As a beta release, this software is bound to be upgraded and changed. Refer to the Web page *http://www.isc.org/dhcp.html* for the most recent information about **dhcpd**. And remember, a DHCP implementation from another vendor will probably be configured in a completely different manner.

Compiling dhcpd

The source code for **dhcpd** can be obtained through the ISC Web site at *www.isc.org* or via anonymous FTP at *ftp://ftp.isc.org/isc/dhcp*. The compressed **tar** file at the time of this writing was *DHCPD-BETA-5.16.tar.gz*, though this name will change as new versions are released. Download, gunzip, and untar the file:

```
> ftp ftp.isc.org
Connected to pub1.bryant.vix.com.
220 pub1.bryant.vix.com FTP server ready.
Name (ftp.isc.org:craig): anonymous
331 Guest login ok, send your complete email address as password.
Password:
230 Guest login ok, access restrictions apply.
ftp> cd isc/dhcp
250 CWD command successful.
ftp> binary
200 Type set to I.
ftp> get DHCPD-BETA-5.16.tar.gz
```

```
200 PORT command successful.
150 Opening BINARY mode data connection for DHCPD-BETA-5.16.tar.gz
226 Transfer complete.
181892 bytes received in 17 secs (10 Kbytes/sec)
ftp> quit
221 Goodbye.
> gunzip DHCPD-BETA-5.16.tar.gz
> tar -xvf DHCPD-BETA-5.16.tar
DHCPD-BETA-5.16/
DHCPD-BETA-5.16/cf/
DHCPD-BETA-5.16/cf/alphaosf.h
DHCPD-BETA-5.16/cf/bsdos.h
DHCPD-BETA-5.16/cf/freebsd.h
 .
 .
 .
DHCPD-BETA-5.16/includes/
DHCPD-BETA-5.16/includes/netinet/
DHCPD-BETA-5.16/includes/netinet/if_ether.h
DHCPD-BETA-5.16/includes/netinet/ip.h
DHCPD-BETA-5.16/includes/netinet/udp.h
```

Change to the newly created directory, DHCPD-BETA-5.16 in the example, and run **configure**. **configure** determines the type of UNIX system you're running and creates the correct Makefile for that system. If **configure** cannot determine what version of UNIX you're running, you must build your own Makefile by hand. Next, type **make** to compile the daemon. Finally, copy the daemon and the manpages to the correct directories:

```
# cd DHCPD-BETA-5.16
# configure
System Type: linux
# make
cc -g      -c dhcpd.c -o dhcpd.o
cc -g      -c dhcp.c -o dhcp.o
cc -g      -c bootp.c -o bootp.o
 .
 .
 .
nroff -man dhcpd.conf.5 >dhcpd.conf.cat5
# make install
```

The DHCP daemon should compile without errors. If you get compile errors or **configure** cannot determine your system configuration, you should consider abandoning the compile and notifying the support group. Join the support group mailing list by going to *http://www.fugue.com/dhcp*. Once you join, send mail to the *dhcp-server@fugue.com* mailing list describing your configuration and the exact problem you have. The list is read by most of the people using **dhcpd**. Someone may have already solved your problem.

Simply installing **dhcpd** may not be all that is required. Remember, **dhcpd** is beta software. Read the *README* file very carefully. **dhcpd** runs on a wide variety of systems, including OSF/1, most recent BSD derivatives, Solaris, and Linux. It runs best on OSF/1 and BSD. On other systems it may have some limitations. For example, on both Solaris and Linux it can support only one network interface. **dhcpd** also may require some system-specific configuration. Our sample Linux 2.0.0 system is an excellent example of this. To successfully run **dhcpd** we had to add the following entry to the */etc/hosts* table:

```
255.255.255.255                all-ones
```

And we had to add a specific route for the limited broadcast address, 255.255.255.255:

```
# route add -host all-ones dev eth0
```

To reinstall the limited broadcast address in the kernel routing table after each boot, we added the following code to the */etc/rc.d/rc.inet2* startup script:

```
# Install the limited broadcast route and start DHCP
if [ -f /etc/dhcpd.conf ]; then
  echo -n " dhcpd"
  route add -host all-ones dev eth0
  /usr/sbin/dhcpd
fi
```

The information needed to complete these extra configuration steps was clearly defined in the *README* file. Read it before you try to run **dhcpd**.

The dhcpd Command

The syntax of the **dhcpd** command is:

dhcpd [–p *port*] [–f] [–d] [–cf *config-file*] [–lf *lease-file*] [*if0* [... *ifn*]]

dhcpd usually is run without any command-line arguments. Most of the arguments are used only when testing and debugging. Two of the command-line arguments handle special configuration requirements:

–f Runs **dhcpd** in foreground mode. By default, **dhcpd** runs as a background daemon process. Use **–f** when **dhcpd** is started from *inittab* on a System V UNIX system.

if0 [... *ifn*]

Lists the interfaces on which **dhcpd** should listen for BOOTREQUEST packets. This is a whitespace-separated list of interface names. For example, dhcpd ec0 ec1 wd0 tells **dhcpd** to listen to interfaces ec0, ec1, and wd0. Normally this argument is not required. In most cases **dhcpd** locates all installed interfaces and eliminates the non-broadcast interfaces automatically. Use this argument only if it appears that **dhcpd** is failing to locate the correct interfaces.

All of the remaining command-line arguments are used for debugging or testing:

–p *port*

> Causes **dhcpd** to listen to a non-standard port. The well-known port for DHCP is 67. Changing it means that clients cannot talk to the server. On rare occasions this is done during testing.

–d Routes error messages to stderr. Normally error messages are written via syslog with facility set to DAEMON.

–cf *config-file*

> Causes **dhcpd** to read the configuration from the file identified by *config-file* instead of from *dhcpd.conf*. Use this only to test a new configuration before it is installed in *dhcpd.conf*. Use the standard file for production.

–lf *lease-file*

> Causes **dhcpd** to write the address lease information to the file identified by *lease-file* instead of to *dhcpd.leases*. Use this only for testing. Changing the name of the lease file could cause dynamic addresses to be misallocated. Use this argument with caution.

Kill the **dhcpd** daemon with the SIGTERM signal. The process ID (PID) of the **dhcpd** daemon is found in the */var/run/dhcpd.pid* file. For example:

```
# kill -TERM 'cat /var/run/dhcpd.pid'
```

dhcpd uses three files. **dhcpd** writes its PID to */var/run/dhcpd.pid*. It maintains a record of dynamic address leases in */var/db/dhcpd.leases*, and **dhcpd** reads its configuration from */etc/dhcpd.conf*. These last two files are created by you. Create an empty lease file before you run **dhcpd** the first time, e.g., *touch /var/db/dhcpd.leases*. Create a configuration and store it in *dhcpd.conf*.

The dhcpd.conf Configuration File

When it starts, **dhcpd** reads its configuration from the */etc/dhcpd.conf* file. *dhcpd.conf* defines the network being served by the DHCP server and the configuration information the server provides to its clients.

dhcpd.conf is an ASCII text file. Comments in the file begin with a sharp sign (#). Keywords are case-insensitive. Whitespace can be used to format the file. Related statements are enclosed in curly braces. IP address can be entered as numeric addresses or as hostnames that resolve to addresses.

Statements in the configuration file define the topology of the network being served. In the documentation these statements are called "declarations" because they declare something about the network topology. The statements that define the topology are: **server-identifier**, **shared-network**, **subnet**, **group**, and **host**. When used, there is only one server-identifier. All the other statements can appear multiple times in the configuration file. The statements define a hierarchical structure. The **shared-network** contains subnets, and subnets can contain hosts.

Parameters and options can be associated with each of these statements. Parameters define things about the server and the protocol, such as the length of time for an address lease or where the boot file is located. The options provide the clients with values for the standard DHCP configuration options defined by the RFCs: for example, whether the client should enable IP forwarding. Parameters and options specified outside of a specific topology statement apply to all networks served by this server. Those specified in the **group** statement apply to all of the shared networks, subnets or hosts grouped together by the statement. The **shared-network** statement options and parameters apply to all subnets on the shared network. **Subnet** options and parameters apply to everything on the subnet. **Host** options and parameters only apply to the individual host. Options applied at a general level can be overridden by the same option applied at a more specific level. **Subnet** options override global options and **host** options override **subnet** options. This structure allows the network administrator to define configuration information for the entire network and all of its parts.

In the following sections, we examine the syntax of all of the topology statements and of all the parameters and options that can be associated with them. We include many more parameters and options than you will ever use, and there is no need to study them all. Use this reference to look up the details of individual parameters and options when you need them. See Chapter 9 for examples of how these statements, parameters, and options are actually used in a real-world configuration.

Topology Statements

server-identifier *hostname*;

The **server-identifier** statement documents the IP address of the server. It is sometimes used at the start of the file as the first statement of a group of parameter statements and option statements that apply to every network served by this server. The documentation calls these "global parameters."

group {[*parameters*] [*options*]}

The **group** statement groups together **shared-network**, **subnet**, **host**, or other **group** statements to apply a set of parameters or options to all members of the group.

shared-network *name* {[*parameters*] [*options*]}

The **shared-network** statement is used only if more than one IP subnet shares the same physical network. In most cases, different subnets are on different physical networks. The *name*, which must be provided, can be any descriptive name. It is used only in debugging messages. Parameters and options associated with the shared network are declared within the curly braces and apply to all subnets in the shared network. The subnets in a shared network must be defined within the curly braces of the **shared-network** statement. It is assumed that each **shared-network** statement contains at least two subnet statements; otherwise there is no need to use the **shared-subnet** statement. **dhcpd** cannot tell on which subnet of a shared network a client should boot. Therefore, dynamically allocated addresses are taken from the available range of all subnets on the shared network and assigned as needed.

subnet *address* **mask** *netmask* { [*parameters*] [*options*]}

The **subnet** statement defines the IP address and address mask of every subnet the daemon will serve. The address and mask are used to identify the clients that belong to the subnet. The parameters and options defined within the curly braces apply to every client on the subnet. Every subnet physically connected to the server must have a **subnet** statement even if the subnet does not have any clients.

host *hostname* {[*parameters*] [*options*]}

The **host** statement defines parameters and options for individual clients. Every BOOTP client must have a **host** statement in the *dhcpd.conf* file. For DHCP clients, the **host** statement is optional. It is matched to an actual DHCP or BOOTP clients by matching the **dhcp-client-identifier** provided by the client or by matching the hardware parameter to the hardware address of the client. BOOTP clients do not provide a dhcp-client-identifier, so use the hardware address for BOOTP clients. DHCP clients can be identified by either the dhcp-client-identifier or the hardware address.

Configuration Parameters

The parameter statements defined in this section control the operation of the DHCP server and the DHCP protocol. The standard DHCP configuration values that are passed to clients are defined in option statements, which are covered in the next section. Some parameter statements can be associated with any of the topology statements discussed above. Others can only be used with specific statements. These are noted in the description of the parameter.

range [dynamic-bootp] *low-address* [*high-address*];

The **range** parameter defines the scope of addresses that are available for dynamic assignment by defining the lowest and highest IP addresses available for assignment. The **range** parameter must be associated with a **subnet** statement. All addresses in the scope of the **range** parameter must be in the subnet in which the **range** parameter is declared. The *dynamic-bootp* flag is specified if addresses may be automatically assigned to BOOTP clients as well as DHCP clients. The **range** parameter must be defined if you intend to use dynamic address assignment. If the **subnet** statement does not include a **range** parameter, dynamic address assignments are not made to clients on the subnet.

default-lease-time *seconds*;
> The life of an address lease in seconds that is used if the client does not request a specific lease length.

max-lease-time *seconds*;
> The maximum life of an address lease in seconds regardless of the lease length the client requests.

hardware *type address*;
> Defines a client's hardware address. At present, *type* must be either `ethernet` or `token-ring`. *address* must be an appropriate physical address for the type of hardware. The hardware parameter must be associated with a host statement. It is required for a BOOTP client to be recognized. It is optional for DHCP clients for which it is an alternative to the **dhcp-client-identifier** option.

filename *file*;
> Identifies the boot file for diskless clients. *file* is an ASCII string enclosed in quotation marks.

server-name *name*;
> The hostname of the DHCP server that is provided to the client. *name* is an ASCII string enclosed in quotation marks.

next-server *name*;
> The hostname or address of the server from which the boot file is to be loaded.

fixed-address *address*[, *address* ...];
> Assigns one or more fixed IP addresses to a host. The **fixed-address** parameter is valid only when associated with a host statement. If more than one address is supplied, the client is assigned the address that is valid for the subnet on which it is booting. If none of the addresses is valid for the subnet, no configuration data is sent to the client.

dynamic-bootp-lease-cutoff *date*;
> Sets a termination date for addresses assigned to BOOTP clients. BOOTP clients do not have a way of renewing leases and don't know that address leases expire. By default, **dhcpd** assigns permanent address to BOOTP clients.

This parameter changes that behavior. It is used only in special circumstances where the life of all systems is known in advance—for example, on a college campus where it is known that all student systems will be removed by June.

dynamic-bootp-lease-length *seconds*;
Defines the life of an address lease in seconds for an address automatically assigned to a BOOTP client. As noted above, BOOTP clients do not understand address leases. This parameter is used only in special circumstances where clients use a BOOTP boot PROM and run an operating system that supports DHCP. During the boot the client acts as a BOOTP client, but once it boots the client runs DHCP and knows how to renew a lease. Use this parameter, and the previous one, with caution.

boot-unknown-clients *flag*;
Tells **dhcpd** whether or not to dynamically assign addresses to unknown clients. If *flag* is "false," addresses are provided only to clients that have a host statement in the configuration file. By default, the flag is "true" and addresses are dynamically assigned to any client on a valid subnet.

get-lease-hostnames *flag*;
Tells **dhcpd** if it should send a DNS hostname to the client when it dynamically assigns it an IP address. If *flag* is "true," **dhcpd** uses DNS to look up the hostnames for all dynamically assigned addresses, which dramatically slows DHCP performance. By default the *flag* is "false" and no lookups are done.

use-host-decl-names *flag*;
Causes the name provided on the host statement to be supplied to the client as the hostname. If *flag* is "true," the hostname is supplied to the client. By default, the flag is "false."

DHCP Options

The option statements available with **dhcpd** cover all of the standard DHCP configuration options currently defined in the RFCs. Furthermore the syntax of the *dhcpd.conf* option statement is extensible. A new option can be identified by its decimal option code. All options are assigned a decimal option code, either in the RFC that describes the option or in the vendor documentation if it is vendor-specific. The value assigned to the new option can be expressed as a string enclosed in quotes or as a colon-separated list of hexadecimal numbers. Imagine that a new DHCP option is created and assigned an option code of 133. Further, imagine that the value carried by this option is a 16-bit binary mask and that you want your clients to "turn on" the high-order 4-bit and "turn off" all other bits in the mask. You could add the following option to your configuration:

```
option option-133 F0:00
```

All option statements begin with the keyword `option`. The keyword is then followed by the name of the option and the value assigned to the option, in that order. In the example above, the option name is in the form **option-*nnn***, where *nnn* is the decimal option code assigned to the option. In this manner any new option that appears can be added to *dhcpd.conf* file. The value assigned to this imaginary option is F000.

Looking at the huge list of standard options, you may well wonder if they will ever need to be extended. The standard options are listed in the following section. The types of values that are assigned to options are:

Address
>An IP address written in dotted decimal notation or a host name that resolves to an address

String
>A series of characters enclosed in quotation marks

Number
>A numeric value

Flag
>A switch containing either 1 or 0

In this book, the list of options is divided into "Commonly used options" and "Other options."

Commonly used options

option subnet-mask *mask*;
>Specifies the subnet mask in dotted decimal notation. If the subnet mask option is not provided, **dhcpd** uses the network mask from the **subnet** statement.

option time-offset *seconds*;
>Specifies the number of seconds this time zone is offset from Coordinated Universal Time (UTC).

option routers *address*[, *address* . . .];
>Lists the routers the client should use, in order of preference.

option domain-name-servers *address*[, *address* . . .];
>Lists the Domain Name System (DNS) name servers the client should use, in order of preference.

option lpr-servers *address* [, *address* . . .];
>Lists line printer (LPR) servers the client should use, in order of preference.

option host-name *host*;
> Defines the hostname the client should use.

option domain-name *domain*;
> Defines the domain name.

option interface-mtu *bytes*;
> Defines the MTU the client should use. The minimum legal value for the MTU is 68.

option broadcast-address *address*;
> Defines the broadcast address for the client's subnet.

option static-routes *destination gateway*[, *destination gateway*...];
> Lists the static routes the client should use. The default route cannot be specified in this manner. Use the routers option for the default route.

option trailer-encapsulation 0 | 1;
> Specifies if the client should use trailer encapsulation. See the discussion of trailer encapsulation in Chapter 6, *Configuring the Interface*. 0 means "no" the client shouldn't and 1 means "yes" the client should use trailer encapsulation.

option nis-domain *string*;
> A character string that defines the name of the Network Information Services (NIS) domain.

option nis-servers *address*[, *address*...];
> Lists IP addresses of the NIS servers the client should use, in order of preference.

option dhcp-client-identifier *string*;
> Used in the host statement to define the DHCP client identifier. **dhcpd** can use the client identifier to identify DHCP clients in lieu of the hardware address.

Other options

option time-servers *address*[, *address*...];
> Lists the time servers the client should use, in order of preference.

option ien116-name-servers *address*[, *address*...];
> Lists the IEN 116 name servers the client should use, in order of preference. IEN 116 is an obsolete name service. Avoid this and use DNS.

option log-servers *address*[, *address*...];
> Lists the MIT-LCS UDP log servers the client should use, in order of preference.

option cookie-servers *address*[, *address* . . .];

Lists the cookie servers available to the client, in order of preference.

option impress-servers *address*[, *address* . . .];

Lists the Image Impress servers available to the client, in order of preference.

option resource-location-servers *address*[, *address* . . .];

Lists the Resource Location servers the client should use, in order of preference.

option boot-size *blocks*;

The number of 512-octet blocks in boot file.

option merit-dump *path*;

path is a character string that identifies the location of the file the client should dump core to in the event of a crash.

option swap-server *address*;

Specifies the IP address of the client's swap server.

option root-path *path*;

path is a character string that identifies the location of the client's root disk.

option ip-forwarding 0 | 1;

Specifies if the client should do IP forwarding. 0 disables IP forwarding, and 1 enables it.

option non-local-source-routing 0 | 1;

Specifies if the client should allow non-local source routes. Source routes are a potential security problem as they can be used by intruders to route data off the local network in ways not intended by the local network administrator. 0 disables forwarding of non-local source routed datagrams, and 1 enables forwarding. 0 is the more secure setting.

option policy-filter *address mask*[, *address mask* . . .];

Lists the IP addresses and masks that specify the only valid destination/mask pairs for incoming source routes. Any source-routed datagram whose next-hop address does not match one of the filters is discarded by the client.

option max-dgram-reassembly *bytes*;

Defines, in bytes, the largest datagram the client should be prepared to reassemble. The value of *bytes* cannot be less than 576.

option default-ip-ttl *ttl* ;

Defines the default time-to-live (ttl) for outgoing datagrams. See the discussion of **traceroute** in Chapter 11, *Troubleshooting TCP/IP*, for information about ttl.

option path-mtu-aging-timeout *seconds*;

Set the number of seconds for timing out Path MTU values discovered by the mechanism defined in RFC 1191.

option path-mtu-plateau-table *bytes*[, *bytes* . . .];

Defines a table of MTU sizes to use when performing Path MTU Discovery as defined in RFC 1191. The minimum MTU value cannot be smaller than 68.

option all-subnets-local 0 | 1;

Tells the client if all subnets of the local network use the same MTU. 1 means that all subnets share the same MTU. 0 means that some subnets have smaller MTUs.

option perform-mask-discovery 0 | 1;

Specifies if the client should use ICMP to discover the subnet mask. 0 enables ICMP mask discovery, and 1 disables it. Because the DHCP server can provide the correct subnet mask, ICMP mask discovery is rarely used on networks that have a DHCP server.

option mask-supplier 0 | 1;

Specifies if the client should respond to ICMP subnet mask requests. 0 means "no" and 1 means "yes" it should respond.

option router-discovery 0 | 1;

Specifies if the client should use the Router Discovery mechanism defined in RFC 1256 to locate routers. 0 means "no" it shouldn't, and 1 means "yes" the client should perform router discovery. Because the DHCP server provides the correct list of routers, router discovery is rarely used on networks that have a DHCP server.

option router-solicitation-address *address*;

Defines the address to which the client should transmit a router solicitation request if router discovery is enabled.

option arp-cache-timeout *seconds*;

Defines the number of seconds entries are maintained in the ARP cache.

option ieee802-3-encapsulation 0 | 1;

Specifies if the client should use Ethernet II (DIX) or IEEE 802.3 Ethernet encapsulation on the network. 0 tells the client to use Ethernet II and 1 tells the client to use IEEE 802.3 encapsulation.

option default-tcp-ttl *ttl*;

Defines the default TTL for TCP segments. Possible values are 1 to 255.

option tcp-keepalive-interval *seconds*;

The number of seconds TCP should wait before sending a keepalive message.

0 means that TCP should not generate keepalive messages. Keepalive messages are generally discouraged.

option tcp-keepalive-garbage 0 | 1;

Specifies if the client should send TCP keepalive messages with an octet of garbage for compatibility with older implementations. 0 means don't send a garbage octet and 1 means send it. Keepalives are generally discouraged.

option ntp-servers *address*[, *address* . . .];

Lists the IP addresses of the Network Time Protocol (NTP) servers the client should use, in order of preference.

option netbios-name-servers *address*[, *address* . . .];

Lists the NetBIOS name servers (NBNS) the client should use, in order of preference.

option netbios-dd-server *address*[, *address* . . .];

Lists the NetBIOS datagram distribution servers (NBDD) the client should use, in order of preference.

option netbios-node-type *type*;

Defines the NetBIOS node type of the client. A *type* of 1 is a NetBIOS B-node; 2 is a P-node; 4 is an M-node; 8 is an H-node.

option netbios-scope *string*;

A character string that defines the NetBIOS over TCP/IP scope parameter as specified in RFC 1001/1002.

option font-servers *address*[, *address* . . .];

Lists the X Window System Font servers the client should use, in order of preference.

option x-display-manager *address*[, *address* . . .];

Lists the systems running the X Window System Display Manager that the client should use, in order of preference.

E

A sendmail Reference

In this appendix:
- *Compiling sendmail*
- *The sendmail Command*
- *m4 sendmail Macros*
- *More sendmail.cf*
- *Sample Configurations*

This appendix provides details of the syntax of the **sendmail** command, of the *sendmail.cf* file, and of the **m4** macros that can be used to build that file. It also contains excerpts of the sample *sendmail.cf* file described in Chapter 10, *sendmail*. It describes where to obtain the latest source code for sendmail and how to compile it. This appendix is a reference, not a tutorial. Refer to Chapter 10 for a tutorial on sendmail configuration.

We start the appendix with information on locating, downloading, and compiling the latest version of sendmail.

Compiling sendmail

The source code for sendmail is available via anonymous ftp from *ftp.sendmail.org*, where it is stored in the *pub/sendmail* directory. When you change to that directory, an information message tells you about the latest version of sendmail. sendmail is updated constantly. The following examples are based on sendmail V8.8.5. Remember that things will change for future releases. Always read the README files and installation documents that come with new software before beginning an installation.

Download the compressed sendmail **tar** file as a binary file. Uncompress and untar it. Change to the *src* directory in the sendmail directory created by the **tar** file and enter:

```
sh makesendmail
```

According to the documentation, this is all you need to do on most systems. This certainly works on BSD 4.4–based systems. However, it does not work on every system. The two systems used for examples in this book, Solaris 2.5.1 and Slackware 96 Linux, both have problems. The problem with Solaris is that it does not have a C compiler. Before even attempting to install sendmail you must download and install the GNU C compiler, **gcc**. The problem with Slackware is more subtle. Different versions of Linux place files in different locations in the filesystem. Let's look at the details of installing sendmail V8.8.5 on a Slackware 96 system.

First we download the **tar** file and put the sendmail source files into the */usr/src* directory where Slackware 96 keeps various source files:

```
# ftp ftp.sendmail.org
Connected to kohler.CS.Berkeley.EDU.
220 kohler.CS.Berkeley.EDU FTP server ready.
Name (ftp.cs.berkeley.edu:craig): anonymous
331 Guest login ok, send your complete email address as password.
Password: craig@nuts.com
230 Guest login ok, access restrictions apply.
ftp> cd pub/sendmail
250 CWD command successful.
ftp> binary
200 Type set to I.
ftp> get sendmail.8.8.5.tar.gz
200 PORT command successful.
150 Opening BINARY mode data connection.
226 Transfer complete.
992815 bytes received in 187 secs (5.2 Kbytes/sec)
ftp> quit
221 Goodbye.
# gunzip sendmail.8.8.5.tar.gz
# cp sendmail.8.8.5.tar /usr/src
# cd /usr/src
# tar -xvf sendmail.8.8.5.tar
```

Next we run **makesendmail**.

```
# cd sendmail-8.8.5/src
# ./makesendmail
Configuration: os=Linux, rel=2.0.0, rbase=2, rroot=2.0, arch=i586, sfx=
Creating obj.Linux.2.0.0.i586 using Makefile.Linux
Making dependencies in obj.Linux.2.0.0.i586
make: Nothing to be done for 'depend'.
Making in obj.Linux.2.0.0.i586
cc -I. -O -I/usr/local/include -DNDBM -DNEWDB    -c alias.c -o alias.o
cc -I. -O -I/usr/local/include -DNDBM -DNEWDB    -c map.c -o map.o
map.c:42: ndbm.h: No such file or directory
make: *** [map.o] Error 1
```

makesendmail recognizes this is a Linux system, but the Makefile it selects is obviously not correct for the Slackware 96 variant of Linux. All of the Makefiles that **makesendmail** uses are located in the *src/Makefiles* subdirectory. Two of those files, *Makefile.Linux* and *Makefile.Linux.ppc*, are designed for Linux. The *Make-*

file.Linux.ppc is a possible solution to our problem. Move it to *Makefile.Linux* and rerun **makesendmail**:

```
# cd Makefiles
# mv Makefile.Linux Makefile.Linux.orig
# cp Makefile.Linux.ppc Makefile.Linux
# cd ..
# touch *
# ./makesendmail
Configuration: os=Linux, rel=2.0.0, rbase=2, rroot=2.0, arch=i586, sfx=
Making in obj.Linux.2.0.0.i586
cc -I. -O -I/usr/local/include -DNEWDB    -c alias.c -o alias.o
cc -I. -O -I/usr/local/include -DNEWDB    -c version.c -o version.o
cc -o sendmail alias.o ... version.o  -L/usr/local/lib -ldb
groff -Tascii -mandoc aliases.5 > aliases.0
groff -Tascii -mandoc sendmail.8 > sendmail.0
```

That's more like it! sendmail compiled and linked without problems.

A quick look at the differences in the two Makefiles shows that only four lines have been changed. Of those four lines, only two, DBMDEF and LIBS, were actually needed to successfully compile sendmail. Possible values for the database definition (DBMDEF) are shown in Table E-1.

Table E-1: DBMDEF Database Arguments

Argument	Function
NDBM	The dbm format from BSD 4.3 accessed with ndbm(3).
NEWDB	The new BSD 4.4 database format accessed with db(3).
NIS	Sun NIS.
NISPLUS	Sun NIS+.
NETINFO	NeXT's NetInfo.
HESIOD	MIT's Hesiod server.
LDAPMAP	X500 LDAP lookups.

The error displayed by the first **./makesendmail** run stated that *ndbm.h* was not found. This indicates that the NDBM argument on the DBMDEF line is the likely culprit. Further, the comments in the *Makefile.Linux* file recommend using DNEWDB and the ldb library. This suggests that a possible solution is to change DBMDEF to **DBMDEF= -DNEWDB** and LIBS to **LIBS= -ldb**. This is exactly what Paul DuBois did when he created the *Makefile.Linux.ppc* file, and it is what allows sendmail to compile on a Slackware 96 system.

He also changed two other lines, neither of which is critical to the compile, but both of which are indicative of the type of things customized in a Makefile. Paul changed the STDIR variable that defines where the *sendmail.st* file is stored to **STDIR= ${DESTDIR}/var/log**. The location of files is the most commonly modified information in a makefile. He also changed BINGRP to **BINGRP= mail** to use the *mail* group defined by the Slackware 96 system as the group ID for the sendmail binary files.

Once sendmail compiles, it is installed with the following command:

```
# ./makesendmail install
```

One other thing that should be checked before declaring the installation complete is the **makemap** command. This is the command that builds the databases read by sendmail. Given the fact that sendmail encountered trouble while compiling certain types of database support, we are suspicious that compiling makemap will have similar problems.

First change to the *sendmail-8.8.5/makemap* directory and look at the two makefiles located there. One of them, *Makefile.dist*, is the type of makefile supported by Slackware Linux. Copy *Makefile.dist* to Makefile and attempt a compile of makemap:

```
# cd ../makemap
# mv Makefile Makefile.orig
# cp Makefile.dist Makefile
# make
cc -I. -O -I../src -I/usr/sww/include -DNDBM -DNEWDB    -c makemap.c
    -o makemap.o
makemap.c:53: ndbm.h: No such file or directory
make: *** [makemap.o] Error 1
```

Just as we suspected! makemap has the same compile problem as sendmail. Luckily, Paul DuBois's solution to the sendmail problem shows us the changes needed for the DBMDEF and LIBS variables. Additionally, we check all of the directory paths in the Makefile to ensure they are valid for a Slackware 96 system:

```
# grep -v '^#' Makefile | grep '/'
SRCDIR= ../src
INCDIRS=-I${SRCDIR} -I/usr/sww/include
LIBDIRS=-L/usr/sww/lib
BINDIR= ${DESTDIR}/usr/sbin
LINKS= ${DESTDIR}/usr/ucb/newaliases ${DESTDIR}/usr/ucb/mailq
${OBJS}: ${SRCDIR}/conf.h
# ls /usr/sww
ls: /usr/sww: No such file or directory
# ls /usr/ucb
ls: /usr/ucb: No such file or directory
# whereis makemap
makemap: /usr/sbin/makemap
# whereis newaliases
newaliases: /usr/bin/newaliases
# whereis mailq
mailq: /usr/bin/mailq
```

These tests show that, in addition to Paul DuBois's corrections, we need to remove references to the non-existent */usr/sww* and */usr/ucb* directories and insert references to */usr/bin* where **mailq** and **newaliases** really reside. After we make these changes, a **diff** shows the new Makefile code and a rerun of **make** shows that we have fixed the problem:

```
# diff Makefile.dist Makefile
22c22
< DBMDEF=        -DNDBM -DNEWDB
---
> DBMDEF=        -DNEWDB
30c30
< INCDIRS=-I${SRCDIR} -I/usr/sww/include
---
> INCDIRS=-I${SRCDIR}
36c36
< LIBDIRS=-L/usr/sww/lib
---
> LIBDIRS=
39c39
< LIBS= -ldb -ldbm
---
> LIBS= -ldb
53c53
< LINKS=         ${DESTDIR}/usr/ucb/newaliases ${DESTDIR}/usr/ucb/mailq
---
> LINKS=         ${DESTDIR}/usr/bin/newaliases ${DESTDIR}/usr/bin/mailq
# make
cc -I. -O -I../src -DNEWDB    -c makemap.c -o makemap.o
cc -o makemap  makemap.o   -ldb
```

Run **make install** to install the new version of makemap. We're finished. Compiling sendmail wasn't as easy as the documentation implies, but wasn't impossible.

sendmail is now ready to run. The next section describes the syntax of the **sendmail** command.

The sendmail Command

The syntax of the **sendmail** command is deceptively simple:

sendmail [*arguments*] [*address* ...]

The syntax is deceptive because it hides the fact that there are a very large number of command-line arguments. Table E-2 lists all of them.

Table E-2: sendmail Command-Line Arguments

Argument	Function
–U	Indicate initial user submission.
–V*envid*	Set the envelope ID to *envid*.
–N*dsn*	Set delivery status notification to *dsn*.
–M*xvalue*	Set macro *x* to *value*.
–R*return*	Set the part of the message returned with an error.
–B*type*	Set the MIME body type.
–p*protocol*	Set the receiving protocol and hostname.
–X*logfile*	Log all traffic in the indicated log file.
–f*addr*	Sender's machine address is *addr*.
–r *addr*	Obsolete form of –f.
–h *cnt*	Drop mail if forwarded *cnt* times.
–F*name*	Set the full name of this user to *name*.
–n	Don't do aliasing or forwarding.
–t	Send to everyone listed in To:, Cc:, and Bcc:.
–bm	Deliver mail (default).
–ba	Run in arpanet mode.
–bs	Speak SMTP on input side.
–bd	Run as a daemon.
–bt	Run in test mode.
–bv	Verify addresses; don't collect or deliver mail.
–bi	Initialize the alias database.
–bp	Print the mail queue.
–q[*time*]	Process queued mail. Repeat at interval *time*.
–C*file*	Use *file* as the configuration file.
–d*level*	Set debugging level.
–o*xvalue*	Set option *x* to the specified *value*.
–i	Ignore dots in incoming messages.
–m	Send to me, too.
–v	Run in verbose mode.
–s*addr*	Alternate form of –f.

Several of the command-line arguments are covered in Chapter 10. These are:

–f Allows trusted users to override the sender address on outgoing messages. For security reasons, it is disabled on some systems. Obsolete alternative forms of this argument are –r and –s.

–t Reads the To:, Cc: and Bcc: headers from standard input. Used to send a file that contains these headers or when typing in a test message, as in Chapter 10.

–bd

Runs sendmail in background mode, causing it to collect incoming mail. Use this argument on the **sendmail** command in the boot script.

–bt

Used to test sendmail address rewrite rules.

–bi

Initializes the aliases database. This is the same as the **newaliases** command covered in Chapter 10.

–q Sets the time interval at which the mail queue is processed. Use on the **send-mail** command in the boot script.

–C Loads an alternative sendmail configuration file. Use this to test the configuration before moving the new file to *sendmail.cf.*

–v Permits you to view the exchange of SMTP commands in real time.

–bv

Verifies address processing without actually sending mail.

Other than the two arguments (**–bd** and **–q**) used on the **sendmail** command line in the boot script to process incoming mail, the most common use for **sendmail** arguments is debugging. From the list above, **–bt**, **–C**, **–bv**, **–v**, and **–t** are all used in Chapter 10 in debugging examples. Other debugging arguments are:

–bp

Prints a list of mail that is queued for delivery. It is the same as the **mailq** command. Mail is queued when it cannot be delivered immediately because the remote host is temporarily unable to accept the mail. sendmail periodically processes the queue, based on the time interval you set with the **–q** argument, and attempts to deliver the mail in the queue. The queue can grow large enough to impede sendmail's performance if an important remote host is down. **mailq** shows how many items are queued as well as the source and destination of each piece of mail.

When the queue requires immediate processing, invoke **sendmail** using **–q** with no time interval. This processes the entire queue. Some variations of the **–q** argument allow you to selectively process the queue. Use **–qI***queue-id* to process only those queue entries with the specified queue identifier; **–qR***recip-ient* to process only items being sent to the specified recipient; or **–qS***sender* to process only mail sent from the specified sender. The **mailq** command displays the queue identifier, sender address, and recipient address for every item in the queue.

–o Sets a sendmail option for this one instantiation of sendmail, e.g., -oA/tmp/test-**aliases**. Use this argument to test alternative option settings without editing the *sendmail.cf* file. **–o** uses the old sendmail option syntax. An alternate form of the argument is **–O**, which uses the new option syntax, e.g., -OAlias-**File=/tmp/test-aliases**. See *sendmail Options* later in this Appendix.

−d Sets the level of detail displayed when debugging sendmail code. Can be used to debug rewrite rules, e.g., `sendmail -bt -d21.12`. Otherwise **−d** is only useful for sendmail source code debugging.

−h Sets the counter used to determine if mail is looping. By default, it is set to 30, which is a good operational value. When you are debugging a mail loop problem, set the hop count lower, e.g., **−h10**, to reduce the number of times a piece of mail is handled by the system. Otherwise, leave this value alone.

The remaining arguments are rarely used on the command line:

−B Indicates the MIME message body type. Acceptable values are either 7BIT or 8BITMIME.

−N

Requests that the sender be notified of the delivery status of the mail. The default value is FAILURE, DELAY, which notifies the sender when mail delivery fails or is delayed in the queue. Other acceptable values are NEVER, to request that no status notifications be returned to the sender, and SUCCESS, to request notification of successful mail delivery.

−M

Sets a macro value for this instantiation of sendmail. For example, **−MMnuts.com** sets macro M to *nuts.com*.

−p Sets the sending protocol and the sending host. This is equivalent to setting the internal **s** and **r** macros. If a system has more than one external mail protocol, for example, UUCP and SMTP, this forces the system to use a specific protocol for this piece of mail.

−R Sets the amount of information returned to the sender when a message cannot be delivered. This can be either HDRS for headers-only or FULL for the headers and the full message body.

−U Indicates that this mail comes directly from a user interface and was not forwarded from a remote mail handler. At this writing this argument is not yet used, but in the future user agent programs may include it when they pass mail to sendmail.

−V Inserts an "envelop id" into the outbound message that is returned if message delivery fails.

−X Logs all mail messages to the specified log file. This rapidly produces an enormous log file.

−n Disables the processing of aliases and mail forwarding.

−bm

Tells sendmail to deliver mail, which it will do anyway.

−ba

Reads the header From: line to find the sender. Uses three digit reply codes, and ends error lines with <CRLF>. This is an obsolete argument.

−bs

Tells sendmail to use SMTP for incoming mail. When appropriate, sendmail will do this even without the **−bs** argument.

−i   Normally, an SMTP message terminates when a line containing only a dot is encountered. This argument tells sendmail to ignore the dots in incoming messages.

−m

Sends a copy of the mail to the person sending the mail. Normally this is done with a CC: or BCC: header in the message, not with the **−m** argument.

This is a complete list of sendmail command-line arguments at this writing. Some of these arguments were introduced in sendmail 8. Others are considered obsolete in sendmail V8. Check the manpage for your system to find out exactly what arguments are available on your system.

When the **sendmail** command is executed, it reads its configuration from the *sendmail.cf* file. A basic *sendmail.cf* file can be built from **m4** macros that come with the sendmail source code. Chapter 10 provides examples of how this is done. The next section provides a complete list of the **m4** macros that come with the sendmail distribution.

m4 sendmail Macros

The sendmail distribution comes with several sample configuration files. Chapter 10 provides an example of how the *tcpproto.mc* file is modified to produce a configuration file suitable for a Linux system. The prototype files are **m4** macro configuration files that produce useable *sendmail.cf* files as output. The prototype files are located in the *sendmail/cf/cf* directory of the sendmail distribution. All of the **m4** macro configuration files end with the *.mc* file name extension. The *.mc* files can be composed of the following **m4** macros:*

VERSIONID

Defines the version number of the *.mc* source file. RCS or SCCS version numbers are commonly used. This command is optional.

---

* The macro commands are listed in the order they would occur in the configuration file.

OSTYPE

Points to the **m4** source file that contains the operating system–specific information for this configuration. This is required.

DOMAIN

Points to the **m4** source file that contains configuration information specific to this domain. This is optional.

FEATURE

Points to an **m4** source file that defines an optional sendmail feature. This is not required for **m4** to process the *.mc* source file, but many configurations have multiple FEATURE entries.

HACKS

Points to an **m4** source file that contains site-specific configuration information. This is a temporary configuration used to fix a temporary problem. The use of HACKS is discouraged.

SITECONFIG

Points to a source file that contains **m4** SITE commands that define the UUCP sites connected to this host. The format of the command is: **SITECONFIG**(*file*, *local-hostname, class*), which reads the UUCP hostnames from *file* into *class*.

define

Defines a local value. Most "defines" are done in the **m4** source files that are called by the *.mc* file, not in the *.mc* file itself. It can define a value for a *sendmail.cf* macro, option, or other command.

MAILER

Points to an **m4** source file that contains the configuration commands that define a sendmail mailer. A least one MAILER command must appear in the configuration file. Generally more than one MAILER command is used.

LOCAL_RULE_*n*

Heads a section of code to be added to ruleset *n*, where *n* is 0, 1, 2, or 3. The code that follows the LOCAL_RULE_*n* command is composed of standard *sendmail.cf* rewrite rules.* The LOCAL_RULE_*n* command is rarely used.

LOCAL_CONFIG

Heads a section of code to be added to the *sendmail.cf* file after the local information section and before the rewrite rules. The section of code contains standard *sendmail.cf* configuration commands. This macro is rarely used.

---

* The one exception to this is the UUCPSMTP macro that can be used in the local rule. See the *New sendmail Configuration Files* document that come with the sendmail V8 distribution if you have questions about UUCP configuration.

Most of the macros in the *.mc* file point to other **m4** source files. The macro names OSTYPE, DOMAIN, FEATURE, MAILER, HACKS, and SITECONFIG are all names of subdirectories within the *sendmail/cf* directory. The value passed to each of these macros is the name of a file within the specified directory. For example, the command FEATURE(nouucp) tells **m4** to load the file *nouucp.m4* from the *feature* directory and process the **m4** source code found there. The real meat of the sendmail configuration is contained in the source files pointed to by the OSTYPE, DOMAIN, FEATURE, and MAILER commands.

The macro commands HACK, SITECONFIG, LOCAL_RULE_*n*, and LOCAL_CONFIG are rarely used in a macro configuration file. To simplify this appendix, we do not mention them again.* Likewise, for the sake of simplicity we avoid discussing UUCP configuration and concentrate on SMTP. Still, **m4** configuration can appear to be enormously complex. Please remember that this appendix is a reference, and as such lists as many of the **m4** macros as possible. Most of these you will never need to use. Refer to Chapter 10 for a realistic example of how **m4** is used to build a *sendmail.cf* file.

In the following section we provide additional information about the OSTYPE, DOMAIN, FEATURE, and MAILER macros and details of the various commands used to build the **m4** source files they call. Chapter 10 provides an example of building a custom DOMAIN macro source file. The source files can contain any of the macros we have already mentioned as well as the additional ones documented below. The macro configuration (*.mc*) file also can contain any of the commands documented below. In fact, pretty much any macro can appear in any file.

To bring some order out of this chaos, we have organized the commands according to the files they are most likely to appear in, which is similar to the organization found in the documentation that comes with sendmail distribution. Just remember, actual implementation files may have a different organization. We start by examining the **define** macros and the **FEATURE** macros that are the primary building blocks of all the other files.

define

The syntax of the **define** macro is:

> **define(**'*parameter*', '*value*'**)**

Where *parameter* is the keyword name of a sendmail configuration parameter and *value* is the value assigned to that configuration parameter. The *parameter*

---

* To see examples of some of these commands, look at the *ucbvax.mc* sample file that comes with the sendmail V8 distribution.

and the *value* are normally enclosed in single quotes to prevent inappropriate macro expansion.

Many of the configuration parameters that can be set using the **define** command are shown below. Most of the parameters correspond to sendmail options, macros, or classes. The name of the option, macro, or class set by the parameter is listed in the parameter description enclosed in square brackets ([]). Macro names begin with a dollar sign (**$j**), class names begin with a dollar sign and an equal sign (**$=w**), and options are shown with long option names (**SingleThreadDelivery**). To find out more about these parameters, see the descriptions of the macros, options, and classes they represent that are provided later in this appendix.

Because many **define** parameters are equivalent to options, macros, and classes, the command:

```
define('confDOMAIN_NAME', 'peanut.nuts.com')
```

placed in an **m4** source file has the same effect as:

```
Djpeanut.nuts.com
```

placed directly in the *sendmail.cf* file. If you compile and install a new version of sendmail, build your configuration with **m4** and set values for macros, classes, and options with the **m4 define** macro.

The list of **define** parameters is quite long. However, because most of the parameters default to a reasonable value they do not have to be explicitly set in the **m4** source file. The default value of each parameter is shown in the listing—unless there is no default.

confMAILER_NAME
: Default is MAILER-DAEMON. The sender name used on error messages. [$n]

confDOMAIN_NAME
: The full hostname. [$j]

confCF_VERSION
: The configuration file's version number. [$Z]

confFROM_HEADER
: Default is `$?x$x <$g>$|$g$.` . The From: header format.

confRECEIVED_HEADER
: Default is `$?sfrom $s $.$?_($?s$|from $.$_) $.by $j ($v/$Z)$?r with $r$. id $i$?u for $u$.; $b` . The Received: header format.

confCW_FILE
: Default is */etc/sendmail.cw*. The file of local host aliases. [$=w]

confCT_FILE

Default is */etc/sendmail.ct*. The file of trusted usernames. [$=t]

confTRUSTED_USERS

Trusted users name to add to *root*, *uucp*, and *daemon*.

confSMTP_MAILER

Default is esmtp. The mailer used for SMTP connections; must be smtp, smtp8, or esmtp.

confUUCP_MAILER

Default is uucp-old. The default UUCP mailer.

confLOCAL_MAILER

Default is local. The mailer used for local connections.

confRELAY_MAILER

Default is relay. The default mailer name for relaying.

confSEVEN_BIT_INPUT

Default is False. Force input to seven bits. [SevenBitInput]

confEIGHT_BIT_HANDLING

Default is pass8. Defines how 8-bit data is handled. [EightBitMode]

confALIAS_WAIT

Default is 10m. The amount of time to wait for alias file rebuild. [AliasWait]

confMIN_FREE_BLOCKS

Default is 100. The minimum number of free blocks on the queue filesystem that must be available to accept SMTP mail. [MinFreeBlocks]

confMAX_MESSAGE_SIZE

Default is infinite. The maximum message size. [MaxMessageSize]

confBLANK_SUB

The character used to replace unquoted blank characters in email addresses. [BlankSub]

confCON_EXPENSIVE

Default is False. Tells system to hold mail bound for mailers that have the **e** flag set until the next queue run. [HoldExpensive]

confCHECKPOINT_INTERVAL

Default is 10. Tells system to checkpoint the queue files after this number of queued items are processed. [CheckpointInterval]

confDELIVERY_MODE

Default is background. Sets the default delivery mode. [DeliveryMode]

confAUTO_REBUILD

Default is False. Automatically rebuilds alias file. [AutoRebuildAliases]

confERROR_MODE

Default is print. Defines how errors are handled. [ErrorMode]

confERROR_MESSAGE

Points to a file containing a message that is prepended to error messages. [ErrorHeader]

confSAVE_FROM_LINES

Tells system not to discard UNIX From: lines. They are discarded if this is not set. [SaveFromLine]

confTEMP_FILE_MODE

Default is 0600. File mode for temporary files. [TempFileMode]

confMATCH_GECOS

Tells system to match the email username to the GECOS field. This match is not done if this is not set. [MatchGECOS]

confMAX_HOP

Default is 25. The counter used to determine mail loops. [MaxHopCount]

confIGNORE_DOTS

Default is False. Tells system to ignore dots in incoming messages. [IgnoreDots]

confBIND_OPTS

Default is undefined. Sets options for DNS resolver. [ResolverOptions]

confMIME_FORMAT_ERRORS*

Default is True. Tells system to send MIME-encapsulated error messages. [SendMimeErrors]

confFORWARD_PATH

Default is *$z/.forward.$w:$z/.forward*. Places to search for *.forward* files. [ForwardPath]

confMCI_CACHE_SIZE

Default is 2. The number of open connections that can be cached. [ConnectionCacheSize]

confMCI_CACHE_TIMEOUT

Default is 5m. The amount of time inactive open connections are held in the cache. [ConnectionCacheTimeout]

confHOST_STATUS_DIRECTORY

Directory in which host status is saved. [HostStatusDirectory]

confUSE_ERRORS_TO*

> Default is False. Delivers errors using the Errors-To: header. [UserErrorsTo]

confLOG_LEVEL

> Default is 9. Level of detail for the logfile. [LogLevel]

confME_TOO

> Default is False. Sends a copy to the sender. [MeToo]

confCHECK_ALIASES

> Default is False. Looks up every alias during alias file build. [CheckAliases]

confOLD_STYLE_HEADERS*

> Default is True. Treats headers without special chars as old style. [OldStyle-Headers]

confDAEMON_OPTIONS

> SMTP daemon options. [DaemonPortOptions]

confPRIVACY_FLAGS

> Default is authwarnings. These flags restrict the use of some mail commands. [PrivacyOptions]

confCOPY_ERRORS_TO

> Address to receive copies of error messages. [PostmasterCopy]

confQUEUE_FACTOR

> Default is 600000. Used to calculate when a loaded system should queue mail instead of attempting delivery. [QueueFactor]

confDONT_PRUNE_ROUTES

> Default is False. Don't prune route-addresses to the minimum possible. [Dont-PruneRoutes]

confSAFE_QUEUE

> Create a queue file, then attempt delivery. This is not done unless this paramter is specified. [SuperSafe]

confTO_INITIAL

> Default is 5m. Maximum time to wait for the initial connect response. [Timeout.initial]

confTO_CONNECT

> Default is 0. Maximum time to wait for a connect to complete. [Timeout.connect]

confTO_ICONNECT

> Maximum time to wait for the very first connect attempt to a host. [Timeout.iconnect]

confTO_HELO

> Default is 5m. Maximum time to wait for a HELO or EHLO response. [Timeout.helo]

confTO_MAIL

> Default is 10m. Maximum time to wait for a MAIL command response. [Timeout.mail]

confTO_RCPT

> Default is 1h. Maximum time to wait for a RCPT command response. [Timeout.rcpt]

confTO_DATAINIT

> Default is 5m. Maximum time to wait for a DATA command response. [Timeout.datainit]

confTO_DATABLOCK

> Default is 1h. Maximum time to wait for a block during DATA phase. [Timeout.datablock]

confTO_DATAFINAL

> Default is 1h. Maximum time to wait for a response to the terminating ".". [Timeout.datafinal]

confTO_RSET

> Default is 5m. Maximum time to wait for a RSET command response. [Timeout.rset]

confTO_QUIT

> Default is 2m. Maximum time to wait for a QUIT command response. [Timeout.quit]

confTO_MISC

> Default is 2m. Maximum time to wait for other SMTP command responses. [Timeout.misc]

confTO_COMMAND

> Default is 1h. Maximum time to wait for a command to be issued. [Timeout.command]

confTO_IDENT

> Default is 30s. Maximum time to wait for an IDENT query response. [Timeout.ident]

confTO_FILEOPEN

> Default is 60s. Maximum time to wait for a file open. [Timeout.fileopen]

confTO_QUEUERETURN

> Default is 5d. Time until a message is returned from the queue as undeliverable. [Timeout.queuereturn]

confTO_QUEUERETURN_NORMAL

> "Undeliverable" timeout for normal priority messages. [Timeout.queuereturn.normal]

confTO_QUEUERETURN_URGENT

> "Undeliverable" timeout for urgent priority messages. [Timeout.queuereturn.urgent]

confTO_QUEUERETURN_NONURGENT

> "Undeliverable" timeout for low priority messages. [Timeout.queuereturn.non-urgent]

confTO_QUEUEWARN

> Default is 4h. Time until a "still queued" warning is sent about a message. [Timeout.queuewarn]

confTO_QUEUEWARN_NORMAL

> Time until a "still queued" warning is sent for normal priority messages. [Timeout.queuewarn.normal]

confTO_QUEUEWARN_URGENT

> Time until a "still queued" warning is sent for urgent priority messages. [Timeout.queuewarn.urgent]

confTO_QUEUEWARN_NONURGENT

> Time until a "still queued" warning is sent for low priority messages. [Timeout.queuewarn.non-urgent]

confTO_HOSTSTATUS

> Default is 30m. Timer for stale host status information. [Timeout.hoststatus]

confTIME_ZONE

> Default is USE_SYSTEM. Sets time zone from the system (USE_SYSTEM) or the TZ variable (USE_TZ). [TimeZoneSpec]

confDEF_USER_ID

> Default is 1:1. Default user ID and group ID. [DefaultUser]

confUSERDB_SPEC

> Path of the user database file. [UserDatabaseSpec]

confFALLBACK_MX

> Backup MX host. [FallbackMXhost]

confTRY_NULL_MX_LIST

Default is False. Instructs system to connect to the remote host directly if the MX point to the local host. [TryNullMXList]

confQUEUE_LA

Default is 8. Sends mail directly to the queue when this load average is reached. [QueueLA]

confREFUSE_LA

Default is 12. Refuses incoming SMTP connections at this load average. [RefuseLA]

confMAX_DAEMON_CHILDREN

If set, refuses connection when this number of children is reached. [MaxDaemonChildren]

confCONNECTION_RATE_THROTTLE

Maximum number of connections permitted per second, if set. [ConnectionRateThrottle]

confWORK_RECIPIENT_FACTOR

Default is 30000. Factor used to lower the priority of a job for each additional recipient. [RecipientFactor]

confSEPARATE_PROC

Default is False. Delivers messages with separate processes. [ForkEachJob]

confWORK_CLASS_FACTOR

Default is 1800. The factor used to favor a high-priority job. [ClassFactor]

confWORK_TIME_FACTOR

Default is 90000. Factor used to lower the priority of a job for each delivery attempt. [RetryFactor]

confQUEUE_SORT_ORDER

Default is Priority. Sorts queue by Priority or Host order. [QueueSortOrder]

confMIN_QUEUE_AGE

Default is 0. Minimum time a job must be queued. [MinQueueAge]

confDEF_CHAR_SET

Default is unknown-8bit. Default character set for unlabeled 8-bit MIME data. [DefaultCharSet]

confSERVICE_SWITCH_FILE

Default is */etc/service.switch*. The path to the service switch file. [ServiceSwitchFile] confHOSTS_FILE

> Default is */etc/hosts*. The path to the hostnames file. [HostsFile]

confDIAL_DELAY

> Default is 0s. Amount of time to delay before retrying a "dial on demand" connection. 0s means "don't retry". [DialDelay]

confNO_RCPT_ACTION

> Default is **none**. Handling for mail with no recipient headers: do nothing (**none**); add To: header (**add-to**); add Apparently-To: header (**add-apparently-to**); add a Bcc: header (**add-bcc**); add "To: undisclosed-recipients" header (**add-to-undisclosed**). [NoRecipientAction]

confSAFE_FILE_ENV

> Default is undefined. **chroot()** to this directory before writing files. [SafeFileEnvironment]

confCOLON_OK_IN_ADDR

> Default is True. Treats colons as regular characters in addresses. [ColonOkInAddr]

confMAX_QUEUE_RUN_SIZE

> Default is 0. Limits the number of entries processed in a queue run. 0 means no limit. [MaxQueueRunSize]

confDONT_EXPAND_CNAMES

> Default is False. If true, don't convert nicknames to canonical names. False means "do convert." [DontExpandCnames]

confFROM_LINE

> Default is From $g $d. The format of the UNIX From: line. [UnixFromLine]

confOPERATORS

> Default is .:%@!^/[]+. Address operator characters. [OperatorChars]

confSMTP_LOGIN_MSG

> Default is *$j sendmail $v/$Z; $b*. The SMTP greeting message. [SmtpGreetingMessage]

confDONT_INIT_GROUPS

> Default is False. If true, disable the initgroups(3) routine. False means "use the initgroups(3) routine. [DontInitGroups]

confUNSAFE_GROUP_WRITES

> Default is False. If true, don't reference programs or file from group-writable *:include:* and *.forward* files. [UnsafeGroupWrites]

confDOUBLE_BOUNCE_ADDRESS

> Default is *postmaster*. When errors occur sending an error message, send the second error message to this address. [DoubleBounceAddress]

confRUN_AS_USER

> Default is undefined. Run as this user to read and deliver mail. [RunAsUser]

confSINGLE_THREAD_DELIVERY

> Default is False. Force single threaded mail deliver when set with HostStatus-Directory. [SingleThreadDelivery]

define macros are the most common macros in the **m4** source files. The next most commonly used macro is the FEATURE macro.

FEATURE

The FEATURE macro processes **m4** source code from the *cf/feature* directory. Source files in that directory define optional sendmail features that you may wish to include in your configuration. The syntax of the FEATURE macro is:

    FEATURE(*name*, [*argument*])

The FEATURE source file can be called with or without an optional argument. If an argument is passed to the source file the argument is used by the source file to generate code for the *sendmail.cf* file. For example:

    FEATURE(mailertable, dbm /usr/lib/mailertable)

generates the code for accessing the mailertable and defines that table as being a dbm database located in the file */usr/lib/mailertable*.

There are several features available in sendmail V8. They are all listed in Table E-3. The table provides the name of each feature and its purpose.

Table E-3: sendmail V8 Features

Name	Purpose
use_cw_file	Load $=w from */etc/sendmail.cw*.
use_ct_file	Load $=t from */etc/sendmail.ct*.
redirect	Support the .REDIRECT pseudo-domain.
nouucp	Don't include UUCP address processing.
nocanonify	Don't convert names with $[. . . $] syntax.
stickyhost	Treat "user" different than "user@local.host".[a]
mailertable	Mail routing using a mailer table.
domaintable	Domain name mapping using a domain table.
bitdomain	Use a table to map bitnet hosts to Internet addresses.
uucpdomain	Use a table to map UUCP hosts to Internet addresses.

Table E-3: sendmail V8 Features (continued)

Name	Purpose
always_add_domain	Add the local hostname to all locally delivered mail.
allmasquerade	Also masquerade recipient addresses.
limited_masquerade	Only masquerade hosts listed in **$=M**.
masquerade_entire_domain	Masquerade all hosts within the masquerading domains.
genericstable	Use a table to rewrite local addresses.
virtusertable	Maps virtual domain names to real mail addresses.
nodns	Don't include DNS support.
nullclient	Forwarding all mail to a central server.
local_procmail	Use procmail as the local mailer.
bestmx_is_local	Accept mail as local when it is addressed to a host that lists us as its MX server.
smrsh	Use **smrsh** as the prog mailer.

a. See the discussion of "stickyhost" in the "DOMAIN" section later in this appendix.

The **use_cw_file** and the **use_ct_file features** are equivalent to **Fw/etc/sendmail.cw** and **Fw/etc/sendmail.ct** commands in the *sendmail.cf* file. See Chapter 10 for descriptions of host aliases (**$=w**) and trusted users (**$=t**).

The .REDIRECT pseudo-domain code returns an error message to the sender telling them to try a new address for the recipient. This is used to handle mail for people who no longer read mail at your site but who are still getting mail sent to a very old address. Enable this feature with the **FEATURE(redirect)** command and then add aliases for each obsolete mailing address in the form:

```
    old-address          new-address.REDIRECT
```

For example: assume that Edward Winslow is no longer a valid user of *almond.nuts.com*. His old username, *ed*, should no longer accept mail. His new mailing address is *WinslowE@industry.com*. We enter the following alias in the */etc/aliases* file:

```
    ed               WinslowE@industry.com.REDIRECT
```

Now when mail is to the *ed* account on *almond*, the following error is returned to the sender:

```
    551 User not local; please try <WinslowE@industry.com>
```

Several of the FEATURE macros actually remove features from the *sendmail.cf* file instead of adding them. nouucp removes the code to handle UUCP addresses for systems that do not have access to UUCP networks, and nodns removes the code for DNS lookups for systems that do not have access to DNS. nocanonify, which is rarely used, disables the **$[**name**]$** syntax that converts nicknames and IP addresses; see Table 10-7. Finally, the nullclient feature strips everything out of the configuration except for the ability to forward mail to a single mail server via a local SMTP link. The name of the mail server is provided as the argument on the nullclient command line. For example, **FEATURE(nullclient, ms.big.com)** forwards all mail to *ms.big.com* without any local mail processing.

Several features relate to mail relaying and masquerading. They are: stickyhost, all-masquerade, limited_masquerade and masquerade_entire_domain. All of these features are covered in the "DOMAIN" section later in this appendix.

Several of the features define databases that are used to perform special address processing. All of these features accept an optional argument that defines the database. (See the sample **mailertable** command at the beginning of this section for an example of defining the database with the optional argument.) If the optional argument is not provided the database description always defaults to **hash** −o /etc/*filename*, where *filename* matches the name of the feature. For example: **mailertable** defaults to the definition `hash  -o  /etc/mailertable`. The database features are:

mailertable

Maps host and domain names to specific mailer:host pairs.* If the host or domain name in the recipient addresses matches a key field in the mailertable database, it returns the mailer and host for that address. The format of mailertable entries is:

        domain-name   mailer:host

where *domain-name* is either a full hostname (host plus domain) or a domain name. If a domain name is used it must start with a dot (.), and it will match every host in the specified domain.

domaintable

Converts an old domain name to a new domain name. The old name is the key and the new name is the value returned for the key.

bitdomain

Converts a Bitnet hostname to an Internet hostname. The Bitnet name is the key and the Internet hostname is the value returned. The **bitdomain** program that comes with sendmail V8 can be used to build this database.

uucpdomain

Converts a UUCP name to an Internet hostname. The key is the UUCP host name and the value returned is the Internet hostname.

---

* See Chapter 10 for a description of the mailer, host, and user triple returned by ruleset 0.

generictable

Converts a sender email address. The key to the database is either a username or a full email address (username and hostname). The value returned by the database is always a full email address. If the value specified in the database is not a full address, **genericstable** appends the value from **$j** to the value to force it to be a full address. **genericstable** converts the same address as those processed for masquerading and the features that affect masquerading affect the **genericstable** conversion in exactly the same way. See Chapter 10 for an example of using the **genericstable** and see the "DOMAIN" section later in this appendix for information on masquerading. Note that if you use the **generic-stable** and you don't use masquerading, you can still get the functionality of the MASQUERADE_DOMAIN and the MASQUERADE_DOMAIN_FILE by using GENERICS_DOMAIN and GENERICS_DOMAIN_FILE. These commands have the same function and are used in the same way as their masquerade counterparts, which are described in the following section.

virtusertable

Aliases incoming email addresses. Essentially, this is an extended alias database for aliasing addresses that are not local to this host. The key to the database is a full email address or a domain name. The value returned by the database is the recipient address to which the mail is delivered. If a domain name is used as a key, it must begin with an at-sign (@). Mail addressed to any user in the specified domain is sent to the recipient defined by the virtusertable database. Any host name used as a key in the virtusertable database must also be defined in class w.

Two of the remaining FEATURE commands relate to domains. The **always_add_domain** macro makes sendmail add the local hostname to all locally delivered mail, even to those pieces of mail that would normally have just a username as an address. The **bestmx_is_local** feature accepts mail addressed to a host that lists the local host as its preferred MX server as if the mail was local mail. If this feature is not used, mail bound for a remote host is sent directly to the remote host even if its MX record lists the local host as its preferred MX server. The **bestmx_is_local** feature should not be used if you use a wildcard MX record for your domain.

The last two features are used to select optional programs for the local and the prog mailers. local_procmail selects **procmail** as the local mailer. Provide the path to **procmail** as the argument in the FEATURE command. The **smrsh** feature selects the sendmail Restricted SHell (**smrsh**) as the prog mailer. **smrsh** provides improved security over /bin/sh, which is normally used as the prog mailer. Provide the path to **smrsh** as the argument in the FEATURE command.

The FEATURE commands discussed in this section and the **define** macros discussed previously are used to build the **m4** source files. The remainder of this section describes the purpose and structure of the OSTYPE, DOMAIN, and MAILER source files.

OSTYPE

The source file for the OSTYPE macro defines operating system–specific parameters. Many operating systems are pre-defined. Look in the *sendmail/cf/ostype* directory for a full listing of the systems that are already defined.

OSTYPE source files are mostly composed of **define** macros. Table E-4 lists the **define** parameters most frequently associated with the OSTYPE source file and the function of each parameter. The default value assigned to each parameter is shown enclosed in square brackets after its functional description, if the parameter has a default value.

Table E-4: OSTYPE Defines

Parameter	Function
ALIAS_FILE	Name of the alias file. [*/etc/aliases*]
HELP_FILE	Name of the help file. [*/usr/lib/sendmail.hf*]
QUEUE_DIR	Directory containing queue files. [*/var/spool/mqueue*]
STATUS_FILE	Name of the status file. [*/etc/sendmail.st*]
LOCAL_MAILER_PATH	The local mail delivery program. [*/bin/mail*]
LOCAL_MAILER_FLAGS	Local mailer flags added to "lsDFM". [**rmn**]
LOCAL_MAILER_ARGS	Arguments for local mail delivery. [**mail –d $u**]
LOCAL_MAILER_MAX	Maximum size of local mail.
LOCAL_MAILER_CHARSET	Character set for local 8-bit MIME mail.
LOCAL_SHELL_PATH	Shell used to deliver piped email. [*/bin/sh*]
LOCAL_SHELL_FLAGS	Flags added to lsDFM for the shell mailer. [**eu**]
LOCAL_SHELL_ARGS	Arguments for the "prog" mail. [**sh -c $u**]
LOCAL_SHELL_DIR	Directory which the shell should run. [*$z:/*]
USENET_MAILER_PATH	Program used for news. [*/usr/lib/news/inews*]
USENET_MAILER_FLAGS	Usenet mailer flags. [**rlsDFMmn**]
USENET_MAILER_ARGS	Arguments for the usenet mailer. [**–m –h –n**]
USENET_MAILER_MAX	Maximum size of usenet mail messages. [100000]
SMTP_MAILER_FLAGS	Flags added to "mDFMUX" for all SMTP mailers.
SMTP_MAILER_MAX	Maximum size of messages for all SMTP mailers.
SMTP_MAILER_ARGS	smtp mailer arguments. [**IPC $h**]
ESMTP_MAILER_ARGS	esmtp mailer arguments. [**IPC $h**]
SMTP8_MAILER_ARGS	smtp8 mailer arguments. [**IPC $h**]
RELAY_MAILER_ARGS	relay mailer arguments. [**IPC $h**]
SMTP_MAILER_CHARSET	Character set for SMTP 8-bit MIME mail.

Table E-4: OSTYPE Defines (continued)

Parameter	Function
UUCP_MAILER_PATH	Path to the UUCP mail program. [*/usr/bin/uux*]
UUCP_MAILER_FLAGS	Flags added to "DFMhuU" for the UUCP mailer.
UUCP_MAILER_ARGS	UUCP mailer arguments.
	[*uux - -r -z -a$g -gC $h!rmail ($u)*]
UUCP_MAILER_MAX	Maximum size for UUCP messages. [100000]
UUCP_MAILER_CHARSET	Character set for UUCP 8-bit MIME mail.
FAX_MAILER_PATH	Path to the FAX program. [*/usr/local/lib/fax/mailfax*]
FAX_MAILER_ARGS	FAX mailer arguments. [**mailfax $u $h $f**]
FAX_MAILER_MAX	Maximum size of a FAX. [100000]
POP_MAILER_PATH	Path of the POP mailer. [*/usr/lib/mh/spop*]
POP_MAILER_FLAGS	Flags added to "lsDFM" for the POP mailer. [**Penu**]
POP_MAILER_ARGS	POP mailer arguments. [**pop $u**]
PROCMAIL_MAILER_PATH	Path to the procmail program. [*/usr/local/bin/procmail*]
PROCMAIL_MAILER_FLAGS	Flags added to "DFMmn" for the Procmail mailer. [**Shu**]
PROCMAIL_MAILER_ARGS	Procmail mailer arguments. [**procmail −m $h $f $u**]
PROCMAIL_MAILER_MAX	Maximum size message for the Procmail mailer.
MAIL11_MAILER_PATH	Path to the mail11 mailer. [*/usr/etc/mail11*]
MAIL11_MAILER_FLAGS	Flags for the mail11 mailer. [**nsFx**]
MAIL11_MAILER_ARGS	mail11 mailer arguments. [**mail11 $g $x $h $u**]
PH_MAILER_PATH	Path to the phquery program. [*/usr/local/etc/phquery*]
PH_MAILER_FLAGS	Flags for the phquery mailer. [**ehmu**]
PH_MAILER_ARGS	phquery mailer arguments. [**phquery −− $u**]
CYRUS_MAILER_FLAGS	Flags added to "lsDFMnP" for the cyrus mailer. [**A5@**]
CYRUS_MAILER_PATH	Path to the cyrus mailer. [*/usr/cyrus/bin/deliver*]
CYRUS_MAILER_ARGS	cyrus mailer arguments. [**deliver −e −m $h −− $u**]
CYRUS_MAILER_MAX	Maximum size message for the cyrus mailer.
CYRUS_MAILER_USER	User and group used to the cyrus mailer. [*cyrus:mail*]
CYRUS_BB_MAILER_FLAGS	Flags added to "lsDFMnP" for the cyrusbb mailer.
CYRUS_BB_MAILER_ARGS	cyrusbb mailer arguments. [**deliver −e −m $u**]

Despite the long list of parameters in Table E-4, most OSTYPE macros are very short. The largest OSTYPE file in the sendmail V8 distribution contains only eight **define**s. There are a few reasons for this. First, many of the parameters in the table are redundant. They define the same things for different mailers, and no operating systems uses all of the mailers. Second, the default values are often correct. A **define** only needs to be made if the operating system requires a value different than the default.

DOMAIN

The DOMAIN source file defines configuration parameters that are related to the local domain. Chapter 10 provides an example of a DOMAIN file built for the imaginary *nuts.com* domain.

Table E-5 shows some **define** macros that commonly appear in DOMAIN files. (See the syntax of the **define** macro earlier.) This table lists the parameters and the function of each parameter. All of these parameters are used to define mail relay hosts. The value provided for each parameter is either a hostname, i.e., the name of a mail relay server, or a mailer:hostname pair where the mailer is the internal name of a local sendmail mailer and the hostname is the name of the remote mail relay server. If only a hostname is used, the mailer defaults to *relay*, which is the name of the SMTP relay mailer. If no values are provided for these parameters, the BIT-NET, DECNET, and FAX pseudo-domains are not used, and the local host must be able to handle its own UUCP and "local" mail.

Table E-5: Mail Relay Defines

Parameter	Function
UUCP_RELAY	Server for UUCP-addressed email
BITNET_RELAY	Server for BITNET-addressed email
DECNET_RELAY	Server for DECNET-addressed email
FAX_RELAY	Server for mail to the .FAX pseudo-domain[a]
LOCAL_RELAY	Sever for unqualified names
LUSER_RELAY	Server for apparently local names that really aren't local
MAIL_HUB	Server for all incoming mail
SMART_HOST	Server for all outgoing mail

a. The "fax" mailer overrides this value.

The precedence of the relays defined by these parameters is from the most specific to the least specific. If both the BITNET_RELAY and the SMART_HOST relay are defined, the BITNET_RELAY is used for outgoing BITNET mail even though the SMART_HOST relay is defined as handling "all" outgoing mail. If you define both LOCAL_RELAY and MAIL_HUB, you must also use the FEATURE(stickyhost) command to get the expected behavior.

When the stickyhost feature is specified, LOCAL_RELAY handles all local addresses that do not have a host part, and MAIL_HUB handles all local addresses that do have a host part. If stickyhost is not specified and both relays are defined, the LOCAL_RELAY is ignored and MAIL_HUB handles all local addresses.

In addition to the defines shown in Table E-5, there are a group of macros that relate to masquerading and relaying that also appear in the DOMAIN source file. Some of these are used in the examples in Chapter 10. The macros are:

LOCAL_USER(*usernames*)
> Defines local usernames that should not be relayed even if LOCAL_RELAY or MAIL_HUB are defined. This command is the same as adding usernames to class L in the *sendmail.cf* file.

MASQUERADE_AS(*host.domain*)
> Converts the host portion of the sender address on outgoing mail to the domain name defined by *host.domain*. Sender addresses that have no hostname or that have a hostname found in the w class are converted. This has the same as effect as defining *host.domain* for the M macro in the *sendmail.cf* file. See examples of MASQUERADE_AS and macro M in Chapter 10.

MASQUERADE_DOMAIN(*otherhost.domain*)
> Converts the host portion of the sender address on outgoing mail to the domain name defined by the MASQUERADE_AS command, if the host portion of the sender address matches *otherhost.domain*. This command must be used in conjunction with MASQUERADE_AS. Its effect is the same as adding hostnames to class M in the *sendmail.cf* file. See Chapter 10.

MASQUERADE_DOMAIN_FILE(*filename*)
> Loads *otherhost.domain* hostnames from the file identified by *filename*. This can be used in place of multiple MASQUERADE_DOMAIN commands. Its effect is the same as loading class M from a file by using the **FM***filename* command in the *sendmail.cf* file.

EXPOSED_USER(*username*)
> Disables masquerading when the user portion of the sender address matches *username*. Some usernames, such as root, occur on many systems and are therefore not unique across a domain. For those usernames, converting the host portion of the address makes it impossible to sort out where the message really came from and makes replies impossible. This command prevents the MASQUERADE_AS command from having an effect on the sender addresses for specific users. This is the same as setting the values in class E in the *sendmail.cf* file.

There are several features that affect relaying and masquerading. We have already discussed FEATURE(stickyhost). Others are:

FEATURE(masquerade_envelope)
> Causes envelop addresses to be masqueraded in the same way that sender addresses are masqueraded. See Chapter 10 for an example of this command.

FEATURE(allmasquerade)

Causes recipient addresses to be masqueraded in the same way that sender addresses are masqueraded. Thus, if the host portion of the recipient address matches the requirements of the MASQUERADE_AS command, it is converted.

Don't use this feature unless you are positive that every alias known to the local system is also known to the mail server that handles mail for the masquerade domain.

FEATURE(limited_masquerade)

Limits masquerading to those hosts defined in class M. The hosts defined in class w are not masqueraded.

FEATURE(masquerade_entire_domain)

Causes MASQUERADE_DOMAIN to be interpreted as referring to all hosts with an entire domain. If this feature is not used, only an address that exactly matches the value defined by MASQUERADE_DOMAIN is converted. If this feature is used, all addresses that end with the value defined by MASQUERADE_DOMAIN are converted.

For example, assume that the options MASQUERADE_AS(nuts.com) and MASQUERADE_DOMAIN(sales.nuts.com) are defined. If FEATURE (masquerade_entire_domain) is set, every hostname in the *sales.nuts.com* domain is converted to *nuts.com* on outgoing email. Otherwise only the hostname *sales.nuts.com* is converted.

See the "FEATURE" section earlier in this chapter for more information on the available features.

MAILER

It is possible that you will need to customize a file location in an OSTYPE file or that you will need to define domain specific information in a DOMAIN file, but unless you develop your own mail delivery program you will not need to create a MAILER source file. Instead, you will need to invoke one or more existing files in your macro configuration file.

The available MAILER files are listed in Table E-6. This table lists each MAILER value and its function. These are invoked using the MAILER(*value*) command in the macro configuration (*.mc*) file, where *value* is one of the mailer names from the table.

Table E-6: MAILER Values

Name	Function
local	The local and prog mailers
smtp	All SMTP mailers: smtp, esmtp, smtp8, and relay
uucp	All UUCP mailers: uucp-old (uucp) and uucp-new (suucp)
usenet	Usenet news support
fax	Fax support using FlexFAX software
pop	Post Office Protocol (POP) support
procmail	An interface for procmail
mail11	The DECnet mail11 mailer
phquery	The phquery program for CSO phone book
cyrus	The cyrus and cyrusbb mailers

Your macro configuration file should have a MAILER(local) and a MAILER(smtp) entry. This gives you the local and prog mailers required by sendmail, the smtp mailer for standard SMTP mail, the esmtp mailer for Extended SMTP, the smtp8 mailer for 8-bit MIME mail, and the relay mailer for the various mail relay servers mentioned in the "DOMAIN" section of this appendix. Selecting **local** and **smtp** provides everything you need for a standard TCP/IP installation.

Of all the remaining mailers, only uucp is widely used. uucp provides UUCP mail support for systems directly connected to UUCP networks. The uucp-old mailer supports standard UUCP mail and the uucp-new mailer is used for remote sites that can handle multiple recipients in one transfer. The system needs the mailer that is correct for the capabilities of the remote site. Use class U to define the host-names of systems that need the old mailer and class Y for the names of remote systems that can work with the new mailer. Specify MAILER(uucp) after the MAILER(smtp) entry if your system has both TCP/IP and UUCP connections. Ordering the MAILER statements in this way adds two more mailers to the two standard UUCP mailers: the uucp-dom mailer to support standard domain names, and the uucp-uudom mailer to support standard domain names with a standard UUCP envelop.

The other mailers are rarely used:

usenet

> Modifies the sendmail rewrite rules to send local mail that contains ".usenet" in the username to the program inews. Instead of this mailer, choose a user mail agent that supports Usenet news. Don't hack sendmail to handle it.

fax

> This is still experimental in sendmail V8, though built-in fax support could be useful when it is ready.

pop

> On most systems, POP support is provided separately by the **popd** daemon, and the MAILER(pop) command is not used.

procmail

> Only provides an interface to procmail for use in the mailertable. The send-mail V8 distribution does not provide procmail. Even when procmail is used as the local mailer, as it is in Slackware Linux, the **MAILER(procmail)** command is not required.

mail11

> Only used on DECNET mail networks that use the mail11 mailer.

phquery

> Provides a name lookup program for the CSO phone book (ph) directory ser-vice. User directory services are usually configured in the user mail agent, not in sendmail.

cyrus

> This is a local mail delivery program with a mailbox architecture. cyrus and cyrusbb mailers are not widely used.

This concludes our discussion of **m4** macros. The output of all of the files and commands that go into the **m4** processor is a *sendmail.cf* file. The remainder of this appendix provides additional details about the *sendmail.cf* configuration and excerpts from a *sendmail.cf* file. The bulk of information about *sendmail.cf* is found in Chapter 10.

More sendmail.cf

Many options and flags can be used in configuring the *sendmail.cf* file. All of the important configuration parameters are covered in Chapter 10. But if you are unlucky enough to have a configuration that requires you to tweak one of the more obscure parameters, you will find all of them in the following tables.

sendmail Classes

sendmail has many internal macros. As of sendmail V8, it also has some internal classes. Some of these classes (e, n, q, and s) have been added to support new MIME mail features. A few (k, m, and w) hold the multiple hostnames and domains associated with a well-connected host. The last one (t) holds the list of trusted users. The full list of internal classes is shown in Table E-7.

Table E-7: Internal sendmail Classes

Name	Stores
e	Supported MIME Content-Transfer-Encodings. Initialized to *7bit*, *8bit*, and *binary*
k	The system's UUCP node names
m	All local domains for this host
n	MIME body types that should never be 8- to 7-bit encoded. Initialized to *multipart/signed*
q	MIME Content-Types that should not be Base64-encoded. Initialized to *text/plain*
s	MIME message subtypes that can be processed recursively. Initialized to *rfc822*
t	The list of trusted users
w	All hostnames this system will accept as its own

sendmail Options

A large number of sendmail options can be set inside of the **sendmail** configuration file. Chapter 10 provides the syntax of the option command in Table 10-1 and several examples of options. The complete list of options is:

AliasFile=[*class***:]***file***, [***class***:]***file* . . .

Identify the alias file(s). *class* is optional and defaults to "implicit". Valid classes are "implicit", "hash", "dbm", "stab" (internal symbol table) or "nis". The selected database class must be a database type that was compiled into **sendmail** on your system. *file* is the pathname of the alias file.

AliasWait=*timeout*

Wait *timeout* minutes for an "@:@" entry to appear in the alias database before starting up. When *timeout* expires, automatically rebuild the database if **AutoRebuildAliases** is set; otherwise, issue a warning.

AllowBogusHELO

Accept illegal **HELO SMTP** commands that don't contain a hostname.

AutoRebuildAliases

Automatically rebuild the alias database when necessary. The preferred method is to rebuild the alias database with an explicit **newaliases** command.

BlankSub=*c*

Use *c* as the blank substitution character to replace unquoted spaces in addresses. The default is to leave the spaces unchanged.

CheckAliases

Check that the delivery address in each aliases is valid when rebuilding the alias database. Normally this check is not done. Adding this check slows the database build substantially. This is a Boolean.

CheckpointInterval=n

Checkpoint the queue after every n items are processed to simplify recovery if your system crashes during queue processing. The default is 10.

ClassFactor=$fact$

The multiplier used to favor messages with a higher value in the Priority: header. Defaults to 1800.

ColonOkInAddr

Accept colons in email addresses (e.g., *host:user*). Colons are always accepted in pairs in mail routing (*nodename::user*) or in an RFC 822 group constructs (groupname: member1, member2, . . . ;). By default, this option is "on" if the configuration version level is less than 6.

ConnectionCacheSize=n

The number of connections that can be held open (cached) by this instantiation of sendmail. The default is 1. The maximum is 4. 0 causes connections to closed immediately after the data is sent, which is the traditional way sendmail operated.

ConnectionCacheTimeout=$timeout$

The amount of time an inactive cached connection is held open. After *timeout* minutes of inactivity it is closed. The default is 5 minutes.

ConnectionRateThrottle=n

Limit the number of incoming connections accepted in any 1-second period to n. The default is 0, which means no limit.

DaemonPortOptions=$options$

Set SMTP server options. The *options* are key=value pairs. The options are:

- **Port=$portnumber$**, where *portnumber* is any valid port number. It can be specified with the number or the name found in */etc/services*. The default is port 25, smtp.

- **Addr=$mask$**, where *mask* is an IP address mask specified either in dotted decimal notation or as a network name. The default is INADDR-ANY, which accepts all addresses.

- **Family=$addressfamily$**, where *addressfamily* is a valid address family (see the **ifconfig** command). The default is INET, which allows IP addresses to be used.

- **Listen=**n, where n is a the number of queued connections allowed. The default is 10.

- **SndBufSize=**n, where n is the send buffer size.

- **RcvBufSize=**n, where n is the receive buffer size.

DefaultCharSet=*charset*

The character set placed in the Content-Type: header when 8-bit data is converted to MIME format. The default is "unknown-8bit". This option is overridden by the Charset= field of the mailer descriptor.

DefaultUser=*user*[:*group*]

The default user ID and group ID for mailers without the S flag in their definitions. If *group* is omitted, the group associated with *user* in the */etc/passwd* file is used. The default is 1:1.

DeliveryMode=*x*

Deliver in mode *x*, where *x* is i (interactive delivery), b (background delivery), q (queue the message), or d (defer until the queue run). The default is b.

DialDelay=*delaytime*

Delay *delaytime* seconds before redialing a failed connection on dial-on-demand networks. The default is 0 (no redial).

DontExpandCnames

Disable the $[*name*$] syntax used to convert nicknames to canonical names.

DontInitGroups

Don't use the initgroups(3) call. This setting reduces NIS server load, but limits a user to the group associated with that user in */etc/passwd*.

DontPruneRoutes

Don't optimize explicit mail routes. Normally, sendmail makes a route as direct as possible. However, optimizing the route may not be appropriate for systems located behind a firewall.

DoubleBounceAddress=*error-address*

Send the report of an error that occurs when sending an error message to *error-address*. The default is "postmaster".

EightBitMode=*action*

Handle undeclared 8-bit data by following the specified *action*. The possible actions are: **s** (strict), reject undeclared 8-bit data; **m** (mime), convert it to MIME; and **p** (pass), pass it through unaltered.

ErrorHeader=*file-or-message*

Prepend *file-or-message* to outgoing error messages. If *file-or-message* is the path to a text file that is to be prepended, it must begin with a slash. If this option is not defined, nothing is prepended to error messages.

ErrorMode=*x*

Handle errors messages according to *x*, where *x* is: **p** (print messages); **q** (give exit status but no messages); **m** (mail back messages); **w** (write messages to the user's terminal); **e** (mail back messages and always give zero exit status). If this option is not defined, error messages are printed.

FallbackMXhost=*fallbackhost*

Use *fallbackhost* as a backup MX server for every host.

ForkEachJob

Run a separate process for every item delivered from the queue. This option reduces the amount of memory needed to process the queue.

ForwardPath=*path*

The *path* to search for .forward files. Multiple paths can be defined by separating them with colons. The default is *$z/.forward*.

HelpFile=*file*

The path to the *help* file.

HoldExpensive

Queue mail for outgoing mailers that have the **e** (expensive) mailer flag. Normally mail is delivered immediately.

HostsFile=*path*

The path to the hosts file. The default is */etc/hosts*.

HostStatusDirectory=*path*

Directory in which host status information is stored so that it can be shared between **sendmail** processes. Normally, the status of a host or connection is only known by the process that discovers that status. To function, this option requires that ConnectionCacheSize be set to at least 1.

IgnoreDots

Ignore dots in incoming messages. Dots cannot be ignored by SMTP mail because they are used to mark the end of a mail message.

LogLevel=*n*

n indicates the level of detail stored in the log file. *n* defaults to 9, which is normally plenty of detail.

MatchGECOS

Check the username from the email address against the GECOS field of the *passwd* file if it was not found in the alias database or in the username field of the *passwd* file. This option is not recommended.

MaxDaemonChildren=*n*

Refuse connections when *n* children are processing incoming mail. Normally **sendmail** sets no arbitrary limit on child processes.

MaxHopCount=*n*

Assume a message is looping when it has been processed more than *n* times. The default is 25.

MaxHostStatAge=*n*

Retain host status information for *n* minutes.

MaxMessageSize=*n*

The maximum message size advertised in response to the ESMTP EHLO. Messages larger than this are rejected.

MaxQueueRunSize=*n*

The maximum number of item that can be processed in a single queue run. The default is no limit.

MeToo

Send a copy to the sender.

MinFreeBlocks=*n*

Don't accept incoming mail unless *n* blocks are free in the queue filesystem.

MinQueueAge=*n*

Don't process any jobs that have been in the queue less than *n* minutes.

MustQuoteChars=*s*

The list of characters added to the set "@,;:\()[]" that must be quoted when used in the username part of an address. If **MustQuoteChars** is specified without an *s* value, it adds "." to the standard set of quoted characters.

NoRecipientAction=*action*

The *action* taken when a message has no valid recipient headers. *action* can be **none** to pass the message on unmodified, **add-to** to add a To: header using the recipient addresses from the envelope, **add-apparently-to** to add an Apparently-To: header, **add-to-undisclosed** to add a "To: undisclosed-recipients:;" header, or **add-bcc** to add an empty Bcc: header.

OldStyleHeaders

Allow spaces to delimit names. Normally, commas delimit names.

OperatorChars=*charlist*

The list of operator characters that are normally defined in macro **o**. The default is the standard set of operators. See the discussion of rewrite tokens, and the use of operators in determining tokens, in Chapter 10.

PostmasterCopy=*username*

Copy error messages to *username*. The default is not to send copies of error messages to the postmaster.

PrivacyOptions=*options*

Set SMTP protocol *options*, where *options* is a comma-separated list containing one or more of these keywords:

- **public**: allow all commands

- **needmailhelo**: require HELO or EHLO before MAIL

- **needexpnhelo**: require HELO or EHLO before EXPN

- **noexpn**: disable EXPN

- **needvrfyhelo**: require HELO or EHLO before VRFY

- **novrfy**: disable VRFY

- **restrictmailq**: restrict **mailq** to users with group access to the queue directory

- **restrictqrun**: only *root* and the owner of the queue directory are allowed to run the queue

- **noreceipts**: don't return successful delivery messages

- **goaway**: disable all SMTP status queries

- **authwarnings**: put X-Authentication-Warning: headers in messages

QueueDirectory=*directory*

directory is the pathname of the queue directory.

QueueFactor=*factor*

The factor used with the difference between the current load and the load average limit and with the message priority to determine if a message should be queued or sent immediately. The idea is to queue low-priority messages if the system is currently heavily loaded. It defaults to 600000.

QueueLA=*n*

Queue messages when the system load average exceeds *n*. The default is 8.

QueueSortOrder=*sequence*

Sort the queue in the *sequence* specified, where *sequence* is: **h** (hostname sequence); **t** (submission time sequence); or **p** (message priority order). Priority ordering is the default.

ResolverOptions=*options*

>   Set resolver *options*. Available option values are: **debug, aaonly, usevc, pri-**
>   **mary, igntc, recurse, defnames, stayopen,** and **dnsrch**. The option can be pre-
>   ceded by a plus (+) to turn it on or a minus (–) to turn it off. One other
>   option, **HasWildcardMX**, is specified without a + or –. Simply adding **HasWild-**
>   **cardMX** turns the option on.

RunAsUser=*userid*[:groupid]

>   Run sendmail under this user ID and group ID instead of under *root*. This may
>   enhance security when the sendmail is running on a well maintained firewall.
>   On general purpose systems, this may decrease security because it requires
>   that many files be readable or writable by this user ID.

RecipientFactor=*factor*

>   The priority of a job is lowered by this factor for each recipient, so that jobs
>   with large numbers of recipients have lower priority. Defaults to 30000.

RefuseLA=*n*

>   Refuse incoming SMTP connections when the system load average exceeds *n*.
>   The default is 12.

RetryFactor=*factor*

>   The factor used to decrease the priority of a job every time it is processed, so
>   that mail that cannot be delivered does not keep popping to the top of the
>   queue. The default is 90000.

SafeFileEnvironment=*directory*

>   chroot(2) to *directory* before writing a file and refuse to deliver to sym-
>   bolic links.

SaveFromLine

>   Save UNIX-style From: lines at the front of headers. Normally they are dis-
>   carded.

SendMIMEErrors

>   Send error messages in MIME format.

ServiceSwitchFile=*path*

>   The *path* to a file that lists the of methods used for various services. The Ser-
>   viceSwitchFile contains entries that begin with the service name followed by
>   the service method. sendmail checks for services named "aliases" and "hosts"
>   and supports "dns", "nis", "nisplus", or "files" as possible service methods,
>   assuming that support for all of these methods is compiled into this copy of
>   sendmail. ServiceSwitchFile defaults to */etc/service.switch*. If that file does not
>   exist, sendmail uses the following service methods: aliases are looked up in
>   the aliases files, and hosts are looked up first using dns, then nis, and finally

the hosts file. If the operating system has a built-in service switch feature, it is used and this option is ignored. See the description of the *nsswitch.conf* file in Chapter 9, *Configuring Network Servers*. It is a service switch file.

SevenBitInput

Strip input to 7 bits for compatibility with old systems. This shouldn't be necessary.

SingleLineFromHeader

For compatibility with some versions of Lotus Notes, unwrapped From: lines that have embedded newlines into one long line.

SingleThreadDelivery

Don't open more than one SMTP connections to a remote host at the same time. This option requires the HostStatusDirectory option.

SmtpGreetingMessage=*message*

The greeting sent to the remote host when it connects to the SMTP server port. This is the value defined in macro e.

StatusFile=*file*

Log summary statistics in *file*. By default, summary statistics are not logged.

SuperSafe

Create a queue file, even when attempting immediate delivery.

TempFileMode=*mode*

Use *mode* to set the access permissions for queue files. *mode* is an octal value. It defaults to 0600.

Timeout.*type*=*timeout*

Set timeout values, where *type* is the thing being timed and *timeout* is the time interval before the timer expires. Table E-8 lists the valid *type* values, the event being timed and the default *timeout* value for each type.

Table E-8: Timeout Types

Type	Waiting For	Default
initial	Initial greeting message	5m
helo	Reply to HELO or EHLO command	5m
mail	Reply to MAIL command	10m
rcpt	Reply to RCPT command	1h
datainit	Reply to DATA command	5m
datablock	Data block read	1h
datafinal	Reply to terminating "."	1h
rset	Reply to RSET command	5m
quit	Reply to QUIT command	2m

Table E-8: Timeout Types (continued)

Type	Waiting For	Default
misc	Reply to NOOP and VERB commands	2m
ident	IDENT protocol response	30s
fileopen	Open on a *.forward* or *:include:* file	60s
command	Command read	1h
queuereturn	Returning a queued message as undeliverable	5d
queuewarn	Warning that a message is still queued	none
hoststatus	Removing stale host status	30m

TimeZoneSpec=`tzinfo`

> Set the local time zone information to `tzinfo`. If **TimeZoneSpec** is not set, the system default is used; if set to null, the user's **TZ** variable is used.

TryNullMXList

> Connect directly to any remote host that lists the local system as its most preferred MX server, as if the remote host had no MX records. You are discouraged from using this option.

UnixFromLine=`fromline`

> Defines the format for UNIX-style From: lines. This is the same as the value stored in macro l.

UnsafeGroupWrites

> Group writable *:include:* and *.forward* files cannot reference programs or write directly to files. World-writable files always have these restrictions.

UseErrorsTo

> Send error messages to the addresses listed in the Errors-To: header. Normally, errors are sent to the sender address form the envelope.

UserDatabaseSpec=`udbspec`

> The user database specification.

UserSubmission

> Indicates that this is not relayed mail, but an initial submission directly from a Mail User Agent.

Verbose

> Run in verbose mode.

Older versions of sendmail use a different option syntax:

```
oxvalue
```

In this syntax o is the command, *x* is a single character option name, and *value* is the value passed to sendmail to set the option. Some options are Booleans that require no input value. Table E-9 lists all of the old-style options.

Table E-9: Old-Style sendmail Options

Name	Function
A*file*	Define the name of the alias file.
a*N*	Wait *N* minutes for @:@; then rebuild the alias file.
B*c*	Define the blank substitution character.
c	Queue mail for expensive mailers.
D	Rebuild the alias database.
db	Deliver in background mode.
di	Deliver interactively.
dq	Deliver during the next queue run.
ee	Mail error messages and always return 0 exit status.
em	Mail back error messages.
ep	Print error messages.
eq	Just return exit status, not error messages.
ew	Write back error messages.
F*n*	Set permissions for temporary files to *n*.
f	Retain UNIX-style From: lines.
g*n*	Set the default group ID for mailers to *n*.
H*file*	Define the name of the SMTP help file.
I	Use the BIND name server to resolve all hostnames.
i	Ignore dots in incoming messages.
L*n*	Set the level of logging to *n*.
M*xval*	Set macro *x* to *val*.
m	Send to me, too.
N*net*	Define the name of the home network.
o	Accept old format headers.
Q*dir*	Define the name of the queue directory.
q*n*	Define a factor *n* used to decide when to queue jobs.
r*t*	Set interval *t* for read timeout.
S*file*	Define the name of the statistics log file.
s	Always create the queue file before attempting delivery.
T*t*	Set the queue timeout to *t*.
u*n*	Set the default user ID for mailers to *n*.
v	Run in verbose mode.
W*pass*	Define password used for remote debugging.
X*l*	Refuse SMTP connections if load average exceeds *l*.
x*l*	Queue messages if load average exceeds *l*.
Y	Deliver each queued job in a separate process.
y*n*	Lower priority of jobs by *n* for each recipient.

Table E-9: Old-Style sendmail Options (continued)

Name	Function
Z*n*	Decrease a job's priority by *n* each time it is run.
z*n*	Factor used with precedence to determine message priority.

See Chapter 10 for examples of setting options with both styles of syntax.

sendmail Mailer Flags

Mailer flags are declared in the F field of the mailer definition. Each mailer flag is set by a single character that represents that flag. For example: **F=lsDFMe** sets six different flags. Table E-10 lists the single character name and function of each flag.

Table E-10: sendmail Mailer Flags

Name	Function
C	Add *@domain* to addresses that do not have an @.
D	The mailer wants a Date: header line.
E	Add > to message lines that begin with From:.
e	This an expensive mailer. See sendmail option c.
F	The mailer wants a From: header line.
f	The mailer accepts a −f flag from trusted users.
h	Preserve uppercase in hostnames.
I	The mailer will be speaking SMTP to another sendmail.
L	Limit the line lengths as specified in RFC821.
l	This is a local mailer.
M	The mailer wants a Message-Id: header line.
m	The mailer can send to multiple users in one transaction.
n	Don't insert a UNIX-style From: line in the message.
P	The mailer wants a Return-Path: line.
R	Use the MAIL FROM: return-path rather than the return address.
r	The mailer accepts a −r flag from trusted users.
S	Don't reset the userid before calling the mailer.
s	Strip quotes off of the address before calling the mailer.
U	The mailer wants UNIX-style From: lines.
u	Preserve uppercase in usernames.
X	Prepend a dot to lines beginning with a dot.
x	The mailer wants a Full-Name: header line.

See Chapter 10 for examples of mailer flag declaration within mailer definitions.

The sendmail K Command

The sendmail K command is used to define a database within the *sendmail.cf* file. The K command syntax is:

```
Kname type [arguments]
```

Chapter 10 provides examples of defining and using a sendmail database, and it describes the K command syntax. This appendix lists the valid *type* values and *arguments* that can be used with a K command.

The type field of the K command identifies what kind of database is being defined. There are several internal database types that are specific to sendmail and several external types that rely on external database libraries. Support for the external database types must be compiled into sendmail by explicitly specifying the supported database types in the DBMDEF variable in the Makefile used to build sendmail. See the example of compiling sendmail earlier in this appendix.

The possible values for type are:

dbm

The "new dbm" database format. It is accessed using the ndbm(3) library. Only supported if sendmail is compiled with NDBM defined.

btree

The btree database format. It is accessed using the Berkeley db(3) library. Only supported if sendmail is compiled with NEWDB defined.

hash

The hash database format. It is accessed using the Berkeley db(3) library. Only supported if sendmail is compiled with NEWDB defined.

nis NIS server lookups. sendmail must be compiled with NIS defined to support this.

nisplus

NIS+ server lookups. sendmail must be compiled with NISPLUS defined to support this.

hesiod

MIT hesiod server lookups. Support requires that sendmail is compiled with HESIOD defined.

ldapx

X500 directory searches using LDAP. sendmail must be compiled with LDAPMAP defined to support this. sendmail supports most of the standard command line arguments of the ldapsearch program.

netinfo

> NeXT NetInfo lookups. Only supported if sendmail is compiled with NETINFO defined.

text

> Text file lookups. Requires no external database libraries or compile options. The format of the text database is defined with the key field, value field, and field delimiter flags. See the next section for a description of the K command flags.

stab

> An internal symbol table database.

implicit

> The default internal sendmail format used for an alias file, if no type is defined for the file.

user

> A special sendmail type used to verify the existence of a user by using getpw-nam(3).

host

> A special sendmail type used to convert nicknames and IP addresses to canonical names via the domain name server. This is an alternative form of the $[*name*]$ syntax.

sequence

> A special sendmail type used to define the order in which previously defined databases are searched. For example, assume that three databases (file1, file2, and file3) are defined by K commands. It is possible to add a fourth K command, **Kallfiles sequence file3 file1 file2**, that "combines" them together as *allfiles* and specifies that file3 is searched first, file1 second, and file2 third.

switch

> A special sendmail type that uses the service switch file to set the order in which database files are searched. The `argument` on a K command with a `type` of "switch" must be the name of a service in the service switch file. The values associated with the service name in the service switch file are used to create the names of databases that are searched in the order in which they are defined. For example: the command **Kali switch aliases** looks up the service switch entry for `aliases`. If it contains the values `nis files`, sendmail searches databases named *ali.nis* and *ali.files* in that order.

dequote

> A special sendmail type used to strip unwanted double quotes (`"`) from email addresses.

The argument that follows most database types is a filename. The filename identifies the external file that contains the database. Only the basic filename is provided. sendmail adds an extension appropriate for the database type. For example: `Krealname dbm /usr/etc/names` becomes */usr/etc/names.db* because *.db* is the correct extension for dbm databases.

In addition to a filename, the arguments field can contain optional flags:

−o This is an optional database. sendmail proceeds without error if the file is not found.

−N

Valid database keys are terminated with a NULL character.

−O

Valid database keys are never terminated with a NULL character. Never specify both −N and −O, which indicates that no keys are valid! It is safest to avoid both −N and −O and let sendmail determine the correct key structure unless you are positive about the correct flag.

−a*x*

Append the string *x* to the value return by a successful match.

−f Do not convert uppercase to lowercase before attempting to match the key.

−m

Check that the key exists in the database, but do not replace the key with the value returned by the database.

−k*keycol*

The location of the key within a database entry. For most databases the key is the first field and this flag is not needed. For text file lookups this flag is required and *keycol* is the column number in which the key begins.

−v*valcol*

The location of the value within a database entry. For most databases, the value follows the key and the **−v** flag is not used. For text file lookups, this flag is required and specifies the column in which the value field begins.

−z*delim*

The character that delimits fields within the database. By default, it is whitespace.

−t Allow database lookups that depend on remote servers to fail instead of queuing the mail for later processing. This is primarily used when you have DNS server problems. Normally when a remote server fails to respond the mail is put in the queue for later delivery. Setting this flag causes the mail to be immediately returned to the sender as undeliverable.

−s*spacesub*

Use *spacesub* to replace space characters after processing an address against the dequote database.

The full lists of database types and flag provided in this appendix will help you understand the K commands inserted into the *sendmail.cf* file by the **m4** processor. Your own K commands will be much simpler. You will stick with a database type that is supported by your **sendmail** and **makemap** commands, and you will build simple databases designed to fulfill specific purposes. Chapter 10 provides examples of such databases, and the next section contains some simple scripts used to build those example databases.

Sample script

In Chapter 10, the *realnames* database is used to rewrite login usernames to the "firstname dot lastname" format for outbound email. The script shown below builds the *realnames* database from the */etc/passwd* file.

```
#! /bin/sh
#
# Eliminate "non-login" accounts
grep -v ':*:' /etc/passwd | \
# Eliminate "exposed" usernames, i.e. usernames defined
#  in class E as names that should not be re-written
grep -v '^root:' | \
# Replace delimiting colons with whitespace
sed 's/:/ /g' | \
# Output the username followed by firstname.lastname
awk '{ print $1, $5"."$6 }' > realnames
# Build the realnames database
makemap dbm realnames < realnames
```

Building *realnames* from the *passwd* file is completely dependent on the format of that file. The *passwd* file *must* have a consistent format for the GECOS field and a consistent way to identify a "non-user" account. A "non-user" account is not accessed by a user to log in or to collect email. It is normally a system account used by system or application software. A classic example is the *uucp* account. Every system has some way to mark that these accounts are not used for user logins. Some systems use an asterisk in the password field, while others use an exclamation mark, the letters NP, an x, or something else. The sample script assumes that an asterisk is used, which is the case on my Linux system. (My Solaris systems uses an x.) Print out your *passwd* file to find out what it uses and modify the script accordingly.

The sample script also assumes that the first two values in the GECOS field are the user's first and last name separated by a blank. If the beginning of the GECOS field is in any other format, the script produces garabage. The procedure you use to add new users to your system should produce a consistent GECOS field. Inconsistency is the enemy of automation. The sample below shows a file that has inconsistencies and the bad data it produces:

```
% cat /etc/passwd
root:oRd1L/vMzzxno:0:1:System Administrator:/:/bin/csh
nobody:*:65534:65534::/:
daemon:*:1:1::/:
sys:*:2:2::/:/bin/csh
bin:*:3:3::/bin:
uucp:*:4:8::/var/spool/uucppublic:
news:*:6:6::/var/spool/news:/bin/csh
ingres:*:7:7::/usr/ingres:/bin/csh
audit:*:9:9::/etc/security/audit:/bin/csh
craig:1LrpKlz8sYjw:198:102:Craig Hunt:/home/craig:/bin/csh
dan:RSU.NYlKuFqzh2:214:885:Dan Scribner:/home/dan:/bin/csh
becca:monfTHdnjj:101:102:"Becky_Hunt":/home/becca:/bin/csh
dave:lniuhugfds:121:885:David H. Craig:/home/dave:/bin/csh
kathy:TUVigddehh:101:802:Kathleen S McCafferty:/home/kathy:/bin/csh
% build.realnames
% cat realnames
craig Craig.Hunt
dan Dan.Scribner
becca "Becky_Hunt"./home/becca
dave David.H.
kathy Kathleen.S
```

Your *passwd* file may have grown over time under the control of several different system administrators. It may be full of inconsistencies. If it is, clean it up before you run the script to build email aliases, and then maintain it consistently.

Sample Configurations

In Chapter 10 we develop a sendmail configuration. The configuration has these characteristics:

- It runs on a Linux system.

- The hostname of the sending system is rewritten to the domain name on all out-bound mail. The hostname is rewritten in the message headers and the envelope headers.

- The sender's username on all outgoing mail is rewritten to the user's first name and last name.

We use two approaches to produce this configuration. First, we use the sample m4 source files that come with sendmail to create a custom macro configuration file. Next, we created the same configuration by directly modifying the sample *sendmail.cf* file that comes with Slackware 96 Linux. In this section we recap both sample configurations.

To many system administrators, the simpliest way to create the configuration is to use the **m4** macro source files. The macro source files are very short, and many people feel they are easier to read than the *sendmail.cf* file. If you download and compile sendmail, it is a good idea to use the macro files because the features in those files will match the downloaded sendmail release.

We name the macro file we create in Chapter 10 *linux.mc*. The file contains these macros:

```
VERSIONID('@(#)tcpproto.mc     8.5 (Berkeley) 3/23/96')
OSTYPE(linux)
DOMAIN(nuts.com)
FEATURE(nouucp)
MAILER(local)
MAILER(smtp)
```

It is identical to the *tcpproto.mc* file delivered with sendmail, with two modifications. First, we change the OSTYPE macro to define Linux as the operating system. Next we add a `DOMAIN(nuts.com)` line to invoke a "domain-specific" macro file we create and name *nuts.com.m4*. The *nuts.com.m4* file contains the following lines:

```
MASQUERADE_AS(nuts.com)
FEATURE(masquerade_envelope)
FEATURE(genericstable)
```

These three lines peform all of the functions we required of our configuration. The `MASQUERADE_AS` statement rewrites the hostname to the domain name. The `FEATURE(masquerade_envelope)` statement ensures that the hostname is rewritten in the envelope headers as well as the message headers. The `FEATURE(generictable)` statement causes the username to be processed through the **genericstable**, which is the database we use to convert it to the user's first and last name.

All of the functions we require of our configuration are accomplished in five lines. Modifying the *sendmail.cf* file directly requires much more effort. However, the the **m4** source files can only be used if they match the version of sendmail. For this reason, **m4** is most often used by administrators who download and install sendmail themselves. Most administrators who use the sendmail that comes with their system also use the *sendmail.cf* file that comes with the system. In Chapter 10, we use the *linux.smtp.cf* file that comes with the Slackware 96 version of Linux 2.0. The detailed modifications of the file are explained in Chapter 10. Excerpts from the modified file are listed in this appendix and are heavily commented to make the modifications more understandable. A full listing of the *sendmail.cf* file would consume 15 pages. Compare that to the listing of the **m4** files shown above.

The *linux.smtp.cf* file is not identical to the configuration file produced by **m4**, even when you follow the example in the "Building a sendmail.cf with m4 Macros" section of Chapter 10. The configurations are similar but not identical. Use this text as a general guide to the structure and function of configuration file. Don't expect the details to match your file exactly.

This excerpt shows the entire local information section because it is discussed extensively in Chapter 10:

```
#++++++++++++++++++++++++++++++++++++++++++++++++++++++++++++++++++++++++
# The V command defines the configuration syntax version level.
# Level 6 was supported by sendmail-8.7.5, which was the release
# of sendmail that came with Slackware 96 Linux 2.0.  The vendor
# name Berkeley means that the standard syntax of the Berkeley
# distribution is supported.
#++++++++++++++++++++++++++++++++++++++++++++++++++++++++++++++++++++++++
# level 6 config file format
V6/Berkeley


#++++++++++++++++++++++++++++++++++++++++++++++++++++++++++++++++++++++++
#Like most sendmail configuration files, the first sections of the file
#contain the data that is most likely to require custom configuration.
#In this file, the section is titled "Local info".  Note that we moved
#things around in this section to bring related items together.  They
#don't really occur in this sequence in the linux.smtp.cf file.
#++++++++++++++++++++++++++++++++++++++++++++++++++++++++++++++++++++++++


##################
#   local info   #
##################
#++++++++++++++++++++++++++++++++++++++++++++++++++++++++++++++++++++++++
#If your host is known by more than one hostname, the multiple host
#names are defined in class "w", which contains all of the names for
#which your host will accept mail.
#++++++++++++++++++++++++++++++++++++++++++++++++++++++++++++++++++++++++
Cwlocalhost


#++++++++++++++++++++++++++++++++++++++++++++++++++++++++++++++++++++++++
The j macro is correctly define by the system.  No need to set it here.
#++++++++++++++++++++++++++++++++++++++++++++++++++++++++++++++++++++++++
# my official domain name
# ... define this only if sendmail cannot automatically determine
# your domain
#Dj$w.Foo.COM


#++++++++++++++++++++++++++++++++++++++++++++++++++++++++++++++++++++++++
#Class P is used to store pseudo domains.  It is only used in this
#file to store a dot (.) used to identify canonical names.  The dot
#(.) class, which is supposed to be used to identify canonical names,
#is not referenced anywhere else in the file.
#++++++++++++++++++++++++++++++++++++++++++++++++++++++++++++++++++++++++
CP.
```

```
# a class with just dot (for identifying canonical names)
C..

#++++++++++++++++++++++++++++++++++++++++++++++++++++++++++++++++++++++
#Several different mail relay servers can be defined.  We don't use any
#in this sample configuration.  The L macro and the L class are only
#significant if relay servers are defined for handling "local" mail.
#++++++++++++++++++++++++++++++++++++++++++++++++++++++++++++++++++++++
# "Smart" relay host (may be null)
DS

# who I send unqualified names to (null means deliver locally)
DR

# who gets all local email traffic ($R has precedence for unqualified names)
DH

# place to which unknown users should be forwarded
#Kuser user -m -a<>
#DLname_of_luser_relay

# class L: names that should be delivered locally, even if we have a relay
#CL root

#++++++++++++++++++++++++++++++++++++++++++++++++++++++++++++++++++++++
#Sample K commands are included in the linux.smtp.cf file.  Of these,
#only the dequote database is active.  The others are commented out by
#default.  The purpose of each of these databases is explained earlier
#in this appendix.
#++++++++++++++++++++++++++++++++++++++++++++++++++++++++++++++++++++++
# Mailer table (overriding domains)
#Kmailertable dbm /etc/mailertable

# Domain table (adding domains)
#Kdomaintable dbm /etc/domaintable

# dequoting map
Kdequote dequote

#++++++++++++++++++++++++++++++++++++++++++++++++++++++++++++++++++++++
#Several lines relate to address "masquerading".  Macro M defines the
#hostname that should be used in place of the system's real hostname
#on outgoing mail.  The M class defines other hostnames that should be
#converted to the macro M hostname.  Class E defines usernames for which
#the hostname should not be converted to $M.
#++++++++++++++++++++++++++++++++++++++++++++++++++++++++++++++++++++++
# class E: names that should be exposed as from this host, even if
# we masquerade
CE root
# class M: domains that should be converted to $M
#CM

# who I masquerade as (null for no masquerading) (see also $=M)
DMnuts.com
```

```
#+++++++++++++++++++++++++++++++++++++++++++++++++++++++++++++++++++++++++
#We added this K command to define a database that we created that converts
#username to the user's real first and last names.
#+++++++++++++++++++++++++++++++++++++++++++++++++++++++++++++++++++++++++
# define a database to map login names to firstname.lastname
Krealnames dbm /tmp/realnames

# operators that cannot be in local usernames (i.e., network indicators)
CO @ %

# my name for error messages
DnMAILER-DAEMON


#+++++++++++++++++++++++++++++++++++++++++++++++++++++++++++++++++++++++++
#Macro Z contains the configuration file's version number.  Modify it
#every time the file is updated.  Keep a record of your modifications.
#+++++++++++++++++++++++++++++++++++++++++++++++++++++++++++++++++++++++++
#  R1.0 - modified for peanut by Craig
#       - cleaned up the comments in the local info section
#  R1.1 - modified macro M to use nuts.com instead of the
#          hostname in outgoing mail
#  R2.0 - added rule a to S11 & S31 to rewrite to first.last format
DZ8.7.3R2.0
```

In Chapter 10 we modified ruleset 94 to enable masquerading for envelope
addresses.

```
####################################################################
###  Ruleset 94 -- convert envelope names to masqueraded form   ###
####################################################################
#+++++++++++++++++++++++++++++++++++++++++++++++++++++++++++++++++++++++++
#To enable "envelop" address masquerading we "uncommented" the first line
#in this ruleset so that it now calls ruleset 93.
#+++++++++++++++++++++++++++++++++++++++++++++++++++++++++++++++++++++++++
S94
R$+                    $@ $>93 $1
R$* < @ *LOCAL* > $*   $: $1 < @ $j . > $2
```

The mailers do not usually require modification. However, in Chapter 10, we made
some changes to the S rulesets of the "smtp" mailer. We made changes to both
ruleset 11 and ruleset 31.

```
#+++++++++++++++++++++++++++++++++++++++++++++++++++++++++++++++++++++++++
#In Chapter 10 we added a single rule to the end of this ruleset to lookup
#the username in the "realnames" database we created and return the
#user's real first and last names.
#+++++++++++++++++++++++++++++++++++++++++++++++++++++++++++++++++++++++++
#
#   envelope sender rewriting
#
S11
R$+                    $: $>51 $1              sender/recipient common
R$* :; <@>             $@                      list:; special case
R$*                    $: $>61 $1              qualify unqual'ed names
```

```
R$+                       $: $>94 $1                       do masquerading
# when masquerading convert login name to firstname.lastname
R$- < @ $M . > $*         $: $(realnames $1 $) < @ $M . > $2  user=>first.last


#
#   envelope recipient rewriting --
#   also header recipient if not masquerading recipients
#
S21
R$+                       $: $>51 $1                       sender/recipient common
R$+                       $: $>61 $1                       qualify unqual'ed names

#++++++++++++++++++++++++++++++++++++++++++++++++++++++++++++++++++++++++++++
#In Chapter 10 we added a single rule to the end of this ruleset to look up
#the username name in the "realnames" database we created and return the
#user's real first and last names.  This is the same modification made
#above.  Often more than one ruleset is modified to add a single new
#feature.
#++++++++++++++++++++++++++++++++++++++++++++++++++++++++++++++++++++++++++++
#
#   header sender and masquerading header recipient rewriting
#
S31
R$+                       $: $>51 $1                       sender/recipient common
R:; <@>                   $@                               list:; special case

# do special header rewriting
R$* <@> $*                $@ $1 <@> $2                     pass null host through
R< @ $* > $*              $@ < @ $1 > $2                   pass route-addr through
R$*                       $: $>61 $1                       qualify unqual'ed names
R$+                       $: $>93 $1                       do masquerading
# when masquerading convert login name to firstname.lastname
R$- < @ $M . > $*         $: $(realnames $1 $) < @ $M . > $2   user=>first.last
```

F

Selected TCP/IP Headers

In Chapter 11, *Troubleshooting TCP/IP*, several references are made to specific TCP/IP headers. Those headers are documented here. This is not an exhaustive list of headers; only the headers used in the troubleshooting examples in Chapter 11 are covered:

* IP Datagram Header, as defined in RFC 791, *Internet Protocol*

* TCP Segment Header, as defined in RFC 793, *Transmission Control Protocol*

* ICMP Parameter Problem Message Header, as defined in RFC 792, *Internet Control Message Protocol*

Each header is presented using an excerpt from the RFC that defines the header. These are not exact quotes; the excerpts have been slightly edited to better fit this text. However, we still want to emphasize the importance of using primary sources for troubleshooting protocol problems. These headers are provided here to help you follow the examples in Chapter 11. For real troubleshooting, use the real RFCs. You can obtain your own copies of the RFCs by following the instructions in Chapter 13, *Internet Information Resources*.

IP Datagram Header

This description is taken from pages 11 to 15 of RFC 791, *Internet Protocol*, by Jon Postel, Information Sciences Institute, University of Southern California.

```
Internet Header Format


 0                   1                   2                   3
 0 1 2 3 4 5 6 7 8 9 0 1 2 3 4 5 6 7 8 9 0 1 2 3 4 5 6 7 8 9 0 1
+-+-+-+-+-+-+-+-+-+-+-+-+-+-+-+-+-+-+-+-+-+-+-+-+-+-+-+-+-+-+-+-+
|Version|  IHL  |Type of Service|          Total Length         |
+-+-+-+-+-+-+-+-+-+-+-+-+-+-+-+-+-+-+-+-+-+-+-+-+-+-+-+-+-+-+-+-+
```

```
|            Identification           |Flags|      Fragment Offset      |
+-+-+-+-+-+-+-+-+-+-+-+-+-+-+-+-+-+-+-+-+-+-+-+-+-+-+-+-+-+-+-+-+
|  Time to Live |    Protocol    |         Header Checksum         |
+-+-+-+-+-+-+-+-+-+-+-+-+-+-+-+-+-+-+-+-+-+-+-+-+-+-+-+-+-+-+-+-+
|                        Source Address                           |
+-+-+-+-+-+-+-+-+-+-+-+-+-+-+-+-+-+-+-+-+-+-+-+-+-+-+-+-+-+-+-+-+
|                      Destination Address                        |
+-+-+-+-+-+-+-+-+-+-+-+-+-+-+-+-+-+-+-+-+-+-+-+-+-+-+-+-+-+-+-+-+
|                        Options                  |    Padding    |
+-+-+-+-+-+-+-+-+-+-+-+-+-+-+-+-+-+-+-+-+-+-+-+-+-+-+-+-+-+-+-+-+
```

Version: 4 bits

  The Version field indicates the format of the internet header.
  This document describes version 4.

IHL: 4 bits

  Internet Header Length is the length of the internet header in 32
  bit words. The minimum value for a correct header is 5.

Type of Service: 8 bits

  The Type of Service indication the quality of service desired.
  The meaning of the bits is explained below.

    Bits 0-2: Precedence.
    Bit   3: 0 = Normal Delay,   1 = Low Delay.
    Bits   4: 0 = Normal Throughput, 1 = High Throughput.
    Bits   5: 0 = Normal Reliability 1 = High Reliability.
    Bit 6-7: Reserved for Future Use.

```
      0     1     2     3     4     5     6     7
   +-----+-----+-----+-----+-----+-----+-----+-----+
   |     |     |     |     |     |     |     |     |
   |  PRECEDENCE     |  D  |  T  |  R  |  0  |  0  |
   |     |     |     |     |     |     |     |     |
   +-----+-----+-----+-----+-----+-----+-----+-----+
```

    Precedence

      111 - Network Control
      110 - Internetwork Control
      101 - CRITIC/ECP
      100 - Flash Override
      011 - Flash
      010 - Immediate
      001 - Priority
      000 - Routine

Total Length: 16 bits

  Total Length is the length of the datagram, measured in octets
  (bytes), including internet header and data.

Identification: 16 bits

   An identifying value assigned by the sender to aid in assembling
   the fragments of a datagram.

Flags: 3 bits

   Various Control Flags.   The Flag bit are explained below:

      Bit 0: reserved, must be zero
      Bit 1: (DF) 0 = May Fragment, 1 = Don't Fragment.
      Bit 2: (MF) 0 = Last Fragment, 1 = More Fragments.

```
        0   1   2
      +---+---+---+
      |   | D | M |
      | 0 | F | F |
      +---+---+---+
```

Fragment Offset: 13 bits

   This field indicates where in the datagram this fragment belongs.
   The fragment offset is measured in units of 8 octets (64 bits).
   The first fragment has offset zero.

Time to Live: 8 bits

   This field indicates the maximum time the datagram is allowed to
   remain in the internet system.

Protocol: 8 bits

   This field indicates the Transport Layer protocol that the data
   portion of this datagram is passed to.   The values for various
   protocols are specified in the "Assigned Numbers" RFC.

Header Checksum: 16 bits

   A checksum on the header only.   Since some header fields change
   (e.g., time to live), this is recomputed and verified at each
   point that the internet header is processed.   The checksum
   algorithm is:

   The checksum field is the 16 bit one's complement of the one's
   complement sum of all 16 bit words in the header.   For purposes
   of computing the checksum, the value of the checksum field is
   zero.

Source Address: 32 bits

   The source IP address.   See Chapter 2, *Delivering the Data*, for a
   description of IP addresses.

```
Destination Address:   32 bits

   The destination IP address.   See Chapter 2 for a description of IP
   addresses.

Options:  variable

   The options may or may not appear in datagrams, but they must be
   implemented by all IP modules (host and gateways).   No options
   were used in any of the datagrams examined in Chapter 11.
```

TCP Segment Header

This description is taken from pages 15 to 17 of RFC 793, *Transmission Control Protocol*, by Jon Postel, Information Sciences Institute, University of Southern California.

```
TCP Header Format

    0                   1                   2                   3
    0 1 2 3 4 5 6 7 8 9 0 1 2 3 4 5 6 7 8 9 0 1 2 3 4 5 6 7 8 9 0 1
   +-+-+-+-+-+-+-+-+-+-+-+-+-+-+-+-+-+-+-+-+-+-+-+-+-+-+-+-+-+-+-+-+
   |          Source Port          |       Destination Port        |
   +-+-+-+-+-+-+-+-+-+-+-+-+-+-+-+-+-+-+-+-+-+-+-+-+-+-+-+-+-+-+-+-+
   |                        Sequence Number                        |
   +-+-+-+-+-+-+-+-+-+-+-+-+-+-+-+-+-+-+-+-+-+-+-+-+-+-+-+-+-+-+-+-+
   |                     Acknowledgment Number                     |
   +-+-+-+-+-+-+-+-+-+-+-+-+-+-+-+-+-+-+-+-+-+-+-+-+-+-+-+-+-+-+-+-+
   |  Data |           |U|A|P|R|S|F|                               |
   | Offset| Reserved  |R|C|S|S|Y|I|            Window             |
   |       |           |G|K|H|T|N|N|                               |
   +-+-+-+-+-+-+-+-+-+-+-+-+-+-+-+-+-+-+-+-+-+-+-+-+-+-+-+-+-+-+-+-+
   |           Checksum            |         Urgent Pointer        |
   +-+-+-+-+-+-+-+-+-+-+-+-+-+-+-+-+-+-+-+-+-+-+-+-+-+-+-+-+-+-+-+-+
   |                    Options                    |    Padding    |
   +-+-+-+-+-+-+-+-+-+-+-+-+-+-+-+-+-+-+-+-+-+-+-+-+-+-+-+-+-+-+-+-+
   |                             data                              |
   +-+-+-+-+-+-+-+-+-+-+-+-+-+-+-+-+-+-+-+-+-+-+-+-+-+-+-+-+-+-+-+-+

Source Port:  16 bits

   The source port number.

Destination Port:  16 bits

   The destination port number.

Sequence Number:  32 bits

   The sequence number of the first data octet (byte) in this segment
   (except when SYN is present). If SYN is present the sequence
   number is the initial sequence number (ISN) and the first data
   octet is ISN+1.
```

Acknowledgment Number: 32 bits

    If the ACK control bit is set, this field contains the value of
the next sequence number the sender of the segment is expecting to
receive. Once a connection is established this is always sent.

Data Offset: 4 bits

    The number of 32 bit words in the TCP Header. This indicates
where the data begins. The TCP header (even one including options)
is an integral number of 32 bits long.

Reserved: 6 bits

    Reserved for future use. Must be zero.

Control Bits: 6 single-bit values (from left to right):

    URG: Urgent Pointer field significant
    ACK: Acknowledgment field significant
    PSH: Push Function
    RST: Reset the connection
    SYN: Synchronize sequence numbers
    FIN: No more data from sender

Window: 16 bits

    The number of data octets (bytes) the sender of this segment is
willing to accept.

Checksum: 16 bits

    The checksum field is the 16 bit one's complement of the one's
complement sum of all 16 bit words in the header and text.

Urgent Pointer: 16 bits

    This field contains the current value of the urgent pointer as a
positive offset from the sequence number in this segment. The
urgent pointer points to the sequence number of the octet
following the urgent data. This field is only be interpreted
in segments with the URG control bit set.

Options: variable

    Options may occupy space at the end of the TCP header and are a
multiple of 8 bits in length.

ICMP Parameter Problem Message Header

This description is taken from pages 8 and 9 of RFC 792, *Internet Control Message Protocol*, by Jon Postel, Information Sciences Institute, University of Southern California.

```
Parameter Problem Message

    0                   1                   2                   3
    0 1 2 3 4 5 6 7 8 9 0 1 2 3 4 5 6 7 8 9 0 1 2 3 4 5 6 7 8 9 0 1
   +-+-+-+-+-+-+-+-+-+-+-+-+-+-+-+-+-+-+-+-+-+-+-+-+-+-+-+-+-+-+-+-+
   |     Type      |     Code      |          Checksum             |
   +-+-+-+-+-+-+-+-+-+-+-+-+-+-+-+-+-+-+-+-+-+-+-+-+-+-+-+-+-+-+-+-+
   |    Pointer    |                   unused                      |
   +-+-+-+-+-+-+-+-+-+-+-+-+-+-+-+-+-+-+-+-+-+-+-+-+-+-+-+-+-+-+-+-+
   |      Internet Header + 64 bits of Original Data Datagram      |
   +-+-+-+-+-+-+-+-+-+-+-+-+-+-+-+-+-+-+-+-+-+-+-+-+-+-+-+-+-+-+-+-+
```

Type

    12

Code

    0 = pointer indicates the error.

Checksum

    The checksum is the 16-bit ones's complement of the one's
    complement sum of the ICMP message starting with the ICMP Type.
    For computing the checksum , the checksum field should be zero.

Pointer

    If code = 0, identifies the octet where an error was detected.

Internet Header + 64 bits of Data Datagram

    The internet header plus the first 64 bits of the datagram that
    elicited this error response.

Index

Symbols

; (see semicolon (;))
* (see asterisk (*))
# (see sharp sign (#))
: (see colon (:))
"" (see quotes, pair (""))
" (see apostrophes, pair ("))
() (see parentheses ())
.. (see dots, pair (..))
\ (see backslash (\)
– (see minus sign (–))
{} (see curly ({))
-> (see hyphen-greater than (->))
@ (see at sign (@))

Numbers

6-bit serial lines, running over, 111
7bit encoding type, 68
8bit encoding type, 68

A

ABORT keyword, 446
Abstract Syntax Notation One (ASN.1), 359
access control, 393-403
    levels of, 229
    services to place under, listed, 394
    software for, 393
ACKD command, in POP, 64
Acknowledgment (ACK) bit set, 19
Acknowledgment Number field, 20
adaptive protocol value, 155

Address Resolution Protocol (ARP), 40, 47, 72
    command, 40, 114
        in troubleshooting, 323, 329-332
    enabling, 133
    proxy server for, 114
    support in BSD, 115
    table, 434
        viewing contents of, 329
addresses
    allocating
        dynamically, 75
        manually, 75
    assigning
        in blocks, 87
        in contiguous blocks, 28, 495
        in DHCP, 75
    broadcast, 31, 41, 80, 124, 128
        limited, 73
        setting, 131
        specifying, 90
    classes of, 25-27, 83
        class rules, 177
    converting, 303
    email
        processing, 302
        simplified, 288
    gateway (see gateway)
    getting in pppd, 143
    host, 26
        assigning, 87
    Internet-style, 306

Y

ypbind, 246
ypcat, 247
    −x command, 246
ypmatch, 247
ypserv, 246
ypwhich, 247

Z

zone, 203
    files, 203
        in named, 503-517
    transfer, 59, 204, 212, 223

About the Author

Craig Hunt has worked with computer systems for the last 25 years. He spent the first few years after receiving his B.A. from American University running an outdoor camp for inner-city kids, but the call of the computer was stronger than the call of the wild. Craig went to work for the federal government as a programmer and then as a systems programmer. He left the government to work for Honeywell on the WWMCCS network in the days before TCP/IP, back when the network used NCP. After Honeywell, Craig went to work for the National Institute of Standards and Technology. He's still there today and currently leads the Advanced Network Technologies Division. Craig is a member of the Federal Networking Council, the Large Scale Network Working Group, and the Next Generation Internet Implementation Team. He taught a course on TCP/IP network administration at Montgomery College in the 1980s and currently teaches a tutorial on the subject at Networld+Interop. In addition to *TCP/IP Network Administration*, he wrote *Networking Personal Computers with TCP/IP* and Appendix C of *Building Internet Firewalls*. He is currently working on a version of *TCP/IP Network Administration* for Windows NT.

Craig lives with his wife and children in Gaithersburg, Maryland. He loves the outdoors, splitting vacation time between the mountains and the sea, and he has a passion for rock and roll music.

Colophon

Our look is the result of reader comments, our own experimentation, and feedback from distribution channels.

Distinctive covers complement our distinctive approach to technical topics, breathing personality and life into potentially dry subjects. UNIX and its attendant programs can be unruly beasts. Nutshell Handbooks help you tame them.

The animal featured on the cover of *TCP/IP Network Administration, Second Edition*, is a land crab. Land crabs are found in tropical America, West Africa, and the Indo-Pacific region where they can be found living in burrows in fields, swamps, and mangrove thickets. They occasionally are found as far as five miles inland, returning to the sea to spawn. Land crabs are a subgroup of over 4,500 species of crabs. Classified with shrimp, lobster, and crayfish, crabs differ from these in their tail structure. Unlike the rest of their order, crabs' tails are curled under their thorax. In addition, their carapaces tend to be unusually broad. Though land crabs in the United States commonly grow to weigh no more than

18 ounces and measure 4 or 5 inches across, crabs in general range in size from less than a centimeter across to the largest, the Japanese spider crab, whose claws can span 12 feet.

Edie Freedman designed the cover of this book, using a 19th-century engraving from the Dover Pictorial Archive. The cover layout was produced with Quark XPress 3.3 using the ITC Garamond font.

The inside layout was designed by Edie Freedman and Nancy Priest and implemented in gtroff by Lenny Muellner. The text and heading fonts are ITC Garamond Light and Garamond Book. Figures were created by Robert Romano in Macromedia Freehand 5.0 and Adobe Photoshop.

Whenever possible, our books use RepKover™, a durable and flexible lay-flat binding. If the page count exceeds RepKover's limit, perfect binding is used.

More Titles from O'Reilly

Network Administration

DNS and BIND, 3rd Edition

By Paul Albitz & Cricket Liu
3rd Edition September 1998
502 pages, ISBN 1-56592-512-2

DNS and BIND discusses one of the Internet's fundamental building blocks: the distributed host information database that's responsible for translating names into addresses, routing mail to its proper destination, and many other services. The third edition covers BIND 4.9, on which most commercial products are currently based, and BIND 8, which implements many important new features and will be the basis for the next generation of commercial name servers.

The Networking CD Bookshelf

By O'Reilly & Associates, Inc.
1st Edition March 1999
ISBN 1-56592-523-8, Features CD-ROM

Network administrator alert! Six bestselling O'Reilly Animal Guides are now available on CD-ROM, easily accessible with your favorite Web browser: *TCP/IP Network Administration, 2nd Edition; sendmail, 2nd Edition; sendmail Desktop Reference; DNS and BIND, 3rd Edition; Practical UNIX & Internet Security, 2nd Edition;* and *Building Internet Firewalls.* As a bonus, the new hardcopy version of *DNS and BIND, 3rd Edition* is also included.

Virtual Private Networks, 2nd Edition

By Charlie Scott, Paul Wolfe & Mike Erwin
2nd Edition December 1998
228 pages, ISBN 1-56592-529-7

This book explains how to plan and build a Virtual Private Network (VPN), a collection of technologies that creates secure connections or "tunnels" over regular Internet lines. It discusses costs, configuration, and how to install and use VPN technologies that are available for Windows NT and UNIX, such as PPTP and L2TP, Altavista Tunnel, Cisco PIX, and the secure shell (SSH). New features in the second edition include SSH and an expanded description of the IPSec standard.

Internet Core Protocols: The Definitive Guide

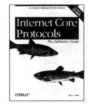

By Eric Hall
1st Edition June 2000 (est.)
480 pages (est.), Includes CD-ROM
ISBN 1-56592-572-6

Internet Core Protocols: The Definitive Guide provides the nitty-gritty details of TCP, IP, and UDP. Many network problems can only be debugged by working at the lowest levels – looking at all the bits traveling back and forth on the wire. This guide explains what those bits are and how to interpret them. It's the only book on Internet protocols written with system and network administrators in mind.

Internet Application Protocols: The Definitive Guide

By Eric Hall
1st Edition June 2000 (est.)
700 pages (est.), Includes CD-ROM
ISBN 1-56592-606-4

Internet Application Protocols: The Definitive Guide covers HTTP, SMTP, POP3, IMAP, FTP, DNS, and other key application protocols that do the work of the Internet. Together with *Internet Core Protocols: The Definitive Guide*, this book forms the foundation of a series that provides network administrators with practical reference material to help them troubleshoot their networks. Includes the Surveyor Lite protocol analyzer on CD-ROM.

sendmail, 2nd Edition

By Bryan Costales & Eric Allman
2nd Edition January 1997
1050 pages, ISBN 1-56592-222-0

sendmail, 2nd Edition, covers sendmail Version 8.8 from Berkeley and the standard versions available on most systems. This cross-referenced edition offers an expanded tutorial and solution-oriented examples, plus topics such as the #error delivery agent, sendmail's exit values, MIME headers, and how to set up and use the user database, mailertable, and smrsh.

Network Administration

Managing Mailing Lists

By Alan Schwartz
1st Edition March 1998
298 pages, ISBN 1-56592-259-X

This book covers four mailing list packages (Majordomo, LISTSERV, Listproc, and SmartList) and tells you everything you need to know to set up and run a mailing list, from writing the charter to dealing with bounced messages. It discusses creating moderated lists, controlling who can subscribe, offering digest subscriptions, and archiving list postings.

Managing Usenet

By Henry Spencer & David Lawrence
1st Edition January 1998
508 pages, ISBN 1-56592-198-4

Usenet, also called Netnews, is the world's largest discussion forum, and it is doubling in size every year. This book, written by two of the foremost authorities on Usenet administration, contains everything you need to know to administer a Netnews system. It covers C News and INN, explains the basics of starting a Netnews system, and offers guidelines to help ensure that your system is capable of handling news volume today – and in the future.

Using & Managing PPP

By Andrew Sun
1st Edition March 1999
444 pages, ISBN 1-56592-321-9

This book is for network administrators and others who have to set up computer systems to use PPP. It covers all aspects of the protocol, including how to set up dial-in servers, authentication, debugging, and PPP options. In addition, it contains overviews of related areas, like serial communications, DNS setup, and routing.

Managing IP Networks with Cisco Routers

By Scott M. Ballew
1st Edition October 1997
352 pages, ISBN 1-56592-320-0

This practical guide to setting up and maintaining a production network covers how to select routing protocols, configure protocols to handle most common situations, evaluate network equipment and vendors, and set up a help desk. Although it focuses on Cisco routers, and gives examples using Cisco's IOS, the principles discussed are common to all IP networks.

Networking Personal Computers with TCP/IP

By Craig Hunt
1st Edition July 1995
408 pages, ISBN 1-56592-123-2

This book offers practical information as well as detailed instructions for attaching PCs to a TCP/IP network and its UNIX servers. It covers the challenges you'll face and offers general advice on how to deal with them, basic TCP/IP configuration information for some of the popular PC operating systems, advanced configuration topics and configuration of specific applications such as email, and integrating NetWare with TCP/IP.

Protecting Networks with SATAN

By Martin Freiss
1st Edition May 1998
128 pages, ISBN 1-56592-425-8

SATAN performs "security audits," scanning host computers for security vulnerabilities. This book describes how to install and use SATAN, and how to adapt it to local requirements and increase its knowledge of specific security vulnerabilities.

UNIX Tools

The UNIX CD Bookshelf

By O'Reilly & Associates, Inc.
1st Edition November 1998
444 pages, Includes CD-ROM
ISBN 1-56592-406-1

The UNIX CD Bookshelf contains six books from O'Reilly plus the software from *UNIX Power Tools* – all on a convenient CD-ROM. A bonus hard-copy book, *UNIX in a Nutshell: System V Edition*, is also included. The CD-ROM contains *UNIX in a Nutshell: System V Edition*; *UNIX Power Tools, 2nd Edition* (with software); *Learning the UNIX Operating System, 4th Edition*; *Learning the vi Editor, 5th Edition*; *sed & awk, 2nd Edition*; and *Learning the Korn Shell*.

sed & awk, 2nd Edition

By Dale Dougherty & Arnold Robbins
2nd Edition March 1997
432 pages, ISBN 1-56592-225-5

sed & awk describes two text manipulation programs that are mainstays of the UNIX programmer's toolbox. This edition covers the sed and awk programs as they are mandated by the POSIX standard and includes discussion of the GNU versions of these programs.

lex & yacc, 2nd Edition

By John Levine, Tony Mason & Doug Brown
2nd Edition October 1992
366 pages, ISBN 1-56592-000-7

Shows programmers how to use two UNIX utilities, lex and yacc, in program development. You'll find tutorial sections for novice users, reference sections for advanced users, and a detailed index. Major MS-DOS and UNIX versions of lex and yacc are explored in depth. Also covers Bison and Flex.

Managing Projects with make, 2nd Edition

By Andrew Oram & Steve Talbott
2nd Edition October 1991
152 pages, ISBN 0-937175-90-0

make is one of UNIX's greatest contributions to software development, and this book is the clearest description of make ever written. It describes all the basic features and provides guidelines on meeting the needs of large, modern projects. Also contains a description of free products that contain major enhancements to make.

Writing GNU Emacs Extensions

By Bob Glickstein
1st Edition April 1997
236 pages, ISBN 1-56592-261-1

This book introduces Emacs Lisp and tells you how to make the editor do whatever you want, whether it's altering the way text scrolls or inventing a whole new "major mode." Topics progress from simple to complex, from lists, symbols, and keyboard commands to syntax tables, macro templates, and error recovery.

UNIX Power Tools, 2nd Edition

By Jerry Peek, Tim O'Reilly & Mike Loukides
2nd Edition August 1997
1120 pages, Includes CD-ROM
ISBN 1-56592-260-3

Loaded with practical advice about almost every aspect of UNIX, this second edition of *UNIX Power Tools* addresses the technology that UNIX users face today. You'll find thorough coverage of POSIX utilities, including GNU versions, detailed bash and tcsh shell coverage, a strong emphasis on Perl, and a CD-ROM that contains the best freeware available.

UNIX Tools

Learning the bash Shell, 2nd Edition

By Cameron Newham & Bill Rosenblatt
2nd Edition January 1998
336 pages, ISBN 1-56592-347-2

This second edition covers all of the features
of bash Version 2.0, while still applying to
bash Version 1.x. It includes one-dimensional
arrays, parameter expansion, more pattern-
matching operations, new commands, security
improvements, additions to ReadLine, improved configuration and
installation, and an additional programming aid, the bash shell
debugger.

MySQL & mSQL

By Randy Jay Yarger, George Reese & Tim King
1st Edition July 1999
506 pages, ISBN 1-56592-434-7

This book teaches you how to use MySQL
and mSQL, two popular and robust database
products that support key subsets of SQL
on both Linux and UNIX systems. Anyone
who knows basic C, Java, Perl, or Python can
write a program to interact with a database, either as a stand-alone
application or through a Web page. This book takes you through the
whole process, from installation and configuration to programming
interfaces and basic administration. Includes ample tutorial material.

Applying RCS and SCCS

By Don Bolinger & Tan Bronson
1st Edition September 1995
528 pages, ISBN 1-56592-117-8

Applying RCS and SCCS is a thorough
introduction to these two systems, viewed
as tools for project management. This book
takes the reader from basic source control
of a single file, through working with multiple
releases of a software project, to coordinating multiple developers.
It also presents TCCS, a representative "front-end" that addresses
problems RCS and SCCS can't handle alone, such as managing
groups of files, developing for multiple platforms, and linking
public and private development areas.

Programming with GNU Software

By Mike Loukides & Andy Oram
1st Edition December 1996
260 pages, Includes CD-ROM
ISBN 1-56592-112-7

This book and CD combination is a complete
package for programmers who are new to
UNIX or who would like to make better use
of the system. The tools come from Cygnus
Support, Inc., and Cyclic Software, companies that provide support
for free software. Contents include GNU Emacs, gcc, C and C++
libraries, gdb, RCS, and make. The book provides an introduction
to all these tools for a C programmer.

Software Portability with imake, 2nd Edition

By Paul DuBois
2nd Edition September 1996
410 pages, ISBN 1-56592-226-3

This handbook is ideal for X and UNIX
programmers who want their software
to be portable. The second edition covers
version X11R6.1 of the X Window System,
using imake for non-UNIX systems such as
Windows NT, and some of the quirks about using imake under
OpenWindows/Solaris.

Practical Internet Groupware

By Jon Udell
1st Edition October 1999 (est.)
384 pages (est.), ISBN 1-56592-537-8

This revolutionary book tells users,
programmers, IS managers, and system
administrators how to build Internet
groupware applications that organize the
casual and chaotic transmission of online
information into useful, disciplined, and documented data.

O'REILLY®

TO ORDER: **800-998-9938** • *order@oreilly.com* • *http://www.oreilly.com/*
OUR PRODUCTS ARE AVAILABLE AT A BOOKSTORE OR SOFTWARE STORE NEAR YOU.
FOR INFORMATION: **800-998-9938** • **707-829-0515** • *info@oreilly.com*

UNIX Basics

Learning the UNIX Operating System, 4th Edition

By Jerry Peek, Grace Todino & John Strang
4th Edition December 1997
106 pages, ISBN 1-56592-390-1

If you are new to UNIX, this concise introduction will tell you just what you need to get started and no more. The new fourth edition covers the Linux operating system and is an ideal primer for someone just starting with UNIX or Linux, as well as for Mac and PC users who encounter a UNIX system on the Internet. This classic book, still the most effective introduction to UNIX in print, now includes a quick-reference card.

Learning the vi Editor, 6th Edition

By Linda Lamb & Arnold Robbins
6th Edition October 1998
348 pages, ISBN 1-56592-426-6

This completely updated guide to editing with vi, the editor available on nearly every UNIX system, now covers four popular vi clones and includes command summaries for easy reference. It starts with the basics, followed by more advanced editing tools, such as ex commands, global search and replacement, and a new feature, multi-screen editing.

Learning the Korn Shell

By Bill Rosenblatt
1st Edition June 1993
360 pages, ISBN 1-56592-054-6

A thorough introduction to the Korn shell, both as a user interface and as a programming language. This book provides a clear explanation of the Korn shell's features, including ksh string operations, co-processes, signals and signal handling, and command-line interpretation. *Learning the Korn Shell* also includes real-life programming examples and a Korn shell debugger (kshdb).

Learning GNU Emacs, 2nd Edition

By Debra Cameron, Bill Rosenblatt &
Eric Raymond
2nd Edition September 1996
560 pages, ISBN 1-56592-152-6

Learning GNU Emacs is an introduction to Version 19.30 of the GNU Emacs editor, one of the most widely used and powerful editors available under UNIX. It provides a solid introduction to basic editing, a look at several important "editing modes" (special Emacs features for editing specific types of documents, including email, Usenet News, and the World Wide Web), and a brief introduction to customization and Emacs LISP programming. The book is aimed at new Emacs users, whether or not they are programmers. Includes quick-reference card.

Using csh and tcsh

By Paul DuBois
1st Edition August 1995
242 pages, ISBN 1-56592-132-1

Using csh and tcsh describes from the beginning how to use these shells interactively to get your work done faster with less typing. You'll learn how to make your prompt tell you where you are (no more pwd); use what you've typed before (history); type long command lines with few keystrokes (command and filename completion); remind yourself of filenames when in the middle of typing a command; and edit a botched command without retyping it.

Volume 3M: X Window System User's Guide, Motif Edition, 2nd Edition

By Valerie Quercia & Tim O'Reilly
2nd Edition January 1993
956 pages, ISBN 1-56592-015-5

The X Window System User's Guide, Motif Edition orients the new user to window system concepts and provides detailed tutorials for many client programs, including the xtermterminal emulator and the twm, uwm, and mwmwindow managers. Later chapters explain how to customize the X environment. Revised for Motif 1.2 and X11 Release 5.

O'REILLY®

TO ORDER: **800-998-9938** • *order@oreilly.com* • *http://www.oreilly.com/*
OUR PRODUCTS ARE AVAILABLE AT A BOOKSTORE OR SOFTWARE STORE NEAR YOU.
FOR INFORMATION: **800-998-9938** • **707-829-0515** • *info@oreilly.com*

UNIX System Administration

Essential System Administration, 2nd Edition

By AEleen Frisch
2nd Edition September 1995
788 pages, ISBN 1-56592-127-5

Covering all major versions of UNIX, this second edition of *Essential System Administration* provides a compact, manageable introduction to the tasks faced by everyone responsible for a UNIX system. Whether you use a standalone UNIX system, routinely provide administrative support for a larger shared system, or just want an understanding of basic administrative functions, this book is for you. Offers extensive sections on networking, electronic mail, security, and kernel configuration.

The Perl CD Bookshelf

By O'Reilly & Associates, Inc.
1st Edition July 1999
Features CD-ROM
ISBN 1-56592-462-2

Perl programmer alert! Six bestselling O'Reilly Animal Guides are now available on CD-ROM, easily accessible with your favorite Web browser: *Perl in a Nutshell*; *Programming Perl, 2nd Edition*; *Perl Cookbook*; *Advanced Perl Programming*; *Learning Perl*; and *Learning Perl on Win32 Sytems*. As a bonus, the new hard-copy version of *Perl in a Nutshell* is also included.

UNIX Backup & Recovery

By W. Curtis Preston
1st Edition October 1999 (est.)
732 pages (est.), Includes CD-ROM
ISBN 1-56592-642-0

This guide provides a complete overview of all facets of UNIX backup and recovery and offers practical, affordable backup and recovery solutions for environments of all sizes and budgets. It explains everything from freely available backup systems to large-scale commercial utilities.

Managing NFS and NIS

By Hal Stern
1st Edition June 1991
436 pages, ISBN 0-937175-75-7

Managing NFS and NIS is for system administrators who need to set up or manage a network filesystem installation. NFS (Network Filesystem) is probably running at any site that has two or more UNIX systems. NIS (Network Information System) is a distributed database used to manage a network of computers. The only practical book devoted entirely to these subjects, this guide is a "must-have" for anyone interested in UNIX networking.

Volume 8: X Window System Administrator's Guide

By Linda Mui & Eric Pearce
1st Edition October 1992
372 pages, ISBN 0-937175-83-8

This book focuses on issues of system administration for X and X-based networks — not just for UNIX system administrators, but for anyone faced with the job of administering X (including those running X on stand-alone workstations).

Using Samba

By Bob Eckstein,
David Collier-Brown, & Peter Kelly
1st Edition October 1999 (est.)
424 pages (est.), Includes CD-ROM
ISBN 1-56592-449-5

Samba turns a UNIX or Linux system into a file and print server for Microsoft Windows network clients. This complete guide to Samba administration covers basic 2.0 configuration, security, logging, and troubleshooting. Whether you're playing on one note or a full three-octave range, this book will help you maintain an efficient and secure server. Includes a CD-ROM of sources and ready-to-install binaries.

O'REILLY®

TO ORDER: **800-998-9938** • *order@oreilly.com* • *http://www.oreilly.com/*

OUR PRODUCTS ARE AVAILABLE AT A BOOKSTORE OR SOFTWARE STORE NEAR YOU.

FOR INFORMATION: **800-998-9938** • **707-829-0515** • *info@oreilly.com*

Hand-held Computing

Palm Programming: The Developer's Guide

By Neil Rhodes & Julie McKeehan
1st Edition December 1998
482 pages, Includes CD-ROM
ISBN 1-56592-525-4

Emerging as the bestselling hand-held
computers of all time, PalmPilots have
spawned intense developer activity and a
fanatical following. Used by Palm in their
developer training, this tutorial-style book shows intermediate
to experienced C programmers how to build a Palm application
from the ground up. Includes a CD-ROM with source code and
third-party developer tools.

PalmPilot: The Ultimate Guide, 2nd Edition

By David Pogue
2nd Edition June 1999
624 pages, Includes CD-ROM
ISBN 1-56592-600-5

This new edition of O'Reilly's runaway
bestseller is densely packed with previously
undocumented information. The bible for
users of Palm VII and all other Palm models,
it contains hundreds of timesaving tips and surprising tricks,
plus an all-new CD-ROM (for Windows 9x, NT, or Macintosh)
containing over 3,100 PalmPilot programs from the collection
of palmcentral.com, the Internet's largest Palm software site.

O'REILLY®

TO ORDER: **800-998-9938** • **order@oreilly.com** • *http://www.oreilly.com/*
OUR PRODUCTS ARE AVAILABLE AT A BOOKSTORE OR SOFTWARE STORE NEAR YOU.
FOR INFORMATION: **800-998-9938** • **707-829-0515** • **info@oreilly.com**

How to stay in touch with O'Reilly

1. Visit Our Award-Winning Web Site

http://www.oreilly.com/

★ "Top 100 Sites on the Web" —*PC Magazine*
★ "Top 5% Web sites" —*Point Communications*
★ "3-Star site" —*The McKinley Group*

Our web site contains a library of comprehensive product information (including book excerpts and tables of contents), downloadable software, background articles, interviews with technology leaders, links to relevant sites, book cover art, and more. File us in your Bookmarks or Hotlist!

2. Join Our Email Mailing Lists

New Product Releases

To receive automatic email with brief descriptions of all new O'Reilly products as they are released, send email to:
listproc@online.oreilly.com
Put the following information in the first line of your message (*not* in the Subject field):
subscribe oreilly-news

O'Reilly Events

If you'd also like us to send information about trade show events, special promotions, and other O'Reilly events, send email to:
listproc@online.oreilly.com
Put the following information in the first line of your message (*not* in the Subject field):
subscribe oreilly-events

3. Get Examples from Our Books via FTP

There are two ways to access an archive of example files from our books:

Regular FTP

* ftp to:
  ftp.oreilly.com
  (login: anonymous
  password: your email address)
* Point your web browser to:
  ftp://ftp.oreilly.com/

FTPMAIL

* Send an email message to:
  ftpmail@online.oreilly.com
  (Write "help" in the message body)

4. Contact Us via Email

order@oreilly.com
To place a book or software order online. Good for North American and international customers.

subscriptions@oreilly.com
To place an order for any of our newsletters or periodicals.

books@oreilly.com
General questions about any of our books.

software@oreilly.com
For general questions and product information about our software. Check out O'Reilly Software Online at **http://software.oreilly.com/** for software and technical support information. Registered O'Reilly software users send your questions to: **website-support@oreilly.com**

cs@oreilly.com
For answers to problems regarding your order or our products.

booktech@oreilly.com
For book content technical questions or corrections.

proposals@oreilly.com
To submit new book or software proposals to our editors and product managers.

international@oreilly.com
For information about our international distributors or translation queries. For a list of our distributors outside of North America check out:
http://www.oreilly.com/www/order/country.html

O'Reilly & Associates, Inc.
101 Morris Street, Sebastopol, CA 95472 USA
TEL   707-829-0515 or 800-998-9938
          (6am to 5pm PST)
FAX   707-829-0104

Titles from O'Reilly

WEB

Advanced Perl Programming
Apache: The Definitive Guide,
    2nd Edition
ASP in a Nutshell
Building Your Own Web Conferences
Building Your Own Website™
CGI Programming with Perl
Designing with JavaScript
Dynamic HTML:
    The Definitive Reference
Frontier: The Definitive Guide
HTML: The Definitive Guide,
    3rd Edition
Information Architecture
    for the World Wide Web
JavaScript Pocket Reference
JavaScript: The Definitive Guide,
    3rd Edition
Learning VB Script
Photoshop for the Web
WebMaster in a Nutshell
WebMaster in a Nutshell,
    Deluxe Edition
Web Design in a Nutshell
Web Navigation:
    Designing the User Experience
Web Performance Tuning
Web Security & Commerce
Writing Apache Modules

PERL

Learning Perl, 2nd Edition
Learning Perl for Win32 Systems
Learning Perl/TK
Mastering Algorithms with Perl
Mastering Regular Expressions
Perl5 Pocket Reference, 2nd Edition
Perl Cookbook
Perl in a Nutshell
Perl Resource Kit—UNIX Edition
Perl Resource Kit—Win32 Edition
Perl/TK Pocket Reference
Programming Perl, 2nd Edition
Web Client Programming with Perl

GRAPHICS & MULTIMEDIA

Director in a Nutshell
Encyclopedia of Graphics
    File Formats, 2nd Edition
Lingo in a Nutshell
Photoshop in a Nutshell
QuarkXPress in a Nutshell

USING THE INTERNET

AOL in a Nutshell
Internet in a Nutshell
Smileys
The Whole Internet for Windows95
The Whole Internet:
    The Next Generation
The Whole Internet
    User's Guide & Catalog

JAVA SERIES

Database Programming with
    JDBC and Java
Developing Java Beans
Exploring Java, 2nd Edition
Java AWT Reference
Java Cryptography
Java Distributed Computing
Java Examples in a Nutshell
Java Foundation Classes in a Nutshell
Java Fundamental Classes Reference
Java in a Nutshell, 2nd Edition
Java in a Nutshell, Deluxe Edition
Java I/O
Java Language Reference, 2nd Edition
Java Media Players
Java Native Methods
Java Network Programming
Java Security
Java Servlet Programming
Java Swing
Java Threads
Java Virtual Machine

UNIX

Exploring Expect
GNU Emacs Pocket Reference
Learning GNU Emacs, 2nd Edition
Learning the bash Shell, 2nd Edition
Learning the Korn Shell
Learning the UNIX Operating System,
    4th Edition
Learning the vi Editor, 6th Edition
Linux in a Nutshell
Linux Multimedia Guide
Running Linux, 2nd Edition
SCO UNIX in a Nutshell
sed & awk, 2nd Edition
Tcl/Tk in a Nutshell
Tcl/Tk Pocket Reference
Tcl/Tk Tools
The UNIX CD Bookshelf
UNIX in a Nutshell, System V Edition
UNIX Power Tools, 2nd Edition
Using csh & tsch
Using Samba
vi Editor Pocket Reference
What You Need To Know:
    When You Can't Find Your
    UNIX System Administrator
Writing GNU Emacs Extensions

SONGLINE GUIDES

NetLaw   NetResearch
NetLearning   NetSuccess
NetLessons   NetTravel

SOFTWARE

Building Your Own WebSite™
Building Your Own Web Conference
WebBoard™ 3.0
WebSite Professional™ 2.0
PolyForm™

SYSTEM ADMINISTRATION

Building Internet Firewalls
Computer Security Basics
Cracking DES
DNS and BIND, 3rd Edition
DNS on WindowsNT
Essential System Administration
Essential WindowsNT
    System Administration
Getting Connected:
    The Internet at 56K and Up
Linux Network Administrator's Guide
Managing IP Networks with
    Cisco Routers
Managing Mailing Lists
Managing NFS and NIS
Managing the WindowsNT Registry
Managing Usenet
MCSE: The Core Exams in a Nutshell
MCSE: The Electives in a Nutshell
Networking Personal Computers
    with TCP/IP
Oracle Performance Tuning,
    2nd Edition
Practical UNIX & Internet Security,
    2nd Edition
PGP: Pretty Good Privacy
Protecting Networks with SATAN
sendmail, 2nd Edition
sendmail Desktop Reference
System Performance Tuning
TCP/IP Network Administration,
    2nd Edition
termcap & terminfo
The Networking CD Bookshelf
Using & Managing PPP
Virtual Private Networks
WindowsNT Backup & Restore
WindowsNT Desktop Reference
WindowsNT Event Logging
WindowsNT in a Nutshell
WindowsNT Server 4.0 for
    Netware Administrators
WindowsNT SNMP
WindowsNT TCP/IP Administration
WindowsNT User Administration
Zero Administration for Windows

X WINDOW

Vol. 1: Xlib Programming Manual
Vol. 2: Xlib Reference Manual
Vol. 3M: X Window System
    User's Guide, Motif Edition
Vol. 4M: X Toolkit Intrinsics
    Programming Manual,
    Motif Edition
Vol. 5: X Toolkit Intrinsics
    Reference Manual
Vol. 6A: Motif Programming Manual
Vol. 6B: Motif Reference Manual
Vol. 8 : X Window System
    Administrator's Guide

PROGRAMMING

Access Database Design and
    Programming
Advanced Oracle PL/SQL
    Programming with Packages
Applying RCS and SCCS
BE Developer's Guide
BE Advanced Topics
C++: The Core Language
Checking C Programs with lint
Developing Windows Error Messages
Developing Visual Basic Add-ins
Guide to Writing DCE Applications
High Performance Computing,
    2nd Edition
Inside the Windows 95 File System
Inside the Windows 95 Registry
lex & yacc, 2nd Edition
Linux Device Drivers
Managing Projects with make
Oracle8 Design Tips
Oracle Built-in Packages
Oracle Design
Oracle PL/SQL Programming,
    2nd Edition
Oracle Scripts
Oracle Security
Palm Programming:
    The Developer's Guide
Porting UNIX Software
POSIX Programmer's Guide
POSIX.4: Programming
    for the Real World
Power Programming with RPC
Practical C Programming, 3rd Edition
Practical C++ Programming
Programming Python
Programming with curses
Programming with GNU Software
Pthreads Programming
Python Pocket Reference
Software Portability with imake,
    2nd Edition
UML in a Nutshell
Understanding DCE
UNIX Systems Programming for SVR4
VB/VBA in a Nutshell: The Languages
Win32 Multithreaded Programming
Windows NT File System Internals
Year 2000 in a Nutshell

USING WINDOWS

Excel97 Annoyances
Office97 Annoyances
Outlook Annoyances
Windows Annoyances
Windows98 Annoyances
Windows95 in a Nutshell
Windows98 in a Nutshell
Word97 Annoyances

OTHER TITLES

PalmPilot: The Ultimate Guide
Palm Programming:
    The Developer's Guide

O'REILLY®

TO ORDER: **800-998-9938** • *order@oreilly.com* • *http://www.oreilly.com/*
OUR PRODUCTS ARE AVAILABLE AT A BOOKSTORE OR SOFTWARE STORE NEAR YOU.
FOR INFORMATION: **800-998-9938** • **707-829-0515** • *info@oreilly.com*

International Distributors

UK, EUROPE, MIDDLE EAST AND AFRICA (EXCEPT FRANCE, GERMANY, AUSTRIA, SWITZERLAND, LUXEMBOURG, LIECHTENSTEIN, AND EASTERN EUROPE)

INQUIRIES
O'Reilly UK Limited
4 Castle Street
Farnham
Surrey, GU9 7HS
United Kingdom
Telephone: 44-1252-711776
Fax: 44-1252-734211
Email: josette@oreilly.com

ORDERS
Wiley Distribution Services Ltd.
1 Oldlands Way
Bognor Regis
West Sussex PO22 9SA
United Kingdom
Telephone: 44-1243-779777
Fax: 44-1243-820250
Email: cs-books@wiley.co.uk

FRANCE

ORDERS
GEODIF
61, Bd Saint-Germain
75240 Paris Cedex 05, France
Tel: 33-1-44-41-46-16 (French books)
Tel: 33-1-44-41-11-87 (English books)
Fax: 33-1-44-41-11-44
Email: distribution@eyrolles.com

INQUIRIES
Éditions O'Reilly
18 rue Séguier
75006 Paris, France
Tel: 33-1-40-51-52-30
Fax: 33-1-40-51-52-31
Email: france@editions-oreilly.fr

GERMANY, SWITZERLAND, AUSTRIA, EASTERN EUROPE, LUXEMBOURG, AND LIECHTENSTEIN

INQUIRIES & ORDERS
O'Reilly Verlag
Balthasarstr. 81
D-50670 Köln
Germany
Telephone: 49-221-973160-91
Fax: 49-221-973160-8
Email: anfragen@oreilly.de (inquiries)
Email: order@oreilly.de (orders)

CANADA (FRENCH LANGUAGE BOOKS)
Les Éditions Flammarion ltée
375, Avenue Laurier Ouest
Montréal (Québec) H2V 2K3
Tel: 00-1-514-277-8807
Fax: 00-1-514-278-2085
Email: info@flammarion.qc.ca

HONG KONG
City Discount Subscription Service, Ltd.
Unit D, 3rd Floor, Yan's Tower
27 Wong Chuk Hang Road
Aberdeen, Hong Kong
Tel: 852-2580-3539
Fax: 852-2580-6463
Email: citydis@ppn.com.hk

KOREA
Hanbit Media, Inc.
Sonyoung Bldg. 202
Yeksam-dong 736-36
Kangnam-ku
Seoul, Korea
Tel: 822-554-9610
Fax: 822-556-0363
Email: hant93@chollian.dacom.co.kr

PHILIPPINES
Mutual Books, Inc.
429-D Shaw Boulevard
Mandaluyong City, Metro
Manila, Philippines
Tel: 632-725-7538
Fax: 632-721-3056
Email: mbikikog@mnl.sequel.net

TAIWAN
O'Reilly Taiwan
No. 3, Lane 131
Hang-Chow South Road
Section 1, Taipei, Taiwan
Tel: 886-2-23968990
Fax: 886-2-23968916
Email: taiwan@oreilly.com

CHINA
O'Reilly Beijing
Room 2410
160, FuXingMenNeiDaJie
XiCheng District
Beijing, China PR 100031
Tel: 86-10-86631006
Fax: 86-10-86631007
Email: beijing@oreilly.com

INDIA
Computer Bookshop (India) Pvt. Ltd.
190 Dr. D.N. Road, Fort
Bombay 400 001 India
Tel: 91-22-207-0989
Fax: 91-22-262-3551
Email: cbsbom@giasbm01.vsnl.net.in

JAPAN
O'Reilly Japan, Inc.
Kiyoshige Building 2F
12-Bancho, Sanei-cho
Shinjuku-ku
Tokyo 160-0008 Japan
Tel: 81-3-3356-5227
Fax: 81-3-3356-5261
Email: japan@oreilly.com

ALL OTHER ASIAN COUNTRIES
O'Reilly & Associates, Inc.
101 Morris Street
Sebastopol, CA 95472 USA
Tel: 707-829-0515
Fax: 707-829-0104
Email: order@oreilly.com

AUSTRALIA
WoodsLane Pty., Ltd.
7/5 Vuko Place
Warriewood NSW 2102
Australia
Tel: 61-2-9970-5111
Fax: 61-2-9970-5002
Email: info@woodslane.com.au

NEW ZEALAND
Woodslane New Zealand, Ltd.
21 Cooks Street (P.O. Box 575)
Waganui, New Zealand
Tel: 64-6-347-6543
Fax: 64-6-345-4840
Email: info@woodslane.com.au

LATIN AMERICA
McGraw-Hill Interamericana
Editores, S.A. de C.V.
Cedro No. 512
Col. Atlampa
06450, Mexico, D.F.
Tel: 52-5-547-6777
Fax: 52-5-547-3336
Email: mcgraw-hill@infosel.net.mx

O'REILLY®